N.O. Lit

200 Years of New Orleans Literature

Edited by

Nancy Dixon

N.O. Lit: 200 Years of New Orleans Literature

ISBN 978-1-935084-52-5

Library of Congress Control Number
2013954137

Book Design: Bill Lavender
Typesetting: Creighton Durrant
Copy Editors: Erica Mattingly, Megan Burns, Lauren Capone

This book has been made possible, in part, through generous grants from the Louisiana Endowment for the Humanities, a state affiliate of the National Endowment for the Humanities, and the New Orleans Jazz & Heritage Foundation. The opinions expressed in this book do not necessarily represent the views of either of these agencies.

Lavender Ink
New Orleans
lavenderink.org

LES
CENELLES.

Choix de Poesies indigenes.

Et de ces fruits qu'un Dieu prodigue dans nos bois
Heureux, si j'en ai su faire un aimable choix !

A. MERCIER.

NOUVELLE ORLEANS.
Imprimé par H. Lauve et Compagnie.

1845.

Frontispiece to the 1845 edition of *Les Cenelles*

N.O. Lit: 200 Years of New Orleans Literature

Acknowledgements

Note: Formal acknowledgements appear as footnotes in the body of the text.

I would first like to thank Dr. George Reinecke, the foremost New Orleans scholar, for sometimes not-so-gently nudging me in the direction of New Orleans literature when I was writing my M.A. thesis at the University of New Orleans. I owe much of my knowledge of this city's literature and my love for research to him. I missed George every day while working on this project and channeled him often. I also want to thank the UNO English Department for assigning me three excellent research assistants: Kat Stromquist, Rich Goode, Laura McKnight—thank you.

I would not have been able to complete this project without the generous grants from the New Orleans Jazz and Heritage Foundation and the Louisiana Endowment for the Humanities In particular, I would like to thank Dr. Michael Sartisky, President and Executive Director of LEH, for his support during the course of this project, and Brian Boyles for his guidance.

There are several colleagues whom I would like to thank, including Moira Crone for agreeing to read and evaluate the text; Dr. Kenneth Holditch, for his gracious help and attention to this project; Dr. Carol Gelderman, Elizabeth Lewis and Reggie Poche, for their suggestions for the table of contents. Thanks also to Creighton Durrant, Megan Burns, Lauren Capone, and Erica Mattingly for their hard work and expertise in preparing the manuscript. Thanks also to C.W. Cannon, Michael Mizell-Nelson, Rosemary James and John H. Lawrence for comments and suggestions.

I also want to thank the English instructors at UNO who urged me to complete this project, largely due to the fact that there is no text for the New Orleans literature course we taught for so many years. My students at UNO and now Dillard University are still the driving force behind this book, and I want to thank my Dillard colleagues, especially Cortheal Clark, Ray Vrazel and Zena Ezeb for their unwavering support and for making me feel at home in the Dillard School of Humanities.

There are many in the city to whom I am indebted for introducing me to writers and their works, like Dr. Jerry Ward, Dar Wolnik, Rosemary James, Jarret Lofstead and Susan Larson. Thanks also to those writers who generously allowed their works to be reprinted here: Shirley Ann Grau, Richard Ford, Andrei Codrescu, Valerie Martin, John Biguenet, Moira Crone and Fatima Shaik. Thanks to Walter Dent for permission to use his brother's work and to Dr. Jerry Ward and Chakula Cha-Jua for their support. Thanks to Regine Latortue for permission to use her translations of *Les Cenelles*. Thanks also to Ella Camburnbeck, Beauregard-Keyes House Director, for her assistance. And a special thanks to all the New Orleans poets and to librarians all over the city who are so often overlooked.

My family has always inspired and continues to inspire me to work harder, especially you, Dad. Thanks to Roxy and Celeste for letting me know what's really important, and to Will and Beth and Ben for welcoming me into your loving family. And to my own sisters and brothers and their partners and children, thanks for always being there for me.

Finally, to publisher Bill Lavender of Lavender Ink, whose love and support for me is a constant source of surprise, inspiration, and strength, thanks is not enough. To Bill, my heart.

—Nancy Dixon, New Orleans, November, 2013

For my mother, Helen Dixon, 1929-2012,
and for my father James Dixon.

Editor's Introduction

Between 1778 and 1783, some ten years after the French Louisianians rebelled against Spanish rule under Governor Ulloa (Antonio de Ulloa y de la Torre-Girault)—the subject of Thomas Wharton Collens' play *The Martyr Patriots, or Louisiana in 1769*—nearly 2000 Canary Islanders, or *Isleños*, arrived in Louisiana. The Louisiana colony, at the time under the Spanish rule of Governor Bernardo de Galvez, needed these new recruits and their families in order to populate the territory and defend it against the British during the American Revolution. And it was no accident that Galvez turned to the Canary Islands to find these soldiers and their families, for the harsh natural setting of Tenerife—the largest of the archipelago—had forced them to live in isolation much as they would in the swamps of the Louisiana Territory. Enough Isleños were persuaded to emigrate that four major settlements were established on both sides of the Mississippi River. The one in St. Bernard Parish, named after Bernardo de Galvez, remains a cohesive community today, and many of the Isleño descendants still make their living off the land, fishing, trapping, and farming oysters, as they have for centuries.

New Orleans itself was geographically isolated up until the mid-19th century, surrounded and accessible only by water. It was also socially, culturally, and legally cut off by being the only territory ruled first by the French, then the Spanish, then again the French, before being purchased by the United States. The citizens spoke French, as some still do. Even under Spanish rule they refused to conform and were reluctant to speak English, but they had little choice when, after the Louisiana Purchase, it became the legal language of the state. Nonetheless, they did refuse to adopt the British system of common law practiced in the rest of the nation, and still today Louisiana is the only state in the nation whose legal system is based on French civil law. Until very recently, the city was one of only two that celebrated Mardi Gras (Mobile, Alabama lays claim to the first American Mardi Gras in 1703, fifteen years before New Orleans was founded.).

The city and its citizens may be set apart from the rest of the nation, but for centuries artists have been drawn to this bend in the Mississippi River. Tennessee Williams claimed that New Orleans provided the creative tension vital to his writing, and many other writers, only some of whom are collected here, have agreed.

New Orleans is, as Eudora Welty writes in "No Place for You, My Love," the "terminus of never." Like many of our nation's great cities, it is not on the way to somewhere; it is rather the destination. One might, for example, drive through Sacramento en route to San Francisco, or Trenton, New Jersey, on the way to New York City, but one does not go through New Orleans on the way to someplace else. In fact, Amtrak advertises its Crescent route as offering "Convenient Daily Trips from the Big Apple to the Big Easy" without mentioning a stopping point in between.

New Orleans is still surrounded by water; we bury our dead above ground because most of the city lies below sea level; Mardi Gras is still a holiday; many people still speak French; and the architecture is decidedly Spanish, especially in the French Quarter, oddly enough.

The Canary Island settlers created ten-verse songs called "décimas" to document their lives in the new world. They sang of love, war, fishing, trapping, essentially recording their own history. After studying for decades to compile this collection, I have discovered that much of the work we might call New Orleans literature accomplishes just what the Isleños set out to do; it captures the city's life in writing.

New Orleans has always been culturally cut off from the rest of the nation, and this is reflected in its literature. George Washington Cable repeatedly writes that both black and white Creoles felt a closer connection to each other than they did to outsiders like Americans and other "immigrants" to the city. He illustrates the cohesion of the Creoles and their sense of superiority in his short story "'Tite Poulette," in which the Dutch Kristin Koppig is ridiculed repeatedly for his rough manners and clumsy French. When he sends a letter in French to his beautiful Creole neighbors, Madame John and 'Tite Poulette, Cable writes: "A letter by a Dutchman in French! – what can be made of it...." Even marrying 'Tite Poulette does not entitle him to forgo his outsider status.

New Orleans has also been, more so than the hinterland, subject to whims of weather. Hurricanes remain a threat to the region, and their destruction can isolate communities but also bring survivors together. In his novella, *Chita*, Lafcadio Hearn writes of the hurricane of 1856 that wiped out the resort island, "Isle Dernier" (Last Island), and the characters in Kate Chopin's *The Awakening* attend mass on Chenier Caminada, a Louisiana barrier island leveled by a hurricane in 1893 and abandoned for good after one in 1915. In the 20th century New Orleans withstood Audrey, Betsy, and Camille, but was not prepared for Hurricane Katrina in 2005, when the flood waters turned us all into Isleños, physically surrounded by water for weeks, even months, and socially and economically cut off from the rest of the nation as well. The outpouring of creativity that ensued to help respond, to understand and to simply cope with that disaster was unparalleled in every artistic medium, but especially in literature, much like the early Spanish settlers' décimas.

The earliest literature of the city is about war, with or among the Native Americans, or with the colonial ruling bodies of the time. From the Louisiana Purchase to the Civil War, slavery and racism become the focus. In what is often considered the golden age of New Orleans literature, the late 19th century, the racial debate becomes both more public and personal. The early 20th century ushers in a new bohemia for some of the finest writers of the time, and that trend continues right on through to the 21st century. *N.O. Lit* is the first collection of literature to span the 200 years of this city since the Louisiana Purchase, and much of that literature has been written by Pulitzer Prize winners, Tony and Oscar winners, historians, and housewives, but also by soldiers, slaves, slave owners, drunks, immigrants, pill freaks and ne'er-do-wells, many of them as fascinating as the literature they produced.

New Orleans is a city of excess that appeals to the creative sort, and many writers are seduced by its siren charms. In the summer it rains every day, and not a simple afternoon mist, but alligator tears. The area is so fecund that for two thirds of the year the lush, green vegetation turns the ambient light of the city an often dazzling blue, an attraction for visual artists. Because of the warm climate—and in the summer that is putting it mildly—much of the city's social life occurs outside in bars and cafes, or at parades and second lines led by brass bands, a tradition that dates back to the slaves in Congo Square. We don't just have storms; we have hurricanes that wipe whole towns and islands off the map. In fact, the Louisiana coastline is disappearing at a faster rate than any on the planet! And our city, state, and national leaders continue to do what they have done for most of the last two centuries—very little.

The city has many monikers, the Crescent City, the Big Easy, the City that Care Forgot, and readers will discover that the tolerance of political corruption, the aversion to work, the excessive drinking and celebration, and violence took root in the city's earliest days. In his book, *The World that Made New Orleans: From Spanish Silver to Congo Square*, Ned Sublette writes:

> With slaves to do the work, and winters that were short and relatively mild, those New
> Orleanians who were prosperous had ample time for leisure, something that became
> practically the stereotype of the New Orleans Creole.... The libertine population, from the
> wealthy few to the many poor, continued celebrating with their dances, their masquerades,
> their drinking, their gambling, their fighting, and their couplings, especially during the

Carnival season but also during a year-round schedule of festivals, parties, and balls.[1]

We come by many of our traditions honestly—or dishonestly—and they are reflected in the literature of the city.

The oldest extant play written by a citizen and performed in New Orleans, Paul LeBlanc de Villeneufve's *The Festival of the Young Corn, or the Heroism of Poucha-Houmma* (1809), offers readers historical insight into violence fueled by booze that is still such a problem today in New Orleans. Young, rash Cala-be, the son of Poucha-houmma, the wise chief of the Houmma Indians, got drunk with his friend, the son of the neighboring Tchacta (Choctaw) chief and murdered him. LeBlanc writes: "…the effects of the burning liquid./ …clouded my reason. Filled with horrible thoughts,/ I [Cala-be] seized a dagger, and my merciless hand/Put an end to the days of a Tchacta, a friend." Such a senseless crime is echoed in Tom Dent's play, *Ritual Murder* (1967), nearly two hundred years later. In Dent's play, a young African American, Joe Brown Jr., gets drunk one Saturday night with his best friend James Roberts and murders him. The narrator explains: "When murder occurs for no apparent reason, but happens all the time, as in our race on a Saturday night, it is ritual murder." Unfortunately, this ritual is repeated almost daily in this city.

Racism is also the subject of this city's literature from the beginning. LeBlanc blames the European colonists for their ill treatment of the Native Americans, and by the middle of the 19th century, the Creole poets of Les Cenelles (The Mayhaws), all free men of color, lament their unfair treatment and that of the free women of color in their poems. From the other side of the racial divide, Charles Gayarré and Grace King both publicly attack George Washington Cable for his stand against slavery, and many of the early white writers, like Alfred Mercier, Alcée Fortier, and Ruth McEnery Stuart, perpetuate the myth of the "happy plantation negro" in their works.

While much of the early literature is written by and about the wealthy and white ruling classes, the poets of Les Cenelles, led by Armand Lanusse, composed the first anthology of African American literature here in New Orleans! In their poetry they examine their second-class standing in the Creole community, as we see in their title poem:

Les Cenelles

Fate gave you
The work of gathering again
The mayhaws to keep their
Flowers for all the world.
In darkness like the noble
Heart of French Louisiana
It will be your courage
that will guide our history
to more fruitful fields.
The mayhaws. They grow
Once again, strong and beautiful
Like your faithful Creole love.

It was up to the educated free Creoles of color—*gens de couleur libres*—to defend their culture, which was under attack after the United States purchased the Louisiana Territory from France in 1803

---

1   Ned Sublette, *The World that Made New Orleans: From Spanish Silver to Congo Square* (New Orleans: Lawrence Hill Press, 2008), 80.

and later, in the decades leading up to and following the Civil War. Armand Lanusse, the editor of the anthology, *Les Cenelles*, even fought for the Confederacy in the Civil War; however, after he saw how blacks were treated, he dedicated his life to educating and uplifting African Americans in New Orleans, in keeping with Les Cenelles' mission statement.

In contrast to Lanusse, however, some of the more established white Creoles, like Alfred Mercier and Alcée Fortier, cloak a thinly disguised condescension toward African Americans in their animal tales. Fortier translated and compiled Creole folktales, many of them as told to him by Creoles of color. Mercier's "Miss Calinda's Marriage" is a reworking of Aesop's "The Tortoise and the Hare." In Mercier's version, the hare wins by cheating, then they all celebrate by eating and drinking to excess, not a very flattering picture of this animal community meant to represent African Americans of the time.

In some of the nonfiction selections in the book, the fight against racism becomes more overt and very public. Cable's 1885 article, "The Freedman's Case in Equity," prompted Charles Gayarré's response, "Mr. Cable's 'Freedman's Case in Equity'," in which he first disparages Cable's writing style—ironic, since Cable is one of the city's finest writers—then violently opposes the mixing of any races, dating back to the Norman Invasion, also ironic, as he was accused of fathering a mixed-race child himself. In the end, Cable was all but run out of town for his abolitionism, but his writing did prompt another of New Orleans' finest writers to take pen to paper. Grace King was a staunch supporter of Gayarré and one of Cable's most vocal adversaries.

Racism finds its way into 20th-century New Orleans literature as well in works like Shirley Ann Grau's "Miss Yellow Eyes," but she leaves Jim Crow behind and writes about the inequality in the city under which African Americans suffer, a topic that will be taken up again by Fatima Shaik, who writes of growing up in the city as an African American Creole during the fight for Civil Rights.

Our high water table and above-ground mausoleums are a constant reminder of the ghosts that haunt the city, and often writers from outside New Orleans capture the spiritual nature of the region in their works. Tennessee Williams and Molly Moore (M.E.M.) Davis come to mind. In Williams' *Vieux Carré* ghosts of family members return—or never leave; in this case the spirit of Tom's grandmother visits him in his run-down Toulouse Street rooming house, offering comfort and acceptance. In M.E.M. Davis' "At La Glorieuse," a young lover, Richard, is haunted by the spirit of the once beautiful Hélène, only to repeat her mistakes in his hopeless pursuit of her daughter, Felice. He finally realizes that he is not haunted by Helene but in love with Felice. Unfortunately, he comes to this realization just in time to see her taking her final vows of poverty, chastity, and obedience. Star-crossed lovers such as these appear often in the literature of the city. When John Dimitry's dashing hero of "Le Tombeau Blanc," Fernand, at his engagement party, discovers that he is leprous, his fiancée Blanche, another good Catholic, also rushes to the convent.

Catholicism is a driving force behind many of these authors and their characters. Several of the Les Cenelles poets wrote about the church, specifically the schism in the St. Louis Cathedral in the mid-19th century, when the lay wardens of the cathedral were trying to wrest control away from the Vatican. Adrien Rouquette became a priest rather late in life in order to serve the Choctaw on the North shore of Lake Pontchartrain. Many of the décimas are Isleños' prayers to keep the trappers and fishers safe in the precarious slip of land that is St. Bernard Parish, and the reader will see references to saints and feast days throughout this collection.

The visitation of Mary provides a much needed alibi in Sallie Rhett Roman's "Bastien," while carnival balls, held just before the Lenten season, are central to Frances Parkinson Keyes' "...And She Wore Diamond Earrings." Manuela, the protagonist of Alice Dunbar Nelson's "The Goodness of St. Rocque," prays devotedly to St. Rocque in order to win her man back from her rival, Clarisse. However, she also seeks the help of the local voodoo priestess to make certain that her prayers are answered.

The 1791 slave revolt in St. Domingue (present day Haiti) sent many blacks, both free and escaped slaves, to Louisiana, and in New Orleans they added to the already large population of free people of color in the city, making it the largest in the nation. These Haitian immigrants brought with them their religious practice of voodoo, which originated in West Africa. As in Haiti, in New Orleans voodoo and Catholicism fused to some extent. Particularly obvious is the veneration of saints that they share, as many of the Catholic saints correspond to those in voodoo, or vice versa. So it comes as no surprise that we see both belief systems represented in the literature of the city, as they are, to this day, in the culture.

Many of our cultural traditions, although they come from other shores—including Africa, Europe, West Indies, or even Canada—are peculiar to New Orleans and are celebrated in its literature. Dancing is one tradition that is ubiquitous in this collection beginning with the very first work, LeBlanc's *The Heroism of Poucha-Houmma*. Whitman writes "A Night at the Terpsichore Ball," during his stint at the *New Orleans Crescent*. Fernand, the protagonist of Dimitry's "Le Tombeau Blanc" is an accomplished dancer, perhaps too accomplished, according to his male rivals in the story. Many works include weddings and other events celebrated by dancing, but in works like Cable's "'Tite Poulette," when Madame John is forced to perform at the quadroon balls in order to support her daughter, dancing emerges as a much more illicit practice. In Kate Chopin's "At the 'Cadian Ball," we see the fais-do-do lead to an adulterous affair in that story's sequel, "The Storm." Dancing is almost as compromising in Alice Dunbar Nelson's "The Goodness of Saint Rocque" and Eudora Welty's "No Place for You, My Love," when it becomes an outward manifestation of desire, a theme that many of these writers explore, beginning with the poets of Les Cenelles.

Tennessee Williams' iconic 1947 play, *A Streetcar Named Desire*, forever linked New Orleans and the theme of desire, but this theme was well entrenched by the time his play appeared. More often than not, of course, as in Williams' classic, desire leads to no good. Les Cenelles write of the forbidden, yet nonetheless practiced, desire of wealthy white Creoles for young women of color. Fernand's desire is thwarted when he discovers that he is a leper in Dimitry's "Le Tombeau Blanc," and the little convent girl, in Grace King's story of the same title, is the result of that forbidden desire, which in the end leads to her death.

Like *Streetcar* before it, one of Williams' last plays, the 1977 *Vieux Carré*, included here, treats the subject of homosexual desire, and as a playwright, he was a pioneer bringing that subject to the stage. *Vieux Carré* is an autobiographical play, or what Williams called a "memory play," like his first success, *The Glass Menagerie*. In fact, *Vieux Carré* picks up where *The Glass Menagerie* leaves off. The protagonist, Tom (Williams' given name) leaves St. Louis and heads for New Orleans and a job as a writer for the WPA.

The earliest French writers were sent to New Orleans by the crown, but like Williams, many of the 19th and 20th century writers came here for employment. Walt Whitman worked as a journalist for the *New Orleans Crescent*. Lafcadio Hearn came to New Orleans on an assignment for the *Cincinnati Commercial* to write a piece on New Orleans, but he ended up staying and writing for the local *Daily City Item* and later the *Times Democrat* before moving permanently to Japan. Sallie Rhett Roman also wrote for the *Times Democrat*, coming here from Charleston, South Carolina with her new husband, Alfred Roman. O. Henry was in New Orleans on the lam after being indicted for theft while working at a bank in Austin, Texas. Other writers who called New Orleans home temporarily read like a list in *Who's Who*: William Faulkner, Alice Dunbar Nelson, Sherwood Anderson, Francis Parkinson Keyes, Truman Capote, Richard Ford, Everette Maddox, Andrei Codrescu. Similarly, the list of writers who are native to the city but moved elsewhere to continue their careers is just as striking: George Washington Cable, Hamilton

Basso, Valerie Martin, Fatima Shaik.

All of these writers find inspiration in the city's history and culture, from the Native Americans who helped the first western settlers—both black and white—survive, to the city's Spanish and French architecture, to Creole cooking, dance, music, Congo Square, Catholicism, voodoo, hurricanes, *plaçage*, slavery, racism, the Civil War, swamps, plantations, the French Quarter, the Mississippi River, cemeteries, political corruption, and the list goes on. All of it inspires the city's writers and much of this list is the subject of their works collected here.

One of the most difficult aspects of compiling a collection of this breadth is the selection process. I decided that the collection would begin with literature after the Louisiana Purchase, when the territory was under American rule, so many earlier writers, like poet Julien Poydras, who wrote in the 1770s and '80s, are not found here. Naturally, not all the writers whose works appear here live in New Orleans or are natives of the city, but all of them did live here for a time and were inspired by and wrote about the place. I purposefully selected writers and their works that would reveal the city's history, beginning with the French settlers' dealings with the Native American Choctaws in LeBlanc's play and the French Insurrection of 1768 against the first Spanish governor, Ulloa, in Thomas Wharton Collens' *The Martyr Patriots; or, Louisiana in 1769*. After the Louisiana Purchase, Les Cenelles write of the plight of free people of color under American rule. Walt Whitman gives us an outsider's look at the city in 1848, one that resonates in Lafcadio Hearn's writing some thirty years later. The end of the 19th century ushers in the golden age of New Orleans literature, represented here by writers like Grace King, Ruth McEnery Stuart, Alice Dunbar Nelson and George Washington Cable. Notable writers, such as Sherwood Anderson, William Faulkner, and O. Henry, were drawn here at the beginning of the 20th century for one reason or another, and the Isleños' décimas tell their history in song beginning about that time. Near the middle of that century more blockbusters arrive, like Tennessee Williams and Truman Capote. Most of the writers of the mid-to-late 20th century included here are still very active in their craft, like Valerie Martin, Moira Crone, John Biguenet, Richard Ford and Fatima Shaik.

The last comprehensive historical collection of New Orleans literature, *The World from Jackson Square: A New Orleans Reader*, was published in New York in 1848, and edited by Etolia Basso, New Orleans writer Hamilton Basso's wife, and though there have been many other very significant compilations of New Orleans literature published since then, it is high time for another look at the literary evolution of the city. I consulted many of those fine collections in order to compile this one. The 1992, *New Orleans Stories: Great Writers on the City*, edited by John Miller, is a fascinating book comprised of many of the writers included here, like Walt Whitman, Truman Capote, and Tennessee Williams. Judy Long's 2000, *Literary New Orleans* is another invaluable collection of the city's literature, as is the 2003 *French Quarter Fiction*, edited by Joshua Clark, and more recently, the 2006 *My New Orleans: Ballads to the Big Easy by her Sons, Daughters, and Lovers*, edited by Rosemary James. Naturally, there is some overlap in the writers included in these various compendiums, but I decided early on that this would be a collection of *short* literature of the city, hence the abbreviated title, *N.O. Lit*. Thus, also, there are no excerpts from novels or longer works, so some major writers who appear in other New Orleans literary collections are not found here, like Mark Twain, John Kennedy Toole, Zora Neale Hurston, and Walker Percy.

This collection is not intended to be all-inclusive. Instead, I have edited a collection of New Orleans literature in much the same way one curates an art collection. My focus is decidedly historical. I want the literature of New Orleans to tell the city's story, which is why the emphasis is not on current writing. Indeed, the current literary milieu in New Orleans, in nonfiction, fiction, poetry, and drama, is so vibrant that an entire collection could be devoted to the writing of the 21st century alone.

After Katrina and the ensuing flood, so many of the city's writers took pen to paper. Even those outside of the city naturally felt compelled to write about it. And the flood also prompted a new wave of "immigrants" to the city. Latino workers came or were brought here to clean up the destruction the flood left behind, promoting, among their many cultural contributions, a new influx of Spanish language publications. Construction workers came from all over the world to help rebuild the city, as did college students and church groups. The city had an influx of teachers to work in the Recovery School District, and many of those newcomers remained to become a vital part of this rebuilt city. And even though Louisiana is losing its battle against coastal erosion, the state is disappearing, and New Orleans is on the verge of becoming an island in more than a cultural sense, that is not the focus of this collection.

I discovered that the amount of good writing going on in and inspired by this city is never-ending, luckily for readers and lovers of New Orleans literature, but difficult to corral into a book of manageable size. I wanted to create a book that would offer readers the literary evolution of the city through a variety of short genres, including poetry, essays, plays, short stories, and journalism, written by a wide variety of authors in those respective genres. Readers can read the oldest extant play in New Orleans, but also find many of the themes that LeBlanc addresses in that play in Tom Dent's 20th-century, *Ritual Murder*.

Most historians cite the industrialization of the modern world and the two World Wars of the 20th century as the principal causes of the Isleños becoming "Americanized." However, they acknowledge that Katrina and the flood did more to disperse their close-knit community in St. Bernard Parish than any other natural or man-made disaster up to that time, including several U.S. wars and countless hurricanes. In fact, very few Isleño descendants remain who can speak their Spanish language or carry on their tradition of writing and performing décimas. Their island has become smaller and smaller over the years, and so has New Orleans, geographically speaking. Once the largest, most vibrant city in the South, an economic powerhouse boasting one of the world's largest ports, it can now claim only one Fortune 500 Company. With the post-Katrina influx of young teachers, IT workers, artists, oil field workers, and people from all over the world, the city is changing, and like the Isleños community of St. Bernard, is becoming smaller and more assimilated, more Americanized. The literature of New Orleans records times past, and that seems paramount right now, before, as musician Benny Grunch writes of such local institutions as K&B, Krauss, Maison Blanche, Mr. Bingle, Godchaux's, Schwegmann's, Pontchartrain Beach, etc., it "Ain't Dere No More."

Paul Louis LeBlanc De Villeneufve (ca. 1734–1815)

According to the *Dictionary of Louisiana Biography* and the editor and translator of *The Heroism of Poucha-Houmma*, Mathé Allain, this is the earliest extant play performed in Louisiana and written by a Louisiana citizen. It premiered at the Théâtre de la Rue St. Pierre in New Orleans on February 15, 1809, and was published five years later. The author died the year after its publication.

LeBlanc was born in Crest, France to Balthazar LeBlanc in 1734, and he tells us in his introduction to the play that his father died when he was only thirteen years old and that soon thereafter he lost his family fortune. Like many young men of prominent families no longer graced with the attending riches, he joined the French military and was sent to America in 1750. He states that he lived among the "Tchacta" Indians for seven years and that he had only been in Louisiana for a few days when he heard that Poucha-Houmma, the hero of his play, had sacrificed his life for his son, Cala-be. Almost sixty years later, LeBlanc writes this play. He does state in his preface that he talked with Cala-be several times over the years about the death of his father, which is interesting in light of the fact that it seems as if there were no Cala-be exactly.

LeBlanc was a devoted French subject until the Spanish rule of the Louisiana Territory in 1762. When the first Spanish governor, Ulloa arrived in New Orleans in 1766, he was not well received and two years later the citizens rebelled. LeBlanc then worked with acting French governor Aubry to help Spain regain control of the territory. Finally, in 1803, when the French sold the territory to the United States, LeBlanc then pledged his allegiance to that country. However, throughout his military career, he was called on by all the administrations to work with the Native Americans in Louisiana.

In her introduction to LeBlanc's play, Allain writes that since New Orleans newspapers of the time did not review plays, there remains no record of how the play was received by the audience. However, she does translate the theater's enthusiastic announcement of the play on February 15, 1809, in *Le Moniteur de la Louisiane:* "A trait of heroic fatherly love is the subject of this interesting work. The most respected law among the savages is based on reciprocity: a murderer is punished by death. Cala-be, the son of Poucha-houmma, the chief of the Hoummas, killed a Tchacta while drunk. The law condemned him, but the father sacrificed his life to redeem that of his son." Allain seems to believe that since there is no extant record of the performance, the audience reception may have been rather cool. She also states that Governor Claiborne sent a manuscript of the play to then President Thomas Jefferson, but since it does not appear in the 1959 five-volume, *Catalogue of the Library of Thomas Jefferson* that Jefferson, like the New Orleans audience, was not impressed by the play. However, the play is listed among Jefferson's papers on the 2004 website "The Papers of Thomas Jefferson, Retirement Series," thus far a twenty-three volume online collection, and although we do not know what Jefferson thought of LeBlanc's play, or if he even read it, we do know that he thought enough of it to keep it among his papers.[1]

Readers today will certainly find LeBlanc's writing style, the twelve-syllable alexandrine, to be inelegant, but it was the most popular measure in French poetry at the time. More problematic is the slow moving plot of the five-act play. All critics agree that it adheres—perhaps too rigidly—to the Aristotelian unities, but it does so by sacrificing much of the suspense so vital to dramatic tragedy. As Allain notes, the real action of the play takes place in only two of the five acts, Acts III and IV, and that in Acts I and II "the action… is foreshadowed, foreseen, and forecast… then mulled over for an entire act of recapitulation and conclusion," in Act V. Therefore, the plot is predictable, as is the formulaic characterization.

The crime occurs among neighboring Choctaw tribes, which LeBlanc refers to as the Houmma and Tchacta. Poucha-Houmma, the wise and noble Houmma chief, makes the ultimate sacrifice of his own life for that of his rash, young son, Cala-be, who capitulates rather too readily to his father's selfless plan. In fact, once Cala-be is apprised of his father's intent in Act III, Scene iii, he speaks only ten lines in protest of the plan before rationalizing, "Since I betrayed the gods and deserved their anger,/ I must at least obey the will of my father." He

---

1   "The Papers of Thomas Jefferson, Retirement Series," *The Jefferson Monticello, Feb. 2003*,
14 Feb. 2010, http://www.monticello.org/site/research-and-collections/papers.

does not appear again until after his father has been killed.

More interesting than the style or plot of the play is much of its historical value. As LeBlanc notes, this play is based on true events, and he himself was present when the French governor Vaudreuil's Choctaw interpreter delivered the official report of an Indian chief who offered his life in exchange for his son's. However, historian Gordon Sayre, in his 2005 book *The Indian Chief as Tragic Hero*, makes a strong claim that the Indian chief was not a Houma but a Colapissa, that his son was named Tichou Mingo and not Cala-be, and that this account first appeared in Jean-Bernard Boussu's 1768 *Nouveaux Voyages en Louisiane*. According to Bernard, Tichou Mingo murdered a Choctaw Indian who called the Colapissa "dogs of the French." LeBlanc never mentions this incident nor Bernard's book, and in LeBlanc's play he changes the Colapissa to the Houmma Indians. He does not specify the insult that provokes the young Cala-be to murder; however, the Indian customs remain the same.[1]

Cala-be, drunk on "the burning liquid..../Put an end to the days of a Tchacta, a friend," and as custom dictated, the Tchactas would exact revenge by taking Cala-be's life. Alcohol and drunkenness play a large role in New Orleans literature and in the city's culture even today. Pat O'Brien's serves more alcohol than any bar on the planet, and Bourbon Street is world famous. It is still surprising to discover that liquor played such an important part in this city's literary history from the very beginning. But as ignoble as Cala-be might seem, his father is truly the man of "primitive integrity" of whom LeBlanc writes in his dedication.

LeBlanc dedicates his play to Madame De Laussat, the wife of Pierre-Clement De Laussat, the French emissary chosen by Napoleon to reclaim Louisiana for France.[2] Laussat arrived in New Orleans in March of 1803 for the transfer of Louisiana from Spain, an act which was delayed until November of that year, and the following month he officially represented France in the transfer of Louisiana to the United States. Naturally, he and his wife Marie were feted in grand New Orleans style, and she must have made quite an impression on LeBlanc, for he dedicated his play to her some six years later. And having the support of a popular diplomat's wife can only help to insure the success of the play. Interestingly, the Laussat Society exists in New Orleans today.

According to LeBlanc, Madame De Laussat shared his admiration for the Native Americans in Louisiana. He recalls her generosity to "a family of these unhappy people who are called barbaric, whom prejudice rejects, whom pride despises, but whom a soul like yours appreciates and pities." LeBlanc even goes so far as to blame the Europeans for any suffering these tribes have sustained and entreats her to "be their advocate." He writes this play in order to restore them to their former greatness, to proclaim their "generous hospitality" and "most commendable virtues," and he declares that Chief Poucha-Houmma embodies just those admirable qualities that "foreign customs corrupted." In his play, LeBlanc also writes of some of the dubious Indian customs at the time, particularly the "festival of the young corn," the play's alternate title.

LeBlanc describes that festival in his preface:

> Its object was to offer to the Sun the first fruits of their crops. The ceremony of the day consisted essentially of blowing flour made from the new grain three times toward the East. Then they ate some of the flour and danced till the next day. This festival, generally marked by great joy, toward the end became quite unpleasant for the children since they, who otherwise were never beaten no matter what faults they committed, were then cruelly flogged by their own mothers.... Alas! So does custom tyrannize over helpless men in the four parts of the world.

The dramatic staging of this part of the festival reads much like his description in his preface, and he even mentions his own explanation in the stage directions as the mothers leave the stage to beat their children.

LeBlanc claims that the Louisiana Native Americans are far from perfect. He states in his preface that he is more interested in presenting the truth than suppressing objectionable practices, such as flogging their children for no reason other than the fact that, in the words of Poucha-Houmma, "Our fathers have followed this custom/

---

1   Gordon Sayre, *The Indian Chief as Tragic Hero: Native Resistance and the Literatures of America, from Moctezuma to Tecumseh* (Chapel Hill: U of NC Press, 2005), 228.

2   For more on Laussat see Pierre Clément De Laussat, Agnes-Josephine (Mary Barnard) Pastwa, trans., *Napoleon and the United States: an Autobiography of Pierre-Clément De Laussat (1756-1835)* (Lanham, Maryland: University Press of America, 1989).

Ruthlessly prescribed by a grim prophecy." LeBlanc's version of the truth has historical value, to be sure, but that does not always make for an interesting dramatic performance. Indeed, modern readers might find this play often difficult to read, but what LeBlanc has created is a remarkable historical play that captures the European impression of the Native American community during the earliest days of French occupation in South Louisiana.

The Festival of the Young Corn, or The Heroism of Poucha-Houmma[1] A Tragedy in Five Acts[2]

Preface

The Houmma tribe, about which this work is written, was still living thirty years ago on the left bank of the Micha-Sepe,[3] twenty leagues above New Orleans. It sprang from the Natchez nation, being one of its colonies.

I will not speak here of the horrible catastrophe which wiped the Natchez off the earth. But I must say that it was the most civilized and the most hospitable of the tribes which were then known and the only one with a religious cult. Imitating the Ancients whose vanity led them to attribute their origin to some god, the Natchez called themselves the Children of the Sun. They had a temple dedicated to the sun, and there they kept their sacred fire. The Hoummas had carefully preserved the customs and uses of their country; they especially remembered the nobility of their origin. Among their festivals was that of the Young Corn, which they celebrated with true religious fervor. Its object was to offer to the Sun the first fruits of their crops. The ceremony of the day consisted essentially of blowing flour made from the new grain three times toward the East. Then they ate some of the flour and danced till the next day. This festival, generally marked by great joy, toward the end became quite unpleasant for the children since they, who otherwise were never beaten no matter what faults they committed, were then cruelly flogged by their own mothers. No one could explain the custom: "Our fathers," said the savages, "had us flogged harshly at this time. We have our children flogged the same way. If we are wrong, custom is to blame." Alas! So does custom tyrannize over helpless men in the four parts of the world.

In my play I have given the flogging a plausible motive, but, in the interest of truth, I did not suppress it.

I had been in Louisiana but a few days when Poucha-houmma, the hero of my play, sacrificed his life. This chief had often been to New Orleans where he was much admired. His death was talked about, and many versions circulated. The governor of the colony, the Marquis de Vandreuil, who esteemed him greatly for his good qualities and his loyalty to our flag, decided to find out the truth. He sent his interpreter to the scene, and I was present when the governor heard the report.

Sent shortly afterward among the Tchactas, I easily learned their language. This language is spoken by most of the tribes of the region. I have since conversed several times with Cala-be about the details of his father's death. These details are engraved in my memory, and I have written only that which the facts aver.

---

1   Translated by Mathé Allain. From: Mathé Allain, ed. *The Festival of the Young Corn or The Heroism of Poucha-Houmma* by LeBlanc de Villeneufve. (Lafayette: University of Southwest Louisiana Press, 1964), 2-54. Rep. by permission.

2   Author's note: *The Young Corn* is a kind of corn, smaller than ordinary corn, which ripens much earlier. Since it was used for this feast, the festival bore its name.

3   Author's note: *Micha-Sepe:* Transformed into Mississippi, means in the Mobilian language, "the old man far away."

CAST OF CHARACTERS

POUCHA-HOUMMA, *the red manitou*[1], chief of the Houmma nation.

CALA-BE, *the one who won in the game of lacrosse*, son of Poucha-houmma.

TCHILITA-BE, *the one who killed the wicked one,* war chief, younger brother of Poucha-houmma.

FOUCHI, *the bird,* wife of Cala-be.

OULITA-HOUMMA, *the strong red one*, Tchacta envoy.

TASCA-AU-PAYE, *the warrior of warriors*, Tchacta envoy.

NACHOUBA, *the wolf,* scout for the Houmma nation.

WARRIORS of the Houmma nation.

AN ELDER

The scene is set in the village of the Hoummas, on one of the banks of the Micha-Sepe.

ACT I
SCENE I

POUCHA-HOUMMA, TCHILITA-BE, THE TRIBESMEN

POUCHA-HOUMMA: Most noble descendants of a peerless race,
Illustrious children of children of the Sun,
The day of the harvest has come at last.
As you know, our fathers ranked this day
Foremost among the happiest of days.
Never yet, in all my sixty years
Have I failed to celebrate this feast.
Let your contented hearts express themselves in song.
The fertile earth has spread her bounty before you:
Make your offering to our protector.
May he accept gladly your fervent sacrifice!
As for me, sad plaything of a most cruel fate,
I cannot preside over the solemn rite.
Let one of the elders replace me.
I beg this boon of you: allow me to withdraw.
[*Aside*] How wretched I am. That dream pursues me....
TCHILITA-BE: Brother, what sorrow overcomes your reason?
Your tears were flowing long before daylight;
And when the sun appeared, your tears were still flowing.
What reason for alarm disturbs your noble heart?
POUCHA-HOUMMA: Question me not: respect my sorrow.
TCHILITA-BE: What! You will not tell me the cause of your concern?
You want me to watch you in silence as you weep
And shame us by a display of failing courage?

---

1   Author's note: *Manitou*: Fetish, protective god; each nation has its own manitou. Usually it is a bird, a beaver, a squirrel, etc. That of the Hoummas was an eagle.

My brother, my leader, where is your valor?
What did your Manitou say to arouse your grief?
Speak! Conceal nothing of the pain that moves you.

POUCHA-HOUMMA: His ferocious look pursues me everywhere.
I question him in vain. He is deaf to my voice,
And this dreadful bird brooding over the earth,
Somber and still, persists in his silence.

TCHILITA-BE: It is true that we once thought such omens portentous,
But time has schooled us; let us not be deceived.
From that young nation which our fathers favored,
From the French, in a word, let us seek wisdom.
Did we ever see them, calumet[1] in hand
Consulting a bird about peace, about war?
Did we ever see them deceived by oracles,[2]
Or sounding the future that no man can know?
I grieve to see you blinded by error.
You know that I love you. I shall open my heart.
Would that I could banish this poison from your mind,
This evil prejudice, this superstition,
Which blinds you and bewitches you.
I am forced to confess— forgive me—
That I blush secretly at your great weakness.
Your torment stems from error and illusion.
You change in a moment from dejection to hope;
This lifeless eagle, the idol you worship,
Torments you and, as quickly, consoles you.
My brother, assured that nothing on this earth
Can give us foreknowledge of evil or of good,
Let us live the present and have no fear of the future.
Destiny has only feeble arms against us
For man can elude fate at any instant
And is doomed to sorrow only when he fears death.

POUCHA-HOUMMA: Withdraw, Hoummas… and proceed
To prepare yourselves for the ceremony.

SCENE II

POUCHA-HOUMMA, TCHILITA-BE

POUCHA-HOUMMA: You censure unjustly my extreme sorrow.
Know then the dreadful grief which tears my heart.

---

1   Author's note: *Calumet*: A pipe made of stone or earth, the long stem of which is adorned with feathers. No ceremony takes place without the calumet, nor without smoking tobacco.

2   Author's note: *Deceived by oracles*: The village chief is always entrusted with the religious cult. He is the high priest, the magician; he takes auspices and interprets as he wishes the signs which he thinks he saw in his stuffed manitou.

I am compelled to speak and reveal the peril
That threatens us; my patience has wearied.
Be not deceived nor think that, easily alarmed,
I allow unreal fears to crush my spirit.
Who could defend himself against dread such as mine?
Even you, my brother, will flinch when you hear.

TCHILITA-BE: You know me ill if you can believe
That I would flinch in the face of danger.
My soul stands fast and firm against the blows of fate;
I can defy death because I despise life.
Would that the tragedy which makes you so fearful
Could spare our nation and crush me only!
Speak without delay. You may surprise me,
But not frighten me. I can bear anything.

POUCHA-HOUMMA: Your proud and fierce courage has blinded your reason.

TCHILITA-BE: Your Manitou always misleads your reason.

POUCHA-HOUMMA: I know well your error; it will soon disappear.
Brother, at long last, you must learn to know me.
Forty years have I been prophet of our gods
And ruled in their name and governed our land.
Respected minister of our somber cult,
I received my power from our forefathers.
But do not be deceived. My dejected spirit
Has made a virtue of necessity.
I know the hollowness of this foolish worship
And despise secretly the idol and the cult.
You are surprised... I see your amazement.

TCHILITA-BE: I have cause for surprise and do not deny it!
Your conduct has always belied your language.
Why are you denying the gods that you serve?

POUCHA-HOUMMA: Know my secret; I shall disclose it.
I now have no reason to conceal it from you.
The people, forever thirsting for novelty,
Need ceaseless guidance toward righteousness.
We must impose firmly our authority
And must use deception to achieve mastery.
Superstitious from birth, they live like children
Who find contentment in their want of knowledge.
If ever enlightened, they become enraged,
Violate the laws and overthrow the gods.
We must therefore subdue their tottering reason
And make them respectful of imposed prescriptions.
By blurring their judgment, we show them their duty;
We sustain their hope while making them tremble;
On their benumbed senses we force our prestige

In order to prolong their dumb aberration;

We keep them forever in a state of blindness

And flatter their weakness to enslave them better.

TCHILITA-BE: This discourse is indeed a complete surprise.

Do I understand the words you have uttered?

But if you recognize the falseness of your cult,

How could any omen burden your heart today?

POUCHA-HOUMMA: Before your eyes I blush at my extreme weakness.

O wretched Cala-be, guilty son whom I love!

Barely was I tasting the sweetness of slumber…

O night, horrible night… O dread awakening!

Why, why, O why is it, that my weak and dim eyes

Can open still and see… O fatal sunshine,

Refuse, if you can, to brighten such a day,

A day of disaster that I have long dreaded!

TCHILITA-BE: You do not trust my heart and think me a coward.

I cannot understand. Your grief insults me.

Cease distressing me with ambiguous words

And learn to judge better my faithful devotion.

Let me hear, at least, what it is I must do.

Rely on my ardor, rely on my courage.

POUCHA-HOUMMA: O most horrible dream,[1] not without reasons

Do you pour on my heart a most lethal poison!

TCHILITA-BE: Now I breathe again, for despite your protests,

I no longer doubt: it is a dream you fear.

That is the conclusion of your lengthy discourse.

A simple wisp of fog has changed your state of mind;

Your happiness depends on a vain chimera.

You dream; that is enough to make you curse the day;

Your moans of agony are heard through the temple;

Alarm spreads in the tribe; and your brother blushes.

POUCHA-HOUMMA: Augment, if you will, the torment I endure;

Reject my affection, deny our natural bond,

Triumph in my sorrow, add to my grievous care,

Humiliate my old age, tear my heart asunder.

Hardened and cruel heart, no compassion moves you.

Call and bitter reproach are ever on your lips

And all I find in you, unhappy though I be,

Is a stubborn censor who compounds my sorrow!

TCHILITA-BE: In this woeful moment when your sorrowing soul

Delights in draining a venomous potion,

You cannot judge fairly, nor with all your reason,

A brother, a friend who loves you tenderly.

---

1   Author's note: *O most horrible dream*: The savages are great dreamers and believe in dreams. This is a trait they seem to share with civilized nations, with this difference, that the savages dream only when asleep.

I wanted to recall your distracted spirit.
I am a blunderer, a cruel barbarian
Whose zeal, misunderstood by you,
Appears harshly and odiously officious.
I betray my duty and the call of nature
And I have become an infamous traitor.

POUCHA-HOUMMA: Have I understood well? What hateful day has come?
I have offended you! Horror pursues me!
Forgive, if you can. Forgive my weakness,
But an excessive grief is worse than drunkenness.
Do not abandon me in this piteous state.
My brother and my friend, receive me in your arms.

[*He throws himself into the arms of his brother who holds him tenderly and sheds a few tears.*]

TCHILITA-BE: Clasped to my faithful heart, you know I forgive you.
O moment of gladness in the midst of sorrow
When my grieving brother finds refuge in my arms!
Cruel fate, do your worst, or fulfill my wishes
And overpower me to display your power.
I dare defy you! Try my constancy.
Brother, you who were first to see me shed tears,
If I am able to share your burning pain,
Let me learn, at least, this care which crushes you,
This hideous portent, this horrible dream.
Speak without delay and unveil your secrets.

POUCHA-HOUMMA: You want it. I must speak. You shall be satisfied.
Yes, you shall learn the cause of my violent sorrow:
Yesterday, the sun was completing its course
And the dimming luster of its glittering fire
Crowned the West with a pallid glimmer.
I was watching from here the dying sunlight
When my eyes were, alas, closed by a deep slumber.
And then... I remember... O cruel memory....
The earth under my feet seemed to split wide open.
An abyss all at once gaped before my eyes.
Suddenly a vapor, sickening, disgusting,
Surged through the air and flung down by my side
A blood-stained body. Terror seized my heart.
I wanted to be gone when some whimpering words
Spoken in a low moan struck my attentive ear.
"Wretched one, would you flee? I only ask your glance.
Look upon my side and see that gaping wound;
That is the shameful deed of your son Cala-be.
I am Ittela-ia, the victim of his wrath.
The wretch came upon me; in his fierce anger,
He struck repeatedly and at last pierced my heart.

You know that in these climes an immutable law
Demands a slayer's life in payment for his crime.
Tomorrow will be the day long expected
When his blood must be shed before the fall of night."
My weary existence, overwhelmed by horror,
Seemed ready to escape from its enfeebled bonds.
Finally the body disappeared from my eyes
And my dreadful slumber, to my relief, ended.

    TCHILITA-BE: That horrible vision, that sinister portent
May be only the work of your ceaseless worry.
Since the day Cala-be became a criminal,
Peace fled forever from your paternal heart.
Daylight holds no more charms for your sorrowing eyes;
Every day, every hour increases your alarm;
At night your spirit, warped by constant fear,
May have reflected the worries of the day.

    POUCHA-HOUMMA: In vain does your friendship, which I prize greatly,
Try to pour on my wounds a soothing ointment.
A dark premonition, engraved deep in my heart,
Rejects the solace of your solicitude.

    TCHILITA-BE: If you must surrender your agitated soul
To that ceaseless torment, surrender with courage.
Whatever be the end of the day which dawns,
Confront it with a peaceful countenance.
I am not convinced that on this festive day,
The sorrow you foresee will disturb your life.
Cala-be, thanks to you, escaped from the Tchactas
And is at this moment with the Attac-Apas.
I know that he has won the friendship of their chief,
Panchi, your dear friend, whose respect he has earned.
That tribe looks on him with very kindly eyes
And speaks already about an adoption;
They say that your friend received him in his home
And plans secretly to give him his daughter.

    POUCHA-HOUMMA: I know it well, yet I fear. You have had no children
And could never conceive the torment I endure.

SCENE III

POUCHA-HOUMMA, TCHILITA-BE, A WARRIOR

    THE WARRIOR: I have come to announce that with some impatience
The tribe already awaits you at the temple.
We see them, their hearts filled with love and respect
For the divine father who has begotten us.

Moreover a canoe approaches our shores.

Its occupants three times have signalled in friendship

And several already have recognized your son.

   Poucha-houmma: You say that… Cala-be….

   The Warrior: Yes, Cala-be, himself.

Our whole nation rejoices at his sight.

   Poucha-houmma: O unexpected blow! Instant all too fatal!

How well justified was my dark foreboding!

   [*He brings his hand to his brow, seems to meditate a moment, then tells the warrior*]

That is enough. Leave me. I have nothing to say.

My son has returned home; I can barely breathe.

Scene IV

Poucha-houmma, Tchilita-be

   Poucha-houmma: Who could ever explain the strange premonitions

Which sometimes reveal the secrets of our fate

And, disclosing to us our sad destinies,

Make us suffer in anticipation?

You see, brother, heaven in its anger,

Brings back to me this son I believed safe afar.

Already I relive the course of my dream!

   Tchilita-be: I can see no evil in such an occurrence.

Your son came to see you and will soon depart,

As soon as tomorrow if that is essential.

But let us wait a while; we shall see him later.

You must conceal from him the sorrow you endure.

   Poucha-houmma: Ah! Indeed, I must! But how to hide it,

This sorrow that my heart cannot learn to conquer?

ACT II
Scene I

Poucha-houmma, Tchilita-be, the Tribe

   Poucha-houmma: I hear that my son, no doubt unwisely,

Sails toward our shores in a hurried course.

Whatever his reason, his imprudent return

Will delay a little the day's festivities.

I want to see him first. My eager impatience

Brooks no delay. Here he comes toward us.

Kind and merciful God, our benefactor,

Protect us from sorrow on this most solemn day;

Deign to watch over us and dissipate the storm

Which threatens to darken our sky, our land.

Scene II

Poucha-houmma, Tchilita-be, the Tribe, Cala-be, Fouchi

Cala-be [*Throwing himself into his father's arms*]
My father, I have returned to you at last!
    Poucha-houmma: In order to cause me a mortal pain, my son.
Have you forgotten that cruel nation
Thirsts for your blood to the very last drop?
That the mighty Tchactas, angered by refusals,
Could at any instant.... But let us say no more,
And forget, if we can, the fatal memory
Which has poisoned the peace of my remaining days.
Who is the young maiden whom I see at your side?
    Cala-be: Panchi's daughter whom I love above all.
I could never tell you how dear she is to me.
Take her into your arms. Let her find a father.
    [*He leads her toward his father who receives her with demonstrations of lively affection.*]
    Poucha-houmma: What tender sentiment do I feel in my breast?
How pleasant it is! How it swells my heart!
I forget at this time even my worst fears.
My daughter, in your arms let me shed joyful tears.
They flow from happiness. Happy would I be....
Alas! May your eyes never know any tears.
    Fouchi: I followed my husband and walked without fear.
I braved the changing moods of violent elements;
I left my country, my parents, and my gods
And abandoned all things to follow my husband.
I lacked only one thing for complete happiness:
The gracious welcome that you have given me.
May our creator, our sole protector,
Watch with attentive care over all your days.
    Cala-be: Father, you hear her! Her soul is sweet and pure,
And admits sentiments that nature sanctifies.
She will love you well, and loving both of us,
Will fill her fortunate husband with happiness.
    Poucha-houmma: [*Aside*] In what amazement my soul plunges again!
Unexpected pleasure, are you only a dream?
Will I have discovered the joy of their presence
Only better to feel my desperate anguish?
[*Aloud*] My children, my mind seems almost delirious.
My senses are disturbed; I am happy; I sigh....
Let us leave this subject. Relate to me, my son,
What troubles assailed you upon leaving these shores.
    Cala-be: You must remember well when, trapped, defenseless,

I escaped with your help from a revengeful foe.
A single instant lost could change my fate:
I was obliged to choose between flight and death.
The immense vault, of night shrouded the sky.
I fled. To the sunset I directed my steps;
Into the deep waters I plunged frequently
To attain my goal more directly.
It was in this manner that without mishap
I concealed my tracks from the swift Tchactas.
The first rays of the sun, which finally appeared,
Lighted my footsteps and ended my terror.

      Poucha-houmma: O Sun, finish your task and show forth your power,
Remove from all hearts the harsh thirst for vengeance.
Deign to fulfill my wish, O God of my people.
Can you accept, alas…? I do listen, my son.

      Cala-be: After twenty days of effort and of pain,
I discovered at last the Attac-Apas' plain.
I advanced wearily. Weariness and hunger
Threatened already to end my life.
Banished from my people, exiled from my father,
And seeking the help of a foreign nation,
I wandered hopelessly in the midst of forests.
Pursued relentlessly by consuming remorse,
I could have faced death with great indifference.
No courage can prevail against excessive grief:
My fortitude, broken, no longer sustained me.
I would have surrendered to my sad destiny
When all at once I saw under a maple tree
A venerable man seated among warriors.
With a serene look he observed my course.
I stopped immediately. All things revealed my pain.
Livid and disfigured, at anyone's mercy,
I could not have inspired mistrust in anyone.
A young man suddenly advanced toward me.
He had a gentle look and, extending his hand,
"Friend," said he, "you seem very disturbed.
We can help you, but first: what purpose brings you here?
My chief sends me to you to ascertain your aim;
Conceal nothing from us, whatever be your hopes."
I answered him: "Alas! you see my misery.
I was born a Houmma; my father is their chief.
My life endangered, I fled to this country….
Such is the truth, without lie or deceit."
After this confession we walked in silence,
And soon I found myself before the proud elder.

Having learned who I was, he appeared satisfied;
His gestures and his glance expressed his interest.
He spoke immediately and to my great surprise
Uttered these words in a most loving tone:
"Stranger, whom a strange and severe destiny
Has led to our land, through a hundred perils.
Be reassured, I beg you. Fear not an evil fate.
You may assume a place among us today:
Your fellow citizens taught me in other times
The immutable laws of hospitality.
Conceal nothing from us; speak forth in complete trust.
Why have you been banished from the land of your birth?"
"Chief," I answered him, "I shall open my heart.
I need conceal nothing of my dreadful sorrow.
You know the effects of the burning liquid.
It clouded my reason. Filled with horrible thoughts,
I seized a dagger, and my merciless hand
Put an end to the days of a Tchacta, a friend.
Unhappy violator of the laws of the tribe,
I fled from my country to protect my life."
Then, as I remembered my wretched trouble,
My tears began to flow and flowed without restraint.
Their mute language, my pain, my frankness, my remorse
Soon became the cause of a pleasing surprise.
Tears escaped from the eyes of the noble elder.
He drew me to his breast and, blessing the gods,
"Listen to me," he said, "Young brave whom I admire,
And share, if possible, my extreme happiness.
In you I discover the son of my friend
And can repay, at last, many acts of kindness.
If your father ever recounted to you
Our wars, our battles, and his great victories,
You know that by him I was liberated,
I who was his captive. For my name is Panchi."
At these words I was filled with a great happiness
And held out my arms. We embraced each other.
This fortunate instant, reawakening hope,
Held for me promises of a happy future.
After eight days of rest, I regained my strength,
And we proceeded toward Panchi's village.
His tribe received me with shows of affection
And the happy morrow witnessed my adoption.
Your friend received me into his family.
He paid his debt to you when he gave me his child.
In this way, father, has a harsh destiny

After great suffering brought me to happiness.

POUCHA-HOUMMA: O my son, destiny is impenetrable
And often betrays us when it seems most gracious.
You should not put your trust in a flattering hope.
It is easy to stray when the path is not clear:
The road to happiness is only seen faintly
And frequently exists only in our dreams.

SCENE III

PRECEDING ACTORS, A WARRIOR

THE WARRIOR: The father of our race, object of our cult,
Has climbed already to the height of heaven.
He goes down now. His swift disappearance
Will soon leave only night in the vast emptiness.
We see regretfully that the hour passes,
Appointed for the feast which you must celebrate.
The council of elders, sparked by a divine fire,
Dispatched me towards you to bring you the tidings.

POUCHA-HOUMMA: Return immediately and inform the elders
That I shall soon perform my pious duties.
Warriors, go before me. Be ready in your places
And announce my coming. I shall follow your steps.
Delay not, my son, and follow the warriors.
Take Fouchi with you. Do not abandon her.
To you Tchilita-be, I need give no order.
However, I do have something to tell you.
I must for a moment, without any disguise,
Discuss here with you my darkest forebodings.

SCENE IV

POUCHA-HOUMMA, TCHILITA-BE

POUCHA-HOUMMA: How changed are the times! Once, this festive day
Fulfilled the desires of my satisfied heart.
Today, pierced to the core by a sinister fear,
I feel my soul besieged by a cruel portent.
I seem to see rivers of the blood of Houmma
Flowing over the land in a dreadful slaughter.
Cries of pain, mournful tones seem to sound in my ears
And my soul responds to so sad a vision.

TCHILITA-BE: With thoughts colored by your fears,
You yield too readily to your distraught reason;
You surrender yourself without a struggle

And fall weakly before a mere shadow;
You no longer feel hope, and your wandering eyes
See a ghost behind you, dogging your every step.
The zeal and the valor of our brave warriors
Can no longer dispel the terror in your heart.
You choose to ignore me and I am naught to you!
You weaken my strong arm and you slight my courage.
In your crushing sorrow, you remember no more
That vanquished enemies have perished at my feet.
Forgive me at this time my lack of modesty.
It is not willingly that I vaunt my prowess.

    POUCHA-HOUMMA: You have failed utterly to understand the fear
Which agitates my heart in this cruel instant.
I know only too well your pride and your courage.
It is the thing I fear; it is the black portent
Which weighs upon my heart and which makes me shudder.
Your proud disposition could never be softened.
The savage arts of war which are your chief delights
Could lead to reverses fatal to the nation.
You would not surrender, even when outnumbered,
And would at any price save the life of my son.
All this traces for me a doleful picture.
Alas! There is one hope that is still left to me:
Since the laws condemn me, I shall abide by them.
I owe my people peace and happiness.
Let us end the struggle; let us pay the debt.
Justice clamors for blood and wants a sacrifice,
But since I will not yield the life of my dear son,
Can I not offer mine, which time will soon ravish?

    TCHILITA-BE: I had not expected this amazing offer.
It is noble, indeed, well worthy of praise.
But I know other means which we can, if need be,
Use to good advantage. It will be my care
To tell you about them at another moment.
Enough. Too long has the tribe waited.
Let us go quickly. Forget your cares a while.
The awaiting nation calls for your presence.
Let us go my brother, let us go assuage
The just impatience which is devouring them.

ACT III
SCENE I

ALL THE ACTORS ARE ON STAGE.

POUCHA-HOUMMA: [*Assisted by two of the elders*]
Nation that I cherish, on this solemn feast day,
Let your ardent prayers rise toward the heavens.
Abundance has rewarded your harassing labors;
Let your hearts open in profound gratitude.
We have now been freed from the fear of hunger:
Our wives and children will no more be driven
To search for nourishment in the thick of forests.
For such great benefits, offer you: first fruits
To our creator. Thank him fervently.
Women, do not delay. Come as I have bid you.
Let everyone of you present her offerings.
Show your respect and your submission
By fulfilling the task with humble mien.

[*The women come. The first carries a large basket which she places on the altar before Poucha-houmma. Those who follow bear little baskets filled with corn flour which they pour into the large basket. They assemble at the left.*]

TCHILITA-BE: Warriors, draw closer. Your awesome countenance
Will impose reverence upon the multitude.
Let your vigilant care repress in this forest
Whatever might disturb the religious ritual.

[*The warriors assemble at the right, Tchilita-be at their head. They carry only their tapinas, a sort of wooden club.*]

[*To the women*] Join to our voices the sweetness of your songs,
You whose attentive care produced the fields of corn,
Whose assiduous work made nature more fruitful.
Gather close to you the youngest of your sons
That, all together, our blended voices
May rise in thankful praise to the best of fathers.

[*At the same time he takes a handful of flour which he throws toward the East by blowing on it. He repeats the same ceremony three times, each time singing a stanza of the following hymn, repeating the refrain.*]

Hymn to the Sun [*To the tune of "Quand le fier Baron d'Etange"*]

Pure and unchanging being,
Sole creator of the world,
Clear and delectable source
From which our happiness flows,
We offer to you the fruits
Which have grown in our fields.

O sole ruler of the world,
Deign to receive our gifts.

Whenever your shining disk
Drives away the somber night,
We worship you in silence
And Nature smiles back at you.
We offer to you the fruits
Which have grown in our fields.
O sole ruler of the world,
Deign to receive our gifts.

Sun, during this festive day,
We offer to you our hope:
Fulfill all our wishes
And scatter our enemies.
We offer to you the fruits
Which have grown in our fields.
O sole ruler of the world,
Deign to receive our gifts.

To impress this feast on the innocent beings
Who grow before our eyes and delight our age,
A dreadful duty must be fulfilled now.
Mothers, you must obey that cruel command:
Let your youngest children be chastised by your hands
Though everyone of them be innocent of wrong.
Alas! Our fathers have followed this custom
Ruthlessly prescribed by a grim prophecy.
In this important rite which you will now perform
Forget, if possible, whom you are chastising.
Probably our God, in his profound wisdom,
Wants to know if your hearts are strong in his service.
    [*The women leave and take with them their smallest children. A little later they should be heard screaming from pain, and all the actors on stage should manifest a sadness mixed with awe. In the Preface I spoke of this dreadful ceremony.*]
The sun is setting and soon his last radiance
Will gild the green foliage of our dark forest.
We are now allowed, without any offence,
To restore our bodies weakened by the long fast.[1]
[*To the women*] Have some of the new grain served immediately
To appease the hunger of elders and children.
[*To Tchilita-be*] Above all, in this day of happy rejoicing,

---

1   Author's note: *...the long fast*: The fasting of savages is very strict. On some occasions they take absolutely nothing for three days.

Curb the eagerness of our impatient youths.

Scene II

Preceding actors, Nachouba

Poucha-houmma: You return this early! What tidings do you bring?
Nachouba, I fear much. Speak without delay.
You appear bewildered; my sad and fearful heart
Already has portents of what you will recount.

Nachouba: In order to obey your secret commands
I have walked the forests since the sun first appeared.
Not far from the river, in the midst of some ferns,
I noticed a foot print, barely perceptible.
Worried, I followed it. I walked very slowly;
My eyes attentively glanced far ahead of me.
After much wandering, in a well favored place,
I saw a fearful group of Tchacta warriors.
With many precautions I approached the group
To ascertain their chief and their position.
At last I recognized, seeing his cruel eyes,
Oulitacha-mingo.... Forgive me if my lips
Dare not pursue further a painful recounting.
Two of his envoys follow upon my steps.

Poucha-houmma: Two envoys, did you say? What purpose brings them here?
I can breathe no longer. Your report torments me.
Finish. What do you know about their intentions?

Nachouba: Since they often mentioned your son, Cala-be,
I fear that in this place where we hold our feast
They will soon appear clamoring for his head.

Poucha-houmma: I am deeply grateful for the zeal you showed.
You may withdraw for now. In this sad moment
I must take precautions and give a few commands.
If I have need of you, I shall send you orders.
[*To his brother*] So, they have come near, these hateful Tchactas!
I shall have to endure their presence on my land.
For the second time their odious presence
Will startle our souls with a cry of revenge.
At the mere thought of it, I shudder; and my heart
Becomes filled with anger and with wrathful fury.
I renounce forever my fears and my alarms.
I shall be first, brother, to take up my weapons.
Let heaven, if it will, end my life today!
I shall at least die with a dagger in my hand.

Tchilita-be: I admire your anger and your virile fury,

But you must remember that as the highest priest
Of our gods, you may not desecrate
The hands with which daily you adorn their altars.
The task is mine, brother! I shall dispel the storm.
You know well the courage of our fierce warriors:
Entrust to our care the task of humbling
Anyone who dares defy us on our land.
However, I believe that we should lend an ear
To the deputation which is coming here.
Oulitacha-mingo has plans that we must learn,
And then we can pursue our best interest.

   Poucha-houmma: I shall yield, if I must, to my impatience.
Destiny has always, alas, deceived my hopes.
I shall see them again, those inhuman beings,
Those cowards, those thieves, these infamous killers
Who only take action in the dark of the night,
Or if they outnumber defenseless enemies.
At the slightest success they forget their own gods;
Yet the slightest defeat makes them devout again.[1]
But, we must dissemble. We may, in justice,
Resort to artifice and tempt their greedy souls.
In some situations it is not a disgrace
To seek devious ways to achieve a purpose.
Let us spread my treasures before their loathsome eyes.
I shall surrender all of my possessions,
Since my people, I hope, will still tend to my needs.
But I must first of all consult our nation.
O Nature! Lend me your most sublime language!
[*To the people*] My people who ever have shared in my sorrows,
You whom forty winters I have ruled lovingly,
Who entrust to my care your life and happiness,
You can serve your leader while serving your nation.
To save a citizen, to snatch him from death,
Deserves a generous gesture on your part.
You know the sordid greed of the vile Tchacta.
He is ever avid to take and to receive;
He will break sacred laws, and forget promises;
And his lust for revenge dies before rich presents.
My son is in danger: that will tell you clearly
What my heart wants from you at a time such as this.

   An Elder: O unhappiest of chiefs, repress any terror.
The people cherish you; rely upon their faith.
Satisfied with their fate, happy under your care,

---

1 Author's note: *Yet the slightest defeat makes them devout again*: Man is the same everywhere. In prosperity the native neglects his manitou.

They will without regret make any sacrifice.

POUCHA-HOUMMA: [*Kneeling*] Our common father whom I kneel to implore,
Keep your anger ever away from my people.
Witness of my hopes, you who have seen my fears
Deliver my tribe from the violence of war.
[*Getting up*] My fellow citizens, my children, my friends,
We must postpone again the pleasures of this day.
Our sky has clouded, but may yet clear again.
I must now consult my son and my brother.
Leave us a moment. I would ward off the blows
The treacherous Tchactas could inflict upon you.

[*The tribe leaves.* FOUCHI *withdraws to the wings and listens.*]

SCENE III

POUCHA-HOUMMA, TCHILITA-BE, CALA-BE

POUCHA-HOUMMA: Past examples always must guide our conduct.
Their notable lessons are there to instruct us.
Is there need to recall the baneful night
The memory of which forever pursues me
When the black treachery of the sly Tchactas
Set fire to our land in the shadow of peace?
This hideous action clearly evinces
That we have cause to fear from their revengeful ire.
Cala-be must depart instantly from these shores;
It is the only way to lighten my burden.
My brother, in your hands I commend my son:
Go to the other shore without tarrying.
Each minute is precious; the storm thunders near us;
Waste no time in your flight across our river
And when at last you think that he is in safety,
Hurry back to comfort by your loving presence
The dreadful anxiety of my disturbed mind.
My son without delay, flee from your native land
And receive the farewell of your grieving father. [*He embraces him.*]

CALA-BE: I cannot go. Father, I beg you, have mercy
And change a decision which pains me grievously.
In this cruel struggle, should I play the coward
And deprive my tribe of the help of my arm?
On this day, your honor forbids that I flee
Since it is for my sake that blood may be shed.
Am I not the culprit who crowns the affliction
Of a nation that must abhor my name?
My father, I must be the one to give my life.

Would that a Tchacta knife had taken it before!

Scene IV

Preceding actors, Fouchi

Fouchi: [*Kneeling before Poucha-houmma*]
Father of my husband, if my intense sorrow
Deserves your compassion in this cruel moment,
Cast a look of pity on your tearful daughter.
You shall see her a prey to fearful despair,
If you do not revoke that most cruel decree
Paternal affection has dictated to you.
Nature protests in you, but let honor move you!
To save Cala-be, would you make him abject?
Ah! If ever my eyes must look upon his death,
At least let him perish with his honor intact.
Let a most glorious death put an end to his life.
The daughter of Panchi, weeping at your feet,
Hopes that you will grant the wish of her husband.
She would rather bear, in the eyes of her tribe,
The despair of his death than of his dishonor.

Tchilita-be: Her noble sentiments, her charming candor,
Her sorrowful accents, and her extreme pain,
The respect that you owe her noble origin,
And the danger less close than you seem to believe,
All things command you to desist from your plan.
Besides, can man hinder the decrees of fate?

Poucha-houmma: Your sentiments and mine are ever opposed.
True, we cannot avoid the anger of heaven,
But we can soften it by watchful precaution
And sometimes, moreover, can escape from its blows.
[*To Fouchi*] My daughter, I am grieved to see your tears flow.
Though honor has laws, prudence also has charms,
And we can reconcile both of them today.
Prudence weighs carefully advantages and risks
And gives assistance to a real honor.
One yields sometimes without lacking courage.
It is treachery which threatens your husband.
Would you have him exposed to treacherous blows?
Withdraw and leave me here filled with hope
To satiate the Tchactas' desire for revenge.
This distasteful duty you must entrust to me.
I shall ward off the blow; and if necessary,
[*To Cala-be*] You shall come back my son, to show by your courage

That your heart is at least worthy of your race.

May you deserve today the prompt aid of the gods!

For the last time, my son, I bid you farewell.

>   [*He embraces him a second time.*]

>   Cala-be: Since I betrayed the gods and deserved their anger,

I must at least obey the will of my father. [*They leave*.]

ACT IV
Scene I

>   Poucha-houmma: I have sent them away; they have gone at last.

Without my brother and my son, I am free

To follow the dictates of my heart.

Let us try to learn the plans of the Tchactas;

Let us cover the blood[1] and spread before their eyes

The most precious treasures possessed by my people.

Let us put an end, it is time, to my fears.

The worst of suffering comes from uncertainty

And today at last, free to act out my plans,

I shall alter my fate or end my life.

I must spare my people the horrors of warfare;

I must not allow blood to be spilled on this land.

How can I, who should be the shield of my people,

Let them spill their blood in defense of my own?

If today the Tchactas demand a sacrifice,

At least, let it be one that justice would approve.

Unhappy Cala-be, what will you do, alas,

When you learn of my plan…?

Scene II

Poucha-houmma, Nachouba

>   Nachouba: I have come to warn you

That the two envoys whom we were awaiting

Ask to be admitted in your presence, my chief.

What are your wishes? Will you receive them

Or tell me at what time you will want to see them?

>   Poucha-houmma: They have waited longer than I should have wished.

I want to see them now and learn for myself

What results to fear from their vengeful anger.

Nachouba, the tribe must be present here.

Summon them, if you please. I hope by their presence

---

1   *To cover the dead or the blood of the dead:* That is to pay the relatives for the life of the murdered man. The relatives do not always accept this substitute.

To inspire confidence and to command respect.

Yet, our warriors in this critical time

Should prepare themselves for any contingence.

I entrust to you the post of my brother.

We must always mistrust that unsteady nation

Which covers its design and knows no other law

Than the shameful rights acquired through treachery.

You may withdraw. And may your diligence

Be great enough to suit my eager impatience.

Scene III

POUCHA-HOUMMA: So it has come at last this expected moment

Which should liberate me from my cruel torment.

Alas, how wrong we are to treasure life

Which is filled with worry, pain, and bitterness.

Life seems to me a horrendous abyss.

I feel only hatred for its slow moving course,

And death, whose very name disturbs our life,

Seems a happy haven of silence and peace,

Of calm and rest. Dead, we forget our pain,

And death puts an end to our erring ways.

We live but a short time; youth soon flies away.

Its frivolous pleasures yield to maturity,

Quickly followed by decrepitude

Which brings a thousand woes harder to bear than death.

Dreaded senility! Pitiful victim

Of age which benumbs you, you have only breath left;

You have only time to lament your sorrows;

Your paltry condition is less even than death.

Why then should you fear to see your journey's end?

Is it necessary that life run its full course?

And when the blow of fate strikes us repeatedly,

Should we, like cowards, accept to endure them?

But when we are bereft of that pure essence

Which infused life and thought into the being—

—That being from whom sprang the nations of the earth—

Whom a creator once fashioned with his hands,

What becomes of that soul, the source of his thought

Which makes him superior to the degraded beast?

When, as swift as lightning it escapes from the flesh,

Does it evaporate into the thin ether?

Or being free at last from the impure matter,

Is it reunited with the God of nature?

How much this cruel doubt stirs me and disturbs me!

O you who limited our understanding
And displayed before us your infinite power,
Your goodness gives us hope of an immortal life.
Your works could never be dissolved to nothingness:[1]
A secret voice gives us a dim premonition.
This hope is not empty! It sustains my courage.
A serene appearance will be mine when I die.
This is the conclusion of my meditation.
I feel stronger now; my doubts have left me.
However, let us see what wealth may accomplish.
Kind deeds can sometimes smother vengeful thoughts.
But if my gifts should fail, my decision is made:
You will live, Cala-be, but I know at what price.

[*The tribesmen come on stage, each Houmma carrying precious gifts. The warriors carrying their tapinas come also.*]

SCENE IV

POUCHA-HOUMA, THE NATION, THE WARRIORS

POUCHA-HOUMMA: Descendants of the Sun, children of his love,
Sustain my courage in this unhappy day.
Forgive me if my eyes at this painful moment
Reveal the suffering of my wounded heart.
Cala-be has never been a real criminal.

---

1   *Your works could never be dissolved to nothingness:* I was crossing a fairly large and uninhabited forest; I had with me only a Tchacta; the heat was excessive and water very scarce. Thirst devoured us. My young guide was rolling a ball in his mouth. I understood that it was to refresh his mouth. I put one in my mouth and immediately felt much better. (I mention this only as a piece of useful advice.) Toward evening on the second day of our trek we reached a much frequented spring. We quenched our thirst, and I started lighting a fire to cook our meager supper. My young guide went in search of wood. He had not been gone more than ten minutes when I saw him come back, running as fast as he could, toward the place where we had deposited our little baggage. He seized his package, took his gun, and disappeared like lightning without saying a word. Amazed by his flight, I thought he had seen some enemies and that it would be prudent to imitate him. Consequently I rushed after him. My man was very swift, and despite all my effort I was losing hope of catching up with him when he stopped at last, after running a full quarter of a mile. Having joined him I asked him, all out of breath and a trifle nettled, what had prompted him to run so fast. "A *soulombich*, my Frenchman," answered he, still frozen with fear.

This is the fact: some hunters, who had preceded us at the spot we had left so swiftly, had lost a man, and, according to custom, had exposed him on a scaffold while waiting for his family to come to gather his bones. Chance led my companion toward this terrible scaffold. In the darkness, deepened still by the shadows of the forest, he had seen it only when he found himself underneath it. He told me that then he had felt a numbness penetrating his limbs, a numbness which rendered him motionless. First he closed his eyes, but having opened them involuntarily he had seen the *soulombich* wandering over the corpse, occasionally emitting sparks of fire similar to those produced by grains of powder sprinkled on burning coals. Having at last reminded himself that he was a man, he decided he should not be afraid, but that he should leave as quickly as possible for the *soulombich* was growing angry.

It is possible that my young guide may really have seen in part the phenomenon he had described. Without being a physicist one can conceive it. Whatever it was, considering what I have just related, I had to believe that the Tchactas at least have some notion of the immortality of the soul. The *soulombichs* are visible only after sunset and are not to be feared by day. The bravest Tchactas would not dare spend the night near the hut in which the bodies of the dead are deposited.

You know him, my friends, worthy of your esteem.
He has shared your play and shared your labors,
Followed you in battle and triumphed before you.
Guileless, obedient to the ancestral cult,
He was my joy during happier days:
Those days are no longer. He flees from these shores,
Abandoned to his grief, tormented by remorse.
That is indeed the price one should pay for a crime.
But the crime of my son was not willfully done.
Bereft of reason, he became a slayer:
The fiery water maddened him, steered his hand.
Yet the Tchactas, unjust in their hatred,
Want him to suffer a murderer's death.
On this horrible day, too slow to end, alas,
I have little hope to soften their wrath.
Whatever happens, rely on my prudence:
My heart holds in horror the violence of warfare,
And if blood is needed to appease our foes,
Be assured that I know whose blood should be shed.
Let us another time endure their presence,
Their pride, their aspect which alone quickens wrath;
Let us bear meekly their arrogant manner;
And with our presents let us tempt their eyes.
We must adapt our ways to circumstances!
Here they are. Heaven, uphold my courage,
And allow the excess of my frightening woe
To excite their pity and affect their hearts!

Scene V

PRECEDING ACTORS, TASCA-AU-PAYNE, OULITA-HOUMMA

[*They shake hands with Poucha-houmma and then with the other actors. They sit down; someone gives them a pipe; then, this ceremony over, Tasca-au-paye arises and speaks.*]

TASCA-AU-PAYE: Most fortunate nation whom fate ever favored,
Forgive the blunt frankness of a Tchacta warrior.
We all know that the French, softening your manners,
Are your protectors and your benefactors.
But do not imagine that, forgetting justice,
That generous nation will be your accomplice.
You know well that they too make a noble effort
To punish murderers with infamy and death.
Safety requires it and Nature herself
Engraved in every heart that supreme sentiment.
I have not come here to obtain your assent

Through the rambling of idle discourses.
Fortune, believe me, may yet deceive your hopes;
She has showed you favors, but she is inconstant.
From her heights quite often man is hurled into pain,
And must suffer her blows and endure her whims.
You enjoy her favor, fear then her sudden change:
A clear and happy day sometimes precedes a storm.
I have spoken enough; you understand my wish.
You know that if we must we shall meet you again;
If you do not wish me to remain on your land,
Surrender to me the head of Cala-be.
Only by such a price will our desire be filled
And peace reign again between our nations.

     NACHOUBA: We regret to see you; we shudder to hear you.
What hope has misled you? What do you dare expect?
Cala-be did no wrong to your nation
Save a crime committed when deprived of reason.
However, to the law we are all obedient
And offer to make you masters of all you see.
     [*He shows the presents on stage.*]
This should suffice, I think, to compensate his crime.
Take it all. May we never see you again.
Farewell. May the Tchactas enjoy the sight of you.

     TASCA-AU-PAYE: [*Aside*] I can breathe no longer, my soul is so angered!
[*Aloud*] If I had had to speak to the fierce Talapouch,
I would have said nothing but with weapons in hand.
Before the Hoummas, I thought I could expect
Courteous attention, not offensive words.
I had praised too much the virtue of their hearts;
I had not known the truth. I see my error now!
[*To Nachouba*] And you, who shows pride worthy of a warrior,
Think you to frighten me by so violent a speech?
Do you know who I am? Do you know the Tchactas?
Go. Keep your fierceness for the days of fighting.
There you will be able to satisfy your ire,
Defying your foes and serving your country.
Master yourself better in council, I advise,
For pride when displayed there arouses but contempt!

     POUCHA-HOUMMA: Worthy warriors who witness my terror,
If my dreadful sorrow does not delight you,
If my state of despair and my violent torment
In this cruel instant can touch your compassion,
In this young warrior who has disobeyed me
See but the expression of an excessive zeal.
I shall quickly repress, by a just show of wrath,

A misguided violence which grieves all the Hoummas.
But you who among us come to demand justice,
Making pressing demands for the grim sacrifice
Of a head which you say we must yield to your hands,
Do you honestly think we must give it to you?
Can a man be guilty when bereft of reason?
Could your law be cruel to such extreme degree?
I cannot believe it. Do you really deny
That where no reason dwells, no crime is committed?
Nevertheless I will cover the blood shed
And quench in some manner your desire for revenge.
Please accept our gifts. Let peace reign between us
And let angry discord be laid down forever.

OULITA-HOUMMA: My nation has always been faithful to its laws
And would never suspect that you were rebellious.
Even I at this time cannot fully believe
That you wish to deny the power of the laws.
Among us the Hoummas were believed sage and wise.
Is justice no longer dwelling in your village?
What! Even though an evil murderer
Wielded his dagger with a merciless hand,
You want to exchange wealth for our vengeance,
To buy our dead and leave him unavenged?
You would bury the dead and choke in our soils
The voice which arouses the wrath of our hearts!
Do not flatter yourselves. In vain with your great skill
Will you spread before us the temptation of wealth
And attempt to disarm our lawful anger
By dazzling our eyes and tempting our hearts.
In a violent fit of insane despair,
You hold us base enough to be seduced by gifts!
We have not left behind our wives and children
To blush when we return loaded with your presents.
You who listen to me, you of a divine race,
Do not degrade your illustrious birth.
Always honor justice, and the torch of heaven
Will shine on your nation with undying brightness.
You venerable chief, made desperate by fate,
Sorrowing being, most unhappy father,
I share your suffering and feel your pain;
But a sacred duty must dictate to my heart.
Forgive my harshness before your broken heart.
Nature shudders in me; but call on your courage
And listen to its voice. Let a noble effort....

POUCHA-HOUMMA: [*Aside*] I listen no longer. I go to my death!

[*To the people*] Withdraw please, my people. Let us end this council.
I must finish alone this melancholy day.
[*After they leave*] I shall endure my fate and yield to destiny.
Most exacting Tchactas, you shall be satisfied.
Without any fears and without delay,
My blood will seal the peace between our nations.
Yes, my blood must be shed in repayment of yours.
I can fulfill quietly that painful duty.
You appear dumbfounded. Listen to me again,
Since I am determined. I can explain to you
That to save my son's life, I yield myself to you.
My head will fall beneath your blows.
Let us go swiftly. Time passes and presses.
Tear an aging warrior from the pains of old age.
By delaying a day you may lose your revenge.
You will see me die with a firm countenance;
As for my son, listen, you may lose any hope
Of sacrificing him to the god of revenge.
He has gone far from here; and I hope that never
Will anyone see you triumphing over him.
Tell me now, if any among you are fathers,
If you have children, should the anger of fate
Try suddenly today to ravish them from you,
To force you to watch them slaughtered under your eyes,
Would you help to fulfill so cruel a decree?
Would you relinquish them to a murderous sword?
Look into your heart. Listen to its dictates.
Your eyes are turned away, I can see you shudder.
Your courage has vanished. A simple example
Reawakened in you the voice of nature.
My head will fall. My friends, you cannot refuse it,
And I shall die content after saving my son.
Let us go to your camp. My word binds me to you.

     OULITA-HOUMMA: O generous father, your courage humbles me
And makes me feel loathing in this dreadful moment
For the blundering oath I took before the gods.
I swore it. That is all. And I shall be faithful,
But I shall spare nothing to soothe my angry tribe.

     POUCHA-HOUMMA: I shall take my farewell forever of this place
For it is death, my friends, death for which I yearn!

ACT V
Scene 1

Tchilita-be, Cala-be, Fouchi

Tchilita-be: [*Appearing at the back of the stage*]
What surprise they will feel at our prompt return!
However, Cala-be, in this time of crisis
We should never have left the land of our people
When we know that there rules a sore anxiety.
These are such times that a severe duty
Admits no obedience to a father's will.
Yours has deceived us. Master of his secret,
He meditates upon a most awesome project.
[*He reaches the front of the stage and says with surprise*]
What an amazing change happened in our absence!
What are we to conclude from this dreary silence?
We see no one here! Have the Tchactas
Spared us alone of all our nation?
Or have the wrathful gods, decreeing our ruin,
Destroyed completely our divine nation?
My judgment fails me in such circumstances
And cannot comprehend so sudden a change,
But I must confess that I have lost all hope
Of ever seeing here your unhappy father.

Cala-be: I also am disturbed, and also confused,
But see all too clearly that everything is lost.
Such a brief absence! Yet such fatal absence!
Untimely departure! Unfortunate return!
My father, my people, I have caused your sorrow
And yet, alas, I live! But I detest myself.

Fouchi: What does this violence mean? Is my husband yielding
To a cruel despair which stupefies his soul?
I believed till now that a warlike courage
Would remain impassive under the blows of fate.
Yes, Cala-be, I had always thought so.
But now you show me how mistaken I was!
[*Disdainfully*] Worthless courage, you are a mere phantom;
You do not sustain us in our days of trial.
You betray us as soon as sorrow crushes us,
And to our weakness you give victory.
In my eyes you are but a brilliant illusion
Which needs but an instant to vanish into mist.

Cala-be: Your words, Fouchi, like a streak of lightning,
Have passed into my heart through my distraught senses.

I was stripped of courage, but now I am reborn
And see the light of day for the second time.
Do not fear to see me wandering helplessly;
You have restored me to my former courage.
But have you not discerned that too ardent a zeal
Made you carelessly harsh toward your husband?

  Tchilita-be: Because of her motives I approve her frankness.
Advice that is friendly should never be disguised.
Does it matter that the fruit be bitter,
If it quiets the sorrow and dissipates the pain?

  Cala-be: Let us listen. A noise has struck my ear.

  Tchilita-be: [*Ironically*] And are we not living in a land of wonders?
We must distrust in a place such as this
Everything that we see, everything that we hear!

  Cala-be: I am not mistaken. This increasing clamor
Presages the approach of a cause for distress.
But at last the elder whom I see hurrying
Will enlighten us about the happenings.
I recognize him now. Alas, in other days,
He was the one to soothe my over-eager youth.
He seems crushed by the weight of a violent sorrow
Which tells me already what affliction is ours.

  [*A few women and wailing children follow the elder.*]

Scene II

Tchilita-be, Cala-be, Fouchi, the Elder

  Tchilita-be: Respectable elder, friend whom I revere,
Speak the entire truth. Where is my brother?
And where have disappeared our wives and children
Who no longer dwell near our abandoned hearths?
What fearful disaster has struck our shelter?

  The Elder: Let me breathe a little. Happiness is fragile.

  Tchilita-be: Ah! I expect the worst. Your sorrow betrays you.

  The Elder: Alas! Do you not know of our misfortune?

  Tchilita-be: From all that I can see I should understand it,
But no one has yet related it to me.

  The Elder: Why can I not conceal from you forever
The source of my sorrow and of all my regrets?

  Tchilita-be: Silence for a while your superfluous grief.

  The Elder: Hardly on the waters had we lost sight of you
When two Tchacta envoys appeared suddenly here.
First to your brother they held out their hand;
And then they went around our assembly

And shook hands with all, even with the children.
Though extremely surprised by this friendly gesture,
We welcomed the envoys with affability
And we smoked together: The quiet conversation
Seemed to herald a surprising accord.
We had hopes that perhaps our splendid presents
Would terminate at last our long quarrel.
Futile hopes! The Tchactas, with threatening gestures,
Rejected our gifts and our friendliness.
Carried away by wrath, they cried furiously
"Blood always by blood must be compensated."
Afterward, one of them let his anger soften
And addressed this discourse to your grieving brother:
"Unfortunate elder, though I may rend your heart,
I share your sorrow, I feel your bitter pain.
Sent here as envoy, I was forced to report
The demands my nation felt entitled to make,
And I can change nothing of its cruel decree."
Then Poucha-houmma asked us to withdraw.
His features were serene and never had his soul
Seemed to be burning with a more brilliant flame.
What power does virtue assume over men!
A single look from him made us all submissive.
He seemed to be saying: "Trust in me, my friends;
Alone I will achieve a peaceful solution."
Without suspicion, without any foresight,
We surrendered our chief to executioners.
        CALA-BE: O what burning remorse must ever follow crime!
Direct your anger against my anguished heart
And shortening the course of a lingering life,
Dry forevermore the source of my tears!
        TCHILITA-BE: We should always hope for a happy future
And must with prudence devise our plans,
But when the blows of fate are inescapable,
We must show fortitude, at least, in bearing them.
We see with regret a vacillating soul
Sometimes bearing grief, sometimes lamenting it.
During the course of life nothing should surprise us.
Friend, we are listening. Please continue your tale.
        THE ELDER: Our suspicions allayed, we felt untroubled
And continued sitting in our assembly.
Suddenly a death cry, heard in the distance,
Opened our eyes and disturbed our minds.
We soon learned the reason for this fearful cry.
The Hoummas aroused, each warrior took his arms;

Following the warriors, our weary old men
Gathered together with women and children.
Futile agitation! We were aroused in vain.
Nachouba who swiftly had rushed across the plain
Arrived at the instant when the cruel Tchactas
Were giving the death blow to your kneeling brother.
He who was a witness will recount the event.
He comes toward us. As for me, I withdraw.

SCENE III

PRECEDING ACTORS, NACHOUBA

[*A few women and children arrive, one after another, and looking stunned.*]
    NACHOUBA: Leader of our tribe, deadly to our foes,
What great sorrows will spring from your absence!
Happiness, eclipsed, has left our land,
And we must now endure the horrors of warfare.
All is ended, alas, our tribe from this day
Is forevermore plunged in desolation.
Have you learned our grief? Have you learned what happened?
    TCHILITA-BE: Happiness might still come to dwell among us,
But when no palliative remains for our pain,
We must obey reason and think no more of it.
It is in great sorrow that one shows great courage.
Without copying the wrath of the vile fiends,
I shall make them regret the crime they committed
If ever fate should show the opportunity.
However, Nachouba, without losing hope,
One should in evil days show more constancy.
One can feel profoundly a woeful sentiment
And yet refuse to yield to discouraged thoughts.
Calm your distraught spirit and then recount for us
The odious actions of the odious Tchactas.
    CALA-BE: Conceal nothing from us. The greater the sorrow,
The more every detail becomes of importance.
Do not fear to burden a wretched culprit.
Sorrow from this day can no longer touch me.
Feelings can no longer penetrate my heart,
For my fate has placed me beyond any grief.
    NACHOUBA: Can I master enough my confused emotions?
What are you asking me? What am I to tell you?
You make it your duty to berate my sorrow,
But, had you only seen what I have just beheld!
O detestable day! Dreadful day! Fatal day!

This is all that remains of the best of leaders.

    [*He throws a bloody shirt on the stage.*]

He is dead. It is done. He defied destiny.

His enemies were loath to give the fatal blow.

The hand was raised to strike; the hatchet was ready.

I arrived. What a sight! It startled my eyes.

"O Tchactas, stay your hand!" I called immediately.

But your brother whose visage was serene

Said to me: "Come nearer," and with perfect control

Explained he had yielded his life to the Tchactas,

That he had to respect the laws of his nation,

But died well satisfied since he could save his son.

"Go back," he continued, "tarry here no longer.

My death will guarantee peace for our nation.

Tell my son that now he no more has foes,

That my blood has paid the purchase price of peace.

Tell him, especially, he must by his just rule

Husband the good fortune of his noble nation.

Farewell. Withdraw. Too long has this discourse

Delayed the end of my final moments."

The amazed Tchacta was touched by this language

And his hideous eyes seemed to grow less cruel.

Merciful gentleness, wont to soften sorrow,

For the first time, perhaps, penetrated his heart.

The whole camp felt pity and each within himself

Felt the subjugation of a mighty power.

Even their own leader, that stormy chief of war,

Seemed quite astonished as tears flowed from his eyes.

      Tchilita-be: What? So cruel a man is capable of tears?

      Nachouba: He felt the sweet sorrow of tender emotion,

And he appeared thoughtful. He seemed undecided.

One might have believed him subdued by your brother.

His merciful hand, with no hesitation,

Seemed ready to release the bonds of the victim.

How, briefly it lived, this illusory hope!

"What!" said Poucha-houmma, taking a severe tone,

"Is this the way for you to fulfill your duty?

What right have you, I ask, to determine the fate

Of the head that I came to surrender to you?

Since I had to yield it into your power,

It is a sacred trust, beyond your command.

Would you choose to ignore the wish of your nation,

To deceive its hope and betray its interest?

This I cannot believe. You will be faithful.

Let us end, as we must, our ancient quarrel.

A moment will end it. You fear to shed my blood:
Fear rather to shed the blood of innocents.
Avoid, as you must, new causes for vengeance.
Have no doubt about it. Peace demands that I die.
Tchactas, come nearer; watching me today
You will learn, at least, how a man should die."
Their wounded vanity reawakened their ire,
And as a confused noise is heard before the storm
Thus this vile nation, this fickle nation,
Announced its fury by a loud outburst.
All its arms were raised. I shuddered and I sighed,
And your smiling brother died by their cruel hand.
In this bitter instant, his eyes searched for mine
And seemed to entrust me with his woeful farewell.
Suddenly a Tchacta, boastful of his success,
Severed our chief's head from his wounded body.
And I, I seized this bloody relic.

    [*He shows the shirt he has thrown on the stage.*]

    TCHILITA-BE: This dreadful account, this gory sacrifice,
Will be the torment of your heart, Cala-be,
Yet do not let the pain obscure our awareness
Of the great duties that remain before us.

Charles Gayarré (1805–1895)

Charles Gayarré was born Charles Etienne Arthur Gayarré in New Orleans, Louisiana, on January 9, 1805.[1] Gayarré's father, Carlos Estevan Gayarré, as his name suggests, was of Spanish origin. Charles Gayarré's great-grandfather, Don Estevan de Gayarré, was a royal emissary from Spain, who accompanied the first Spanish governor Don Antonio de Ulloa when he took possession of the colony of Louisiana for King Carlos III of Spain. Long after Ulloa was expelled from Louisiana, and Don Estevan returned to his native Spain, Charles Gayarré's grandfather, Don Juan Antonio Gayarré, remained and was appointed by then Spanish Governor O'Reilly, Commissary of War, at only eighteen years old. Don Juan Antonio was later appointed *Contador Real* of Acapulco, Mexico, where he died and where Charles Gayarré's father, Carlos Estevan, was born. Charles Gayarré's mother, Marie Elizabeth de Boré Gayarré, was the daughter of one of New Orleans' most prominent plantation owners, Etienne de Boré, who was responsible for successfully introducing sugar cane as a staple crop of Louisiana, but moreover, for perfecting the granulation process, making him one of the wealthiest men in the region. In fact, Gayarré's first memories hark back to his childhood and the years he passed on Etienne Boré's sugar plantation, some six miles upriver from New Orleans, what would now be situated along the Mississippi River between Napoleon Avenue and Audubon Park.

Gayarré was first educated in a small schoolhouse on the neighboring Foucher plantation, upriver, on the site of what is now Audubon Park, and later sent to board in the Collège d' Orleans, where he stayed until he moved to Philadelphia, to study law. After being admitted to the Pennsylvania Bar in 1828, he returned to Louisiana and began practicing law. Gayarré also began his literary career at this time. Right out of Collège d' Orleans, at the age of twenty, he published his first pamphlet on the Louisiana legal code, in opposition to abolishing capital punishment in the state. However, his first work of significance was his 1830, *Essai Historique sur la Louisiane,* thought by many readers to be a more lively retelling, or even an abstract, of Supreme Court Justice Francois Xavier Martin's *History of Lousisiana,* the first history of the state written in English.[2] On the other hand, Gayarré's four-volume *History of Louisiana* is still today one of the most comprehensive historical accounts of the state, if a little whitewashed and romanticized. The volumes were originally published separately beginning in 1854 and not published as one set until 1879.

Upon his return from Pennsylvania, Gayarré was elected to the state legislature to represent New Orleans in 1830, and the following year he was appointed Assistant Attorney General. By 1835, he was elected to the United States Senate. Unfortunately, his political career at this time was cut short due to a mysterious illness. For the next eight years he sought medical care in France, thereby resigning his Senate seat. He did continue to write while in Paris, completing his *Histoire de la Louisiane,* the history of the state written in French.

Back in New Orleans, Gayarré resumed his political career. He served twice as the New Orleans state representative, and twice he was appointed Secretary of State, but he also continued writing his state history. Gayarré did not turn to writing fiction until after the Civil War. Naturally, he was in favor of secession, but he spent the war years on his family plantation in St. Helena Parish, Roncal, named after his family's Spanish ancestral home in the province of Navarre in northern Spain. While there, he turned to writing his first works of fiction.

In the 1850s, Gayarré wrote two plays, both of which are all but unreadable, *The School for Politics* (1854), and *Dr. Bluff in Russia* (1865), and in 1866 he produced his first work of fiction, *The New Orleans Boot-black: A Tale,* a fictionalized account of his dealings with a Mrs. M.C. Daigre, of Mulberry Grove Plantation near Baton Rouge, to whom his wife lent a considerable amount of money. After the Civil War, Gayarré, like so many white, southern landowners, was broke, and upon discovering that his wife had lent Mrs. Daigre such a large sum of

---

1   For more on Charles Gayarré and the source of much of the biographical information given here, see Edward M. Socola's *Charles Gayarré, A Biography,* diss.U of Pennsylvania, 1954 (Ann Arbor: UMI, 1977), and Grace King's "Charles Gayarré, A Biographical Sketch," *Charles Gayarré, Louisiana Historian and Politician* (New York: Publishers Marketing Research Associations, 1998), 159-89.

2   Socola, *Gayarré,* 39.

money, he tried desperately to get it back. However, she claimed that she too had fallen on hard financial times so she could not repay the loan. Once he discovered that Mrs. Daigre had sold her plantation yet still managed to avoid paying Gayarré, he responded in the only way available to him. He wrote and published a fictional account of the entire affair, which might have been satisfying, but he never did see a payment from Mrs. Daigre. He later wrote two novels, *Fernando de Lemos, Truth and Fiction* (1872) and *Aubert Dubayet* (1882). Gayarré's creative writing proves that essays were indeed his strongest genre. Included here are two: "The Old Eden" and "Mr. Cable's 'Freedman's Case in Equity.'"

The first essay, "The Old Eden," is a rather humorous account of the way in which Louisiana managed to be settled at all. Gayarré first exaggerates the bounty of the territory, in much the same way the early governor Cadillac and financier Crozat must have in trying to lure folks to populate the area in the early 1700s. He writes of the "inexhaustible mines of gold and silver" and that the "fountain of eternal youth had been discovered." But the second half of the essay is concerned with the colony of Louisiana after its financial control had been transferred to John Law and the capitol moved from Biloxi to New Orleans in 1721. The tone decidedly changes. During this time, voluntary migration to Louisiana was not what the French government hoped it would be, so it is true that many undesirables, including prisoners and prostitutes, were sent here often against their will. However, just as the streets here were not paved with gold as the original leaders of this colony would have liked the French to think, nor was Louisiana "a vile compound of marshes, lagoons, swamps, bayous, fens, bogs, endless prairies, inextricable and gloomy forests, peopled with every monster of the natural and mythological world." In fact, the truth lies somewhere in between. Gayarré maintains his satiric, hyperbolic tone throughout in much the same way—but perhaps not as effectively—as Jonathan Swift does in "A Modest Proposal."

The second essay, "Mr. Cable's 'Freedman's Case in Equity,'" is in response to George Washington Cable's essay, "The Freedman's Case in Equity," first published in *Century* magazine in January, 1885, and which is also included in this collection. In his essay, Cable discusses the plight of the freed slaves, especially in the South and in his native Louisiana. One of the compromises of the Hayes-Tilden election of 1876 was the removal of federal troops from the South, effectively signaling the end of Reconstruction and ushering in the Jim Crow era. The freed blacks in the South were on their own, and Cable argues that the "Southern slave has within two decades risen from slavery to freedom, from freedom to citizenship, passed on into political ascendency, and fallen again from that eminence," and that if the nation does not act as a whole, politically and morally, then former slaves will remain shackled, to some degree. Cable's argument is often hidden in overblown prose, and Gayarré, in his response to Cable's essay, dedicates the first half to Cable's desultory writing style, saying that "[i]t reminds us of an artichoke, whose eatable substance cannot be reached without patiently removing the numerous prickly scales that envelop the fleshy base which is sought after," and that "[w]e read Mr. Cable's article three times, with extreme fatigue, before we could have a very clear conception of what it meant." And even though Gayarré's writing style more often than not resembles Cable's, again his biting sarcasm is amusing, and at one point he does admit that "Mr. Cable is a Louisianian, and has talent." However, he spends the latter half of his essay arguing against the mixing of any races, historically speaking, dating back to the Norman invasion of England. And his argument is all the more interesting because he himself fathered a child in 1825 by a free woman of color.[1] Finally, he also sets forth the very southern notion of *noblesse oblige:* "It (the racial inferiority of blacks) will be… an additional reason for the superior race to assist the inferior with increasing kindness and enlightened humanity."

Gayarré's views on racial superiority did not change before his death nine years after he published his response to Cable's article, and little was done in the South for African Americans until the Civil Rights movement some seventy-five years later. Charles Gayarré died at his family home, Roncal, on February 11, 1895, just weeks after his ninetieth birthday, and he is still considered one of the state's noted historians.

---

1   Socola, *Gayarré*, 320-321.

The Old Eden[1]

In the early days of Louisiana, France was flooded with pamphlets describing the advantages which it offered to emigrants. The luxuriant imaginations of prolific writers were taxed to clothe Louisiana with all the perfections they could invent. It was more than the old Eden, so long lost to mankind. The picturesque was happily blended with the fertile, and abundance smiled on rocky mountains as on the alluvial plains of the valleys. The climate was such that all the vegetables of the globe existed there, or could be introduced with success. All the fruits known were to be gathered in profusion from the forests, all the year round, and the most luscious peaches, pears, apples, and other delicacies, dropping from their parent boughs, were piled up in heaps under cool shades and on the velvet banks of bubbling streams. There, dust and mud were equally excluded, as the ground was lined in all seasons with a thick carpet of flowers, endless in variety, and perfuming the air. The finest breed of all domestic or useful animals was to be found there in all the primitive vigor and gentleness of their antediluvian perfection. The poor peasant who, during a long life in France, had never dreamed of eating meat, would there feed on nothing less than wild ducks, venison, pheasants, snipes and woodcocks. The birds kept up a never-ceasing concert, which would have shamed the opera singing of Paris. The rivers and lakes were stocked with fish, so abundant that they would suffice to nourish millions of men, so delicate that no king ever had any such on his table.

The seasons were so slightly marked that the country might be said to be blessed with a perpetual spring. None but gentle winds fluttered over this paradise. The sky was brighter, the sun more gorgeous, the moon more chastely serene and pure, and the nights more lovely than anywhere else. Heaven itself seemed to bend down upon earth in conjugal dalliance. There, it is true, it could not be said to have been positively ascertained that the fountain of eternal youth had been discovered, but the Indians were known to retain the appearance of youth even after having attained five or six hundred years. Those very Indians had conceived such attachment for the white men, whom they considered as gods, that they would not allow them to labor, and insisted on performing themselves all the work that might be necessary for the comfort of their pale-faced brethren. It was profanation in their eye not to minister to all the wants of their idolized guests.

More enticing than all that were the inexhaustible mines of gold and silver, which, however, it would not be necessary to work by the usual tedious process, because the whole surface of the country was strewn with lumps of gold, and when the waters of the lakes and rivers were filtered, particularly the thick water of the Mississippi, it yielded an invaluable deposit of gold. As to silver, it was common that it would become of no value and would have to be used in the shape of square stones, to pave the public roads. The fields were covered with an indigenous plant which was gifted with the most singular property. The dew which gathered within the perfumed cups of its flowers would, in the course of a single night, be converted into a solid diamond; and the soft texture of the flowers, bursting open and dropping down under the weight of its contents, would leave the precious gem resting on the stem, reflecting the rays of the morning sun. What is written on California in our day would appear tame when compared to the early publications on Louisiana.

By the time the capitol of the colony had been transferred to New Orleans, however, there had been a shift of opinion concerning the colony. It was no longer described as the land of promise, but as a terrestrial representation of Pandemonium. The whole country was nothing else, it was said, but a vile compound of marshes, lagoons, swamps, bayous, fens, bogs, endless prairies, inextricable and gloomy

---

1   "The Old Eden" appears in: Etolia S. Basso, Ed. *The World from Jackson Square, a New Orleans Reader,* (New York: Farrar, Straus and Co., 1948).

forests, peopled with every monster of the natural and of the mythological world. The Mississippi rolled onward a muddy and thick substance, which hardly deserved the name of water and which was alive with every insect and every reptile. Enormous trunks, branches and fragments of trees were swept down by the velocity of the current, and in such quantity as almost to bridge over the bed of the river, and they prevented communication from one bank to the other, by crushing every bark or canoe that attempted the passage. At one epoch of the year, the whole country was overflowed by that mighty river, and then, all the natives betook themselves to the tops of trees, where they roosted and lived like monkeys, and jumped from tree to tree in search of food, or they retired to artificial hills of shells, piled up by preceding generations, where they starved, or fed as they could by fishing excursions.

In many of its parts (the legend of disenchantment continued), the country was nothing but a thin coat, one foot thick, of alluvial soil, kept together on the surface of the water by the intermingled teguments of bind-weeds and the roots of other plants, so that if one walked on this crust, he made it, by the pressure of the weight of his body, heave up around him, in imitation of the waves of the sea, and great was the danger of sinking through this weak texture. Tempting-looking fruits and berries invited the taste, it is true, but they were all poisonous. The sun was so intensely hot, that at noon it could strike a man dead as if with a pistol shot— it was called a stroke of the sun. Its fiery breath drew from the bogs, fens, and marshes the most pestilential vapors, engendering disease and death. The climate was so damp, that in less than a week a bar of iron would be coated over with rust and eaten up. The four seasons of the year would meet in one single day, and a shivering morning was not unfrequently succeeded by a sultry evening. The ear was, by day and by night, assailed by the howls of wolves, and by the croakings of frogs so big that they swallowed children and could bellow as loud as bulls. Sleep, sweet sleep, was disturbed, if not altogether made impossible, by the buzz and sting of myriads of mosquitoes which thickened the atmosphere and incorporated themselves with the very air which the lungs inhaled.

It is easy to conceive the startling effects produced by such malicious misrepresentations. The tide of emigration which was pouring onward rolled back, and the prospect of establishing a powerful colony in Louisiana, which at first had appeared so feasible, was nipped in the bud and looked upon as an impossibility. Under the exaggerated and gloomy apprehensions of the moment, no actual tender of money, no promise of future reward, could have tempted anybody to embark for Louisiana. So universal was the terror inspired by the name of the Mississippi, that it became even a bugbear of the nursery. For half a century after the explosion of Law's great Mississippi scheme, when French children were unruly and unmanageable, and when all threats had proved ineffectual, the mother would, in the last resort, lift up her finger impressively, and in a whispering tone, as if afraid of speaking too loud of something so horrible, would say with a shudder, and with pale lips to her rebellious progeny: "Hush! or I will send you to the Mississippi!"

However, the Western or Mississippi Company (headed by John Law,) having contracted the obligation to colonize Louisiana and to transport thither within a fixed time a certain number of emigrants, found itself under the necessity, in order to comply with the terms of its contract, to have recourse to the most iniquitous and unlawful means. As it was indispensable that there should be emigration— when it ceased to be voluntary, it was necessary that it should be forced. Thus violence was resorted to, and throughout France agents were dispatched to kidnap all vagrants, beggars, gipsies, or people of the like description, and women of bad repute. Unfortunately, the power given by the government to these agents of the Company was abused in the most infamous manner. It became in their hands an engine of peculation, oppression, and corruption. It is incredible what a number of respectable people of both sexes were put, through bribery, in the hands of these satellites of an arbitrary government, to gratify private malice and the dark passions or interested views of men in power. A purse of gold slipped into the hand, and a whisper in the ear, went a great way to get rid of obnoxious persons, and many a fearful tale of revenge, of hatred, or of cupidity, might be told of persons who were unsuspectedly seized and carried away to the banks of the Mississippi, before their voices could be heard when crying for justice; or for protection. The dangerous rival, the hated wife or troublesome husband, the importuning creditor, the prodigal son, or the too long-lived father, the one who happened to be an obstacle to an expected inheritance, or crossed the path of the wealthy or of the powerful, became the victims of their position, and were soon hurried away with the promiscuous herd of thieves, prostitutes, vagabonds, and all sorts of wretches of bad fame who had been swept together, to be transported to Louisiana.

Guarded by a merciless soldiery, they, on their way to sea-ports, crowded the public roads of France like droves of cattle, and as they were hardly furnished with means of subsistence or with clothing by their heartless conductors, who speculated on the food and other supplies with which they were bound to provide their prisoners, they died in large numbers, and their unburied corpses, rotting above ground, struck with terror the inhabitants of the districts through which the woe-begone caravan had passed. At night, they were locked up in barns, when any could be found, and if not, they were forced, the better to prevent escape, to lie down in heaps at the bottom of ditches and holes, and sentinels were put round to watch over them. Hunger and cold pinched the miserable creatures, and their haggard looks, emaciated bodies, and loud wailings carried desolation everywhere. Such sights, added to the horrifying descriptions which were given of Louisiana, made its name more terrifying to the minds of the people of France than that of the celebrated Bastille and its dark dungeons.

Mr. Cable's "Freedman's Case in Equity"[1]

We take notice of Mr. Cable's *Freedman's Case in Equity* published in the December *Century*. We depart from the workshop of fiction and caricature, and we enter the solemn temple of justice, where Mr. Cable appears as a self-constituted attorney "in the equity case" which he upholds, on behalf of the colored race, against the systematically oppressing, tyrannically inclined, and perjured white race of the whole South, that continues to be oblivious of its most solemnly sworn obligations. We beg Mr. Cable to keep in mind that it is he who attacks, and he who puts us on the defence.

We read Mr. Cable's article three times, with extreme fatigue, before we could have a very clear conception of what it meant. In every phrase the words are so unnecessarily and densely crowded, in chaotic confusion, round the sense intended to be conveyed! It reminds us of the artichoke, whose eatable substance cannot be reached without patiently removing the numerous prickly scales that envelop the fleshy base which is sought after. It was not an easy road for us to travel, before arriving at Mr. Cable's conclusions, and tasting on the tip of our tongue the panacea which he trumpets forth to cure our Southern leprosies, and guard us against the social, political, moral, judicial, and legislative iniquities that threaten us with another bloody revolution and final perdition. What beating of the bush it requires to make Mr. Cable's rabbit run out of its shelter of briars! It is a timid animal. It shows first the tip of its whiskers, or of its long ears; then one half-concealed foot, or perhaps a peep at its tail may be permitted, before it ventures out in full view of the hunter and dares his shot. We much prefer the open and bold position of the anarchist, the socialist, the communist, and the nihilist. They tell us plainly the extent of destruction which they meditate. They are levellers; Mr. Cable, the would-be regenerator, is a mere plasterer, or patcher.

---

1   "Mr. Cable's 'Freedman's Case in Equity'" was first published in the *Times-Democrat*, Jan. 1885. Note that this essay is a response to George Washington Cable's "The Freedman's Case in Equity," below.

Mr. Cable delights in raving promulgations of new and startling principles, in the utterances of tempestuous expressions against his supposed antagonists, however respectable they may be for intellect and virtue. But his most violent denunciations, in his epileptic fits of periodical indignation at the condition of our prisons and of the tortured negro, are generally accompanied by velvety reticences to escape from too perilous responsibilities. He seems to speculate in sensational attitudes and stage effect, on whose financial success he confidently relies. His style is peculiar; it is emphatically his own *in equity*, by the right of invention. He cannot be accused of servile imitation. It is not the English to which we have been accustomed, and therefore we solicit his indulgence if we in any way misunderstand and misstate his premises and the deductions resulting from their acceptance. We are not sure that we can ascertain to our satisfaction the true quality and nature of the driftwood which he hurries on to market, and which floats indistinctly on a foggy stream of illogical reasonings and more than doubtful statements. He evidently aims at a new language to enunciate new principles. Be it so; but we object to its obscurity and to the writer's chronic mania of entangling and twisting every sentence like a cat playing with a spool of cotton. It gives much trouble to the reader, who is anxious to profit, without too much study and a headache, by the discoveries of that learned professor of ethics and Darwinian evolver of equities, on which a new order of society is to be established under his auspices. Mr. Cable is a Louisianian, and has talent. We might be disposed to admire him if he understood the propriety of being less incisive, not to say insulting, in his admonitions, and if he had the modesty to assume a less lofty tone of moral and intellectual superiority in his dictations over a vast number of his fellow-citizens, whom, in the face of the world, without the slightest hesitation and without the least sign of regret, he proclaims as guilty of the basest malignancy, the most systematic tyranny, and the most drivelling imbecility. As to imbecility, we personally plead guilty; for we confess that, while one page of Addison's or of Edmund Burke's refreshes and brightens our intellect, the complicated sentences of Mr. Cable obscure and fatigue it to the utmost. If we were, as a professional critic, to qualify the style of this author, we would call it Labyrinthine. It imposes too much groping and wandering before discovering the bull in his hiding-place and taking him by the horns. We think, however, that we have at last, after considerable labor, succeeded in obtaining a clear view of the four-footed beast in all its proportions.

Mr. Cable begins his article with this assertion: "The greatest problem before the American people to-day is, as it has been for a hundred years, the presence among us of the negro." We fully agree with him on this point, and we do not hesitate to add: That the problem resulting now from the presence of the freedman entails on us of the white race a question more difficult to solve satisfactorily, than the one which formerly proceeded from his presence as a slave.

We further aver, with the deepest conviction, that the existence in the same country of two races, as different as day and night in their physical and spiritual endowments, and apparently incapable of fusing into a homogeneous whole, is the most dreadful calamity that ever could befall a community. History tells us the terrible struggles that have always resulted from the meeting of even two white races on the same soil, notwithstanding the practicability, in the course of centuries, of their gradually forming a unit by intermarriage. All the various records of mankind contain a long recital of the total annihilation or expulsion of races by races. In many parts of civilized Europe, at this day, where different white races have been inhabiting the same territory for ages, they still entertain toward one another a deadly enmity, which fatally breaks out like the lava of a volcano, whenever the opportunity presents itself.

In England it was a disgrace, during a long time, even for a poor Norman knight to marry a rich Saxon princess. At least, so thought the Norman dames. For them she was the mulattress of the epoch, although as white as new-fallen snow. In their eye such a mesalliance could be palliated only by the necessity of complying with the exigencies of worldly policy and ambition, if not prompted by sordid interest.

But Normans and Saxons could fuse, and they did fuse at last, although the latter had been considered by the former as hardly better than swine. Another striking instance is what happened in Spain. The ancient population of that country and the invading Goths soon merged into an harmonious nationality. The two races had entertained no instinctive repugnance for each other. Next came the swarthy Arabs and the darker-hued Moors, very distinct in color from the descendants of the Goths. What followed? Assimilation! Fusion! No. Eight hundred years of bloody conflicts, until one of the races exterminated the other. What is now taking place in Algeria? Are the Arabs becoming French, or the French turning Arabs? Or are the two races breeding hybrids? No. It is not long since an Arab chief said to a French officer, his friend: "If a Frenchman and an Arab were boiled down together, so that there remained only their bones, those bones would instantly separate." Therefore, the fact that the population of our State is about equally divided between the Caucasian race and the African must be considered as presenting a question of an awful nature, if examined by the light of history and of undeniable precedents. Surely it is a question to be anxiously studied with the calm reason, the profound knowledge, the sagacious foresight, of a statesman, and is not to be superficially treated with the unpardonable flippancy of a sentimental aspirant to notoriety, the arrogant superciliousness of an improvised pedagogue, the exorbitant conceit of a self-worshipping censor of public and private morals, or with the raving imprecations, the bowlings, and the maniac gesticulations of an Orlando Furioso.

Let us now glance rapidly at the probable future of the freedman in Louisiana, and only glance, because we are to confine ourselves within the limits assigned to this essay. That future will depend on the relative position of inferiority, equality, or superiority which the black race is to occupy toward the white one—three things as powerful to settle this question as the three mythological sisters who of yore wove the destinies of man.

Should the black race not have been favored by nature with the same letters patent of nobility which it has granted to the white, it will be vain to attempt to remove the inferiority by artificial means. Should this race inferiority be the fiat of Providence, the blacks although they should be put in possession of all the political, social and civil rights which they may desire, although given, as equally as to the whites, the same encouragement and advantages for education and for the acquisition of wealth in any department of industry, will not keep pace with their Caucasian competitors. In that case, they will sink to their proper level and become the mudsills of the social edifice. It will be, however, an additional reason for the superior race to assist the inferior with increasing kindness and enlightened humanity. But, in spite of this protection, the negro, in all probability, will gradually disappear. As to the hybrids, those in whom the line of color no longer exists apparently will continue, as they do daily, to creep into the Caucasian ranks, where their traces will soon be lost sight of and forever obliterated. It must be kept in mind, in connection with this subject, that the negro hates the hybrid; and the hybrid, despising the negro, is more averse than the white man to associate with him, except for political purposes. As to the female quadroons, there are few of them that would not belabor with a broomstick the leveller and trader in new principles who should propose to them to marry a negro. Thereby hangs a tale, which we offer to the consideration of Mr. Cable.

We cannot admit the possibility of the future superiority and domination of the black race over the white in Louisiana, and the consequent extinction of the latter; it is too absurd. But let us suppose that both races become equal in energy, knowledge, wealth, and number. Should they keep systematically apart and form two distinct camps, with no social intercourse between them, it is fearful to think of the inevitable consequences in the struggle that would ensue for power and government, and from other causes.

Probably this is the state of things which Mr. Cable anticipates, as he believes in the equality of the races. For the purpose of averting those anticipated evils, we should be happy to join him heartily, in honest, sincere, and patriotic efforts to provide for the best possible means to increase the kind relations now existing between the two races, and secure their common welfare by the reciprocal exercise of lasting amity, as much as this may be within the reach of human power, outside of miscegenation, which we abhor. We are convinced that those relations are as harmonious as they could be under the conditions which the past has created for us, but the way to prolong their existence indefinitely is not by inflammatory and false descriptions of the present intolerable oppression of the negroes in the South—an oppression which, in Mr. Cable's opinion, would justify them, if they had Caucasian energy, to inundate the country with blood by cutting the throats of the white devils by whom they are tortured. "We could hardly trust in the correctness of our eyesight when we read his furious denunciations.... Let Mr. Cable be judged by the evidence furnished by himself."

In support of the semi-cloudy position occupied by Mr. Cable, I transcribe the following lines from his December effusion: "We hear much about race instinct. The most of it, I fear, is pure twaddle. It may be there is such a thing. We do not know. It is not proved. And even if it were established, it would not be necessarily a proper moral guide. We subordinate instinct to society's best interests as apprehended in the light of reason." If we have misinterpreted Mr. Cable's oracular dictum, we beg to be corrected

Thomas Wharton Collens (1812–1879)

Thomas Wharton Collens[1] was born in New Orleans on June 23, 1812 to Marie de Tabiteau and John Wharton Collens. He spent much of his boyhood in Wharton, Louisiana, a town across Lake Ponchartrain from New Orleans that his father had established in 1813. The name was soon changed to its present one, Covington, after General Leonard Covington, the hero of the War of 1812. Collens' father died in 1817, when Thomas Collens was only five years old, leaving the land in St. Tammany Parish to Thomas and his mother Marie. As a young man, Thomas sold off much of his land and moved to New Orleans where he began his short-lived career as a printer's devil, only the first of his many jobs.

In 1833, he became an associate editor of the *True American*, a Whig newspaper. That year he also married Ameraide Milbrou, and they went on to have eight children together. Some two years later he was admitted to the bar and served as clerk and translator of French and Spanish to the Louisiana Senate. He also served as a clerk of the United States Court in 1836, the year that he wrote *The Martyr Patriots, or Louisiana in 1769.* After that he continued public service as District Attorney for Orleans District in 1840, a member of the State Convention in 1852, and Judge of the First District Court of New Orleans in 1861. Though he was opposed to secession, he supported the Confederacy, and in 1862, ahead of General Butler's arrival, he left New Orleans to live in exile in Pass Christian until the war's end.

In 1910, 22 years after his death in 1879 at the age of 67, a portrait of Collens was donated to the Supreme Court of Louisiana, where Justice Frank McGloin spoke a few words about his former friend and colleague, saying that after little formal education, Collens extended his knowledge of literature and art over a wide field through "a persevering course of patient reading and study," and also noting that his most notable works aside from this play include *Humanics,* a philosophical study which Collens defined as the "science of man through deist eyes," published in 1860, and *Eden of Labor or Christian Utopia,* a much more religious philosophical work published in 1876, just three years before his death.

As a young man, Collens turned his back on his Catholic faith and studied utopian socialists popular at the time, such as Robert Owen and Charles Fourier. Later in life, however, he embraced the Catholic Church, and at the end of his life was a regular contributor to the New Orleans Archdiocesan newspaper. He wrote philosophical tracts such as those mentioned above and published works in newspapers and periodicals throughout his life. He was also interested in literature and history, as this play suggests.

The Martyr Patriots, or Louisiana in 1769 is the second historical play included in this anthology, but that is where the similarities end. Whereas Paul Leblanc's *Festival of the Young Corn, or The Heroism of Poucha-Houmma* is slow moving, to say the least, with all the action occurring in only two of the five acts, Collens' play is action-packed. We have in this play a conjure woman and her secret potions, a young abandoned orphan who is nurtured by a prominent white family only to be rejected later because of his dark hair and complexion, poisoning, betrayal of a commander, a father, a son, a brother, a love triangle, all set in a key historical period of Louisiana history.

To explain the context briefly, after the Treaty of Paris in 1763, Louisiana was transferred from France, by Louis XV, to Spain, under Carlos III. However, news of the transfer did not reach Louisiana until a year later, and the French colonists were shocked and angry. The following year, Spain sent the new governor, Ulloa (Antonio de Ulloa y de la Torre-Girault, 1716–95), to New Orleans, where he worked closely with the senior military officer, Aubry, who figures prominently in Collens's play. The Superior Council of Louisiana met in 1768, and decided to reject the deal made by the two monarchs, eventually ousting Ulloa and remaining under their own rule until Spain sent the next governor, O'Reilly (Alejandro, Conde de O'Reilly, 1722–94).

Although that is what happened historically, Collens's play is a work of fiction. In it, Aubry is a jealous backstabbing murderer, and although he was loyal to the French throne while working with Ulloa, there is little

---

1   All the biographical information presented here is from the Thomas Whatron Collens papers at the Historic New Orleans Collection.

evidence that he was the evil character Collens creates here. Similarly, Collens takes liberty with dates and events. The Superior Council did indeed meet, but in October of 1768, and not mere days before the arrival of O'Reilly but almost a year before. However, as we saw with Leblanc's play, popular drama of the time adhered strictly to the Aristotelean unities of action, time, and place, and Collens does so in this play as well. The young French patriots were brave, but they were also brash and headstrong. Five were sentenced to death, including Lafrenière, who was hung, not immediately after being captured as in the play, but some four months later. Six others were sentenced to prison in the Morro Castle in Havana, Cuba. After less than a year, they were released, but they were never allowed to return to Louisiana.

Collens wrote a historical play, but unlike Leblanc, he was not bound by history in his work of fiction and did not sacrifice popular appeal in order to be, as he claimed, historically faithful. This work is also chock full of local color, such as the fortune teller who lives in the swamp and sells a potion that disfigures Adeleaide Villere, Lafrenière's love interest in the play. Collens is also one of the first New Orleans authors to address racism in the character of Garidel, who was found by Villeré after being abandoned as a baby and raised by him as his own son. Garidel explains it best:

> He picked me up, and had me nursed with care,
> And, cheated by the fairness of my skin,
> He thought me one of Europe's sickly race,
> And did adopt me as his son, and strove
> To teach me science and morality,
> But now I am among his servants classed;
> For soon as I grew up my figure changed;
> And this black hair, and eye, and bronzed face
> Proclaimed me one of that dread tribe of men
> Whose birthplace is the unbridled wild.

In the end, Collens offers a racist depiction of Garidel, as he is bound by his race to commit the crimes he does, including murder.

All this makes for a fascinating retelling of a momentous time in Louisiana history, one that coincided with the revolution of the original thirteen colonies, which Collens also romanticizes. In Lafrenière's initial rabble-rousing speech he cries out, "Then let our Country be Louisiana! Let's be Americans!" which is odd, since the French colonists were hardly overjoyed when they came under American rule at the time of the Louisiana Purchase. Collens was born in 1812 and wrote this play 33 years after the Louisiana Purchase, so perhaps a certain homage to American rule seemed appropriate. The play was first performed the year in which it was published, 1836, at the St. Charles Theatre.

The Martyr Patriots, or Louisiana in 1769
An Historical Tragedy in Five Acts[1]

DRAMATIS PERSONÆ

CREOLES

LAFRENIÈRE, VILLERÉ [PRONOUNCE VIL-RA], AUBRY, GARIDEL, ADELAIDE, MRS. VILLERÉ, DENOYANT, MILHET, MARQUIS, CARRERE, SURGEON, A CREOLE SOLDIER, A CROWD OF CITIZENS.

---

1   From: Thomas M'Caleb, ed. *The Louisiana Book: Selections from the Literature of the State.* (New Orleans: R.F. Straughan. 1894). 421-72.

SPANIARDS

Herald, First Judge, A Spanish Soldier, A Spaniard, A Scribe, Ruffian, Judges, Sailors, Soldiers.

ACT I
SCENE 1

A public place [trees on the sides, a church in the background]
    [Lafrenière *enters, holding an open letter.*]
    Laf: [*refers to his letter*]
'Tis well— 'tis well— these things will serve the cause
Of Freedom; and though our mother spurns us
From her bosom, we gain our Liberty
By that unnatural deed. My country,
My noble country, yes, thou shalt be free!
Thou ne'er canst brook the shame of slavery;
Thou wilt not tamely thus be bartered off.
What! sold like cattle?— treated with disdain!
No! Louisiana's sons can never bear
Such foul disgrace. And when I'll tell them all,
Of every insult, and the shame which thus
This reckless King would heap upon their heads,
Twill put a burning fagot to their pride,
'Twill blow their indignation into flame;
And like the fire on our grass-grown plains,
By raging winds devouring driven,
'Twill spread, in blazing waves, e'en to the edge
And utmost limit of the land; and then,
Proud Kings, beware! lest e'en within the bounds
Of Europe's slave-trod vales the blaze should catch,
Sweep despots and their thrones away, and like
Unprofitable weeds consume them all.
Ay! and how happy this occurrence!
'Twill aid my *own* ambitious views; and while
The cause of freedom prospers, so shall I.
For 'tis my aim, in this young colony,
To be the first among the free— to lead
Them on in war, and rule by equal laws
A land of liberty. Oh! could I see
The Independence of my native land,
Myself its Liberator and its Chief—
Not Caesar's glory nor his power would
One moment be my envy. O lovely,
Glorious picture of futurity
Which now my young imagination draws
In brilliant hues of glittering hope,

Thou dazzlest e'en thy painter!
    But Villeré
Comes not. I must tell him all my plans,
And gain his sanction to them, or I fear
They'll not succeed. In such respect are held
His silvered head and sage advice, that once
Unto me his adherence gained, most sure
The people's warm approval I'll obtain,
And all that hope doth promise soon possess.
Ah! but here comes my Adelaide. O love!
Thou hast a power which we cannot break!
But though thy chains are strong, and bind us tight,
Yet they brace us up, and give us double strength
For action; and the bold hero oft achieves
His noblest deed when ere the doubtful fight
He kneels to thee.
    [*Enter* ADELAIDE.]
    ADELAIDE: Ah, Lafrenière,
What brings thee out so soon? The god of day
Hath scarcely risen in the east, nor hath
His morning rays as yet dissolved the drops—
The diamond drops, which, shaken from the veil
Of humid night, are sparkling in the rose,
Or on the breast of some blue violet.
    LAF: How could I stay at home, my Adelaide,
And, like an owl, hide myself from light,
When, like the early lark, I fain would seek,
Impatient to behold, thy sunny eyes, and bask
Beneath their cheering beams!
    ADE: Nay, but the owl
Is Wisdom's chosen bird. Thou shouldst be wise,
And copy her.
    LAF: I would be happy first.
    ADE: Smooth flatterer! Enough of honeyed words,
Which sportingly, and with a cruel joy,
Make but a plaything of a woman's heart.
Tell me, what news from France? Since early dawn
My father seeks thee through the town. 'Tis said
Thou hast late tidings of Lesassier.
    LAF: Nay,
Sweet Adelaide— disturb not now thy soul
With cares of politics, which 'tis the lot
Of womankind, much happier than our own,
Ne'er to be troubled with.
    ADE: Thou wrong'st our sex.

Think ye that women have such hardened souls
As not to feel their country's sufferings?
True, they mind not (as do some silly men)
On which poor courtier kingly smiles are turned,
Nor do they calculate each changing shade
Of policy of jealous nations 'twixt
Each other; but when a woman sees
That pending dangers, thickening round,
Threaten the land where Heaven casts her lot,
Then is each throb her father— brother— feels
Reechoed in her breast.
    LAF: Well, let us hence
Unto thy father's dwelling; as we go,
Thy gentle ear shall hear the painful news.
    [*As* LAFRENIÈRE *and* ADELAIDE *go out,* AUBRY *enters.*]
    AUBRY: Ay, there they go, smiling on each other—
She with many looks of tender love,
He with the gaze of conquering passion;
And I am left despised, without a hope
Save that of dire revenge; and that I'll have,
Cost what it may, ten thousand crimes,
Toil, pain, and years of time. I'll persevere
Until I tread upon his very neck,
Nor yield, though seas of bitter tears are shed.
I'll have a sacrifice of human blood
Unto my hate paid up. And am I wrong?
He thwarts me daily at the council board,
Resists the plans I lay to serve and gain
The favor of the Spanish Governor.
His very reputation is my bane—
It points invidiously at my own,
And has more power in this colony
Than I can claim as legal Governor.
Ha! here cometh one I have enlisted
In my cause, and who doth serve me well.
    [*Enter* GARIDEL.]
Ah, Garidel, I'm glad we meet to-day!
You find me in a flowing humor for our work.
Hast thou performed the charge I gave thee?
    GARIDEL: Yes—
I put the letter on her toilet table.
    AUB: Well, what result?
    GAR: None— she has not seen it.
But prithee, Master Aubry, why not use
Some means more certain in effect to part

These foolish lovers? These letters, well wrought
And plausible, 'tis true, can they reduce
Love's hottest flame? They may cause some pouting;
But oaths and tears soon quell the anger raised
By cloaked accusers 'gainst the one we love.
      Aub: 'Tis well to try this method first; and then,
If not successful, I have other plans.
      Gar: And they are?
      Aub: Listen, Garidel. Art thou
An honest fellow, and can I be sure
That if I give thee *all* my confidence,
Thou'lt not deceive me?
      Gar: What, Master Aubry,
And do *you* ask me that? But yesterday
We did acknowledge to each other
That nature round our hearts had wound a tie
Of sympathy. Have you not often said,
That, in the darkness of my brow, there was
A something most congenial to thyself?
      Aub: But answer, wilt thou aid me against Villeré,
And Villeré's house to all extremity?
      Gar: Pshaw!
Do not anger me. Have I not advised
The use of stronger measures 'gainst them? True,
Villeré has been a father to me.
He found me, when an infant, in a ditch,
Thrown there by an inhuman mother.
He picked me up, and had me nursed with care,
And, cheated by the fairness of my skin,
He thought me one of Europe's sickly race,
And did adopt me as his son, and strove
To teach me science and morality.
But now I am among his servants classed;
For soon as I grew up my figure changed;
And this black hair, and eye, and bronzed face
Proclaimed me one of that dread tribe of men
Whose birthplace is the undivided wild,
Whose law is in the power of their arms,
Whose hate is trusted to a poisoned knife,
Whose thirst is for the white man's blood,
And whose ambition is to sweep away
Those pale usurpers of this land
Who seek to pen the freeborn Indian up
And set a bound'ry to his roving steps.
Listen, Aubry! I feel as if the red man's God

Had cast my lot amidst thy race to be
An agent of our nation's vengeance.
Think ye I'll shrink from such a sacred task?
Though Villeré still should call me his own son,
I would begin with him. I'll end, perhaps,
With you.

    AUB: With me!

    GAR: Nay, speak not of yourself,
But parley to your purposes. You have
My service now; use it while you may.

    AUB: [*aside*] A dreadful fellow this; but I must bend
Awhile unto his temper.
[*To* GARIDEL.] Well, I see
Thou art the man I sought for, Garidel.
I'll trust thee to the whole. Listen! If I fail
To gain my end by superstition's aid;
If calumny, with her venom, don't succeed
In turning their sweet loves into bitter
Jealousy— why, Garidel, I'll then attack
That very beauty which enslaves my heart
And causes all my pain; ay, and to which
Lafrenière kneels. I swear by Heaven
I'll destroy it, and what *I* could not gain
No other man shall feast upon. Look here!
This vial holds a subtle poison
Which, rubbed against the rose and lily
Of her face, will raise it full of blots
And biles, ulcers and putrid sores— make her
Disgusting to every one around her,
And even to herself. Tell me; think ye
He'll love her then?

    GAR: [*taking the vial*] Trust it to my hands.
I will apply it. But is its venom sure?
Say, from what propitious fiend of hell
Did you the drug procure?

    AUB: From that old witch,
That bride of Lucifer, the fortune-teller
Who lives midst the miasmas of the swamp.
Do you not know her?

    GAR: No, but tell me
How to find her; for, if she sells such drugs
As this, her traffic might be profited
By my acquaintance.

    AUB: Near the rotting trunk
Of that dead cypress tree which stands,

Like a giant skeleton, behind the common
Burial ground, without the city,
Her hut she has erected. It seems a heap
Of half-burned logs, and boards, and earth
Thrown there by accident. She chose the spot
For it is solitary, and near the fens
Where toads, and snakes, and poisonous weeds
Are trod upon at every step. 'Tis near
The graves and crumbling tombs from whence she gets
Most fit ingredients for the hellish spells
She deals in. The day she gave me that,
I found her in her low and dingy cabin
Crouched on the humid earth— watching,
With a curious care, some working spell
Which crackled 'midst the smoking embers.
A reddened light fell o'er the African;
Her twisted hair, white as a maiden's shroud,
Contrasted with her ebon skin; and her limbs,
Shrivelled by age, were but half covered 'neath
Some filthy, partly-colored rags.
A laugh, which sounded like a tiger's growl;
A smile, as when he shows his bloody teeth—
Her heavy lips relaxed, while, searching mine,
She raised her serpent eyes. I tremble
Even now.

    GAR: And I rejoice.

    AUB: By Heaven!
How can I reward thee?

    GAR: Teach me more crimes—
They give me joy enough! Continue on;
Detail your full intention unto me.
What would you do 'gainst Villeré, and 'gainst young
Lafrenière? I pant to deal with men.

    AUB: [*taking a dagger from his bosom*]
Here is a dagger I would trust with thee;
Its point is more envenomed than the bite
Of any serpent in thy native woods.
If thou couldst only touch them with its point—
They die, and I am happy.

    GAR: [*takes the dagger*] I take it,
And will do the deed; and though, with prudence,
You have steeped the dagger's point in poison,
Yet the wise precaution shall be useless;
For, when I strike the oppressors of my race,
The blow shall reach their hearts.

Aub: Hush! be careful!

Villeré approaches.

[*Enter* Villeré.]

Ah! Sir Villeré,
We meet in proper time. This way I came
To give you notice, that, at twelve to-day,
The council meets; and you, of course, must come:
For your opinions, ever wise, will aid us much
In acting on the matters strange we must
Discuss to-day.

Vil: Whatever wisdom, sir,
Heaven may have endowed me with
Is at the service of the colony.
But tell me, sir, what strange occurrence this,
Which is so greatly to engage our minds?

Aub: Excuse me, sir; this public place ill suits
The tale. Already have seditious men
Summoned the crowd to meet them here, and soon
The hour fixed will strike. Adieu, sir;
We shall expect you.

[*Exit* Aubry *and* Garidel *severally.*]

Vil: Strange this,
The people and the council both—

[*Enter* Lafrenière.]

Laf: Father,
For thus I love to call thee—

Vil: Lafrenière,
What stir is this, my son? Why is this
Meeting of the people called?

Laf: Ah, Villeré,
I have got such news 'twill turn your blood
To fire. What think ye— France— France has spurned us,
She has disowned us! We have lost the name—
The glorious name of Frenchmen.

Vil: What!
Has the King refused our prayer?

Laf: Ay, insists
That he will sell us like a gang of slaves,
And give us the treacherous Spaniard
For a master.

Vil: Can it be so? O France!
How couldst thou treat thy children thus? But say,
Lafrenière, is there no hope remaining?

Laf: None but in ourselves.

Vil: Speak, what can we do?

LAF: Have we not freeborn souls, stout hearts,
And sinewy arms?

VIL: We have; what then?

LAF: What! dost thou ask it? Can we stand thus,
With folded arms, and with our swords still sheathed,
And see our country trampled in disgrace—
Sold to a Spanish tyrant, be made
Spanish slaves— and not a single effort make
To gain our liberty?

VIL: Liberty?

LAF: Ay, Liberty!
The word sounds strangely in your ear; but soon
Will come a day, when, after father, mother, God,
That word will be the first one taught
To prattling babes; and even now
I'd have it make each brave Louisianian
Thrill with a godlike sentiment,
And like the electric shock
Strike to his ardent soul, and wake him up
To deeds of honor and renown.

VIL: But do I understand thee well?
Ha! hast thou pleased thy fancy with a dream
Of Greek republics, or of a Roman commonwealth?

LAF: Then must slavery be our choice.
Would ye have us bear the yoke of Spain, and
Call her tyrant *our* king and master, and
Her treacherous sons our countrymen?

VIL: Ah, much rather would I die than bear
Such shame.

LAF: And why not rather then be free?
There is no middle stand between two.
Ungrateful France has bartered us away;
We should from her ask help no more; but now
Must pass from one proud master to another,
Or rise at once like men, and boldly strike
For freedom.

VIL: I fear, my son, that thou art right.
But be exact. What are thy plans?

LAF: Already
Have I sent Garidel around, to call
Together our most worthy citizens.
I would have them, now, disclaim all foreign
Power, govern themselves; and take up arms
Should France or Spain invade the land.

VIL: But stay,

Lafrenière, dost thou not dread a failure?

    Laf: I dread *dishonor* more.

    Vil: We are few, and all
Undisciplined.

    Laf: Our cause is just. That— and
An able leader— will insure us victory.

    Vil: But France and Spain are powerful; they'll pour
Upon us armies, fleets. Could we resist
Such mighty strength as theirs?

    Laf: Well, should we fail,
What then? We will have done our duty;
But should we yield without a struggle,
Not only chains we'll bear, but fame will brand us—
Cowards!

    Vil: Thou hast gained me; and now with thee
This compact do I make— to fight, and die
Or triumph by thy side.

    Laf: Come, let us haste
And make some preparation for the meeting.

    [*Exit* Lafrenière *and* Villeré.]

    [*Enter* Denoyant, Milhet, Marquis, *and* Carrere.]

    Denoy: 'Tis my opinion that our deputation
Will meet with full success. Louis can never
Thus abandon his faithful subjects,
And his richest province in the western world.

    Car: Well, I confess I have strong doubts;
'Tis probable, I think, that all our hopes
Will be deceived, and that the Spaniard
Will reign in Louisiana yet.

    Denoy: Never!
Were I but sure that such a day would come,
I'd quit my native land, home, and possessions—
All— and hie me to some distant shore,
Where I'd not see nor even hear it told.

    Milh: For me, far rather would I drain this heart
Of all the blood that rushes to it now,
Than see my country for one moment suffer
Such foul disgrace.

    Marq: And I reecho that,
If e'er a Spanish tyrant treads on me,
Twill be upon a lifeless corpse.

    Car: Well, well! That
Such sentiments are highly noble
I don't deny. But are they not in vain?
Resistance will serve us nothing; we must

Be conquered. Should we take up arms,
Our stubbornness will but increase
The tyrant's rancor.

    [*During the dialogue* CROWDS OF CITIZENS *enter from every side.*]

    MARQ: Here comes Lafrenière.

    [*Enter* LAFRENIÈRE *and* VILLERÉ.]

    [*Voices.*] What news? What news?

    LAF: Fellow-citizens, most painful tidings
Do I bring you. All, all our hopes are crushed.
A letter from our friend Lesassier,
Chief of the deputation we have sent
To lay our griefs before the King, and beg
The revocation of the shameful treaty
Of which we have such reason to complain,
Informs me he could not even reach
The royal presence— that the ministers
Refuse to listen to our just demands,
And that we, at our gates, may soon expect
A Spanish army.

    [*Voices.*] Shame! What degradation!

    LAF: My friends, there is not one of you, I hope,
Whose soul feels not its indignation rise,
And all its anger conflagrated burn,
To hear of the high contempt with which
Licentious Louis treats our prayer. Countrymen,
Shall our native land, our honors and our lives,
Be humbled to strange laws— laws
Made by tyrants and by slaves enforced?

    [*Voices.*] No, never.

    DENOY: What can we do?

    LAF: I'd have ye
Take up arms—yes, die or triumph—
And never yield submission to the yoke.
When ills have reached their last extremity,
Despair must give the remedy that cures
Their strong intensity.

    CAR: Can we resist
Our pending fate? Can we contend 'gainst Spain's
Unnumbered hordes?

    LAF: Why ask ye not if hearts
We have, of temper bold and brave, and souls
Which labor to be free? Why count ye numbers?
Say, do ye fear to die, or care ye if
Your death doth come from one or from
Ten thousand hands?

Vil: I think Lafrenière right.
Our numbers are but few, but still we may,
By courage and determination, intimidate
Spain's mercenary hordes and free our shores
From vile pollution.

    Marq: My life, my fortune,
Freely would I give, to save my country
From this bondage.

    Denoy: And I!

    Milh: And I!

    Car: And I!

    Laf: My countrymen! I knew ye could not brook
This much-detested change. Soon would our
Patriot breasts be strangers in the land
Where once they breathed their natal air,
If we should try to join the variance wide
Which parts us from the arrogant Spaniard.
His morals, manners, character, all vary
From our own. Frenchmen will now disown us;
Spaniards we can never be, nor Englishmen;
But shall we be without a name? Of what
Nation will ye call yourselves? Old Europe
Has not a name to fit ye. Then let our
Country be Louisiana! Let's be Americans!

    Citizens. Yes, yes! Americans!

    Laf: Ay, that's a name
That will be ours; that none can take away.
Already has the cry of liberty
Resounded in the North. The colonies
Of Britain, the thirteen provinces, have risen
'Gainst a despot's tyranny; already
Has their blood flowed in the sacred cause.
Let's mix *our* blood with theirs,
And doubtless victory will coronate
The sacred pact. The Indian will help us;
For he has heard, e'en in the trackless woods,
Of mines, where Indians find a living tomb;
Of all the Inquisition's horrors dark;
Of blood-stained Gothic institutions, and
Of feudal slavery. Let us resist, I say!
Remember well, that Fortune's favored ones
Are noble, daring in audacious bravery.

    Citizens: We'll not submit! No, never! never!

    [Enter Garidel.]

    Gar: The Spaniards have reached our shores! A fleet

Bearing in it full five thousand men sails
Swiftly up the river.

LAF: Now! now,
My countrymen! now is the time to prove
Our firm resolve! Let us haste and arm, and
Drive them back as we did the ignoble
Don Ulloa! Soon must we give our liberty
Its baptism of blood! Prepare to die or be
Triumphant! Ay, let's take a sacred oath—
A solemn pledge, of victory or death!
Swear, countrymen! to die or to be free!

CITIZENS: [*simultaneously stretching out their right hands*]
We swear!

ACT II

SCENE 1

THE COUNCIL CHAMBER. AUBRY, VILLERÉ, MILHET, DENOYANT, MARQUIS, CARRERE,
AND OTHER MEMBERS OF THE COUNCIL SITTING ROUND A TABLE.

AUB: Gentlemen, matter of great consequence
Unites us here to-day in grave debate.
Deliberate measures must we take, and
Prudence more than anything to-day should guide
And dictate all our actions. No reckless
Resolutions, or undertaking rash,
By us adopted, should this fair province,
And ourselves, in risks and danger plunge.
You have already been informed that this
Fair colony has, by our gracious King,
Louis the beloved, been surrendered
Unto his Majesty the sovereign Charles
Of Spain. I need not tell you of the greatness,
The clemency and wisdom, of this prince.
Obedience to him is our duty.
Long have I waited with impatience,
That o'er us should begin his rule. At last
My longing wishes are all satisfied.

[*Enter* LAFRENIÈRE, *who remains in front.*]
O'Reilly, with full powers from his King,
Ascends the river and will soon be here.
'Tis true, that moved by futile hope, and strong
Attachment for the mother country,
Our citizens did drive good Don Ulloa
From their native shore; but of this wrong deed
They have, I hope, repented. Ambitious

Factions and discontented men, I know,
Have, by their cunning and exciting speeches,
Stirred their noble spirits to rebellion;
But quick submission will, I hope, soon show
That 'tis but a moment's aberration
Which leads them thus, with folly, to disown
The will and power of their rightful king.

     Laf: [*aside*] Base hypocrite! lying traitor!

     Vil: Indeed!

Your Excellence will pardon me, if my
Opinion differs from your own. I think
Our citizens are not thus unsteady;
Nor are they guided by a blind caprice.
What they have done, was calmly done, and not
In headlong haste. They have resolved to rise,
And desperate resistance to oppose
To the invading horde; and their honor
They have pledged, at price of blood, to save
Their country from oppression.

     Laf: [*aside*] Ay, tremble,
Ye traitors, for they'll keep that sacred oath.

     Aub: Much does it hurt me to confess the great
Displeasure I do feel, Sir Villeré, now
To find that you, whose discreet judgments have
So often shed benignant influence o'er
This council board, should thus have joined the voice,
The raging of the factious few, whose acts,
Thoughtless and criminal, ere long might bring
An evil scourge upon Louisiana,
And on themselves complete destruction.

     Laf: [*aside*] God!
Restrain me, or I'll kill the wretch!

     Aub: Remember,
Villeré, that when the Mississippi's wave,
With mighty force, and waters running high,
Threatens to crumble down our feeble dykes,
The prudent planter seeks to prop the banks
Or mend the widening breach. I fondly thought
That you, in this event, would seek to set
The barrier of your wisdom up against
The unruly current of this folly—
This rash presumption which menaces now
To sweep you with it, and destroy you.

     Laf: [*aside*] Oh, the bribed scoundrel!

     Vil: Aubry, I care not

How soon this white head of mine is felled; still
Persist I in my first opinion. Wisdom,
You say, has until now her breath infused
Into my words; she has not quit my side.
No factious counsel have I given; but
The people— the whole people— have arisen,
And Spain's mercenaries shall dye their swords
In Creole blood, and tread upon an host
Of slain, before they gain the city's walls.

  Denoy: Ay, Aubry; and I have joined them too, and
Have pledged my honor also with the rest;
And to redeem the promise I have made,
My sword must triumph in the battle, or
My life be paid a tribute to the grave.

  Milh: And mine!

  Marq: [*to Aubry*] Sir, we'll never yield!

  Denoy: No, never.

  Aub: Gentlemen! This is rebellion— treason!
France has made a formal resignation—

  Car: I do deny the right—

  Denoy: We all deny it.

  Aub: The people here cannot assume a voice.

  Laf: [*to Aubry*] Thou liest, dog! The people *will* assume
That right—

  Milh: Yes, and they'll maintain it too!

  Laf: Ah! hear you that, your Excellence? Thought ye
These men were bought by dirty Spanish gold?
You've called them traitors— *you* are the traitor!
Do you not hold a correspondence close
With the governor of Havana, say?
And sent you not unto the court of Spain
The names of those who led the noble band
Which drove proud Don Ulloa from our shore?
I tell you, Aubry, *you* are the traitor.

  Aub: Gentlemen, do you suffer this?

  Laf: Suffer!
Do you appeal to them? Go, call your friends,
The treacherous Spaniards.

  Aub: I'll call my guard.
I'll have you all arrested. [*The members rise and draw.*]

  Laf: What!—guard! arrest!
I do defy you to attempt it. Ha!
Pronounce one word, and round us I will bring
The assembled city, all up in arms,
To tear thy worthless soldiery to pieces,

And destroy thee with them.

    Aub: [*softening*] Excuse me, sirs,

But 'twas my duty which commanded me.

I meant no insult, nor was I in earnest—

    Laf: [*to Aubry*] Silence!

[*To the members*] Gentlemen! The people send me to you.

My message is, that they have made me chief,

And all authority have placed in me,

Until invaders shall no more pollute

The air we breathe. This council is dissolved;

And you, my friends, it is expected, will

Unite your strength with ours, to repel

The horde of bandits who, advancing fast,

Approach with angry cries our walls.

    Vil: Whate'er

Our fellow-citizens ordain, we'll do.

    Denoy: And we are happy, Lafrenière, that you

Have been selected to command.

    Milh: Success

Is thus insured.

    Marq: And confidence inspired.

    Aub: I do protest against this whole proceeding.

It is illegal.

    Laf: [*to Aubry*] Silence, I tell thee, thou perfidious

Coward. [*To the members*]

My friends, it is my ardent wish

That your great trust in me should be maintained.

All my best energies I'll use to gain

The franchise we aspire to. The aid

Of your advice, good gentlemen, will be

Of great assistance to me, and I hope

That 'twill be given with profusion. Come,

Let us haste; our forces must be formed.

And we must march to-night.

    [*Exeunt* Lafrenière, Villeré, *and members.*]

    Aub: A coward! Yes,

I know I am a coward; but, rash youth,

With all thy bravery, I'll overcome thee.

Ay! trust thee to honor, strength, and courage.

Cunning will overset thee with a straw.

Aubry will teach thee lessons so severe

They'll make you feel as a well-punished child

Scorching 'neath his tutor's whip. I'll teach him,

Young, presuming dog! to know his fellow-men—

Their falsehood, and the little trust to place

In all their oaths and protestations loud.
To-morrow's dawn shall ope to disappoint
His proud ambition and his brilliant plans.

SCENE 2:— ADELAIDE'S APARTMENT.

[*Enter* GARIDEL.]

GAR: 'Tis now my glowing Indian blood doth flow
With all its vigor through my beating veins.
How high it leaps at thoughts of gratified
Revenge! [*Holds up the vial of poison.*]

All hail, thou elixir of hell!
Poison to her, and balm to me for every wound
Inflicted by her father. Now's the time—
No one observes me— none will dare suspect.

[*Takes up a vial from the toilet table.*]
This is her favorite essence; 'tis the
Sweet cologne of wide reputed virtue—
Its purity unsullied as descending dew,
Its odor fragrant as a garden's breath,
Its healing power most miraculous.

[*Pours the vial of poison into it.*]
Neither its odor nor its color change.
Thou God! it will succeed! Ha! how she'll look!—
Her beauty gone and horror in its place!
I see her raving at its loss; and he,
Distracted by the dreadful blow, shall writhe
Beneath the vengeful stroke. Her father, too!—
Ha! how he will feel it, when this goddess—
This queen of beauty he so dotes upon,
Will fall upon his neck all withered o'er
By sullying disease! Ha! and perhaps
He'll shrink away, and dread to kiss that cheek
On which so often he has pressed the lip—
The fervent lip, of warm parental love.
Ah! and her mother— what will she do? Oh,
She will die!. For 'tis beyond conception
That she should bear the dreadful agony
That this will bring upon her. They come—
I must not here be seen. O happy hour!
Brim full of secret pleasure.

[*Exit* GARIDEL.]

[*Enter* ADELAIDE *and* MRS. VILLERÉ.]

MRS. VIL: My Adelaide,
Thy choice, indeed, doth satisfaction give

To thy fond mother. Of all the noble
Youths who crowd to catch one softened ray
From those bright eyes of thine, more worthy none
Than young Lafrenière is to be thy lord;
His form is cast in manly beauty's mould,
His heart is virtue's richest, purest gem,
His mind a palace genius lighteth up.

 Ade: Ah, mother, thou dost almost natter him.

 Mrs. Vil: Faultless, I do not say he is.

 Ade: Some faults
He has; but, like clouds around the sun,
They're gilded over by the shining rays
Cast from the brightness of his qualities,
And only serve to give a high relief
To all the splendor of his virtue.

 Mrs. Vil: Say,
Think ye not he is presumptuous?

 Ade. No, no.
Presumption is, I think, the distance 'tween
What men themselves believe to be the worth,
The virtue, talent, power, they possess,
And what their real value is. Pray, then,
To what has young Lafrenière yet pretended
In which he overprized himself?

 Mrs. Vil: Thou dost
Defend him well, and with an eloquence
Near equal to his own.

 Ade: My heart doth prompt it.

 [*Trumpets, drums, and shouts are heard without, distantly.*]

 Mrs. Vil: Hark to these sounds!

 Ade: [*opening a window*] See, mother, 'tis the proud
Array of war; and, while we talk of love,
Our youths abandon now their chosen fair,
And court the favor of less tender dames:
Glory and carnage, and bright liberty,
Are now the mistresses to whom they bow,
And deck their forms in warlike garb to woo.
Think, mother, that our verdant fields will soon
In gory streams be soaked; and that many friends
We love, 'neath hostile swords may sink. Ah! think,
That my father, too, may fall amidst the fight,
Pouring his life-blood on his native soil—
Dying— all gashed and pierced and trampled o'er
By charging horses and the reckless feet
Of rushing thousands. [*The noises are repeated.*]

Mrs. Vil: Ah! my Adelaide,
Thou bringest on me thoughts which shake my soul
E'en to its inmost dwelling.
    [*Enter* Villeré]
    Ade: Father!
    Mrs. Vil: Husband!
    Vil: My wife— my child!
    Mrs. Vil: Villeré,
I read my fate already in thine eye.
Thou art called to risk thy life, so precious
To our hearts, in battle's dreadful fury.
And must we now, when years of quiet and
Content have blessed our union, part with fear
Of never meeting more?
    Vil: Not so, my spouse.
Let not thus fear victorious hold the sway
Of thy true heart. Let rather pleasing hopes
Dispel thy cloudy bodings of the future.
No share to me is granted in the fight
Which is to fix my country's destiny;
And, though I begged a station to obtain
In its defenders' ranks, my prayer was vain.
Lafrenière, whom the people have appointed
Leader, sends me amongst the settlements
To call in all Louisiana's force,
And gain the succor of our red allies.
From thence, in haste, I'll wend my lengthened way
To ask assistance of that noble race
Who dwell along Atlantic's western shore,
And who are now, in proud array, opposed
To proud Britannia's tyranny.
    Mrs. Vil: Thanks to Lafrenière for this happy care.
Much will I try, the pleasure now he gives
This sorrowing breast, in double fold to pay.
    Ade: But, father, dost thou leave us e'en to-day?
    Vil: Yes, all is ready, and I go e'en now;
My steed awaits me at the gate.
    Mrs. Vil: My love,
Why haste you thus? Oh, wait until the morn!
Stay with us yet this day.
    Vil: Each minute counts.
Come, then, embrace thy husband e'er he goes. [*They embrace.*]
My country needs the promptest services,
And I must fly upon the wings of haste.
My daughter, go, tell Garidel prepare

To start upon this voyage with me.

    [*Exit* Adelaide.]

Come, my love, be not depressed. I'll send thee news
Of all that doth befall me as I go.

    Mrs. Vil: And must it then be so? But, Villeré, say,
Wilt thou be absent long?

    Vil: But six short weeks
Will suffice for my duty. I'll then return;
And Heaven grant I find my country free,
The Spaniards beaten, and untroubled peace
Around our happy fireside! And then,
My wife, the long retarded union of
Our child with Lafrenière once solemnized,
In tranquil solitude we'll pass the days
Of our last years.

    [*Reenter* Adelaide.]

    Ade. Father, thy bidding's done; Garidel is ready.

    Vil: I thank thee, child;
But come before thy father goes, and take his blessing.

[*He kisses her forehead, and she kneels.*]

My daughter, Heaven bless thee,
Ward off all dangers from this lovely head,
Keep thy fragile frame from pain or sickness,
Preserve thee to console my coming age,
And make thee thy Lafrenière's worthy bride. [*She rises.*]
Remember oft thy father; in thy prayers,
Each eve and morn, send up to God's high throne
An earnest supplication for success
To all his labor, and his safe return.

    Ade: Oh! could I forget that duty, Father?
Oh, may my faint petition reach the ear
Of Him who holds our fate within His hand!
He'll not refuse what asks a guileless heart:
He'll shield thee, father, and will keep thee for us.

    Mrs. Vil: Nay, go not yet.

    Vil: Indeed, I must depart.
My country calls. Adieu!

    [*They embrace and part.*]

    Ade: Adieu!

    Mrs. Vil: Adieu!

    [*Exit* Villeré.]

Ade: O mother, I am faint! This unforewarned
Departure of my father striketh hard
Upon my heart, and makes me feel quite sick.

Mrs. Vil: [*wetting her kerchief from the vial*]

Here, my daughter, here; respire this, my love,

And pour it o'er thy cheeks, and neck, and temples;

'Twill spur the blood that stoppeth in thy veins.

    [*As* Mrs. Villeré *gives the kerchief and vial to her daughter,* Garidel *enters.*]

    Gar: [*aside*] Ha! [*To Mrs.* Villeré.]

Dear madam, I come to bid adieu

To you and kind Miss Adelaide.

    Mrs. Vil: Thank thee,

Garidel, for this attention. Good-by.

I wish thee a pleasant voyage, and hope

That nought but good will come across thy path.

    Gar: Thank thee, good lady; but is Miss Adelaide

Unwell?— she looks quite pale.

    Ade: A little faint—

'Tis nothing— *this* will drive it soon away.

But, Garidel, take good care of father—

Let nothing do him harm.

    Gar: Long as this arm

Can move, it shall be lifted to protect

My benefactor. Adieu!

    [Garidel *shakes the hands of both.*]

    [*Exit* Garidel.]

Mrs. Vil: Indeed, Garidel is well worthy of the care

That on him Villeré has bestowed; but say,

My daughter, art thou still unwell?

Ade: 'Tis past—

I'm quite recovered.

Mrs. Vil: Well, then, I leave thee;

I have some duties to attend to. [*They kiss.*]

    [*Exit* Mrs. Villeré.]

Ade: Ah!

How full of pain this hour is, and how

My feeble heart doth throb with suffering!

    [*Sees a letter on the toilet.*]

Ah, a letter!— 'Tis addressed to me. What can

It be? [*Opens it and reads.*] "Adelaide, thy love's bestowed

On one unworthy; and the hot passion

He pretends, a false heart disguises.

His high ambition and his secret plans

Force him to seek an union which will gain

A strong support to all his wild designs.

And, lady, though he feels no spark of love,

Yet still he woos thee for thy name, and will

Perhaps e'en yet sufficient power have

To make thee spurn the warning of a friend."

Ah! can this be true, or is it calumny?

O Lafrenière, couldst thou deceive me thus?

Oh, double blow of pitiless misfortune!

    [*Enter* Lafrenière.]

        Laf: Ah, Adelaide! thou seem'st unwell, my love.

Say, what weighs thee down so heavily?

What! is't on *me* thy angry frowns are bent?

What have I done to merit such reception?

        Ade: Leave me this instant, sir!

        Laf: Nay, say not so.

Thou art not serious, Adelaide. Ah,

That blush which cloth suffuse thy lovely cheek

Methinks doth tell another tale!

        Ade: Blush, sir!

The red that rose upon my brow doth mark

My great displeasure at the sight of thee.

        Laf: Heaven! what crime have I committed?

        Ade: Say,

Art thou not false, and is not Ambition

The only dame whose favors thou dost court

When thou dost kneel to me?

        Laf: 'Tis true I am

Ambitious; but, my Adelaide, I swear

Thou'rt joined with my ambition's brightest dream;

And laurels, riches, fame, I'd cast away

As childish baubles, nor would I aspire

To aught above the name of honest man,

Did I not think to share these things with thee.

        Ade: Most bravely, frankly, said; and thou too canst

Thine honor and thy truth both lay aside

With her whose weakness ye'd beguile. Sir,

I have friends who o'er my welfare watch,

And whose kind care detected have thy plans—

Thy wily, base, ungenerous plots.

        Laf: [*kneeling*] Upon my knees I pray thee, Adelaide,

Tell me what whim is this. What black falsehood

Hast thou heard which makes thee doubt, what ne'er

Until to-day hath been impeached by woman or

By man— Lafrenière's honor?

        Ade: Ay, 'tis thus

With all your sex: ye kneel and cringe;

With cheating words, and oaths, and promises,

And whining prayers, ye do triumph o'er

Our unsuspecting hearts; and when we own

Your power, and our love— to masters change;

Poor feeble woman's duty then becomes
To watch each caprice of a tyrant's will—
Live in his smile and wither 'neath his frown.

    Laf: [*who has risen*]

Lady, I've done. Thou'lt hear from me no more
Words prompted by my passion's ardor. Yet
Do not think the fire that burns within
This breast will cease to burn. Though smothered,
'Twill not die, and, thus confined, 'twill torture
None but me. My countrymen await me.
Oh, may I lead *them* unto victory,
And may I meet with death!

    [*Exit* Lafrenière.]

    Ade: What have I done?

Why did I not show him this?— Laf— Ah, no!
I must not call him back; he would exult
As in a victory. Proud of the strong
Seductions of his mien and eloquence,
He'd look upon me as a conquered slave.
No, no: I'm full of love, yet I'm as proud
As he. Ah, my mother! To thee I'll haste
For consolation to my stricken breast.[*Exit.*]

Scene 3:— A Wood [Night]

[Enter Aubry, accompanied by Ruffians.]

    Aub: Yes; this is the place fixed by Garidel—

His note describes it well. Go ye and hide
Behind these trees; and, when I the signal give,
Rush on Sir Villeré— ye know him all. Mind,
Shed not one drop of blood, or ye shall not
Be paid a single sou. Remember well,
That he that's with him is a friend. Go.

    [*Exit* Ruffians.]

                 Now,

Villeré, I think I'll make thee much repent
This morning's insult, thrown with heedless hand
Into my face. Villeré my prisoner,
My favor with the Spanish chief is doubly
Sure; and thus both interest and my hate
I serve at once; and yet I will myself
Be safe, nor stand the danger of a blow.
'Tis thus with prudence men should ever act,
Nor rashly jeopardize their own lives
In open combats of uncertain end.

It is not all to serve the spite one feels,
But most maturely should we weigh results.
None would I hurt who useful to me are,
Though I should hate them with a poisoned hate.
But if I loved a man— though that can't be—
I'd have him murdered if he barred my plans.
These fights, done in the world's wide eye, create
To one an host of angry enemies;
But 'tis the midnight blow, the killing draught,
Which yield revenge while safety is not risked;
And on to-morrow I can give this hand
Into the brother of the man it kills
To-night.

    GAR: [*outside*] 'Tis a fit place. Good Sir Villeré,
Let us here dismount and seek the path: on foot
We'll find it easier. Our steeds are tired—
Let's give them rest a while.

    AUB: Ah, here they come,
I must conceal myself; I'll not approach
Until he's well secured and bound.

    [*Exit* AUBRY.]

    [*Enter* GARIDEL *and* VILLERÉ.]

    VIL: Well, Garidel,
With thy fancy for a shorter path,
We're lost, and now must pass the dreary night
In this cold morass.

    GAR: I promise it, good sir,
That in a healthy bed you'll sleep this night,
And 'neath a shelter most secure. [*Thunder.*]

    VIL: Hear that!
And we shall have a storm to make the night
Most comfortably romantic. [*Lightning and thunder.*]

    GAR: Indeed,
Sir Villeré, walk with me but some few steps:
Surely I'll meet with friends.

    [*Enter* RUFFIANS *slowly creeping behind.*]

    VIL: Pshaw! seest thou not
That we are in the very swamp itself?
This delay distracts me. Oh, my country!
May Heaven shield thee till I send thee help.
I fear the battle, on which turns thy fate,
Will be decided e'er I send thee succor;
And that thy little band will be o'erwhelmed.

    GAR: Come. This swampy air doth chill your blood.

    VIL: [*turning, sees the* RUFFIANS *and draws*] Ah, see.

Garidel! through the darkness I discover
Some human figures lurking.
  Gar: Ah! doubtless
They are black, runaways! Give me your sword,
For I am young and strong; take these instead.
[*They exchange arms.* Villeré *gives* Garidel *his sword, who returns a brace of pistols. The* Ruffians *rush on* Villeré, *who attempts to fire, but the pistols snap. The* Ruffians *seize him.*]
  Vil: Treachery! Wretches! slaves! unhand me!
[*The curtain falls.*]

ACT III.
Scene 1:— The interior of Lafrenière's tent.

  [*Enter* Lafrenière.]
Laf: I like the plan; it will, I think, secure
A glorious victory. On one side
The deep, broad, rapid Mississippi rolls;
And, on the other, impenetrable swamps
Prevent approaches of the foe. Our front
Protected by a breastwork and a fosse,
We can defy the well-drilled troops of Spain,
Bring all our force to bear, and though unused
To battle (yet, in savage forests trained
To use, with fatal aim, the carabine),
Americana's brave and hardy sons
Will strew the field with dead, make the Spaniard
Shrink away with dread, and victory insure.
Yes, I like the plan; it answers well;
It is the only one by which the rising
City of my birth, Louisiana's pride,
Can be defended 'gainst invading hordes
Who seek for rapine and for slaughter.
  [*Enter* Aubry.]
Aubry! What wouldst coward, traitor, here?
Hast thou repented— hast thou brave become,
And wouldst thou aid thy country in the fight?
Or dost thou come, a cunning spy, to watch
Our movements, and give the Spaniards notice?
  Aub: Lafrenière, I am no traitor. I ne'er
Acknowledged thy authority, nor that
Of those who rashly made you chief: I owe
Allegiance to the Spanish king; and I
Do show obedience to the plain command
Of Louis, by whose decree and gracious will
I held the rule o'er this fair colony.

I have protested, but in vain 'twas done,
'Gainst thine and the people's usurpation
Of the power which belonged to me. But since
My proclamation is disdained,
I ask thee— chief of this rebel army—
      Laf: [*offers to strike him*] Rebel! vile traitor, had I not pity
On thy helplessness, I'd shake thy limbs apart
For this insulting insolence.
      Aub: Nay, sir,
Excuse my words; no insult did I mean,
And hope it is not taken so. The words
Came of themselves upon my lip: I called
Them not with wish of giving you offence;
But rebels, fear I, ye will still be named,
Unless victorious in the coming fight— [Lafrenière *offers to draw.*]
Nay, sir—I beg—I would not anger you—
There's no insult meant.
      Laf: Speak! What wouldst thou?
      Aub: I pray that, since I owe you no submission,
Since enrolment with you is but voluntary,
Since 'tis the duty of the rank I hold,
Since my proclamation has been vain,
That you would let me, at this hour, repair
Unto the Spanish camp, and there remain,
And all the rights of war partake as do
The other subjects of the Iberian king.
      Laf: Pshaw! Think'st thou that we do want thee 'mongst us?
Go, sir! The service thou canst render Spain
Will do us little injury. Go, sir!
And bow thy servile head unto the slave
Of Europe's vilest despot. Go, sir!
We want not cowards, traitors, 'mongst us;
We'll dread thee less when in the Spanish camp.
      Aub: I thank you, sir— I go; but—
      Laf: Mind thee, sir,
Thou'lt run much risk to cross this camp; for if
One of the citizens discover thee,
Thou'lt soon be torn into a thousand parts.
      Aub: I know that; for I heard them cursing me,
As I passed through them to you. I dread not
Such detection; this cloak doth hide me well.
But can I pass the outposts?
      Laf: Thou couldst not,
Unless thou hadst the word. But that would make
Thee tremble, but to hear it spoken out;

'Twould choke thy utterance to speak the word;
'Twas made for braves and freemen to pronounce.
Without there! citizen!

[*Enter* SOLDIER.]

Conduct this
Man beyond the outposts, and leave him free.

[*Exit* SOLDIER *and* AUBRY, *who bows to* LAFRENIÈRE *as he goes out.*]

O man! thou art a creature strange indeed!
Who can explain the workings of thy heart?
Aubry is insolent, yet cowardly—
A traitor, who killeth while caressing you;
And yet how many other men are mild,
Yet brave and true, who scorn a crime!
'Tis strange—
Some men have virtue, others vice; and while
Each beast has some peculiar character,
Man cannot say that he is so or so.
The tiger is bloody, false, and cowardly;
The lion is bold and generous; but men
Have souls of various makes, so many
That they not even know themselves.
But Villeré—
I get no news of him; what can it mean?
'Tis now a week since I have sent him hence,
And yet he does not send intelligence;
No succors do arrive. Why lags he thus?
Are the settlements indisposed to join?
Is he neglectful? No! That cannot be.
I know not what to think.

[*Enter* MRS. VILLERÉ.]

MRS. VIL: Lafrenière!

LAF: Madam! What can bring you here?
What has occurred? Your look is full of pain.

MRS. VIL: Where is my husband, Lafrenière?

LAF: Thy husband!
Lady, I sent him to the settlements
To gather forces for the army.

MRS. VIL: Have you got news? Where— how fares my husband?

LAF: Lady, I'll not deceive you— I know not.
Daily I've waited for some messenger—
Yet none from him has arrived. I tremble
Lest some accident has befallen him.

MRS. VIL: Ah! 'Tis this I have trembled should occur.
Ah! 'Twas thy unquiet spirit led him on,
And brought thy country into dangers vain.

LAF: Madam, reproach me not. Do you not teach
Your beauteous daughter, by your precepts wise,
That honor's palm is more, in real worth,
Than the gaudiest diadem which e'er was placed
Upon the brows of shameless votaries—
That death is better than a tarnished fame?
And wouldst thou see thy loved husband, lady,
Or I, or any of thy countrymen,
Bend to a stranger's pride? Say, should we live
To blush to own that we *do* live? Ah, lady, no!
It cannot be that Villeré's wife doth utter
Words which would make her husband blush to hear.

MRS. VIL: True, true. Lafrenière, thou dost speak it right.
Pardon me— I am distracted. Heaven
Is witness that I love my husband's fame;
But I could love him with that fame all lost.

LAF: Cheer up, good madam!

[*Enter* FIRST SOLDIER.]

What wouldst thou, soldier?

SOLD: A deserter from the Spanish camp asks
For admittance near you. He doth assert
That he has business pressing and important
To lay before our chief.

LAF: Bring him to me.

[*Enter a* SPANIARD, *exit* SOLDIER.]

Approach, good fellow! Art thou from the camp
Of Spain?

SPAN: I am; I hope it will please you, sir,
I'm charged to bear this letter to you.

LAF: Ha! Thou God! It is Villeré's writing!

MRS. VIL: Villeré!
Read! Read! Read! What does he say?

LAF: [*reading*] "My dear friend:
To him who bears this I have promised safety,
And from you a rich reward. Garidel
Has proved a traitor! Plotted with Aubry!
And since six long days I've been confined
On board a Spanish ship. Console my wife
And gentle Adelaide!"

[MRS. VILLERÉ *faints and falls into the arms of the* SPANIARD, *while* LAFRENIÈRE *exclaims.*]
Eternal God!
He has escaped me! O Aubry! Aubry!
Hadst thou but come an hour later! What can I do?
I have no prisoners who are worth him;
I'd have to force the Spanish camp to reach

The ship. My troops are much too raw. Distraction!

MRS. VIL: [*recovering*]

Oh, my poor heart! Thou art quite hard to burst.

[*To the* SPANIARD.] Where is the ship?— the Spanish ship which holds

My husband— the man who sent you here?

SPAN: A mile

Below the other camp, and near the shore,

It lies.

[*Exit* MRS. VILLERÉ.]

LAF: [*who has not seen what has passed, but who is still musing*]

Yes, that's the only way to save him— yes.

To-night, assisted by th' obscurity,

I go, in a well-armed boat, below,

To burn the ship, and save my aged friend—

Ah! Where is the lady gone?

SPAN: She went out

In sorrow overwhelmed.

LAF: Poor, good lady!

She hastes too much to tell the fatal news

Unto her daughter and her friends. Follow!

[*Exeunt.*]

SCENE 2:— *A SPANISH SHIP AT ANCHOR IN THE MISSISSIPPI, NEAR THE BANK / TWO BOATS ALONGSIDE; SAILORS LOUNGING IN DIFFERENT POSTURES; THE SUN SETTING; AUBRY AND GARIDEL ON DECK.*

AUB: The fool! He thinks that bravery alone

Can the Spaniards in this crisis serve. Ha!

I know a secret path meandering

Through the swamp, by which I can, with every ease,

Bring in his rear half of the Spanish host,

While in his front the other half doth charge.

GAR: Ha! ha! How will his helter-skelter band

Oppose Spain's compact legions then? But say,

How has the poison worked? Did you inquire?

AUB: Yes; while roving about the city's streets,

I met a slave of theirs. The thing works well,

But slowly; each day a change for worse is seen.

It will soon break out in all its frightfulness.

GAR: I saw her use it ere I started thence—

Perhaps she does so even now. I felt

A strange pleasure when I saw it. Aubry,

Thou didst discover regions in my soul

Which ere thou cam'st were yet untrodden. Thanks

Be to thee for thy keen perception. I've found

My element; soon wilt thou see me swimming
In a sea of blood.

 Aub: [*arising*] Garidel, adieu,
This hour must I meet O'Reilly— he'll not
Be driven off as Don Ulloa was.
To-night I lead the Spanish troops around;
And to-morrow shall Lafrenière's blood
Stream out with bubbling force, and I shall laugh
To see it flow. [*He enters a boat.*]

 Gar: Adieu, good master Aubry;
I wish thee much success. I'll be with you
If my duty here is done in good time.
I've yet to hang old father Villeré;
I think he'll not take long to die. Adieu.

 [*Exit* Aubry.]
Well, now that darkness has commenced, I may
Begin this old rascal's execution.
My men! To work! Prepare the rope— bring up
That fellow from the cabin. We shall see
How he can dance in air; from yonder mast
We'll swing him off. Ha! here he comes! I'll try
The temper of his soul, in this dread hour,
E'en in its tenderest part.

 [*Enter* Villeré, *led up in chains.*]
Sir Villeré,
Good news I bring you— your child and lady
Soon you'll see.

 Vil: O Garidel! Though thou hast
Betrayed me, and most ungrateful proved;
Though thou hast e'en upbraided me for all
The very kindness I've heaped upon thee—
Yet I would pardon all, and die with joy,
Could I but clasp them once— but once— again,
With these weak, shackled arms!

 Gar: Well, then, 'tis gained;
Soon will I have thy pardon, benefactor.
Ye'll meet them not with shackled arms, and not
To quit them soon again. Come, will you go?

 Vil: Indeed!

 Gar: I do assure you!

 Vil: [*kneeling*] I thank thee
With lowly and confounded wonder, God!
God of the helpless, receive my fervent
Thanks.

 Gar: Amen!

[*All the* Sailors *together.*] Amen!

 Vil: [*rising*] Well, Garidel!

Do I go now, or when?

  Gar: Yes, even now.

  Vil: Take off my chains.

  Gar: Not yet; but ye shall not

Have them when you meet your wife and child.

  Vil: Well, well, that's all I care for; say, go I

Within that boat?

  Gar: No! By a shorter road.

  [*Pointing to the rope prepared to hang* Villeré.]

See! Yon rope shall bear thee to them.

Thy wife and child will meet thee in the grave.

  [Garidel *and the* Sailors *burst into a loud laugh.*]

Vil: [*after standing a while confounded*] Wretches!

  [*Enter* Mrs. Villeré, *on the bank.*]

  Mrs. Vil: My husband!

  Vil: God! is this a dream?

  Gar: No, it is no dream! 'Tis triumph! Glory!

Woman, prepare to see thy husband die!

  Mrs. Vil: [*kneeling*] Oh, spare him, Garidel! Oh, remember,

He saved thee when a child from want and death,

He was a father to thee in thy youth,

He loves thee with paternal love! Oh, stay!

O Garidel, have pity!

  Gar: Pity? I know not

What you mean. [Mrs. Villeré *faints.*]

  Vil: Nay, trifle not so roughly;

This can't be serious; 'tis a cruel play.

I will go to my wife; she awaits me there.

  Gar: Ha! ha! The gallows 'tis awaits you, sir!

Come, prepare the rope— despatch!

  Vil: The gallows! [*Striking* Garidel.]

Slave! Durst thou thus insult me?

  Gar: [*drawing a dagger*] Ha, Villeré!

This dagger was given me for thee! [*Stabs* Villeré *several times.*]

  Vil: [*falling*] God!

I'm dying! My child! My wife! My country! [*Dies.*]

  Mrs. Vil: [*recovering*] Where is my husband? Did he not call me?

  Gar: [*steeping a kerchief in* Villeré's *blood*]

Thy husband, woman! Here is his blood!

  [*Throws the kerchief to her.*]

  Mrs. Vil: [*staggering*] Oh!

  Gar: Art thou not satisfied? Go, join him, then!

  [*Fires a pistol at her; she falls and dies.*]

[*At that moment* LAFRENIÈRE *rushes in along the shore, accompanied by armed followers.*]

LAF: Stop, murderers! Ah, ye have done your work!

But mine begins! Fire! [*The soldiers fire;* GARIDEL *staggers.*]

GAR: [*falling*] Lafrenière, I die!

But I await thee at the gates of hell. [*Falls.*]

ACT IV.

SCENE 1.— LAFRENIÈRE'S CAMP. LAFRENIÈRE'S TENT IN THE BACKGROUND- THE BODIES
OF MR. AND MRS. VILLERÉ LAID OUT ON A LITTER; LAFRENIÈRE GAZING UPON THEM.

LAF: There— there is what is left of noble man

And virtuous woman. There Villeré lies,

The wise, the brave, the generous— a man

Respected, loved; he had a crowd of friends,

Who shook his hands and clasped him in their arms:

Now they would loathe e'en to put their finger

On his dead, but stately, brow; they'd stand round

In silence, as if they feared to wake him

From the marble sleep of death, and look on

With eyes and faces which would seem to say,

Can he be dead? What! can *this* be the man—

The living man we saw but yesterday?

To-day, God! what could have done this?

By some slight gashes on his side he lieth there

The senseless mockery of what he was!

And on his human faculties is placed

A seal as lasting as eternity.

[*Enter* ADELAIDE, *extremely pale and emaciated; he does not see her.*]

Thou God! what will I say to Adelaide?

I'd tremble 'neath the look of that poor girl,

And feel, though pure, as guilty of a crime.

ADE: Lafrenière!

LAF: Heavens! What voice is that?

No, no, it cannot be— thou art not Adelaide!

ADE: O Lafrenière! speak not such dreadful words.

I know it— I am no more that beauteous

Adelaide on whom ye once did fix the gaze

Of love; but though now but the ghost of what

I was— the tattered remnant of a robe

Which once was rich and graceful— oh, let not

This new deformity drive away the love

Which once was fostered in thy breast

For me! Oh, make me not loathe e'en myself!

Know'st thou not thine Adelaide? Say, has she lost

All semblance to herself?

LAF: My Adelaide! [*They embrace.*]

ADE: Lafrenière! Ah! well mayst thou look with wide
Astonished eyes upon me. Look, look on;
But try to look with love and not disgust.
Seest thou these sunken, tarnished eyes— this
Deadened skin which leaves the unhealthy flesh—
These lips, which thou didst oft compare, whene'er
Amidst the bloom of spring we roved, to every
Crimson flower thou didst pluck— these lips,
Like those now withered flowers, have faded too.

LAF: Nay; rave not so, my own dear Adelaide,
'Tis only passing sickness— thou'lt be well
In some few days.

ADE: No, no; believe it not.
I thought so too; but I did hear them say,
In whispers which they thought I did not hear,
'Twas poison—

LAF: Poison?

ADE: Yes, a cankering
Drug, well known by its fell workings on me,
Which on my skin perfidious hands have put,
And which will soon (oh, wilt thou love me then?)
Break out in putrid sores and leaking biles.
Nay, do not seem thus horror-struck.

LAF: O God!
It cannot be, my Adelaide. Who could have done
So infamous a deed? What hast thou done—
Who harmed— that one should seek thee out and thus
Deface thy cheek with his polluted hands?

ADE: Ah, was it not a wanton crime?

LAF: O man! what can exceed thy wickedness?
That enemy of every breathing thing,
The serpent of the woods, will raise his head,
Hiss, and shake his rattles at the approach
Of unsuspecting feet. But man, the greatest
Enemy of man, rejoiceth in the blood
Of innocence; and, while wild beasts destroy
To get their food, man— savage man— doth kill
To kill, and doth amusement find to see
The blood ooze out of wounds his hand has made.
And laughs when victims writhe in death's last agony.

ADE: Ah, Lafrenière, say dost thou love me still?

LAF: If I do love thee, Adelaide? Ask me
If this warm heart still beats; for till its throbs
Do cease, its highest bound will be for thee.

ADE: We parted last in anger. 'Twas silly;
But thou wilt not chide me, Lafrenière,
Though 'twas a jealous whim, for sorrow now
Inflicts the punishment upon me. Think,
I blush to tell thee, some rival enemy
Of thine— he cannot be thy rival now,
For thy love hangs not on the flesh as doth
The love of common men— yes, that rival
Wrote me this, and I believed it— ah, wilt
Thou love me less?
     LAF: Astonishment! Yes, yes,
'Tis Aubry's secret hand with which he wrote
That false perfidious note he once addressed
To Don Ulloa, full of monstrous lies
Against his countrymen. Aubry! Aubry!
Thy deeds will soon encounter punishment.
Thou God, turn on him his own faithless arms;
Bring on him, though not from Lafrenière's hands,
The lying snares he knows so well to lay—
The poisoned blades he can so well direct.
ADE: [*seeing the bodies, but not recognizing*]
Ah, what! has the war so soon been fatal?
Perhaps some orphan o'er each body there will weep
A father slain. Who are they, Lafrenière?
     LAF: [*aside*] Thou God, what can I do to ward this blow away?
     ADE: Say, were they good and virtuous?
     LAF: They were indeed.
     ADE: O death! why dost thou not— whose arm
Guides in its rapid flight the fatal ball,
Directs the impending sabre where to strike—
Why dost thou not, while ruling o'er the field,
Select such victims of the battle's strife
As *should* be punished by thy bloody scythe?
Preserve the father for his anxious child,
And pierce the heart whose wishes, could they kill,
Would slay a husband and a widow make.
Say, had they children? I would fain console them
In their pains, for I can feel how strong must be
The pangs which tear a son's or daughter's soul
When parted from a father's love forever.
     LAF: My Adelaide, look not so on that dark
Display of man's frail destiny, but come,
For much emotion suits not thy weak health.
Within my tent thou mayest rest awhile.
The travel from the town must have fatigued

Thee much.

 ADE: True. But is my mother there?

 LAF: Thy mother?

 ADE: Yes. What startles you so much?
Where is my mother? I must find her straight.
She went from home to seek thee, and inquire
If news you had of my father's uncertain fate.
She promised, when she left my filial arms,
In three short hours to be back again.
But what disturbs thy countenance, and shakes
Thy body thus? Some accident, I fear,
Hath to my mother here occurred.

 LAF: No, no.
'Tis the humid breath of evening which makes
Me feel unwell. Come, come, let's hasten in.

 ADE: Nay, nay! I came to seek my mother here.
Where is my mother?

 LAF: My gentle Adelaide,
Why wilt thou fret so much? What wouldst thou, girl,
Should happen to thy mother here?

 ADE: Cruel!
Part not a mother from her child. Oh, sir,
What harm has crossed her path? Shall I not look
Again upon her features— kiss her cheek?
Oh, I pray you by the love to me you've sworn,
Give— give me back my mother!

 LAF: Adelaide,
Have courage, girl. How can I tell thee all
Unless thou hast a stouter heart?

 ADE: Oh, yes!
I see it now! Some fatal accident
Has robbed me of her! Oh, my mother!
Where— O Lafrenière, where is my mother?
Let me embrace her even if she's dead. [*She turns to the bodies.*] Ha!
Can it be!— those bodies! [*She runs towards them.*]

 LAF: Adelaide!

 ADE: [*uncovering one of the bodies*] Oh! [*Faints.*]

 LAF: [*taking her in his arms*]
Too tender maid, canst thou withstand this shock?
Or has it, like the fiery bolt from high,
Destroyed the beating life within thy breast,
And borne thy soul upon its wings to God?
Halloo, within there!

 [*Enter* FIRST SOLDIER.]
Go, call the surgeon

Of the army— fly! Tell him it presses much!

    [*Exit* FIRST SOLDIER.]

    [*Exit* LAFRENIÈRE, *bearing Adelaide into his tent.*]

    [*Enter* DENOYANT.]

    DEN: Yes, yes, it must be so; the troops I see

Advancing in our rear are certainly

The promised succors from the country sent;

They have a martial mien, appear well ranged,

And firm within their ranks. [*A trumpet sounds distantly.*]

Do I hear,

Or are my ears deceived? A Spanish march

Methinks they sound. I do remember well

The tune. [*The trumpet sounds again.*]

    [*Enter* MARQUIS.]

    MARQ: We are lost! we are lost! undone!

    DEN: Friend, what hast thou?

    MARQ: The Spaniards, on our rear,

Approach with half their force. See them advance!

Come, let us haste and arm.

    [*Exeunt.*]

    [*Enter* LAFRENIÈRE.]

    LAF: Thank God, she breathes!

But, oh! she will not long survive the hour

Which loosed the band which held on earth the soul

Of parents, whom as much the girl did love

As the woodland flower doth the earth and shade

By which 'tis nourished and 'neath which it grows.

Once taken from that native soil, it pines,

Nor can attentive hands revive its drooping life—

No man-made showers, nor artificial warmth,

Can stop its fading or arrest its death. [*Enter* DENOYANT.]

    DEN: See, Lafrenière, see! the Spaniards come!

    LAF: Nay, Denoyant! seest thou not they come

Upon the rear? How could the Spaniards pass

The morass on our left, the river on our right?

These are doubtless succors, come at last.

    DEN: Nay, sir. Observe their discipline, their dress,

[*The distant trumpet sounds again.*]

And listen to that march.

    LAF: My doubts are gone.

    DEN: And Louisiana's lost.

    LAF: Not so, sir!

She is not lost! Are our hands chopped off?

Are we not Louisianians yet?

The coming fight will show you, sir, what can

Men, by the love of Liberty impelled,
'Gainst venal hirelings to tyrants sold.

    DEN: On our front too— see, sir— the enemy
Is marshalling his men.

    LAF: To arms! to arms!
Haste thee, Denoyant, and bear the order.
Let the drum beat the call to arms. Send here
The chief commander of each regiment.

    [*Exit* DENOYANT.]

[*Kneeling.*] Eternal God! thou knowest all the deep
Sincerity of this uncorrupted heart;
And though 'mongst men my bearing has been proud,
Before thy throne I've always humbly bowed.
God! thou who pourest out, with equal hand,
Into the current of unstaying time,
Joy's limpid stream and sorrow's cup of brine,
Send not to me an unalloyed draught of gall,
But let some sweet be mingled with the pain
Which of late days has fallen to my share.
But if against me only thou art angered,
Then let thy wrath descend on me alone;
And save my country from the ills which I
Should suffer by thy wisdom's stern decree.
God! By thy strong will our struggles aid,
And send confusion through the ranks of those
Who make Thy name a frightening password
To the greatest crimes. God, I pray thee for
My country's liberty. Liberty, the gift
Which thou didst give to man e'en from his birth,
Shall it be wrested from his hand to-day?
Thou didst not destine him for slavery
When thou didst make him like unto thyself,
And stamped him in the holy, perfect mould
Of thine own intelligence and beauty.
Shall this proud soul which liveth here, and which,
By thine own lungs, was breathed into this breast,
Be cramped within the carcass of a slave?
It cannot be! I feel thine impulse now;
And victory for us will soon make this day
A day of record on our grateful hearts. [*Rises.*]

    [*Enter several officers, among whom are* MARQUIS, MILHET, *and* CARRERE.]
[*The drums beat the call, and the cry is heard.*]
To arms! to arms! to arms! to arms! to arms!

    [*Enter* DENOYANT.]

    DEN: A herald from the Spanish line awaits.

LAF: Bring him to me.

[*Enter a* SPANISH HERALD.]

Well, Spaniard, what wouldst thou?

HER: Dost thou command these hostile bands?

LAF: I do.

HER: I come a messenger of peace. If you
And yours surrender ere the fight, ye shall
Be treated with humanity, and all
Your vain rebellion pardoned.

LAF: What! pardoned!
Sirrah! Go, tell your master 'tis in vain
He thinks to cheat us with his futile tricks.
We know how far a Spaniard we can trust.
His rancor can be only cooled with blood;
His falsehood teaches him to kill the man
He hates, e'en while he greets him with a kiss.
Go, tell your chief that pardon we ne'er ask,
But from our God for sins against his law.
Pardon, indeed! We disdain his offer;
And rather much would give him our blood
Than take his favors, though he tenders life.

HER: Then must I tell you that without delay
The battle will begin on our part.

LAF: We are prepared.

[*Exit* HERALD.]

[*To the officers.*] Is all ready, gentlemen,
To face the enemy? Can I depend
Upon the bravery and the firmness
Of the men of all your companies?

OFFICERS: You can! you can!

LAF: Well, then, the word shall be,
Charge on for liberty! When ye return,
And take the head, each of his separate band,
Ye'll tell the soldiers that it is my plan
To break the foe who pens us in the rear,
And then to intrench again beyond them.
Tell them that if we fail in this design,
Our country's lost, and, what is ten times worse,
We lose our freedom, ne'er to get it back.
Try ye to inspire each soldier with a firm
Resolve to die or to be free. Remember,
That on our arms to-day depends the fame,
The future reputation of our country;
And on this day we heroes make ourselves,
Or gain the base and ignominious name

Of slaves. Sirs, remember that! and when ye charge
Upon those Spanish dogs, shout the loud cry
Of Liberty into their ears. 'Twill make
The rascals shrink and fly; and like the damned,
Whose power fails when saints appeal to Christ,
These slaves will prostrate fall, when high are raised
The voice and arm of patriots unstained,
For martyrdom prepared.
      [*Exeunt.*]
      [*Enter* ADELAIDE *and* SURGEON *from the tent.*]
      SURG: Lady! Lady!
You need for rest. Why will you leave your bed,
To strain yourself by this exertion great?
This hard struggle 'gainst your weakness now
Will hurt you much, and may be fatal to you.
      ADE: I pray to God, good surgeon, that it will.
Death cannot come too soon upon me now,
For now he parts me from my parents dear.
The blow which struck them reached the feeble thread
On which my life doth hang; and now I'll knock
With arm untiring at the door of Death,
Until he gives me entrance through that gate
At whose dread portal has been left the dust
Of those who were my dearest love on earth.
[*She goes to the bodies; drums beat the charge, firing and shouts are heard.*]
      SURG: Lady! lady! for heaven's sake, retire.
The battle's raging, and some straying ball
May strike you dead. Come; I will bring you
To some safer place, where, from these flying deaths,
You'll sheltered be. [*Firing, drums, and shouts.*]
      ADE: Not so. Here let me weep,
And call on Death. He'll hear the better here,
For he is near me in an hundred shapes.
O father! mother! why are the deadly strokes,
Which fell on ye so lavishly, withheld
From me, whose heart would leap to meet them now?
[*Firing, drums, and shouts.*] [*Enter* LAFRENIÈRE.]
      LAF: [*throwing away his sword*]
Go from my hand, thou useless trash! Lost! lost!
Thrice did our soldiers charge, and thrice repulsed;
They strive in vain to form their broken ranks;
By myriads stopped, though myriads they have slain,
'Twere vain to try to bring them on again.
In small detachments scattered o'er the field,
They fight surrounded by the compact lines

Of mercenary troops— full ten times more
In numbers. God! God! Can I not something do
To turn the current of the day? Ah, yes!
There— there— I see a rallied regiment! [*Shouts.*]
Nay! nay! nay! poor weakened eyes, they're Spanish troops. [*Shouts.*]
Yes, ye demons, stretch forth your glutted throats,
Which gurgle with the blood to-day ye've drank.
Let it be heard 'midst hell's eternal fires,
And let the damned reecho up the cry,
Turned to a shout of victory 'gainst God! [*Spanish soldiers rush in.*]

    First Spanish Soldier: Kill him! it is their chief.

    Ade: [*rushing forward and shielding* Lafrenière] Nay, nay! not so!
Ye cowards! ye shall kill a woman first!

[*The curtain drops.*]

Dream Of Lafrenière [between the fourth and fifth acts]

    Lafrenière appears sleeping in a prison.

The prison vanishes, and a landscape appears; a wide river flows through the centre; and on each side of it, extensive forests and uncultivated fields are seen. On one side stands a throne, on which a personification of Europe is seated, holding a sceptre, and having a lash and fetters lying at her feet. A personification of Louisiana sits weeping, chained to the throne; plaintive music, and pantomime expressive of the distress of Louisiana, and of the despotism and cruelty of Europe.

    The music gradually changes to more stern and threatening tones; the sky darkens; clouds appear; the thunder is heard, and the lightning flashes.

    A thunderbolt strikes the throne, which crumbles to pieces, while Europe is thrown prostrate on the earth.

    The gloom is dispelled, the clouds disappear, the music is joyful, and Louisiana exults.

    Liberty appears descending from above, bearing the American flag. Above the head of Liberty seventeen stars [representing the number of States of the Union at the time Louisiana was admitted] appear arranged in a circle around the words "Constitution," "Union."

    Liberty approaches and takes off the fetters of Louisiana, saying: "*Arise, my child, rejoin thy sisters. Thou art free.*" They embrace each other, while Liberty points to the Star of Louisiana rising in the sky, and ranging itself with the others.

    "*Hail, Columbia*" breaks forth, and to that tune the fields flourish, cities rise, boats and ships ply upon the river, and busy crowds of people thicken on the landscape.

    The prison resumes awhile its appearance, and again disappears to give place to a dark curtain, on which suddenly appears a circle of portraits [drawn in white] representing the Revolutionary heroes and worthies, with Washington in the centre.

ACT V.

Scene 1:— A Prison. Lafrenière fettered, and chained to a ring in the wall.

    Laf: O Liberty, thou art not invincible!
Slaves by plunder baited have o'erthrown thee,
And thus it seems, that hearts inclined to crime

Do feel for crime as great enthusiasm,
As souls which take their fire from the skies
Do in the acting of a virtuous deed.
O my country! and art thou then like me
Chained, fettered, and beneath a tyrant's foot?
Ah! was green America sought in vain
By Pilgrim Fathers, flying 'cross the main
To seek a refuge from oppression's rod?
Were its wide forests, where untutored men
Live 'neath the shade of the tall magnolia—
Were its broad rivers, 'gainst whose current nought
But the Indian's light canoe can ply—
Was its free soil, from whence civilization's foot
Not yet treads down and wears the verdure off—
Were these unto degrading slavery doomed?
Oh, no; it cannot be! And still I hope.
Last night, when dragged across the horrid field,
Where hundreds of my countrymen laid dead,
Pierced by mercenary swords and balls,
I was thrown here, within this dungeon dark—
Long did I weep Louisiana's fall,
Till sorrow's fount was drained all dry:
Sleep came at last, and closed my heavy eyes
To ope imagination's lids on worlds
Unknown, and in prophetic dreams to wake
Midst future days. I saw, though Death methought
Did press me down with his unbending arm,
My country in a veil of darkness wrapped,
Her wrists and ankles worn by clinching chains,
Her back all marked with deep and bleeding stripes,
And moaning 'midst her sufferings. But soon
The darkness vanished, and a brilliant light
Dispersed the clouds which hung around in gloom;
And forth appeared, in shining radiance,
A youth whose air spoke Freedom, and whose frame
Was built with strength and grace; in his right hand
A palm and sword he held, and in his left
A scroll on which eternal truths were written,
And a floating banner, where, in beauty
Blended, were the white, and blue, and red,
In fulgent stars and flowing stripes disposed,
He broke her bonds, and with his manly voice
Exclaimed, "Go, join thy sisters; thou art free."
     [*Enter* Adelaide.]
Adelaide! What miracle has oped the door

Of this gloomy dungeon to let thee in?
     Ade: Lafrenière, I bring thee news of freedom!
With gold— what Spaniard can resist its lure?—
I've gained thy jailer, and to-night thou flyest.
     Laf: Fly! Lady, no! Here will I stay, and meet
My fate, whate'er it be.
     Ade: And that is death,
If thou dost here remain.
     Laf: A brave man's death
Is better than a coward's flight.
     Ade: 'Tis true.
Couldst thou defend thyself, I'd rather see
Thee fighting sword in hand, than aid thy flight;
But here assassination doth await thee,
And, while thou sleepest, treachery will plunge
His poisoned knife into thy noble heart.
     Laf: I care not how these Spaniards end my life;
My destiny is fixed. In freedom's cause
To die, is greater, in my estimation,
Than dragging out in vile obscurity
An useless life. To-day it is the richest prize
My country's conquerors have gained.
Well, let them have it, while 'tis worth a crime.
Thy father, girl, is laid among the martyrs
Who yesterday did shed their blood and die
For liberty. What! Shall *I* shrink away
And dread the example he has set me?
     Ade: *Then* there was hope, but now—
     Laf: Honor and glory
Yet remain to be completely gained.
     Ade: Nay,
Lafrenière, if thou lovest me, leave these vain
Aspirings. Listen. There is an aged
African, who seeing, as I passed by,
The threatened dissolution of my features,
Offered to give me certain antidotes
For the evil which afflicts me now.
Lafrenière, thou art now the only prop
Round which my life's weak vine will twine itself:
My father— mother— both have been snapped off,
And if thou fallest, Adelaide falls too.
     Laf: God, give me strength to meet this trial hard!
     Ade: I will fly with thee to some distant land;
And there, in wedded love, we'll live in peace,
Blest by contentment and a quiet home.

LAF: 'Tis wrong to put into my hands thy fate;
Why with dilemma thus surround me;
On one side, honor, the fame I cherish,
Call me to stay and die; on the other,
My love, thy happiness and threatened life,
Unite to make me swerve from duty's path.
Adelaide, thou art unjust; assist me
Rather to preserve my fame unspotted,
And tempt me not to play a shameful part.

ADE: 'Tis said the northern colonies have raised,
And threaten rebellion against England.
Go, join them, and for freedom fight with them.

LAF: I've sworn to free my country or to die!

ADE: Dost thou refuse?

LAF: I do. [*She sinks down upon a seat.*]
Nay, Adelaide,
Sustain thyself with better courage.

[*Enter* AUBRY.]

Aubry here!

AUB: Ha! ha! Well, my good sir, what say you now?
Ha! You have struck— heaped insults on me—
Called me a coward. Well, you spoke the truth.
Say, what think ye of a coward's vengeance?

[*Lafrenière rushes at him, but is stopped by the chain.*]
No, no! I had these chains too well prepared.

ADE: Monster!

AUB: Ha! Foolish wench! What dost thou here?
Well, 'tis a double blow I'll strike. Listen.
Ye know not all I've done against you both.
'Twas I seduced that rascal Garidel
To place his master in the Spaniard's hand,
To pour a poison over this maiden's beauty,

[LAFRENIÈRE *strains to break his chains, and sinks down in the effort, trembling with rage.*]
Keep cool, good sir, that is not half. 'Twas I
Who made him plunge a dagger in the heart
Of Villeré.

ADE: God! God! [*Faints.*]

AUB: What! Faint already?
Halloo without there! [*Enter* JAILER.] Here, jailer, take out
This foolish girl, and throw her in the ditch. [*Exit* JAILER *bearing out* ADELAIDE.]
So, sir, you have freed your country, have you?
A great and mighty general indeed!
Poor— foolish— vain— rash— green— hot-headed— boy!
What! Did you think to thwart a man like me?
Thy wild ambition showed the crazy youth,

And not a man to lead an army on.
Why were not the outskirts of your army
Better guarded? I led the Spaniards round
And came upon your rear, nor even met
A single scout until our drums ye heard.
Ay, sir! To me you owe your fall. Say,
What think you of the puny coward now?

  Laf: [*rising*] Aubry, I do despise thee still, and still
I do defy thee! Do thy worst! All's not done—
I still exist. Why am I not murdered?
Ye cannot lack for those who'd do the deed;
The country's full of Spaniards now.

  Aub: Be sure
I will not leave my work unfinished thus,
Nor can you teach me how to do it, boy.
Ye shall not be murdered in the dark. No!
I'll have you ended on the public square.
I'll have you tried, condemned in form, and shot!
You shall have company; four of your friends,
Denoyant, Carrere, Milhet, and Marquis,
Have been already sentenced.

  Laf: Wretch!

  Aub: They come.
Your judges here advance; and, what is more,
I am their colleague named.

  Laf: Thou!

  Aub: Yes, sir, I!

  [*Enter two* Judges *and a* Scribe. *They seat themselves at a table together with Aubry.*]

  First Judge: Is this the man?

  Aub: It is.

  First Judge: Of heinous crimes,
Against your rightful king, you are accused.
You have upraised sedition in this province;
You have been the chief of discontented bands;
You have led them on against the army
Sent by his Majesty Most Catholic,
Our gracious lord and master, Charles the Third,
By grace of God King of Spain and India,
To take possession of his proper claim,
And legal acquisition— in one word,
High treason is your crime.

  Laf: Most wise judges,
Do I well hear your words? Is it to judge
Ye come, or, most sage and sapient judges,
Am I condemned already? Mark your words:

"You *have* upraised sedition in this land,
You *have* been the chief of discontented bands,
You have"— "You have," good sirs, be not so swift;
Convict me first, and then my sentence read.

    Aub: Colleague, proceed in better form. Ask first
His name.

    Laf: You're right, let it be done in form,
Let me be murdered legally.

    First Judge: Mind, sir,
With more respect your judges treat. Speak,
But no insulting language use. Say,
What is your name?

    Laf: Great Judge! That very name
Is the greatest insult I can speak
When I address ye; and by to-morrow
'Twill be a greater insult still. It is—
For I am proud to speak it— Lafrenière!

    First Judge: [*To* Secretary.]Write. [*To* Lafrenière.]
Your birthplace?

    Laf: Most pleased am I to answer.
I am a Creole, born in New Orleans.

    First Judge: Your profession?

    Laf: An advocate.

    First Judge: Your age?

    Laf: Out, dastards! I'll parley no more with ye.
Ye know me— who I am, and what I am;
And I plead guilty in every point
On which ye do accuse me — ay, guilty!
And glory in what ye call a crime. Go!
I hate your nation and your tyrant King,
I weep that I cannot destroy ye all,
I moan my country's enslaved destiny,
I pant to die ere ye have washed your hands
Of all the blood ye shed on yesterday.
Go! I have enough of mockery.

    Aub: Ye hear,
He doth confess.

    First Judge: [*to* Scribe] Proceed! Read the sentence.

    Laf: What! Was it ready written up? Why, ye ape
But ill your parts.

    Scribe: [*reading*] "Lafrenière, found guilty,
In due form, of high treason 'gainst the King,
Is by this honorable court condemned,
Within an hour hence, to die."

    Laf: Thank ye, kind gentlemen, ye could not more

Give pleasure to me; know, I kiss your hands,
Ye grant me e'en my heart's core wish.

    [*Exit* Aubry, Scribe, *and* Judges.]

Oh, yes;
To-day my name is written in the sacred book—
The purest, chosen page of history.
From now my cherished name will live
Immortal in the hearts of freemen—
The Louisianian's future pride.
He'll shout my name unto the skies;
He'll place it first upon the monument
His heart will raise to virtue, surrounded
By a glorious halo! Eternal God!
I come— I come— already crowned before thee,
The unstained martyr of bright Liberty!
Liberty! the first and greatest dogma
Thou dost teach us in thy book of nature.

    [*Enter* First Spanish Soldier, *accompanied by other soldiers, with reversed muskets; and the* Jailer.
    The drum beats a dead march.]

    First Spanish Soldier: Art thou prepared to go? Hast made thy prayer?

    Laf: What I have asked of God, ye grant me now.

[*Jailer takes off the chains.*]

    [*Exeunt.*]

Scene 2:— The Public Square.

[*Enter a* Ruffian.]

    Ruf: The citizens have fled as if a pestilence
Infected all this section of the city;
The place is desolate e'en as 'twere night.
'Tis here they'll shoot the Creole chief to-day.
A fine time this to rob some straying fool:
If some rich scoundrel now would only pass
Across this green, how quick I'd murder him,
And rob him of his gold! Ah, someone comes!
By the Holy Virgin, it is Aubry,
For whom we seized the old man in the forest!
He's loaded, doubtless, with the riches gained
By turning traitor to his countrymen.
I'm tempted strong to let him pass along,
For he is one of us who kill and steal
And take false oath. Ha! he lets fall a purse.
Pshaw! he picks it up. Saints! 'tis full of gold!
By the holy cross, I'll have it! [*Retires.*]

    [*Enter* Aubry.]

AUB: 'Tis well!

My work is done. I am revenged, and now,

With all the riches I have gained, I'll go

To Europe and enjoy myself. But

I must behold Lafrenière e'er I go.

To-day he takes his crown of glory, and

'Tis my purpose here to calculate, with care,

The different value of his gain from mine. [*Holding up the purse.*]

Money! who'd not worship thee is but a fool.

What is fame, honors, titles, place, to thee?

Though I'm a coward and a criminal,

More men will bow to me, and envy me,

And yield to my desires, than will e'er recall

The memory of this great Lafrenière.

Learn to make money, and then ye may

Dispense with further knowledge. Gain riches;

It decks the bearer more than wisdom would,

It is the power of a mighty prince,

It is a brilliant title to one's name.

See! It has no smell nor pleasing taste,

'Tis rigid to the touch, and yonder flower

Which blooms unnoticed in the grass

Exceeds it far in beauty; yet I

Have been as false and cruel as the tiger

To obtain it, and still I think the prize

Was quickly, cheaply gained.

Why come they not?

I'll go and see whence this delay.

[*Exit* AUBRY, *followed cautiously by the* RUFFIAN.]

AUBRY: [*without*] Murder! Oh!

[*The drum is heard beating a dead march, gradually approaching— the orchestra plays soft and mournful music. Enter* LAFRENIÈRE *escorted as before, and accompanied by* DENOYANT, MILHET, MARQUIS, *and* CARRERE; *the soldiers range themselves on the right side.*]

LAF: 'Tis triumph! more glorious than the pomp

Which glittered round a Roman conqueror.

I envy not the wreath that Caesar wore

When, from Pharsalia's field, he trod on Rome.

His coronet was steeped in freemen's blood,

Mine shall be wet with their regretful tears;

He sought to fetter Rome in slavery,

I tried to make my native country free;

He died with usurpation's hand outstretched,

I fall the martyr of bright liberty.

And could *I* envy Caesar now? Oh, no!

Like him I failed to gain a prize most dear,

Yet do I die more proudly than he died;
For this I leave behind— a virtuous name.
[*To his companions.*] My friends, I greet you joyfully
As parties to a festive revelry,
As bridegrooms on their wedding day,
As saints who take their crown of sanctity!
This day the blood we'll here together spill
Will rise into a monument of fame,
Will nourish seeds of freedom in this soil,
And bless our country with five patriot names.
Denoyant, say! since Freedom's cause is lost,
Couldst thou wish aught more glorious than this,
The death of freemen for their country slain?

    Den: Ay, and who still defy the tyrant's power;
For though he slay us, and revengefully
Should drag our bodies in ignoble dust,
Yet, here or hence, our souls are ever free,
And spurn the mandates of his tyranny.

    Marq: Unto us now the value of this life
Is wholly lost; a foreign master treads
Upon our native land.

    Mil: How could we live
Beneath the rule of such inhuman slaves?
Their hands are red with Villeré's honored blood.

    Car: To me now death has all of freedom's charms;
For death will burst oppressive chains.

    Laf: 'Tis well!
Dear friends, now let us yield our ready breasts
Unto the bullets of these murderers,
Who bring disgrace upon the soldier's garb.
[*To the* First Spanish Soldier.]
Come! why lag you thus your duty to perform?
[The Soldier *offers to bandage his eyes.*]
Not so! Think ye we cannot look on death?
Thou hast already seen us look it in the face.
Where shall we stand?

    First Spanish Soldier: Yonder, between the trees.

    Laf: And now, my native land, but one more glance,
And then I'll close my eyes in death with joy.
Adieu, blue sky and verdant foliage,
'Neath which, when but a child, I loved to play
With bounding limbs and fluttering heart,
Adieu! I look no more with pleasure on ye—
Ye are no more what I did love ye for.

    [*While* Lafrenière *is speaking, his companions retire behind the scenes on the left. Exit* Lafrenière, *same side.*]

LAF: [*without*] Now— now! with hand in hand we'll fall at once

For right and liberty!

FIRST SPANISH SOLDIER: Are you prepared?

LAF: [*outside*] We are!

FIRST SPANISH SOLDIER: Soldiers, attention! Ready! Aim!

LAF: [*outside*] Liberty forever!

FIRST SPANISH SOLDIER: Fire!

[*As the soldiers fire,* ADELAIDE *rushes in between them and* LAFRENIÈRE, *and falls wounded.* LAFRENIÈRE *staggers in, mortally wounded in several parts of the body, and falters towards her.*]

LAF: God! she is killed.

Adelaide! Adelaide!

ADE: I thank that ball—

By my torn side— it lets in death— ah— love—

Dost thou still live?— Lafrenière, I've news— news! [LAFRENIÈRE *sinks down.*]

Nay, live awhile to hear me— e'er you die—

Aubry, Aubry— is dead— murdered— murdered

By a *Spaniard* for his gold— the gold he got

From Spaniards to betray us— Adieu! [*She dies.*]

LAF: Great God! [*Rises.*]

FIRST SPANISH SOLDIER: Load, load your guns again, and finish him!

LAF: 'Tis useless— I feel the cold hand of death

Press from my heart its last— last drop of blood.

Louisianians, by my example learn

How great— how noble— is a freeman's death! [*Falls and dies.*]

The Poets of Les Cenelles

Armand Lanusse (1812-1867), a free Creole of color in New Orleans, was a writer and educator who published the first collection of poetry by African Americans in the United States in 1845, *Les Cenelles (The Mayhaws¹)*, of which he was a founding member. *Les Cenelles* was a group of seventeen free Creoles of color, many of whom were the product of *plaçage*, the arrangement of a union between young Creole women of color and white men of means, a practice that resulted in a unique class of wealthy, educated, Creole men of color, like the men of *Les Cenelles*. The seventeen contributors to the collection *Les Cenelles* were Valcour B., Bowers (Bo...rs), Jean Boise, Louis Boise, Pierre Dalcour, Desormes Dauphin, Nelson Desbrosses, Armand Lanusse, Numa Lanusse, Mirtil-Ferdinand Liotau, August Populus, Joanni Questi (Joanni), Nicol Riquet, Michel Saint-Pierre, Victor Séjour, Manual Sylva, and Camille Thierry.² Included here are the works of Armand Lanusse, Mirtil-Ferdinand Liotau, Michel Saint-Pierre, Camille Thierry, and Victor Séjour.

In 1843, a time when the most popular form of literature published by people of color in this country was the slave narrative, Armand Lanusse, an educator, poet, and publisher, began *L'Album Littéraire, Journal des Jeunes Gens, Amateurs de Literature!*, a monthly journal of literature in New Orleans penned by free Creoles of color. Although the journal was short lived, it did inspire Lanusse to publish *Les Cenelles* two years later. Many of the poems in the latter collection are clearly inspired by the French Romantic style popular at the time, but they also address very serious issues facing the free Creoles of color in New Orleans. In the mid-nineteenth century, New Orleans had the largest number of free people of color of any city in the South, in large part due to the emigration of free blacks from Saint-Domingue (now Haiti), but also thanks to the practice of plaçage. Lanusse and his fellow poets were fiercely proud of their Creole heritage, which is apparent in much of their poetry, but they were also concerned with the dubious tradition of "placing" young, Creole women of color in these sham marriages, thus diminishing their roles as wives and mothers in the black Creole community.

Up to the 1830s, New Orleans was unique in its three-tiered racial hierarchy: whites, free people of color, and black slaves. According to the editors of *Louisiana: A History*, after *"Walker's Appeal,* the plea of a free black man in Boston that the slaves of the South rise in revolt, had made its appearance in New Orleans in 1829... it became a capital crime in Louisiana not only to distribute printed matter which might incite insurrection, but also even to say anything from pulpit, bar, stage, bench or anywhere else that might breed discontent or encourage rebellion."³ Therefore, nonwhites in New Orleans, including free Creoles of color, could say nothing to criticize whites or any of their dubious practices, such as plaçage and slavery. The laws passed in 1830 placed such restrictions on the writing of Les Cenelles that their works are sometimes difficult to follow, particularly for readers outside of New Orleans.

Armand Lanusse is the editor and largest contributor to the collection and in his dedicatory poem, "To The Fair Sex of Louisiana," he lauds the virtue of the women of the state, or more specifically the young, Creole women, who are a subject not only of his poetry, but of his short story, "A Marriage of Conscience." In his poems, "To Elora," "The Priest and the Young Girl," and "Epigram" he laments the lost virtue of young Creole women of color and criticizes the Catholic Church for its role in "placing" these young women with the wealthy, white Creole men in a union neither recognized by the church nor the state. He addresses the topic humorously in his poem "Epigram," in which a mother assures a priest that she wishes to renounce Satan, but before doing so asks, "Why can't I, father—what?—*establish* my daughter?" In his poems, he also chastises mothers for the roles they

---

1   In 1953, Edward Larocque Tinker, in his book *Creole City,* translated *Les Cenelles* as *The Hollyberries,* but New Orleans historian, Jerah Johnson, in his 1990 article *"Les Cenelles:* What's in a Name?" convincingly describes the springtime practice of young men gathering mayhaws in Louisiana to offer to their mothers, sisters, sweethearts to make the coveted mayhaw jelly, in much the same way Armand Lanusse of *Les Cenelles* offered up their collection of 84 poems "To The Fair Sex of Louisiana" (Jerah Johnson, *"Les Cenelles:* What's in a name?," *Louisiana History* 31.4 [1990]: 407-410).

2   For more biographical information on members of Les Cenelles, see the introduction to Latortue, *Les Cenelles,* xxii-xxx; or the *Dictionary of Louisiana Biography Online* (Louisiana Historical Association, 2008).

3   Bennett H. Wall et al., *Louisiana, a History* (Arlington Heights: Illinois: the Forum Press, 1984), 123.

play in the corruption of their daughters.

Michel Saint-Pierre wrote six poems for *Les Cenelles*, and he too laments the pitfalls of plaçage for young Creole women in "The Dying Young Girl." He writes of the dying girl's mother "finding a suitor who better fit her plans" than the sixteen-year-old dying girl's lover. Saint-Pierre congratulates the young girl for taking with her to her grave, "innocence and honor!"

Both Lanusse and Liotau address the state of the Catholic church—particularly the St. Louis Cathedral—in the 1830s, Lanusse in his short story, "A Marriage of Conscience" and Liotau in his poem included here, "An Impression." At that time, the newly appointed Bishop Antoine Blanc had refused to capitulate to the lay "wardens" of the cathedral who claimed that they had the right to name their own pastor, so these wardens withheld all church revenue from the diocese. In response, Bishop Blanc withdrew all priests, and therefore all sacraments, including baptism and marriage, from the cathedral. The wardens sued, lost, and a new Archdiocese of Louisiana was formed with Blanc as the first archbishop.[1] New Orleans readers would have understood Liotau's lament for the "Church of Saint-Louis… /empty and deserted!" but few others would have. Both authors raise the issue of the church's moral failings when it comes to race and slavery in New Orleans.

Camille Thierry was himself a product of plaçage, with an octoroon mother and white French father, from whom he inherited a small fortune. He turned to writing poetry and at the age of 37 left New Orleans for Paris to escape the stifling racism in the city, a topic he addresses in his poem "The Sailor," in which the narrator begs his lover to flee with him to escape her father, who "refused your hand to me/And vilified my race." In his poem "Farewell," he laments having to leave New Orleans, the city he has come to love, and in fact, he never did return, dying in Bordeaux in 1874.

The last writer, and perhaps the most well known, Victor Séjour, was born in New Orleans in 1817 to a Haitian father and New Orleans mother, both free people of color. He left New Orleans in 1834 to live in France, where he remained until his death. There he became friends with Alexandre Dumas, and also became secretary to Napoleon, who attended at least one of his plays. In his only poem included in *Les Cenelles*, "The Return of Napoleon," a lavish encomium to the former emperor, in which he calls him "…grand, superb, and handsome too," he chastises France for exiling Napoleon to Saint Helena and pleads for the emperor's body to be returned to France. Indeed, Séjour is the only Les Cenelles poet to identify so strongly with the French. He considers himself a Frenchman when he blames France for Napoleon's death: "Ah! Our honor, Frenchmen, is linked to his death throes!" Séjour's short story, "The Mulatto," is considered to be the first written by an African American.

Armand Lanusse and the rest of the writers of Les Cenelles, proud Catholics themselves, some even children of *placées*, were fiercely protective of their heritage and standing as *gens de couleur libres* or free Creoles of color; yet they criticized the church and its role in the mixing of the races, truly a complicated stand and one not made any easier for readers to interpret due to the racist laws imposed upon them at the time.

Armand Lanusse (1812-1867)

The Fair Sex of Louisiana[2]

Please accept these modest Cenelles
Our heart offers you with sincerity;

---

1   For more on the Catholic Church in the 1830s, see Wall et al., *Louisiana: A History*, 66-8.
2   All the poems in this section are translations from the French, taken from: Regine Latortue and Gleason R.W. Adams, trans. *Les Cenelles, A Collection of Poems by Creole Writers of the Early Nineteenth Century*. (Boston: G. K. Hall & Co., 1979.) Rep. by permission of Regine Latortue.

A single glance fallen from your virtuous eyes
Will mean as much as glory and immortality.

Epigram

"You really do not want to renounce Satan,"
A good preacher was saying to a certain zealot
Who, every year, came to present him
Her interminable list of rather mortal sins.
"I do want to renounce him," says she, "for ever,
"But before grace sparkles in my soul,
"To remove henceforth all incentive to sin,
"Why can't I, father"—What?—"*establish* my daughter?"

To Elora

This child, without her mother, would maybe have been wise,
As wife, to her husband she would have given care;
Mother, she'd have seen to the needs of her young.

Verjux

Enlighten, Elora, my increduluous mind
On the secret rumour which is presently circulating;
It is everywhere whispered that unfaithful to the vow
Which engaged your heart to that of a lover
Whose only desire awaits the blessed hour
When by a sacred bond you will be united to him;
It is whispered, but undoubtedly, Elora, by mistake,
That self-interest has opposed another your heart,
That you are fleeing marriage and its severe laws
To adopt other laws less sure but more lenient.
I wish not to believe it and blame with anger
This misdeed that they impute to you.
But if it happens, however, that seduced by other examples,
You weigh the advantages of both destinies,
In order to strengthen you in your first contemplation,
Listen to this story which is bound to make you weep;
Do you remember young, pretty Noemie
Whom you once called your very best friend?
Her mother, without remorse, was an accomplice
To the corruption of her innocent mind.
And Noemie, alas, displayed triumphantly
These trifles which came from an ignominious source;
Some new furniture, a dazzling jewel-case
Had captured the heart of that poor child;

Proud to be admired in her new silk dress,
She forgot all the shame and appeared quite happy.
But soon, Elora, the giver disappeared;
A new affair was again quickly arranged;
Then a few months later, urged by necessity,
The young girl turned to vice, holding low her head;
Fallen prey to passions whose excess will kill her,
Noemie today… I'll stop here, Elora!—
This is too often the fate of many young girls
Who form loosely these impure liaisons.
In vain palaces displaying their splendor
Would they like to hide this horrible ugliness,
Those who live in the lap of luxury
Have, printed on their forehead: indignity, disgrace!

The Priest and the Young Girl

Silent shadows invade these walls
And envelope everything in lugubrious vesture;
And the lamp which nightly sheds its soft rays
Will soon illuminate on His cross the Man-God.
Where is Leosida, my faithful dove,
Why isn't she yet in the confessional box?
Who can be retarding the devout flight
   Of this angel's zeal?

Will I have to leave this sanctuary
Without having heard her? In vain the wind brings me
The noise of a few steps, they are not hers;
Her walk is a concert of aerial chords!
What am I saying? What demon is taking hold of my soul?
From where does this thought come to me, priest of Jesus?
In the passion which leads me astray, His law, my vows,
   I no longer remember.

But then this law is far too cruel!
Do these vows correspond with our nature?
Cold theology, where is the evil
In admiring the most perfect of God's creations?
When Saint Paul declares by the authority of the gospel
That a preacher can form a conjugal bond,
Must the decrees of an inhuman council
   Take this privilege away from us?

When she arrives here, with a troubled voice

Let me hear these words: "Father, I have sinned,"
I immediately want to forgive her everything
In order to say to her: "I am also guilty.
Yes, everyone in this world, needs leniency.
No one is capable of feeling only pure sentiments,
You must know, Leosida, that your presence
          Always troubles my senses."

Let me be silent and try to control this delirium
Which makes me deserve the ire of angered Heaven.
But Leosida is coming, because my excited heart
Leaps like the skiff blown about by the storm!
To banish far from me these thoughts,
Let me try to pray, to weep—Here she comes!
Go far away from me, worldly thoughts of mine!
          My God! Protect her, please!

Michel St. Pierre (1810–1852)

The Dying Young Girl

How lucky you are, how worthy of envy!
You are leaving, young lady, leaving this life
You will enjoy in peace a happier abode
Taking with you innocence and honor!
Go without regret, God is calling you,
Dry eyed and calm, fly up to Him;
Nothing is certain down here, pleasure is deceptive,
Hope is fleeting and so is happiness!
Love, they told me—and still upon your face
That grief spoils, that sadness devours—
Yes love—I see it now, cruel verity!—
Promised you pure joy and sheer happiness!
Leaning over your bed, his eyes filled with tears,
Your lover is overwhelmed by mournful lament;
How he had hoped and wished that one day
Blessed nuptials would fulfill his vows and his love.
But who knows if fate, or rather your mother,
Distrusting the sincere ardor of his heart
Or finding a suitor who better fit her plans
Would not have cruelly interposed herself?
I, like you, have known virtuous young ladies,

Made most unhappy by overzealous parents
Young ladies who, finding no cure for their ills,
Seek some respite in the Temple of God.
Farewell—I see death approaching, advancing—
Your eyes now grow dim—we are all afraid—
One last minute then, one last long sigh,—
And you will be no more than ash and memory!—
Goodbye then forever, to you who evoke
To me a sister, a friend, as gentle as lovely,
Which death had struck down at age sixteen,
In spite of my wishes, my tears, my laments.
If, among those beauties, those angels of light,
Where you will take your place upon leaving this earth,
You see her chanting praises to God,
Bid her for me a belated farewell!

Mirtil-Ferdinand Liotau (ca. 1800–1847)

An Impression

Church of Saint-Louis, old temple, shrine
You are today empty and deserted!
Those who were entrusted in this world to your care,
Scorning the needs of the sacred tabernacle,
Have led the Christian army elsewhere.
Until each one has realized his mistake,
On your stones, alas! Will we no longer see
Kneeling down the children of Jesus
Who, their ear attentive and their soul trembling
Relished the sacred words of the preacher?
And in your sanctuary, sacred abode,
Incense will no longer send its perfume to Heaven!
Your splendid altars, your ancient images,
Your crosses, your ornaments, your sacred relics.
Will alas! Remain in profound oblivion
Which is already enveloping them in its immense folds!
O Divine temple, final resting place
Of respected men still mourned by the people,
And who, perhaps, feeling also all your unhappiness,
Are moaning like us from inside their graves,
O shrine which saw me as a child within these walls

Receive on my forehead the signs of baptism
Alas! Did I grow up to see you today
Deserted, abandoned perhaps forever?
Pure and august asylum where one's soul is delighted
When sacred liturgy is sung in chorus,
Will you always remain bereft of honors?
Since we never pray to the Almighty in vain,
Christians, let us unite; when this tutelary God
Had shed all His blood for you on Calvary,
Let us hope that today, all mighty and strong,
Granting our prayers, He will change our destiny;
Let us pray if, through His mercy we wish Him
To destroy among us hatred and discord.
Has not this hope, in drying up our tears,
Already poured balm on our wounded hearts?
Have not we seen the crowd of New Orleans,
When came the Noble Feast, at ease in the old temple?
Then, true happiness was shining in all eyes,
For all was forgotten in that joyous moment!
Christians, another effort will tip the scale
Undoubtedly toward peace, we can be sure of that;
And we will see again, as in the past,
The people every day fill up the forsaken temple!

Camille Thierry (1814–1875)

The Sailor

Let us mingle our sighs, our sweet words intertwine—
        Let us talk, O my love!
Let us talk, that our speech arouse the old echoes
        Of the sleeping cavern.

Under my hand I felt your lovely body move.
        O favorable portent!
The winds may rise indeed; the waves too may sing out,
        On the beach I will stay.

What does it matter if upon the foaming sea
        My ship is captainless?
What importance! To you my soul. Such bliss know I
        In this grotto with you!

Fear not, fear not today to give your heart to me,
    To give your life to me.
Our lone observers are the coolness and shadows
    Of this lovely grotto.

Were he to appear, that savage, hoary man
    Titled by your father;
My face would darken and my dagger, long and keen
    Would play his lullaby.

Were he to here appear to openly show forth
    His darkly raging soul,
Then would I dig for him near some deserted path
    A deep concealing grave!

That man, that hoary man refused your hand to me
    And vilified my race,
Therefore all thoughts humane for that senile old fool
    Are from my soul wiped clean!

I see pearl-like within the depths of your black eyes
    A white tear start to form;
I see your body shake because my deep despair
    Alarms you, young maiden.

Let us flee, let us flee these shores!—to plow the seas.
    My ship is ever set.
Let us flee—I will find some small deserted isles
    As shelters for my head!

Farewell

Carondelet Canal, the north wind forces me
    To flee your shores today.
Farewell, for I shall seek a station near the hearth
    As shelter for my form.
Along your powdery path, green crickets are no more
    Nor lovely butterflies,
There only is the noise which comes at intervals
    To die within your shrubs.

But not unlike the lover who far from his beloved
    Ceaselessly cries and groans,
Far away from you my voice can only moan,

And my days will be worthless.
I will again recall the music soft and sweet
    Which floats up from your reeds,
When in a summer's eve the breezes trouble them,
    Incline them o'er your flow.
And come the season when the hummingbird returns,
    When the flower reappears,
To you will I pour out the tales of the cruel nymph
    Who makes of me a dreamer.

Yes, I will talk to you of that fantastic love
    I treasure in my heart,
Which at times causes my bewildered mind
    To brew an evil scheme!

If my mind is ravaged, if my pain's augmented
    By dreams most hideous,
'Tis that I cannot see the single drop of dew
    Which refreshes our hearts.
O unfortunate bard, I have broken the Mandola
    Which I held in my hands.
Of what use is singing when she whom I adore
    Remains deaf to my voice?
Farewell!—I do not fear that these days of absence
    Will make me forget you;
I love remembering, and memories of you
    Will I have, near the hearth!

Victor Séjour (1817–1874)

The Return of Napoleon

Always him! Him everywhere! Burning or frozen, / His image ceaselessly disintegrates my thoughts.
                                        Victor Hugo (*Les Orientates*)

I

Like the immeasurable sea roaring in the tropics,
The people surged onto the public meeting place,
    While crying there he is!
A coffin!—Oh Misery! —A coffin for that man,
That man who of his homeland made a second Rome!
    Oh Misery! 'Tis all there.

When before, to our shores, triumphant he returned,
His head encircled with the fruits of victory
    Simple in his grandeur;
These crowds, alas! the same, pressed him along his way,
Cheered at his arrival, glorified his courage,
    Reflected his splendor.

Oh! it was at that time that France most winsome was!
She only had to pass and kings bent o'er her path
Like slender stalks of wheat before a breath of wind
She went and not unlike the tempest did she go,
With the world, fragmented, becoming her conquest,
    Behind, and her in front.

Now nothing.—It is done.—Greetings, O my captain;
Greetings to my consul, you of the noble face.
August were you, and grand, superb and handsome too;
Your mien transcended even Pompey's or Hannibal's,
Europe was submissive to the weight of your sword—
How then can you possibly fit within that narrow tomb?

Weep, people, weep; for he is there, sad, pale,
Not unlike the linen which makes up his death bed;
Weep then for your caesar, the dauntless warrior;
Weep.—For a soldier dies on the field of battle,
Swept away, arm in hand, by the artillery;
    He died a prisoner.

Ah! When, alone and pensive, on Saint Helena he stood,
His eyes turned toward France, far, far away,
    As toward a golden star;
His face was luminous with the fires of memory;
He cried out: "Oh my God, I would give up my soul,
    To see her once again.

No, no, it is not I whom the unworthy English
Like a captive lion keep locked up on this isle.
    It is you, noble France,
It is you, your future, your power, your glories,
Your twenty years of combat, your twenty years of conquest;
    Not I, not I, not I!"

        II

    Oh! Don't allow that man, Oh France,

To vainly wait to be set free—
Strap on your shield, take up your sword,
Awaiting you is your steed;
Swiftly, swiftly, like the thunder
Go now and free the prisoner.

Awake, people, awake, let's make the alarms sound out—
Soldiers, veterans too, take up again your arms.
In the name of your honor,
Frenchmen, let's not allow our hate to fall asleep;
Two prisoners have we on the rock called Saint Helena:
Glory and the Emperor.

III

But no, it is too late; on the new Calvary
Death has now struck down the popular giant;
He is dead, he is dead!
Stricken and abandoned, betrayed by his country;
Sighing: "I die, my France, O my beloved France,
And in spite of myself, I weep over your fate."

IV

They give his coffin to us—What piercing irony!
Ah! our honor, Frenchmen, is linked to his death throes!
We should blush, we should blush, for his executioner,
Having, under his feet, a deep abyss carved out,
Having, of the victim, the precious blood drunk down,
Now gives as alms the tomb to us.

We should surely blush, a people of great renown,
To make bold to approach the corpse of this great man,
With the affront on our brows;
To dare to raise our eyes, when with a Punic hand,
They give us, on one side, his most heroic remains;
On the other, an insult.

Shame on us! He should have been left on his island;
Far from our weaknesses, he rested tranquil there—
Or, to have him again, him, covered with laurels,
Him, victor at Austerlitz, him, son of glory,
He should, weapon in hand, guided by victory,
Have been brought back to our land.

That would have been fitting and just!—the drum, the cannon salute.
Our military men still warm from some great battle,
The powder and the cannon,

Our France again raised up, and England, infamous,
Atoning for her wrongs, both knees upon the ground—
  Thus should have been feted the great Napoleon.

What matters it, he is here! Courage, noble France.
Your shame, your suffering, cannot long be extended
  For on the marble of the tomb.
Reviving in our hearts our truncated hatred,
We will go, young and old, to hone again our swords
  Dulled at Waterloo! ! !

Adrien Rouquette ("Chahta–Ima") (1813–1887)

A drien-Emmauel Rouquette was born in New Orleans on February 26, 1813, to Dominique and Louise Cousin Rouquette. Adrien's father, Dominique, a native of France, moved to New Orleans in 1800, and prospered as an importer of French wines to the then Spanish ruled Louisiana territory. Adrien, the couple's fifth surviving child, grew up in the fashionable house at what is now 413 Royal Street, and on his mother's large estate on Bayou St. John, now the rectory for Our Lady of Holy Rosary Catholic church.[1] In much of Adrien Rouquette's writing, when he reminisces about his home during his youth, he is referring to the estate on the bayou. His father, Dominique died of yellow fever when Adrien was only six years old, leaving his mother to raise him, his three brothers, François, Felix, and Térence, and his sister, Antoinette, and the family moved from the French Quarter home out to the more spacious home on the bayou.

In the early 1800s, Bayou St. John was not considered part of the city, but rather a scenic setting where wealthy New Orleanians set up their retreats from city life. It was also a common belief that living out of the city and on the more rural bayou was a healthy way to escape the yellow fever epidemics that continuously plagued the city. Even more significant than the natural setting to Adrien Rouquette was the fact that the Choctaw Indians populated much of that area, and there he began his association with them that would last throughout his life.

According to Rouquette biographer, Dagmar LeBreton, his mother let Adrien and his brothers have free reign at the Bayou St. John home and on her Cousin family home on the North Shore of Lake Pontchartrain on the banks of Bayou Lacombe in St. Tammany Parish. So by the time he began his formal education in 1821, he spoke Choctaw as well as French. His literary career also began on the banks of Bayous St. John and Lacombe with his brothers and Cousin cousins, who called themselves the "Bards of Bonfouca."[2]

Adrien Rouquette began his studies like so many young, white men of wealthy Creole families in New Orleans at the Collège d'Orléans; however, he did not excel there, so his mother sent him and his brother Felix to Transylvania University in Lexington, Kentucky, also popular among the Creole ruling class of the time. Studying in Kentucky was more agreeable to young Adrien, and his time there helped inspire his first verse collection, *Les Savanes* (*The Savannas*). At fifteen, Rouquette was sent to study in Philadelphia, and a year later would find him in France. According to LeBreton, he chose to study in Nantes in part because Brittany was the home of Chateaubriand, a favorite French romantic poet of so many 19th-century New Orleans writers, including Les Cenelles, John Dimitry, and Alfred Mecier. While in France, Rouquette began to turn from academics to more Christian studies. Nonetheless, after briefly returning to Louisiana, he went back to France to study law, a profession he would soon be forced to abandon after telling the Supreme Court during his examinations in New Orleans: "All that I know is that I know nothing."[3]

1841 was a big year for Rouquette. *Les Savanes* was published both in Paris and New Orleans, and he decided to pursue his priestly vocation. He wanted to preach, though, not to the parish of New Orleans, but to the Choctaw Indians, of St. Tammany, much to Bishop Blanc's chagrin. Blanc was named the first Archbishop of New Orleans after resolving the "schism" in the St. Louis Cathedral, which Les Cenelles

---

1   In the French Quarter home at 413 Royal Street, the decorative family initials "DR" are visible in the wrought iron second-floor balcony. The large family home on the Bayou is now 1324 Moss Street.

2   Dagmar Renshaw LeBreton, *Chahta-Ima: The Life of Adrien-Emmanuel Rouquette* (Baton Rouge: LSU Press. 1947), 15. Bayou Bonfouca is also in St. Tammany Parish in what is now the Big Branch Marsh Wildlife Reserve.

3   LeBreton, 80.

also write about. This was a difficult time in the church's history, and Blanc expected Rouquette's assistance in the parish diocese soon after his ordination in 1845. In fact, Rouquette was the first native priest to be ordained in the state of Louisiana.[1] While ministering to the Choctaw Indians Rouquette was given the name, Chahta-Ima, or "Choctaw-like," since he had lived among them since childhood.

During this time he also published his second poetry collection, *Wild Flowers, Sacred Poetry,* inspired by nature, particularly that of Bayou Lacombe, but in an ecclesiastical sense, which is typical of Rouquette's poetry. In his paean, "The Wild Lily and the Passion-Flower," he extols the lily, "The queen of solitude, / The image bright / Of grace-born maidenhood," while lamenting the passion flower as "dark-colored... solemn, awful, sad!" Yet he recognizes that "Such is our life—/ Alternate joys and woes / Short peace, long strife, / Few friends, and many foes." He believes, however, that such is life here on Earth until we reach the "realms above." In "To Nature, My Mother" he writes about "Nature, mother, still the same," perhaps because his mother died when he was but thirteen, and in fact he was as much raised by the natural setting of the south Louisiana prairie as by his parents. Likewise, in "Bayou St. John" he praises God's natural setting, which "Lifts up the soul to the heavens serene." He again finds salvation in nature.

Throughout his life, Rouquette published verse, religious and otherwise; newspaper articles; a novel, *The New Atala,* inspired by Chateaubriand's *Atala;* and even a biography of Napoleon. In his novel, *Aboo and Caboo,* Rouquette, like so many other prominent New Orleans Creoles, such as Grace King, attacks George Washington Cable after his publication of *The Grandissimes.*

He built many simple retreats on the North Shore where he lived and said mass to the Choctaws, some of which still stand today. He was one of the foremost authorities on their language and worked to translate the bible into Choctaw. He died in New Orleans at Hotel Dieu Hospital on July 15, 1887, and is buried in St. Louis Cemetery No. 2.

The Wild Lily and the Passionate Flower[2]

Sweet flow'r of light,
The queen of solitude,

The image bright
Of grace-born maidenhood,

Thou risest tall,
Midst struggling weeds that droop:

Thy lieges all,
They humbly bow and stoop!

Dark-colored flow'r,
How solemn, awful, sad!—

---

1   Ibid., 95.

2   "The Wild Lily and the Passion-Flower" and "To Nature, My Mother" were published in Rouquette's second collection of poetry, *Wild Flowers, Sacred Poetry* (New Orleans, 1848). Other important sources of both poems and biographical information can be found in Susan B. Elder's *The Life of Abbé Adrien Rouquette, Chahta-Ima* (New Orleans, 1913) and Dagmar Renshaw LeBreton's *Chahta-Ima: The Life of Adrien-Emmanuel Rouquette* (Baton Rouge, 1947).

I feel thy pow'r,
O king, in purple clad

With head recline,
Thou art the emblem dear

Of woes divine;
The flow'r I most revere!

The lily white,
The purple passion-flow'r,

Mount Thabor bright,
The gloomy Olive-bow' r.

Such is our life—
Alternate joys and woes,

Short peace, long strife,
Few friends, and many foes!

My friend, away
All wailings here below:

The ROYAL WAY

To realms above is woe!

To Nature, My Mother

Dear Nature is the kindest mother still. (Byron)

O nature, pow'rful, smiling, calm,
To my unquiet heart,
Thy peace, distilling as a balm,
Thy mighty life impart.
O nature, mother still the same,
So lovely mild with me,
To live in peace, unsung by fame, —
Unchanged, I come to thee;
I come to live as Saints have lived,
I fly where they have fled,
By men unholy never grieved,
In pray'r my tears to shed.
Alone with thee, from cities far,
Dissolved each earthly tie,
By some divine, magnetic star,
Attracted still on high,
Oh! that my heart, inhaling love
And life with ecstasy,
From this low world to worlds above,
Could rise exultingly!

Charles Alfred Mercier (1816–1894)

Alfred Mercier,[1] as he preferred to be called, was born on June 3, 1816, in McDonoghville, Louisiana, on the Westbank of New Orleans, a settlement that has since been incorporated by the cities of Algiers and Gretna. His father, Jean-Baptiste Mercier, was a Louisiana French Creole, and his mother, Marie-Héloïse Leduc, a Canadian, and like most young Creole men of the time, he was sent to Paris, France, where he attended the *Lycée Louis-le-grand,* for a more formal and traditional education than he could receive in New Orleans; he was only fourteen at the time. While there he became fascinated with Latin and Greek literature, a passion which would last his lifetime. He returned to the United States to study English in Boston in 1839, but four years later he returned to Paris where he published his first works, the verse narrative, *La Rose de Smyrne (The Rose of Smyrna)* and the dramatic mystery, *L'Ermite du Niagara (The Hermit of Niagara),* which were both well received.

Soon after his first modest literary success, Mercier traveled extensively throughout Europe, from France to Switzerland, Spain, Belgium, England, and finally on a walking tour of Italy. Two years after the French Revolution of 1848, he decided to pursue a more stable career and studied medicine. After receiving his degree in 1855, he returned to New Orleans, where he practiced medicine but also continued to pursue his interests in literature.

Mercier did not believe in the institution of slavery; however, he did believe in the Confederacy and returned to Paris at the outbreak of the Civil War in order to plead with the French to support the cause. He returned to New Orleans after the war's end and remained there until his death in 1894, practicing medicine and writing and discussing literature with some of the leading literary figures of the day.

In 1876, Mercier, along with his brother, Armand Mercier, General P.G.T. Beauregard, and Alcée Fortier, founded the literary society, *L'Athénée Louisianais,* a society to promote French literature in Louisiana. According to Alcée Fortier, a lifelong friend of Mercier, and whose work is also included in this collection, Mercier's knowledge of literature was most extraordinary, and not only his knowledge of classical Greek and Latin literature, but also of French, Spanish, Italian, and English. Nonetheless, even though Mercier acknowledged that in Louisiana English was the language of business and politics, he believed that in writing, the French Creoles should not abandon the language of their ancestors, and there remains today very little of his work in translation, even though he was very popular in post-Civil War Louisiana.[2]

Perhaps his most enduring work is *L'Habitation Saint-Ybars (St. Ybar's House),* a novel that evokes the bygone southern plantation life. Fortier was a great admirer of this novel, and he even compares it to Harriet Beecher Stowe's wildly popular *Uncle Tom's Cabin.* But like most southerners, Fortier condemns Stowe for her portrayal of the cruel slave master, and states that Mercier knows that "they were not all monsters like Legree."[3]

Included here are two of his shorter works that draw on his love of classical literature. "Miss Calinda's Marriage," first appeared in the journal of *L'Athénée Louisianais* in 1880, and is a reworking of Aesop's "The Tortoise and the Hare." It too is an animal tale, but unlike Aesop's version, "Brother Deer" and "Brother Tortoise" are vying for Calinda's hand in marriage. She cannot decide between the more "valiant" Brother Deer or the "good-natured" Brother Tortoise, so she decides to marry whoever wins the mile-and-a-half race. The tortoise in both versions wins the race; however, unlike Aesop's tale in which the slow, deliberate tortoise wins by never losing sight of his goal, Mercier has a neighboring lawyer, "Monsieur Avocat," devise a complicated plan involving several tortoises planted throughout the course in order to fool Brother Deer and assure that victory goes to Brother Tortoise. It is odd for us today to read about cheaters being rewarded with victory, but that is just what happens in this fable, with the help of an underhanded lawyer. Also odd is that last line of the story: "Brother Tortoise married Miss Calinda the following Saturday, and everybody ate until they were stuffed and drank so

---

1   For more on Alfred Mercier see Alcée Fortier, *Athénée Louisianais, Séance Speciale du 18 Mai, 1894, Homage à la Mémoire du Dr. Alfred Mercier, Secrétaire Perpétual* (Athenian Society of Louisiana, Special Meeting on May 18, 1894, in Memory of Dr. Alfred Mercier, Permanent Secretary) Print.

2   Ibid., 7.

3   Ibid., 12. Translated by author.

much they got drunk." So not only does Mercier celebrate cheating, but drunken excess as well. Both the trickery and excess are also elements of the very popular, if racist, plantation narratives of the time.

The second story included here, "The Banquet," appeared in Thomas Caleb's *The Louisiana Book: Selections from the Literature of the State* in 1894, the year Mercier died. This story is more reminiscent of an Asian parable or even a Medieval dream vision. An exhausted laborer is worried that his life of drudgery will result in his untimely death causing his wife and family to fend for themselves. Such a notion consumes him, until, so weary from the weight he carries up a mountain, he falls asleep and dreams of a joyous banquet. At this banquet he sees his wife, daughters, sons, as well as "kings and queens, ferocious looking soldiers, diplomats with astute smiles, beggars in rags, sailors, priests, pale nuns, laborers, courtiers, and suspicious looking gentry; in short people from every tribe, race, and country." But he also sees a "Spectre" who acts as the finger of death, tapping those whose time has come, all of whom accept their fate. When the laborer awakens, he realizes that death is inevitable and that he should enjoy life while he can, no matter how dreary it may sometimes seem.

Although Alfred Mercier is not, today, a household name like some of his contemporaries, such as Cable, Chopin and Hearn, he was very popular at the time for his writings in French. Little has been translated, especially of his longer works, and that might account for his obscurity. He died in New Orleans on May 12, 1894, at the age of 78, leaving behind his wife and three children.

Miss Calinda's Marriage[1]

Many years ago Brother Deer and Brother Tortoise were both courting Miss Calinda. Miss Calinda preferred Brother Deer because he was the most valiant, but she liked Brother Tortoise, too, because he was so good-natured.

Miss Calinda's father told her: "young lady, it's time for you to get married, choose the one you want."

The next day both Brother Deer and Brother Tortoise stopped by Miss Calinda's house.

Miss Calinda, who had thought about it all night long, announced to them: "Brother Deer and Brother Tortoise, my father wants me to get married. I don't want to say no to either of you. So next Sunday, you'll race a mile and a half, and I'll marry whoever wins."

They both left, Brother Deer with a happy heart, but Brother Tortoise was lost in thought: "a long time ago my granddaddy beat Brother Rabbit in a race but I don't know what I'm going to do to beat Brother Deer."

In those days, an old, old crocodile—more than sixty years old—lived nearby. He was so crafty that everybody called him Papa Avocat.

Night came. Brother Tortoise ran to see Papa Avocat to tell him all about his problems with the race. Papa Avocat told him: "I want to help you, my son; we're part of the same family; the earth and water are the same for you and me. I'll think about this business. Come see me tomorrow morning and I'll tell you what you need to do."

Brother Tortoise ran home to go to bed but he didn't sleep much. He was so worried! The next morning he hurried over to see Papa Avocat.

Papa Avocat was already up and having a cup of coffee.

"Good morning, Monsieur Avocat."

"Morning, my son. Your problem has really given me fits, but I think you'll beat Brother Deer, if you do what I tell you.

---

1   Translated by D.A. Kress. From: Mercier, Charles A. *Comptes Rendus de L'Athénée* (Louisianais, Juillet: 1880), 378-383.

"Today go find a judge who will measure the road along the bayou. Every 800 feet, drive in a pole; Brother Deer will run on land and you'll go by water. Do you understand what I'm telling you?

"Oh yes, Papa Avocat, I'm listening to everything you're saying."

"The night before the race, when it gets dark, go get nine of your friends and hide one of them near each of the poles. As for you, you'll hide near Miss Calinda's house. Do you understand what I'm telling you?"

"Oh yes, Papa Avocat, I understand perfectly well what you're telling me!"

"Well, go get ready to uphold our nation's honor!"

Brother Tortoise went to see Brother Deer and arranged everything just like Papa Avocat had told him. Brother Deer was so sure of winning the race that he said yes to everything that Brother Tortoise wanted. The next day, bright and early, everybody who lived along the bayou gathered to see the big race.

When the moment came, Brother Deer and Brother Tortoise were both ready. The judge yelled: "Go!" and they took off at a galop.

When Brother Deer reached the first pole, he shouted: "Hey, Brother Tortoise!"

"Here I am, Brother Deer."

When they reached the second pole, Brother Deer whistled: "Whewww!"

Brother Tortoise answered, "Croakkkk!"

Passing the third pole, Brother Tortoise was still snout to muzzle with Brother Deer.

"What the devil! This tortoise swims faster than a steamboat; I gotta get myself in gear."

When Brother Deer reached the ninth pole, he saw Brother Tortoise diving into the water. He had raced as hard as he could, all for nothing; before he could reach the finish line, he heard everybody shouting: "Hurrah! hurrah for Brother Tortoise!"

When he reached the finish line, he saw Brother Tortoise on the porch kissing Miss Calinda. It hurt so much he ran off into the woods.

Brother Tortoise married Miss Calinda the following Saturday, and everybody ate until they were stuffed and drank so much they got drunk.

The Banquet[1]

I

N ight was approaching.

    A laborer, heavily laden, was slowly ascending a mountain; exhausted by the weight he carried, he sat upon a rock near the road, and sighing deeply, said:

"How unfortunate I am. After so many years of relentless toil I can scarcely provide the necessaries of life for my family. I know I am strong still, but I am continually tormented by the fear of what the future has in store for us; and the thought that I may die leaving my wife and children penniless makes me shudder. That fear tortures me and poisons the very well spring of my happiness."

Such were the laborer's lamentations.

He bent his head to his chest; the fever of weariness seized him, and he fell half asleep, while his thoughts unconsciously wandered in the indefinite land of dreams.

He felt himself uplifted and transported far away.

Suddenly he was seated at an immense banquet, in a hall dazzling with lights and gold. The table,

---

1   Translation unattributed. From: Thomas M'Caleb, ed., *The Louisiana Book: Selections from the Literature of the State.* (New Orleans: R.F. Straughan, 1894), 373-75.

surrounded by guests, extended itself from the rising to the setting of the sun, and there he saw people of every description; men and women, young and old, children, kings and queens, ferocious looking soldiers, diplomats with astute smiles, beggars in rags, sailors, priests, pale nuns, laborers and suspicious looking gentry; in short, people from every race and country; some nearly naked, others covered with silks precious stones.

Looking at his right, the dreamer recognized his wife and son; at his left were his daughters, surrounded by young men who them in pure and loving language.

Waiters, crowned with myrtles and roses, went from one guest the other, giving to each a drink that not only was palatable, but also had the property of reviving.

Opposite the laborer one could see a large gallery, on the top which stairs of black marble rested, and their upper portions were lost in the skies.

II

From the summit of the stairs came a Spectre that was veiled robed in white.

And the Spectre, approaching a king who was speaking to his ministers about his plans of war, touched him with the tip of its fingers.

The king rose, went on the gallery, ascended the stairs, and returned not.

And the Spectre touched two lovers in the act of taking their betrothal kiss.

The lovers left the table and disappeared forever.

A miser had just won an enormous amount of gold, and knew not how to take it all with him; the Spectre stopped and made a sign to him.

Astonished and trembling, the miser obeyed. As he walked, his gold dropped from his pockets to the resounding floor; he would have stopped, but could not, and vanished like a vapor that leaves naught to detect it.

Then the Spectre with its right hand drew a great circle around a group of happy children, who were listening to the tales of an octogenarian.

The aged man directed his steps towards the mysterious hall; the children followed playfully.

A mathematician of universal renown was calculating the chances of the future and promising a long career to several capitalists, who wondered at his knowledge; he did not heed an old hag, who also wanted to know how long she had to live.

Looking around suddenly, as if they heard someone call them, the capitalists saw the Spectre shaking its head in the affirmative.

Surprised and frightened, they left the table, and their friends waited for them in vain.

Two young men rose, each with a cup in his hand. Joy and love were depicted on the one's face; the other looked very sad.

Said the former: "Let us enjoy life! Here's to my mistress—and to the happy days we have before us!"

Said the latter: "Happiness is a lie; the spring of my life has brought me but bitter delusions. I empty this cup as a farewell to every vain hope."

But the youths did not have time to drink; the cups slipped from their fingers without the loss of a single drop of wine; and suspended in the air, like feathers carried by the wind, were wafted towards the hal. The Spectre commanded the two young men to follow, and they departed, as the others had previously done, forever.

III

The laborer became frightened. Wildly clasping his arms around his wife and children, he pressed them to his heart.

New guests took the place of departed ones. The meats and drinks were always renewed, and the banquet always continued.

Time fled rapidly, and the dreamer's hair had whitened. It seemed to him that he had reached life's last degree, and that his daughters, who had borne children several times, smiled on him; while his aged wife leaned on her grandson's arm.

And when the Spectre approached him at last, he fearlessly rose and said:

"I am ready. Now I understand what is meant. The banquet is Life; and thou art Fate's messenger, that calls each of us at his turn. We must neither rely on, nor despair of, the morrow. Young or old, happy or unhappy, we all obey thy mandates; and man should live in peace with himself, and take calmly what every day brings.

"Hail to thee, O Death! Thou commandest that I leave this banquet, which I have attended longer than I should have expected. I go cheerfully. I have carried my burden without complaint, and I deposit it without regret."

IV

The sleeper opened his eyes and stood up. His courage was revived by what he had seen. He resumed his ascent of the mountain, and, by the sweet light of the stars, reached his modest home, where his wife and children awaited him for the evening meal.

Walt Whitman (1819–1892)

Walt Whitman[1] arrived in New Orleans on February 25, 1848, to work as an editor on the local newspaper, *The Daily Crescent*, and he left the city on June 15, some three and a half months later. His fifteen-year-old brother, Thomas Jefferson (Jeff), accompanied him on his trip to New Orleans, and he too was employed for a time by *The Daily Crescent* as an office boy, earning five dollars a week.[2] According to Emory Holloway in his book *The Uncollected Poetry and Prose of Walt Whitman*, Whitman was given a two-hundred dollar advance to cover his traveling expenses from New York to New Orleans,[3] and his brother Jeff wrote to his parents saying that when his big brother Walt had saved one-thousand dollars, they would return to New York.[4]

Much has been made of Whitman's move to New Orleans as well as his abrupt departure, but Whitman biographer Henry Seidel Canby states that his move was never intended to be more than a visit. According to Canby, only two weeks after being let go from the *Brooklyn Eagle* for supporting the anti-slavery Free Soil Party, Whitman was approached in a Broadway theater lobby by a Mr. McClure of New Orleans, who, during the fifteen-minute intermission over cocktails, offered Whitman a job on his forthcoming New Orleans newspaper, *The Crescent*.[5] It is apparent from Jeff's letters home, which offer the most thorough account of Whitman's stay in New Orleans, that Jeff's homesickness and Whitman's salary squabbles with the owners of *The Crescent* had much to do with their return to New York after a little more than three months. Even though many critics speculate that while in New Orleans Whitman had at least one romantic affair, which is likely, especially since he admits that he was so taken with the Creole women in the city, there is very little solid evidence of it or that such a romance led to his hasty departure. Walt Whitman might have stayed longer had Jeff not been in tow, but immediately upon his return to Brooklyn he was selected as one of fifteen representatives at the Free Soil Convention to represent Kings County, where he heard Frederick Douglass speak, among others, so he did have commitments and every intention of returning to New York after his brief stint with *The Crescent*. He even made enough money in New Orleans to purchase some property in New York shortly after his return.

He was hired by McClure to be one of several news editors for the paper, but in his March 23, 1848 piece, "Daggerdraw and Bowieknife, Esq." he refers to himself as "a chap whose business it is to make 'Sketches,'" and that is primarily what he contributed to the paper. In fact, one of his earliest pieces to appear in the paper was also the only poem that he published during his tenure at *The Crescent*, "The Mississippi at Midnight," which appeared on March 6, 1848. In the poem, Whitman tackles the topic of slavery, in large part because New Orleans was the first city he'd ever spent any time in that actually had a marketplace for buying and selling human beings.

For the most part, however, Whitman wrote short, often humorous, sentimental prose pieces in the style popular at the time. He and Jeff rented rooms at a boarding house in Lafayette, which was then a suburb of New Orleans—or at least of the French Quarter—in what is now Lafayette Square. On May 9, 1848, he wrote a very funny account of a ball he attended "overflowing with the beauty of Lafayette with a sprinkling of Carrollton"—another suburb at the time—entitled, "'A Night at the Terpsichore Ball' By 'You Know Who'." His attempt at humor is a success in this piece, but that is not always the case in his New Orleans sketches.

He also wrote a series entitled "Sketches of the Sidewalks and Levees," in which he focuses on different New Orleans characters whom he encounters in his travels about town. The above "Daggerdraw and Bowieknife, Esq"

1   All the pieces by Walt Whitman are from: Emory Holloway, ed. *The Uncollected Poetry and Prose of Walt Whitman* (Garden City, NY and Toronto: Doubleday, Page & Company, 1921).

2   Thomas Jefferson Whitman, "To Walt Whitman Sr.," the Walt Whitman Archive, eds. Ed Folsom and Kenneth M. Price, http://www.whitmanarchive.org/.

3   Emory Holloway, introduction to *The Uncollected Poetry and Prose of Walt Whitman* (New York: Doubleday, 1972), xiv.

4   Walt Whitman, "To Walt Whitman Sr. and Louisa Van Velsor Whitman," the Walt Whitman Archive, eds. Ed Folsom and Kenneth M. Price, http://www.whitmanarchive.org/.

5   Henry Seidel Canby, *Walt Whitman, an American: a Study in Biography* (Boston: Houghton Mifflin Company, 1943), 73.

is in that collection, as is "Miss Dusky Grisette," about a beautiful Creole woman of color selling flowers to men on the streets. Canby claims that Whitman was fascinated by "most of all the quadroons and octoroons of mixed Negro, French, and Spanish blood, beautiful, sexual creatures, born outside of Puritanism and natural caressers of life," and "Miss Dusky Grisette" seems to support Canby's claim.[1]

By June 15, Whitman and his brother were back in New York, almost four months to the day after their departure. Whitman's journalistic career in New Orleans, while brief, is still very important. Few readers know that he ever resided and worked in New Orleans, and even fewer have read his work in *The Crescent*. While here he wrote not as the outsider that he was, but as a local observer of the city and its denizens. He used French phrases, yet he did not know French and had never lived where it was spoken. He wrote of local customs and folks, such as dueling, masked balls, quadroons, oyster fisherman, sailors, and stevedores, yet he encountered many of these practices and people for the first time in this city. He truly offers up a slice of life in pre-Civil War New Orleans made all the more significant because he is Walt Whitman.

Daggerdraw Bowieknife, Esq.[2]

It is almost with fear and trembling, "I take my pen in hand," to attempt the portraiture of this fearful son of Mars, whose very name is almost enough to

> —"Freeze my young blood, Make each particular hair to stand on end, Like quills upon the fretful porcupine."[3]

We do not say that our hero lives in New Orleans now, but he "used to did," and that's enough for a chap whose business it is to make "Sketches." He lived here once upon a time, and flourished extensively— went to the Legislature and to Congress, for aught we know—that is, the Congress of Texas, while that "lone star" was shining with bedimmed lustre in the political firmament.

Squire Bowieknife emigrated, some years ago, to a village in Mississippi from one of the Carolinas. He was a limb of the law, and by dint of an abundance of swagger, in a short time fought his way into notice. There are parts of Mississippi where a man may graduate into public favor, through the merits of gunpowder, with a rapidity that is astonishing. It requires a peculiar conformation and organization—a fitness of things, as it were—to constitute an individual who can thrive upon sharp steel and patent revolvers, but Bowieknife was the man, and "he went it with a rush."

Thence, he found his way to Orleans, and now has gone to Texas, followed by the ghosts of no less than six hale, hearty men, at least, that were such before his "bloody-minded" shooting irons made daylight shine through them. Never did man stand more upon a point of honor than he did: he would cavil upon the hundredth part of a hair if he thought a bit of a fight was to be got out of his antagonist: and upon the most trifling misunderstanding in the world, he would attack you in a "street fight," or "call you out" and shoot you down, as though your life were of no more value than a cur dog's. Oh, he was a brave fellow, and people were afraid of him, and we cannot wonder at it.

But it so happened, that the Hon. Daggerdraw Bowieknife was not, by any manner of means, so punctual in meeting his own little liabilities as he was in being first upon the ground to take part in the murderous duel—in other words, he was one of those "damned highminded, honorable, clever fellows," who would rather shoot a man than pay him what he owed him. There are such men in the world, and our friend was one of them: they pretend to be the very soul of honor, but an honest debt, such as an

---

1   Canby, *Biography*, 76.

2   From the *Daily Crescent*, March 23, 1848. Note: Text and footnotes of the prose pieces are from Holloway (see note above).

3   Cf. *Hamlet*, I, 5, 16-20.

honest man would pay with entire punctuality, these sons of *honor* "pass by as the idle wind, which they regard not."[1] One day, Daggerdraw sallied out from his office to take a walk into town. He was armed and equipped, though not "according to law," but he was, in common parlance, quite "loaded down to the guards" with fashionable killing tools. In each pantaloons pocket he carried a small loaded pistol: in his bosom, and within reach, was the handle of a large bowie-knife, weighing just one pound and a half, one of those murderous weapons more efficient than the Roman short sword, and equally serviceable at cutting or thrusting. Daggerdraw had done bloody deeds with it in both ways, as more than one individual in Mississippi had experienced to his sorrow. This said big butcher-knife had run the rounds of several street fights, and was the dearly beloved of its dreaded owner. Whether the personal prowess he displayed in its use was a violation of the laws of decency and humanity, and befitted him more for the society of desperadoes and professional cut-throats, is altogether another question. No man doubted the bull-dog courage of this disciple of Blackstone, but whether any of the sympathies of human nature, such as make man the being he is, had an abiding place in his ferocious heart, is not for us to say, though it may well be supposed there were none.

Yes, there he goes! and there is blood upon his shirt now, or at least there is revenge brooding in his thoughts, and ere long the life of some doomed one must pay the forfeit. He is not a bad-looking man either, being gentle enough in his dress and address, but

> "There was a lurking devil in his sneer.
> That raised emotions both of hate and fear."[2]

His eye was wild and restless, and there was a something in his brow that was repulsive. "And the Lord set a mark upon Cain"—can it be true that this modern Cain had his mark set upon him too? And yet there it was, the stamp and the impress of the cruel heart, legibly fixed in the very lineaments of the man's face, and no one loved to gaze upon him, for his features had that about them to freeze the heart of the beholder.

Why is it that a false sense of honor requires men to face in deadly combat such as Daggerdraw, it were hard to divine. Perhaps they suppose, as Bob Acres[3] says, that honor follows them to the grave. We are of opinion with Bob's servant, that this is the very place one might make shift to do without it, and that the honor and applause, such as it is, whips over to the adversary. Very well: Squire, take your grand rounds, and as you walk the streets, feel secure that men are afraid of you, but take good care and don't get afraid of yourself. I've heard strange stories about you—how that you never sleep o' nights—that you pace the long gallery of your boarding-house with restless and uneasy steps, and while others luxuriate in the blessings of "tired nature's sweet restorer,"[4] sleep is a stranger to your eyelids. I have heard that the lone and solemn hour of midnight is a terror to you, and that the ghosts of murdered Banquos will rise mentally to your vision, as a meet reward for your deeds of awful transgression, and your disregard for the injunction, "Thou shalt not kill."

Some men become noted, some are celebrated, and others, again, have the stamp of notoriety fixed to their names: such is the unenviable condition of him whom we have here sketched. He has made his mark through life, but it has been in the spirit of the pestilence and the destroyer.

---

1   Cf. "That they pass by me as the idle wind/ Which I respect not." *Julius Caeser*, IV, 2, 77.

2   A misquotation from Byron's "The Corsair," Canto 1, Stanza ix. It should read: "a laughing Devil."

3   A swaggering coward in Sheridan's "The Rivals." (See Act iv, Sc. 1.)

4   Young's "Night Thoughts," Night I, 1. i.

A Night At The Terpsichore Ball, By "You Know Who"[1]

A strict adherence to the truth compels me to acknowledge that I am a bachelor, whether young or old, handsome or ugly, rich or poor, I will leave your readers to guess. I am, however, like all bachelors, one from inclination, not necessity. As all philosophers have acknowledged that Everyone can be suited to their minds as regards the selection of a wife, why I should be an exception to the general rule arises no doubt from the fact of my being a resident of this city of epidemics, and she somewhere else, with no likelihood of her ever getting here, so I have settled down [to be] as comfortable as circumstances will admit, joined the "Old Bachelor Society," intending to prove my constancy toward her by marrying nobody. If this ain't satisfactory and self-sacrificing on my part, and sufficient to immortalize me, I will keel over and expire.

Japhet in search of his father never had more difficulties to surmount, obstacles to contend against, and incidents to befall him, than I have had in my efforts to find her, I did not cease my labors night nor day, as my portfolio will prove, but all in vain; my supplications were useless, my efforts fruitless, my dreams and fancies of no avail. The following incident befel me in one of my exploring expeditions after her.

'Twas Saturday evening, cool and pleasant, just the kind of night for a dance, as I found myself with a few friends, comfortably seated in the Lafayette car. "Who knows," so ran my mind, "but what I may see her this evening? Nature may repay all my labors by showing me the one she intends to share my lot." And a thousand other fanciful thoughts flitted through my mind, when "Gentlemen will please make room for ladies" assailed my ears from two or three stentorian voices. My gallantry would not allow me to remain one second after this appeal; so I got up on deck as best I could, amidst the yelling of a crowd of b'hoys trying to sing "Old Dan Tucker." I was about taking a seat, but finding some three inches of the thickest kind of dew on the bench, I stood it the balance of the distance.

At length we arrived at the end of our journey. The Trojan horse could scarcely contain more persons than that car; they were pouring out from all sides and in every direction. I followed the crowd. Arriving at the ball-room I imagined all trouble and inconvenience ceased, for that night. Poor deluded being! I forgot I had a hat, and that I should provide a place for it. I did so, but suffered some. The post-office on advertizing days was nothing to it. When I was clear of the crowd, I requested one of my friends to squeeze me into shape again; I felt as flat as a pancake. Did you ever put on white kid gloves—the delicate little creatures—without wishing they were never known? If you did not, I did, that night. In the hurry of the moment I bought sevens instead of nines. I pulled; I pressed and pulled again. No go. I was determined to have them on or burst. After a while I did both. Although my hands looked like cracked dumplings, I didn't care; so I put my hands behind my back and made my first *début* amidst the chivalry, beauty, loveliness, and exquisite grace congregate in that social hall.

The room was overflowing with the beauty of Lafayette, with a sprinkling from New Orleans and Carrollton. A promenade was in order when I entered and I watched each graceful form and lovely face; as they approached like sylphs of some fairy tale, in plain, fancy and mask dresses. Each one, me-thought, was more lovely than the other; but no, the object of my heart,—she who has caused me so many sleepless nights and restless days,—she whom I have seen so often in my dreams and imaginings, was not among the unmasked. I rose from my seat with a heavy heart, walked into the _____ and took a drink of lemonade without any brandy in it. On my return, a cotillion was in motion. I looked upon it with stoic indifference—she was not there, and not being there, the place or persons had no charms for me.

While musing to myself that I would emigrate to Europe or China—get wrecked, perhaps—find her

---

1   From the *Daily Crescent*, May 18, 1848.

on some barren isle, etc.—I caught a glimpse of what I considered the very pink of perfection, in form, grace and movement, in fancy dress. Doctor Collyer would give the world for such a figure. My eyes were riveted on the spot. My head began to swim. I saw none but her. A mist surrounded all the others, while she moved about in bold relief. She turned. I saw her face, radiant with smiles, ecstasy, delight. "'Tis she!" I ejaculated, as if tossed by a pitchfork, and caught the arm of a manager, to introduce me. He didn't know her. It was her first appearance in the ball-room. I imagined it was an auspicious coincidence. It was also my first appearance. Seeing a gentleman conversing with her, I watched my opportunity, and seeing him alone, I requested him to introduce me. Never saw him before in my life; but what cared I— my case was getting desperate. He willingly consented; and off we started toward her. To describe my feelings while approaching her, is impossible. I was blind to all but her.

The agony was over; she spoke; and the deed was done. I found that she was everything that I imagined—accomplished, pleasing in her manners, agreeable in her conversarion, well versed in the authors, from Dryden down to James—including all the intermediate landings—passionately fond of music, she said; and by her musical voice I knew she could sing. I was happy in every sense of the word— delighted beyond measure. She kindly consented to promenade—would carry me through a cotillion if I'd go—but, knowing nothing about the poetry of motion, I had to decline; and she,—noble, generous creature as she was!—preferred rather to talk and walk than dance. I admired her, nay, I will confess, for the first time in my life, I felt the "tender passion" creeping all over me. *I was in love!* I could not restrain myself. Candor compelled me to speak openly—I told her I had been looking for her since I was 18 years of age. "Looking for me!" she exclaimed with astonishment. "If not you," I answered, "someone very much like you." She guessed my object, saw and understood all, and invited me to call and see her.

I was, in my own opinion, as good as a married man—at length my toils and troubles were to cease—I was about to be repaid for my constancy, by having the one for my wife that nature intended. Just at this moment where, in any other place I would have been on my knees, the gentleman who [had] introduced me, came up to us and said —"Wife ain't it time to go home?" "Yes, my dear," she responded. So taking his arm, casting a peculiar kind of look at me, and bidding me good night, they left me like a motionless statue on the floor. The perspiration flowed down my cheeks, like rain drops—the blood rushed to my head—my face was as red as a turkey rooster's—I was insensible. Some of my friends, seeing my situation, carried me into the —, and administered another lemonade with a little brandy in it, which revived me very shortly. I jumped into a cab—in one hour afterwards I was in the arms of Morpheus.

It is very evident that she was the one; and yet it astonishes me how she could take her present husband for me. There is no similarity between us. She was still young, and no chance of being an old maid; while he appeared as careless of his wife's charms as I did of his existence.

I wish them both much happiness, altho' I am the sufferer by it.

Miss Dusky Grisette[1]

M iss Dusky Grisette is the young "lady" who takes her stand of evenings upon the pavement opposite the St. Charles Hotel, for the praiseworthy purpose of selling a few flowers by retail, showing off her own charms meanwhile, in a wholesale manner. She drives a thriving trade when the evenings are pleasant. Her neat basket of choice bouquets sits by her side, and she has a smile and a wink for every one of the passers-by who have a wink and a smile for her.

---

1   From the *Daily Crescent*, March 16, 1848.

Mademoiselle Grisette was "raised" in the city, and is pretty well known as a very pretty *marchande des fleurs*. She can recommend a tasteful bunch of posies with all the grace in the world, and her "buy a broom" style of addressing her acquaintance has, certainly, something very taking about it. She possesses pretty eyes, a pretty chin, and a mouth that many an heiress, grown oldish and faded, would give thousands for. The *em bon point* of her form is full of attraction, and she dresses with simple neatness and taste. She keeps her eyes open and her mouth shut, except it be to show her beautiful teeth—ah, her's are teeth that are teeth. She has sense enough to keep her tongue quiet, and discourses more by "silence that speaks and eloquence of eyes" than any other method—herein she is prudent.

Grisette is not "a blue" by any means, rather a brune, or, more prettily, a brunette—"but that's not much," the vermillion of her cheeks shows through the veil, and her long glossy hair is nearly straight. There are many who affect the brune rather than the blonde, at least when they wish to purchase a bouquet—and as

"Night/ Shows stars and women in a better light,"[1]

they have a pleasant smile and a bewitching glance thrown into the bargain whilst purchasing a bunch of posies.

What becomes of the flower-girl in the day time would be hard to tell: perhaps it would be in bad taste to attempt to find out. She is only interesting in character and association. Standing at, or reclining against, the door-cheeks of a store, with the brilliancy of the gas light falling favorably, and perhaps deceptively, upon her features and upon her person, with her basket of tasteful bouquets at her feet, and some of the choicest buds setting off her own head-dress. As such she looks in character as a *jolie grisette* as she is, and will excite the notice of those who, beneath the light of the sun, and in the noontide gaze of men, would spurn and loathe such familiarities. Poor Grisette therefore slinks away to some retired hole or comer when the witching hours of gas light have passed by, and when the walkers upon the streets have grown tired of wandering, and with noise, [and] have thrown themselves upon their beds for repose. She sells her flowers, and barters off sweet looks for sweeter money; and with her empty basket upon her head, she takes up "the line of march" for her humble home, along with "daddy" who, being ever upon the safe lookout, has come for her.

Perhaps, in the morning, she sells coffee at one of the street corners, to the early draymen, who have an appetite for the regaling draft—becoming "all things to all men" in changing *tout à fait* her set of customers. In this last employment, she sylph-like puts on the air and manner of drudgery. Habited in a plain frock, with a check apron, and with her head "bound about" by a cotton handkerchief, she retails bad coffee at a picayune a cup, with an air of nonchalance entirely suited to the calling and to the customers. Hard-working men like draymen, want coffee and not glances—they need the stomach and not the appetite to be feasted. Grisette, therefore, acts well her part. Flowers and fancy for the upper ten thousand, in the glow and excitement of evening and gas-light—but neither airs nor graces attend her, nor do flowers deck her hair as, by day-light, in the cool of the morning, she repairs to her accustomed stand, with her tin coffee urn upon her head.

During the day, perhaps she assists her mother, in _____ street, who is a very respectable washer-woman, and highly esteemed for those exceedingly desirable qualifications, namely—the rendering of linen white and well starched. And thus, Mademoiselle Grisette fills up a very clever place of usefulness. Instead of degenerating into a mere dowd, as so many beauties become during the unenchanting hours of day-light, lounging the time away, from sofa to rocking-chair, and from rocking-chair back to sofa again, with some trifle of a novel in their hands, Grisette, who does not know a letter in the book, and is thence

---

1   Byron's "Don Juan," Canto II, Stanza 152.

fortunately secure against the seductions of popular literature, betakes herself, with hearty good will, to the washtub; and they do say that her cousin Marie and herself have rare fun whilst splashing among the suds, in detailing the numerous conquests they (poor things!) supposed (themselves) to have made in the flower market the evening before.

The Mississippi at Midnight[1]

How solemn! sweeping this dense black tide!
    No friendly lights i' the heaven o'er us;
A murky darkness on either side,
    And kindred darkness all before us!

Now, drawn nearer, the shelving rim,
    Weird-like shadows suddenly rise;
Shapes of mist and phantoms dim
    Baffle the gazer's straining eyes.

River fiends, with malignant faces!
    Wild and wide their arms are thrown,
As if to clutch in fatal embraces
    Him who sails their realms upon.

Then, by the trick of our swift motion,
    Straight, tall giants, an army vast,
Rank by rank, like the waves of ocean,
    On the shore march stiffly past,

How solemn! the river a trailing pall,
    Which takes, but never again gives back;
And moonless and starless the heaven's arch'd wall,
    Responding an equal black!

Oh, tireless waters! like Life's quick dream,
    Onward and onward ever hurrying—
Like Death in this midnight hour you seem,
    Life in your chill drops greedily burying!

---

1   "The Mississippi at Midnight." *New Orleans Daily Crescent*, (6 March 1848): 2. Revised as "Sailing the Mississippi at Midnight," *Specimen Days & Collect* (1882–83).

Mary Ashley Townsend ("Xariffa") (1832–1901)

In 1882, when Oscar Wilde was touring the southern United States, he stopped in New Orleans, where he was introduced to poet, novelist, playwright, and socialite, Mary Ashley Townsend,[1] not George Washington Cable or Grace King, but Townsend, proving just how popular she was at the time. In fact, she was called on to write the dedicatory poems for the 1884 Cotton Centennial Exposition and also for the setting of the cornerstone of Tulane University's Arts and Science building in 1893. Townsend was also named the Poet Laureate of the esteemed Krewe of Rex twice, once in 1873 and again in 1879.[2] The day after her death in June of 1901, a tribute to Townsend appeared in the *Times-Democrat* stating, "for every public occasion of moment in this city she sent up the silver note of her bugle, and the occasions that now mark the history of the town are recorded in her work."[3] Townsend was also the first woman invited to join the exclusive Mexico City literary club, Liceo Hidalgo, and was the first American member of that club. But as popular as she was at the time, unlike Chopin, King, or Cable, she has been largely forgotten.

Townsend used many pen names over the years, "Mary Ashley," "Crab Crossbones," "Henry Rip," "Michael O'Quilo," but "Xariffa" was the one she used as a poet. The online *Louisiana Anthology* at Louisiana Tech in Ruston very recently published Xariffa's 1857 novel, *The Brother Clerks: A Tale of New Orleans*. The memorial plaque to Townsend at Tulane's Howard Library, however, is now in the archives, and her poetry, for which she was best known, exists primarily in New Orleans newspapers on microfilm and in books out of print. Aside from her novel, she wrote five books of poetry: *Xariffa's Poems* (1870), *The Captain's Story: A Poem* (1874), *Down the Bayou and Other Poems* (1882), *Easter Sunrise* (1889), and *Distaff and Spindle* (1895).

Townsend was born Mary Ashley Van Voorhis in Lyons, New York, on September 24, 1932, to James G. and Catherine Van Winkle Van Voorhis. Her father, her mother's second of three husbands, died when Mary was only one year old. She first came to New Orleans in 1850 to visit her sister, Cephise Slawson, and according to biographer Audry May Meyer, published her first poem, "An Hour out of the City," in the *Daily Delta* in September of that year.[4] She would continue to publish her poetry in the *Delta* for over a decade.

In 1852, Van Voorhis married her cousin, Gideon Townsend, and for a time they lived in Fishkill, New York, and Iowa City, Iowa, before moving permanently to New Orleans in 1860. They had three children: Cora Alice, Adele Cephise, and Daisy Budd. Her oldest daughter, Cora, married José Martin Rascon, the Minister Plenipotentiary from Mexico to Japan, and after residing in Tokyo for a time, they returned to Rascon's native San Luis Potosí, Mexico. Rascon bought Cora's parents a small estate there, *La Chapala*—which Townsend renamed *La Chapelle*—and the couple spent much time there over the years, until Cora's sudden death in 1898 and Gideon's the following year.[5]

Townsend was socially active in New Orleans and counted among her friends most of the local writers of her day: George Washington Cable, Grace King, Sallie Rhett Roman, Eliza Nicholson, and M.E.M. Davis, to name a few. She was one of the founding members of the still active women's literary association, the Quarante Club, and like Davis and King, she held salons at her Garden District home. Like her abovementioned contemporaries, she too wrote for several of the local newspapers. Aside from the *Delta*, she contributed regularly to the New Orleans *Times*, and later the *Times-Democrat*, the *Picayune*, and the New Orleans *Crescent*, the paper that Whitman came to New Orleans to help jumpstart.

Xariffa's best known poem, "Creed," was first published in the *Picayune* on November 1, 1868, and Meyer calls it "the most important single item in her rise to fame."[6] Because it was her most popular, it was republished

---

1   For more on Townsend and the source of much of the biographical information here, see Audrey May Meyer, *Mary Ashley Townshend: Xariffa, 1832-1901* (New Orleans: NP, 1938).

2   Ibid., 17.

3   *New Orleans Times-Democrat*, June 8, 1901.

4   Meyer, *Xariffa*, 9.

5   Ibid., 23.

6   Ibid., 12.

too many times to count. Like so many poets of the time, Xariffa wrote about love, death, nature, art, and religious faith, and the subjects of "Creed" and the other poems included here are no exception.

In "Creed" Xariffa writes of her faith, and in "Down the Bayou," she finds religious rapture in nature, specifically in Louisiana's "cypress swamp." She employs religious imagery throughout the poem, for example, when she describes the "moss-hung branches there/Like congregations rustling down to prayer." In her final sonnet included here, "Her Horoscope," she takes a candid look at the lives women lead, and writes that "Tis true, one half of woman's life is hope/ And one half resignation./ Between there lies/ Anguish of broken dreams,— doubt, dire surprise/ And then is born the strength with all to cope." She ends the poem wondering if women will be remembered "as is for one brief day/ The rose one leaves in some forgotten book," a strikingly sad image.

In contrast to her rise to fame and social success, Townsend's later years were filled with sadness, with the death of her sister Cephise, her mother, her daughter, Cora, and her husband, Gideon, all within a very short time. She was in a railroad accident in 1907, and the complications from that accident contributed to her death on June 7 of that year, in Galveston, Texas, where she was staying with her daughter, Daisy. Like in her poem "Her Horoscope," Townsend too wondered how she would be remembered. Her friend and contemporary, Grace King called Townsend's death "a loss to the Southland."[1]

Creed[2]

I.

I believe if I should die,
And you should kiss my eyelids when I lie
  Cold, dead, and dumb to all the world contains,
The folded orbs would open at thy breath,
And from its exile in the isles of death
  Life would come gladly back along my veins!

II.

I believe if I were dead,
And you upon my lifeless heart should tread,
  Not knowing what the poor clod chanced to be,
It would find sudden pulse beneath the touch
Of him it ever loved in life so much,
  And throb again, warm, tender, true to thee.

III.

I believe if on my grave,
Hidden in woody deeps or by the wave,
  Your eyes should drop some warm tears of regret,
From every salty seed of your dear grief,
Some fair, sweet blossom would leap into leaf,
  To prove death could not make my love forget.

---

1   New Orleans *Times-Democrat*, June 8, 1901.

2   From: Thomas M'Caleb, ed. *The Louisiana Book: Selections from the Literature of the State* (New Orleans: R.F. Straughan. 1894), 547-8.

IV.

I believe if I should fade
Into those mystic realms where light is made,
  And you should long once more my face to see,
I would come forth upon the hills of night
And gather stars, like fagots, till thy sight,
  Led by their beacon blaze, fell full on me.

V.

I believe my faith in thee,
Strong as my life, so nobly placed to be,
  I would as soon expect to see the sun
Fall like a dead king from his height sublime,
His glory stricken from the throne of time,
  As thee unworth the worship thou has won.

VI.

I believe who hath not loved
Hath half the sweetness of his life unproved;
  Like one who, with the grape within his grasp,
Drops it with all its crimson juice unpressed,
And all its luscious sweetness left unguessed,
  Out from his careless and unheeding clasp.

VII.

I believe love, pure and true,
Is to the soul a sweet, immortal dew
  That gems life's petals in its hours of dusk.
The waiting angels see and recognize
The rich crown jewel, love, of paradise,
  When life falls from us like a withered husk.

Down the Bayou[1]

The cypress swamp around me wraps its spell,
With hushing sounds in moss-hung branches there,
Like congregations rustling down to prayer,
While Solitude, like some unsounded bell,
Hangs full of secrets that it cannot tell,
And leafy litanies on the humid air
Intone themselves, and on the tree-trunks bare
The scarlet lichen writes her rubrics well.
The cypress-knees take on them marvellous shapes

---

1   From: Mary Ashley Townsend. *Distaff and Spindle: Sonnets*. (Philadelphia & London: J.B. Lippincott Company, 1895), XLII.

Of pygmy nuns, gnomes, goblins, witches, fays,
The vigorous vine the withered gum-tree drapes,
Across the oozy ground the rabbit plays,
The moccasin to jungle depths escapes,
And through the gloom the wild deer shyly gaze.

Her Horoscope[1]

'Tis true, one half of woman's life is hope
And one half resignation. Between there lies
Anguish of broken dreams,—doubt, dire surprise,
And then is born the strength with all to cope.
Unconsciously sublime, life's shadowed slope
She braves; the knowledge in her patient eyes
Of all that love bestows and love denies,
As writ in every woman's horoscope!
She lives, her heart-beats given to others' needs,
Her hands, to lift for others on the way
The burdens which their weariness forsook.
She dies, an uncrowned doer of great deeds.
Remembered? Yes, as is for one brief day
The rose one leaves in some forgotten book.

At Set of Sun[2]

A scent of guava-blossoms and the smell
Of bruiséd grass beneath the tamarind-trees;
The hurried humming of belated bees
With pollen-laden thighs; far birds that tell
With faint, last notes of night's approaching spell,
While smoke of supper-fires the low sun sees
Creep through the roofs of palm, and on the breeze
Floats forth the message of the evening bell.
Our footsteps pause, we look toward the west,
And from my heart throbs out one fervent prayer:
O love! O silence! ever to be thus,—
A silence full of love and love its best,
Till in our evening years we two shall share
Together, side by side, life's Angelus!

---

1   From: Townsend, *Distaff,* LXVI. The two sonnets, "At Set of Sun" and "Her Horoscope" also appear in Edmund Clarence Stedman, ed. *An American Anthology, 1787–1900* (Boston: Houghton Mifflin, 1900).

2   From: Townsend, *Distaff,* XXIII.

John Dimitry (1835–1901)

John Bull Smith Dimitry[1] was born in Washington D.C. on December 27, 1835, to Alexander and Mary Powell Mills Dimitry. His mother, Mary, was the daughter of Robert Mills, the designer of the Washington Monument, and his father, Alexander Dimitry, was a journalist, educator, and public servant, working as a clerk in the U.S. Post Office at the time of his son John's birth. Alexander Dimitry soon thereafter returned to Louisiana, where he initiated the free school system and served for several years as the Superintendent of Public Education for the state until beginning a career as a U.S. diplomat. Alexander Dimitry was named the U.S. minister to Nicaragua and Costa Rica, where he hired John as his secretary. Both father and son resigned their diplomatic positions to fight in the Civil War.

After being wounded at the Battle of Shiloh, Dimitry, like his father before him, took a job as clerk of the Post Office Department, but in Richmond, Virginia. In 1871, he married Adelaide Stuart of Mississippi, and they soon moved to Barranquilla, Colombia, where he was a professor of English and French at the Colegio Caldas for two years. The couple returned to New Orleans, where John worked as the literary and drama critic for the *Times* for seven years. In the 1880s, he wrote for the *New York Mail and Express* before returning to teaching at Montgomery Preparatory School of West Virginia University in 1895.

Dimitry is best known for his historical scholarship. His book, *Lessons in the History of Louisiana, from its Earliest Settlement to the Close of the Civil War, to Which are Appended Lessons in its Geography and Products* (sic) was published in 1877; five years later, he published a book on 16th-century writer, François Rabelais entitled, *Three Good Giants Whose Famous Deeds Are Recorded in the Ancient Chronicals of François Rebelais* (sic), and in 1899, he published *The Confederate Military History of Louisiana*. He also wrote a historical novel, *Atahualpa's Curtain*, about the last emperor of the Incan empire, and a historical drama, *The Queen's Letters.*

According to the editors of the *Library of Southern Literature,* while working as a journalist for the *New York Mail and Express,* John Dimitry won a $500 prize for "Le Tombeau Blanc," a story which they go on to describe as "a romance of singular power." Indeed it is a powerful and even at times shocking short story.

The story opens with a seemingly innocuous statement that foreshadows alarming events for which today's readers are totally unprepared; however, that might not have been the case for 19th-century readers: "There was no doubt of it. Fernand Torres had the freshest, pinkest complexion of any man in the great city of the Crescent…." What we later discover is that his pink complexion, like that of his mother on her deathbed, is due to the fact that he has leprosy, what is more commonly referred to today as Hansen's Disease.

Up to the time that Dimitry divulges the fact that Fernand, the protagonist, has leprosy, he is portrayed as the typical, dashing romantic hero, almost too dashing and romantic: "This Fernand was a man—and his type is not too often met—whom men could respect without envy, and women love without humiliation." He was handsome, daring, and "[h]e was the heir, as he had been the only child, of a wealthy planter, whose magnificent plantation spread a mile or more along the low banks of the Bayou Lafourche in Louisiana." So it was no surprise that after he rescued Mademoiselle Blanche de Beaumanior—the daughter of the neighboring wealthy plantation owner—from the "rushing waters of the Father-stream" they would fall in love and soon be married. Again, the story follows the typical 19th-century romantic narrative.

However, during their engagement party, a Japanese lantern ignites Blanche's lace shawl, and Fernand races to extinguish the fire. Blanche suffers a few blisters, nothing more, and Fernand amazingly escapes uninjured. Once again he is lauded for his bravery, but the story takes a very dark turn here. He rushes home to change his charred clothes and assures Blanche that he will return soon, but once at home, his devoted servant, Confianza (trusted or reliable in Spanish) after hearing his story and seeing that he suffered no burns, reminds him of a book belonging to his deceased father that tells of "dose who skin no can burn… no can feel notin," lepers. The

---

1   For more on John Dimitry and from where most of this biographical information is taken, see Edwin Anderson Alderman and Joel Chandler Harris, eds, "Dimitry, John (Bull Smith)," *Library of Southern Literature, 1909* (Cornell University: 2001).

revelation is shocking to Fernand and readers alike.

Dimity and his readers would have known such facts about leprosy, but today's readers may not. In fact, Dimitry's son, Dr. T.J. Dimitry, was an expert on the disease and in 1937 wrote an article tracking the history of it in Louisiana for the *New Orleans Medical and Surgical Journal,* "Introduction of Leprosy into Louisiana and the First Leper Hospitals." In his article, he cites the first documented case of leprosy back to 1758. Two doctors before him, Drs. Blanc and Dyer, attribute the then growing number of Hansen Disease patients to the influx of Acadians into the state. T.J. Dimitry questions their theory, instead claiming that slaves from Africa and Haiti introduced the disease to Louisiana. Of course, neither of these theories is correct.

We also know that Louisiana was the last state in the union to have an operating Hansen's Disease Center, in Carville, which only closed in 1998. It was at that time the sole leprosarium in the continental United States, another being in Hawaii. The Carville hospital, founded in 1894, was located upriver from New Orleans, near Baton Rouge, but Dimitry sets his story in Lafourche Parish, south of New Orleans, in the mid-19th century. In fact, his son, T.J. Dimitry writes that "Joseph Jones, President of the Louisiana Board of Health, reported a case of leprosy on the Lower Lafourche" in 1858, so John Dimitry's story may be historically accurate.[1] The rest of the story is much more predictable: Fernand builds a *"tombeau blanc"* (white tomb) in which he is buried alive until his death, and Blanche joins a convent. Nonetheless, the horrific portrayal of the disease and the historical accuracy of the story make it fascinating for readers even today.

It is, however, also one of the most referential texts included in this collection, and even readers of his time would have struggled with some of the arcane allusions. Dimitry writes that Fernand has "the graces of Juan Giron," a 15-century Spanish nobleman, the 4th Count of Ureña, nicknamed "The Saint" after he created Franciscan and Dominican monasteries in Osuña, Spain, in the southern province of Seville. He goes on to say that Fernand "affected the fragrant *Viuditas* of Ambalema" a reference to short-tailed cigars rolled with tobacco from one of the premier growing regions of Colombia, the country Dimitry calls "New Granada." (In a web search today for the Viuditas of Ambalema, the first thing to pop up is an online dating service for Jewish widows—or viuditas!) And these are only two of the several references that appear on the first page of the story.

According to the editors of the *Library of Southern Literature,* John Dimitry, while alive, was probably best known as an author of epitaphs for many prominent people, such as Andrew "Stonewall" Jackson, Edgar Allan Poe, Charlotte Temple, Charles Sumner, Jefferson Davis, and even the Confederate Flag. He died on September 7, 1901, in New Orleans.

Le Tombeau Blanc[2]

I

There was no doubt of it. Fernand Torres had the freshest, pinkest complexion of any man in the great city of the Crescent, wherein those two natural enemies, trade and music, for three-quarters of a century, have worked together in the pleasantest of unions.

This Fernand was a man—and his type is not met too often—whom men could respect without envy, and women love without humiliation. For the men, he had the muscles of Milo and the graces of Juan Giron. It was he who had set the city agog, after a foolish wager, by tooling a six-in-hand pony-trap along the "Shell Road." It was he who had ridden his own "Lightning" in a famous race won by that more famous horse—the proudest victory recorded in the chronicles of the old "Ridge." It was he who had struggled for a brave five minutes with the rushing waters of the Father-stream and brought

---

1   T.J. Dimitry, "Introduction of Leprosy into Louisiana and the First Leper Hospitals." *New Orleans Medical and Surgical Journal.* 90:3 (1937): 113-21.

2   From: Thomas M'Caleb, ed. *The Louisiana Book: Selections from the Literature of the State.* New Orleans: R.F. Straughan (1894), 327-72.

out all dripping by safe, all pale but heroic, a certain Mademoiselle de Beaumanoir. For the rest, he was a pronounce dandy, affected the fragrant *Viuditas* of Ambalema, opened the freest of purses, had the readiest ear for needy friends, and the scantiest memory of favors granted. In short, he was the half of a modern Admirable Chichton, one who would have ridden shoulder to shoulder with the marvelous Scotchman at the tilting matches of the Louvre, although he might not have cared particularly to claim brotherhood with him in the bout with the wise heads of the University of Paris.

"A devilish fine fellow," cried the club men; "but, by Jove! too much of a prig. Why doesn't Fernand drink and gamble like the rest of us?"

"Isn't he handsome?" sighed the society girls, "so strong, so noble-looking, so rich; but, dear me! just a little too good. Why *doesn't* he flirt like the rest of them?"

To speak the truth, Fernand's comrades were not without cause for complaint. He was—in his inmost nature—something more than they were allowed to know; a quite other creature than the courtly man known to society, the stately framer of compliments to fashionable beauties, the breathful swimmer who could cheat even the Mississippi of its prey, and the bold rider who on the Metairie could win heavy stakes and laughingly decline to receive them. Somebody asked lightly, of Fernand's friend, Père Rouquette, what he thought of him.

"*Ce cher* Fernand," quietly replied Chahta-Ima[1], while he pressed back with both hands his long black curls, "is a veritable modern Saint Christopher. He has broad shoulders, you say? *Eh bien*! so had Saint Christopher."

This nut was the very next day presented to Society, which at once tried its teeth on it. "Saint Christopher's shoulders were broad," exclaimed Society; "bon! but what has that to do with Fernand?"

Puzzle or no puzzle, there was one point I wish to make plain, on which everybody agreed. Fernand's complexion was simply perfect. "A surface white as snow touched with the blush of the arbutus," was what a dainty admirer, evidently feminine, had called it. To say the truth, there were some in the circle who were rather envious of that pink blushing in the snow.

Who was Fernand, after all? He was a *campagnard*, not a city man. He was the heir, as he had been the only child, of a wealthy planter, whose magnificent plantation spread a mile of more along the low banks of Bayou Lafourche in Louisiana. A grave old citizen remembered well that, somewhere about the '30s, Torres *père* had taken refuge in this free country from the vengeance of a volcanic government in New Granada. That he was rich was proved by his purchase, cash down, of a splendid estate, house, lands, slaves, and but his subsequent style of living. He recollected perfectly that the wife, a beautiful woman crowned with piety, had died in a few years (he had forgotten how many), and of what disease he had no clear idea.

"As to Camille, he died in 1855," said the grave old citizen, exhaling meditatively, the smoke of his cigarette.

Of the son, he had known nothing until his appearance in the city. What, between those dates, had really become of him? That was soon displayed by the youth himself on several open pages before an eager Society, which turned all its eye-glasses upon them. He had gone to Heidelberg, had not come out ill in its student-quarrels, had returned after an extended tour to receive his dying father's blessing, and had come to pass the winter in New Orleans, which, in the two languages of the Mother State, is known as the "city" and "*la ville*."

About himself there was no mystery—not the smallest. But could the same be said of an old Indian woman, who was his constant companion—who had stood by him in student-quarrels at Heidelberg—

---

1   Author's note: "Chahta-Ima" (Choctaw-like) is a name given by the Indians to Père Adrien Rouquette, the poet-priest of Louisiana, and their apostle.

who would not be left behind during his tour in the East—who insisted on keeping clean his rooms in Paris, London, New York—and who was now doing the same service in his quiet chambers on Royal Street?

Some had chanced to meet Confianza, as she was named—a tall, lean woman, whose head was persistently muffled in a mantilla; a woman who, though unbent with the years that had crowned that head with the glory of old age, had a strong-set, many-wrinkled face; a woman with a swarthy skin, and a wistful look that seemed to tell of inward wrestlings; a woman, in a word, cursed by one absorbing thought.

Here the opened page of Fernand's story came to an end. But there was another page—a tender, timid page, which no one could read save Fernand, Confianza, and a certain fair young girl who lived in his own parish.

A flutter of interest, as sudden as it was temporary, had some time before centred in this very young lady, Mademoiselle Blanche de Beaumanoir, because, as already told, she had, while crossing the ferry to Algiers, lost her balance and fallen overboard in mid-stream. Her preserver, Fernand himself, was thrown forward, at this supreme moment, into the broad glare that falls upon all gallant saviors of endangered beauty.

He did not take over-kindly to the glare. No more did Mademoiselle Blanche, who, however, had never shone more brightly than when friends trooped around her to congratulate her. At last, congratulations ceased perforce. Mademoiselle Blanche, it was given out, had returned to her country home. No one noticed it—yet such was the fact—that, after this incident, Fernand's visits to his plantation were more frequent and more prolonged than before.

Fortunately, there was no icy rigueur of Creole domestic life to block the happiness of these two. It had melted before the priceless services of the suitor. I do not say that the good people on Bayou Lafourche did not suspect this happy idyl dropping its roses among them. To the proverbial walls with ears must be added the proverbial servants with tongues. Gossip flew on free wing around the neighborhood of La Quinta de Bolivar, as Torres pere had named his Southern home, or La Quinte, as the popular ignorance had corrupted it. But it never reached the city.

It was in the spring-time. The magnolia grandiflora was slowly baring her white bosom to the eager sun, while the myrtle tossed him, in odorous coquetry, her plumed crest; the mystic oleander, telling of desert founts and dark-haired Arabian girls, was opening its rosy petals; and when the sun had left his loves lamenting to seek an unknown couch beyond the cypriere, a great, heavy, pervading perfume, coming from under the wings of the night, told of the nearness of the jasmine. But above all these scents there stole over the railings on low, broad balconies fronting the bayou, and in the causeries high and low, the gentle odor of orange blossoms—blossoms that were not real, but were the gracious prophecies of coming happy hours, a sacred altar, and a holy ring.

II

One star-lit night in April, the moon rose clear, full, queenly. She threw the forest into gloom, but touched with silver the broad-spreading fields in front of it. And as the waters of the bayou caught upon their dark and frowning bosom her radiance, they broke into rippling laughter and flowed in smiles gulf ward.

Beaumanoir itself was all brilliant with light, which blazed through the open doors and windows. M. de Beaumanoir had this evening, through a soiree, made a formal announcement of the engagement of Fernand and Blanche. The spacious rooms were crowded. At every door and window the slaves, with open mouths but tender hearts, were watching that mysterious process which was to usher Mamselle into the dignity of Madame. The vast grounds were filled with a motley crowd, because the poorer neighbors and slaves alike had come to catch that light of joy which, like marriage in the Mother Church, comes but once in a lifetime. The veranda was here and there lit by colored lanterns. Through the raised windows was to be caught the flitting of the dancers; and the sound of laughter and music made the outer crowd, under the trees of the avenue, turn round and round in many a fantastic twirl unknown to the guests.

While eyes and ears among the open-mouthed servants at the doors and windows, among the uninvited guests in the garden and on the grounds, are fully occupied, two figures leave the brilliant parlors to take the air.

"*Mais, la M'sieu Fernand*" cries a voice. "Yes," echoes another.

"*M'sieu Fernand* and *Mamselle Blanche*!"

The lookers-on were right. It was Fernand and Blanche who had appeared on the veranda. The conversation was as brief as, judging from signs, it must have been tender. To the horror of gossips female, and to the chuckles and nudgings of veteran gossips male, the watchers without saw a sudden lifting of Mademoiselle Blanche's face and a bend of M'sieu Fernand's. And there was not one of the unseen observers who would not have said that there had been a kiss given and taken on the broad veranda of Beaumanoir, under the blessing of the full moon.

A light form was seen gliding back to the parlors, Fernand remaining behind. One old gossip under the trees thus commented "*Tiens* you see M'sieu Fernand. He stay to tank de *bon Dieu. Ouida! mais il a bon raison.*"

But something else was presently visible; for at a bound Fernand had left his place and was fighting fire—fire that seemed to envelop a woman. A Japanese lantern, hung in the doorway, had caught fire, burnt the cord that upheld it, and had fallen upon the light Spanish wrap worn by Blanche. It was but a moment for Fernand to grasp the filmy lace fastened by a pin, to tear it burning from his darling's form and with his hands and feet to crush out the leaping flames. All told, he had not been sixty seconds at it. But the guests in alarm were now crowding the veranda. Mademoiselle Blanche had come out of it well. Her white neck was slightly blistered. By good fortune her face—that lovely face—had escaped uninjured. And as to Fernand only his clothes had suffered.

"See," he cried, holding out the brave hands which had fought the flames and conquered them, "see, friends, my hands are not even scorched!"

Each guest judged the miracle from his own point of view.

"It takes Fernand to be lucky," called out his acquaintances.

"Monsieur Torres is surely protected by God," echoed Mademoiselle Blanche.

"The most amazing thing I ever heard in my life," shouted that old hero General Victoire. "*Sacre bleu*! What would I not have given to have had that Fernand at Chalmette! and thou, too, Beaumanoir wouldst thou not? Fire enough behind the barricades there for any salamander, eh, *mon brave*?" And the veteran chuckled while he took a huge pinch of Perique *fin*.

"There is something abnormal in this," was Dr. Tousage's professional comment, whispered to himself.

Once again Fernand's cheery voice was heard. Exhibiting wristband and coat-sleeve all charred, leaving the strong muscular arm mocking at the trial by fire, he exclaimed laughingly:

"I am off. It is early—a little past nine o'clock. La Quinte is a bare half-mile away. A sharp gallop, and it will be but a short ten minutes to change my clothes and return. Don't wait for me. Let the dance go on. *Au revoir, mesdames.*"

And with the light limbs of young manhood he was away. He reined his horse where he saw a light in a room—a light that told of the faithful watch of his old nurse. Crazy with joy he burst upon her. Why not? He looked upon his last adventure as the crown of his love. Surely it was he who had been destined from creation to be Blanche's savior. He was full of that proud happiness which is born of danger encountered for one beloved. What true lover would not rejoice if, twice, his love had owed her life to him?

"Here, Confianza, another coat and a clean shirt! I have been fighting fire."

"Fightin' de fire?"

"Yes; see what it has done?"

He laughed as he showed his coat and shirt, both burned and well-nigh sleeveless. The old woman had no eyes for these. She had crept close to him, and was caressing his hands nervously—furtively almost, as it seemed.

"An' de poor hands—dey must hurt you, no?"

"They? Not at all. Why, now I come to think of it, that is the most astonishing part of it all. Old General Victoire was right. I am a real salamander."

"Hijo mio, que está diciendome?" broke forth from the old Indian in her native tongue, as she leaped to her feet, all trembling.

She stood as might some Priestess of the Sun, devoted unto death, when the head of royal Atahualpa deluged with its sacred blood the holy Peanan Stone!

Fernand was struck by the old woman's look. Once before had he seen it—once, when a round, dull white mark had come upon his forehead, stayed for a month, and then, fought by science, had left the tiniest of scars. That was when he was a student at Heidelberg, and holding his own in the fighting-gardens of Zur Hirschgasse. Once afterward it had appeared—this time on his broad breast—but he had said nothing of it to Confianza.

"Don't be crazy, dear old nurse. Look at my hands. Touch them for yourself; there is nothing wrong about them. I said that I fought the fire; I was wrong. I only played with it. Come, kiss your boy, and after that, a clean shirt and another coat!"

She threw her withered arms around Fernand's neck. She pressed her lips to his mouth—one looking on might well think with a touch of sublime defiance. She kissed his two hands—those hands that were so strong and had been so brave. Then she sat on the floor near him, still holding them within her own. She tried to smile; but it was not a smile that would have done one good to see.

"Fernand," she said gently, "tu remember of dat book which tu papa to you gave, when tu has not more of *quince años?*"

"Yes, yes; I have read it a dozen times or more. But what has that to do with my going out? Don't you know Blanche is waiting for me?"

The old woman seemed not to hear him.

"No forget what a book dat was—dose poor peoples?"

She felt the hands on which her tears were now streaming growing cold. They did not tremble, but the chill of the grave had fallen upon them. Still he said nothing, but shivered as though the cold had really struck him on that balmy April night smiling among its roses and gardenias.

"Der' was something 'bout de fire. Dose who sick no can burn 'esef, no can feel notin'—*oh! hijo mio*—have calm!" she pleaded; and he rose to his feet, murmuring:

"My God!—not this—not this!"

He staggered as he rose, and swayed like some tall tree touched by the tempest's wrath. He understood now his doom too well; but he threw off the weakness as he began to pace the room, first slowly, then rapidly. The pink did not leave his cheeks; but his eyes glittered piteously, yet half defiantly, like those of a noble animal caught in a trap unaware. The old woman, still seated on the floor, was reciting her rosary. There were words that came unbidden to the sacred beads, words of a personal application, that, through tears, tell of human pity, and better still, of human trust in the Divine pity: "May God have mercy upon my boy! May God have mercy!" And from the man treading the floor came, in lugubrious response, the wail of that sorrowful Sister of Human Prayer—that Sister, haggard, hopeless, tearless, who knows no invocation to Divine Justice save to call it to judgment:

"My God! what have I done to deserve this?"

Suddenly, in his rapid strides, Fernand halted before the table, on which a lamp was burning. Seizing the lamp, he deliberately circled the heated chimney with his right hand. Then he clasped it with his left hand. Removing the chimney, he kept one hand steadily in the flame. After that, the other.

"You are right, Confianza," he said coldly; "I must not go back to Mademoiselle Blanche."

"*Que Dios tenga piedad de mi hijo!*" (May God have mercy on my boy!) rose again from the praying woman. She knew her boy well. Whosoever might be deceived by his calmness, it was not she who had nursed him—oh, no, not she!

"The fire-test is satisfactory," continued Fernand, in a tone that appalled her. "There can be no illusion here. The leper's skin can burn, but the burn leaves no mark, nor can pain be felt. My hands should have been burned; I feel no pain; it is clear, then, *I am a leper!*"

"*Que Dios tenga piedad de mi hijo! Por Dios! Par su Santis-sima Madre! Por todos los Santos y Santas del cielo!*" (May God have mercy on my boy! For Christ's sake! For His holy Mother's sake! For the sake of all the saints and angels of Heaven!) wailed once more from the floor, like a prayer for a parting soul. It was unheard by Fernand. A bitter smile passed over his lips as he said:

"But come! Blanche must not be forgotten. She must learn this charming finale to our hopes and our loves."

Paper, pen, and ink were before him. Not pausing to cull phrases, much less to think, he wrote a note and put it into an envelope which he sealed. Ringing a bell, a black presented himself.

"Baptiste, take this letter at once to Mademoiselle Blanche. Place it in her own hands. You need not report."

After Baptiste had left, Fernand said:

"My good Confianza, I wish to be alone. Leave me now. Tomorrow, by eight o'clock, let Dr. Tousage be here."

He did not leave the chair through the long black night. He was alone—alone with the sorrowful Sister of Human Prayer. He made no movement, he breathed no sigh, he murmured no word through all the hours, but fell like a death-bell upon the heart of the figure crouched like a faithful dog, on the other side of his chamber door.

And so the bright sun found them.

III

Baptiste' s master had told him that he need not report the result of his visit to Mademoiselle Blanche. But long before noon the next day, Fernand, had he chosen, might have heard his story from a hundred tongues. There was not a guest at Beaumanoir, over night, that had not borne it away, through the darkness and gardenia-scented air, a fearful but delicious burden. There was not a passenger on the boat which had left that morning, who was not carrying Fernand's name, and blasted love, a morsel of the juiciest for the delectation of the great city. His tragic story, too, was in the mouths, and had touched the hearts, and had filled the eyes, of rude but sympathetic workers a-field in the early summer sunshine; and there was a dew that had not fallen from the sky upon many a plough-handle and many an axe-helve. For there was not a slave at Beamnanoir or La Quinte that had not prayed to hear the joyful marriage-bells, which would bring the two plantations under the same master and mistress.

Then too, there were—unhappily, not far off—men and women whom all avoided; men and women hobbling on crutches, crawling aground, moaning on pestiferous beds, who, selfish by nature, had for once been brought together, not in cynicism but pity. To them the gossip was not sweet. It was bitter—as bitter, as abhorrent, as their own flesh. Fernand had been their truest friend and most fearless neighbor. *"Lui, un lépreuz? Mon Dieu!* if he has got it from us, we are accursed indeed," old père Carancro had said; and with blurred eyes and shaking hands, all had concurred.

After all, what had happened at Beaumanoir?

Obedient to his master, Baptiste had sought Mademoiselle Blanche privately. He had found her seated with two friends, Mademoiselle Diane de Monplaisir and Mademoiselle Marie Bonsecour, in a small room giving on the veranda and opening into the parlor through a curtained door. Baptiste, on presenting the note, had simply said:

"Mamselle Blanche, M'sieu Fernand, he tell me to give dis to you."

Mademoiselle Blanche had opened the note eagerly. It could not have been long, nor could its contents have been over-pleasant. So afterward affirmed Mademoiselle Diane, who added that Blanche had turned pale, *"mais oui, pâle comme la mort,"* had uttered a faint moan, and, in attempting to rise from her chair, had fallen back insensible. What had become of the note itself? Mademoiselle Diane had kept her black marmoset eyes fixed upon that. She declared dramatically that Mademoiselle Blanch had thrown it haughtily away after reading it. Mademoiselle Marie, however, did not agree with her. She said that the note, if it had fallen at all, had not fallen until Blanche became unconscious.

Bad news filled the air like electricity. It was scarce a moment before the curtained doors were torn aside, and a crowd of well-bred, though curious, guests came streaming into the room. At their head was the father. He was about approaching his daughter, but, hearing from a mob of angels in white organdie and tulle that she had recovered consciousness, he was turning aside when he felt his arm touched gently. It was Mademoiselle Diane who had touched him. She pointed silently to a letter on the floor. Monsieru de Beaumanoir picked it up. It was strange. He was in a white heat of anger, certainly; but, on reading it, he did not look so much angry as puzzled.

"What can this be?" he muttered. "*Vraiment, un mauvais farceur* is this Fernand. But come, my friends," he called out, in a loud voice, to the crowd of guests who had already thronged the room. "*Mademoiselle ma fille* is in good hands. This note is from Monsieur Torres. She has been somewhat excited by that, and is naturally nervous. The whole affair is a riddle to me. Perhaps some among you may read it for me."

The crowd surged back, still curious-eyed, but clearly more anxious than when it had torn away the curtained door.

Monsieur de Beaumanoir had stationed himself by the mantel, on which blazed, with their double score of waxen lights, the great golden candelabras that had descended, son to son, from that doughty knight, Sieur Kaoul de Beaumanoir, who had died with Bayard hard by the bloody waters of the Sesia. I do not know how it was, but the fair women in gauze and the white-cravatted men seemed to be a court; Blanche forced to be the plaintiff; Fernand, the defendant; and the owner of the mansion the advocate of the—mystery. For mystery in that note there must be, so whispered one to the other, those flurried beauties that circled, in broadening folds, around the mantel, and, as they whispered, turned just a little pale.

For his part, M. de Beaumanoir, a trifle puzzled and unmistakably stirred, seemed nowise anxious. He re-opened the note impetuously.

No date, no address, no signature. Nothing save these words:

"Do not misjudge me; but I must not go back tonight. You have seen the last of me. Oh, my God! to think that I have seen the last of you! I do not know wherein we have offended

Heaven; but God is angry with us. I am what they call—I am—I dare not write what loathsome creature I have become to myself since a half hour. Read Second Chronicles, chapter xxvi., verse 20. That verse speaks for me who cannot. Read it, and you will know why I have hasted to go out from what to me was not a sanctuary of the Father, but higher still, his Paradise."

Nervously removing his spectacles, M. de Beaumanoir turned interrogatively to the brilliant company.

"*Eh Bien!*" said a pert and petted beauty; "*c'est une question de la Bible.* Let us see the Bible."

Mademoiselle uttered the voice of Society.

"Yes, yes; where is the Bible?" cried all.

A youth of tender mustache, and with the reddest of roses granted him by the grace of Mademoiselle Diane, had, at that lady's nod, already sought the great Douay Bible, which rested upon a side table immediately under a sword crossed with its scabbard upon the wall. Without a word he put the book into the hands of M. de Beaumanoir. The gray old man, mustached like a veteran of Chalmette, opened the Holy Book gingerly, as though he did not know, gallant gentleman and ex-sabreur that he was, its quiet pages quite so well as the temper of his sabre. He had seen the volume certainly, but only accidentally, so to speak, as he might be leaning over it to read for the thousandth time the inscription: "Tribute to—*hem!*—by admiring company—*hum!*—patriotic services—*ha!*—January 8, 1815." Written in French, bound in Russia, heavily edged with gold, and published in Paris, the Sacred Word, while being little noticed by the master, had brought comfort to the late Madame de Beaumanoir, as it was, without his knowledge, the daily guide of his daughter.

The company drew nearer to the father. From the press of loveliness, as might a dainty Bourbon rose from a basket of flowers, stepped Mademoiselle Diane de Monplaisir. It was she who crept close to the side of M. de Beaumanoir, and with her jewelled fingers turned the leaves till her index finger rested upon the chapter and the verse which were to reveal the mystery devouring her. With a stately old-fashioned bow, though with no suspicion of the tragic story in verse 20, the old man read these words slowly aloud:

> "*And Azariah, the chief priest, and all the priests, looked upon him, and, behold, he was leprous, and they thrust him out from thence; yea, himself hasted to go out, because the Lord had smitten him.*"

At these words, so passionless yet so vivid, so filled with fire yet so death-cold, a great hush fell upon the company. It was as though a breeze laden with the poisonous breath of poppies had passed through the room. Psychologists tell us that a single thought may work in madness upon a crowd, a thought springing not from a visible danger, but from the spur of a hidden terror. Of such must have been the feeling, which swept like a cyclone over the joyful throng that had been drinking in excitement under the golden lights to the sound of voluptuous music. A thought of flight, certain, no matter how or whither, only that it should be that very instant, out of the house, out of the grounds, out into the open road, shining yellow-white under the full moon—anywhere, anywhere beyond the evil spirit that had seized upon the princely hospitality of Beaumanoir, and was even then draping, by a mystic and awful hand, its laughing walls in mourning.

In the *sauve qui pent* of an army, pride is thrown aside with the knapsack. In the *sauve qui pent* of Society, it is courtesy that is dropped with the slippers.

One by one the courtly company, with its color and its glitter and its laughter, left the salon. One by one, without even a nod to their old host who stood more dazed than indignant on his threshold, they streamed, with burnous and nubias, and what not, snatched pell-mell on the way, down the broad steps of the front veranda, and into the gravelled walk, where were the carriages of the ladies and the horses of their escorts. For once, one may fancy, there was none of that idle talk—none of those soft whispers, those empty phrases, those vaporous compliments, given with an air and received with a blush—that make up the unwritten literature of carriage windows. A mighty fear shook all, and the colored coachmen were told in sharp tones, altogether new to those fatted favorites, to drive fast and stop at nothing. Through the noble avenue of live oaks, famous throughout that section, through the Arcadian scene, under Chinese lanterns, by rustic groups at their simple pleasures, the carriages thundered, and the riders rushed by plying whip and spur.

Among the last that reached her carriage was Mademoiselle Diane de Monplaisir. She was in no sense excited—that young lady was too poised for that, but it had suited her to play with the fears of her friends. Her garments had rustled with the rest down the steps, but, on leaving the salon, she had been particularly careful respectfully to curtsey before her host, as he stood erect at his post like a forgotten sentinel. Having given this lesson of social tact, she thought herself justified in raising her voice to a decorously high pitch, and saying, in the shape of a problem presented to her escorts: "*Ma foi, Messieurs,* is not this a pretty comedy with which Monsieur Torres has favored us?"

Trained though they were in the young lady's imperious service, none of these gallants answered. The call was too sudden, and the danger altogether too pressing for that.

It had not struck eleven o'clock before the mansion, still blazing with the lights of a joyous betrothal, was left to the ghosts destined to haunt its walls so long as they shall stand. Of the hundred who had froufroued that evening up the carpeted steps, who had opened very promising flirtations of their own, who had envied Blanche while they coveted Fernand, not one remained save Dr. Tousage and Mademoiselle Marie Bonsecour. It was not long after that hour that the doctor himself, having seen that Blanche was recovered and in gentle hands, took leave of the old man, who sat crushed and broken under the wasting lights of the great golden candelabras. As he descended the steps, Dr. Tousage said to himself: "I must refer to my abnormal cases. It was what I suspected. There *was* something extraordinary in his insensibility to fire. I shall see Fernand tomorrow."

For that matter, Dr. Tousage, had he chosen, might have suspected years and years before. He had known Fernand's mother. He had attended her in her last illness, and had seen with surprise the antemortal pallor give place to a post-mortal rosiness. The case had been something beyond his experience. He had contented himself with classing among his "Abnormal Cases" this woman who had looked as blooming in her coffin as she had done in her boudoir, and whose roses in death were like the gorgeous blossom plucked from the twin sister of Rappacini's daughter.

The good doctor had taken no account, however, of the fact that La Quinte, fronting broad on the bayou, and spreading deep in smiling fields of sugar-cane, back to the great funereal *cyprière,* bordered perilously on a world ostracized by the world, between which and it there rises a wall broader, deeper, higher, more deadly repellent, than ever Chinese fear raised against Tartar aggression. A world not populous, save in wrecked hopes, harrowing dreams, and mournful shadows. A world of agonized hearts, of putrid ulcers, of flesh dropping from rotting bones, of Selfishness holding a Spartan throne with Horror, of the Divine likeness distorted, year by year, till the very semblance of man, born in His gracious image, comes to be blotted out. A world, the men and women in which are players in a life-tragedy, to which *Hamlet* is a comedy, and the *Duchess of Malfi* a melodrama.

A terrible world this—in short, a world of LEPERS.

In the parish of Lafourche, along Bayou Lafourche, there are lepers as poisonous as Naaman, and as incurable as Uzziah. It is an old story barely touched here, not even surfaced. It is a curse which lawmakers, in these later days, are called upon to rub out or to wall around. Practically, there has always been a walling around this curse—this blot—whatsoever one may choose to call it; practically, because the neighbors of these unhappy people have lost the sentiment of neighborliness. The feeling against them is as old as the first human deformity, and as bitter as the first human prejudice. What has happened to races before them, offending the eye of civilization, has become their fate. Civilization frowns upon her accursed races, her lepers, her Cagots, her Marrons, her Colliberts, her Chuetas. She prescribes for them certain metes and limits, and says to them, "O God-abandoned, pass not beyond these, at your peril."

The doctors prop up with their science this feeling. They agree that a peculiar disease is confined to a certain class of the population living along Bayou Lafourche; declare that disease to be leprosy, and pronounce it cureless. On their side, the sufferers protest vehemently in denial. No one takes their word, while they themselves, when compelled to wander from their fields, creep with furtive look and stealthy step. Like lepers everywhere, those of Bayou Lafourche are the Lemuridae of mankind. After all, what destroys their case is the single fact which separates them absolutely from their fellows—*if once attacked, these people never get well.* Science is not always consistent; but ages ago she pronounced a judgment against herself which still stands. She admitted then, as she admits now, that she is powerless to heal a leper. It needs a Christ to say: "Be thou clean, and the leprosy is cleansed."

The life of these lepers, if a tragedy, has a plot of sorrow simple enough. There are not many of them. They may now count between twenty-five and fifty families, principally poor, all of whom raise their homes of corruption on Bayou Lafourche. They are not bunched together in one settlement, but stretch out along the stream a distance of thirty or forty miles, scenting, at one end, the soft saccharine smell of growing cane, and at the other the sharp saline odor of a mighty gulf. Their awful malady is an inheritance with them; their sufferings are acute; their disfigurement becomes, in time, complete; but their deaths, though from the same disease, do not create an epidemic.

What the Caqueurs were to Bretagne, and the Yaqueros to the Asturias, these lepers are to Bayou Lafourche. Many-sided are the rumors about them; but a wide-spreading, far-reaching tongue adds that there are among them some who are rich in this world's goods, and yet are forced to take this world's refuse.

No one knew all this better than Dr. Tousage. He had been prominent among those brave physicians who strive to be healers. But, as it happened, he was not thinking of Leper-Land while riding slowly towards La Quinte. Honest Baptiste was in wait. There was a mystery about his *p'tit maitre*—so much Baptiste knew. Confianza's eyes were filled with tears, and they dumfounded the simple slave. Traditions of any kind, save the peaceful, oftentimes tender gossip of La Quinte, where two generations of kindly masters had made the furrows of labor almost as full of roses as the "path of dalliance," had never turned Baptiste's brain into a race-track; so, on the doctor's arrival, his eyes were full of a terror inviting inquiry, but above all sympathy. The doctor was pre-occupied; he gave neither.

"Where is your master, Baptiste?" was all he said.

"M'sieu Fernand, he ees in la bibliotec," replied Baptiste, with a certain awe crossing his terror at right angles. Baptiste fervently believed that the ghost of his old master walked that particular room at midnight. And, for that matter, it would have been hard to find any slave within five leagues who did not agree with Baptiste.

"He is there, is he? Then I know the way very well."

Dr. Tousage found Fernand in a small, well-lighted room, divided from the great wide parlors, sombre even at that early hour, by a falling lace curtain. The sunbeams of the morning streamed through the windows, glinting tenderly the backs of books of great thinkers loved by Don Camilo, and cherished for association's sake by his son. It was a chamber rich in windows as it was brilliant in light—a chamber for the strong, not for the weak.

"*Sapristi!*" said the doctor to himself, "open windows are a sign of joy. The case is not so hopeless, after all."

The good doctor was wrong for once. Fernand had lost hope; or, rather, despair had pushed hope from its place, and there brooded. The young man was seated by a table on which were laid two books. One was a copy of the Bible; the other, Maundrel's work on the Syrian leprosy, a very old book, and as rare as it is old. Rising as his old friend entered, for the first time in his life he did not offer his hand.

"Be pleased to take a seat, doctor."

"*Eh Bien!* Fernand, what is all this? You, a Hercules, and sick?"

The attempt at ease, if intended to deceive, was a failure.

The young man faced his visitor.

"Stop, doctor. This is no time for comedy. I am still a Hercules, if brawn and muscle and twenty-five years can make one. But there is a plague about me more deadly to bear than Dejanira's robe."

"And that plague is—?"

"Leprosy!"

"Have you convinced yourself of that?"

"Perfectly; and you also, you need not deny it. I have not studied that kindly face so long without being able to read it."

"To speak frankly, I am not surprised. But does the disease really exist? It is because I wish to assure myself on this point that I have come. Think over my question quietly."

"Look at this, doctor. This may help you to a conclusion."

While saying this he was throwing open his shirt, revealing a small white-reddish sore slowly eating into his brawny chest.

"I have never been, as you know, doctor, much of what you call a thinking man. At any rate, I have taken this to be the mysterious 'date-mark,' which, at some time in his life, pursues and brands each traveller to Bagdad. It first broke out while I was in Paris, some months ago. My old nurse knows nothing of it. I accepted it gayly enough. I argued something in this way. I had not forgotten Bagdad—why should Bagdad forget me?"

While he was speaking, the physician had been examining the ulcer. He grew more thoughtful as he looked.

"Has this increased in size since it first appeared?"

"Yes; but very little."

"Any pain?"

"No, I cannot say that it has pained me, but it has annoyed me considerably. Remember that, until last night, whenever I thought of it, it was solely in connection with Bagdad. With my physique, what else could give it birth? But that is over now. It is not the date-mark. What, then, is it?"

Dr. Tousage knew his young friend's courage. He did for him what he would not have done for a weaker soul. He took refuge in that truth, which is more often a kindness shown by this world's healers than they are given credit for.

" This," he replied slowly, "represents a leprosy already developed."

"And the Salamanderism of last night?"

"Was a strong, although a wholly accidental, proof of its existence."

"Accidental, you think it? I look upon it rather as providential," retorted Fernand, while adding: "You regard my case as hopeless, then?"

"Absolutely, though the danger is not immediate."

"In other words, *cher docteur,* one must pay for being Hercules. A long life, and each knotted muscle prolonging the torture which it doubles, that is the story, eh?" said the young man, bitterly, as he touched a bell on the table.

In response, the old Indian nurse appeared and stood, quietly waiting, near the door.

"Look, and then listen, doctor," said Fernand, as he pointed with his finger to her. "This old woman—you know her?—has fairly haunted me through life. She was the one to receive me at my birth. She tended me through my babyhood. She protected my boyhood. When my mother died, she became mother and nurse in one. She watched me in my plays. She interfered in my disputes. She made me the laughing-stock of my schoolmates until I fought them into respect. As I grew older, I saw that in her love there was a large leaven of anxiety. She showed it during my years at Heidelberg. She grew thin and more despondent during our stay in the East. She hovered around me in Paris. The Quartier Latin, at a very feverish time, could raise no barricade against her. Mabille had no terrors for her. I found her everywhere on watch, and always with her eyes fixed wistfully on myself. It was then I took to thinking of her as a woman cursed with a single thought that had borrowed the intensity of a mania. It is not three months since I began to believe that that single thought might be for me. Last night I knew that I was right. It was she who prevented my returning to Beaumanoir. Such devotion is rare. I say again, look at her, doctor."

Wondering a little, Science scanned Devotion.

The woman was well worth looking at in her brown-skinned, white-haired, brave, honest, faithful old age. A prophetess of evil had she always been, but not of the order of Cassandra. She had foreseen. She had not chosen to foretell.

Fernand resumed in a reckless manner, as though he had something to do that hurt him, and of which he wished to be rid:

"Would you believe after this, doctor, when I am beaten down to the earth, that she refuses to speak? She talks to me in the jargon of my childhood. Last night she reminded me of a book containing the story of a leper. That is her way of telling me that I am one. There lies the book on the table. Have you ever read it? Old Maundrel held a wise pen in his hand. He reports the case of a man in Syria, who knew himself to be leprous by having passed unscorched through flames. Confianza remembered the story, but I wish to know why she recalled it.—Nurse, here is the doctor. He is a friend, and a true one. In his presence, tell me why you have feared for me through all these years."

The old Indian remained silent. Her tongue was bound by a pledge that it could not break. The dead in their graves forge chains indissoluble.

"But I can tell you, Fernand," said the doctor, gravely, " what Confianza, under oath, dares not."

"You! And what—what can you tell?"

"Your mother died a leper!"

IV

The small world about La Quinte had soon a tidbit to roll around its tongue more to its taste than even that delicious morsel from Beaumanoir. Workmen, it heard, were busy building a cottage under the ancient live oak that was old when Iberville's ships sailed through the waters of Manchac, and moss-crowned when simple *Acadiens* from the Northern ice, camping under it, broke out in wild enthusiasm over its knotted knees and spreading boughs, while their children plucked the giant by his frosty beard, and shouted gleefully as they crowned themselves with the mossy theft. The same oak had, for generations, been the pride of the country round. They called it lovingly *le Père Chêne,* the Father Oak. Superstition had added a special charm to its head, grown gray in the circling rings of a thousand years. Lovers' vows, pledged under it, for once ceased to be false, and a happy marriage never failed, it was fervently believed, to follow the kisses for which the old tree had for ages stood sponsor. To build a cottage under the *Père Chêne,* therefore, was a violent shock given to the love, the pride, the superstition of the entire neighborhood. But what could love, pride, or superstition say? The tree itself was private property; the old gray beard stood on land belonging to La Quinte. It was quite clear, therefore, that the owner had ordered the erection of the cottage, and that he had a right to do so.

Mademoiselle de Monplaisir spoke the voice of a critical circle:

"*Ma foi, c'est bien noble de la part de M. Torres.* He wishes to be near his kin."

There was always a sting in the honey vouchsafed by this young lady to her friends. The sting in this particular honey was that Leper-Land began within half a league below the lower terminus of La Quinte.

A low-roofed, broad-verandaed cottage soon nestled under the protecting branches of the old tree. The roof once reached, farm wagons, filled with furniture, stirred up the white dust of the Bayou highway. Then came carts filled with books. The cottage itself was only a three days' wonder, after all. Something came afterward, that was to prove a plethoric, full-mouthed, nine days' talk. After the last cart had deposited its burden, the workmen reappeared. They came in crowds. In an amazingly short time, a great whitewashed brick wall rose high enough to look down upon the cottage, which it had been built to screen. It loomed up full thirty feet in the air, stretching in a square on all sides of the giant oak, whose head, turbaned in mosses, could be seen behind it from the road and from boats passing swiftly on the Bayou. There was nothing cheerful in this strange pile. In the sunlight it looked like a prison; in the moonlight, like a graveyard. The Panteon of Bogota is not more ghost-like.

The wall being finished, but one entrance was left to the interior. This was at the lower end, to the rear, where a strong oak door, iron-bound, challenged the way. On the side of that door was a turn-window in the wall, through which could be passed such articles as might be needed for the dweller within. Close to that window and outside of the wall was a small hut. It was the home of Confianza—martyr to the child of her love in his weakness, as she had been faithful to him in his young strength under the skies of Damascus and on the shining shores of the Mediterranean.

And what did Society, that part of it which whispers its wisdom behind summer fans, think of all this? It only sighed prettily, and itched the more to know all. Fernand's story was an exciting one so far, but society is never wholly satisfied unless it sees the green curtain fall on a tragedy on which it has seen it rise. For the rest, it had been told that he remained shut up in his rooms and had been seen by no one but the doctor and Confianza. It clamored, however, for the end. Somehow, this did not come to it so soon as expected. It was very long after Society had retired, so to speak, from the boxes, and the lights had been put out, that it heard that Fernand, on the very night of the day when the strong oak door was hung on its hinges, had passed through it alone. Little by little it came out, that, for that particular night, an order had been given to all the slaves of La Quinte, somewhat in the fashion of that borne by the herald of Coventry,

"…a thousand summers back."

The old Indian had taken the message through the house and the quarters. "The master is going," she said, "to leave La Quinte tonight for his new home. He is very sick and very unhappy. He knows that his people love him, and he begs them all to go to their cabins early tonight, and not to leave them."

In the old story of Coventry it was a "shameless noon" that, from its hundred towers, clanged the triumph of a peerless sacrifice. In the new one, it was a pitying midnight which, from its hundred shadows, shrouded the sacrifice of a noble life. La Quinte, fertile as she was in sons and daughters, had not bred a "Peeping Tom" among them all; and by nine o'clock there was not one of her children who was not abed.

Fernand had died to the world. So the world, true to its traditions, avenged itself by calling his retreat *Le Tomheau Blanc,* a ghoulish fancy, which had received its inspiration from a remark accredited to Mme. Diane Dragon (nee Monplaisir), while daintily sipping her orgeat, that, "since M. Torres has chosen to bury himself alive, his home is well called The White Tomb." For the rest, Society had no time for a tragic tale already old. Autumn had laughed with Summer over the richness of their common harvest. Winter, which had passed in storm over the parish, had found time—there is a deal of unrecorded kindly blood in these stern old seasons—to press a parting kiss upon Spring's virgin lips, and to whisper: "Be good, my daughter, and spare not thy sweetest blossoms." It scarcely seemed cause for wonder, then, that Society should have forgotten the hermit as completely as though he lay, indeed, stretched cold and dreamless in his last bed.

As to the leper's actual condition, even the old Indian knew but little. He had locked the gate behind him and kept the key with him in his cottage. The turn-window remained the only medium of communication between them. Before burying himself, Fernand had said to her: "You know that I am very sick; what is worse, I am hopeless. My life may be short or long. Whether long or short, I am forced to suffer. I wish to die, but it is my duty to live. Cook my meals and put them twice a day in the turn-window. I shall call for them at eight o'clock in the morning; then again at four in the afternoon." That was all which had passed between the two. It seemed a sorry exhibit enough, this gratitude smothered in the fumes of a gastronomic edict. But the true old woman took it all to herself, and that night, with her worn rosary in hand, she broke into an extra plea of *Paternosters* and *Ave Marias.*

In the meantime, and in his bitter solitude, shuddering and sick at heart, Fernand would turn from his mournful future to the compensation which must be his so long as his skilful hands could win music from the strings of his Cremona. This instrument was a gift to him, when a lad, from Duffeyte, that brilliant tenor whose sweet notes had entranced Creoledom somewhere in the '40's. His power over his gift was not unworthy of the donor. His soul was alive with music as a heated forge is with flame. Compositions of the great masters weighted his music-rack; but memories of Verdi and Donizetti, and melodies of Liszt and Strauss were with him, and through the chords of his Cremona, with an almost human sympathy, spoke tenderly and consolingly to the leper's heart. The cool and quiet of midnight were wont to fall like a dream of peace upon his tortured soul. He had cried with Themistocles, "Give me the art of oblivion!" But the unpitying sun was not his friend. Its torrid glare already revealed that fatal whiteness which separated him from his fellows. He felt that, for him, the moonlight was better than the sunlight; and the night's black mantle friendlier than the day's blazing shield. In his isolation, he learned, too, to acknowledge a comradeship, during the short spring and long summer months, with the whippoorwill, that sad brown bird of the eyprière, which, shunning the haunts of happier men, had been won by the mystic shadows and unbroken silence within the wall, and had come to grieve with him through moonlit nights, coyly hidden, but fearless, among the leaves of the ancient oak.

For in the meantime, Dr. Tousage's judgment had been verified.

Fernand's leprosy was already developed when he fought the flames at Beaumanoir. But when Spring came, in memory of her agreement with Father Winter to drop blossoms on the trees and to fill the black earth with flowers, the second stage was already reached. It was to the credit of the doctor's sincere friendship that not a whisper of this was breathed beyond the old woman's hut. But the fight was held within the wall and under *Père Chêne,* all the while. The old physician's visits were for a time regular. Then, all at once, his knock ceased to be heard at the oak door. Something had taken place between the two—a quarrel, everybody said. Oh, no! not that; only a bit of truth from Science, told in a broken voice, and with great tears streaming down from under the gold spectacles of the leech:

"I can no longer hope to do you good, Fernand, and I may possibly injure others by my visits. The physician does not belong to himself. Your disease, always incurable, has within the last six months become practically contagious. God bless you, my son, and give you courage to bear unto the end."

This was, for Fernand, a dismissal that had long been foreseen. There was death in his heart already, and all that he asked was that he might indeed cease to live, and be at rest forever. But of what he suffered, and of the storm that, raging in him, broke out in bitter rain, all this the great wall hid, as a new and sadder secret, among the branches of its monster oak.

When Dr. Tousage left him, Fernand was fighting with the second stage of his disease. The arbutus-like pink of his complexion had faded out. He had become a "leper white as snow." He saw before him a Calvary on whose *viâ dolorosa* he could hope to meet no Cyrenian to bear his cross. He found himself thinking of a time when the white skin would change into a coarse yellow; when deep into its surface a growth of tubercles would fatten in ulcerous corruption; when the hand that had grown so warm in love might lose the use of its shapely fingers; and when even the face hallowed by the first and last kiss of Blanche, might, if seen in its awful disfigurement, come to frighten timid women in mother's labor. He knew himself to be like another Vivenzio in the castle of Tolfi. His own life, in its decaying physical form, measured for him as surely the year-posts to death as the lessening windows of his iron shroud had for the Italian.

Behind his wall, perhaps in a bitter spirit, perhaps in resignation, he had gauged the world and believed it wanting in remembrance. But he was not forgotten. Old Confianza, at his window, sat day and night, as silently and faithfully watching as Mordecai at the Persian's gate. And there were others. In those dark hours dear to him, there were passers-by along the bayou-road. These were men and women who had learned to make that road a Mecca, because they had loved the kindly man now forced to live a pariah.

The road seemed haunted with ghosts.

For, as the darkness fell upon bayou and swamp, shadows would come stepping softly out of it to mass a moment in fearful silence in front of *Le Tombeau Blanc;* to point out, each to his neighbor, the great ghostly wall, and to raise their black hands in whispered blessing over it; and then, as their creeping-off would drop into a half-trot, they would break out into a wild hymn, which, beginning soft and tremulous, would grow into loudness, drowning the whippoorwill's plaint, and filling the woods with the presence of an uncultured but mighty *miserere*.

Following these ghosts, but avoiding always to meet them, would come others. These would creep from the forest depths lower down, stand for a longer time than the rest staring at the wall; would raise their hands, too, in silent benediction, and, in their turn, retire as noiselessly as the shadows that they were. Lepers in body, the souls of these ghosts were clean. For out of the agony that was Selfishness had bloomed the flower that was Gratitude.

But, after a time, these loving ghosts left the bayou-road to its loneliness. Then a ghost, gaunt and tall, assuming a woman's shape, would step out into the road and stand, looking up with patient sadness. This shape would appear so suddenly after the lepers' flitting that it was clear it had been lying in wait.

Then a special phantom, also a Roman, with strange black robes floating around her, would glide quickly in front of the wall, stop, clasp its hands wildly, with face upturned toward it, as though in supplication; lower its head, with hands still clasped, into the dust of the road, to pray and weep, and weep and pray again.

After a while, the first ghost would draw near, gently touch the shoulder of the kneeling figure, and together both phantoms would become lost in the deeper shadows of Confianza's hut.

Of all these ghosts Fernand knew nothing.

Fernand was a prisoner for life. But the world outside had not, for him or his wall, ceased to move. Action had clutched the scabbard from Argument, and with its right hand drawn the blade. Of the war that had drenched the land in blood, he had heard but once. Men in blue and men in gray had marched past his wall, awed at its height, marvelling at its quaintness, wondering at its use. Then, learning its tragic story, the brave men had turned, somehow, a free and easy route-step into something suspiciously like a double-quick. Confianza herself was mute. A curt order for silence, given by Fernand in the beginning of his malady, had been loyally obeyed by the old Indian; and by long prohibition, no copy of the Picayune had come to tell him that Mars, sword in hand, was sweeping over fields of sugar, corn, and cotton. One day—the date thereof is fixed in the war annals, not in these pages—a single boom was heard under the branches of *le Père Chêne*. Faintly but distinctly, the boom soon came to Fernand's ear—fast, furious, continuous. Evidently a distant cannonade. He could not hear the wild yell, nor the great answering shout that kept time to its martial challenge. But Battle has a voice of its own, and that spoke in the heavy guns of Labadieville.

"What is that, Confianza?" came hoarsely shouted from the turn-window.

"Son las tropas, Señor."

"Troops! men playing at soldiers, you mean."

"Oh, no, *hijo mio!* Dey de troops of the Nort and de Sout. Dey fight demselves togeder. *Ya* ees old *la guerra.*"

Then, with ears alert and eyes distended, she raised herself to listen—listening not to the guns, but to a cry that wailed through the silence—a cry harsh, sinister, discordant, horrible—a cry that was the roar of a wild beast hunted to death in the jungle.

"My God! my God! why cannot I find death among the fighters yonder?"

This was an episode—not the least ghastly among the episodes of that sorrowful time.

Years had passed since then. The leper seemed to have forgotten the day when he had heard from within *Le Tombeau Blanc* the guns of Labadieville. After all, it was time that he should do so. Already he thought of himself as a creature like Moore's "bloodless ghost," speculating bitterly on the day, sure to dawn, when, chained to his bed, he would come to sit by his

"…own pale corpse, watching it."

Bear in mind that it was through all these years from that night at Beaumanoir, through peaceful times, through quiet harvests, through gathering clouds, through deep thunderings, through lightning bursting from those clouds, through a great war, through a noble effort, through a mighty liberation, through a peace that was not a calm and a calm that became peace, that Fernand had changed from the figure of a perfect manhood to what he then was. On the whole, his dread disease had been merciful to him. The muscles, once firm as Samson's, had long since betrayed their strength into eating ulcers. But Gangrene—Death's grimmest lieutenant—still refrained from striking. It hovered with its scythe over the feet, filled with a growth of pustules. It threatened those hands once so strong, so soft, as instinct with music as with daring; but ten fingers still remained to be counted between them. His voice had become *rauque* and broken; but the hair, beard, and eye-brows, although prematurely white, had not yet dropped from their follicles. His features were enlarged, had turned to ghastly grotesqueness, but so far they had escaped the teredo-like borings of leprosy. With all this, he felt himself growing weaker day by day. He had ceased to use Dr. Tousage's medicines, left at intervals on his window. He could have no faith whatsoever in the physician who had none in himself, and who had told him frankly: "Palliatives, not remedies, Fernand, these are all I can promise you." But even these were now beyond his reach—the good old doctor had written his last prescription.

Little by little, Fernand yielded his consolations. A fine dust, settling around the strings of Duffeyte's Cremona, had clogged their melody. Of the wild-beast-like, circular paths around and about the *Tombeau,* no sign remained. The grass had grown thick over them, as well as over that which, night after night, had so long been his road in the old days, to the lowest rung of a ladder by which he had reached the summit of the great solemn wall, and where, condemned like Moses on Pisgah's height, he would direct yearning glances "westward and northward, and southward and eastward," toward the black waters of the bayou swirling by in the darkness, and the shadowy outlines of fertile fields, once his own, and of dark forests which had been his hunting-ground as boy and man.

* * *

There is now but one path in the *Tombeau Blanc.* It was the leper's first, as it will be his last path—the walk which leads from the cottage to the turn-window, which holds, each morning and afternoon, his food and drink.

There are two parts fairly mixed in our humanity when in extremity. One is animal; the other, spiritual. The two cannot live apart, so long as the body itself holds together. Fernand feels this keenly. He seeks his food, as a beast, maimed in the fierce wars of its kind, might crawl to seek it—by habit. But unlike the beast, his spirit, which stands for his pleasures, is confined to his cottage, or, in fair sunny weather, to his seat under the Father Oak. He can no longer find solace in his Cremona. He can no longer see to read. He can only—think, think, think! He totters, while he keeps back the groans, as he now makes the daily trips for food. He remembers how, years, years ago, he had firmly planted his feet on that well-beaten path, hopeless then, but self-poised. Now, he can only creep painfully along it, stopping at intervals to gasp, taking a half-hour where once the half-minute had sufficed. Then, he had clutched his food with the appetite which young manhood gives, even when it knows itself doomed to lingering disease. Now, he puts his hand up for it with loathing, and turns aside with a shudder when he draws it down.

That terrible path! This is what he now most fears. His hands are not of the strongest for the carrying of food, none of the safest for bearing a full pitcher. For over their swollen surface the skin has thickened and stretched tight and hard like a drum's head. His fingers are gradually turning within like a harpy's claws. He is far from sure of them. One day he doubts whether they will be able to take the food without dropping it. The next day he fears that they cannot carry drink without spilling it. The sorrowful truth is that he is growing afraid of himself. He trembles as he looks down at his pustuled feet, now always bare. At times he holds before his eyes in the sunlight his two yellow swollen hands with their curved fingers. Then, indeed, he breaks out into sudden despair; he bows his head upon those fingers, blotting out the tell-tale sun, while through them trickle the scalding scanty tears which lepers weep.

He knows that he is now far in the last stage of his disease; that the end of all this must be impotence. The certainty of his fate haunts him like a spectre. He has marked with a ? that unknown day, soon to come, when he shall be too weak to leave his room. One way or other, he feels that that day, when it does come, must break the self-will which has grown almost marble under the *Père Chêne.* The Church has taught him that suicide is a crime. Though in a tomb, whence he can neither see the blaze of altar-candles, nor hear the chimes in steeple-bells, he believes it from his soul to be one. He is utterly alone in these days. Even Nature, the tried ally of solitary man, has neglected, if it have not altogether forgotten him. For years, that wizard of the forest, the mocking-bird, has cheered him with its "lyric bursts" of unmatched melody. But, true to its own instincts, it has set up its throne in the thickets around Confianza's hut. Outside of, not within, the gloomy Avail is where the singer chooses to reign; and there it reigns, day and night, content if it only knows that the leper within gains from its wondrous notes a single hope. Fernand does not doubt his consoler, I think; or, if he does, his is only the faint shadow of a fainter doubt. Both were bred in the land of the orange and the sugar-cane. In the man's philosophy, born of his old nurse's lullabies, a certain sorcery attaches to this wondrous bird of wondrous song. As he listens in his agony to its joyous bursts, he so bound, it so free, he murmurs half unconsciously, in the wild words of an old Creole hymn of Nature, caught breathing from her by Pere Rouquette:

> "Ah, mokeur! Ah, mokeur shanteur!
> Ah, ah! to gagnin giab dan kor!
> To gagnin tro l'espri, mokeur.
> Mé, shanté: m'a kouté ankor!"[1]

Thus, in its own fashion, is the gray maestro faithful to him. But not so his old shy comrade, the whippoorwill, which has long since left the tree that, in its depths, it haunted, and the master whom, in its coyness, it had seemed to love. The *cyprière* has sent none other of its songsters; and even the little twittering birds, that dote on freedom and space and glitter and company, avoid the mournful Father Oak as though he were a plague. Or, perhaps, these tiny creatures have finer senses than man, and know of the plague that sits and ponders, a breathing corpse, under the grand old tree.

Here it is that Fernand passes hours in figuring over and over again what will come of the inevitable invasion. Confianza must, of course, be admitted. And Blanche? Oh, would that she could! But how foolish all this is, none knows so well as he. He would not let his darling in, no! not were she even to knock at the gate and ask that it be opened unto her. Nor can Blanche—but I had forgotten, there is no longer a Blanche.

There is a *Sceur Angelique* who once bore her name—a fair and sinless woman dedicated to God, of whom her black-robed sisters speak with love and pride. Nothing of all this passes into the *Tombeau Blanc.* Fernand has not forgotten Blanche, but he has no knowledge of *Sceur Angelique.* He is ever intent upon the old problems that vex his waning life. The great iron-bound door, so long closed, must soon turn upon its rusty hinges. Who will dare pass the gate? Who will, having once passed it, dare advance to confront the odor of the charnel-house which fills the square, and which seems to have blasted the green old age of *le Père Chêne* who

The world? No!

His old doctor? No!

His former slaves? No!

Delegates from Leper-Land? Yes!

Forgetfulness forbids the first; death, the second; superstition and "exodus," the third; brotherhood admits the last.

At this prospect, leper as he is, he shudders.

These fancies fill his dark hours. He keeps his failings fastened wearily upon his narrow domain. The grass is growing thick and green over all the paths which he once circled in his madness. It is with eager longing he awaits the day when it shall spring up as thick and green around and over his last walk.

"It took years to cover those," he murmurs hoarsely. "My God! how many weeks will it be before this last one is covered?"

December 25, 187-. A letter just received from my friend, the Mayor of Thibodaux, contains this simple announcement: "Death, the Consoler, has at last come to Fernand."

---

1   Ah, mocking-bird! Ah, mocking songster! / Ah, thou hast the devil in thy heart! / Thou hast too much wit, mocking-bird. / But sing on; I must listen—once more!

Eliza Poitevent Nicholson ("Pearl Rivers") (1843–1896)

Eliza Jane Poitevent Holbrook Nicholson grew up near the Pearl River in Mississippi, which explains her pen name, Pearl Rivers; her childhood, however, like her career, was anything but traditional. She was born on March 11, 1843,[1] to William J. and Mary Russ Poitevent. She had three brothers and three sisters, and most sources report that her mother was very sickly, so at the age of nine, she moved in with her aunt and uncle, Jane and Leonard Kimball, in nearby Hobolochitto, Mississippi (now Picayune), who raised her until she moved to New Orleans to pursue her career as a writer, much to her family's dismay.[2]

Nicholson began writing poetry while living with her foster parents in rural Mississippi, and her poetry often reflects that lush, bucolic setting of her childhood. After only six years of living with the Kimballs, they sent her off to boarding school at the Amite Female Seminary in nearby Amite County, Mississippi, a school with a typical curriculum for young women of the time, which Nicholson later described as "the ordinary useless education women get… without one solitary qualification for earning a living."[3] But she was not sent to the school in order to be armed with the necessary tools with which to make a living. On the contrary, according to Nicholson biographer James Henry Harrison, "a little was enough to equip a girl for a world filled with fashions and social affairs, housekeeping and children. To go deeply into education was to become that odd and unpopular creature, an 'intellectual' woman, hateful alike to men and true 'ladies' of the Southland."[4] Nicholson was sent to Amite Female Seminary in order to become a proper—and moreover, marriageable—young lady. While there, Nicholson did meet and fall for William Cole Harrison, but her foster parents did not approve of the young man and kept them apart. However, even after moving to New Orleans and marrying (twice) Nicholson remained life-long friends with Harrison.[5]

Nicholson graduated from the seminary in 1859, but she did not go to New Orleans until after the Civil War, in 1868, to visit her maternal grandfather, Samuel Potter Russ, and there she met his friend, the editor of the New Orleans *Picayune*, Alva Morris Holbrook, who was at that time still married to Jennie Bronson Holbrook. Eliza had already published some poems in the *Picayune*, and shortly after their meeting, Holbrook offered her the job as literary editor of the paper.[6] Naturally, her family was appalled that she would even consider moving to the city, which had much the same reputation as it does today, as a dangerous, politically corrupt, and sexually liberal urban center fueled by alcohol. To take a job there was unthinkable. Nevertheless, she began working for the paper in 1870; Holbrook divorced his wife in 1871, and he and Eliza were married in 1872, the same year he handed over control of the newspaper to the New Orleans Printing and Publishing Company for $100,000.[7]

Eliza's move to the city and marriage to a divorced man twenty-nine years her senior—older than her father—was scandalous enough for her family, but things would only get worse. Not long after their marriage, Holbrook's ex-wife, Jennie sued unsuccessfully for alimony, prompting her to enter the Holbrook home when Eliza was there alone and shoot at her twice, luckily missing both times. After wrestling the gun away from her, Jennie then grabbed a rum bottle and repeatedly beat Eliza over the head with it before she could escape to a neighbor's house. Naturally, this event caused quite a public stir. Jennie was jailed and subsequently left town, but

---

1   Like many writers in this collection, Nicholson lied about her age; her birth date is published in most sources as 1849.

2   For more on Nicholson, and from where much of this biographical information comes, see Lamar W. Bridges, "Eliza Jane Nicholson and the *Times-Picayune*," *Louisiana History: The Journal of the Louisiana Historical Association* 30, no. 3 (Summer, 1989), 263; and Kenneth W. Holditch, "Eliza Jane Poitevent, Pearl Rivers, and the Old Lady of Camp Street," *Louisiana Literature* IV, (1987), 27.

3   Bridges, 265.

4   James Henry Harrison, *Pearl Rivers, Publisher of the Picayune* (New Orleans: Tulane University Department of Journalism, 1932), 9.

5   Don Wicks, "Eliza Jane Poitevent Holbrook Nicholson (Pearl Rivers), Lecture for the Pearl River Historical Society Meeting, 21 May 2007, *David A. Farrell At-Large.com* (12 May 2009).

6   Harrison, 10.

7   Ibid., 12.

this is not the only calamity the Holbrooks faced soon after their marriage.

A year after their marriage and after selling the *Picayune*, the current owners were having difficulty surviving in the depression, so Holbrook once again took the reins of the newspaper. But before he could manage to turn the failing paper around, he died, in 1876. Eliza's family was hoping that his death would prompt her to sell the paper and return home, but she surprised almost everyone, and on March 26, 1876, the masthead of the *Picayune* read "Mrs. A.M. Holbrook, Proprietor."[1] In so doing, Eliza became the first female editor of a major newspaper in the country, and she worked to make it the most successful daily in the South.

Eliza worked closely with the paper's business manager, George Nicholson in turning the paper around, and very soon after his wife died, he and Eliza married. Eliza Nicholson first turned to her area of expertise and expanded the literary page and added several popular women writers, such as Catherine Cole and Dorothy Dix. She also added a society page and features that would appeal to women and younger readers, but that's not to say that she did not address the more serious issues of her time, like Reconstruction politics, corruption on both the local and national levels, prison reform, public education, and animal abuse.

Readers should not allow Nicholson's success as the first female editor of the newspaper whose masthead boasted the "Largest Circulation in the Southwest,"[2] to eclipse her ability as the poet, Pearl Rivers. In 1873, Lippincott published her first collection of poetry, *Lyrics,* and another collection remained unfinished upon her death. The first poem included here, "The Royal Funeral, (The Body of the Queen Lying in State)" shares much in common with Emily Dickinson's "Because I could not stop for Death—" in that both poets examine mortality as it manifests itself in the natural world around them. In Pearl Rivers' poem, "Spring, the Virgin Queen, is dead," the narrator bemoans the onset of autumn and winter, but like in Dickinson's poem, these seasons are cyclical, a natural passage of time.

"Hagar," was published twenty years later in *Cosmopolitan,* and Pearl Rivers' improved skill as a poet is obvious. "Hagar" is a dramatic monologue, capturing the conversation between the biblical Hagar, who bore a son, Ishmael, with Abraham, upon his wife Sarah's insistence. The poem is remarkable in a biographical sense also, as Pearl Rivers was accused of being the mistress of both of her husbands before she married them. Perhaps not surprisingly, the mistress, Hagar, comes off as the more admirable character in the poem.

George Nicholson already had four grown children when he and Eliza married, and together they went on to have two sons, Leonard and York, whom his daughter Anna raised upon the death of their parents. In February of 1896, George came down with the flu and was dead within a week. Eliza, constantly by his side, also contracted the flu; however, hers progressed to pneumonia, and she died less than two weeks after her husband. The *Picayune* later merged with the competition, the *Times-Democrat,* becoming the *Times-Picayune,* the city's daily paper until just recently, when the current owners, Newhouse Publishing, decided that it would be more cost effective to publish only three days a week on paper and focus on its online presence, an ignominious fate for the paper that once boasted the "Largest Circulation in the Southwest."

The Royal Funeral[3]

The Body of the Queen Lying in State

There is mourning through the valleys,
    There is mourning on the hills,
And I hear a broken music
    In the voice of all the rills.

---

1   Bridges, 266.

2   Patricia Brady, "Eliza Jane Nicholson (1843-1896) New Orleans Publisher," *Louisiana Women, Their Lives and Times* (Athens: University of Georgia Press, 2009), 107.

3   First published in Ida Raymond, ed. *Southland Writers: Biographical and Critical Sketches of the Living Female Writers of the South, with Extracts from their Writings* (Philadelphia: Claxton, Remsen & Heffelfinger, 1870), 640-3.

Spring, the fairest of the seasons,
 Spring, the Virgin Queen, is dead;
And a young voluptuous sister
 Reigns upon her throne instead.

Royal June, with rosy fingers,
 Softly closed her violet eyes,
And within the Court of Nature
 Now in regal state she lies.

Brave old March, her veteran soldier,
 Covered with a tattered fold
Of the banner borne so proudly,
 Lies beside her, dead and cold.

Fair capricious Lady April
 Sleepeth deep and calmly nigh;
Round her mouth a smile still lingers,
 Still a tear-drop in her eye.

On a bier of withered roses
 Lies the tender Lady May,
And her constant loves, the Poets,
 Royal honors to her pay.

Low and reverently kneeling
 Round her lovely form they throng,
And embalm her precious beauty
 With the costly myrrh of song.

Unto each she left a token,
 As a dying pledge of love:
One she gave her azure girdle;
 One she gave her rosy glove;

One she gave her silver sandals,
 Bright with shining gems of dew;
O'er the shoulders of another
 She her holy mantle threw.

But to me, the humble singer,
 Leaning on my harp apart,
From the royal high-coiced Poets,
 She has left a broken heart.

Through the reign of glowing Summer
    Lies the royal dead in state;
High-voiced Poets, humble singer,
    Mournfully keep watch and wait;

Wait! the sober days are coming,
    Sad pall-bearers of the dead;
In the distant Autumn Country
    Hear their slow and solemn tread!

The Procession

With the incense of her glory
    Burning low and sweet and dim,
And the harps of all her minstrels
    Tuned to chant a funeral hymn;

In a robe of fragrance shrouded
    By the spirits of the Flowers,
In a sable hearse of Sorrow,
    Drawn by weary-footed Hours;

From the silent Court of Nature
    Comes the fair dead Queen in state,
O'er the road of Gloomy Weather,
    Leading down to Winter Gate.

And her royal guard of Sunbeams
    Faint and falter through the day,
And at night her Glow-worm footmen
    Drop their lanterns by the way.

And the young Lord Zephyr, sighing,
    Yields his life upon her bier,
While the diamonds of Sir Dew-drop
    Melt away into a tear.

All the trees cast down their garments
    In the way where she will pass,
As the sad procession windeth
    Through the ruined State of Grass

Through the Autumn Country slowly
    Winds the royal funeral now,

And with rue and heavy cypress
 Wreathed upon my thoughtful brow,

By the roadside I stand waiting
 For the Queen, and in the dell
I can hear the solemn pealing
 Of a dreary funeral knell.

She is coming, nearer! Nearer!
 Hark that solemn mournful strain!
Fly to honor her, young minstrel,
 Joining in the funeral train.

The Burial

There is mourning through the valleys,
 There is wailing on the hills,
And I hear a broken music
 In the voice of all the rills.

Nature's heart is sorely troubled,
 And her grief is fierce and wild,
As she chants the funeral service
 O'er her best-beloved child.

Through the dreamy realms of Winter
 Phantom Queens have led the way
To the Land of Gloom and Shadow,
 To the Kingdom of Decay.

From the bier the strong youth North-Wind
 Quickly lifts the Virgin Queen,
While the soft wings of the South-Wind
 Drooping o'er her form are seen.

O'er the bride of his Idea,
 Young King Winter bendeth low,
And around her tender body
 Wraps a winding-sheet of snow.

And his busy silent workmen,
 Frost and Ice, have wrought with care
For the Queen a crystal coffin,
 Covered with devices rare.

Now old Time, the haggard Sexton,
    Opes the deep tomb of the Past;
And my broken heart and lyre
    On the buried Queen I cast.

Hagar[1]

Go back! How dare you follow me beyond
The door of my poor tent? Are you afraid
That I have stolen something? See! my hands
Are empty, like my head. I am no thief!
The bracelets and the golden finger rings
And silver anklets that you gave to me,
I cast upon the mat before my door,
And trod upon them. I would scorn to take
One trinket with me in my banishment
That would recall a look or tone of yours,
My lord, my generous lord, who send me forth,
A loving woman, with a loaf of bread
And jug of water on my shoulder laid,
To thirst and hunger in the wilderness!
                      Go back!

Go back to Sara! See, she stands
Watching us there, behind the flowering date,
With jealous eyes, lest my poor hands should steal
One farewell touch from yours. Go back to her,
And say that Hagar has a heart as proud,
If not so cold, as hers: and, though it break,
It breaks without the sound of sobs, without
The balm of tears to ease its pain. It breaks,
It breaks, my lord, like iron—hard, but clean—
And breaking asks no pity. If my lips
Should let one plea for mercy slip between
These words that lash you with a woman's scorn,
My teeth should bite them off, and I would spit
Them at you, laughing, though all red and warm with blood.
        "Cease!" do you say? No, by the gods
Of Egypt, I do swear that if my eyes should let one tear melt through their burning lids,
My hands should pluck them out; and if these hands,
Groping outstretched in blindness, should by chance
Touch yours, and cling to them against my will,
My Ishmael should cut them off, and blind

---

1   Originally appeared in *Cosmopolitan*, 1893. Collected in Edwin Alderman, et. al., eds. *Library of Southern Literature*, Vol. IX. (New Orleans and Atlanta: Martyn and Hoyt, 1907), 3770-9.

And maimed, my little son should lead me forth
Into the wilderness to die. Go back!
Does Sara love you as I did, my lord?
Does Sara clasp and kiss your feet, and bend
Her haughty head in worship at your knee?
Ah, Abraham, you were a god to me!
If you but touched my hand my foolish heart
Ran down into the palm, and throbbed and thrilled,
Grew hot and cold, and trembled there: and when
You spoke, though not to me, my heart ran out
To listen through my eager ears and catch
The music of your voice and prison it
In memory's murmuring shell. I saw no fault
Nor blemish in you, and your flesh to me
Was dearer than my own. There is no vein
That branches from your heart, whose azure course
I have not followed with my kissing lips.
I would have bared my bosom like a shield
To any lance of pain that sought your breast.
And once, when you lay ill within your tent,
No taste of water or of bread or wine
Passed through my lips; and all night long I lay
Upon the mat before your door to catch
The sound of your dear voice, and scarcely dared
To breathe, lest she, my mistress, should come forth
And drive me angrily away; and when
The stars looked down with eyes that only stared
And hurt me with their lack of sympathy,
Weeping, I threw my longing arms around
Benammi's neck. Your good horse understood
And gently rubbed his face against my head,
To comfort me. But if you had one kind,
One loving thought of me in all that time,
That long, heart-breaking time, you kept it shut
Close in your bosom as a tender bud,
And did not let it blossom into words.
Your tenderness was all for Sara. Through
The door, kept shut against my love, there came
No message to poor Hagar, almost crazed
With grief lest you should die. Ah! you have been
So cruel and so cold to me, my lord;
And now you send me forth with Ishmael,
Not on a journey through a pleasant land
Upon a camel as my mistress rides,
With kisses, and sweet words, and dates and wine,

But cast me off, and sternly send me forth
Into the wilderness with these poor gifts—
A jug of water and—a loaf of bread.
That sound was not a sob; I only lost
My breath and caught it hard again. Go back!
Why do you follow? I am a poor
Bondswoman, but a woman still, and these
Sad memories, so bitter and so sweet,
Weigh heavily upon my breaking heart
And make it hard, my lord, for me to go.
"Your God commands it?" Then my gods, the gods
Of Egypt, are more merciful than yours.
Isis and good Osiris never gave
Command like this, that breaks a woman's heart,
To any prince in Egypt. Come with me,
And let us go and worship them, dear lord.

Leave all your wealth to Sara. Sara loves
The touch of costly linen and the scent
Of precious Chaldean spices, and to bind
Her brow with golden fillets, and perfume
Her hair with ointment. Sara loves the sound
Of many cattle lowing on the hills;
And Sara loves the slow and stealthy tread
Of many camels moving on the plains.
Hagar loves you. Oh, come with me, dear lord!
Take but your staff and come with me! Your mouth
Shall drink my share of water from this jug
And eat my share of bread with Ishmael;
And from your lips I will refresh myself
With love's sweet wine from tender kisses pressed.
Ah, come, dear lord! Oh, come, my Abraham!
Nay, do not bend your cold, stern brows on me
So frowningly; it was not Hagar's voice
That spoke those pleading words.

                                                 Go back! Go back!

And tell your God I have him, and I hate
The cruel, craven heart that worships him
And dares not disobey. Ha! I believe
'Tis not your far-off, bloodless God you fear,
But Sara. Coward! Cease to follow me!
Go back to Sara. See! she beckons now.
Hagar loves not a coward; you do well
To send me forth into the wilderness,
Where hatred hath no weapon keen enough

That held within a woman's slender hand
Could stab a coward to the heart.

                                                  I go!

I go, my lord; proud that I take with me,
Of all your countless herds by Hebron's brook,
Of all your Canaan riches, naught but this—
A jug of water and a loaf of bread.
And now, by all of Egypt's gods, I swear,
If it were not for Ishmael's dear sake,
My feet would tread upon this bitter bread,
My hands would pour this water on the sands,
And leave this jug as empty as my heart
Is empty now of all the reverence
And overflowing love it held for you

                                                  I go!

But I will teach my little Ishmael
To hate his father for his mother's sake.
His bow shall be the truest bow that flies
Its arrows through the desert air; his feet
The fleetest on the desert's burning sands.
Ay! Hagar's son a desert prince shall be,
Whose hand shall be against all other men;
And he shall rule a fierce and mighty tribe,
Whose fiery hearts and supple limbs will scorn
The chafing curb of bondage, like the fleet
Wild horses of Arabia.

                                                  I go!

But like this loaf that you have given me,
So shall your bread taste bitter with my hate;
And like the water in this jug, my lord,
So shall the sweetest water that you draw
From Canaan's wells taste salty with my tears,
Farewell! I go, but Egypt's mighty gods
Will go with me, and my avengers be.
And in whatever distant land your God,
Your cruel God of Israel, is known,
There, too, the wrongs that you have done this day
To Hagar and your first-born, Ishmael,
Shall waken and uncoil themselves, and hiss
Like adders at the name of Abraham.

Sallie Rhett Roman (1844-1921)

A relatively unknown but nonetheless vital addition to the canon of post-bellum Louisiana writers is Sallie Rhett Roman,[1] a turn-of-the-century writer for the New Orleans *Times-Democrat*. Roman was born Sarah Taylor Rhett in 1844, to Elizabeth Burnet and Robert Barnwell Rhett, a firebrand secessionist from Charleston, South Carolina. In 1863, Sallie married Judge Alfred Roman, son of Creole governor of Louisiana, Andre Bienvenu Roman, of Vacherie, Louisiana. Although the couple's marriage seemed by all accounts to be a happy one, their fathers may have arranged it to some degree, as they were political acquaintances at the very least.

After the Civil War, as the political climate of New Orleans shifted, Alfred Roman lost his appointed judgeship, and much of the family sugar plantation, upriver in Vacherie, had been claimed by the Mississippi River and lacked the free workers that slavery provided. Consequently, Sallie entered the workforce in 1889 to help provide for her large family of eleven children, many of whom later entered the workforce as well.

In her writing, Sallie Roman addresses many of the same issues as her Louisiana contemporaries Alice Dunbar Nelson, Grace King, Kate Chopin, and Ruth McEnery Stuart. Bloodlines and ancestry, women's roles, artistic outlets for women, social conventions, marriage, women's independence, and Christianity and spirituality all play important roles in Roman's work. Unlike her more liberal, and by today's standards, enlightened contemporaries, however, Roman also championed such causes as white supremacy, male superiority, and the southern aristocracy.

By the mid-1870s, Roman's husband Alfred finally returned to practicing law. It is probably because of her husband's profession that Roman includes so many heroic lawyers in her fiction. In two of her works, "Bastien: A X-mas in the Great Salt Marshes of Louisiana," included in this anthology, and "Follette of Timbalier Island" the ingenious lawyers work to crack the cases of injustice and literally save the day. She could also be using these exemplary lawyers to pay homage to other lawyers in her family which include her father, brother, and father-in-law.

"Bastien: A X-mas in the Great Salt Marshes of Louisiana" is the only one of Roman's short stories to be published nationally in the popular sporting magazine, *Outing*.[2] "Bastien" embodies many of the themes that Roman addressed in her editorials and earlier fiction, including imminent justice, aristocratic ennui, and Louisiana's natural bounty. She also draws on her life experiences as the conservative wife of a New Orleans lawyer and a rural plantation mistress for much of the plot. "Bastien," like most of Roman's fiction, revolves around members of Louisiana high society and their interaction with the rugged fishing community of the Louisiana Gulf Coast.

Roman's father and husband preceded her in death, and neither of them left her financially secure. So, somewhat ironically, she spent her last years struggling financially and not as one of the wealthy aristocrats of her fiction. She submitted fiction to the *Times-Democrat* until 1910, three years after moving from New Orleans with her sons, Charles and Alfred to Asheville, North Carolina, where she remained for three years. In 1914, she moved to Columbia, South Carolina, where she died in 1921. She continued to write articles that were never published, many of which resemble her early political editorials, including such titles as "The Menace of the Boll Weevil" and "Commercial Importance of Improved Municipal Works." For the last two years of her life, she fought the United States government for her son Rhett's military pension, which she finally did receive. Roman espoused a certain degree of independence among women in her fiction, yet even after supporting herself and her family with her writing, she still tried to depend, usually unsuccessfully, on the men in her family for financial support. She is not the only Louisiana writer whose life and work often seem to contradict one another.

Including Roman in the canon of postbellum Louisiana writers allows us to gain more insight to the lives of women writers and their readers in turn-of-the-century New Orleans and the issues that concerned them. And although Roman has not received the acclaim that her perhaps more deserving peers have, she nonetheless had

---

1   For more on Sallie Rhett Roman and the source of most of the biographical information in this article, see Nancy Dixon, *Fortune and Misery: Sallie Rhett Roman of New Orleans* (Baton Rouge: LSUP, 1999).

2   *Outing*, XXXIII (January, 1899), 375-82.

great appeal and was read by a wider audience than they for over twenty years. We might not agree with Roman's views on such issues as race, classism, women's suffrage, marriage, and male superiority, but her longevity with the newspaper indicates that many of her readers did.

Bastien: A X-mas in the Great Salt Marshes of Louisiana

"Say, Leveque, where are you going to spend Christmas?" I asked, as we sat smoking together at the club one cold, bleak afternoon.

"Dunno," said Dick, with lazy discontent. "Hate all this jollification business, these Christmas and New Year celebrations. Having no family fireside, I feel rather out of it."

"I'll tell you what we'll do, then," I said, having ruminated and evolved an idea. Like Leveque, I was rather out of it this year, my folks being abroad. "We'll go bird shooting, you and I, out at Barataria. You don't mind roughing it, I suppose? I rather like that sort of thing myself, once in a while. It acts like a bracer, after too much office work, civilization, truffles and Cliquot."

"Good," said Leveque, straightening up with an air of some little interest. "I'm a right good shot at snipe and quail. One of the jolliest summers I ever spent was camping out in northwest Canada."

"The deuce! Then you know how to paddle a pirogue?" I asked. "Do I? Like a Nez Perce man," answered Leveque, with increasing liveliness. "How do you get to Barataria? I thought Barataria was a bay, and one would have to take a fishing smack or schooner to get there."

"No," I explained; "we'll cross at the Jackson street ferry, get boats from the fisher folks on the other side of the river, and paddle our way down the old Company's Canal. It will take about six hours' hard, steady work, but we will finally get at the best hunting ground imaginable for duck and snipe."

"All right," said Leveque, with animation; "when will we start?"

"To-morrow afternoon at four sharp. I'll call for you here," I answered.

And so I did. The evening was cold and bright, and everything seemed propitious for a few days of glorious sport.

I had warned Leveque not to bring his man or any extensive trappings along, but just a few provisions, as I was doing--cigars and a brandy flask--and trust to old Bastien, the trapper, to whose house I was taking him, to feast us on whatever game we would bring back at nightfall.

Dick had declared himself charmed, so we started off that December afternoon in high spirits, blue flannel shirts, rough clothes and water-proof boots, glad to be rid temporarily of the city, its clanging electric bells and boisterous Christmas pleasures.

We selected two good canoes; had them scientifically packed with a few necessaries. Our guns lay packed in leather cases and we had ammunition enough to last for a month's sport out in the great prairies and forests of southern Louisiana.

Leveque and I were in for a good time as we shot off down the canal. We sped along past Grandes Coquilles, those curious shell mounds near the old deserted Zeringue sugar plantation; then by Deadman's Point, so named because of a murder some years ago; past Cabanage Francais and through a gloomy swamp, with tall cypress and magnolia trees, swaying moss and hooting owls, until finally we reached the borders of the great salt marshes.

The canal before us cut straight like a knife through the heart of the vast, undulating prairie, gradually dwindling into a thin, black thread between the tall rushes, which grow on either side in one thick, continuous stretch of shaded greens and browns.

On that December afternoon the browns predominated, although the setting sun cast a glow here and a fleck of color there, as it sank behind a mass of flaming clouds.

Sweeping across this unbroken expanse, unbroken except for a small clump of trees in the far distance and the crumbling parapets of old Fort Henry, lying near the borders of the lake, a light wind ruffled the dark water as our pirogues sped along under the even strokes of our long-handled paddles.

A faint mist was rolling up from the horizon, for the short winter afternoon was drawing rapidly to a close, but a distinct paling in the sky suggested that the moon would soon throw her cold, uncertain smile over the tall swaying reeds and the immensity of the solitudes around.

There was something wonderfully restful, I thought, in the silence which enveloped us as we moved steadily forward, with an occasional remark, a jest, or a snatch of song from Dick, who had a good baritone voice and some knowledge of music, while the sough of the wind made a monotonous accompaniment to his singing.

The shrill call of a startled blackbird, plover or sandpiper, as it flew upward in alarm at sounds so unusual, was the only interruption to the still, brooding quiet of the night.

"Say, Barton, where do you suppose this canal leads to? My belief is it runs straight out into the Pacific Ocean. See any likelihood of our getting to the end of it before next year, or to our getting to any stopping place before daybreak to-morrow morning?" queried Dick, finally, suspending his paddle in mid-air, and mopping his face cautiously and with a due regard to the equilibrium of his unreliable canoe.

The night was clear, frosty and cold, but sixteen miles of continuous paddling is good exercise, and is apt to get a man into a comfortable glow.

"Oh, yes," I said reassuringly, letting my canoe drift also. "Look ahead down yonder at that clump of trees. There's a house among them where an old trapper and hunter lives. We'll halt there, and get supper and a good bed."

"Great Scott, man!" said Dick aghast. "Why, that's about thirty miles away! It's in the very center of the prairie. We won't reach those trees for hours."

"By eleven o'clock," I answered. "I've come out here time and again and know all about it."

We resumed our work, and Leveque began to whistle a Mexican march, in tune to the regular dip and gurgle of our paddles.

"Some other fellow is out for duck and snipe shooting besides ourselves," remarked Dick, between the snatches of his tune.

"How do you know that?" I asked in surprise.

"Because while we were resting just now, I heard the faint beat of his paddle behind us," said Dick.

Yes, now that my attention was aroused, I seemed to hear something of the kind, by straining to catch and distinguish the few noises perceptible in the silence of the star-lit night.

"There he comes, just as I said," remarked Dick, looking cautiously backward.

Gliding forward and gradually gaining on us, came a long, slender canoe. It was occupied by a man wearing a felt hat pushed down low over his face, a man young and muscular, apparently, for he outstripped us in the vigor of his strokes, and yet we were skilled paddlers and pretty good athletes.

"Looks as if he was trying to win a race, or, perhaps, somebody is after him," remarked Dick, lighting a cigar, when the slender pirogue had caught up and slid past us, while the man bent determinedly at his work.

For some little time we could discern his boat like a moving shadow glide between the salt rushes; then it vanished suddenly, turning, we supposed, into some one of the winding branches which intersect the great prairies in all directions, making of them a splendid hunting ground for game of various kinds.

"Entrez, messieurs, entrez," said Bastien, with hearty hospitality, holding aloft his lantern so that its light could guide us up the rough wooden steps of his queer house, when we finally got there, some hours later.

It shone full on Bastien, so that Dick, who had never seen him, said to me in a surprised undertone, as we entered a small room in which a fire still smoldered on the hearth:

"Why, what a splendid-looking old fellow! Must have been a soldier."

And certainly old Bastien the trapper, with his close-cut gray hair, searching brown eyes (which would blaze with anger or shine with a pleasant mirth, as the occasion arose), broad forehead and firm-set mouth, the grand build of his massive frame and air of strength, in spite of accumulating years, was a most striking-looking individual.

The thought always occurred to me when I was with Bastien that it must be the solitary freedom of those boundless windswept prairies which gave him his large-hearted nature. Perhaps the blue vault of heaven seemed so close and unmarred by man's small obstructions, that pure and honest thoughts and words grew to be natural to one living out here. For who could detract and slander and falsify, burn with envy, scramble and contend for gold under these great, tranquil skies, before the voiceless majesty of these silent regions?

"La chasse est bonne en ce moment," Bastien continued cheerily, as he lit a lamp, stirred the dying embers of the fire, and put on a kettle to boil, with the quick dexterity of a long habit of housewifery, while a genial smile temporarily effaced some deep lines of care and sorrow which seamed his face.

To bring out lemons, glasses, gin and sugar, then swing up a hammock on two hooks screwed into the woodwork of the room, throw clean blankets on the bed from which our hasty call had evidently just aroused him, was the work of but a few minutes for Bastien.

Nor would he listen to my suggestion that I sleep in his big cane-bottom rocker in front of the fire until daybreak.

"You will take my bed, que diable," he said with kindly decision, "and I will sleep in the grenier. It will not be the first, neither the last time, that Bastien will bivouac in his blanket. I will call you at daybreak, messieurs, when I go to set my traps."

I selected the hammock and Dick took the bed, and, thanks to our trip down Harvey's Canal, we were soon fast asleep.

Truly, Bastien's rude cabin was a cozy enough nest.

Guns and arms of various descriptions hung over the broad mantel, a number of beautiful skins of the spotted panther, badger, wildcat and wolverine were tacked against the walls like tapestry, while deerskins made pretty rugs over the bare floor, and a tall old-fashioned bahut of oak gave quite an air to the small room.

I don't know what aroused me some hours later--the low growl of Bastien's big setter, I suppose--but I suddenly awoke, and, looking up, my gaze went through the unshuttered window, before which my hammock was swung, straight out into the night.

The moon shone bright and clear, and the oak trees, which grew tall and luxuriant on this small oasis in the prairie, were clustered at the back of Bastien's cabin, leaving an unobstructed view of vast marshes stretching out down to the horizon.

Was it imagination, or did I hear a guarded step outside?

"Couche toi, Fauvette! Couche toi, bonne bete!" I heard a man's voice whisper softly and persuasively to the Irish setter on the porch, who, from a growl of distrust, now lapsed into a joyous whine, which the owner of the voice seemed to try to soothe and moderate.

Some friend of old Bastien, I thought, who does not wish to disturb him at this late hour of the night.

Just then a face peered in through the window panes. It was surmounted by a felt hat pulled down low over the eyes.

The man in the pirogue, I mentally ejaculated. He must have cut through some winding creek to get here, instead of coming straight down the canal.

By this time the moon was shining with such brilliancy and intensity that I could distinguish his features, as if in broad daylight.

Good heavens! Why, he was the living image of old Bastien, only younger. His hair was brown instead of white, and he had none of those deep furrows which gave a look of suppressed sorrow to Bastien's noble face.

For no one in all the country-side was so much loved and looked up to as Bastien, the old Acadian trapper--a big-hearted, generous, splendid old fellow, always ready to help misfortune, who would walk twenty miles to get a toy for a sick child, or give his last cent to relieve the want of another.

Who so honest and fearless and so true--qualities which always seem to go together--as Bastien? Never had he turned his back on a comrade or friend in all his life, or failed when called on in the hour of need, in any and every conjuncture, however perilous.

His son, I had been told, a wild, joyous, erratic, handsome young fellow, had disappeared some time ago.

It was the anxiety caused by his turbulent career, and final disappearance, which had traced those sad lines on his father's face.

For Bastien's whole heart and soul were wrapped up in Paul; and when the boy's hunting companion was found dead, with a bullet through his heart, the day after they had started out together across the prairies on a hunting expedition, and Paul had never come home, there were reasons why the presumption of foul play should find some credence.

But old Bastien said he knew his boy too well to doubt him. He said that young Duval's death had surely been accidental, and that his son would one day come and vindicate himself.

There had been a warrant out for Paul's arrest, but, although it was believed the lad was in hiding with the fishermen down on Barataria Bay, he had never been traced.

It crossed my mind like a flash that the peering figure whose voice the startled dog so soon recognized must be Paul, and that it was he who had passed us on the canal. If so, his evident intention was to see his father, for what purpose I could only surmise.

Slipping cautiously and silently out, I motioned for silence with my finger.

Paul, for it was he, whispered some assurance to the dog and led the way into the thick black shadows which veiled the back of the house.

He told me the story of his flight, his life among the fishermen, and that he was here to-night to say good-bye to Bastien, before the officers who were on his track would come up with him, he said.

"Not a single witness, you say? You believe that Duval must have tripped and fallen, his gun going off and shooting him? You had had a quarrel down at the station, and had parted in anger, as the men there knew?" I queried, reflectively. "You only heard of it yourself through a fisherman the next day? Where were you all that night?"

The silence around remained deep and unbroken. The melancholy sighing of the wind in the marshes, and Fauvette the setter's deep breathing, as she slept with her head resting confidingly on Paul's knee, were the only sounds perceptible.

There was a glisten in Paul's brown eyes, but his mouth was firm-set like his father's, in spite of his troubled look.

A light broke on me.

"She is a very pretty child; I remember her well," I said, slowly lighting a cigar with silent caution. For I had more than once in former years stopped at her father's small fisher hut. He was a blind old fisherman, living on the borders of Lake Katawache, twenty miles away, and I remembered how Nanette's photograph was hung up in Paul's room. I had heard they were soon to be married.

Paul gave a great start at my words, then turned squarely facing me, putting his hand gently but firmly on my knee.

It required a very superficial knowledge of life to have reached the deduction I had drawn, or to further conclude that Nanette was wrapped up in the fine-looking, attractive lad before me.

"Does she know?" I queried.

"She believes it is true," said Paul, slowly and resolutely.

"How's that?" I asked, taken aback.

"It had to be," said Paul steadily, "else she would have come forward to try to help. She sees few people beyond the fisher folks down at the lake, and she knows not much, my poor little Nanette. So I had to deceive her, you understand, monsieur."

Does Dame Nature, I thought, in her strange caprice, preach chivalry with the silent breezes of these solitudes? And from the blue, unclouded vault of heaven does she pour down tender, heroic devotion into the hearts of her lonely settlers--sentiments which are befogged by the thick smoke of our crowded cities and the restless turmoil of their inhabitants in the ceaseless grind and pursuit after wealth, which absorbs thought, heart, and energy?

"Poor old Pere!" said Paul, with a half sob. "Would that I could let him know that his son is not red-handed! But, monsieur," he added solemnly, "I have trusted to you honor. No one must know, on account of little Nanette, who is motherless."

I felt certain that, had I the opportunity, I could unravel the mystery; but to obtain this it was clear Paul must not be captured. It was better to avoid a long and expensive defense and the pain of ignominy of imprisonment, at least until I had investigated the evidence at Lake Katawache. If, after that, I was satisfied Paul was guilty, why, of course, he must take his chance, and in all probability he would be ultimately captured. At present I did not intend he should be if I could compass his escape.

I thought I could, and, with the aid of Leveque, the details were soon arranged. Bastien was to be kept in ignorance, and Leveque and I would start out for one day's sport. When in a place of perfect seclusion Paul could join us, don my clothes and paddle away with Leveque as his companion in the day's sport; meanwhile I would return and entertain the officers who would, in all probability, so Paul thought, arrive ere midday.

At daybreak, Bastien softly prepared some inimitable black coffee and broiled bacon and eggs; then called us for our day's sport, in blissful ignorance of our interview with his son or our project.

"Down the winding creek toward the lake," he said, while getting ready his own pirogue and tackle, "you will find wild duck thick and plentiful, teal and mallard, and, deeper in the prairie, snipe and woodcock abound. But stay not late; the day is cold and raw. Au revoir, messieurs!"

The change was soon effected. Leveque and Paul disappeared, leaving me to shoot, but the story and the excitement had spoiled my zest for sport. Besides, the solitude of those lagoons and lonely marshes was not cheering. I was glad to paddle back to Bastien's cozy cottage toward noon.

"Tiens! your friend has left you?" said Bastien in surprise, when he joined me.

"Yes," I said nonchalantly; "had to go back on some pressing business he had forgotten. I went half-way back down the canal with him to keep him company, then turned off after duck, as you see. Aren't they beauties?" I tossed some half-dozen teal and other birds on the porch, from the bottom of my canoe.

"Hello! Who comes here?" queried Bastien, leaving his inspection of my game to look curiously down the canal at a four-oared boat which was approaching.

A dark frown settled on his handsome face, and an ominous fire burned in his great brown eyes as the glint of the sun shone on some police uniforms.

The boat swung up to the steps, the oars were shipped, and three officers sprang out.

Bastien never moved.

Neither did I, except to light a cigar, the first I had smoked since morning, for a man cannot paddle a pirogue, shoot duck and smoke, all at the same time.

"I'm sorry, Bastien," said the corporal, "but I must arrest him, you know. Better tell the boy to come along with us quietly. We know he's here."

"My son has never been here," said old Bastien, proudly. "If he had, you may be sure I would have gone with him to the first magistrate, and spared you the trouble of coming after him, corporal. My boy is innocent. Paul n'a jamais ete un assassin."

"All right. Men, search the premises," said the officer gruffly, shrugging his shoulders.

Then turning to me:

"Have you and your friends been here long?" he asked.

"I hardly see how that can interest you," I said. "But I've no objection to answering your question. We came yesterday." Then I gathered up the game, and moved off toward the kitchen, the officer following me. "Your friends went back to the city to-day?" he said.

"Yes," I answered; "you must have passed them in the canal. Two gentlemen in a skiff, one in a blue hunting suit, the other in gray."

Alas, my extra suit, which I would fain have exchanged for the present moist and muddy apparel I was wearing.

Nor could that astute official guess that Paul's worn and shabby clothes lay wrapped around a brick in twenty feet of water at the foot of Bastien's wooden steps.

Ten minutes was ample time to search the few buildings on Bastien's small inland island.

"Rather a nuisance to take this long row for nothing," I suggested, as the men grouped around the porch and got back discomfited into their boat.

"I envy you not, messieurs," said old Bastien, with stern contempt, leaning against his door-post, with folded arms. "Yours is a sad metier--to hunt men. When you track and hound down a criminal, it is cruel work. But to try to snare and entrap an innocent lad--bah!"

And he turned scornfully on his heel and went indoors.

As the boat shot off, "Good afternoon," I called politely. "You have a long row of it down Harvey's Canal. Pretty tiresome, isn't it?"

"Bastien," I said, as we sat at supper before a steaming roasted mallard, baked trout, potatoes, and one of the bottles Leveque's man had put in his pirogue, "take me down early to-morrow to the fishing settlement on Lake Katawache. I'd like to visit it for special reasons."

"Certes," said Bastien, "avec plaisir."

I was glad to get him away from his cabin to soothe some of his silent, gnawing grief, which gave so pathetic a gloom to this strong, fine face, albeit no complaint issued from his lips.

"You will see there little Nanette, a pretty child who was ever fond of Paul, mon fils," he said, as we approached the few scattering houses which formed the settlement on the lake shore. "She was to be his wife," he added with a stifled sigh.

Joyous and pathetic was Nanette's cry when she saw old Bastien. Then she fell to sore weeping, plying Bastien with hurried questions as to Paul.

"Where was he? Why came he never any more?" But twice had she seen Paul in the past. Once he was gay and joyous, and had given her the pretty ring she wore.

Then, when he came a few days later, he was in deep grief, and said he was accused of killing his friend Duval, and would never see her, Nanette, again.

But Nanette would not believe he had done so evil a thing, and would wait for him ever and ever, to be his wife some day when he would come back.

Nanette had prayed to the Virgin, and knew she would in her goodness help Paul.

"Can you recall the evening when he was so gay and joyous?" I asked.

"Truly," said Nanette, for never since then had her heart been light.

It was on the evening of May the 31st, the chapel being just completed and Monsieur le Cure had service there for the first time. Every one had brought flowers for the Virgin's altar, and it was Paul who had swung the bell for vespers. Then they had had a dance on the beach by the water, and Paul had helped the fishermen with their boats and tackle, and long before daybreak they all had set sail for the Chandeleur Islands.

They told her that Paul had jumped in his pirogue when the fishermen left, and had gone home at daybreak.

"The 31st of May, you say?" I asked slowly.

"Yes," she said with decision, but with a puzzled look, unconscious of the import of the testimony she was giving. "It was the 31st of May, for we crowned the Virgin that evening, and Paul rang the bell, as Monsieur le Cure will tell you."

Old Bastien took Nanette in his arms, and blessed her over and over again, showering words of loving affection on her pretty head.

"Said I not, monsieur, my boy is innocent of the black deed? Paul a murderer! Know I not the lad's heart?"

"A noble boy, Bastien," I said, "and wholly innocent, as we will easily prove, by the testimony of his little fiancee and that of Monsieur le Cure, and the fishermen who went out to the Barataria Bay and the Chandeleur Islands at daybreak on the 31st of May."

"Then," said Bastien, taking my hands in both of his, which trembled with emotion, "you knew, monsieur, but you could not speak—and you came here—"

"Yes," I nodded, "to make his little sweetheart save him. You will shortly have Paul back with you in your windswept prairie, Pere Bastien, but first we will celebrate a gay wedding." But Bastien could only wring my hand in answer and turn aside to wipe away the tears of joy which ran down his furrowed cheeks.

    * * *

"That's all very well for you," said Leveque, spitefully, and with an injured air, as we shook hands at the club some days later. "You had way the best of that expedition. Splendid sport out on those prairies, fine shooting, and lots of game. I had to paddle back to the city to save that handsome fellow Paul from arrest. I missed all the fun and got right into the thick of the Christmas festivities here in town. Found three invitations to Christmas dinner waiting for me, made three enemies by declining them; could get nothing at home, because my cook and butler were naturally out enjoying themselves, and ate a beastly meal all by myself, at a restaurant!

"The next time we go out snipe shooting together, old boy, if there is any tragedy around loose, you'll do the heroic and I'll do the snipe shooting."

"All right," I said; "we'll take a run up Harvey's Canal early next month. We shall be in time for the wedding, Dick; besides, February's fine for woodcock. I'll undertake to let old Bastien know we're coming."

"Good," said Leveque, approvingly, and we went, but, as Rudyard Kipling says, "that is another story."

George Washington Cable (1844–1925)[1]

George Washington Cable is one of the most versatile and talented writers to come out of New Orleans, and arguably the finest nineteenth-century Louisiana writer. Included here are examples of his writing in two different genres. The first, "'Tite Poulette," appeared in his first short story collection, *Old Creole Days*, in 1879. The second is Cable's essay, "The Freedman's Case in Equity," (1885) which prompted the response from Charles Gayarré previously discussed in this collection, and which also prompted Cable's permanent move from New Orleans to Connecticut.

Cable was born in a house on Annunciation Square in New Orleans to George Washington and Rebecca Boardman Cable on October 12, 1844. His father was of German descent and had first settled in Virginia and then in Dearborn County, Indiana, where he met and married Rebecca Boardman in 1834. The family prospered there for the next few years, but in the financial crash of 1837, they lost everything and moved south to New Orleans, where his father worked in the riverboat supply business, and once again they lived a life of ease in a large house in the Garden District, where they owned eight slaves and where Cable was born in 1844. Such prosperity, however, was again fleeting, and by the time young George Cable was five years old, they had to sell the family property. Cable's father would not enjoy such success again, working as a clerk in a customhouse until his death ten years later in 1859. Upon his father's death, Cable was forced to give up his studies and was fortunate to move into his father's position in the customhouse, a position he held until the federal blockade of New Orleans in 1861 closed it down. For the next two years Cable worked as a grocery clerk in order to support his family, until he joined the Confederate Army in 1863.

After the war's end, Cable returned to New Orleans, again in desperate need of a job. He worked for much of the summer of 1865 as a cotton clerk in Kosciusko, Mississippi, but left there to work on a surveying team on the Atchafalaya River, where he contracted malaria and returned to New Orleans. In 1869, he married Louise Stewart Bartlett, a young New Orleans woman whose family hailed from Connecticut, a factor that would play a role in his subsequent move to that state. By this time, Cable had begun to publish, and in 1870 he began to write the weekly "Drop Shot" for the New Orleans *Picayune*, a column much like Whitman's in the *New Orleans Crescent*: a man about town musing on a variety of topics, in Cable's case, topics that interested him, including local characters and events, history, and local flora and fauna. However, as Louis D. Rubin points out, as the columns progressed, they became more literary and political. Although he did return to the cotton business briefly, out of necessity, Cable's writing career had begun, and his first short story "'Sieur George" appeared in *Scribner's Monthly* in October of 1873, and six years later his first collection of short stories, *Old Creole Days*, was published.

Critic John Cleman calls "'Tite Poulette" a sentimental love story made all the more clumsy with the contrived *deus ex machina* conclusion. That seems a bit harsh. Although it is sentimental, it is also Cable's first story to address the race question and the practice of plaçage directly. Moreover, it takes the traditional story of the tragic mulatto and turns it on its head, and that is downright radical! The protagonist, 'Tite Poulette (little chick) is lusted after by the "Creole lads": "So beautiful, beautiful, beautiful! White? –white like a water lily! White—like a magnolia!" These comments hint at her true race, even though she is thought to be the daughter of Madame John, or Zalli, a free woman of color who was once "placed" with a white man, Monsieur John, thought to be 'Tite Poulette's father. Here, like the poets of *Les Cenelles*, Cable points out the dangers of such a system as plaçage. Madame John and 'Tite Poulette are reared as most refined women of the day, both black and white, with "no... education... they knew nothing beyond a little music and embroidery," and like so many free women of color, they have nothing to fall back on once Monsieur John dies, except the exploitative quadroon balls. Their young Dutch neighbor, Kristian Koppig, is in love with 'Tite Poulette, but he writes to his mother of the "proper, horror of mixed blood" even though "if she ('Tite Poulette) were in Holland today, not one of a hundred suitors would detect the hidden blemish." He is forbidden by law to marry her, but he finally disregards her "hidden blemish" of race

---

1   For more on Cable see Louis D. Rubin, *George W. Cable: The Life and Times of a Southern Heretic* (New York: Pegasus, 1969).

and proposes. That is when we discover that 'Tite Poulette is a foundling, the daughter of a Spanish gentleman and his wife who died of yellow fever upon arriving in New Orleans. By making 'Tite Poulette white yet having been reared as a quadroon or even an octoroon, Cable subverts the traditional tragic mulatto tale, thereby illustrating just how ridiculous a system is that bases race and racism on the color of one's skin. He also exposes the evils of plaçage and the plight of free women of color in New Orleans.

According to Cable biographer Louis D. Rubin, Cable's essay included here, "The Freedman's Case in Equity," was his first outright attack on racism in the South. It was also the essay that caused more ire among southern readers than any other of his to date, and it precipitated his permanent move to Connecticut. Although it was not published until 1885 in *Century* magazine, according to Rubin, he had delivered it in some form at the University of Alabama spring commencement a year earlier. One of the compromises resulting from the all but deadlocked Tilden-Hayes election of 1876 was the removal of federal troops from the South, which put an end to Reconstruction and ushered in the Jim Crow era. Southern states were left unchecked in their treatment of the recently freed slaves, which resulted in a segregated South and a North indifferent to the plight of the freed men and women. In this essay, Cable argues for class distinction based on a man or woman's social comportment and character, not on his or her race: "It (the racist system in place in the South) prompts the average Southern white passenger to find less offense in the presence of a profane, boisterous, or unclean white person than in that of a quiet, well-behaved colored man or woman attempting to travel on an equal footing with him without a white master or mistress." In part, Cable was inspired to write this essay due to his own experience on a train ride through Alabama, during which a young mother and her daughter were refused seats in a "white only" car and forced to ride in a car with convicts simply because they were black, hardly separate but equal.

At the time, Cable was one of the nation's most popular writers, and naturally, his militant writing about racism in the South was not well-received. In fact, although he might have garnered some private support for speaking out, publicly in the southern press he was vilified, and it even spilled over to his fiction. He left New Orleans with his family in 1884 for Connecticut, which was not unusual for them during the brutal summer months, but this time, they did not return. That same year he also set out on a popular reading tour with Mark Twain, and Cable continued writing and lecturing around the country for much of the 1880s and '90s. By the early 1900s Cable, now living in Massachusetts, returned to New Orleans almost yearly, and in 1915, he was asked to speak at the Louisiana Historical Society, of which writer Grace King was a member, and one who had very publicly attacked Cable for his stance on race some thirty years earlier. This time, however, her response was different: "The hall was packed. When he finished everybody stood up, and I never heard such applause. I am so glad that at last he got his compliment from New Orleans. He deserved it, not only as a tribute to his genius, but as compensation for the way we treated him."[1] By the end of his career, Cable suffered financial setbacks but continued his frequent visits to New Orleans from his Northampton, Massachusetts home, Tarryawhile, which he purchased in 1892. He died in St. Petersburg, Florida on January 31, 1925.

'Tite Poulette[2]

K ristian Koppig was a rosy-faced, beardless young Dutchman. He was one of that army of gentlemen who, after the purchase of Louisiana, swarmed from all parts of the commercial world, over the mountains of Franco-Spanish exclusiveness, like the Goths over the Pyrenees, and settled down in New Orleans to pick up their fortunes, with the diligence of hungry pigeons. He may have been a German; the distinction was too fine for Creole haste and disrelish.

He made his home in a room with one dormer window looking out, and somewhat down, upon a building opposite, which still stands, flush with the street, a century old. Its big, round-arched windows in a long, second-story row, are walled up, and two or three from time to time have had smaller windows

---

1   *Boston Evening Transcript*, Sept. 29, 1923.

2   From: George W. Cable, *Old Creole Days: A Story of Creole Life.* (New York. Charles Scribner's Sons, 1906), 213-46.

let into them again, with odd little latticed peep-holes in their batten shutters. This had already been done when Kristian Koppig first began to look at them from his solitary dormer window.

All the features of the building lead me to guess that it is a remnant of the old Spanish Barracks, whose extensive structure fell by government sale into private hands a long time ago. At the end toward the swamp a great, oriental-looking passage is left, with an arched entrance, and a pair of ponderous wooden doors. You look at it, and almost see Count O'Reilly's artillery come bumping and trundling out, and dash around into the ancient Plaza to bang away at King St. Charles's birthday.

I do not know who lives there now. You might stand about on the opposite *banquette* for weeks and never find out. I suppose it is a residence, for it does not look like one. That is the rule in that region.

In the good old times of duels, and bagatelle-clubs, and theatre-balls, and Cayetano's circus, Kristian Koppig rooming as described, there lived in the portion of this house, partly overhanging the archway, a palish handsome woman, by the name—or going by the name—of Madame John. You would hardly have thought of her being "colored." Though fading, she was still of very attractive countenance, fine, rather severe features, nearly straight hair carefully kept, and that vivid black eye so peculiar to her kind. Her smile, which came and went with her talk, was sweet and exceedingly intelligent; and something told you, as you looked at her, that she was one who had had to learn a great deal in this troublesome life.

"But!"—the Creole lads in the street would say—"—her daughter!" and there would be lifting of arms, wringing of fingers, rolling of eyes, rounding of mouths, gaspings and clasping of hands. "So beautiful, beautiful, beautiful! White?—white like a water lily! White—like a magnolia!"

Applause would follow, and invocation of all the saints to witness.

And she could sing.

"Sing?" (disdainfully)—"if a mocking-bird can sing! Ha!"

They could not tell just how old she was; they "would give her about seventeen."

Mother and daughter were very fond. The neighbors could hear them call each other pet names, and see them sitting together, sewing, talking happily to each other in the unceasing French way, and see them go out and come in together on their little tasks and errands. "'Tite Poulette," the daughter was called; she never went out alone.

And who was this Madame John?

"Why, you know!—she was"—said the wig-maker at the corner to Kristian Koppig—"I'll tell you. You know?—she was"—and the rest atomized off in a rasping whisper. She was the best yellow-fever nurse in a thousand yards round; but that is not what the wig-maker said.

A block nearer the river stands a house altogether different from the remnant of old barracks. It is of frame, with a deep front gallery over which the roof extends. It has become a den of Italians, who sell fuel by daylight, and by night are up to no telling what extent of deviltry. This was once the home of a gay gentleman, whose first name happened to be John. He was a member of the Good Children Social Club. As his parents lived with him, his wife would, according to custom, have been called Madame John but he had no wife. His father died, then his mother; last of all, himself. As he is about to be off, in comes Madame John, with 'Tite Poulette, then an infant, on her arm.

"Zalli," said he, "I am going."

She bowed her head, and wept.

"You have been very faithful to me, Zalli."

She wept on.

"Nobody to take care of you now, Zalli."

Zalli only went on weeping.

"I want to give you this house, Zalli; it is for you and the little one."

An hour after, amid the sobs of Madame John, she and the "little one" inherited the house, such as it was. With the fatal caution which characterizes ignorance, she sold the property and placed the proceeds in a bank, which made haste to fail. She put on widow's weeds, and wore them still when 'Tite Poulette "had seventeen," as the frantic lads would say.

How they did chatter over her. Quiet Kristian Koppig had never seen the like. He wrote to his mother, and told her so. A pretty fellow at the corner would suddenly double himself up with beckoning to a knot of chums; these would hasten up; recruits would come in from two or three other directions; as they reached the corner their countenances would quickly assume a genteel severity, and presently, with her mother, 'Tite Poulette would pass—tall, straight, lithe, her great black eyes made tender by their sweeping lashes, the faintest tint of color in her Southern cheek, her form all grace, her carriage a wonder of simple dignity.

The instant she was gone every tongue was let slip on the marvel of her beauty; but, though theirs were only the loose New Orleans morals of over fifty years ago, their unleashed tongues never had attempted any greater liberty than to take up the pet name, 'Tite Poulette. And yet the mother was soon to be, as we shall discover, a paid dancer at the *Salle de Conde.*

To Zalli, of course, as to all "quadroon ladies," the festivities of the Conde-street ball-room were familiar of old. There, in the happy days when dear Monsieur John was young, and the eighteenth century old, she had often repaired under guard of her mother—dead now, alas!—and Monsieur John would slip away from the dull play and dry society of Theatre d'Orleans, and come around with his crowd of elegant friends; and through the long sweet hours of the ball she had danced, and laughed, and coquetted under her satin mask, even to the baffling and tormenting of that prince of gentlemen, dear Monsieur John himself. No man of questionable blood dare set his foot within the door. Many noble gentlemen were pleased to dance with her. Colonel De —— and General La ——: city councilmen and officers from the Government House. There were no paid dancers then. Every thing was decorously conducted indeed! Every girl's mother was there, and the more discreet always left before there was too much drinking. Yes, it was gay, gay!—but sometimes dangerous. Ha! more times than a few had Monsieur John knocked down some long-haired and long-knifed rowdy, and kicked the breath out of him for looking saucily at her; but that was like him, he was so brave and kind;—and he is gone!

There was no room for widow's weeds there. So when she put these on, her glittering eyes never again looked through her pink and white mask, and she was glad of it; for never, never in her life had they so looked for anybody but her dear Monsieur John, and now he was in heaven—so the priest said—and she was a sick-nurse.

Living was hard work; and, as Madame John had been brought up tenderly, and had done what she could to rear her daughter in the same mistaken way, with, of course, no more education than the ladies in society got, they knew nothing beyond a little music and embroidery. They struggled as they could, faintly; now giving a few private dancing lessons, now dressing hair, but ever beat back by the steady detestation of their imperious patronesses; and, by and by, for want of that priceless worldly grace known among the flippant as "money-sense," these two poor children, born of misfortune and the complacent badness of the times, began to be in want.

Kristian Koppig noticed from his dormer window one day a man standing at the big archway opposite, and clanking the brass knocker on the wicket that was in one of the doors. He was a smooth man, with his hair parted in the middle, and his cigarette poised on a tiny gold holder. He waited a moment, politely cursed the dust, knocked again, threw his slender sword-cane under his arm, and wiped the inside of his hat with his handkerchief.

Madame John held a parley with him at the wicket. 'Tite Poulette was nowhere seen. He stood at the gate while Madame John went up-stairs. Kristian Koppig knew him. He knew him as one knows a snake. He was the manager of the *Salle de Conde*. Presently Madame John returned with a little bundle, and they hurried off together.

And now what did this mean? Why, by any one of ordinary acuteness the matter was easily understood, but, to tell the truth, Kristian Koppig was a trifle dull, and got the idea at once that some damage was being planned against 'Tite Poulette. It made the gentle Dutchman miserable not to be minding his own business, and yet—

"But the woman certainly will not attempt"—said he to himself—"no, no! she cannot." Not being able to guess what he meant, I cannot say whether she could or not. I know that next day Kristian Koppig, glancing eagerly over the "*Ami des Lois*," read an advertisement which he had always before skipped with a frown. It was headed, "*Salle de Conde*," and, being interpreted, signified that a new dance was to be introduced, the *Danse de Chinois*, and that a young lady would follow it with the famous "*Danse du Shawl*."

It was the Sabbath. The young man watched the opposite window steadily and painfully from early in the afternoon until the moon shone bright; and from the time the moon shone bright until Madame John!—joy!—Madame John! and not 'Tite Poulette, stepped through the wicket, much dressed and well muffled, and hurried off toward the *Rue Conde*. Madame John was the "young lady;" and the young man's mind, glad to return to its own unimpassioned affairs, relapsed into quietude.

Madame John danced beautifully. It had to be done. It brought some pay, and pay was bread; and every Sunday evening, with a touch here and there of paint and powder, the mother danced the dance of the shawl, the daughter remaining at home alone.

Kristian Koppig, simple, slow-thinking young Dutchman, never noticing that he staid at home with his window darkened for the very purpose, would see her come to her window and look out with a little wild, alarmed look in her magnificent eyes, and go and come again, and again, until the mother, like a storm-driven bird, came panting home.

Two or three months went by.

One night, on the mother's return, Kristian Koppig coming to his room nearly at the same moment, there was much earnest conversation, which he could see, but not hear.

"'Tite Poulette," said Madame John, "you are seventeen."

"True, Maman."

"Ah! my child, I see not how you are to meet the future." The voice trembled plaintively.

"But how, Maman?"

"Ah! you are not like others; no fortune, no pleasure, no friend."

"Maman!"

"No, no;—I thank God for it; I am glad you are not; but you will be lonely, lonely, all your poor life long. There is no place in this world for us poor women. I wish that we were either white or black!"—and the tears, two "shining ones," stood in the poor quadroon's eyes.

Tha daughter stood up, her eyes flashing.

"God made us, Maman," she said with a gentle, but stately smile.

"Ha!" said the mother, her keen glance darting through her tears, "Sin made me, yes."

"No," said 'Tite Poulette, "God made us. He made us Just as we are; not more white, not more black."

"He made you, truly!" said Zalli. "You are so beautiful; I believe it well." She reached and drew the fair form to a kneeling posture. "My sweet, white daughter!"

Now the tears were in the girl's eyes. "And could I be whiter than I am?" she asked.

"Oh, no, no! 'Tite Poulette," cried the other; "but if we were only *real white!*—both of us; so that some gentleman might come to see me and say 'Madame John, I want your pretty little chick. She is so beautiful. I want to take her home. She is so good—I want her to be my wife.' Oh, my child, my child, to see that I would give my life—I would give my soul! Only you should take me along to be your servant. I walked behind two young men to-night; they were coming home from their office; presently they began to talk about you."

'Tite Poulette's eyes flashed fire.

"No, my child, they spoke only the best things. One laughed a little at times and kept saying 'Beware!' but the other—I prayed the Virgin to bless him, he spoke such kind and noble words. Such gentle pity; such a holy heart! 'May God defend her,' he said, *cherie*; he said, 'May God defend her, for I see no help for her.' The other one laughed and left him. He stopped in the door right across the street. Ah, my child, do you blush? Is that something to bring the rose to your cheek? Many fine gentlemen at the ball ask me often, 'How is your daughter, Madame John?'"

The daughter's face was thrown into the mother's lap, not so well satisfied, now, with God's handiwork. Ah, how she wept! Sob, sob, sob; gasps and sighs and stifled ejaculations, her small right hand clinched and beating on her mother's knee; and the mother weeping over her.

Kristian Koppig shut his window. Nothing but a generous heart and a Dutchman's phlegm could have done so at that moment. And even thou, Kristian Koppig!—for the window closed very slowly.

He wrote to his mother, thus:

"In this wicked city, I see none so fair as the poor girl who lives opposite me, and who, alas! though so fair, is one of those whom the taint of caste has cursed. She lives a lonely, innocent life in the midst of corruption, like the lilies I find here in the marshew, and I have great pity for her. 'God defend her,' I said to-night to a fellow clerk, 'I see no help for her.' I know there is a natural, and I think proper, horror of mixed blood (excuse the mention, sweet mother), and I feel it, too; and yet if she were in Holland today, not one of a hundred suitors would detect the hidden blemish."

In such strain this young man wrote on trying to demonstrate the utter impossibility of his ever loving the lovable unfortunate, until the midnight tolling of the cathedral clock sent him to bed.

About the same hour Zalli and 'Tite Poulette were kissing good-night.

"'Tite Poulette, I want you to promise me one thing."

"Well, Maman?"

"If any gentleman should ever love you and ask you to marry,—not knowing, you know,—promise me you will not tell him you are not white."

"It can never be," said 'Tite Poulette.

"But if it should," said Madame John pleadingly.

"And break the law?" asked 'Tite Poulette, impatiently.

"But the law is unjust," said the mother.

"But it is the law!"

"But you will not, dearie, will you?"

"I would surely tell him!" said the daughter.

When Zalli, for some cause, went next morning to the window, she started.

"'Tite Poulette!"—she called softly without moving. The daughter came. The young man, whose idea of propriety had actuated him to this display, was sitting in the dormer window, reading. Mother and daughter bent a steady gaze at each other. It meant in French, "If he saw us last night!"—

"Ah! dear," said the mother, her face beaming with fun—

"What can it be, Maman?"

"He speaks—oh! ha, ha!—he speaks—such miserable French!"

It came to pass one morning at early dawn that Zalli and 'Tite Poulette, going to mass, passed a cafe, just as—who should be coming out but Monsieur, the manager of the *Salle de Conde*. He had not yet gone to bed. Monsieur was astonished. He had a Frenchman's eye for the beautiful, and certainly there the beautiful was. He had heard of Madame John's daughter, and had hoped once to see her, but did not but could this be she?

They disappeared within the cathedral. A sudden pang of piety moved him; he followed. 'Tite Poulette was already kneeling in the aisle. Zalli, still in the vestibule, was just taking her hand from the font of holy-water.

"Madame John," whispered the manager.

She courtesied.

"Madame John, that young lady—is she your daughter?"

"She—she—is my daughter," said Zalli, with somewhat of alarm in her face, which the manager misinterpreted.

"I think not, Madame John." He shook his head, smiling as one too wise to be fooled.

"Yes, Monsieur, she is my daughter."

"O no, Madame John, it is only make-believe, I think."

"I swear she is, Monsieur de la Rue."

"Is that possible?" pretending to waver, but convinced in his heart of hearts, by Zalli's alarm, that she was lying. "But how? Why does she not come to our ball-room with you?"

Zalli, trying to get away from him, shrugged and smiled. "Each to his taste, Monsieur; it pleases her not."

She was escaping, but he followed one step more. "I shall come to see you, Madame John."

She whirled and attacked him with her eyes. "Monsieur must not give himself the trouble!" she said, the eyes at the same time adding, "Dare to come!" She turned again, and knelt to her devotions. The manager dipped in the font, crossed himself, and departed.

Several weeks went by, and M. de la Rue had not accepted the fierce challenge of Madame John's eyes. One or two Sunday nights she had succeeded in avoiding him, though fulfilling her engagement in the *Salle*; but by and by pay-day,—a Saturday,—came round, and though the pay was ready, she was loath to go up to Monsieur's little office.

It was an afternoon in May. Madame John came to her own room, and, with a sigh, sank into a chair. Her eyes were wet.

"Did you go to his office, dear mother?" asked 'Tite Poulette.

"I could not," she answered, dropping her face in her hands.

"Maman, he has seen me at the window!"

"While I was gone?" cried the mother.

"He passed on the other side of the street. He looked up purposely, and saw me." The speaker's cheeks were burning red.

Zalli wrung her hands.

"It is nothing, mother; do not go near him."

"But the pay, my child."

"The pay matters not."

"But he will bring it here; he wants the chance."

That was the trouble, sure enough.

About this time Kristian Koppig lost his position in the German importing house where, he had fondly told his mother, he was indispensable.

"Summer was coming on," the senior said, "and you see our young men are almost idle. Yes, our engagement *was* for a year, but ah—we could not foresee"—etc., etc., "besides" (attempting a parting flattery), "your father is a rich gentleman, and you can afford to take the summer easy. If we can ever be of any service to you," etc., etc.

So the young Dutchman spent the afternoons at his dormer window reading and glancing down at the little casement opposite, where a small, rude shelf had lately been put out, holding a row of cigar-boxes with wretched little botanical specimens in them trying to die. 'Tite Poulette was their gardener; and it was odd to see,—dry weather or wet,—how many waterings per day those plants could take. She never looked up from her task; but I know she performed it with that unacknowledged pleasure which all girls love and deny, that of being looked upon by noble eyes.

On this peculiar Saturday afternoon in May, Kristian Koppig had been witness of the distressful scene over the way. It occurred to 'Tite Poulette that such might be the case, and she stepped to the casement to shut it. As she did so, the marvellous delicacy of Kristian Koppig moved him to draw in one of his shutters. Both young heads came out at one moment, while at the same instant—

"Rap, rap, rap, rap, rap!" clanked the knocker on the wicket. The black eyes of the maiden and the blue over the way, from looking into each other for the first time in life, glanced down to the arched doorway upon Monsieur the manager. Then the black eyes disappeared within, and Kristian Koppig thought again, and re-opening his shutter, stood up at the window prepared to become a bold spectator of what might follow.

But for a moment nothing followed.

"Trouble over there," thought the rosy Dutchman, and waited. The manager waited too, rubbing his hat and brushing his clothes with the tips of his kidded fingers.

"They do not wish to see him," slowly concluded the spectator.

"Rap, rap, rap, rap, rap!" quoth the knocker, and M. de la Rue looked up around at the windows opposite and noticed the handsome young Dutchman looking at him.

"Dutch!" said the manager softly, between his teeth.

"He is staring at me," said Kristian Koppig to himself;—"but then I am staring at him, which accounts for it."

A long pause, and then another long rapping.

"They want him to go away," thought Koppig.

"Knock hard!" suggested a street youngster, standing by.

"Rap, rap"—The manager had no sooner recommenced than several neighbors looked out of doors and windows.

"Very bad," thought our Dutchman; "somebody should make him go off. I wonder what they will do."

The manager stepped into the street, looked up at the closed window, returned to the knocker, and stood with it in his hand.

"They are all gone out, Monsieur," said the street-youngster.

"You lie!" said the cynosure of neighboring eyes.

"Ah!" thought Kristian Koppig; "I will go down and ask him"—Here his thoughts lost outline; he was only convinced that he had somewhat to say to him, and turned to go down stairs. In going he became a little vexed with himself because he could not help hurrying. He noticed, too, that his arm holding the stair-rail trembled in a silly way, whereas he was perfectly calm. Precisely as he reached the street-door the manager raised the knocker; but the latch clicked and the wicket was drawn slightly ajar.

Inside could just be descried Madame John. The manager bowed, smiled, talked, talked on, held money in his hand, bowed, smiled, talked on, flourished the money, smiled, bowed, talked on and plainly persisted in some intention to which Madame John was steadfastly opposed.

The window above, too,—it was Kristian Koppig who noticed that,—opened a wee bit, like the shell of a terrapin. Presently the manager lifted his foot and put forward an arm, as though he would enter the gate by pushing, but as quick as gunpowder it clapped—in his face!

You could hear the fleeing feet of Zalli pounding up the staircase.

As the panting mother re-entered her room, "See, Maman," said 'Tite Poulette, peeping at the window, "the young gentleman from over the way has crossed!"

"Holy Mary bless him!" said the mother.

"I will go over," thought Kristian Koppig, "and ask him kindly if he is not making a mistake."

"What are they doing, dear?" asked the mother, with clasped hands.

"They are talking; the young man is tranquil, but 'Sieur de la Rue is very angry," whispered the daughter; and just then—pang! came a sharp, keen sound rattling up the walls on either side of the narrow way, and "Aha!" and laughter and clapping of female hands from two or three windows.

"Oh! what a slap!" cried the girl, half in fright, half in glee, jerking herself back from the casement simultaneously with the report. But the "ahas" and laughter, and clapping of feminine hands, which still continued, came from another cause. 'Tite Poulette's rapid action had struck the slender cord that held up an end of her hanging garden, and the whole rank of cigar-boxes slid from their place, turned gracefully over as they shot through the air, and emptied themselves plump upon the head of the slapped manager. Breathless, dirty, pale as whitewash, he gasped a threat to be heard from again, and, getting round the corner as quick as he could walk, left Kristian Koppig, standing motionless, the most astonished man in that street.

"Kristian Koppig, Kristian Koppig," said Greatheart to himself, slowly dragging up-stairs, "what a mischief you have done. One poor woman certainly to be robbed of her bitter wages, and another—so lovely!—put to the burning shame of being the subject of a street brawl! What will this silly neighborhood say? 'Has the gentleman a heart as well as a hand?' 'Is it jealousy?'" There he paused, afraid himself to answer the supposed query; and then—"Oh! Kristian Koppig, you have been such a dunce!" "And I cannot apologize to them. Who in this street would carry my note, and not wink and grin over it with low surmises? I cannot even make restitution. Money? They would not dare receive it. Oh! Kristian Koppig, why did you not mind your own business? Is she any thing to you? Do you love her? *Of course not!* Oh!—such a dunce!"

The reader will eagerly admit that however faulty this young man's course of reasoning, his conclusion was correct. For mark what he did.

He went to his room, which was already growing dark, shut his window, lighted his big Dutch lamp, and sat down to write. "Something *must* be done," said he aloud, taking up his pen; "I will be calm and cool; I will be distant and brief; but—I shall have to be kind or I may offend. Ah! I shall have to write in French; I forgot that; I write it so poorly, dunce that I am, when all my brothers and sisters speak it so well." He got out his French dictionary. Two hours slipped by. He made a new pen, washed and refilled his inkstand, mended his "abominable!" chair, and after two hours more made another attempt, and another failure. "My head aches," said he, and lay down on his couch, the better to frame his phrases.

He was awakened by the Sabbath sunlight. The bells of the Cathedral and the Ursulines' chapel were ringing for high mass, and a mocking-bird, perching on a chimney-top above Madame John's rooms, was carolling, whistling, mewing, chirping, screaming, and trilling with the ecstasy of a whole May in his throat. "Oh! sleepy Kristian Koppig," was the young man's first thought, "—such a dunce!"

Madame John and daughter did not go to mass. The morning wore away, and their casement remained closed. "They are offended," said Kristian Koppig, leaving the house, and wandering up to the little Protestant affair known as Christ Church.

"No, possibly they are not," he said, returning and finding the shutters thrown back.

By a sad accident, which mortified him extremely, he happened to see, late in the afternoon,—hardly conscious that he was looking across the street,—that Madame John was—dressing. Could it be that she was going to the *Salle de Conde*? He rushed to his table, and began to write.

He had guessed aright. The wages were too precious to be lost. The manager had written her a note. He begged to assure her that he was a gentleman of the clearest cut. If he had made a mistake the previous afternoon, he was glad no unfortunate result had followed except his having been assaulted by a ruffian; that the *Danse du Shawl* was promised in his advertisement, and he hoped Madame John (whose wages were in hand waiting for her) would not fail to assist as usual. Lastly, and delicately put, he expressed his conviction that Mademoiselle was wise and discreet in declining to entertain gentlemen at her home.

So, against much beseeching on the part of 'Tite Poulette, Madame John was going to the ball-room. "Maybe I can discover what 'Sieur de la Rue is planning against Monsieur over the way," she said, knowing certainly the slap would not be forgiven; and the daughter, though tremblingly, at once withdrew her objections.

The heavy young Dutchman, now thoroughly electrified, was writing like mad. He wrote and tore up, wrote and tore up, lighted his lamp, started again, and at last signed his name. A letter by a Dutchman in French!—what can be made of it in English? We will see:

> Madame and Mademoiselle:
> A stranger, seeking not to be acquainted, but seeing and admiring all days the goodness and high honor, begs to be pardoned of them for the mistakes, alas! of yesterday, and to make reparation and satisfaction in destroying the ornaments of the window, as well as the loss of compensation from Monsieur the manager, with the enclosed bill of the *Banque de la Louisiane* for fifty dollars ($50). And, hoping they will seeing what he is meaning, remains, respectfully,
> Kristian Koppig.
> P.S.—Madame must not go to the ball.

He must bear the missive himself. He must speak in French. What should the words be? A moment of study—he has it, and is off down the long three-story stairway. At the same moment Madame John stepped from the wicket, and glided off to the *Salle de Conde*, a trifle late.

"I shall see Madame John, of course," thought the young man, crushing a hope, and rattled the knocker. 'Tite Poulette sprang up from praying for her mother's safety. "What has she forgotten?" she asked herself, and hastened down. The wicket opened. The two innocents were stunned.

"Aw—aw"—said the pretty Dutchman, "aw,"—blurted out something in virgin Dutch,... handed her the letter, and hurried down street.

"Alas! what have I done?" said the poor girl, bending over her candle, and bursting into tears that fell on the unopened letter. "And what shall I do! It may be wrong to open it—and worse not to." Like her sex, she took the benefit of the doubt, and intensified her perplexity and misery by reading and misconstruing the all but unintelligible contents. What then? Not only sobs and sighs, but moaning and beating of little fists together, and outcries of soul-felt agony stifled against the bedside, and temples pressed into knitted palms, because of one who "sought not to be acquainted," but offered money—money!—in pity to a poor—shame on her for saying that!—a poor *nigresse*.

And now our self-confessed dolt turned back from a half-hour's walk, concluding there might be an answer to his note. "Surely Madame John will appear this time." He knocked. The shutter stirred above, and something white came fluttering wildly down like a shot dove. It was his own letter containing the fifty-dollar bill. He bounded to the wicket, and softly but eagerly knocked again.

"Go away," said a trembling voice from above.

"Madame John?" said he; but the window closed, and he heard a step, the same step on the stair. Step, step, every step one step deeper into his heart. 'Tite Poulette came to the closed door.

"What will you?" said the voice within.

"I—I—don't wish to see you. I wish to see Madame John."

"I must pray Monsieur to go away. My mother is at the *Salle de Conde*."

"At the ball!" Kristian Koppig strayed off, repeating the words for want of definite thought. All at once it occurred to him that at the ball he could make Madame John's acquaintance with impunity. "Was it courting sin to go?" By no means; he should, most likely, save a woman from trouble, and help the poor in their distress.

Behold Kristian Koppig standing on the floor of the *Salle de Conde*. A large hall, a blaze of lamps, a bewildering flutter of fans and floating robes, strains of music, columns of gay promenaders, a long row of turbaned mothers lining either wall, gentlemen of the portlier sort filling the recesses of the windows, whirling waltzers gliding here and there—smiles and grace, smiles and grace; all fair, orderly, elegant, bewitching. A young Creole's laugh mayhap a little loud, and—truly there were many sword-canes. But neither grace nor foulness satisfied the eye of the zealous young Dutchman.

Suddenly a muffled woman passed him, leaning on a gentleman's arm. It looked like—it must be, Madame John. Speak quick, Kristian Koppig; do not stop to notice the man!

"Madame John"—bowing—"I am your neighbor, Kristian Koppig."

Madame John bows low, and smiles—a ball-room smile, but is frightened, and her escort,—the manager,—drops her hand and slips away.

"Ah! Monsieur," she whispers excitedly, "you will be killed if you stay here a moment. Are you armed? No. Take this." She tried to slip a dirk into his hands, but he would not have it.

"Oh, my dear young man, go! Go quickly!" she plead, glancing furtively down the hall.

"I wish you not to dance," said the young man.

"I have danced already; I am going home. Come; be quick! we will go together." She thrust her arm through his, and they hastened into the street. When a square had been passed there came a sound of men running behind them.

"Run, Monsieur, run!" she cried, trying to drag him; but Monsieur Dutchman would not.

"*Run*, Monsieur! Oh, my God! it is 'Sieur"—

"*That* for yesterday!" cried the manager, striking fiercely with his cane. Kristian Koppig's fist rolled him in the dirt.

"*That* for 'Tite Poulette!" cried another man dealing the Dutchman a terrible blow from behind.

"And *that* for me!" hissed a third, thrusting at him with something bright.

"*That* for yesterday!" screamed the manager, bounding like a tiger; "That!" "THAT!" "Ha!"

Then Kristian Koppig knew that he was stabbed.

"That!" and "That!" and "That!" and the poor Dutchman struck wildly here and there, grasped the air, shut his eyes, staggered, reeled, fell, rose half up, fell again for good, and they were kicking him and jumping on him. All at once they scampered. Zalli had found the night-watch.

"Buz-z-z-z!" went a rattle. "Buz-z-z-z!" went another.

"Pick him up."

"Is he alive?"

"Can't tell; hold him steady; lead the way, misses."

"He's bleeding all over my breeches."

"This way—here—around this corner."

"This way now—only two squares more."

"Here we are."

"Rap-rap-rap!" on the old brass knocker. Curses on the narrow wicket, more on the dark archway, more still on the twisting stairs.

Up at last and into the room.

"Easy, easy, push this under his head: never mind his boots!"

So he lies—on 'Tite Poulette's own bed.

The watch are gone. They pause under the corner lamp to count profits;—a single bill—*Banque de la Louisiane*, fifty dollars. Providence is kind—tolerably so. Break it at the "Guillaume Tell." "But did you ever hear any one scream like that girl did?"

And there lies the young Dutch neighbor. His money will not flutter back to him this time; nor will any voice behind a gate "beg Monsieur to go away." O, Woman!—that knows no enemy so terrible as man! Come nigh, poor Woman, you have nothing to fear. Lay your strange, electric touch upon the chilly flesh; it strikes no eager mischief along the fainting veins. Look your sweet looks upon the grimy face, and tenderly lay back the locks from the congested brows; no wicked misinterpretation lurks to bite your kindness. Be motherly, be sisterly, fear nought. Go, watch him by night; you may sleep at his feet and he will not stir. Yet he lives, and shall live—may live to forget you, who knows? But for all that, be gentle and watchful; be womanlike, we ask no more; and God reward you!

Even while it was taking all the two women's strength to hold the door against Death, the sick man himself laid a grief upon them.

"Mother," he said to Madame John, quite a master of French in his delirium, "dear mother, fear not; trust your boy; fear nothing. I will not marry 'Tite Poulette; I cannot. She is fair, dear mother, but ah! she is not—don't you know, mother? don't you know? The race! the race! Don't you know that she is jet black. Isn't it?"

The poor nurse nodded "Yes," and gave a sleeping draught; but before the patient quite slept he started once and stared.

"Take her away,"—waving his hand—"take your beauty away. She is jet white. Who could take a jet white wife? O, no, no, no, no!"

Next morning his brain was right.

"Madame," he weakly whispered, "I was delirious last night?"

Zalli shrugged. "Only a very, very, wee, wee trifle of a bit."

"And did I say something wrong or—foolish?"

"O, no, no," she replied; "you only clasped your hands, so, and prayed, prayed all the time to the dear Virgin."

"To the virgin?" asked the Dutchman, smiling incredulously.

"And St. Joseph—yes, indeed," she insisted; "you may strike me dead."

And so, for politeness' sake, he tried to credit the invention, but grew suspicions instead.

Hard was the battle against death. Nurses are sometimes amazons, and such were these. Through the long, enervating summer, the contest lasted; but when at last the cool airs of October came stealing in at the bedside like long-banished little children, Kristian Koppig rose upon his elbow and smiled them a welcome.

The physician, blessed man, was kind beyond measure; but said some inexplicable things, which Zalli tried in vain to make him speak in an undertone. "If I knew Monsieur John?" he said, "certainly! Why, we were chums at school. And he left you so much as that, Madame John? Ah! my old friend John, always noble! And you had it all in that naughty bank? Ah, well, Madame John, it matters little. No, I shall not tell 'Tite Poulette. Adieu."

And another time:—"If I will let you tell me something? With pleasure, Madame John. No, and not tell anybody, Madame John. No, Madame, not even 'Tite Poulette. What?"—a long whistle—"is that possi-ble?—and Monsieur John knew it?—encouraged it?—eh, well, eh, well!—But—can I believe you, Madame John? Oh! you have Monsieur John's sworn statement. Ah! very good, truly, but—you say you have it; but where is it? Ah! to-morrow!" a sceptical shrug. "Pardon me, Madame John, I think perhaps, *perhaps* you are telling the truth.

"If I think you did right? Certainly! What nature keeps back, accident sometimes gives, Madame John; either is God's will. Don't cry. 'Stealing from the dead?' No! It was giving, yes! They are thanking you in heaven, Madame John."

Kristian Koppig, lying awake, but motionless and with closed eyes, hears in part, and, fancying he understands, rejoices with silent intensity. When the doctor is gone he calls Zalli.

"I give you a great deal of trouble, eh, Madame John?"

"No, no; you are no trouble at all. Had you the yellow fever—ah! then!"

She rolled her eyes to signify the superlative character of the tribulations attending yellow fever.

"I had a lady and gentleman once—a Spanish lady and gentleman, just off the ship; both sick at once with the fever—delirious—could not tell their names. Nobody to help me but sometimes Monsieur John! I never had such a time,—never before, never since,—as that time. Four days and nights this head touched not a pillow."

"And they died!" said Kristian Koppig.

"The third night the gentleman went. Poor Senor! 'Sieur John,—he did not know the harm,—gave him some coffee and toast! The fourth night it rained and turned cool, and just before day the poor lady"—

"Died!" said Koppig.

Zalli dropped her arms listlessly into her lap and her eyes ran brimful.

"And left an infant!" said the Dutchman, ready to shout with exultation.

"Ah! no, Monsieur," said Zalli.

The invalid's heart sank like a stone.

"Madame John,"—his voice was all in a tremor,—"tell me the truth. Is 'Tite Poulette your own child?"

"Ah-h-h, ha! ha! what foolishness! Of course she is my child!" And Madame gave vent to a true Frenchwoman's laugh.

It was too much for the sick man. In the pitiful weakness of his shattered nerves he turned his face into his pillow and wept like a child. Zalli passed into the next room to hide her emotion.

"Maman, dear Maman," said 'Tite Poulette, who had overheard nothing, but only saw the tears.

"Ah! my child, my child, my task—my task is too great—too great for me. Let me go now—another time. Go and watch at his bedside."

"But, Maman,"—for 'Tite Poulette was frightened,—"he needs no care now."

"Nay, but go, my child; I wish to be alone."

The maiden stole in with averted eyes and tiptoed to the window—*that window*. The patient, already a man again, gazed at her till she could feel the gaze. He turned his eyes from her a moment to gather resolution. And now, stout heart, farewell; a word or two of friendly parting—nothing more.

"'Tite Poulette."

The slender figure at the window turned and came to the bedside.

"I believe I owe my life to you," he said.

She looked down meekly, the color rising in her cheek.

"I must arrange to be moved across the street tomorrow, on a litter."

She did not stir or speak.

"And I must now thank you, sweet nurse, for your care. Sweet nurse! Sweet nurse!"

She shook her head in protestation.

"Heaven bless you, 'Tite Poulette!"

Her face sank lower.

"God has made you very beautiful, 'Tite Poulette!"

She stirred not. He reached, and gently took her little hand, and as he drew her one step nearer, a tear fell from her long lashes. From the next room, Zalli, with a face of agonized suspense, gazed upon the pair, undiscovered. The young man lifted the hand to lay it upon his lips, when, with a mild, firm force, it was drawn away, yet still rested in his own upon the bedside, like some weak thing snared, that could only not get free.

"Thou wilt not have my love, 'Tite Poulette?"

No answer.

"Thou wilt not, beautiful?"

"Cannot!" was all that she could utter, and upon their clasped hands the tears ran down.

"Thou wrong'st me, 'Tite Poulette. Thou dost not trust me; thou fearest the kiss may loosen the hands. But I tell thee nay. I have struggled hard, even to this hour, against Love, but I yield me now; I yield; I am his unconditioned prisoner forever. God forbid that I ask aught but that you will be my wife."

Still the maiden moved not, looked not up, only rained down tears.

"Shall it not be, 'Tite Poulette?" He tried in vain to draw her.

"'Tite Poulette?" So tenderly he called! And then she spoke.

"It is against the law."

"It is not!" cried Zalli, seizing her round the waist and dragging her forward. "Take her! she is thine. I have robbed God long enough. Here are the sworn papers—here! Take her; she is as white as snow—so! Take her, kiss her; Mary be praised! I never had a child—she is the Spaniard's daughter!"

The Freedman's Case in Equity

The greatest social problem before the American people to-day is, as it has been for a hundred years, the presence among us of the negro.

No comparable entanglement was ever drawn round itself by any other modern nation with so serene a disregard of its ultimate issue, or with a more distinct national responsibility. The African slave was brought here by cruel force, and with everybody's consent except his own. Everywhere the practice was favored as a measure of common aggrandizement. When a few men and women protested, they were mobbed in the public interest, with the public consent. There rests, therefore, a moral responsibility on the whole nation never to lose sight of the results of African-American slavery until they cease to work mischief and injustice.

It is true these responsibilities may not fall everywhere with the same weight; but they are nowhere entirely removed. The original seed of trouble was sown with the full knowledge and consent of the nation. The nation was to blame; and so long as evils spring from it, their correction must be the nation's duty.

The late Southern slave has within two decades risen from slavery to freedom, from freedom to citizenship, passed on into political ascendency, and fallen again from that eminence. The amended Constitution holds him up in his new political rights as well as a mere constitution can. On the other hand, certain enactments of Congress, trying to reach further, have lately been made void by the highest court of the nation. And another thing has happened. The popular mind in the old free States, weary of strife at arm's length, bewildered by its complications, vexed by many a blunder, eager to turn to the cure of other evils, and even tinctured by that race feeling whose grosser excesses it would so gladly see suppressed, has retreated from its uncomfortable dictational attitude and thrown the whole matter over to the States of the South. Here it rests, no longer a main party issue, but a group of questions which are to be settled by each of these States separately in the light of simple equity and morals, and which the genius of American government does not admit of being forced upon them from beyond their borders. Thus the whole question, become secondary in party contest, has yet reached a period of supreme importance.

Before slavery ever became a grave question in the nation's politics,—when it seemed each State's private affair, developing unmolested,—it had two different fates in two different parts of the country. In one, treated as a question of public equity, it withered away. In the other, overlooked in that aspect, it petrified and became the corner-stone of the whole social structure; and when men sought its overthrow as a national evil, it first brought war upon the land, and then grafted into the citizenship of one of the most intelligent nations in the world six millions of people from one of the most debased races on the globe.

And now this painful and wearisome question, sown in the African slave-trade, reaped in our civil war, and garnered in the national adoption of millions of an inferior race, is drawing near a second seed-time. For this is what the impatient proposal to make it a dead and buried issue really means. It means to recommit it to the silence and concealment of the covered furrow. Beyond that incubative retirement no suppressed moral question can be pushed; but all such questions, ignored in the domain of private morals, spring up and expand once more into questions of public equity; neglected as matters of public equity, they blossom into questions of national interest; and, despised in that guise, presently yield the red fruits of revolution.

This question must never again bear that fruit. There must arise, nay, there has arisen, in the South itself, a desire to see established the equities of the issue; to make it no longer a question of endurance between one group of States and another, but between the moral debris of an exploded evil and the duty, necessity, and value of planting society firmly upon universal justice and equity. This, and this only, can give the matter final burial. True, it is still a question between States; but only secondarily, as something formerly participated in, or as it concerns every householder to know that what is being built against his house is built by level and plummet. It is the interest of the Southern States first, and *consequently* of the whole land, to discover clearly these equities and the errors that are being committed against them.

If we take up this task, the difficulties of the situation are plain. We have, first, a revision of Southern State laws which has forced into them the recognition of certain human rights discordant with the sentiments of those who have always called themselves the community; second, the removal of the entire political machinery by which this forcing process was effected; and, third, these revisions left to be interpreted and applied under the domination of these antagonistic sentiments. These being the three terms of the problem, one of three things must result. There will arise a system of vicious evasions eventually ruinous to public and private morals and liberty, or there will be a candid reconsideration of the sentiments hostile to these enactments, or else there will be a division, some taking one course and some the other.

This is what we should look for from our knowledge of men and history; and this is what we find. The revised laws, only where they could not be evaded, have met that reluctant or simulated acceptance of their narrowest letter which might have been expected—a virtual suffocation of those principles of human equity which the unwelcome decrees do little more than shadow forth. But in different regions this attitude has been made in very different degrees of emphasis. In some the new principles have grown, or are growing, into the popular conviction, and the opposing sentiments are correspondingly dying out. There are even some limited districts where they have received much practical acceptance. While, again, other sections lean almost wholly toward the old sentiments; an easy choice, since it is the conservative, the unyielding attitude, whose strength is in the absence of intellectual and moral debate.

Now, what are the gains, what the losses of these diverse attitudes? Surely these are urgent questions to any one in our country who believes it is always a losing business to be in the wrong. Particularly in the South, where each step in this affair is an unprecedented experience, it will be folly if each region, small or large, does not study the experiences of all the rest. And yet this, alone, would be superficial; we would still need to do more. We need to go back to the roots of things and study closely, analytically, the origin, the present foundation, the rationality, the rightness, of those sentiments surviving in us which prompt an attitude qualifying in any way peculiarly the black man's liberty among us. Such a treatment will be less abundant in incident, less picturesque; but it will be more thorough.

First, then, what are these sentiments? Foremost among them stands the idea that he is of necessity an alien. He was brought to our shores a naked, brutish, unclean, captive, pagan savage, to be and remain a kind of connecting link between man and the beasts of burden. The great changes to result from his contact with a superb race of masters were not taken into account. As a social factor he was intended to be as purely zero as the brute at the other end of his plow-line. The occasional mingling of his blood with that of the white man worked no change in the sentiment; one, two, four, eight, multiplied upon or divided into zero, still gave zero for the result. Generations of American nativity made no difference; his children and children's children were born in sight of our door, yet the old notion held fast. He increased to vast numbers, but it never wavered. He accepted our dress, language, religion, all the fundamentals of our civilization, and became forever expatriated from his own land; still he remained, to us, an alien. Our sentiment went blind. It did not see that gradually, here by force and there by choice, he was fulfilling a host of conditions that earned at least a solemn moral right to that naturalization which no one at first had dreamed of giving him. Frequently he even bought back the freedom of which he had been robbed, became a tax-payer, and at times an educator of his children at his own expense; but the old idea of alienism passed laws to banish him, his wife, and children by thousands from the state, and threw him into loathsome jails as a common felon for returning to his native land.

It will be wise to remember that these were the acts of an enlightened, God-fearing people, the great mass of whom have passed beyond all earthly accountability. They were our fathers. I am the son and grandson of slave-holders. These were their faults; posterity will discover ours; but these things must be frankly, fearlessly taken into account if we are ever to understand the true interests of our peculiar state of society.

Why, then, did this notion that the man of color must always remain an alien stand so unshaken? We may readily recall how, under ancient systems, he rose not only to high privileges, but often to public station and power. Singularly, with us the trouble lay in a modern principle of liberty. The whole idea of American government rested on all men's equal, inalienable right to secure their life, liberty, and the pursuit of happiness by governments founded in their own consent. Hence, our Southern forefathers, shedding their blood, or ready to shed it, for this principle, yet proposing in equal good conscience to continue holding the American black man and mulatto and quadroon in slavery, had to anchor that conscience, their conduct, and their laws in the conviction that the man of African tincture was, not by his master's arbitrary assertion merely, but by nature and unalterably, an alien. If that hold should break, one single wave of irresistible inference would lift our whole Southern social fabric and dash it upon the rocks of negro emancipation and enfranchisement. How was it made secure? Not by books, though they were written among us from every possible point of view, but, with the mass of our slave-owners, by the calm hypothesis of a positive, intuitive knowledge. To them the statement was an axiom. They abandoned the methods of moral and intellectual reasoning, and fell back upon this assumption of a God-given instinct, nobler than reason, and which it was an insult to a freeman to ask him to prove on logical grounds.

Yet it was found not enough. The slave multiplied. Slavery was a dangerous institution. Few in the South to-day have any just idea how often the slave plotted for his freedom. Our Southern ancestors were a noble, manly people, springing from some of the most highly intelligent, aspiring, upright, and refined nations of the modern world; from the Huguenot, the French Chevalier, the Old Englander, the New Englander. Their acts were not always right; whose are? But for their peace of mind they had to believe them so. They therefore spoke much of the negro's contentment with that servile condition for which nature had designed him. Yet there was no escaping the knowledge that we dared not trust the slave caste with any power that could be withheld from them. So the perpetual alien was made also a perpetual menial, and the belief became fixed that this, too, was nature's decree, not ours.

Thus we stood at the close of the civil war. There were always a few Southerners who did not justify slavery, and many who cared nothing whether it was just or not. But what we have described was the general sentiment of good Southern people. There was one modifying sentiment. It related to the slave's spiritual interests. Thousands of pious masters and mistresses flatly broke the shameful laws that stood between their slaves and the Bible. Slavery was right; but religion, they held, was for the alien and menial as well as for the citizen and master. They could be alien and citizen, menial and master, in church as well as out; and they were.

Yet over against this lay another root of to-day's difficulties. This perpetuation of the alien, menial relation tended to perpetuate the vices that naturally cling to servility, dense ignorance and a hopeless separation from true liberty; and as we could not find it in our minds to blame slavery with this perpetuation, we could only assume as a further axiom that there was, by nature, a disqualifying moral taint in every drop of negro blood. The testimony of an Irish, German, Italian, French, or Spanish beggar in a court of justice was taken on its merits; but the colored man's was excluded by law wherever it weighed against a white man. The colored man was a prejudged culprit. The discipline of the plantation required that the difference between master and slave be never lost sight of by either. It made our master caste a solid mass, and fixed a common masterhood and subserviency between the ruling and the serving race. Every one of us grew up in the idea that he had, by birth and race, certain broad powers of police over any and every person of color.

All at once the tempest of war snapped off at the ground every one of these arbitrary relations, without removing a single one of the sentiments in which they stood rooted. Then, to fortify the freedman in the tenure of his new rights, he was given the ballot. Before this grim fact the notion of alienism, had it been standing alone, might have given way. The idea that slavery was right did begin to crumble almost at once. "As for slavery," said an old Creole sugar-planter and former slave-owner to me, "it was damnable." The revelation came like a sudden burst of light. It is one of the South's noblest poets who has but just said:

"I am a Southerner;

I love the South; I dared for her
To fight from Lookout to the sea,
With her proud banner over me:
But from my lips thanksgiving broke,
As God in battle-thunder spoke,
And that Black Idol, breeding drouth
And dearth of human sympathy
Throughout the sweet and sensuous South,
Was, with its chains and human yoke,
Blown hellward from the cannon's mouth,
While Freedom cheered behind the smoke!"

With like readiness might the old alien relation have given way if we could only, while letting that pass, have held fast by the other old ideas. But they were all bound together. See our embarrassment. For more than a hundred years we had made these sentiments the absolute essentials to our self-respect. And yet if we clung to them, how could we meet the freeman on equal terms in the political field? Even to lead would not compensate us; for the fundamental profession of American politics is that the leader is servant to his followers. It was too much. The ex-master and ex-slave—the quarter-deck and the fore-castle, as it were—could not come together. But neither could the American mind tolerate a continuance of martial law. The agonies of reconstruction followed.

The vote, after all, was a secondary point, and the robbery and bribery on one side, and whipping and killing on the other, were but huge accidents of the situation. The two main questions were really these: on the freedman's side, how to establish republican State government under the same recognition of his rights that the rest of Christendom accorded him; and on the former master's side, how to get back to the old semblance of republican State government, and—allowing that the freedman was *de facto* a voter—still to maintain a purely arbitrary superiority of all whites over all blacks, and a purely arbitrary equality of all blacks among themselves as an alien, menial, and dangerous class.

Exceptionally here and there someone in the master caste did throw off the old and accept the new ideas, and, if he would allow it, was instantly claimed as a leader by the newly liberated thousands around him. But just as promptly the old master race branded him also an alien reprobate, and in ninety-nine cases out of a hundred, if he had not already done so, he soon began to confirm by his actions the brand on his cheek. However, we need give no history here of the dreadful episode of reconstruction. Under an experimentative truce its issues rest to-day upon the pledge of the wiser leaders of the master class: Let us but remove the hireling demagogue, and we will see to it that the freedman is accorded a practical, complete, and cordial recognition of his equality with the white man before the law. As far as there has been any understanding at all, it is not that the originally desired ends of reconstruction have been abandoned, but that the men of North and South have agreed upon a new, gentle, and peaceable method for reaching them; that, without change as to the ends in view, compulsory reconstruction has been set aside and a voluntary reconstruction is on trial.

It is the fashion to say we paused to let the "feelings engendered by the war" pass away, and that they are passing. But let not these truths lead us into error. The sentiments we have been analyzing, and upon which we saw the old compulsory reconstruction go hard aground—these are not the "feelings engendered by the war." We must disentangle them from the "feelings engendered by the war," and by reconstruction. They are older than either. But for them slavery would have perished of itself, and emancipation and reconstruction been peaceful revolutions.

Indeed, as between master and slave, the "feelings engendered by the war" are too trivial, or at least were too short-lived, to demand our present notice. One relation and feeling the war destroyed: the patriarchal tie and its often really tender and benevolent sentiment of dependence and protection. When the slave became a freedman the sentiment of alienism became for the first time complete. The abandonment of this relation was not one-sided; the slave, even before the master, renounced it. Countless times, since reconstruction began, the master has tried, in what he believed to be everybody's interest, to play on that old sentiment. But he found it a harp without strings. The freedman could not formulate, but he could see, all our old ideas of autocracy and subserviency, of master and menial, of an arbitrarily fixed class to guide and rule, and another to be guided and ruled. He rejected the overture. The old master, his well-meant condescensions slighted, turned away estranged, and justified himself in passively withholding that simpler protection without patronage which any one American citizen, however exalted, owes to any other, however humble. Could the freedman in the bitterest of those days have consented to throw himself upon just that one old relation, he could have found a physical security for himself and his house such as could not, after years of effort, be given him by constitutional amendments, Congress, United States marshals, regiments of regulars, and ships of war. But he could not; the very nobility of the civilization that had held him in slavery had made him too much a man to go back to that shelter; and by his manly neglect to do so he has proved to us who once ruled over him that, be his relative standing among the races of men what it may, he is worthy to be free.

To be a free man is his still distant goal. Twice he has been a freedman. In the days of compulsory reconstruction he was freed in the presence of his master by that master's victorious foe. In these days of voluntary reconstruction he is virtually freed by the consent of his master, but the master retaining the exclusive right to define the bounds of his freedom. Many everywhere have taken up the idea that this state of affairs is the end to be desired and the end actually sought in reconstruction as handed over to the States. I do not charge such folly to the best intelligence of any American community; but I cannot ignore my own knowledge that the average thought of some regions rises to no better idea of the issue. The belief is all too common that the nation, having aimed at a wrong result and missed, has left us of the Southern States to get now such other result as we think best. I say this belief is not universal. There are those among us who see that America has no room for a state of society which makes its lower classes harmless by abridging their liberties, or, as one of the favored class lately said to me, has "got 'em so they don't give no trouble." There is a growing number who see that the one thing we cannot afford to tolerate at large is a class of people less than citizens; and that every interest in the land demands that the freedman be free to become in all things, as far as his own personal gifts will lift and sustain him, the same sort of American citizen he would be if, with the same intellectual and moral caliber, he were white.

Thus we reach the ultimate question of fact. Are the freedman's liberties suffering any real abridgment? The answer is easy. The letter of the laws, with but few exceptions, recognizes him as entitled to every right of an American citizen; and to some it may seem unimportant that there is scarcely one public relation of life in the South where he is not arbitrarily and unlawfully compelled to hold toward the white man the attitude of an alien, a menial, and a probable reprobate, by reason of his race and color. One of the marvels of future history will be that it was counted a small matter, by a majority of our nation, for six millions of people within it, made by its own decree a component part of it, to be subjected to a system of oppression so rank that nothing could make it seem small except the fact that they had already been ground under it for a century and a half.

Examine it. It proffers to the freedman a certain security of life and property, and then holds the respect of the community, that dearest of earthly boons, beyond his attainment. It gives him certain guarantees against thieves and robbers, and then holds him under the unearned contumely of the mass of good men and women. It acknowledges in constitutions and statutes his title to an American's freedom and aspirations, and then in daily practice heaps upon him in every public place the most odious distinctions, without giving ear to the humblest plea concerning mental or moral character. It spurns his ambition, tramples upon his languishing self-respect, and indignantly refuses to let him either buy with money, or earn by any excellence of inner life or outward behavior, the most momentary immunity from these public indignities even for his wife and daughters. Need we cram these pages with facts in evidence, as if these were charges denied and requiring to be proven? They are simply the present avowed and defended state of affairs peeled of its exteriors.

Nothing but the habit, generations old, of enduring it could make it endurable by men not in actual slavery. Were we whites of the South to remain every way as we are, and our six million blacks to give place to any sort of whites exactly their equals, man for man, in mind, morals, and wealth, provided only that they had tasted two years of American freedom, and were this same system of tyrannies attempted upon them, there would be as bloody an uprising as this continent has ever seen. We can say this quietly. There is not a scruple's weight of present danger. These six million freedmen are dominated by nine million whites immeasurably stronger than they, backed by the virtual consent of thirty-odd millions more. Indeed, nothing but the habit of oppression could make such oppression possible to a people of the intelligence and virtue of our Southern whites, and the invitation to practice it on millions of any other than the children of their former slaves would be spurned with a noble indignation.

Suppose, for a moment, the tables turned. Suppose the courts of our Southern States, while changing no laws requiring the impaneling of jurymen without distinction as to race, etc., should suddenly begin to draw their thousands of jurymen all black, and well-nigh every one of them counting not only himself, but all his race, better than any white man. Assuming that their average of intelligence and morals should be not below that of jurymen as now drawn, would a white man, for all that, choose to be tried in one of those courts? Would he suspect nothing? Could one persuade him that his chances of even justice were all they should be, or all they would be were the court not evading the law in order to sustain an outrageous distinction against him because of the accidents of his birth? Yet only read white man for black man, and black man for white man, and that—I speak as an eye-witness—has been the practice for years, and is still so to-day; an actual emasculation, in the case of six million people both as plaintiff and defendant, of the right of trial by jury.

In this and other practices the outrage falls upon the freedman. Does it stop there? Far from it. It is the first premise of American principles that whatever elevates the lower stratum of the people lifts all the rest, and whatever holds it down holds all down. For twenty years, therefore, the nation has been working to elevate the freedman. It counts this one of the great necessities of the hour. It has poured out its wealth publicly and privately for this purpose. It is confidently expected that it will soon bestow a royal gift of millions for the reduction of the illiteracy so largely shared by the blacks. Our Southern States are, and for twenty years have been, taxing themselves for the same end. The private charities alone of the other States have given twenty millions in the same good cause. Their colored seminaries, colleges, and normal schools dot our whole Southern country, and furnish our public colored schools with a large part of their teachers. All this and much more has been or is being done in order that, for the good of himself and everybody else in the land, the colored man may be elevated as quickly as possible from all the debasements of slavery and semi-slavery to the full stature and integrity of citizenship. And it is in the face of all this that the adherent of the old regime stands in the way to every public privilege and place—steamer landing, railway platform, theater, concert-hall, art display, public library, public school, court-house, church, everything—flourishing the hot branding-iron of ignominious distinctions. He forbids the freedman to go into the water until *he* is satisfied that he knows how to swim, and for fear he should learn hangs mill-stones about his neck. This is what we are told is a small matter that will settle itself. Yes, like a roosting curse, until the outraged intelligence of the South lifts its indignant protest against this stupid firing into our own ranks.

I say the outraged intelligence of the South; for there are thousands of Southern-born white men and women in the minority in all these places—in churches, courts, schools, libraries, theaters, concert-halls, and on steamers and railway carriages—who see the wrong and folly of these things, silently blush for them, and withhold their open protests only because their belief is unfortunately stronger in the futility of their counsel than in the power of a just cause. I do not justify their silence; but I affirm their sincerity and their goodly numbers. Of late years, when condemning these evils from the platform in Southern towns, I have repeatedly found that those who I had earlier been told were the men and women in whom the community placed most confidence and pride—they were the ones who, when I had spoken, came forward with warmest hand-grasps and expressions of thanks, and pointedly and cordially justified my every utterance. And were they the young South? Not by half! The gray-beards of the old times have always been among them, saying in effect, not by any means as converts, but as fellow-discoverers, "Whereas we were blind, now we see."

Another sort among our good Southern people make a similar but feebler admission, but with the time-worm proviso that expediency makes a more imperative demand than law, justice, or logic, and demands the preservation of the old order. Somebody must be outraged, it seems; and if not the freedman, then it must be a highly refined and enlightened race of people constantly offended and grossly discommoded, if not imposed upon, by a horde of tatterdemalions, male and female, crowding into a participation in their reserved privileges. Now, look at this plea. It is simply saying in another way that though the Southern whites far outnumber the blacks, and though we hold every element of power in greater degree than the blacks, and though the larger part of us claim to be sealed by nature as an exclusive upper class, and though we have the courts completely in our own hands, with the police on our right and the prisons on our left, and though we justly claim to be an intrepid people, and though we have a superb military experience, with ninety-nine hundredths of all the military equipment and no scarcity of all the accessories, yet with all the facts behind us we cannot make and enforce that intelligent and approximately just assortment of persons in public places and conveyances on the merits of exterior decency that is made in all other enlightened lands. On such a plea are made a distinction and separation that not only are crude, invidious, humiliating, and tyrannous, but which do not reach their ostensible end or come near it; and all that saves such a plea from being a confession of driveling imbecility is its utter speciousness. It is advanced sincerely; and yet nothing is easier to show than that these distinctions on the line of color are really made not from any necessity, but simply for their own sake—to preserve the old arbitrary supremacy of the master class over the menial without regard to the decency or indecency of appearance or manners in either the white individual or the colored.

See its every-day working. Any colored man gains unquestioned admission into innumerable places the moment he appears as the menial attendant of some white person, where he could not cross the threshold in his own right as a well-dressed and well-behaved master of himself. The contrast is even greater in the case of colored women. There could not be a system which when put into practice would more offensively condemn itself. It does more: it actually creates the confusion it pretends to prevent. It blunts the sensibilities of the ruling class themselves. It waives all strict demand for painstaking in either manners or dress of either master or menial, and, for one result, makes the average Southern railway coach more uncomfortable than the average of railway coaches elsewhere. It prompts the average Southern white passenger to find less offense in the presence of a profane, boisterous, or unclean white person than in that of a quiet, well-behaved colored man or woman attempting to travel on an equal footing with him without a white master or mistress. The holders of the old sentiments hold the opposite choice in scorn. It is only when we go on to say that there are regions where the riotous expulsion of a decent and peaceable colored person is preferred to his inoffensive company, that it may seem necessary to bring in evidence. And yet here again it is *prima facie* evidence; for the following extract was printed in the Selma (Alabama) "Times" not six months ago, and not as a complaint, but as a boast:

"A few days since, a negro minister, of this city, boarded the east-bound passenger train of the E. T. V. & G. Railway and took a seat in the coach occupied by white passengers. Some of the passengers complained to the conductor and brakemen, and expressed considerable dissatisfaction that they were forced to ride alongside of a negro. The railroad officials informed the complaintants that they were not authorized to force the colored passenger into the coach set apart for the negroes, and they would lay themselves liable should they do so. The white passengers then took the matter in their own hands and ordered the ebony-hued minister to take a seat in the next coach. He positively refused to obey orders, whereupon the white men gave him a sound flogging and forced him to a seat among his own color and equals. We learned yesterday that the vanquished preacher was unable to fill his pulpit on account of the severe chastisement inflicted upon him. Now (says the delighted editor) the query that puzzles is, 'Who did the flogging?'"

And as good an answer as we can give is that likely enough they were some of the men for whom the whole South has come to a halt to let them get over the "feelings engendered by the war." Must such men, such acts, such sentiments, stand alone to represent us of the South before an enlightened world? No. I say, as a citizen of an extreme Southern State, a native of Louisiana, an ex-Confederate soldier, and a lover of my home, my city, and my State, as well as of my country, that this is not the best sentiment in the South, nor the sentiment of her best intelligence; and that it would not ride up and down that beautiful land dominating and domineering were it not for its tremendous power as the *traditional* sentiment of a conservative people. But is not silent endurance criminal? I cannot but repeat my own words, spoken near the scene and about the time of this event. Speech may be silvern and silence golden; but if a lump of gold is only big enough, it can drag us to the bottom of the sea and hold us there while all the world sails over us.

The laws passed in the days of compulsory reconstruction requiring "equal accommodations," etc., for colored and white persons were freedmen's follies. On their face they defeated their ends; for even in theory they at once reduced to half all opportunity for those more reasonable and mutually agreeable self-assortments which public assemblages and groups of passengers find it best to make in all other enlightened countries, making them on the score of conduct, dress, and price. They also led the whites to overlook what they would have seen instantly had these invidious distinctions been made against themselves: that their offense does not vanish at the guarantee against the loss of physical comforts. But we made, and are still making, a mistake beyond even this. For years many of us have carelessly taken for granted that these laws were being carried out in some shape that removed all just ground of complaint. It is common to say, "We allow the man of color to go and come at will, only let him sit apart in a place marked off for him." But marked off how? So as to mark him instantly as a menial. Not by railings and partitions merely, which, raised against any other class in the United States with the same invidious intent, would be kicked down as fast as put up, but by giving him besides, in every instance and without recourse, the most uncomfortable, uncleanest, and unsafest place; and the unsafety, uncleanness, and discomfort of most of these places are a shame to any community pretending to practice public justice. If any one can think the freedman does not feel the indignities thus heaped upon him, let him take up any paper printer for colored men's patronage, or ask any colored man of known courageous utterance. Hear them:

"We ask not Congress, nor the Legislature, nor any other power, to remedy these evils, but we ask the people among whom we live. Those who *can* remedy them if they *will*. Those who have a high sense of honor and a deep moral feeling. Those who have one vestige of human sympathy left.... Those are the ones we ask to protect us in our weakness and ill-treatments.... As soon as the colored man is treated by the white man as a *man*, that harmony and pleasant feeling which should characterize all races which dwell together, shall be the bond of peace between them."

Surely their evidence is good enough to prove their own feelings. We need not lean upon it here for anything else. I shall not bring forward a single statement of fact from them or any of their white friends who, as teachers and missionaries, share many of their humiliations, though my desk is covered with them. But I beg to make the same citation from my own experience that I made last June in the far South. It was this: One hot night in September of last year I was traveling by rail in the State of Alabama. At rather late bed-time there came aboard the train a young mother and her little daughter of three or four years. They were neatly and tastefully dressed in cool, fresh muslins, and as the train went on its way they sat together very still and quiet. At the next station there came aboard a most melancholy and revolting company. In filthy rags, with vile odors and the clanking of shackles and chains, nine penitentiary convicts chained to one chain, and ten more chained to another, dragged laboriously into the compartment of the car where in one corner sat this mother and child, and packed it full, and the train moved on. The keeper of the convicts told me he should take them in that car two hundred miles that night. They were going to the mines. My seat was not in that car, and I staid in it but a moment. It stank insufferably. I returned to my own place in the coach behind, where there was, and had all the time been, plenty of room. But the mother and child sat on in silence in that foul hole, the conductor having distinctly refused them admission elsewhere because they were of African blood, and not because the mother was, but because she was *not*, engaged at the moment in menial service. Had the child been white, and the mother not its natural but its hired guardian, she could have sat anywhere in the train, and no one would have ventured to object, even had she been as black as the mouth of the coal-pit to which her loathsome follow-passengers were being carried in chains.

Such is the incident as I saw it. But the illustration would be incomplete here were I not allowed to add the comments I made upon it when in June last I recounted it, and to state the two opposite tempers in which my words were received. I said: "These are the facts. And yet you know and I know we belong to communities that, after years of hoping for, are at last taking comfort in the assurance of the nation's highest courts that no law can reach and stop this shameful foul play until we choose to enact a law to that end ourselves." And now the east and north and west of our great and prosperous and happy country, and the rest of the civilized world, as far as it knows our case, are standing and waiting to see what we will write upon the white page of to-day's and to-morrow's history, now that we are simply on our honor and on the mettle of our far and peculiarly famed Southern instinct. How long, then, shall we stand off from such ringing moral questions as these on the flimsy plea that they have a political value, and, scrutinizing the Constitution, keep saying, "Is it so nominated in the bond? I cannot find it; 'tis not in the bond."

With the temper that promptly resented these words through many newspapers of the neighboring regions there can be no propriety in wrangling. When regions so estranged from the world's thought carry their resentment no further than a little harmless invective, it is but fair to welcome it as a sign of progress. If communities nearer the great centers of thought grow impatient with them, how shall we resent the impatience of these remoter ones when their oldest traditions are, as it seems to them, ruthlessly assailed? There is but one right thing to do: it is to pour in upon them our reiterations of the truth without malice and without stint.

But I have a much better word to say. It is for those who, not voiced by the newspapers around them, showed, both then and constantly afterward in public and private during my two days' subsequent travel and sojourn in the region, by their cordial, frequent, specific approval of my words, that a better intelligence is longing to see the evils of the old régime supplanted by a wiser and more humane public sentiment and practice. And I must repeat my conviction that if the unconscious habit of oppression were not already there, a scheme so gross, irrational, unjust, and inefficient as our present caste distinctions could not find place among a people so generally intelligent and high-minded. I ask attention to their bad influence in a direction not often noticed.

In studying, about a year ago, the practice of letting out public convicts to private lessees to serve out their sentences under private management, I found that it does not belong to all our once slave States nor to all our once seceded States. Only it is no longer in practice outside of them. Under our present condition in the South, it is beyond possibility that the individual black should behave mischievously without offensively rearousing the old sentiments of the still dominant white man. As we have seen, too, the white man virtually monopolizes the jury-box. Add another fact: the Southern States have entered upon a new era of material development. Now, if with these conditions in force the public mind has been captivated by glowing pictures of the remunerative economy of the convict-lease system, and by the seductive spectacle of mines and railways, turnpikes, and levees, that everybody wants and nobody wants to pay for, growing apace by convict labor that seems to cost nothing, we may almost assert beforehand that the popular mind will—not so maliciously as unreflectingly—yield to the tremendous temptation to hustle the misbehaving black man into the State prison under extravagant sentence, and sell his labor to the highest bidder who will use him in the construction of public works. For ignorance of the awful condition of these penitentiaries is extreme and general, and the hasty, half-conscious assumption naturally is, that the culprit will survive this term of sentence, and its fierce discipline "teach him to behave himself."

But we need not argue from cause to effect only. Nor need I repeat one of the many painful rumors that poured in upon me the moment I began to investigate this point. The official testimony of the prisons themselves is before the world to establish the conjectures that spring from our reasoning. After the erroneous takings of the census of 1880 in South Carolina had been corrected, the population was shown to consist of about twenty blacks to every thirteen whites. One would therefore look for a preponderance of blacks on the prison lists; and inasmuch as they are a people only twenty years ago released from servile captivity, one would not be surprised to see that preponderance large. Yet, when the actual numbers confront us, our speculations are stopped with a rude shock; for what is to account for the fact that in 1881 there were committed to the State prison at Columbia, South Carolina, 406 colored persons and but 25 whites? The proportion of blacks sentenced to the whole black population was one to every 1488; that of the whites to the white population was but one to every 15,644. In Georgia the white inhabitants decidedly outnumber the blacks; yet in the State penitentiary, October 20, 1880, there were 115 whites and 1071 colored; or if we reject the summary of its tables and refer to the tables themselves (for the one does not agree with the other), there were but 102 whites and 1083 colored. Yet of 52 pardons granted in the two years then closing, 22 were to whites and only 30 to blacks. If this be a dark record, what shall we say of the records of lynch law? But for them there is not room here.

A far pleasanter aspect of our subject shows itself when we turn from courts and prisons to the school-house. And the explanation is simple. Were our educational affairs in the hands of that not high average of the community commonly seen in jury-boxes, with their transient sense of accountability and their crude notions of public interests, there would most likely be no such pleasant contrast. But with us of the South, as elsewhere, there is a fairly honest effort to keep the public-school interests in the hands of the State's most highly trained intelligence. Hence our public educational work is a compromise between the unprogressive prejudices of the general mass of the whites and the progressive intelligence of their best minds. Practically, through the great majority of our higher educational officers, we are fairly converted to the imperative necessity of elevating the colored man intellectually, and are beginning to see very plainly that the whole community is sinned against in every act or attitude of oppression, however gross or however refined.

Yet one thing must be said. I believe it is wise that all have agreed not to handicap education with the race question, but to make a complete surrender of that issue, and let it find adjustment elsewhere first and in the schools last. And yet, in simple truth and justice and in the kindest spirit, we ought to file one exception for that inevitable hour when the whole question must be met. There can be no more real justice in pursuing the freedman's children with humiliating arbitrary distinctions and separations in the schoolhouses than in putting them upon him in other places. If, growing out of their peculiar mental structure, there are good and just reasons for their isolation, by all means let them be proved and known; but it is simply tyrannous to assume them without proof. I know that just here looms up the huge bugbear of Social Equality. Our eyes are filled with absurd visions of all Shantytown pouring its hordes of unwashed imps into the company and companionship of our own sunny-headed darlings. What utter nonsense! As if our public schools had no gauge of cleanliness, decorum, or moral character! Social Equality? What a godsend it would be if the advocates of the old Southern regime could only see that the color line points straight in the direction of social equality by tending toward the equalization of all whites on one side of the line and of all blacks on the other. We may reach the moon some day, not social equality; but the only class that really effects anything toward it are the makers and holders of arbitrary and artificial social distinctions interfering with society's natural self-distribution. Even the little children everywhere are taught, and begin to learn almost with their A B C, that they will find, and must be guided by, the same variations of the social scale in the public school as out of it; and it is no small mistake to put them or their parents off their guard by this cheap separation on the line of color.

But some will say this is not a purely artificial distinction. We hear much about race instinct. The most of it, I fear, is pure twaddle. It may be there is such a thing. We do not know. It is not proved. And even if it were established, it would not necessarily be a proper moral guide. We subordinate instinct to society's best interests as apprehended in the light of reason. If there is such a thing, it behaves with strange malignity toward the remnants of African blood in individuals principally of our own race, and with singular indulgence to the descendants of—for example—Pocohontas. Of mere race *feeling* we all know there is no scarcity. Who is stranger to it? And as another man's motive of private preference no one has a right to forbid it or require it. But as to its being an instinct, one thing is plain: if there is such an instinct, so far from excusing the malignant indignities practiced in its name, it furnishes their final condemnation; for it stands to reason that just in degree as it is a real thing it will take care of itself.

It has often been seen to do so; whether it is real or imaginary. I have seen in New Orleans a Sunday-school of white children every Sunday afternoon take possession of its two rooms immediately upon their being vacated by a black school of equal or somewhat larger numbers. The teachers of the colored school are both white and black, and among the white teachers are young ladies and gentlemen of the highest social standing. The pupils of the two schools are alike neatly attired, orderly, and in every respect inoffensive to each other. I have seen the two races sitting in the same public high-school and grammar-school rooms, reciting in the same classes and taking recess on the same ground at the same time, without one particle of detriment that any one ever pretended to discover, although the fiercest enemies of the system swarmed about it on every side. And when in the light of these observations I reflect upon the enormous educational task our Southern States have before them, the inadequacy of their own means for performing it, the hoped-for beneficence of the general Government, the sparseness with which so much of our Southern population is distributed over the land, the thousands of school districts where, consequently, the multiplication of schools must involve both increase of expense and reduction of efficiency, I must enter some demurer to the enforcement of the tyrannous sentiments of the old régime until wise experiments have established better reasons than I have yet heard given.

What need to say more? The question is answered. Is the freedman a free man? No. We have considered his position in a land whence nothing can, and no man has a shadow of right to, drive him, and where he is multiplying as only oppression can multiply a people. We have carefully analyzed his relations to the finer and prouder race, with which he shares the ownership and citizenship of a region large enough for ten times the number of both. Without accepting one word of his testimony, we have shown that the laws made for his protection against the habits of suspicion and oppression in his late master are being constantly set aside, not for their defects, but for such merit as they possess. We have shown that the very natural source of these oppressions is the surviving sentiments of an extinct and now universally execrated institution; sentiments which no intelligent or moral people should harbor a moment after the admission that slavery was a moral mistake. We have shown the outrageousness of these tyrannies in some of their workings, and how distinctly they antagonize every State and national interest involved in the elevation of the colored race. Is it not well to have done so? For, I say again, the question has reached a moment of special importance. The South stands on her honor before the clean equities of the issue. It is no longer whether constitutional amendments, but whether the eternal principles of justice, are violated. And the answer must—it shall—come from the South. And it shall be practical. It will not cost much. We have had a strange experience: the withholding of simple rights has cost us much blood; such concessions of them as we have made have never yet cost a drop. The answer is coming. Is politics in the way? Then let it clear the track or get run over, just as it prefers. But, as I have said over and over to my brethren in the South, I take upon me to say again here, that there is a moral and intellectual intelligence there which is not going to be much longer beguiled out of its moral right of way by questions of political punctilio, but will seek that plane of universal justice and equity which it is every people's duty before God to seek, not along the line of politics,—God forbid!—but across it and across it and across it as many times as it may lie across the path, until the whole people of every once slaveholding State can stand up as one man, saying, "Is the freedman a free man?" and the whole world shall answer, "Yes."

Ruth McEnery Stuart (1849–1917)

Ruth McEnery, the oldest of eight children, was born Mary Routh McEnery in Marksville, Louisiana, in 1849, to her Scottish mother, Mary Routh Stirling and Irish father, James McEnery. She changed the spelling of her name to Ruth after she began her literary career, which was remarkable, as she published over fifteen volumes of primarily short fiction. When we think of late 19th- and early 20th-century Louisiana women writers, Kate Chopin and Grace King usually come to mind; however, according to an article in the 1904 literary journal, *The Bookman*, Stuart was a more popular and accomplished writer than her female contemporaries.[1] Nonetheless, she still remains more obscure than her contemporaries today.

When she was only three years old, the McEnery's moved from rural Marksville in Avoyelles Parish to New Orleans, where Ruth was educated in private and public schools. After the Civil War, it was necessary that she find employment in those same schools, so she taught at the Loquet-LeRoy Institute, a finishing school for young women. She remained in New Orleans until 1879 when she married Alfred Oden Stuart, a widower twenty-eight years her senior and father of eleven children, and they moved to his plantation in Washington, Arkansas, a place that became the inspiration for much of her fiction.

Ruth and Alfred had one son, Stirling, in 1883, but unfortunately, Alfred died later that same year, and like Kate Chopin, she turned to writing to make a living when she was widowed. Five years later, Stuart published "Uncle Mingo's Speculations," in *New Princeton Review,* followed by "Lamentations of Jeremiah Johnson" later that same year in *Harper's New Monthly Review.* Her writing career had taken off, and also that same year, 1888, she moved with her son and her sister Sarah to New York City, where she lived and wrote until her death in 1917.

Most critics agree that her early short fiction is her strongest, particularly her works capturing the black plantation workers based on those she came to know in Arkansas. Plantation fiction, like that of Charles Waddell Chesnutt and Joel Chandler Harris, was wildly popular at the time, yet Harris, the most widely read author of plantation fiction, wrote to Stuart saying, "You have got nearer the heart of the negro than any of us."[2] Her best writing relies heavily on the African-American dialect of the time, so it is difficult for some readers today, but she captures what she felt was a realistic picture of "the Southern Negro." Today it seems a racist and overly romanticized version of the life of poor freed slaves after the Civil War, and it might have seemed that way at the time too for her Northern readers.

Stuart, a young widow herself, often addresses marriage and widowhood in her fiction, and one of her best stories to do so is "The Widder Johnsing," published in her 1898 collection, *Golden Wedding and Other Tales.* Robert Bush calls Lize Ann, the protagonist of this short story, Stuart's Wife of Bath, and she is indeed the marrying kind. The story opens with the funeral of her third husband, Jake, whom she wooed away from his wife and son, who attend the wake. Throughout most of the story, readers, like the townsfolk, see no reason to doubt Lize Ann's sincere grief over Jake's death; however, by the end of the story, we discover that she has been plotting to snare the finest catch in town, the Reverend Mr. Langford. Her female protagonists are often very cunning and resourceful in providing for themselves: no victims here.

Stuart's later writing career suffered perhaps due to the tragedy of losing her only son in 1905. She continued writing, and her last work, *The Cocoon,* a novella, was published in 1915. She died two years later in New York, and was buried in New Orleans, where, two years before her death, the Ruth McEnery Stuart Clan, a women's literary and social club, was founded by Judith Hyams Douglas, a friend of Stuart's. The clan is still active today and now has male members as well. There has also been a recent resurgence of interest in Stuart's writing. Many of her books are now available in bookstores and online, much more accessible than they were just a decade or two ago.

---

1   Robert Bush, "Louisiana Prose Fiction, 1870-1900." (Diss: Iowa State U, 1957), 303-55. Print. Much of the biographical information presented here can be found in Bush.

2   Ibid., 303-4.

The Widder Johnsing

"**M**onkey, monkey, bottle o' beer, How many monkeys have we here? One, two, three; out goes she!"

"No use ter try ter hoi' 'er. She des gwine f'om fits ter convulsions, and f'om convulsions back inter fits!"

Sister Temperance Tias raised her hands and spoke low. She had just come out of the room of sorrow.

Jake Johnson was dead, and Lize Ann Johnson again a widow. The "other room" in the little cabin was crowded with visitors the old, the young, the pious, the thoughtless, the frivolous all teeming with curiosity, and bursting into expressions of sympathy, each anxious to look upon the ever-interesting face of death, everyone eager to " he'p hoi' Sis' Lize Ann."

But Temperance held sway on this as on all similar occasions on the plantation, and no one would dare to cross the threshold from "the other room " until she should make the formal announcement, "De corpse is perpared ter receive 'is frien's," and even then there would be the tedium of precedence to undergo.

It was tiresome, but it paid in the end, for long before midnight every visitor should have had his turn to pass in and take a look. Then would begin an informal, unrestricted circulation between the two rooms, when the so-disposed might " choose pardners," and sit out on the little porch, or in the yard on benches brought in from the church, and distributed about for that purpose.

Here they would pleasantly gather about in groups with social informality, and freely discuss such newly discovered virtues of the deceased as a fresh retrospect revealed, or employ themselves with their own more pressing romances, as they saw fit.

There were many present, inside and at the doors, who eagerly anticipated this later hour, and were even now casting about for "pardners;" but Sister Temperance was not one of these. Now was the hour of her triumph. It was she alone, excepting the few, selected by herself, who were at this moment making a last toilet for the departed, who had looked upon the face of the dead.

She was even ahead of the doctors, who, as the patient had died between visits, did not yet know the news.

As she was supreme authority upon the case in all its bearings, whenever she appeared at the door between the two rooms the crowd pressed eagerly forward. They were so anxious for the very latest bulletin.

"F'om convulsions inter fits! Umh!" repeated the foremost sister, echoing Temperance's words.

"Yas, an' back ag'in!" reiterated the oracle. "She des come thoo a fit, an' de way she gwine orn now, I s'picion de nex' gwine be a reverind convulsion! She taken it hard, I tell yer!" And Sister Temperance quietly, cruelly closed the door, and withdrew into the scene of action,

"Sis' Lize Ann ought ter be helt," ventured a robust sister near the door.

"Or tied, one," added another.

"I knowed she keered mo' fur Brer Jake 'n she let orn," suggested a third. "Lize Ann don't mean no harm by her orf-handed ways. She des kep' 'er love all ter 'erse'f."

So ran the gossip of "the other room," when Temperance reappeared at the door.

"Sis' Calline Taylor, yo' services is requi'ed." She spoke with a suppressed tone of marked distinctness and a dignity that was inimitable, where upon a portly dame at the farthest corner of the room began to elbow her way through the crowd, who regarded her with new respect as she entered the chamber of death, a shrill scream from the new-made widow adding its glamour to her honors, as, with a loud groan, she closed the door behind her.

A stillness now fell upon the assembly, disturbed only by an occasional moan, until Sister Phyllis, a leader in things spiritual, broke the silence.

"Sis' Calline Taylor is a proud han' ter hoi' down fits, but I hope she'll speak a word in season fur sperityal comfort."

"Sis' Tempunce callin' out Scripture ev'y time she see 'er ease up," said old Black Sal. "Lize Ann in good han's, po' soul! Look like she is got good 'casion ter grieve. Seem like she's born ter widderhood."

"Po' Jake! Ycr reck'n she gwine bury 'im 'longside ol' Alick an' Steve?"—her former husbands.

"In co'se. 'Tain' no use dividin' up grief an' sowin' a pusson's sorrer broadcas', 'caze."

The opening door commanded silence again.

"Brer Jake's face changin' mightily!" said Temperance, as she stood again before them. "De way hit's a-settlin', I b'lieve he done foun' peace ter his soul."

"Is 'is eyes shet?"

"De lef' eye open des a leetle teenchy tinechy bit."

"Look fur a chile ter die nex' a boy chile. Yer say de lef eye open, ain't yer!"

"Yas de one todes de chimbly. He layin' catti-cornders o' de baid, wid 'is foots ter de top."

"Catti-cornders! Fmh!"

"Yas, an' wid 'is haid down todes de foot."

"Eh, Lord! Haids er foots is all one ter po' Jake now."

"Is yer gwine plat 'is fingers, Sis' Tempunce?"

"His fingers done platted, an' do way I done twissen 'em in an' out, over an' under, dee gwine stay tell Gab'iel call fur 'is ban'!"

"Umh!"

"Eh, Lord! An' is yer done comb 'is haid, Sis' Tempunce?"

"I des done wropp'n an' twissen it good, an' I 'low' ter let it out fur de fun'al to-morrer. I knowed Jake 'd be mo' satisfider ef he knowed it 'd be in its f us' granjer at the fun'al an' Sis' Lize Ann too. She say she 'ain't nuver is had no sec- on'-class buryin's, an' she ain' gwine have none. Time Alick died she lay in a trance two days, an' de brass ban' at de fun'al nuver fazed 'er! An' y' all ricollec' how she taken ter de woods an' had ter be ketched time Steve was kilt, an' now she des a-stavin' it orf brave as she kin on convulsions an' fits! Look like when a pusson taken sorrer so hard, Gord would sho'ly spare de scourgin' rod."

"Yas, but yer know what de preacher say 'Gord sen' a tempes' o' win' ter de shorn lamb;'"

"Yas indeedy," said another, a religious celebrity, "an' we daresn't jedge de Jedge!"

"Maybe sometimes Gord sen' a tempes' o' win' ter de shorn lamb ter meek it run an' hide in de Shepherd's fol'. Pray Gord dis searchin' win' o' jedgmint gwine blow po' Sis' Lize Ann inter de green pastures o' de kingdom!"

"Amen!" came solemnly from several directions.

An incisive shriek from within, which startled the speakers into another awe-stricken silence, summoned Temperance back in haste to her post.

Crowds were gathering without the doors now, and the twinkle of lanterns approaching over the fields and through the wood promised a popular attendance at the wake, which, after much tedious waiting, was at last formally opened. Temper ance herself swung wide the dividing door, and hesitating a moment as she stood before them, that the announcement should gain in effect by a prelude of silence, she said, with marked solem nity:

"De corpse is now perpared ter receive 'is frien's! Ef," she continued, after another pause "ef so be any pusson present is nigh kin ter de lately deceased daid corpse, let 'em please ter step in fust at de haid o' de line."

A half-minute of inquiring silence ensued, and that the first to break it by stepping forward was a former discarded wife of the deceased caused no comment. She led by the hand a small boy, whom all knew to be the dead man's son, and it was with distinct deference that the crowd parted to let them pass in. Just as they were entering, a stir was heard at the outer door.

"Heah comes de corpse's mammy and daddy," one said, in an audible whisper.

It was true. The old parents, who lived some miles distant, had just arrived. The throng had fallen well back now, clearing a free passage across the room. With a loud groan and extend ed arms, Temperance glided down the opening to meet the aged couple, who sobbed aloud as they tremulously followed her into the presence of the dead.

The former wife and awe-stricken child had already entered, and that they all, with the new- made widow, who rocked to and fro at the head of the corpse, wept together, confessed sharers in a common sorrow, was quite in the natural order of things.

The procession of guests now began to pass through, making a circuit of the table on which the body lay, and as they moved out the door, someone raised a hymn. A group in the yard caught it up, and soon the woods echoed with the weird rhythmic melody. All night long the singing continued, carried along by new recruits as the first voices grew weary and dropped out. If there was some giggling and love-making among the young people, it was discreetly kept in the shadowy corners, and wounded no one's feelings.

The widow took no rest during the night. When exhausted from violent emotion, she fell into a rhythmic moan, accompanied by corresponding swaying to and fro of her body a movement at once unyielding and restful.

The church folk were watching her with a keen interest, and indeed so were the worldlings, for this was Lize Ann's third widowhood within the short space of five years, and each of the other funerals had been practically but an inaugural service to a most remarkable career. As girl first, and twice as widow, she had been a conspicuous and, if truth must be told, rather a notorious figure in colored circles. Three times she had voluntarily married into quiet life, and welcomed with her chosen partner the seclusion of wedded domesticity; but during the intervals she had played promiscuous havoc with the matrimonial felicity of her neighbors, to such an extent that it was a confessed relief when she had finally walked up the aisle with Jake Johnson, as, by taking one woman's husband, she had brought peace of mind to a score of anxious wives.

It is true that Jake had been lawfully wedded to the first woman, but the ceremony had occurred in another parish some years before, and was practically obsolete, and so the church, taking its cue from nature, which does not set eyes in the back of one's head, made no indiscreet retrospective investigations, but, in the professed guise of a peace-maker, pronounced its benediction upon the new pair.

The deserted wife had soon likewise repaired her loss, whether with benefit of clergy or not, it is not ours to say, but when she returned to mourn at the funeral, it was not as one who had refused to be comforted. She felt a certain secret triumph in bringing her boy to gaze for the last time upon the face of his father. It was more than the childless woman, who sat, acknowledged chief mourner, at the head of the corpse could do.

There was a look of half -savage defiance upon her face as she lifted the little fellow up and said, in an audible voice: "Take one las' look at yo' daddy, Jakey. Dat's yo' own Gord-blessed father, an' you ain't nuver gwine see 'im no mo', tell yer meet 'im in de King dom come, whar dey ain't no marryin', neither gimrib in marriage"; and she added, in an undertone, with a significant sniffle, "nur borryin', nuther."

She knew that she whom it could offend would not hear this last remark, as her ears were filled with her own wails, but the words were not lost upon the crowd.

The little child, frightened and excited, began to cry aloud.

"Let 'im cry," said one. "D'ain't nobody got a better right."

"He feel his loss, po' chile!"

"Blood's thicker'n water ev'y time."

"Yas, blood will tell. Look like de po' chile's heart was rendered in two quick's he looked at 'is pa."

Such sympathetic remarks as these, showing the direction of the ultimate sentiment of the people, reached the mother's ears, and encouraged her to raise her head a fraction higher than before, as, pacifying the weeping child, she passed out and went home.

The funeral took place on the afternoon following, and, to the surprise of all, the mourning widow behaved with wonderful self-control during all the harrowing ceremony.

Only when the last clod fell upon the grave did she throw up her hands, and with a shriek fall over in a faint, and have to be "toted" back to the wagon in which she had come.

If some were curious to see what direction her grief would take, they had some time to wait. She had never before taken long to declare herself, and on each former occasion the declaration had been one of war, a worldly, rioting, rollicking war upon the men.

During both her previous widowhoods she had danced longer and higher, laughed oftener and louder, dressed more gaudily and effectively, than all the women on three contiguous plantations put together; and when, in these well-remembered days, she had passed down the road on Sunday evenings, and chosen to peep over her shoulders with dreamy half-closed eyes at some special man whom it pleased her mood to ensnare, he had no more been able to help following her than he had been able to help lying to his wife or sweetheart about it afterward.

The sympathy expressed for her at Jake's funeral had been sincere. No negro ever resists any noisy demonstration of grief, and each of her moans and screams had found responsive echo in more than one sympathetic heart.

But now the funeral was over, Jake was dead and gone, and the state of affairs so exact a restoration to a recent well-remembered condition that it was not strange that the sisters wondered with some concern what she would do.

They had felt touched when she had fainted away at the funeral, and yet there were those, and among them his good wife, who had not failed to observe that she had fallen squarely into Pete Richards's arms.

Now everyone knew that she had once led Pete a dance, and that for a time it seemed a question whether he or Jake Johnson should be the coming man.

Of course this opportune fainting might have been accidental, and it may be that Pete's mother was supercensorious when, on her return from the funeral, she had said, as she lit her pipe:

"Dat gal Lize Ann is a she-devil."

But her more discreet daughter-in-law, excepting that she thrashed the children all round, gave no sign that she was troubled.

For the first few months of her recovered widowhood Lize Ann was conspicuous only by her absence from congregations of all sorts, as well as by her mournful and persistent refusal to speak with any one on the subject of her grief, or, indeed, to speak at all.

There was neither pleasure nor profit in sitting down and looking at a person who never opened her lips, and so, after oft-repeated but ineffectual visits of condolence, the sisters finally stopped visiting her cabin.

They saw that she had philosophically taken up the burden of practical life again, in the shape of a family washing, which she carried from the village to her cabin poised on her head, but the old abandon had departed from her gait, and those who chanced to meet her in the road said that her only passing recognition was a groan.

Alone in her isolated cabin, the woman so recently celebrated for her social proclivities ranged her wash-tubs against the wall; alone she soaked, washed, rinsed, starched, and ironed; and, when the week's routine of labor was over, alone she sat within her cabin door to rest.

For a long time old Nancy Price or Hester Ann Jennings, the two superannuated old crones on the plantation, moved by curiosity and an irresistible impulse to "talk erligion"to so fitting a subject, had continued occasionally to drop in to see the silent woman, but they always came away shaking their heads and declining to stake their reputations on any formulated prophecy as to just how, when, where, or in what direction Lize Ann would come out of her grief. That she was deliberately poising herself for a spring they felt sure, and yet their only prognostications were always prudently ambiguous.

When, however, the widow had consistently for five long months maintained her position as a broken-hearted recluse not to be approached or consoled, the people began to regard her with a degree of genuine respect; and when one Sunday morning the gathering congregation discovered her sitting in church, a solitary figure in black, on the very last of the Amen pews in the corner, they were moved to sympathy.

She had even avoided a sensational entrance by coming early. Her conduct seemed really genuine, and yet it must be confessed that even in view of the doleful figure she made, there were several women present who were a little less comfortable beside their lovers and husbands after they saw her.

If the wives had but known it, however, they need have had no fear. Jake's deserted wife and child had always weighed painfully upon Lize Ann's consciousness. Even after his death they had come in, diverting and intercepting sympathy that she felt should have been hers. When she married again she would have an unencumbered, free man, all her own.

As she was first at service to-day, she was last to depart, and so pointedly did she wait for the others to go, that not a sister in church had the temerity to approach her with a welcoming hand, or to join her as she walked home. And this was but the beginning. From this time forward the little mourning figure was at every meeting, and when the minister begged such as desired salvation to remain to be prayed for, she knelt and stayed. When, however, the elders or sisters sought her out, and, kneeling beside her, questioned her as to the state of her soul, she only groaned and kept silence.

The brethren were really troubled. They had never encountered sorrow or conviction of sin quite so obstinate, so intangible, so speechless, as this. The minister, Brother Langford, had remembered her sorrowing spirit in an impersonal way, and had colored his sermons with tender appeals to such as mourned and were heavy-laden with grief.

But the truth was, the Reverend Mr. Langford, a tall, handsome bachelor of thirty years or there abouts, was regarded as the best catch in the parish, and had he been half so magnetic in his personality or half so persuasive of speech, all the dusky maids in the country would have been setting their feathered caps for him.

When he conducted the meetings there were always so many boisterous births into the Kingdom all around him, when the regenerate called aloud as they danced, swayed, or swooned for "Brother Langford," that he had not found time to seek out the silent mourners, and so had not yet found himself face to face with the widow. Finally, however, one Sunday night, just as he passed before her, Lize Ann heaved one of her very best moans.

He was on his knees at her side in a moment. Bending his head very low, he asked, in a voice soft and tender, laying his hand the while gently upon her shoulder, "'Ain't you foun' peace yit, Sis' Johnsing?"

She groaned again.

"What is yo' mos' chiefes' sorrer, Sister John- sing? Is yo' heart mo' grieveder f 'om partin' wid yo' dear belovin' pardner, or is yo' soul weighted down wid a sense o' inhuman guilt? Speak out an' tell me, my sister, how yo' trouble seem ter shape itse'f."

But the widow, though she turned up to him her dry beseeching eyes, only groaned again.

"Can't you speak ter yo' preacher, Sis' John- sing? He crave in 'is heart ter he'p you."

Again she looked into his face, and now, with quivering lip, began to speak: "I can't talk'heah, Brer Langford; I ain't fittin'; my heart's clean broke. I ain't nothin' but des a miser'ble out- cas'. Seem lak even Gord 'isse'f done cas' me orf. I des comes an' goes lak a hongry suck-aig dorg wha' nobody don't claim, a-skulkin' roun' heah in a back seat all by my lone se'f, tryin' ter pick up a little crumb wha' fall f'om de table. But seem lak de feas' is too good fur me. I goes back ter my little dark cabin mo' harder-hearted an' mo' sinf uler 'n I was bef o'. Des de ve'y glimsh o' dat empty cabin seem lak hit turn my heart tev stone."

She dropped her eyes, and as she bent forward, a tear fell upon the young man's hand.

His voice was even tenderer than before when he spoke again. "It is a hard lot, my po' sister, but I am positive sho' dat de sisters an' brers o' de chu'ch would come ter you an' try ter comfort yo' soul ef you would give 'em courage fur ter do so."

"You don't know me, Brer Langford, er you wouldn't name sech a word ter me. I's a sinner, an' a sinner what love sin. Look lak de wus a sin is, de mo' hit tas'es lak sugar in my mouf. I can't trus' myse'f ter set down an' talk wid dese heah brers an' sisters wha' I knows is one-half sperit- yal an' fo'-quarters playin' ketcher wid de devil. I can't trust myse'f wid' em tell Gord set my soul free f'om sin. I'd soon be howlin' happy on de devil's side des lak I was befo', facin' two-forty on de shell road ter perditiom."

"I see, my po' sister I see whar yo' trouble lay."

"Yas, an' dat's huccome I tooken to yer, 'caze I knowed you is got de sperityal eye to see it. You knows I's right when I say ter you dat I ain't gwine set down in my cabin an' hoi' speech wid nobody less'n 'tis a thoo-an'-thoo sperityal pusson, lak a preacher o' de gorspil, tell my soul is safe. An' dey ain't no minister o' de sperit wha' got time ter come an' set down an' talk wid a po' ongordly widder pusson lak me. I don't sped 'em ter do it. De shepherds can't teck de time to run an' haid orf a ole frazzled-out black sheep lak I is, what M be a disgrace ter de fol', anyway. Dey 'bleege ter spen' dey time a-coaxin' in de purty sleek yo'ng friskin' lambs, an' I don't blame 'em."

"Don't talk dat-a-way, Sis' Jolmsing don't talk dat-a-way. Sence you done specified yo' desire, I'll call an' see you, an' talk an' pray wid you in yo' cabin whensomever you say de word. I knows yo' home is kivered by a cloud o' darkness an' sorrer. When shill I come to you?"

"De mos' lonesomes' time, Brer Langford, an' de time what harden my heart de mos', is in de dark berwilderin' night-times when I fus' goes home. Seem lak ef I c'd des have some reel Gordly man ter come in wid me, an' maybe call out some little passenger o' Scripture to comfort me, tell I c'd des ter say git usen ter de lone- someness, I c'd maybe feel mo' cancelized ter de Divine will. But, co'se, I don't expec no yo'ng man lak you is ter teck de trouble ter turn out'n yo' path fur sech as me."

"I will do it, Sis' Johnsing, an' hit will be a act o' pleasurable Christianity. When de meet'n' is over, ef you will wait, er ef you will walk slow, I will overtaken you on de road quick as I shets up de church-house, an' I pray Gord to give me de seasonable word fur yo' comfort. Amen, an' Gord bless yer!"

Lize Ann had nearly reached her cabin when the reverend brother, stepping forward, gallantly placed his hand beneath her elbow, and aided her to mount the one low step which led to her door.

As they entered the room, he produced and struck a match, while she presented a candle, which he lit and placed upon the table. Neither had yet spoken. If he had his word ready, the season for its utterance seemed not to have arrived.

"'Scuse my manners, Brer Langford," she said, finally, "but my heart is so full, seem lak I can't one speech. Take a rock'n'-cheer an' set down tell I stirs de fire ter meek you welcome in my po' little shanty."

The split pine which she threw upon the coals brought an immediate illumination, and as the young man looked about the apartment he could hardly believe his eyes, so thorough was its transformation since he had seen it on the day of the funeral.

The hearth, newly reddened, fairly glowed with warm color, and the gleaming white pine floor seemed fresh from the carpenter's plane. Dainty white muslin curtains hung before the little square windows, and from the shelves a dazzling row of tins reflected the blazing fire a dozen times from their polished surfaces.

The widow leaned forward before him, stirring the fire; and when his eyes fell upon her, his astonishment confirmed his speechlessness. She had removed her black bonnet, and the heavy shawl, which had enveloped her figure, had fallen behind her into her chair. What he saw was a round, trig, neatly clad, youngish woman, whose face, illumined by the flickering fire, was positively charming in its piquant assertion of grief. Across her shapely bosom lay, neatly folded, a snowy kerchief, less white only than her pearly teeth, as, smiling through her sadness, she exclaimed, as she turned to her guest:

"Lor' bless my soul, ef I 'ain't raked out a sweet 'tater out'n deze coals! I 'feerd you'll be clair disgusted at sech onmannerly doin's, Brer Lang- ford; but when dey ain't no company heah, I des kivers up my 'taters wid ashes an' piles on de live coals, an' let 'em cook. I don't reck'n you'd even ter say look at a roas' 'tater, would you, Brer Langford?"

The person addressed was rubbing his hands together and chuckling. "Ef yer tecks my jedg-mint, Sis' Johnsing, on de pretater question, roas'in' is de onies way to cook 'em."

His hostess had already risen, and before he could remonstrate she had drawn up a little table, lifted the potato from its bed, and laid it on a plate before him.

"Ef you will set down an' eat a roas' 'tater in my miser'ble little cabin, Brer Langford, I 'clar' fo' gracious hit'll raise my sperits mightily. Gord knows I wushes I had some'h'n good to offer you, a-comin' in out'n de col'; but ef you'll please, sir, have de mannerliness ter hoi' de candle, I'll empty my ole cupboard clean inside outen but I'll fin' you somdin 'nother to spressif y yo' welcome."

Langford rose, and as he held the light to the open safe, his eyes fairly glared. He was hungry, and the snowy shelves were covered with open vessels of tempting food, all more or less broken, but savory as to odor, and most inviting.

"I 'clare, Sis' Johnsing I 'clare!"were the only words that the man of eloquent speech found to express his appreciation and joy, and his entertainer continued:

"Dis heah cupboard mecks me 'shame', Brer Langford. Dey ain't a thing fittin' fur sech as you in it. Heah's a pan o' col' 'tater pone an' some cabbage an' side meat, an' dis heah's a few ords an' eens o' fried chicken an' a little passel o' spare-ribs, piled in wid co'n-brade scraps. Hit don't look much, but hit's all clean. Heah, you gimme de candle, an' you retch 'em all down, please, sir; an' I ain't shore, but ef I don't disre- member, dey's de bes' half a loaf o' reeson-cake 'way back in de fur corner. Dat's hit. Now, dat's some'h'n like. An' now pass down de but ter; an' ef yer wants a tumbler o' sweet milk wid yo' 'tater, you'll haf ter hop an' go fetch it. Lis'n ter me, fur Gord sake, talkin' ter Brer Langford same as I'd talk ter a reg'lar plantation nigger!"

Langford hesitated. "Less'n you desires de sweet milk, Sis' Johnsing."

"I does truly lak a swaller o' sweet milk wid my 'tater, Brer Langford, but seem lak 'fo' I'd git itfurmyse'f I'd do widout it. Won't you, please, sir, teck de candle an' fetch it fur me? Go right thoo my room. Hit's in a bottle, a-settin' outside de right-han' winder des as you go in."

Langford could not help glancing about the widow's chamber as he passed through. If the other room was cozy and clean, this one was charming. The white bed, dazzling in its snowy fluted frills, reminded him of its owner, as she sat in all her starched freshness to-night. The polished pine floor here was nearly covered with neatly fringed patches of carpet, suggestive of housewifely taste as well as luxurious comfort.

He had returned with the bottle, and was seating himself, when the disconsolate widow actually burst into a peal of laughter.

"Lord save my soul!" she exclaimed, "ef he 'ain't gone an' fetched a bottle o' beer! You is a caution, Brer Langford! I wouldn't 'a' had you know I had dat beer in my house fur nothin'. When I was feelin' so po'ly in my f us' grief, seem lak I craved sperityal comfort, an' I went an' bought a whole lot o' lager-beer. I 'lowed maybe I c'd drink my sorrer down, but 'twarn't no use. I c'd drink beer all night, an' hit wouldn't nuver bring nobody to set in dat rockin'-cheer by my side an' teck comfort wid me. Does you think fur a perfesser ter teck a little beer ur wine when he feels a nachel faintiness is a fatal sin, Brer Langford?"

"Why, no, Sis' Johnsing. Succumstances alter cases, an' hit's de succumstances o' drinkin' what mecks de altercations an' de way I looks at it, a Christian man is de onies pusson who oughter dare to trus' 'isse'f wid de wine cup, 'caze a sinner don' know when ter stop."

"Dat soun' mighty reason'ble, Brer Langford. An' sence you fetched de beer, now you 'bleege ter drink it. But please, sir, go, lak a good man, an' bring my milk, on de tother side in de winder."

The milk was brought, and the Rev. Mr. Langford was soon smacking his lips over the best supper it had been his ministerial good fortune to enjoy for many a day.

As the widow raked a second potato from the fire, she remarked, in a tone of inimitable pathos:

"Seem lak I can't git usen ter cookin' fur one. I cooks fur two ev'y day, an' somehow I fines a little spec o' comfort in lookin' at de odd po'tion, even ef I has ter eat it myse'f. De secon' 'tater on de hyearth seem lak hit stan's fur company. Seein' as you relishes de beer, Brer Langford, I's proud you made de mistake an' fetched it. Gord knows somebody better drink it! I got a whole passel o' bottles in my trunk, an' I don't know what ter do wid 'em. A man what wuck an' talk an' preach hard as you does, he need a little some- 'h'n' 'nother ter keep 'is cour'ge up."

It was an hour past midnight when finally the widow let her guest out the back door, and as she directed him how to reach home by a short-cut through her field, she said, while she held his hand in parting:

"Gord will bless you fur dis night, Brer Lang- ford, fur you is truly sakerficed yo'se'f fur a po' sinner; an' I b'lieve dey's mo' true 'ligion in com- fortin' a po' lonely widderless 'oman lak I is, what 'ain't got nobody to stan' by 'er, dan in all de ser mons a-goin'; an' now I gwine turn my face back todes my lonely fireside wid a better hope an' a firmer trus' 'caze I knows de love o' Gord done sont you ter me. My po' little brade an' meat warn't highfalutin' nur fine, but you is shared it wid me lak a Christian, an' I gi'n it ter you wid a free heart."

Langford returned the pressure of her hand, and even shook it heartily during his parting speech:

"Good-night, my dear sister, an' Gord bless you! I feels mo' courageous an' strenk'n'd my- se'f sence I have shared yo' lonely fireside, an', please Gord, I will make it my juty as well as my pleasure to he'p you in a similar manner when- somever you desires my presence. I rejoices to see that you is tryin' wid a brave heart to rise f'om yo' sorrer. Keep good cheer, my sister, an' remember dat the Gord o' Aberham an' Isaac an' Jacob de patriots o' de Lord is also de friend ter de fatherless an' widders, an' to them that are desolate an' oppressed."

With this beautiful admonition, and a last distinct pressure of the hand, the Rev. Mr. Langford disappeared in the darkness, carefully fastening the top button of his coat as he went, as if to cover securely the upper layer of raisin-cake which still lay, for want of lower space, just beneath it within.

He never felt better in his life. The widow watched his retreating shadow until she dimly saw one dark leg rise over the rail as he scaled the garden fence; then coming in, she hooked the door, and throwing herself on the floor, rolled over and over, laughing until she cried, verily.

"Stan' back, gals, stan' back!"she exclaimed, rising. "Stan' back, I say! A widder done haided yer off wid a cook-pot!"With eyes fairly dancing, she resumed her seat before the fire. She was too much elated for sleep yet. "I 'clare 'fo' gra cious, I is a devil!"she chuckled. "Po' Alick an' po' Steve an' po' Jake!"she continued, pausing after each name with something that their spiritual presences might have interpreted as a sigh if they were affectionately hovering near her. "But,"she added, her own thoughts supplying the connection, "Brer Langford gwine be de stylishes' one o' de lot."And then she really sighed. "I mus' go buy some mo' beer. Better git two bottles. He mought ax fur mo', bein' as I got a trunkful."And here alone in her cabin she roared aloud. "I does wonder huccome I come ter be sech a devil, anyhow? I 'lowed I was safe ter risk de beer. Better git a dozen bottles, I reck'n; give 'im plenty rope, po' boy! Well, Langford honey, good-night fur to-night! But perpare, yo'ng man, perpare!"And chuc kling as she went, she passed into her own room and went to bed.

The young minister was as good as his promise, and during the next two months he never failed to stop after every evening meeting to look after the spiritual condition of the "widder Johnsing," while she, with the consummate skill of a practised hand, saw to it that without apparent fore thought her little cupboard should always supply a material entertainment, full, savory, and varied. If on occasion she lamented a dearth of cold dishes, it was that she might insist on sharing her breakfast with her guest, when, producing from her magic safe a ready-dressed spring chicken or squirrel, she would broil it upon the coals in his presence, and the young man would depart thoroughly saturated with the odor of her delightful hospitality.

Langford had heard things about this woman in days gone by, but now he was pleased to realize that they had all been malicious inventions prompted by jealousy. Had he commanded the adjectives, he would have described her as the most generous, hospitable, spontaneous, sympathetic, vivacious, and witty, as well as the most artless of women. As it was, he thought of her a good deal between visits; and whether the thought moved backward or forward, whether it took shape as a memory or an anticipation, he somehow unconsciously smacked his lips and swallowed. And yet, when one of the elders questioned him as to the spiritual state of the still silent mourner, he knit his brow and answered, with a sigh:

"It is hard ter say, my brothers it is hard ter say. De ole lady do nourish an' cherish 'er grief mightily; but yit, ef we hoi' off an' don't crowd 'er, I trus' she'll come thoo on de Lord's side yit."

If there had been the ghost of a twinkle in his interlocutor's eye, it died out, abashed at itself at this pious and carefully framed reply. The widow was indeed fully ten years Langford's senior a discrepancy as much exaggerated by outward circumstances as it was minimized in their fire side relations.

So matters drifted on for a month longer. The dozen bottles of beer had been followed by a second, and these again by a half-dozen. This last reduced purchase of course had its meaning. Langford was reaching the end of his tether. At last there were but two bottles left. It was Sunday night again.

The little cupboard had been furnished with unusual elaboration, and the savory odors which emanated from its shelves would have filled the room but for the all-pervading essence of bergamot with which the widow had recklessly deluged her hair. Indeed, her entire toilet betrayed exceptional care tonight.

She had not gone to church, and as it was near the hour for dismissal, she was a trifle nervous, feeling confident that the minister would stop in, ostensibly to inquire the cause of her absence. She had tried this before, and he had not disappointed her. Finally she detected his familiar announcement, a clearing of his throat, as he approached the door.

"Lif up de latch an' walk in, Brer Wolf,"she laughingly called to him; and as he entered she added, "Look lak you come in answer to my thoughts, Brer Langford."

"Is dat so, Sis' Johnsing?"he replied, chuckling with delight. "I knowed some'fi'n' 'nother drawed me clean over f 'om de chu'ch in de po'in'-down rain."

"Is it a-rainin'? I 'clare, I see yer bring yo' umberella but sett'n' heah by de fire, I nuver studies 'bout de elemints. I been studyin' 'bout some'h'n mo'n rain or shine, I's tell yer."

"Is yer, Sis' Johnsing? What you been studyin' 'bout?"

"What I been studyin' 'bout? Nemmine what I been studyin' 'bout! I studyin' 'bout Brer Langford now. De po' man look so tired an' frazzled out, 'is eyes looks des lak dorg-wood blor-soms. You is des nachelly preached down, Brer Langford, an' you needs a morsel o' some'h'n' 'nother ter stiddy yo' cornstitutiom." She rose forthwith, and set about arranging the young man's supper.

"But you 'ain't tol' me yit huccome you 'ain't come ter chu'ch ter-night, Sis' Johnsing?"

"Nemmine 'bout dat now. I ain't studyin' 'bout gwine ter chu'ch now. I des studyin' 'bout how ter induce de size o' yo' eyes down ter dey nachel porportiora. Heah, teck de shovel, an' rake out a han'ful o' coals, please, sir, an' I'll set dis pan o' rolls ter bake. Dat's hit. Now kiver de led good wid live coals an' ashes. Dat's a man! Now time you wrastle wid de j'ints o' dis roas' guinea-hen, an' teck de corkscrew an' perscribe fur dis beer bottle, and go fetch de fresh butter out'n de winder, de rolls'll be a-singin.' ' Now is de accepted time!' "

It was no wonder the young man thought her charming.

Needless to say, the feast, seasoned by a steady flow of humor, was perfect. But all things earthly have an end, and so, by-and-by, it was all over. A pattering rain without served to enhance the genial in-door charm, but it was time to go.

"Well, Sis' Johnsing, hit's a-gittin' on time fur me ter be a-movin',"said the poor fellow at length, for he hated to leave.

"Yas, I knows it is, Brer Langford,"the hostess answered, with a tinge of sadness, "an' dat ain't de wust of it."

"How does you mean, Sis' Johnsing?"

"'Ain't I tol' yer, Brer Langford, ter-night dat my thoughts was wid you? Don't look at me so quizzical, please, sir, 'caze I got a heavy sorrer in my heart."

"A sorrer 'bout me, Sis' Johnsing? How so?"

"Brer Langford I been thinkin' 'bout you all day, an' an' ter come right down ter de p'int, I, I..."She bit her lip and hesitated. "I 'feerd I done put off what I ought ter said ter you tell look lak hit'll 'mos' bre'k my heart to say it."

"Speak out, fur Gord sake, Sis' Johnsing, an' ease yo' min'! What is yo' trouble?"

She seemed almost crying. "You you you mustn't come heah no mo', Brer Langford."

"Who me? Wh-wh-what is I done, Sis' Johnsing?"

"My Gord! how kin I say it? You 'ain't done nothin', my dear frien'. You has been Gord's blessin' ter me; but but I 'clare 'fo' Gord, how kin I say de word? But don't you see yo'se'f how de succumstances stan'? You is a yo'ng man li'ble to fall in love wid any lakly yo'ng gal any day, an' ter git married, an', of co'se, dat's right; but don't you see dat ef a po' lonesome 'oman lak me put too much 'pendence orn a yo'ng man lak you is, de time gwine come when he gwine git tired a-walkin' all de way f'om chu'ch in de po'in'-down rain des fur charity ter comfort a lonely sinner pusson lak I is; an' an' settin' heah by myse'f ternight, I done made up my min' dat I gwine scuse you f'om dis task while I kin stand it. Of co'se I don't say but hit'll be hard. You is tooken me by de ban' an' he'ped me thoo a dark cloud, but you an' me mus' say far'well ter- night, an' you you mustn't come back no mo'."

Her face was buried in her hands now, and so she could not see her guest's storm-swept visage as he essayed to answer her.

"You you you you talkin' 'bout you c'n stan' it, Sis' Johnsing, an' an' seem lak you 's forgitt'n' all "bout me"His voice was trembling. ' I I knows I ain't nothin' but a no-'count yo'ng striplin', so ter speak, an' you is a mannerly lady o' speunce, but hit do seem lak 'fo' you'd send me away, des lak ter say a yaller dorg, you'd you'd ax me could I stan' it; an' an', tell de trufe, I can't stan' it, an' I ain't gwine stan' it, 'less'n you des nachelty, p'int-blank, out an' out, shots de do' in my face."

"Brer Langford…"

"Don't you say Brer Langford ter me no mo',' ef you please, ma'am; an' an' I ain't gwine call you Sis' Johnsing no mo', nuther. You is des, so fur as you consents, hencefo'th an' fo'ever mo', in season an' out'n season des my Lize Ann. You knows yo'se'f dat we is come ter be each one-'n'ners heart's delight." He drew his chair nearer, and, leaning forward, seized her hand, as he continued: "Leastwise, dat's de way my heart language hit-se'f. I done tooken you fur my sweetness 'fo' ter- night, Lize Ann, my honey."

But why follow them any further? Before he left her, the widow had consented, with becoming reluctance, that he should come to her on the following Sunday with the marriage license in his pocket, on one condition, and upon this condition she insisted with unyielding pertinacity. It was that Langford should feel entirely free to change his mind, and to love or to marry any other woman within the week ensuing.

Lize Ann arrived late at service on the following Sunday evening. Her name had just been announced as a happy convert who rejoiced in new found grace; and when she stepped demurely up the aisle, arrayed in a plain white dress, her face beaming with what seemed a spiritual peace, the congregation were deeply touched, and, eager to welcome her into the fold, began to press forward to extend the right hand of fellowship to one who had come in through so much tribulation. It was a happy time all round, and no one was more jubilant than the young pastor, who seemed, indeed, to rejoice more over this recovered lamb than over the ninety-and-nine within the fold who had not gone astray.

The young girl converts of recent date, never slow to respond to any invitation which led to the chancel, were specially demonstrative in their affectionate welcome, some even going so far as to embrace the new "sister,"while others were moved to shout and sing as they made the tour of the aisles.

When, however, as soon as congratulations were over, it was formally announced that this identical convert, Mrs. Eliza Ann Johnsing, was then and there to be joined in the holy estate of matrimony to the Reverend Julius Caesar Langford, the shock was so great that these same blessed damosels looked blankly one upon the other in mute dismay for the space of some minutes, and when presently, as a blushing bride, Lize Ann again turned to them for congratulations, it is a shame to have to write it, but they actually did turn their backs and refuse to speak to her.

The emotions of the company were certainly very much mixed, and the two old crones, Nancy Price and Hester Ann Jennings, sitting side by side in a front pew, were seen to nudge each other as, their old sides shaking with laughter, they exclaimed:

"What I tol' yer, Sis' Host' Ann?"

"What I tol' yer, Sis' Nancy?"

"Dat's des what we tol' one-'n'ner Lize Ann gwine do!"

Though no guests were bidden to share it, the wedding supper in the little cabin that night was no mean affair, and when Langford, with a chuckling, half-embarrassed, new-proprietary air drew the cork from the beer bottle beside his plate, Lize Ann said, "Hit do do me good ter see how you relishes dat beer."

But she did not mention that it was the last bottle, and maybe it was just as well.

Lafcadio Hearn (1850–1904)

Lafcadio Hearn[1] was born Patricio Lafcadio Tessima Carlos Hearn on June 27, 1850, to his Anglo-Irish father, Charles Hearn, and Italian-Roma-Greek mother, Rosa Antonia Cassimati Hearn. His father was a British Army surgeon assigned to the Ionian Islands in 1846, where, two years later, he met Rosa Cassimati. Lafcadio was named after the island on which he was born, Leucadia, also called Lefkada in Greek and Santa Maura in Italian. He was Charles and Rosa's second child. His older brother, George, however, would die not long after Lafcadio's birth. Later that same year his father was transferred to the islands of Dominica and Grenada in the West Indies, and two years later Lafcadio left the Greek islands, for Dublin, with his mother, never to return. His parents were briefly reunited in Dublin, in 1853, but the marriage was doomed. After the death of her first child, his mother suffered mentally, and she was simply too "foreign" for the Hearn family. In 1854, she left Dublin, again pregnant, and returned to Greece where she gave birth to Hearn's younger brother, James Daniel. In 1856, Charles Hearn had the marriage annulled, and both of Lafcadio's parents remarried. They also both agreed to renounce their sons, Lafcadio and James, leaving them with Hearn relatives in Dublin, while Rosa stayed in Greece, and Charles moved to India. The two boys never saw either of their parents again. Rosa had two more sons and two daughters in Greece, but there is no evidence that Lafcadio ever met them, and his father, with his new wife, went on to have three daughters in India: Elizabeth, Minnie, and Posey. Later in life, Lafcadio Hearn would maintain a written correspondence with only two of his siblings, his brother James and his half-sister Minnie Hearn Atkinson.

Being shuffled about as a child from parent to parent to relatives probably had much to do with Hearn's peripatetic life. When his father left him in Dublin, in 1857, Lafcadio spent most of his young life living with his great aunt, the wealthy, widowed, childless Sarah Holmes Brenane, who took a liking to Lafcadio, and as a devout Catholic, she also took Rosa's side in the dissolution of the Hearn's marriage and disinherited Charles. In 1862, she sent Hearn to study in France, where he soon became fluent in French, both speaking and writing, and the following year he was sent to St. Cuthbert's College in Ushaw, England.

The most significant event to happen at St. Cuthbert's would mark Hearn for life. At age sixteen, while playing some sort of rope game with his classmates outside, he was struck in the eye with the knotted end of the rope, and the already myopic Hearn subsequently and permanently lost the use of his left eye. He never completed his studies at St. Cuthbert's, but the reason for that is uncertain and is probably a result of several factors combined, the loss of eyesight in his left eye being one of them. According to Hearn biographer Nina H. Kennard, in a letter from Hearn to his brother James, he admitted that he "was not even Catholic" so that might be another reason for his having left St. Cuthbert's early.[2] But perhaps the biggest blow was his great aunt having been swindled out of her fortune by a distant relative, Henry Hearn Molyneux. Soon thereafter she also lost her mind, so, penniless, Hearn moved to London to live with Sarah Brenane's former servant, Catherine Delaney, and her husband, a dockworker, and from there to Paris. In the end, all that Molyneux was willing to give Hearn was the money for one-way passage to the United States where he was being sent to Molyneux's brother-in-law in Cincinnati. He would never return to Europe.

In Cincinnati, Hearn first worked as a printer's devil for Mr. Watkin, with whom he would have a

---

1   For more on Lafcadio Hearn and from where most of the biographical information presented here is taken, see Robert Gale, *A Lafcadio Hearn Companion* (Westport, Connecticut: Greenwood Press, 2002).

2   Nina H Kennard, *Lafcadio Hearn* (Port Washington, New York: Kennikat Press, 1967), 57.

lifelong friendship, but times were hard for the penniless Hearn. He did begin to write for the *Cincinnati Enquirer* and *Commercial* newspapers, but he was paid very little. Nonetheless, this is where he began his journalistic career that would last until his death. Also significant about his time is Cincinnati, was his marriage in 1874, to Alethea Foley, an African American woman, thereby making the marriage illegal. They separated the following year, and two years later Hearn left for New Orleans.

In New Orleans, Hearn continued his journalistic writing, contributing to the *Item, Democrat,* and later the *Times-Democrat;* however, he was still living in abject poverty. According to Kennard, the deadly yellow fever outbreak of 1878, was actually responsible for Hearn attaining full-time employment. There were many vacancies due to the city's high death rate, so Hearn was offered an assistant editorship at the *Item,* a position which allowed him much more time for his own literary pursuits, one of which was his New Orleans masterpiece, *Chita: A Memory of Last Island.*[1]

A year after Hearn had left New Orleans for good, *Chita* was published in *Harpers* in April of 1888. Hearn's letters in 1884 describe his vacation in Grand Isle, one of Louisiana's largest barrier islands, which was the inspiration for Hearn's short novel as well as Kate Chopin's *The Awakening.* In the 19th century, Last Island (*L'Ile Dernier*), a barrier island like Grand Isle, was also a fashionable vacation spot for wealthy New Orleanians, but in 1856, one of the strongest hurricanes in recorded history wiped out the island, killing more than one hundred residents and tourists. Surely when Hearn visited Grand Isle, there were many survivors of that hurricane still willing to talk of it, and *Chita* is a fictional account of the storm told in three parts.

Most striking about Part I of *Chita,* "The Legend of *L'Ile Derniere,*" is Hearn's vivid and impressionistic description of the disappearing Louisiana wetlands, particularly so in light of Hurricane Katrina in 2005, and the BP oil spill of 2010:

> Year by year that rustling strip of green land grows narrower; the sand spreads and sinks, shuddering and wrinkling like a living brown skin; and the last standing corpses of the oaks, ever clinging with naked, dead feet to the sliding beach, lean more and more out of the perpendicular. As the sands subside, the stumps appear to creep; their intertwisted masses of snakish roots seem to crawl, to writhe,—like the reaching arms of cephalopods.

We have since learned just how vital these wetlands are to South Louisiana, and indeed to the entire Gulf Coast, and even over one hundred fifty years ago, their disappearance was disturbing, as Hearn goes on to note: "Grand Terre is going: the sea mines her fort, and will before many years carry the ramparts by storm. Grand Isle is going—slowly but surely: the Gulf has eaten three miles into her meadowed land. Last Island has gone!" Hearn goes on to describe the hurricane that would wipe out Last Island and its aftermath in Part I, before moving on to the narrative in Part II, "Out of the Sea's Strength," where we meet the Spanish fisherman, Feliu Viosca and his wife Carmen.

Much like in Sallie Rhett Roman's "Bastien," Feliu is shaped by the rugged coast to which he and his wife moved after losing their first child in Barcelona. Feliu is the strongest and most capable in this settlement of immigrant fishermen at Viosca's Point. Only he can distinguish a small child and her dead mother floating on the horizon, and only he can rescue the helpless child. The superstitious Carmen, of course, finds the appearance of Eulalie Brierre to be a sign from God that her deceased child, Concha, has returned to her, so she names her Conchita. In this section, the mystery of Chita is solved and we discover that although her mother, Adele did perish, her father Julien Brierre is very much alive, and six months later, much to his family's dismay, "He had come back to find strangers in his home, relatives at law concerning his estate, and himself regarded as an intruder among the living—an unlucky guest,

---

1   Ibid., 123-124.

a *revenant*" (ghost). Like his family, however, he wishes he had died, but only because he is too grief stricken to carry on.

The final section, Part III, "The Shadow of the Tide," reunites Julien and Eulalie, but only briefly. Also in this section, Hearn has a deadly yellow fever epidemic sweep through the city of New Orleans, much like the one he lived through in 1878. Finally, Julien is forced to flee the city for the healthier coast, but by the time he arrives at Viosca's Point, it is too late. He does recognize his child, but by this time he is delirious and Carmen keeps Chita from him. In the end, only Carmen knows that young Chita has lost both her parents, as she prays to Jesus for compassion.

In this novel, Hearn captures the local landscape and its inhabitants so common in local color fiction of the 19th century, but he also includes a gripping story of love, betrayal, and loss while establishing just how vital a role Louisiana's rugged coastal wetlands play in the survival of the city of New Orleans, even some one-hundred-fifty years ago. He only lived here for ten years before moving on to Martinique and finally settling in Japan, where he died in 1904, but in a very short time he embraced the culture of the city and its surrounding natural environment, which he never seemed to accomplish in Cincinnati. Perhaps that is the source of his most-quoted phrase, known by heart to so many New Orleanians: "…it is better to live here in sack cloth and ashes, than to own the whole state of Ohio."

Chita: A Memory of Last Island[1]

"But Nature whistled with all her winds,
Did as she pleased, and went her way."   —Emerson

To my friend, Dr. Rodolfo Matas of New Orleans.

The Legend of L'Ile Derniere

I

Traveling south from New Orleans to the Islands, you pass through a strange land into a strange sea, by various winding waterways. You can journey to the Gulf by lugger if you please; but the trip may be made much more rapidly and agreeably on some one of those light, narrow steamers, built especially for bayou-travel, which usually receive passengers at a point not far from the foot of old Saint-Louis Street, hard by the sugar-landing, where there is ever a pushing and flocking of steam craft—all striving for place to rest their white breasts against the levee, side by side,—like great weary swans. But the miniature steamboat on which you engage passage to the Gulf never lingers long in the Mississippi: she crosses the river, slips into some canal-mouth, labors along the artificial channel awhile, and then leaves it with a scream of joy, to puff her free way down many a league of heavily shadowed bayou. Perhaps thereafter she may bear you through the immense silence of drenched rice-fields, where the yellow-green level is broken at long intervals by the black silhouette of some irrigating machine;—but, whichever of the five different routes be pursued, you will find yourself more than once floating through sombre mazes of swamp-forest,—past assemblages of cypresses all hoary with the parasitic tillandsia, and grotesque as gatherings of fetich-gods. Ever from river or from lakelet the steamer glides again into canal or bayou,—from bayou or canal once more into lake or bay; and sometimes the swamp-forest visibly thins away from these shores into wastes of reedy morass where, even of breathless nights, the quaggy soil trembles

---

1   From: Lafcadio Hearn, *Chita: A Memory of Last Island*. (New York: Harper & Brothers, 1889).

to a sound like thunder of breakers on a coast: the storm-roar of billions of reptile voices chanting in cadence,—rhythmically surging in stupendous crescendo and diminuendo,—a monstrous and appalling chorus of frogs!

Panting, screaming, scraping her bottom over the sand-bars,—all day the little steamer strives to reach the grand blaze of blue open water below the marsh-lands; and perhaps she may be fortunate enough to enter the Gulf about the time of sunset. For the sake of passengers, she travels by day only; but there are other vessels which make the journey also by night—threading the bayou-labyrinths winter and summer: sometimes steering by the North Star,—sometimes feeling the way with poles in the white season of fogs,—sometimes, again, steering by that Star of Evening which in our sky glows like another moon, and drops over the silent lakes as she passes a quivering trail of silver fire. Shadows lengthen; and at last the woods dwindle away behind you into thin bluish lines;—land and water alike take more luminous color;—bayous open into broad passes;—lakes link themselves with sea-bays;—and the ocean-wind bursts upon you,—keen, cool, and full of light. For the first time the vessel begins to swing,—rocking to the great living pulse of the tides. And gazing from the deck around you, with no forest walls to break the view, it will seem to you that the low land must have once been rent asunder by the sea, and strewn about the Gulf in fantastic tatters....

Sometimes above a waste of wind-blown prairie-cane you see an oasis emerging,—a ridge or hillock heavily umbraged with the rounded foliage of evergreen oaks:—a cheniere. And from the shining flood also kindred green knolls arise,—pretty islets, each with its beach-girdle of dazzling sand and shells, yellow-white,—and all radiant with semi-tropical foliage, myrtle and palmetto, orange and magnolia. Under their emerald shadows curious little villages of palmetto huts are drowsing, where dwell a swarthy population of Orientals,—Malay fishermen, who speak the Spanish-Creole of the Philippines as well as their own Tagal, and perpetuate in Louisiana the Catholic traditions of the Indies. There are girls in those unfamiliar villages worthy to inspire any statuary,—beautiful with the beauty of ruddy bronze,—gracile as the palmettoes that sway above them.... Further seaward you may also pass a Chinese settlement: some queer camp of wooden dwellings clustering around a vast platform that stands above the water upon a thousand piles;—over the miniature wharf you can scarcely fail to observe a white sign-board painted with crimson ideographs. The great platform is used for drying fish in the sun; and the fantastic characters of the sign, literally translated, mean: "Heap—Shrimp—Plenty.".... And finally all the land melts down into desolations of sea-marsh, whose stillness is seldom broken, except by the melancholy cry of long-legged birds, and in wild seasons by that sound which shakes all shores when the weird Musician of the Sea touches the bass keys of his mighty organ....

II

Beyond the sea-marshes a curious archipelago lies. If you travel by steamer to the sea-islands to-day, you are tolerably certain to enter the Gulf by Grande Pass—skirting Grande Terre, the most familiar island of all, not so much because of its proximity as because of its great crumbling fort and its graceful pharos: the stationary White-Light of Barataria. Otherwise the place is bleakly uninteresting: a wilderness of wind-swept grasses and sinewy weeds waving away from a thin beach ever speckled with drift and decaying things,—worm-riddled timbers, dead porpoises.

Eastward the russet level is broken by the columnar silhouette of the light house, and again, beyond it, by some puny scrub timber, above which rises the angular ruddy mass of the old brick fort, whose ditches swarm with crabs, and whose sluiceways are half choked by obsolete cannon-shot, now thickly covered with incrustation of oyster shells.... Around all the gray circling of a shark-haunted sea...

Sometimes of autumn evenings there, when the hollow of heaven flames like the interior of a chalice, and waves and clouds are flying in one wild rout of broken gold,—you may see the tawny grasses all covered with something like husks,—wheat-colored husks,—large, flat, and disposed evenly along the lee-side of each swaying stalk, so as to present only their edges to the wind. But, if you approach, those pale husks all break open to display strange splendors of scarlet and seal-brown, with arabesque mottlings in white and black: they change into wondrous living blossoms, which detach themselves before your eyes and rise in air, and flutter away by thousands to settle down farther off, and turn into wheat-colored husks once more... a whirling flower-drift of sleepy butterflies!

Southwest, across the pass, gleams beautiful Grande Isle: primitively a wilderness of palmetto (latanier);—then drained, diked, and cultivated by Spanish sugar-planters; and now familiar chiefly as a bathing-resort. Since the war the ocean reclaimed its own;—the cane-fields have degenerated into sandy plains, over which tramways wind to the smooth beach;—the plantation-residences have been converted into rustic hotels, and the negro-quarters remodelled into villages of cozy cottages for the reception of guests. But with its imposing groves of oak, its golden wealth of orange-trees, its odorous lanes of oleander, its broad grazing-meadows yellow-starred with wild camomile, Grande Isle remains the prettiest island of the Gulf; and its loveliness is exceptional. For the bleakness of Grand Terre is reiterated by most of the other islands,—Caillou, Cassetete, Calumet, Wine Island, the twin Timbaliers, Gull Island, and the many islets haunted by the gray pelican,—all of which are little more than sand-bars covered with wiry grasses, prairie-cane, and scrub-timber. Last Island (*L'Ile Derniere*),—well worthy a long visit in other years, in spite of its remoteness, is now a ghastly desolation twenty-five miles long. Lying nearly forty miles west of Grande Isle, it was nevertheless far more populated a generation ago; it was not only the most celebrated island of the group, but also the most fashionable watering-place of the aristocratic South;—to-day it is visited by fishermen only, at long intervals. Its admirable beach in many respects resembled that of Grande Isle to-day; the accommodations also were much similar, although finer: a charming village of cottages facing the Gulf near the western end. The hotel itself was a massive two-story construction of timber, containing many apartments, together with a large dining-room and dancing-hall. In rear of the hotel was a bayou, where passengers landed—"Village Bayou" it is still called by seamen;—but the deep channel which now cuts the island in two a little eastwardly did not exist while the village remained. The sea tore it out in one night—the same night when trees, fields, dwellings, all vanished into the Gulf, leaving no vestige of former human habitation except a few of those strong brick props and foundations upon which the frame houses and cisterns had been raised. One living creature was found there after the cataclysm—a cow! But how that solitary cow survived the fury of a storm-flood that actually rent the island in twain has ever remained a mystery...

III

On the Gulf side of these islands you may observe that the trees—when there are any trees—all bend away from the sea; and, even of bright, hot days when the wind sleeps, there is something grotesquely pathetic in their look of agonized terror. A group of oaks at Grande Isle I remember as especially suggestive: five stooping silhouettes in line against the horizon, like fleeing women with streaming garments and wind-blown hair,—bowing grievously and thrusting out arms desperately northward as to save themselves from falling. And they are being pursued indeed;—for the sea is devouring the land. Many and many a mile of ground has yielded to the tireless charging of Ocean's cavalry: far out you can see, through a good glass, the porpoises at play where of old the sugar-cane shook out its million bannerets; and shark-fins now seam deep water above a site where pigeons used to coo. Men build dikes; but the besieging tides bring up their battering-rams—whole forests of drift—huge trunks of water-oak and weighty cypress. Forever the yellow Mississippi strives to build; forever the sea struggles to destroy;—and amid their eternal strife the islands and the promontories change shape, more slowly, but not less fantastically, than the clouds of heaven.

And worthy of study are those wan battle-grounds where the woods made their last brave stand against the irresistible invasion,—usually at some long point of sea-marsh, widely fringed with billowing sand. Just where the waves curl beyond such a point you may discern a multitude of blackened, snaggy shapes protruding above the water,—some high enough to resemble ruined chimneys, others bearing a startling likeness to enormous skeleton-feet and skeleton-hands,—with crustaceous white growths clinging to them here and there like remnants of integument. These are bodies and limbs of drowned oaks,—so long drowned that the shell-scurf is inch-thick upon parts of them. Farther in upon the beach immense trunks lie overthrown. Some look like vast broken columns; some suggest colossal torsos imbedded, and seem to reach out mutilated stumps in despair from their deepening graves;—and beside these are others which have kept their feet with astounding obstinacy, although the barbarian tides have been charging them for twenty years, and gradually torn away the soil above and beneath their roots. The sand around,—soft beneath and thinly crusted upon the surface,—is everywhere pierced with holes made by a beautifully mottled and semi-diaphanous crab, with hairy legs, big staring eyes, and milk-white claws;—while in the green sedges beyond there is a perpetual rustling, as of some strong wind beating among reeds: a marvellous creeping of "fiddlers," which the inexperienced visitor might at first mistake for so many peculiar beetles, as they run about sideways, each with his huge single claw folded upon his body like a wing-case. Year by year that rustling strip of green land grows narrower; the sand spreads and sinks, shuddering and wrinkling like a living brown skin; and the last standing corpses of the oaks, ever clinging with naked, dead feet to the sliding beach, lean more and more out of the perpendicular. As the sands subside, the stumps appear to creep; their intertwisted masses of snakish roots seem to crawl, to writhe,—like the reaching arms of cephalopods....

… Grande Terre is going: the sea mines her fort, and will before many years carry the ramparts by storm. Grande Isle is going,—slowly but surely: the Gulf has eaten three miles into her meadowed land. Last Island has gone! How it went I first heard from the lips of a veteran pilot, while we sat one evening together on the trunk of a drifted cypress which some high tide had pressed deeply into the Grande Isle beach. The day had been tropically warm; we had sought the shore for a breath of living air. Sunset came, and with it the ponderous heat lifted,—a sudden breeze blew,—lightnings flickered in the darkening horizon,—wind and water began to strive together, and soon all the low coast boomed. Then my companion began his story; perhaps the coming of the storm inspired him to speak! And as I listened to him, listening also to the clamoring of the coast, there flashed back to me recollection of a singular Breton fancy: that the Voice of the Sea is never one voice, but a tumult of many voices—voices of drowned men,—the muttering of multitudinous dead,—the moaning of innumerable ghosts, all rising, to rage against the living, at the great Witch call of storms....

IV

The charm of a single summer day on these island shores is something impossible to express, never to be forgotten. Rarely, in the paler zones, do earth and heaven take such luminosity: those will best understand me who have seen the splendor of a West Indian sky. And yet there is a tenderness of tint, a caress of color, in these Gulf-days which is not of the Antilles,—a spirituality, as of eternal tropical spring. It must have been to even such a sky that Xenophanes lifted up his eyes of old when he vowed the Infinite Blue was God;—it was indeed under such a sky that De Soto named the vastest and grandest of Southern havens Espiritu Santo,—the Bay of the Holy Ghost. There is a something unutterable in this bright Gulf-air that compels awe,—something vital, something holy, something pantheistic: and reverentially the mind asks itself if what the eye beholds is not the Pneuma indeed, the Infinite Breath, the Divine Ghost, the great Blue Soul of the Unknown. All, all is blue in the calm,—save the low land under your feet, which you almost forget, since it seems only as a tiny green flake afloat in the liquid eternity of day. Then slowly, caressingly, irresistibly, the witchery of the Infinite grows upon you: out of Time and Space you begin to dream with open eyes,—to drift into delicious oblivion of facts,—to forget the past, the present, the substantial,—to comprehend nothing but the existence of that infinite Blue Ghost as something into which you would wish to melt utterly away forever....

And this day-magic of azure endures sometimes for months together. Cloudlessly the dawn reddens up through a violet east: there is no speck upon the blossoming of its Mystical Rose,—unless it be the silhouette of some passing gull, whirling his sickle-wings against the crimsoning. Ever, as the sun floats higher, the flood shifts its color. Sometimes smooth and gray, yet flickering with the morning gold, it is the vision of John,—the apocalyptic Sea of Glass mixed with fire;—again, with the growing breeze, it takes that incredible purple tint familiar mostly to painters of West Indian scenery;—once more, under the blaze of noon, it changes to a waste of broken emerald. With evening, the horizon assumes tints of inexpressible sweetness,—pearl-lights, opaline colors of milk and fire; and in the west are topaz-glowings and wondrous flushings as of nacre. Then, if the sea sleeps, it dreams of all these,—faintly, weirdly,—shadowing them even to the verge of heaven.

Beautiful, too, are those white phantasmagoria which, at the approach of equinoctial days, mark the coming of the winds. Over the rim of the sea a bright cloud gently pushes up its head. It rises; and others rise with it, to right and left—slowly at first; then more swiftly. All are brilliantly white and flocculent, like loose new cotton. Gradually they mount in enormous line high above the Gulf, rolling and wreathing into an arch that expands and advances,—bending from horizon to horizon.

A clear, cold breath accompanies its coming. Reaching the zenith, it seems there to hang poised awhile,—a ghostly bridge arching the empyrean,—upreaching its measureless span from either underside of the world. Then the colossal phantom begins to turn, as on a pivot of air,—always preserving its curvilinear symmetry, but moving its unseen ends beyond and below the sky-circle. And at last it floats away unbroken beyond the blue sweep of the world, with a wind following after. Day after day, almost at the same hour, the white arc rises, wheels, and passes...

... Never a glimpse of rock on these low shores;—only long sloping beaches and bars of smooth tawny sand. Sand and sea teem with vitality;—over all the dunes there is a constant susurration, a blattering and swarming of crustacea;—through all the sea there is a ceaseless play of silver lightning,—flashing of myriad fish. Sometimes the shallows are thickened with minute, transparent, crab-like organisms,—all colorless as gelatine. There are days also when countless medusae drift in—beautiful veined creatures that throb like hearts, with perpetual systole and diastole of their diaphanous envelops: some, of translucent azure or rose, seem in the flood the shadows or ghosts of huge campanulate flowers;—others have the semblance of strange living vegetables,—great milky tubers, just beginning to sprout. But woe to the human skin grazed by those shadowy sproutings and spectral stamens!—the touch of glowing iron is not more painful... Within an hour or two after their appearance all these tremulous jellies vanish mysteriously as they came.

Perhaps, if a bold swimmer, you may venture out alone a long way—once! Not twice!—even in company. As the water deepens beneath you, and you feel those ascending wave-currents of coldness arising which bespeak profundity, you will also begin to feel innumerable touches, as of groping fingers—touches of the bodies of fish, innumerable fish, fleeing towards shore. The farther you advance, the more thickly you will feel them come; and above you and around you, to right and left, others will leap and fall so swiftly as to daze the sight, like intercrossing fountain-jets of fluid silver. The gulls fly lower about you, circling with sinister squeaking cries;—perhaps for an instant your feet touch in the deep something heavy, swift, lithe, that rushes past with a swirling shock. Then the fear of the Abyss, the vast and voiceless Nightmare of the Sea, will come upon you; the silent panic of all those opaline millions that flee glimmering by will enter into you also…

From what do they flee thus perpetually? Is it from the giant sawfish or the ravening shark?—from the herds of the porpoises, or from the grande-ecaille,—that splendid monster whom no net may hold,—all helmed and armored in argent plate-mail?—or from the hideous devilfish of the Gulf,—gigantic, flat-bodied, black, with immense side-fins ever outspread like the pinions of a bat,—the terror of luggermen, the uprooter of anchors? From all these, perhaps, and from other monsters likewise—goblin shapes evolved by Nature as destroyers, as equilibrists, as counterchecks to that prodigious fecundity, which, unhindered, would thicken the deep into one measureless and waveless ferment of being… But when there are many bathers these perils are forgotten,—numbers give courage,—one can abandon one's self, without fear of the invisible, to the long, quivering, electrical caresses of the sea…

V

Thirty years ago, Last Island lay steeped in the enormous light of even such magical days. July was dying;—for weeks no fleck of cloud had broken the heaven's blue dream of eternity; winds held their breath; slow waves caressed the bland brown beach with a sound as of kisses and whispers. To one who found himself alone, beyond the limits of the village and beyond the hearing of its voices,—the vast silence, the vast light, seemed full of weirdness. And these hushes, these transparencies, do not always inspire a causeless apprehension: they are omens sometimes—omens of coming tempest. Nature,—incomprehensible Sphinx!—before her mightiest bursts of rage, ever puts forth her divinest witchery, makes more manifest her awful beauty…

But in that forgotten summer the witchery lasted many long days,—days born in rose-light, buried in gold. It was the height of the season. The long myrtle-shadowed village was thronged with its summer population;—the big hotel could hardly accommodate all its guests;—the bathing-houses were too few for the crowds who flocked to the water morning and evening. There were diversions for all,—hunting and fishing parties, yachting excursions, rides, music, games, promenades. Carriage wheels whirled flickering along the beach, seaming its smoothness noiselessly, as if muffled. Love wrote its dreams upon the sand…

Then one great noon, when the blue abyss of day seemed to yawn over the world more deeply than ever before, a sudden change touched the quicksilver smoothness of the waters—the swaying shadow of a vast motion. First the whole sea-circle appeared to rise up bodily at the sky; the horizon-curve lifted to a straight line; the line darkened and approached,—a monstrous wrinkle, an immeasurable fold of green water, moving swift as a cloud-shadow pursued by sunlight. But it had looked formidable only by startling contrast with the previous placidity of the open: it was scarcely two feet high;—it curled slowly as it neared the beach, and combed itself out in sheets of woolly foam with a low, rich roll of whispered thunder. Swift in pursuit another followed—a third—a feebler fourth; then the sea only swayed a little, and stilled again. Minutes passed, and the immeasurable heaving recommenced—one, two, three, four… seven long swells this time;—and the Gulf smoothed itself once more. Irregularly the phenomenon continued to repeat itself, each time with heavier billowing and briefer intervals of quiet—until at last the whole sea grew restless and shifted color and flickered green;—the swells became shorter and changed form. Then from horizon to shore ran one uninterrupted heaving—one vast green swarming of snaky shapes, rolling in to hiss and flatten upon the sand. Yet no single cirrus-speck revealed itself through all the violet heights: there was no wind!—you might have fancied the sea had been upheaved from beneath...

And indeed the fancy of a seismic origin for a windless surge would not appear in these latitudes to be utterly without foundation. On the fairest days a southeast breeze may bear you an odor singular enough to startle you from sleep,—a strong, sharp smell as of fish-oil; and gazing at the sea you might be still more startled at the sudden apparition of great oleaginous patches spreading over the water, sheeting over the swells. That is, if you had never heard of the mysterious submarine oil-wells, the volcanic fountains, unexplored, that well up with the eternal pulsing of the Gulf-Stream...

But the pleasure-seekers of Last Island knew there must have been a "great blow" somewhere that day. Still the sea swelled; and a splendid surf made the evening bath delightful. Then, just at sundown, a beautiful cloud-bridge grew up and arched the sky with a single span of cottony pink vapor, that changed and deepened color with the dying of the iridescent day. And the cloud-bridge approached, stretched, strained, and swung round at last to make way for the coming of the gale,—even as the light bridges that traverse the dreamy Teche swing open when luggermen sound through their conch-shells the long, bellowing signal of approach.

Then the wind began to blow, with the passing of July. It blew from the northeast, clear, cool. It blew in enormous sighs, dying away at regular intervals, as if pausing to draw breath. All night it blew; and in each pause could be heard the answering moan of the rising surf,—as if the rhythm of the sea moulded itself after the rhythm of the air,—as if the waving of the water responded precisely to the waving of the wind,—a billow for every puff, a surge for every sigh.

The August morning broke in a bright sky;—the breeze still came cool and clear from the northeast. The waves were running now at a sharp angle to the shore: they began to carry fleeces, an innumerable flock of vague green shapes, wind-driven to be despoiled of their ghostly wool. Far as the eye could follow the line of the beach, all the slope was white with the great shearing of them. Clouds came, flew as in a panic against the face of the sun, and passed. All that day and through the night and into the morning again the breeze continued from the north. east, blowing like an equinoctial gale...

Then day by day the vast breath freshened steadily, and the waters heightened. A week later sea-bathing had become perilous: colossal breakers were herding in, like moving leviathan-backs, twice the height of a man. Still the gale grew, and the billowing waxed mightier, and faster and faster overhead flew the tatters of torn cloud. The gray morning of the 9th wanly lighted a surf that appalled the best swimmers: the sea was one wild agony of foam, the gale was rending off the heads of the waves and veiling the horizon with a fog of salt spray. Shadowless and gray the day remained; there were mad bursts of lashing rain. Evening brought with it a sinister apparition, looming through a cloud-rent in the west—a scarlet sun in a green sky. His sanguine disk, enormously magnified, seemed barred like the body of a belted planet. A moment, and the crimson spectre vanished; and the moonless night came.

Then the Wind grew weird. It ceased being a breath; it became a Voice moaning across the world,—hooting,—uttering nightmare sounds,—Whoo!—whoo!—whoo!—and with each stupendous owl-cry the mooing of the waters seemed to deepen, more and more abysmally, through all the hours of darkness. From the northwest the breakers of the bay began to roll high over the sandy slope, into the salines;—the village bayou broadened to a bellowing flood... So the tumult swelled and the turmoil heightened until morning,—a morning of gray gloom and whistling rain. Rain of bursting clouds and rain of wind-blown brine from the great spuming agony of the sea.

The steamer Star was due from St. Mary's that fearful morning. Could she come? No one really believed it,—no one. And nevertheless men struggled to the roaring beach to look for her, because hope is stronger than reason...

Even today, in these Creole islands, the advent of the steamer is the great event of the week. There are no telegraph lines, no telephones: the mail-packet is the only trustworthy medium of communication with the outer world, bringing friends, news, letters. The magic of steam has placed New Orleans nearer to New York than to the Timbaliers, nearer to Washington than to Wine Island, nearer to Chicago than to Barataria Bay. And even during the deepest sleep of waves and winds there will come betimes to sojourners in this unfamiliar archipelago a feeling of lonesomeness that is a fear, a feeling of isolation from the world of men,—totally unlike that sense of solitude which haunts one in the silence of mountain-heights, or amid the eternal tumult of lofty granitic coasts: a sense of helpless insecurity.

The land seems but an undulation of the sea-bed: its highest ridges do not rise more than the height of a man above the salines on either side;—the salines themselves lie almost level with the level of the flood-tides;—the tides are variable, treacherous, mysterious. But when all around and above these ever-changing shores the twin vastnesses of heaven and sea begin to utter the tremendous revelation of themselves as infinite forces in contention, then indeed this sense of separation from humanity appalls... Perhaps it was such a feeling which forced men, on the tenth day of August, eighteen hundred and fifty-six, to hope against hope for the coming of the Star, and to strain their eyes towards far-off Terrebonne. "It was a wind you could lie down on," said my friend the pilot.

... "Great God!" shrieked a voice above the shouting of the storm,—"she is coming!"... It was true. Down the Atchafalaya, and thence through strange mazes of bayou, lakelet, and pass, by a rear route familiar only to the best of pilots, the frail river-craft had toiled into Caillou Bay, running close to the main shore;—and now she was heading right for the island, with the wind aft, over the monstrous sea. On she came, swaying, rocking, plunging,—with a great whiteness wrapping her about like a cloud, and moving with her moving,—a tempest-whirl of spray;—ghost-white and like a ghost she came, for her smoke-stacks exhaled no visible smoke—the wind devoured it! The excitement on shore became wild;—men shouted themselves hoarse; women laughed and cried. Every telescope and opera-glass was directed upon the coming apparition; all wondered how the pilot kept his feet; all marvelled at the madness of the captain.

But Captain Abraham Smith was not mad. A veteran American sailor, he had learned to know the great Gulf as scholars know deep books by heart: he knew the birthplace of its tempests, the mystery of its tides, the omens of its hurricanes. While lying at Brashear City he felt the storm had not yet reached its highest, vaguely foresaw a mighty peril, and resolved to wait no longer for a lull. "Boys," he said, "we've got to take her out in spite of Hell!" And they "took her out." Through all the peril, his men stayed by him and obeyed him. By midmorning the wind had deepened to a roar,—lowering sometimes to a rumble, sometimes bursting upon the ears like a measureless and deafening crash. Then the captain knew the Star was running a race with Death. "She'll win it," he muttered;—"she'll stand it... Perhaps they'll have need of me to-night."

She won! With a sonorous steam-chant of triumph the brave little vessel rode at last into the bayou, and anchored hard by her accustomed resting-place, in full view of the hotel, though not near enough to shore to lower her gang-plank... But she had sung her swan-song. Gathering in from the northeast, the waters of the bay were already marbling over the salines and half across the island; and still the wind increased its paroxysmal power.

Cottages began to rock. Some slid away from the solid props upon which they rested. A chimney fumbled. Shutters were wrenched off; verandas demolished. Light roofs lifted, dropped again, and flapped into ruin. Trees bent their heads to the earth. And still the storm grew louder and blacker with every passing hour.

The Star rose with the rising of the waters, dragging her anchor.

Two more anchors were put out, and still she dragged—dragged in with the flood,—twisting, shuddering, careening in her agony. Evening fell; the sand began to move with the wind, stinging faces like a continuous fire of fine shot; and frenzied blasts came to buffet the steamer forward, sideward. Then one of her hog-chains parted with a clang like the boom of a big bell. Then another!... Then the captain bade his men to cut away all her upper works, clean to the deck. Overboard into the seething went her stacks, her pilot-house, her cabins,—and whirled away. And the naked hull of the Star, still dragging her three anchors, labored on through the darkness, nearer and nearer to the immense silhouette of the hotel, whose hundred windows were now all aflame. The vast timber building seemed to defy the storm. The wind, roaring round its broad verandas,—hissing through every crevice with the sound and force of steam,—appeared to waste its rage. And in the half-lull between two terrible gusts there came to the captain's ears a sound that seemed strange in that night of multitudinous terrors... a sound of music!

VI

... Almost every evening throughout the season there had been dancing in the great hall;—there was dancing that night also. The population of the hotel had been augmented by the advent of families from other parts of the island, who found their summer cottages insecure places of shelter: there were nearly four hundred guests assembled. Perhaps it was for this reason that the entertainment had been prepared upon a grander plan than usual, that it assumed the form of a fashionable ball. And all those pleasure seekers,—representing the wealth and beauty of the Creole parishes,—whether from Ascension or Assumption, St. Mary's or St. Landry's, Iberville or Terrebonne, whether inhabitants of the multi-colored and many-balconied Creole quarter of the quaint metropolis, or dwellers in the dreamy paradises of the Teche,—mingled joyously, knowing each other, feeling in some sort akin—whether affiliated by blood, connaturalized by caste, or simply interassociated by traditional sympathies of class sentiment and class interest. Perhaps in the more than ordinary merriment of that evening something of nervous exaltation might have been discerned,—something like a feverish resolve to oppose apprehension with gayety, to combat uneasiness by diversion. But the hours passed in mirthfulness; the first general feeling of depression began to weigh less and less upon the guests; they had found reason to confide in the solidity of the massive building; there were no positive terrors, no outspoken fears; and the new conviction of all had found expression in the words of the host himself,—"Il n'y a rien a mieux a faire que de s'amuser!" Of what avail to lament the prospective devastation of cane-fields,—to discuss the possible ruin of crops? Better to seek solace in choregraphic harmonies, in the rhythm of gracious motion and of perfect melody, than hearken to the discords of the wild orchestra of storms;—wiser to admire the grace of Parisian toilets, the eddy of trailing robes with its fairy-foam of lace, the ivorine loveliness of glossy shoulders and jewelled throats, the glimmering of satin-slippered feet,—than to watch the raging of the flood without, or the flying of the wrack...

So the music and the mirth went on: they made joy for themselves—those elegant guests;—they jested and sipped rich wines;—they pledged, and hoped, and loved, and promised, with never a thought of the morrow, on the night of the tenth of August, eighteen hundred and fifty-six. Observant parents were there, planning for the future bliss of their nearest and dearest;—mothers and fathers of handsome lads, lithe and elegant as young pines, and fresh from the polish of foreign university training;—mothers and fathers of splendid girls whose simplest attitudes were witcheries. Young cheeks flushed, young hearts fluttered with an emotion more puissant than the excitement of the dance;—young eyes betrayed the happy secret discreeter lips would have preserved. Slave-servants circled through the aristocratic press, bearing dainties and wines, praying permission to pass in terms at once humble and officious,—always in the excellent French which well-trained house-servants were taught to use on such occasions.

... Night wore on: still the shining floor palpitated to the feet of the dancers; still the piano-forte pealed, and still the violins sang,—and the sound of their singing shrilled through the darkness, in gasps of the gale, to the ears of Captain Smith, as he strove to keep his footing on the spray-drenched deck of the Star.

—"Christ!" he muttered,—"a dance! If that wind whips round south, there'll be another dance!... But I guess the Star will stay."

Half an hour might have passed; still the lights flamed calmly, and the violins trilled, and the perfumed whirl went on... And suddenly the wind veered!

Again the Star reeled, and shuddered, and turned, and began to drag all her anchors. But she now dragged away from the great building and its lights,—away from the voluptuous thunder of the grand piano, even at that moment outpouring the great joy of Weber's melody orchestrated by Berlioz: l'Invitation a la Valse,—with its marvellous musical swing! —"Waltzing!" cried the captain. "God help them!—God help us all now!... The Wind waltzes to-night, with the Sea for his partner!"...

O the stupendous Valse-Tourbillon! O the mighty Dancer! One—two—three! From northeast to east, from east to southeast, from southeast to south: then from the south he came, whirling the Sea in his arms...

... Some one shrieked in the midst of the revels;—some girl who found her pretty slippers wet. What could it be? Thin streams of water were spreading over the level planking,—curling about the feet of the dancers... What could it be? All the land had begun to quake, even as, but a moment before, the polished floor was trembling to the pressure of circling steps;—all the building shook now; every beam uttered its groan. What could it be?...

There was a clamor, a panic, a rush to the windy night. Infinite darkness above and beyond; but the lantern-beams danced far out over an unbroken circle of heaving and swirling black water. Stealthily, swiftly, the measureless sea-flood was rising.

—"Messieurs—mesdames, ce n'est rien. Nothing serious, ladies, I assure you... Mais nous en avons vu bien souvent, les inondations comme celle-ci; ca passe vite! The water will go down in a few hours, ladies;—it never rises higher than this; il n'y a pas le moindre danger, je vous dis! Allons! il n'y a—My God! what is that?"

For a moment there was a ghastly hush of voices. And through that hush there burst upon the ears of all a fearful and unfamiliar sound, as of a colossal cannonade rolling up from the south, with volleying lightnings. Vastly and swiftly, nearer and nearer it came,—a ponderous and unbroken thunder-roll, terrible as the long muttering of an earthquake.

The nearest mainland,—across mad Caillou Bay to the sea-marshes,—lay twelve miles north; west, by the Gulf, the nearest solid ground was twenty miles distant. There were boats, yes!—but the stoutest swimmer might never reach them now!

Then rose a frightful cry,—the hoarse, hideous, indescribable cry of hopeless fear,—the despairing animal-cry man utters when suddenly brought face to face with Nothingness, without preparation, without consolation, without possibility of respite... Sauve qui peut! Some wrenched down the doors; some clung to the heavy banquet-tables, to the sofas, to the billiard-tables:—during one terrible instant,—against fruitless heroisms, against futile generosities,—raged all the frenzy of selfishness, all the brutalities of panic. And then—then came, thundering through the blackness, the giant swells, boom on boom!... One crash!—the huge frame building rocks like a cradle, seesaws, crackles. What are human shrieks now?— the tornado is shrieking! Another!—chandeliers splinter; lights are dashed out; a sweeping cataract hurls in: the immense hall rises,—oscillates,—twirls as upon a pivot,—crepitates,—crumbles into ruin. Crash again!—the swirling wreck dissolves into the wallowing of another monster billow; and a hundred cottages overturn, spin in sudden eddies, quiver, disjoint, and melt into the seething.

… So the hurricane passed,—tearing off the heads of the prodigious waves, to hurl them a hundred feet in air,—heaping up the ocean against the land,—upturning the woods. Bays and passes were swollen to abysses; rivers regorged; the sea-marshes were changed to raging wastes of water. Before New Orleans the flood of the mile-broad Mississippi rose six feet above highest water-mark. One hundred and ten miles away, Donaldsonville trembled at the towering tide of the Lafourche. Lakes strove to burst their boundaries. Far-off river steamers tugged wildly at their cables,—shivering like tethered creatures that hear by night the approaching howl of destroyers. Smoke-stacks were hurled overboard, pilot-houses torn away, cabins blown to fragments. And over roaring Kaimbuck Pass,—over the agony of Caillou Bay,—the billowing tide rushed unresisted from the Gulf,—tearing and swallowing the land in its course,—ploughing out deep-sea channels where sleek herds had been grazing but a few hours before,—rending islands in twain,—and ever bearing with it, through the night, enormous vortex of wreck and vast wan drift of corpses…

But the Star remained. And Captain Abraham Smith, with a long, good rope about his waist, dashed again and again into that awful surging to snatch victims from death,—clutching at passing hands, heads, garments, in the cataract-sweep of the seas,—saving, aiding, cheering, though blinded by spray and battered by drifting wreck, until his strength failed in the unequal struggle at last, and his men drew him aboard senseless, with some beautiful half-drowned girl safe in his arms. But well-nigh twoscore souls had been rescued by him; and the Star stayed on through it all. Long years after, the weed-grown ribs of her graceful skeleton could still be seen, curving up from the sand-dunes of Last Island, in valiant witness of how well she stayed.

VII

Day breaks through the flying wrack, over the infinite heaving of the sea, over the low land made vast with desolation. It is a spectral dawn: a wan light, like the light of a dying sun.

The wind has waned and veered; the flood sinks slowly back to its abysses—abandoning its plunder,—scattering its piteous waifs over bar and dune, over shoal and marsh, among the silences of the mango-swamps, over the long low reaches of sand-grasses and drowned weeds, for more than a hundred miles. From the shell-reefs of Pointe-au-Fer to the shallows of Pelto Bay the dead lie mingled with the high-heaped drift;—from their cypress groves the vultures rise to dispute a share of the feast with the shrieking frigate-birds and squeaking gulls. And as the tremendous tide withdraws its plunging waters, all the pirates of air follow the great white-gleaming retreat: a storm of billowing wings and screaming throats.

And swift in the wake of gull and frigate-bird the Wreckers come, the Spoilers of the dead,—savage skimmers of the sea,—hurricane-riders wont to spread their canvas-pinions in the face of storms; Sicilian and Corsican outlaws, Manila-men from the marshes, deserters from many navies, Lascars, marooners, refugees of a hundred nationalities,—fishers and shrimpers by name, smugglers by opportunity,—wild channel-finders from obscure bayous and unfamiliar chenieres, all skilled in the mysteries of these mysterious waters beyond the comprehension of the oldest licensed pilot…

There is plunder for all—birds and men. There are drowned sheep in multitude, heaped carcasses of kine. There are casks of claret and kegs of brandy and legions of bottles bobbing in the surf. There are billiard-tables overturned upon the sand;—there are sofas, pianos, footstools and music-stools, luxurious chairs, lounges of bamboo. There are chests of cedar, and toilet-tables of rosewood, and trunks of fine stamped leather stored with precious apparel. There are objets de luxe innumerable. There are children's playthings: French dolls in marvellous toilets, and toy carts, and wooden horses, and wooden spades, and brave little wooden ships that rode out the gale in which the great Nautilus went down. There is money in notes and in coin—in purses, in pocketbooks, and in pockets: plenty of it! There are silks, satins, laces, and fine linen to be stripped from the bodies of the drowned,—and necklaces, bracelets, watches, finger-rings and fine chains, brooches and trinkets... "Chi bidizza!—Oh! chi bedda mughieri! Eccu, la bidizza!" That ball-dress was made in Paris by—But you never heard of him, Sicilian Vicenzu... "Che bella sposina!" Her betrothal ring will not come off, Giuseppe; but the delicate bone snaps easily: your oyster-knife can sever the tendon... "Guardate! chi bedda picciota!" Over her heart you will find it, Valentino—the locket held by that fine Swiss chain of woven hair—"Caya manan!"

And it is not your quadroon bondsmaid, sweet lady, who now disrobes you so roughly; those Malay hands are less deft than hers,—but she slumbers very far away from you, and may not be aroused from her sleep. "Na quita mo! dalaga!—na quita maganda!"... Juan, the fastenings of those diamond ear-drops are much too complicated for your peon fingers: tear them out!—"Dispense, chulita!"...

... Suddenly a long, mighty silver trilling fills the ears of all: there is a wild hurrying and scurrying; swiftly, one after another, the overburdened luggers spread wings and flutter away.

Thrice the great cry rings rippling through the gray air, and over the green sea, and over the far-flooded shell-reefs, where the huge white flashes are,—sheet-lightning of breakers,—and over the weird wash of corpses coming in.

It is the steam-call of the relief-boat, hastening to rescue the living, to gather in the dead.

The tremendous tragedy is over!

Out of the Sea's Strength

I

There are regions of Louisiana coast whose aspect seems not of the present, but of the immemorial past—of that epoch when low flat reaches of primordial continent first rose into form above a Silurian Sea. To indulge this geologic dream, any fervid and breezeless day there, it is only necessary to ignore the evolutional protests of a few blue asters or a few composite flowers of the coryopsis sort, which contrive to display their rare flashes of color through the general waving of cat-heads, blood-weeds, wild cane, and marsh grasses. For, at a hasty glance, the general appearance of this marsh verdure is vague enough, as it ranges away towards the sand, to convey the idea of amphibious vegetation,—a primitive flora as yet undecided whether to retain marine habits and forms, or to assume terrestrial ones;—and the occasional inspection of surprising shapes might strengthen this fancy. Queer flat-lying and many-branching things, which resemble sea-weeds in juiciness and color and consistency, crackle under your feet from time to time; the moist and weighty air seems heated rather from below than from above,—less by the sun than by the radiation of a cooling world; and the mists of morning or evening appear to simulate the vapory exhalation of volcanic forces,—latent, but only dozing, and uncomfortably close to the surface. And indeed geologists have actually averred that those rare elevations of the soil,—which, with their heavy coronets of evergreen foliage, not only look like islands, but are so called in the French nomenclature of the coast,—have been prominences created by ancient mud volcanoes.

The family of a Spanish fisherman, Feliu Viosca, once occupied and gave its name to such an islet, quite close to the Gulf-shore,—the loftiest bit of land along fourteen miles of just such marshy coast as I have spoken of. Landward, it dominated a desolation that wearied the eye to look at, a wilderness of reedy sloughs, patched at intervals with ranges of bitter-weed, tufts of elbow-bushes, and broad reaches of saw-grass, stretching away to a bluish-green line of woods that closed the horizon, and imperfectly drained in the driest season by a slimy little bayou that continually vomited foul water into the sea. The point had been much discussed by geologists; it proved a godsend to United States surveyors weary of attempting to take observations among quagmires, moccasins, and arborescent weeds from fifteen to twenty feet high. Savage fishermen, at some unrecorded time, had heaped upon the eminence a hill of clam-shells,—refuse of a million feasts; earth again had been formed over these, perhaps by the blind agency of worms working through centuries unnumbered; and the new soil had given birth to a luxuriant vegetation. Millennial oaks interknotted their roots below its surface, and vouchsafed protection to many a frailer growth of shrub or tree,—wild orange, water-willow, palmetto, locust, pomegranate, and many trailing tendrilled things, both green and gray. Then,—perhaps about half a century ago,—a few white fishermen cleared a place for themselves in this grove, and built a few palmetto cottages, with boat-houses and a wharf, facing the bayou. Later on this temporary fishing station became a permanent settlement: homes constructed of heavy timber and plaster mixed with the trailing moss of the oaks and cypresses took the places of the frail and fragrant huts of palmetto. Still the population itself retained a floating character: it ebbed and came, according to season and circumstances, according to luck or loss in the tilling of the sea. Viosca, the founder of the settlement, always remained; he always managed to do well.

He owned several luggers and sloops, which were hired out upon excellent terms; he could make large and profitable contracts with New Orleans fish-dealers; and he was vaguely suspected of possessing more occult resources. There were some confused stories current about his having once been a daring smuggler, and having only been reformed by the pleadings of his wife Carmen,—a little brown woman who had followed him from Barcelona to share his fortunes in the western world.

On hot days, when the shade was full of thin sweet scents, the place had a tropical charm, a drowsy peace. Nothing except the peculiar appearance of the line of oaks facing the Gulf could have conveyed to the visitor any suggestion of days in which the trilling of crickets and the fluting of birds had ceased, of nights when the voices of the marsh had been hushed for fear. In one enormous rank the veteran trees stood shoulder to shoulder, but in the attitude of giants over mastered,—forced backward towards the marsh,—made to recoil by the might of the ghostly enemy with whom they had striven a thousand years,—the Shrieker, the Sky-Sweeper, the awful Sea-Wind!

Never had he given them so terrible a wrestle as on the night of the tenth of August, eighteen hundred and fifty-six. All the waves of the excited Gulf thronged in as if to see, and lifted up their voices, and pushed, and roared, until the cheniere was islanded by such a billowing as no white man's eyes had ever looked upon before. Grandly the oaks bore themselves, but every fibre of their knotted thews was strained in the unequal contest, and two of the giants were overthrown, upturning, as they fell, roots coiled and huge as the serpent-limbs of Titans. Moved to its entrails, all the islet trembled, while the sea magnified its menace, and reached out whitely to the prostrate trees; but the rest of the oaks stood on, and strove in line, and saved the habitations defended by them...

II

Before a little waxen image of the Mother and Child,—an odd little Virgin with an Indian face, brought home by Feliu as a gift after one of his Mexican voyages,—Carmen Viosca had burned candles and prayed; sometimes telling her beads; sometimes murmuring the litanies she knew by heart; sometimes also reading from a prayer-book worn and greasy as a long-used pack of cards. It was particularly stained at one page, a page on which her tears had fallen many a lonely night—a page with a clumsy wood cut representing a celestial lamp, a symbolic radiance, shining through darkness, and on either side a kneeling angel with folded wings. And beneath this rudely wrought symbol of the Perpetual Calm appeared in big, coarse type the title of a prayer that has been offered up through many a century, doubtless, by wives of Spanish mariners,—Contra las Tempestades.

Once she became very much frightened. After a partial lull the storm had suddenly redoubled its force: the ground shook; the house quivered and creaked; the wind brayed and screamed and pushed and scuffled at the door; and the water, which had been whipping in through every crevice, all at once rose over the threshold and flooded the dwelling. Carmen dipped her finger in the water and tasted it. It was salt! And none of Feliu's boats had yet come in;—doubtless they had been driven into some far-away bayous by the storm. The only boat at the settlement, the Carmencita, had been almost wrecked by running upon a snag three days before;—there was at least a fortnight's work for the ship-carpenter of Dead Cypress Point. And Feliu was sleeping as if nothing unusual had happened—the heavy sleep of a sailor, heedless of commotions and voices. And his men, Miguel and Mateo, were at the other end of the cheniere.

With a scream Carmen aroused Feliu. He raised himself upon his elbow, rubbed his eyes, and asked her, with exasperating calmness, "Que tienes? que tienes?" (What ails thee?)

—"Oh, Feliu! the sea is coming upon us!" she answered, in the same tongue. But she screamed out a word inspired by her fear: she did not cry, "Se nos viene el mar encima!" but "Se nos viene LA ALTURA!"—the name that conveys the terrible thought of depth swallowed up in height,—the height of the high sea.

"No lo creo!" muttered Feliu, looking at the floor; then in a quiet, deep voice he said, pointing to an oar in the corner of the room, "Echame ese remo."

She gave it to him. Still reclining upon one elbow, Feliu measured the depth of the water with his thumb nail upon the blade of the oar, and then bade Carmen light his pipe for him. His calmness reassured her. For half an hour more, undismayed by the clamoring of the wind or the calling of the sea, Feliu silently smoked his pipe and watched his oar. The water rose a little higher, and he made another mark;—then it climbed a little more, but not so rapidly; and he smiled at Carmen as he made a third mark. "Como creia!" he exclaimed, "no hay porque asustarse: el agua baja!" And as Carmen would have continued to pray, he rebuked her fears, and bade her try to obtain some rest:

"Basta ya de plegarios, querida!—vete y duerme." His tone, though kindly, was
imperative; and Carmen, accustomed to obey him, laid herself down by his side, and soon,
for very weariness, slept.

It was a feverish sleep, nevertheless, shattered at brief intervals by terrible sounds, sounds magnified by her nervous condition—a sleep visited by dreams that mingled in a strange way with the impressions of the storm, and more than once made her heart stop, and start again at its own stopping. One of these fancies she never could forget—a dream about little Concha,—Conchita, her firstborn, who now slept far away in the old churchyard at Barcelona. She had tried to become resigned,—not to think. But the child would come back night after night, though the earth lay heavy upon her—night after night, through long distances of Time and Space. Oh! the fancied clinging of infant-lips!—the thrilling touch of little ghostly hands!—those phantom-caresses that torture mothers' hearts!… Night after night, through many a month of pain. Then for a time the gentle presence ceased to haunt her,—seemed to have lain down to sleep forever under the high bright grass and yellow flowers. Why did it return, that night of all nights, to kiss her, to cling to her, to nestle in her arms?

For in her dream she thought herself still kneeling before the waxen Image, while the terrors of the tempest were ever deepening about her,—raving of winds and booming of waters and a shaking of the land. And before her, even as she prayed her dream-prayer, the waxen Virgin became tall as a woman, and taller,—rising to the roof and smiling as she grew. Then Carmen would have cried out for fear, but that something smothered her voice,—paralyzed her tongue. And the Virgin silently stooped above her, and placed in her arms the Child,—the brown Child with the Indian face. And the Child whitened in her hands and changed,—seeming as it changed to send a sharp pain through her heart: an old pain linked somehow with memories of bright windy Spanish hills, and summer scent of olive groves, and all the luminous Past;—it looked into her face with the soft dark gaze, with the unforgotten smile of... dead Conchita!

And Carmen wished to thank the smiling Virgin for that priceless bliss, and lifted up her eyes, but the sickness of ghostly fear returned upon her when she looked; for now the Mother seemed as a woman long dead, and the smile was the smile of fleshlessness, and the places of the eyes were voids and darknesses... And the sea sent up so vast a roar that the dwelling rocked.

Carmen started from sleep to find her heart throbbing so that the couch shook with it. Night was growing gray; the door had just been opened and slammed again. Through the rain-whipped panes she discerned the passing shape of Feliu, making for the beach—a broad and bearded silhouette, bending against the wind. Still the waxen Virgin smiled her Mexican smile,—but now she was only seven inches high; and her bead-glass eyes seemed to twinkle with kindliness while the flame of the last expiring taper struggled for life in the earthen socket at her feet.

III

Rain and a blind sky and a bursting sea. Feliu and his men, Miguel and Mateo, looked out upon the thundering and flashing of the monstrous tide. The wind had fallen, and the gray air was full of gulls. Behind the cheniere, back to the cloudy line of low woods many miles away, stretched a wash of lead-colored water, with a green point piercing it here and there—elbow-bushes or wild cane tall enough to keep their heads above the flood. But the inundation was visibly decreasing;—with the passing of each hour more and more green patches and points had been showing themselves: by degrees the course of the bayou had become defined—two parallel winding lines of dwarf-timber and bushy shrubs traversing the water toward the distant cypress-swamps. Before the cheniere all the shell-beach slope was piled with wreck—uptorn trees with the foliage still fresh upon them, splintered timbers of mysterious origin, and logs in multitude, scarred with gashes of the axe. Feliu and his comrades had saved wood enough to build a little town,—working up to their waists in the surf, with ropes, poles, and boat-hooks. The whole sea was full of flotsam. Voto a Cristo!—what a wrecking there must have been! And to think the Carmencita could not be taken out!

They had seen other luggers making eastward during the morning—could recognize some by their sails, others by their gait,—exaggerated in their struggle with the pitching of the sea: the San Pablo, the Gasparina, the Enriqueta, the Agueda, the Constanza. Ugly water, yes!—but what a chance for wreckers!... Some great ship must have gone to pieces;—scores of casks were rolling in the trough,—casks of wine. Perhaps it was the Manila,—perhaps the Nautilus!

A dead cow floated near enough for Mateo to throw his rope over one horn; and they all helped to get it out. It was a milch cow of some expensive breed; and the owner's brand had been burned upon the horns:—a monographic combination of the letters A and P. Feliu said he knew that brand: Old-man Preaulx, of Belle-Isle, who kept a sort of dairy at Last Island during the summer season, used to mark all his cows that way. Strange!

But, as they worked on, they began to see stranger things,—white dead faces and dead hands, which did not look like the hands or the faces of drowned sailors: the ebb was beginning to run strongly, and these were passing out with it on the other side of the mouth of the bayou;—perhaps they had been washed into the marsh during the night, when the great rush of the sea came. Then the three men left the water, and retired to higher ground to scan the furrowed Gulf;—their practiced eyes began to search the courses of the sea-currents,—keen as the gaze of birds that watch the wake of the plough. And soon the casks and the drift were forgotten; for it seemed to them that the tide was heavy with human dead—passing out, processionally, to the great open. Very far, where the huge pitching of the swells was diminished by distance into a mere fluttering of ripples, the water appeared as if sprinkled with them;—they vanished and became visible again at irregular intervals, here and there—floating most thickly eastward!—tossing, swaying patches of white or pink or blue or black each with its tiny speck of flesh-color showing as the sea lifted or lowered the body. Nearer to shore there were few; but of these two were close enough to be almost recognizable: Miguel first discerned them. They were rising and falling where the water was deepest—well out in front of the mouth of the bayou, beyond the flooded sand-bars, and moving toward the shell-reef westward. They were drifting almost side by side. One was that of a negro, apparently well attired, and wearing a white apron;—the other seemed to be a young colored girl, clad in a blue dress; she was floating upon her face; they could observe that she had nearly straight hair, braided and tied with a red ribbon. These were evidently house-servants,—slaves. But from whence? Nothing could be learned until the luggers should return; and none of them was yet in sight. Still Feliu was not anxious as to the fate of his boats, manned by the best sailors of the coast. Rarely are these Louisiana fishermen lost in sudden storms; even when to other eyes the appearances are most pacific and the skies most splendidly blue, they divine some far-off danger, like the gulls; and like the gulls also, you see their light vessels fleeing landward. These men seem living barometers, exquisitely sensitive to all the invisible changes of atmospheric expansion and compression; they are not easily caught in those awful dead calms which suddenly paralyze the wings of a bark, and hold her helpless in their charmed circle, as in a nightmare, until the blackness overtakes her, and the long-sleeping sea leaps up foaming to devour her.

—"Carajo!"

The word all at once bursts from Feliu's mouth, with that peculiar guttural snarl of the "r" betokening strong excitement,—while he points to something rocking in the ebb, beyond the foaming of the shell-reef, under a circling of gulls. More dead? Yes—but something too that lives and moves, like a quivering speck of gold; and Mateo also perceives it, a gleam of bright hair,—and Miguel likewise, after a moment's gazing. A living child;—a lifeless mother. Pobrecita! No boat within reach, and only a mighty surf-wrestler could hope to swim thither and return! But already, without a word, brown Feliu has stripped for the struggle;—another second, and he is shooting through the surf, head and hands tunnelling the foam hills... One—two—three lines passed!—four!—that is where they first begin to crumble white from the summit,—five!—that he can ride fearlessly!... Then swiftly, easily, he advances, with a long, powerful breast-stroke,—keeping his bearded head well up to watch for drift,—seeming to slide with a swing from swell to swell,—ascending, sinking,—alternately presenting breast or shoulder to the wave; always diminishing more and more to the eyes of Mateo and Miguel,—till he becomes a moving speck, occasionally hard to follow through the confusion of heaping waters... You are not afraid of the sharks, Feliu!—no: they are afraid of you; right and left they slunk away from your coming that morning you swam for life in West-Indian waters, with your knife in your teeth, while the balls of the Cuban coast-guard were purring all around you. That day the swarming sea was warm,—warm like soup—and clear, with an emerald flash in every ripple,—not opaque and clamorous like the Gulf today... Miguel and his comrade are anxious. Ropes are unrolled and inter-knotted into a line. Miguel remains on the beach; but Mateo, bearing the end of the line, fights his way out,—swimming and wading by turns, to the further sandbar, where the water is shallow enough to stand in,—if you know how to jump when the breaker comes.

But Feliu, nearing the flooded shell-bank, watches the white flashings,—knows when the time comes to keep flat and take a long, long breath. One heavy volleying of foam,—darkness and hissing as of a steam-burst; a vibrant lifting up; a rush into light,—and again the volleying and the seething darkness. Once more,—and the fight is won! He feels the upcoming chill of deeper water,—sees before him the green quaking of unbroken swells,—and far beyond him Mateo leaping on the bar,—and beside him, almost within arm's reach, a great billiard-table swaying, and a dead woman clinging there, and... the child.

A moment more, and Feliu has lifted himself beside the waifs... How fast the dead woman clings, as if with the one power which is strong as death,—the desperate force of love! Not in vain; for the frail creature bound to the mother's corpse with a silken scarf has still the strength to cry out:—"Maman! maman!" But time is life now; and the tiny hands must be pulled away from the fair dead neck, and the scarf taken to bind the infant firmly to Feliu's broad shoulders,—quickly, roughly; for the ebb will not wait...

And now Feliu has a burden; but his style of swimming has totally changed;—he rises from the water like a Triton, and his powerful arms seem to spin in circles, like the spokes of a flying wheel. For now is the wrestle indeed!—after each passing swell comes a prodigious pulling from beneath,—the sea clutching for its prey.

But the reef is gained, is passed;—the wild horses of the deep seem to know the swimmer who has learned to ride them so well. And still the brown arms spin in an ever-nearing mist of spray; and the outer sand-bar is not far off,—and there is shouting Mateo, leaping in the surf, swinging something about his head, as a vaquero swings his noose!... Sough! splash!—it struggles in the trough beside Feliu, and the sinewy hand descends upon it. Tiene!—tira, Miguel! And their feet touch land again!...

She is very cold, the child, and very still, with eyes closed.

—"Esta muerta, Feliu?" asks Mateo.

—"No!" the panting swimmer makes answer, emerging, while the waves reach whitely up the sand as in pursuit,—"no; vive! respira todavia!"

Behind him the deep lifts up its million hands, and thunders as in acclaim.

IV

—"Madre de Dios!—mi sueno!" screamed Carmen, abandoning her preparations for the morning meal, as Feliu, nude, like a marine god, rushed in and held out to her a dripping and gasping baby-girl,— "Mother of God! my dream!" But there was no time then to tell of dreams; the child might die. In one instant Carmen's quick, deft hands had stripped the slender little body; and while Mateo and Feliu were finding dry clothing and stimulants, and Miguel telling how it all happened—quickly, passionately, with furious gesture,—the kind and vigorous woman exerted all her skill to revive the flickering life. Soon Feliu came to aid her, while his men set to work completing the interrupted preparation of the breakfast. Flannels were heated for the friction of the frail limbs; and brandy-and-water warmed, which Carmen administered by the spoonful, skilfully as any physician,—until, at last, the little creature opened her eyes and began to sob. Sobbing still, she was laid in Carmen's warm feather-bed, well swathed in woollen wrappings. The immediate danger, at least, was over; and Feliu smiled with pride and pleasure.

Then Carmen first ventured to relate her dream; and his face became grave again. Husband and wife gazed a moment into each other's eyes, feeling together the same strange thrill—that mysterious faint creeping, as of a wind passing, which is the awe of the Unknowable. Then they looked at the child, lying there, pink checked with the flush of the blood returning; and such a sudden tenderness touched them as they had known long years before, while together bending above the slumbering loveliness of lost Conchita.

—"Que ojos!" murmured Feliu, as he turned away,—feigning hunger...

(He was not hungry; but his sight had grown a little dim, as with a mist.) Que ojos! They were singular eyes, large, dark, and wonderfully fringed. The child's hair was yellow—it was the flash of it that had saved her; yet her eyes and brows were beautifully black. She was comely, but with such a curious, delicate comeliness—totally unlike the robust beauty of Concha... At intervals she would moan a little between her sobs; and at last cried out, with a thin, shrill cry: "Maman!—oh! maman!" Then Carmen lifted her from the bed to her lap, and caressed her, and rocked her gently to and fro, as she had done many a night for Concha,—murmuring,—"Yo sere tu madre, angel mio, dulzura mia;—sere tu madrecita, palomita mia!" (I will be thy mother, my angel, my sweet;—I will be thy little mother, my doveling.) And the long silk fringes of the child's eyes overlapped, shadowed her little cheeks; and she slept—just as Conchita had slept long ago,—with her head on Carmen's bosom.

Feliu re-appeared at the inner door: at a sign, he approached cautiously, without noise, and looked.

—"She can talk," whispered Carmen in Spanish: "she called her mother"—ha llamado a su madre.

—"Y Dios tambien la ha llamado," responded Feliu, with rude pathos;—"And God also called her."

—"But the Virgin sent us the child, Feliu,—sent us the child for Concha's sake."

He did not answer at once; he seemed to be thinking very deeply;—Carmen anxiously scanned his impassive face.

—"Who knows?" he answered, at last;—"who knows? Perhaps she has ceased to belong to any one else."

One after another, Feliu's luggers fluttered in,—bearing with them news of the immense calamity. And all the fishermen, in turn, looked at the child. Not one had ever seen her before.

V

Ten days later, a lugger full of armed men entered the bayou, and moored at Viosca's wharf. The visitors were, for the most part, country gentlemen,—residents of Franklin and neighboring towns, or planters from the Teche country,—forming one of the numerous expeditions organized for the purpose of finding the bodies of relatives or friends lost in the great hurricane, and of punishing the robbers of the dead. They had searched numberless nooks of the coast, had given sepulture to many corpses, had recovered a large amount of jewelry, and—as Feliu afterward learned,—had summarily tried and executed several of the most abandoned class of wreckers found with ill-gotten valuables in their possession, and convicted of having mutilated the drowned. But they came to Viosca's landing only to obtain information;—he was too well known and liked to be a subject for suspicion; and, moreover, he had one good friend in the crowd,—Captain Harris of New Orleans, a veteran steamboat man and a market contractor, to whom he had disposed of many a cargo of fresh pompano, sheep's-head, and Spanish-mackerel... Harris was the first to step to land;—some ten of the party followed him. Nearly all had lost some relative or friend in the great catastrophe;—the gathering was serious, silent,—almost grim,—which formed about Feliu.

Mateo, who had come to the country while a boy, spoke English better than the rest of the cheniere people;—he acted as interpreter whenever Feliu found any difficulty in comprehending or answering questions; and he told them of the child rescued that wild morning, and of Feliu's swim. His recital evoked a murmur of interest and excitement, followed by a confusion of questions. Well, they could see for themselves, Feliu said; but he hoped they would have a little patience;—the child was still weak;—it might be dangerous to startle her. "We'll arrange it just as you like," responded the captain;—"go ahead, Feliu!"...

All proceeded to the house, under the great trees; Feliu and Captain Harris leading the way. It was sultry and bright;—even the sea-breeze was warm; there were pleasant odors in the shade, and a soporific murmur made of leaf-speech and the hum of gnats. Only the captain entered the house with Feliu; the rest remained without—some taking seats on a rude plank bench under the oaks—others flinging themselves down upon the weeds—a few stood still, leaning upon their rifles. Then Carmen came out to them with gourds and a bucket of fresh water, which all were glad to drink.

They waited many minutes. Perhaps it was the cool peace of the place that made them all feel how hot and tired they were: conversation flagged; and the general languor finally betrayed itself in a silence so absolute that every leaf-whisper seemed to become separately audible.

It was broken at last by the guttural voice of the old captain emerging from the cottage, leading the child by the hand, and followed by Carmen and Feliu. All who had been resting rose up and looked at the child.

Standing in a lighted space, with one tiny hand enveloped by the captain's great brown fist, she looked so lovely that a general exclamation of surprise went up. Her bright hair, loose and steeped in the sun-flame, illuminated her like a halo; and her large dark eyes, gentle and melancholy as a deer's, watched the strange faces before her with shy curiosity. She wore the same dress in which Feliu had found her—a soft white fabric of muslin, with trimmings of ribbon that had once been blue; and the now discolored silken scarf, which had twice done her such brave service, was thrown over her shoulders. Carmen had washed and repaired the dress very creditably; but the tiny slim feet were bare,—the brine-soaked shoes she wore that fearful night had fallen into shreds at the first attempt to remove them.

—"Gentlemen," said Captain Harris,—"we can find no clew to the identity of this child. There is no mark upon her clothing; and she wore nothing in the shape of jewelry—except this string of coral beads. We are nearly all Americans here; and she does not speak any English... Does any one here know anything about her?"

Carmen felt a great sinking at her heart: was her new-found darling to be taken so soon from her? But no answer came to the captain's query. No one of the expedition had ever seen that child before. The coral beads were passed from hand to hand; the scarf was minutely scrutinized without avail. Somebody asked if the child could not talk German or Italian.

—"Italiano? No!" said Feliu, shaking his head.... One of his luggermen, Gioachino Sparicio, who, though a Sicilian, could speak several Italian idioms besides his own, had already essayed.

—"She speaks something or other," answered the captain—"but no English. I couldn't make her understand me; and Feliu, who talks nearly all the infernal languages spoken down this way, says he can't make her understand him. Suppose some of you who know French talk to her a bit... Laroussel, why don't you try?"

The young man addressed did not at first seem to notice the captain's suggestion. He was a tall, lithe fellow, with a dark, positive face: he had never removed his black gaze from the child since the moment of her appearance. Her eyes, too, seemed to be all for him—to return his scrutiny with a sort of vague pleasure, a half savage confidence... Was it the first embryonic feeling of race-affinity quickening in the little brain?—some intuitive, inexplicable sense of kindred? She shrank from Doctor Hecker, who addressed her in German, shook her head at Lawyer Solari, who tried to make her answer in Italian; and her look always went back plaintively to the dark, sinister face of Laroussel,—Laroussel who had calmly taken a human life, a wicked human life, only the evening before.

—"Laroussel, you're the only Creole in this crowd," said the captain; "talk to her! Talk gumbo to her!... I've no doubt this child knows German very well, and Italian too,"—he added, maliciously—"but not in the way you gentlemen pronounce it!"

Laroussel handed his rifle to a friend, crouched down before the little girl, and looked into her face, and smiled. Her great sweet orbs shone into his one moment, seriously, as if searching; and then... she returned his smile. It seemed to touch something latent within the man, something rare; for his whole expression changed; and there was a caress in his look and voice none of the men could have believed possible—as he exclaimed:—

—"Fais moin bo, piti."

She pouted up her pretty lips and kissed his black moustache.

He spoke to her again:—

—"Dis moin to nom, piti;—dis moin to nom, chere."

Then, for the first time, she spoke, answering in her argent treble:

—"Zouzoune."

All held their breath. Captain Harris lifted his finger to his lips to command silence.

—"Zouzoune? Zouzoune qui, chere?"

—"Zouzoune, a c'est moin, Lili!"

—"C'est pas tout to nom, Lili;—dis moin, chere, to laut nom."

—"Mo pas connin laut nom."

—"Comment ye te pele to maman, piti?"

—"Maman,—Maman 'Dele."

—"Et comment ye te pele to papa, chere?"

—"Papa Zulien."

—"Bon! Et comment to maman te pele to papa?—dis ca a moin, chere?"

The child looked down, put a finger in her mouth, thought a moment, and replied:—

—"Li pele li, 'Cheri'; li pele li, 'Papoute.'"

—"Aie, aie!—c'est tout, ca?—to maman te jamain pele li daut' chose?"

—"Mo pas connin, moin."

She began to play with some trinkets attached to his watch chain;—a very small gold compass especially impressed her fancy by the trembling and flashing of its tiny needle, and she murmured, coaxingly:—

—"Mo oule ca! Donnin ca a moin."

He took all possible advantage of the situation, and replied at once:—

—"Oui! mo va donnin toi ca si to di moin to laut nom."

The splendid bribe evidently impressed her greatly; for tears rose to the brown eyes as she answered:

—"Mo pas capab di' ca;   mo pas capab di' laut nom… Mo oule; mo pas capab!"

Laroussel explained. The child's name was Lili,—perhaps a contraction of Eulalie; and her pet Creole name Zouzoune. He thought she must be the daughter of wealthy people; but she could not, for some reason or other, tell her family name. Perhaps she could not pronounce it well, and was afraid of being laughed at: some of the old French names were very hard for Creole children to pronounce, so long as the little ones were indulged in the habit of talking the patois; and after a certain age their mispronunciations would be made fun of in order to accustom them to abandon the idiom of the slave-nurses, and to speak only French. Perhaps, again, she was really unable to recall the name: certain memories might have been blurred in the delicate brain by the shock of that terrible night. She said her mother's name was Adele, and her father's Julien; but these were very common names in Louisiana,—and could afford scarcely any better clew than the innocent statement that her mother used to address her father as "dear" (Cheri),— or with the Creole diminutive "little papa" (Papoute). Then Laroussel tried to reach a clew in other ways, without success. He asked her about where she lived,—what the place was like; and she told him about fig-trees in a court, and galleries, and banquettes, and spoke of a faubou',—without being able to name any street. He asked her what her father used to do, and was assured that he did everything—that there was nothing he could not do. Divine absurdity of childish faith!—infinite artlessness of childish love!… Probably the little girl's parents had been residents of New Orleans—dwellers of the old colonial quarter,—the faubourg, the faubou'.

—"Well, gentlemen," said Captain Harris, as Laroussel abandoned his cross-examination in despair,—"all we can do now is to make inquiries. I suppose we'd better leave the child here. She is very weak yet, and in no condition to be taken to the city, right in the middle of the hot season; and nobody could care for her any better than she's being cared for here. Then, again, seems to me that as Feliu saved her life,—and that at the risk of his own,—he's got the prior claim, anyhow; and his wife is just crazy about the child—wants to adopt her. If we can find her relatives so much the better; but I say, gentlemen, let them come right here to Feliu, themselves, and thank him as he ought to be thanked, by God! That's just what I think about it."

Carmen understood the little speech;—all the Spanish charm of her youth had faded out years before; but in the one swift look of gratitude she turned upon the captain, it seemed to blossom again;—for that quick moment, she was beautiful.

"The captain is quite right," observed Dr. Hecker: "it would be very dangerous to take the child away just now." There was no dissent.

—"All correct, boys?" asked the captain… "Well, we've got to be going. By-by, Zouzoune!"

But Zouzoune burst into tears. Laroussel was going too!

—"Give her the thing, Laroussel! she gave you a kiss, anyhow—more than she'd do for me," cried the captain.

Laroussel turned, detached the little compass from his watch chain, and gave it to her. She held up her pretty face for his farewell kiss…

VI

But it seemed fated that Feliu's waif should never be identified;—diligent inquiry and printed announcements alike proved fruitless. Sea and sand had either hidden or effaced all the records of the little world they had engulfed: the annihilation of whole families, the extinction of races, had, in more than one instance, rendered vain all efforts to recognize the dead. It required the subtle perception of long intimacy to name remains tumefied and discolored by corruption and exposure, mangled and gnawed by fishes, by reptiles, and by birds;—it demanded the great courage of love to look upon the eyeless faces found sweltering in the blackness of cypress-shadows, under the low palmettoes of the swamps,—where gorged buzzards started from sleep, or cottonmouths uncoiled, hissing, at the coming of the searchers. And sometimes all who had loved the lost were themselves among the missing. The full roll call of names could never be made out; extraordinary mistakes were committed. Men whom the world deemed dead and buried came back, like ghosts,—to read their own epitaphs…. Almost at the same hour that Laroussel was questioning the child in Creole patois, another expedition, searching for bodies along the coast, discovered on the beach of a low islet famed as a haunt of pelicans, the corpse of a child. Some locks of bright hair still adhering to the skull, a string of red beads, a white muslin dress, a handkerchief broidered with the initials "A.L.B.,"—were secured as clews; and the little body was interred where it had been found.

And, several days before, Captain Hotard, of the relief-boat Estelle Brousseaux, had found, drifting in the open Gulf (latitude 26 degrees 43 minutes; longitude 88 degrees 17 minutes),—the corpse of a fair-haired woman, clinging to a table. The body was disfigured beyond recognition: even the slender bones of the hands had been stripped by the nibs of the sea-birds-except one finger, the third of the left, which seemed to have been protected by a ring of gold, as by a charm. Graven within the plain yellow circlet was a date,—"JUILLET—1851"; and the names,—"ADELE + JULIEN,"—separated by a cross. The

Estelle carried coffins that day: most of them were already full; but there was one for Adele.

Who was she?—who was her Julien?... When the Estelle and many other vessels had discharged their ghastly cargoes;—when the bereaved of the land had assembled as hastily as they might for the du y of identification;—when memories were strained almost to madness in research of names, dates, incidents— for the evocation of dead words, resurrection of vanished days, recollection of dear promises,—then, in the confusion, it was believed and declared that the little corpse found on the pelican island was the daughter of the wearer of the wedding ring: Adele La Brierre, nee Florane, wife of Dr. Julien La Brierre, of New Orleans, who was numbered among the missing.

And they brought dead Adele back,—up shadowy river windings, over linked brightnesses of lake and lakelet, through many a green glimmering bayou,—to the Creole city, and laid her to rest somewhere in the old Saint-Louis Cemetery. And upon the tablet recording her name were also graven the words:

AUSSI A LA MEMOIRE DE SON MARI;

JULIEN RAYMOND LA BRIERRE,

NE A LA PAROISSE ST. LANDRY,

LE 29 MAI; MDCCCXXVIII;

ET DE LEUR FILLE,

EULALIE,

AGEE DE 4 AS ET 5 MOIS,—

QUI TOUS PERIRENT

DANS LA GRANDE TEMPETE QUI

BALAYA L'ILE DERNIERE, LE

10 AOUT, MDCCCLVI

... + ...

PRIEZ POUR EUX!

VII

Yet six months afterward the face of Julien La Brierre was seen again upon the streets of New Orleans. Men started at the sight of him, as at a spectre standing in the sun. And nevertheless the apparition cast a shadow. People paused, approached, half extended a hand through old habit, suddenly checked themselves and passed on,—wondering they should have forgotten, asking themselves why they had so nearly made an absurd mistake.

It was a February day,—one of those crystalline days of our snowless Southern winter, when the air is clear and cool, and outlines sharpen in the light as if viewed through the focus of a diamond glass;— and in that brightness Julien La Brierre perused his own brief epitaph, and gazed upon the sculptured name of drowned Adele. Only half a year had passed since she was laid away in the high wall of tombs,— in that strange colonial columbarium where the dead slept in rows, behind squared marbles lettered in black or bronze. Yet her resting-place,—in the highest range,—already seemed old. Under our Southern sun, the vegetation of cemeteries seems to spring into being spontaneously—to leap all suddenly into luxuriant life! Microscopic mossy growths had begun to mottle the slab that closed her in;—over its face some singular creeper was crawling, planting tiny reptile-feet into the chiselled letters of the inscription; and from the moist soil below speckled euphorbias were growing up to her,—and morning glories,—and beautiful green tangled things of which he did not know the name.

And the sight of the pretty lizards, puffing their crimson pouches in the sun, or undulating athwart epitaphs, and shifting their color when approached, from emerald to ashen-gray;—the caravans of the ants, journeying to and from tiny chinks in the masonry;—the bees gathering honey from the crimson blossoms of the crete-de-coq, whose radicles sought sustenance, perhaps from human dust, in the decay of generations:—all that rich life of graves summoned up fancies of Resurrection, Nature's resurrection-work—wondrous transformations of flesh, marvellous bans migration of souls!... From some forgotten crevice of that tomb roof, which alone intervened between her and the vast light, a sturdy weed was growing. He knew that plant, as it quivered against the blue,—the chou-gras, as Creole children call it: its dark berries form the mockingbird's favorite food... Might not its roots, exploring darkness, have found some unfamiliar nutriment within?—might it not be that something of the dead heart had risen to purple and emerald life—in the sap of translucent leaves, in the wine of the savage berries,—to blend with the blood of the Wizard Singer,—to lend a strange sweetness to the melody of his wooing?...

... Seldom, indeed, does it happen that a man in the prime of youth, in the possession of wealth, habituated to comforts and the elegances of life, discovers in one brief week how minute his true relation to the human aggregate,—how insignificant his part as one living atom of the social organism. Seldom, at the age of twenty-eight, has one been made able to comprehend, through experience alone, that in the vast and complex Stream of Being he counts for less than a drop; and that, even as the blood loses and replaces its corpuscles, without a variance in the volume and vigor of its current, so are individual existences eliminated and replaced in the pulsing of a people's life, with never a pause in its mighty murmur. But all this, and much more, Julien had learned in seven merciless days—seven successive and terrible shocks of experience. The enormous world had not missed him; and his place therein was not void— society had simply forgotten him. So long as he had moved among them, all he knew for friends had performed their petty altruistic roles,—had discharged their small human obligations,—had kept turned toward him the least selfish side of their natures,—had made with him a tolerably equitable exchange of ideas and of favors; and after his disappearance from their midst, they had duly mourned for his loss—to themselves! They had played out the final act in the unimportant drama of his life: it was really asking too much to demand a repetition... Impossible to deceive himself as to the feeling his unanticipated return had aroused:—feigned pity where he had looked for sympathetic welcome; dismay where he had expected surprised delight; and, oftener, airs of resignation, or disappointment ill disguised,—always insincerity, politely masked or coldly bare. He had come back to find strangers in his home, relatives at law concerning his estate, and himself regarded as an intruder among the living,—an unlucky guest, a revenant... How hollow and selfish a world it seemed! And yet there was love in it; he had been loved in it, unselfishly, passionately, with the love of father and of mother, of wife and child... All buried!—all lost forever!... Oh! would to God the story of that stone were not a lie!—would to kind God he also were dead!...

Evening shadowed: the violet deepened and prickled itself with stars;—the sun passed below the west, leaving in his wake a momentary splendor of vermilion... our Southern day is not prolonged by gloaming. And Julien's thoughts darkened with the darkening, and as swiftly. For while there was yet light to see, he read another name that he used to know—the name of RAMIREZ... Nacio en Cienfuegos, isla de Cuba... Wherefore born?—for what eternal purpose, Ramirez,—in the City of a Hundred Fires? He had blown out his brains before the sepulchre of his young wife... It was a detached double vault, shaped like a huge chest, and much dilapidated already:—under the continuous burrowing of the crawfish it had sunk greatly on one side, tilting as if about to fall. Out from its zigzag fissurings of brick and plaster, a sinister voice seemed to come:—"Go thou and do likewise!... Earth groans with her burthen even now,—the burthen of Man: she holds no place for thee!"

VIII

… That voice pursued him into the darkness of his chilly room,—haunted him in the silence of his lodging. And then began within the man that ghostly struggle between courage and despair, between patient reason and mad revolt, between weakness and force, between darkness and light, which all sensitive and generous natures must wage in their own souls at least once—perhaps many times—in their lives. Memory, in such moments, plays like an electric storm;—all involuntarily he found himself reviewing his life.

Incidents long forgotten came back with singular vividness: he saw the Past as he had not seen it while it was the Present;—remembrances of home, recollections of infancy, recurred to him with terrible intensity,—the artless pleasures and the trifling griefs, the little hurts and the tender pettings, the hopes and the anxieties of those who loved him, the smiles and tears of slaves… And his first Creole pony, a present from his father the day after he had proved himself able to recite his prayers correctly in French, without one mispronunciation—without saying crasse for grace,—and yellow Michel, who taught him to swim and to fish and to paddle a pirogue;—and the bayou, with its wonder-world of turtles and birds and creeping things;—and his German tutor, who could not pronounce the j;—and the songs of the cane-fields,—strangely pleasing, full of quaverings and long plaintive notes, like the call of the cranes… Tou', tou' pays blanc!… Afterward Camaniere had leased the place;—everything must have been changed; even the songs could not be the same. Tou', tou' pays blare!—Danie qui commande… And then Paris; and the university, with its wild under-life,—some debts, some follies; and the frequent fond letters from home to which he might have replied so much oftener;—Paris, where talent is mediocrity; Paris, with its thunders and its splendors and its seething of passion;—Paris, supreme focus of human endeavor, with its madnesses of art, its frenzied striving to express the Inexpressible, its spasmodic strainings to clutch the Unattainable, its soarings of soul-fire to the heaven of the Impossible…

What a rejoicing there was at his return!—how radiant and level the long Road of the Future seemed to open before him!—everywhere friends, prospects, felicitations. Then his first serious love;—and the night of the ball at St. Martinsville,—the vision of light! Gracile as a palm, and robed at once so simply, so exquisitely in white, she had seemed to him the supreme realization of all possible dreams of beauty… And his passionate jealousy; and the slap from Laroussel; and the humiliating two-minute duel with rapiers in which he learned that he had found his master. The scar was deep. Why had not Laroussel killed him then?… Not evil-hearted, Laroussel,—they used to salute each other afterward when they met; and Laroussel's smile was kindly. Why had he refrained from returning it? Where was Laroussel now?

For the death of his generous father, who had sacrificed so much to reform him; for the death, only a short while after, of his all-forgiving mother, he had found one sweet woman to console him with her tender words, her loving lips, her delicious caress. She had given him Zouzoune, the darling link between their lives,—Zouzoune, who waited each evening with black Eglantine at the gate to watch for his coming, and to cry through all the house like a bird, "Papa, lape vini!—papa Zulien ape vini!"… And once that she had made him very angry by upsetting the ink over a mass of business papers, and he had slapped her (could he ever forgive himself?)—she had cried, through her sobs of astonishment and pain:—"To laimin moin?—to batte moin!" (Thou lovest me?—thou beatest me!) Next month she would have been five years old. To laimin moin?—to batte moin!…

A furious paroxysm of grief convulsed him, suffocated him; it seemed to him that something within must burst, must break. He flung himself down upon his bed, biting the coverings in order to stifle his outcry, to smother the sounds of his despair. What crime had he ever done, oh God! that he should be made to suffer thus?—was it for this he had been permitted to live? had been rescued from the sea and carried round all the world unscathed? Why should he live to remember, to suffer, to agonize? Was not

Ramirez wiser?

How long the contest within him lasted, he never knew; but ere it was done, he had become, in more ways than one, a changed man. For the first,—though not indeed for the last time,—something of the deeper and nobler comprehension of human weakness and of human suffering had been revealed to him,—something of that larger knowledge without which the sense of duty can never be fully acquired, nor the understanding of unselfish goodness, nor the spirit of tenderness. The suicide is not a coward; he is an egotist.

A ray of sunlight touched his wet pillow,—awoke him. He rushed to the window, flung the latticed shutters apart, and looked out.

Something beautiful and ghostly filled all the vistas,—frost-haze; and in some queer way the mist had momentarily caught and held the very color of the sky. An azure fog! Through it the quaint and checkered street—as yet but half illumined by the sun,—took tones of impossible color; the view paled away through faint bluish tints into transparent purples;—all the shadows were indigo. How sweet the morning!—how well life seemed worth living! Because the sun had shown his face through a fairy veil of frost!...

Who was the ancient thinker?—was it Hermes?—who said:—"The Sun is Laughter; for 'tis He who maketh joyous the thoughts of men, and gladdeneth the infinite world.".…

The Shadow of the Tide

I

Carmen found that her little pet had been taught how to pray; for each night and morning when the devout woman began to make her orisons, the child would kneel beside her, with little hands joined, and in a voice sweet and clear murmur something she had learned by heart. Much as this pleased Carmen, it seemed to her that the child's prayers could not be wholly valid unless uttered in Spanish;—for Spanish was heaven's own tongue,—la lengua de Dios, el idioma de Dios; and she resolved to teach her to say the Salve Maria and the Padre Nuestro in Castilian—also, her own favorite prayer to the Virgin, beginning with the words, "Madre santisima, toda dulce y hermosa.".…

So Conchita—for a new name had been given to her with that terrible sea christening—received her first lessons in Spanish; and she proved a most intelligent pupil. Before long she could prattle to Feliu;—she would watch for his return of evenings, and announce his coming with "Aqui viene mi papacito?"—she learned, too, from Carmen, many little caresses of speech to greet him with. Feliu's was not a joyous nature; he had his dark hours, his sombre days; yet it was rarely that he felt too sullen to yield to the little one's petting, when she would leap up to reach his neck and to coax his kiss, with—"Dame un beso, papa!—asi;—y otro! otro! otro!" He grew to love her like his own;—was she not indeed his own, since he had won her from death? And none had yet come to dispute his claim. More and more, with the passing of weeks, months, seasons, she became a portion of his life—a part of all that he wrought for. At the first, he had had a half-formed hope that the little one might be reclaimed by relatives generous and rich enough to insist upon his acceptance of a handsome compensation; and that Carmen could find some solace in a pleasant visit to Barceloneta. But now he felt that no possible generosity could requite him for her loss; and with the unconscious selfishness of affection, he commenced to dread her identification as a great calamity.

It was evident that she had been brought up nicely. She had pretty prim ways of drinking and eating, queer little fashions of sitting in company, and of addressing people. She had peculiar notions about colors in dress, about wearing her hair; and she seemed to have already imbibed a small stock of social prejudices not altogether in harmony with the republicanism of Viosca's Point. Occasional swarthy visitors,—men of the Manilla settlements,—she spoke of contemptuously as negues-marrons; and once she shocked Carmen inexpressibly by stopping in the middle of her evening prayer, declaring that she wanted to say her prayers to a white Virgin; Carmen's Senora de Guadalupe was only a negra! Then, for the first time, Carmen spoke so crossly to the child as to frighten her. But the pious woman's heart smote her the next moment for that first harsh word;—and she caressed the motherless one, consoled her, cheered her, and at last explained to her—I know not how—something very wonderful about the little figurine, something that made Chita's eyes big with awe. Thereafter she always regarded the Virgin of Wax as an object mysterious and holy.

And, one by one, most of Chita's little eccentricities were gradually eliminated from her developing life and thought. More rapidly than ordinary children, because singularly intelligent, she learned to adapt herself to all the changes of her new environment,—retaining only that indescribable something which to an experienced eye tells of hereditary refinement of habit and of mind:—a natural grace, a thorough-bred ease and elegance of movement, a quickness and delicacy of perception.

She became strong again and active—active enough to play a great deal on the beach, when the sun was not too fierce; and Carmen made a canvas bonnet to shield her head and face. Never had she been allowed to play so much in the sun before; and it seemed to do her good, though her little bare feet and hands became brown as copper. At first, it must be confessed, she worried her foster-mother a great deal by various queer misfortunes and extraordinary freaks;—getting bitten by crabs, falling into the bayou while in pursuit of "fiddlers," or losing herself at the conclusion of desperate efforts to run races at night with the moon, or to walk to the "end of the world." If she could only once get to the edge of the sky, she said, she "could climb up." She wanted to see the stars, which were the souls of good little children; and she knew that God would let her climb up. "Just what I am afraid of!"—thought Carmen to herself;—"He might let her climb up,—a little ghost!" But one day naughty Chita received a terrible lesson,—a lasting lesson,—which taught her the value of obedience.

She had been particularly cautioned not to venture into a certain part of the swamp in the rear of the grove, where the weeds were very tall; for Carmen was afraid some snake might bite the child.

But Chita's bird-bright eye had discerned a gleam of white in that direction; and she wanted to know what it was. The white could only be seen from one point, behind the furthest house, where the ground was high. "Never go there," said Carmen; "there is a Dead Man there, will bite you!" And yet, one day, while Carmen was unusually busy, Chita went there.

In the early days of the settlement, a Spanish fisherman had died; and his comrades had built him a little tomb with the surplus of the same bricks and other material brought down the bayou for the construction of Viosca's cottages. But no one, except perhaps some wandering duck hunter, had approached the sepulchre for years. High weeds and grasses wrestled together all about it, and rendered it totally invisible from the surrounding level of the marsh.

Fiddlers swarmed away as Chita advanced over the moist soil, each uplifting its single huge claw as it sidled off;—then frogs began to leap before her as she reached the thicker grass;—and long-legged brown insects sprang showering to right and left as she parted the tufts of the thickening verdure. As she went on, the bitter-weeds disappeared;—jointed grasses and sinewy dark plants of a taller growth rose above her head: she was almost deafened by the storm of insect shrilling, and the mosquitoes became very wicked. All at once something long and black and heavy wriggled almost from under her naked feet,—squirming so horribly that for a minute or two she could not move for fright. But it slunk away somewhere, and hid itself; the weeds it had shaken ceased to tremble in its wake; and her courage returned. She felt such an exquisite and fearful pleasure in the gratification of that naughty curiosity!

Then, quite unexpectedly—oh! what a start it gave her!—the solitary white object burst upon her view, leprous and ghastly as the yawn of a cotton-mouth. Tombs ruin soon in Louisiana;—the one Chita looked upon seemed ready to topple down. There was a great ragged hole at one end, where wind and rain, and perhaps also the burrowing of crawfish and of worms, had loosened the bricks, and caused them to slide out of place. It seemed very black inside; but Chita wanted to know what was there. She pushed her way through a gap in the thin and rotten line of pickets, and through some tall weeds with big coarse pink flowers;—then she crouched down on hands and knees before the black hole, and peered in. It was not so black inside as she had thought; for a sunbeam slanted down through a chink in the roof; and she could see!

A brown head—without hair, without eyes, but with teeth, ever so many teeth!—seemed to laugh at her; and close to it sat a Toad, the hugest she had ever seen; and the white skin of his throat kept puffing out and going in. And Chita screamed and screamed, and fled in wild terror,—screaming all the way, till Carmen ran out to meet her and carry her home. Even when safe in her adopted mother's arms, she sobbed with fright. To the vivid fancy of the child there seemed to be some hideous relation between the staring reptile and the brown death's-head, with its empty eyes, and its nightmare-smile.

The shock brought on a fever,—a fever that lasted several days, and left her very weak. But the experience taught her to obey, taught her that Carmen knew best what was for her good. It also caused her to think a great deal. Carmen had told her that the dead people never frightened good little girls who stayed at home.

—"Madrecita Carmen," she asked, "is my mamma dead?"

—"Pobrecita!... Yes, my angel. God called her to Him,—your darling mother."

—"Madrecita," she asked again,—her young eyes growing vast with horror,—"is my own mamma now like That?"... She pointed toward the place of the white gleam, behind the great trees.

—"No, no, no! my darling!" cried Carmen, appalled herself by the ghastly question,—"your mamma is with the dear, good, loving God, who lives in the beautiful sky, above the clouds, my darling, beyond the sun!"

But Carmen's kind eyes were full of tears; and the child read their meaning. He who teareth off the Mask of the Flesh had looked into her face one unutterable moment:—she had seen the brutal Truth, naked to the bone!

Yet there came to her a little thrill of consolation, caused by the words of the tender falsehood; for that which she had discerned by day could not explain to her that which she saw almost nightly in her slumber. The face, the voice, the form of her loving mother still lived somewhere,—could not have utterly passed away; since the sweet presence came to her in dreams, bending and smiling over her, caressing her, speaking to her,—sometimes gently chiding, but always chiding with a kiss. And then the child would laugh in her sleep, and prattle in Creole,—talking to the luminous shadow, telling the dead mother all the little deeds and thoughts of the day... Why would God only let her come at night?

... Her idea of God had been first defined by the sight of a quaint French picture of the Creation,—an engraving which represented a shoreless sea under a black sky, and out of the blackness a solemn and bearded gray head emerging, and a cloudy hand through which stars glimmered. God was like old Doctor de Coulanges, who used to visit the house, and talk in a voice like a low roll of thunder... At a later day, when Chita had been told that God was "everywhere at the same time "—without and within, beneath and above all things,—this idea became somewhat changed. The awful bearded face, the huge shadowy hand, did not fade from her thought; but they became fantastically blended with the larger and vaguer notion of something that filled the world and reached to the stars,—something diaphanous and incomprehensible like the invisible air, omnipresent and everlasting like the high blue of heaven...

II

... She began to learn the life of the coast.

With her acquisition of another tongue, there came to her also the understanding of many things relating to the world of the sea She memorized with novel delight much that was told her day by day concerning the nature surrounding her,—many secrets of the air, many of those signs of heaven which the dwellers in cities cannot comprehend because the atmosphere is thickened and made stagnant above them—cannot even watch because the horizon is hidden from their eyes by walls, and by weary avenues of trees with whitewashed trunks. She learned, by listening, by asking, by observing also, how to know the signs that foretell wild weather:—tremendous sunsets, scuddings and bridgings of cloud,—sharpening and darkening of the sea-line,—and the shriek of gulls flashing to land in level flight, out of a still transparent sky,—and halos about the moon.

She learned where the sea-birds, with white bosoms and brown wings, made their hidden nests of sand,—and where the cranes waded for their prey,—and where the beautiful wild-ducks, plumaged in satiny lilac and silken green, found their food,—and where the best reeds grew to furnish stems for Feliu's red-clay pipe,—and where the ruddy sea-beans were most often tossed upon the shore,—and how the gray pelicans fished all together, like men—moving in far-extending semicircles, beating the flood with their wings to drive the fish before them.

And from Carmen she learned the fables and the sayings of the sea,—the proverbs about its deafness, its avarice, its treachery, its terrific power,—especially one that haunted her for all time thereafter: Si quieres aprender a orar, entra en el mar (If thou wouldst learn to pray, go to the sea). She learned why the sea is salt,—how "the tears of women made the waves of the sea,"—and how the sea has ii no friends,—and how the cat's eyes change with the tides.

What had she lost of life by her swift translation from the dusty existence of cities to the open immensity of nature's freedom? What did she gain?

Doubtless she was saved from many of those little bitternesses and restraints and disappointments which all well-bred city children must suffer in the course of their training for the more or less factitious life of society:—obligations to remain very still with every nimble nerve quivering in dumb revolt;—the injustice of being found troublesome and being sent to bed early for the comfort of her elders;—the cruel necessity of straining her pretty eyes, for many long hours at a time, over grimy desks in gloomy school-rooms, though birds might twitter and bright winds flutter in the trees without;—the austere constrains and heavy drowsiness of warm churches, filled with the droning echoes of a voice preaching incomprehensible things;—the progressively augmenting weariness of lessons in deportment, in dancing, in music, in the impossible art of keeping her dresses unruffled and unsoiled. Perhaps she never had any reason to regret all these.

She went to sleep and awakened with the wild birds;—her life remained as unfettered by formalities as her fine feet by shoes. Excepting Carmen's old prayer-book,—in which she learned to read a little,—her childhood passed without books,—also without pictures, without dainties, without music, without theatrical amusements. But she saw and heard and felt much of that which, though old as the heavens and the earth, is yet eternally new and eternally young with the holiness of beauty,—eternally mystical and divine,—eternally weird: the unveiled magnificence of Nature's moods,—the perpetual poem hymned by wind and surge,—the everlasting splendor of the sky.

She saw the quivering pinkness of waters curled by the breath of the morning—under the deepening of the dawn—like a far fluttering and scattering of rose-leaves of fire;—

Saw the shoreless, cloudless, marvellous double-circling azure of perfect summer days—twin glories of infinite deeps inter-reflected, while the Soul of the World lay still, suffused with a jewel-light, as of vaporized sapphire;—

Saw the Sea shift color,—"change sheets,"—when the viewless Wizard of the Wind breathed upon its face, and made it green;—

Saw the immeasurable panics,—noiseless, scintillant,—which silver, summer after summer, curved leagues of beach with bodies of little fish—the yearly massacre of migrating populations, nations of sea-trout, driven from their element by terror;—and the winnowing of shark-fins,—and the rushing of porpoises,—and the rising of the grande-ecaille, like a pillar of flame,—and the diving and pitching and fighting of the frigates and the gulls,—and the armored hordes of crabs swarming out to clear the slope after the carnage and the gorging had been done;—

Saw the Dreams of the Sky,—scudding mockeries of ridged foam,—and shadowy stratification of capes and coasts and promontories long-drawn out,—and imageries, multicolored, of mountain frondage, and sierras whitening above sierras,—and phantom islands ringed around with lagoons of glory;—

Saw the toppling and smouldering of cloud-worlds after the enormous conflagration of sunsets,—incandescence ruining into darkness; and after it a moving and climbing of stars among the blacknesses,—like searching lamps;—

Saw the deep kindle countless ghostly candles as for mysterious night-festival,—and a luminous billowing under a black sky, and effervescences of fire, and the twirling and crawling of phosphoric foam;—

Saw the mesmerism of the Moon;—saw the enchanted tides self-heaped inmuttering obeisance before her.

Often she heard the Music of the Marsh through the night: an infinity of flutings and tinklings made by tiny amphibia,—like the low blowing of numberless little tin horns, the clanking of billions of little bells;—and, at intervals, profound tones, vibrant and heavy, as of a bass viol—the orchestra of the great frogs! And interweaving with it all, one continuous shrilling,—keen as the steel speech of a saw,—the stridulous telegraphy of crickets.

But always,—always, dreaming or awake, she heard the huge blind Sea chanting that mystic and eternal hymn, which none may hear without awe, which no musician can learn,—

Heard the hoary Preacher,—El Pregonador,—preaching the ancient Word, the word "as a fire, and as a hammer that breaketh the rock in pieces,"—the Elohim—Word of the Sea!...

Unknowingly she came to know the immemorial sympathy of the mind with the Soul of the World,—the melancholy wrought by its moods of gray, the reverie responsive to its vagaries of mist, the exhilaration of its vast exultings—days of windy joy, hours of transfigured light.

She felt,—even without knowing it,—the weight of the Silences, the solemnities of sky and sea in these low regions where all things seem to dream—waters and grasses with their momentary wavings, woods gray-webbed with mosses that drip and drool,—horizons with their delusions of vapor,—cranes meditating in their marshes,—kites floating in the high blue... Even the children were singularly quiet; and their play less noisy—though she could not have learned the difference—than the play of city children. Hour after hour, the women sewed or wove in silence. And the brown men,—always barefooted, always wearing rough blue shirts,—seemed, when they lounged about the wharf on idle days, as if they had told each other long ago all they knew or could ever know, and had nothing more to say. They would stare at the flickering of the current, at the drifting of clouds and buzzard:—seldom looking at each other, and always turning their black eyes again, in a weary way, to sky or sea. Even thus one sees the horses and the cattle of the coast, seeking the beach to escape the whizzing flies;—all watch the long waves rolling in, and sometimes turn their heads a moment to look at one another, but always look back to the waves again, as if wondering at a mystery...

How often she herself had wondered—wondered at the multiform changes of each swell as it came in—transformations of tint, of shape, of motion, that seemed to betoken a life infinitely more subtle than the strange cold life of lizards and of fishes,—and sinister, and spectral. Then they all appeared to move in order,—according to one law or impulse;—each had its own voice, yet all sang one and the same everlasting song. Vaguely, as she watched them and listened to them, there came to her the idea of a unity of will in their motion, a unity of menace in their utterance—the idea of one monstrous and complex life! The sea lived: it could crawl backward and forward; it could speak!—it only feigned deafness and sightlessness for some malevolent end. Thenceforward she feared to find herself alone with it. Was it not at her that it strove to rush, muttering, and showing its white teeth,… just because it knew that she was all by herself?… Si quieres aprender a orar, entra en el mar! And Concha had well learned to pray. But the sea seemed to her the one Power which God could not make to obey Him as He pleased. Saying the creed one day, she repeated very slowly the opening words,—"Creo en un Dios, padre todopoderoso, Criador de cielo y de la tierra,"—and paused and thought. Creator of Heaven and Earth? "Madrecita Carmen," she asked,—"quien entonces hizo el mar?" (who then made the sea?).

—"Dios, mi querida," answered Carmen.—"God, my darling… All things were made by Him" (todas las cosas fueron hechas por El).

Even the wicked Sea! And He had said unto it: "Thus far, and no farther."… Was that why it had not overtaken and devoured her when she ran back in fear from the sudden reaching out of its waves? Thus far…? But there were times when it disobeyed—when it rushed further, shaking the world! Was it because God was then asleep—could not hear, did not see, until too late?

And the tumultuous ocean terrified her more and more: it filled her sleep with enormous nightmare;—it came upon her in dreams, mountain-shadowing,—holding her with its spell, smothering her power of outcry, heaping itself to the stars.

Carmen became alarmed;—she feared that the nervous and delicate child might die in one of those moaning dreams out of which she had to arouse her, night after night. But Feliu, answering her anxiety with one of his favorite proverbs, suggested a heroic remedy:—

—"The world is like the sea: those who do not know how to swim in it are drowned;—and the sea is like the world," he added… "Chita must learn to swim!"

And he found the time to teach her. Each morning, at sunrise, he took her into the water. She was less terrified the first time than Carmen thought she would be;—she seemed to feel confidence in Feliu; although she screamed piteously before her first ducking at his hands. His teaching was not gentle. He would carry her out, perched upon his shoulder, until the water rose to his own neck; and there he would throw her from him, and let her struggle to reach him again as best she could. The first few mornings she had to be pulled out almost at once; but after that Feliu showed her less mercy, and helped her only when he saw she was really in danger. He attempted no other instruction until she had learned that in order to save herself from being half choked by the salt water, she must not scream; and by the time she became habituated to these austere experiences, she had already learned by instinct alone how to keep herself afloat for a while, how to paddle a little with her hands. Then he commenced to train her to use them,—to lift them well out and throw them forward as if reaching, to dip them as the blade of an oar is dipped at an angle, without loud splashing;—and he showed her also how to use her feet. She learned rapidly and astonishingly well. In less than two months Feliu felt really proud at the progress made by his tiny pupil: it was a delight to watch her lifting her slender arms above the water in swift, easy curves, with the same fine grace that marked all her other natural motions. Later on he taught her not to fear the sea even when it growled a little,—how to ride a swell, how to face a breaker, how to dive. She only needed practice thereafter; and Carmen, who could also swim, finding the child's health improving marvellously under this new discipline, took good care that Chita should practice whenever the mornings were not too cold, or the water too rough.

With the first thrill of delight at finding herself able to glide over the water unassisted, the child's superstitious terror of the sea passed away. Even for the adult there are few physical joys keener than the exultation of the swimmer;—how much greater the same glee as newly felt by an imaginative child,—a child, whose vivid fancy can lend unutterable value to the most insignificant trifles, can transform a weed-patch to an Eden!... Of her own accord she would ask for her morning bath, as soon as she opened her eyes;—it even required some severity to prevent her from remaining in the water too long. The sea appeared to her as something that had become tame for her sake, something that loved her in a huge rough way; a tremendous playmate, whom she no longer feared to see come bounding and barking to lick her feet. And, little by little, she also learned the wonderful healing and caressing power of the monster, whose cool embrace at once dispelled all drowsiness, feverishness, weariness,—even after the sultriest nights when the air had seemed to burn, and the mosquitoes had filled the chamber with a sound as of water boiling in many kettles. And on mornings when the sea was in too wicked a humor to be played with, how she felt the loss of her loved sport, and prayed for calm! Her delicate constitution changed;— the soft, pale flesh became firm and brown, the meagre limbs rounded into robust symmetry, the thin cheeks grew peachy with richer life; for the strength of the sea had entered into her; the sharp breath of the sea had renewed and brightened her young blood...

... Thou primordial Sea, the awfulness of whose antiquity hath stricken all mythology dumb;— thou most wrinkled diving Sea, the millions of whose years outnumber even the multitude of thy hoary motions;—thou omniform and most mysterious Sea, mother of the monsters and the gods,—whence shine eternal youth? Still do thy waters hold the infinite thrill of that Spirit which brooded above their face in the Beginning!—still is thy quickening breath an elixir unto them that flee to thee for life,—like the breath of young girls, like the breath of children, prescribed for the senescent by magicians of old,— prescribed unto weazened elders in the books of the Wizards.

III

... Eighteen hundred and sixty-seven;—midsummer in the pest-smitten city of New Orleans.

Heat motionless and ponderous. The steel-blue of the sky bleached from the furnace-circle of the horizon;—the lukewarm river ran yellow and noiseless as a torrent of fluid wax. Even sounds seemed blunted by the heaviness of the air;—the rumbling of wheels, the reverberation of footsteps, fell half-toned upon the ear, like sounds that visit a dozing brain.

Daily, almost at the same hour, the continuous sense of atmospheric oppression became thickened;—a packed herd of low-bellying clouds lumbered up from the Gulf; crowded blackly against the sun; flickered, thundered, and burst in torrential rain—tepid, perpendicular—and vanished utterly away. Then, more furiously than before, the sun flamed down;—roofs and pavements steamed; the streets seemed to smoke; the air grew suffocating with vapor; and the luminous city filled with a faint, sickly odor,—a stale smell, as of dead leaves suddenly disinterred from wet mould,—as of grasses decomposing after a flood. Something saffron speckled the slimy water of the gutters; sulphur some called it; others feared even to give it a name! Was it only the wind-blown pollen of some innocuous plant?

I do not know; but to many it seemed as if the Invisible Destruction were scattering visible seed!... Such were the days; and each day the terror-stricken city offered up its hecatomb to death; and the faces of all the dead were yellow as flame!

"DECEDE—"; "DECEDEE—"; "FALLECIO;"—"DIED."... On the door-posts, the telegraph-poles, the pillars of verandas, the lamps,—over the government letter-boxes,—everywhere glimmered the white annunciations of death. All the city was spotted with them. And lime was poured into the gutters; and huge purifying fires were kindled after sunset.

The nights began with a black heat;—there were hours when the acrid air seemed to ferment for stagnation, and to burn the bronchial tubing;—then, toward morning, it would grow chill with venomous vapors, with morbific dews,—till the sun came up to lift the torpid moisture, and to fill the buildings with oven-glow. And the interminable procession of mourners and hearses and carriages again began to circulate between the centres of life and of death;—and long trains and steamships rushed from the port, with heavy burden of fugitives.

Wealth might flee; yet even in flight there was peril. Men, who might have been saved by the craft of experienced nurses at home, hurriedly departed in apparent health, unconsciously carrying in their blood the toxic principle of a malady unfamiliar to physicians of the West and North;—and they died upon their way, by the road-side, by the river-banks, in woods, in deserted stations, on the cots of quarantine hospitals. Wiser those who sought refuge in the purity of the pine forests, or in those near Gulf Islands, whence the bright sea-breath kept ever sweeping back the expanding poison into the funereal swamps, into the misty lowlands. The watering-resorts became overcrowded;—then the fishing villages were thronged,—at least all which were easy to reach by steamboat or by lugger. And at last, even Viosca's Point,—remote and unfamiliar as it was,—had a stranger to shelter: a good old gentleman named Edwards, rather broken down in health—who came as much for quiet as for sea-air, and who had been warmly recommended to Feliu by Captain Harris. For some years he had been troubled by a disease of the heart.

Certainly the old invalid could not have found a more suitable place so far as rest and quiet were concerned. The season had early given such little promise that several men of the Point betook themselves elsewhere; and the aged visitor had two or three vacant cabins from among which to select a dwelling-place. He chose to occupy the most remote of all, which Carmen furnished for him with a cool moss bed and some necessary furniture,—including a big wooden rocking-chair. It seemed to him very comfortable thus. He took his meals with the family, spent most of the day in his own quarters, spoke very little, and lived so unobtrusively and inconspicuously that his presence in the settlement was felt scarcely more than that of some dumb creature,—some domestic animal,—some humble pet whose relation to the family is only fully comprehended after it has failed to appear for several days in its accustomed place of patient waiting,—and we know that it is dead.

IV

Persistently and furiously, at half-past two o'clock of an August morning, Sparicio rang Dr. La Brierre's night-bell. He had fifty dollars in his pocket, and a letter to deliver. He was to earn another fifty dollars—deposited in Feliu's hands,—by bringing the Doctor to Viosca's Point. He had risked his life for that money,—and was terribly in earnest.

Julien descended in his under-clothing, and opened the letter by the light of the hall lamp. It enclosed a check for a larger fee than he had ever before received, and contained an urgent request that he would at once accompany Sparicio to Viosca's Point,—as the sender was in hourly danger of death. The letter, penned in a long, quavering hand, was signed,—"Henry Edwards."

His father's dear old friend! Julien could not refuse to go,—though he feared it was a hopeless case. Angina pectoris,—and a third attack at seventy years of age! Would it even be possible to reach the sufferer's bedside in time? "Due giorno,—con vento,"—said Sparicio. Still, he must go; and at once. It was Friday morning;—might reach the Point Saturday night, with a good wind... He roused his housekeeper, gave all needful instructions, prepared his little medicine-chest;—and long before the first rose-gold fire of day had flashed to the city spires, he was sleeping the sleep of exhaustion in the tiny cabin of a fishing-sloop.

... For eleven years Julien had devoted himself, heart and soul, to the exercise of that profession he had first studied rather as a polite accomplishment than as a future calling. In the unselfish pursuit of duty he had found the only possible consolation for his irreparable loss; and when the war came to sweep away his wealth, he entered the struggle valorously, not to strive against men, but to use his science against death. After the passing of that huge shock, which left all the imposing and splendid fabric of Southern feudalism wrecked forever, his profession stood him in good stead;—he found himself not only able to supply those personal wants he cared to satisfy, but also to alleviate the misery of many whom he had known in days of opulence;—the princely misery that never doffed its smiling mask, though living in secret, from week to week, on bread and orange-leaf tea;—the misery that affected condescension in accepting an invitation to dine,—staring at the face of a watch (refused by the Mont-de-Piete) with eyes half blinded by starvation;—the misery which could afford but one robe for three marriageable daughters,—one plain dress to be worn in turn by each of them, on visiting days;—the pretty misery— young, brave, sweet,—asking for a "treat" of cakes too jocosely to have its asking answered,—laughing and coquetting with its well-fed wooers, and crying for hunger after they were gone. Often and often, his heart had pleaded against his purse for such as these, and won its case in the silent courts of Self. But ever mysteriously the gift came,—sometimes as if from the hand of a former slave; sometimes as from a remorseful creditor, ashamed to write his name. Only yellow Victorine knew; but the Doctor's housekeeper never opened those sphinx-lips of hers, until years after the Doctor's name had disappeared from the City Directory...

He had grown quite thin,—a little gray. The epidemic had burthened him with responsibilities too multifarious and ponderous for his slender strength to bear. The continual nervous strain of abnormally protracted duty, the perpetual interruption of sleep, had almost prostrated even his will. Now he only hoped that, during this brief absence from the city, he might find renewed strength to do his terrible task.

Mosquitoes bit savagely; and the heat became thicker;—and there was yet no wind. Sparicio and his hired boy Carmelo had been walking backward and forward for hours overhead,—urging the vessel yard by yard, with long poles, through the slime of canals and bayous. With every heavy push, the weary boy would sigh out,—"Santo Antonio!—Santo Antonio!" Sullen Sparicio himself at last burst into vociferations of ill-humor:—"Santo Antonio?—Ah! santissimu e santu diavulu!... Sacramentu paescite vegnu un asidente!—malidittu lu Signuri!" All through the morning they walked and pushed, trudged and sighed and swore; and the minutes dragged by more wearily than the shuffling of their feet. "Managgia Cristo co tutta a croce!"... "Santissimu e santu diavulu!"...

But as they reached at last the first of the broad bright lakes, the heat lifted, the breeze leaped up, the loose sail flapped and filled; and, bending graciously as a skater, the old San Marco began to shoot in a straight line over the blue flood. Then, while the boy sat at the tiller, Sparicio lighted his tiny charcoal furnace below, and prepared a simple meal,—delicious yellow macaroni, flavored with goats' cheese; some fried fish, that smelled appetizingly; and rich black coffee, of Oriental fragrance and thickness. Julien ate a little, and lay down to sleep again. This time his rest was undisturbed by the mosquitoes; and when he woke, in the cooling evening, he felt almost refreshed. The San Marco was flying into Barataria Bay. Already the lantern in the lighthouse tower had begun to glow like a little moon; and right on the rim of the sea, a vast and vermilion sun seemed to rest his chin. Gray pelicans came flapping around the mast;—sea-birds sped hurtling by, their white bosoms rose-flushed by the western glow... Again Sparicio's little furnace was at work,—more fish, more macaroni, more black coffee; also a square-shouldered bottle of gin made its appearance. Julien ate less sparingly at this second meal; and smoked a long time on deck with Sparicio, who suddenly became very good-humored, and chatted volubly in bad Spanish, and in much worse English. Then while the boy took a few hours' sleep, the Doctor helped delightedly in maneuvering the little vessel. He had been a good yachtsman in other years; and Sparicio declared he would make a good fisherman. By midnight the San Marco began to run with a long, swinging gait;—she had reached deep water. Julien slept soundly; the steady rocking of the sloop seemed to soothe his nerves.

—"After all," he thought to himself, as he rose from his little bunk next morning,—"something like this is just what I needed."... The pleasant scent of hot coffee greeted him;—Carmelo was handing him the tin cup containing it, down through the hatchway. After drinking it he felt really hungry;—he ate more macaroni than he had ever eaten before. Then, while Sparicio slept, he aided Carmelo; and during the middle of the day he rested again. He had not had so much uninterrupted repose for many a week. He fancied he could feel himself getting strong. At supper-time it seemed to him he could not get enough to eat,—although there was plenty for everybody.

All day long there had been exactly the same wave-crease distorting the white shadow of the San Marco's sail upon the blue water;—all day long they had been skimming over the liquid level of a world so jewel-blue that the low green ribbon-strips of marsh land, the far-off fleeing lines of pine-yellow sand beach, seemed flaws or breaks in the perfected color of the universe;—all day long had the cloudless sky revealed through all its exquisite transparency that inexpressible tenderness which no painter and no poet can ever reimage,—that unutterable sweetness which no art of man may ever shadow forth, and which none may ever comprehend,—though we feel it to be in some strange way akin to the luminous and unspeakable charm that makes us wonder at the eyes of a woman when she loves.

Evening came; and the great dominant celestial tone deepened;—the circling horizon filled with ghostly tints,—spectral greens and grays, and pearl-lights and fish-colors... Carmelo, as he crouched at the tiller, was singing, in a low, clear alto, some tristful little melody. Over the sea, behind them, lay, black-stretching, a long low arm of island-shore;—before them flamed the splendor of sun-death; they were sailing into a mighty glory,—into a vast and awful light of gold.

Shading his vision with his fingers, Sparicio pointed to the long lean limb of land from which they were fleeing, and said to La Brierre:—

—"Look-a, Doct-a! Last-a Islan'!"

Julien knew it;—he only nodded his head in reply, and looked the other way,—into the glory of God. Then, wishing to divert the fisherman's attention to another theme, he asked what was Carmelo singing. Sparicio at once shouted to the lad:—

—"Ha!... ho! Carmelo!—Santu diavulu!... Sing-a loud-a! Doct-a lik-a! Sing-a! sing!"... "He sing-a nicee,"—added the boatman, with his peculiar dark smile. And then Carmelo sang, loud and clearly, the song he had been singing before,—one of those artless Mediterranean ballads, full of caressing vowel-sounds, and young passion, and melancholy beauty:—

> M'ama ancor, belta fulgente,
> Come tu m'amasti allor;—
> Ascoltar non dei gente,
> Solo interroga il tuo cor....

—"He sing-a nicee,—mucha bueno!" murmured the fisherman. And then, suddenly,—with a rich and splendid basso that seemed to thrill every fibre of the planking,—Sparicio joined in the song:—

> M'ama pur d'amore eterno,
> Ne deilitto sembri a te;
> T'assicuro che l'inferno
> Una favola sol e."...

All the roughness of the man was gone! To Julien's startled fancy, the fishers had ceased to be;—lo! Carmelo was a princely page; Sparicio, a king! How perfectly their voices married together!—they sang with passion, with power, with truth, with that wondrous natural art which is the birthright of the rudest Italian soul. And the stars throbbed out in the heaven; and the glory died in the west; and the night opened its heart; and the splendor of the eternities fell all about them. Still they sang; and the San Marco sped on through the soft gloom, ever slightly swerved by the steady blowing of the southeast wind in her sail;— always wearing the same crimpling-frill of wave-spray about her prow,—always accompanied by the same smooth-backed swells,—always spinning out behind her the same long trail of interwoven foam. And Julien looked up. Ever the night thrilled more and more with silent twinklings;—more and more multitudinously lights pointed in the eternities;—the Evening Star quivered like a great drop of liquid white fire ready to fall;—Vega flamed as a pharos lighting the courses ethereal,—to guide the sailing of the suns, and the swarming of fleets of worlds. Then the vast sweetness of that violet night entered into his blood,—filled him with that awful joy, so near akin to sadness, which the sense of the Infinite brings,—when one feels the poetry of the Most Ancient and Most Excellent of Poets, and then is smitten at once with the contrast-thought of the sickliness and selfishness of Man,—of the blindness and brutality of cities, whereinto the divine blue light never purely comes, and the sanctification of the Silences never descends… furious cities, walled away from heaven… Oh! if one could only sail on thus always, always through such a night—through such a star-sprinkled violet light, and hear Sparicio and Carmelo sing, even though it were the same melody always, always the same song!

… "Scuza, Doct-a!—look-a out!" Julien bent down, as the big boom, loosened, swung over his head. The San Marco was rounding into shore,—heading for her home. Sparicio lifted a huge conch-shell from the deck, put it to his lips, filled his deep lungs, and flung out into the night—thrice—a profound, mellifluent, booming horn-tone. A minute passed. Then, ghostly faint, as an echo from very far away, a triple blowing responded…

And a long purple mass loomed and swelled into sight, heightened, approached—land and trees black-shadowing, and lights that swung… The San Marco glided into a bayou,—under a high wharfing of timbers, where a bearded fisherman waited, and a woman. Sparicio flung up a rope.

The bearded man caught it by the lantern-light, and tethered the San Marco to her place. Then he asked, in a deep voice:

—"Has traido al Doctor?"

—"Si, si!" answered Sparicio… "Y el viejo?"

—"Aye! pobre!" responded Feliu,—"hace tres dias que esta muerto."

Henry Edwards was dead!

He had died very suddenly, without a cry or a word, while resting in his rocking-chair,—the very day after Sparicio had sailed. They had made him a grave in the marsh,—among the high weeds, not far from the ruined tomb of the Spanish fisherman. But Sparicio had fairly earned his hundred dollars.

V

So there was nothing to do at Viosca's Point except to rest. Feliu and all his men were going to Barataria in the morning on business;—the Doctor could accompany them there, and take the Grand Island steamer Monday for New Orleans. With this intention Julien retired,—not sorry for being able to stretch himself at full length on the good bed prepared for him, in one of the unoccupied cabins. But he woke before day with a feeling of intense prostration, a violent headache, and such an aversion for the mere idea of food that Feliu's invitation to breakfast at five o'clock gave him an internal qualm. Perhaps a touch of malaria. In any case he felt it would be both dangerous and useless to return to town unwell; and Feliu, observing his condition, himself advised against the journey. Wednesday he would have another opportunity to leave; and in the meanwhile Carmen would take good care of him... The boats departed, and Julien slept again.

The sun was high when he rose up and dressed himself, feeling no better. He would have liked to walk about the place, but felt nervously afraid of the sun. He did not remember having ever felt so broken down before. He pulled a rocking-chair to the window, tried to smoke a cigar. It commenced to make him feel still sicker, and he flung it away. It seemed to him the cabin was swaying, as the San Marco swayed when she first reached the deep water.

A light rustling sound approached,—a sound of quick feet treading the grass: then a shadow slanted over the threshold. In the glow of the open doorway stood a young girl,—gracile, tall,—with singularly splendid eyes,—brown eyes peeping at him from beneath a golden riot of loose hair.

—"M'sieu-le-Docteur, maman d'mande si vous n'avez besoin d'que'que chose?"... She spoke the rude French of the fishing villages, where the language lives chiefly as a baragouin, mingled often with words and forms belonging to many other tongues. She wore a loose-falling dress of some light stuff, steel-gray in color;—boys' shoes were on her feet.

He did not reply;—and her large eyes grew larger for wonder at the strange fixed gaze of the physician, whose face had visibly bleached,—blanched to corpse-pallor. Silent seconds passed; and still the eyes stared—flamed as if the life of the man had centralized and focussed within them.

His voice had risen to a cry in his throat, quivered and swelled one passionate instant, and failed—as in a dream when one strives to call, and yet can only moan... She! Her unforgotten eyes, her brows, her lips!—the oval of her face!—the dawn-light of her hair!... Adele's own poise,—her own grace!—even the very turn of her neck, even the bird-tone of her speech!... Had the grave sent forth a Shadow to haunt him?—could the perfidious Sea have yielded up its dead? For one terrible fraction of a minute, memories, doubts, fears, mad fancies, went pulsing through his brain with a rush like the rhythmic throbbing of an electric stream;—then the shock passed, the Reason spoke:—"Fool!—count the long years since you first saw her thus!—count the years that have gone since you looked upon her last! And Time has never halted, silly heart!—neither has Death stood still!"

... "Plait-il?"—the clear voice of the young girl asked. She thought he had made some response she could not distinctly hear.

Mastering himself an instant, as the heart faltered back to its duty, and the color remounted to his lips, he answered her in French:—

"Pardon me!—I did not hear... you gave me such a start!"... But even then another extraordinary fancy flashed through his thought;—and with the tutoiement of a parent to a child, with an irresistible outburst of such tenderness as almost frightened her, he cried: "Oh! merciful God!—how like her!... Tell me, darling, your name;... tell me who you are?" (Dis-moi qui tu es, mignonne;—dis-moi ton nom.)

... Who was it had asked her the same question, in another idiom ever so long ago? The man with the black eyes and nose like an eagle's beak,—the one who gave her the compass. Not this man—no!

She answered, with the timid gravity of surprise:—

—"Chita Viosca"

He still watched her face, and repeated the name slowly,—reiterated it in a tone of wonderment:—"Chita Viosca?—Chita Viosca!"

—"C'est a dire..." she said, looking down at her feet,—"Concha—Conchita." His strange solemnity made her smile,—the smile of shyness that knows not what else to do. But it was the smile of dead Adele.

—"Thanks, my child," he exclaimed of a sudden,—in a quick, hoarse, changed tone. (He felt that his emotion would break loose in some wild way, if he looked upon her longer.) "I would like to see your mother this evening; but I now feel too ill to go out. I am going to try to rest a little."

—"Nothing I can bring you?" she asked,—"some fresh milk?"

—"Nothing now, dear: if I need anything later, I will tell your mother when she comes."

—"Mamma does not understand French very well."

—"No importa, Conchita;—le hablare en Espanol."

—"Bien, entonces!" she responded, with the same exquisite smile.

"Adios, senor!"...

But as she turned in going, his piercing eye discerned a little brown speck below the pretty lobe of her right ear,—just in the peachy curve between neck and cheek... His own little Zouzoune had a birthmark like that!—he remembered the faint pink trace left by his fingers above and below it the day he had slapped her for overturning his ink bottle... "To laimin moin?—to batte moin!"

"Chita!—Chita!"

She did not hear... After all, what a mistake he might have made! Were not Nature's coincidences more wonderful than fiction? Better to wait,—to question the mother first, and thus make sure.

Still—there were so many coincidences! The face, the smile, the eyes, the voice, the whole charm;— then that mark,—and the fair hair. Zouzoune had always resembled Adele so strangely! That golden hair was a Scandinavian bequest to the Florane family;—the tall daughter of a Norwegian sea captain had once become the wife of a Florane. Viosca?—who ever knew a Viosca with such hair? Yet again, these Spanish emigrants sometimes married blonde German girls... Might be a case of atavism, too. Who was this Viosca? If that was his wife,—the little brown Carmen,—whence Chita's sunny hair?...

And this was part of that same desolate shore whither the Last Island dead had been drifted by that tremendous surge! On a clear day, with a good glass, one might discern from here the long blue streak of that ghastly coast... Somewhere—between here and there... Merciful God!...

... But again! That bivouac-night before the fight at Chancellorsville, Laroussel had begun to tell him such a singular story... Chance had brought them,—the old enemies,—together; made them dear friends in the face of Death. How little he had comprehended the man!—what a brave, true, simple soul went up that day to the Lord of Battles!... What was it—that story about the little Creole girl saved from Last Island,—that story which was never finished?... Eh! what a pain!

Evidently he had worked too much, slept too little. A decided case of nervous prostration. He must lie down, and try to sleep.

These pains in the head and back were becoming unbearable. Nothing but rest could avail him now.

He stretched himself under the mosquito curtain. It was very still, breathless, hot! The venomous insects were thick;—they filled the room with a continuous ebullient sound, as if invisible kettles were boiling overhead. A sign of storm... Still, it was strange!—he could not perspire...

Then it seemed to him that Laroussel was bending over him—Laroussel in his cavalry uniform. "Bon jour, camarade!—nous allons avoir un bien mauvais temps, mon pauvre Julien." How! bad weather?— "Comment un mauvais temps?"... He looked in Laroussel's face. There was something so singular in his smile. Ah! yes,—he remembered now: it was the wound!... "Un vilain temps!" whispered Laroussel. Then he was gone... Whither?

—"Cheri!"...

The whisper roused him with a fearful start... Adele's whisper! So she was wont to rouse him sometimes in the old sweet nights,—to crave some little attention for ailing Eulalie,—to make some little confidence she had forgotten to utter during the happy evening... No, no! It was only the trees. The sky was clouding over. The wind was rising... How his heart beat! how his temples pulsed! Why, this was fever! Such pains in the back and head!

Still his skin was dry,—dry as parchment,—burning. He rose up; and a bursting weight of pain at the base of the skull made him reel like a drunken man. He staggered to the little mirror nailed upon the wall, and looked. How his eyes glowed;—and there was blood in his mouth! He felt his pulse spasmodic, terribly rapid. Could it possibly—?... No: this must be some pernicious malarial fever! The Creole does not easily fall a prey to the great tropical malady,—unless after a long absence in other climates. True! he had been four years in the army! But this was 1867... He hesitated a moment; then,—opening his medicine chest, he measured out and swallowed thirty grains of quinine.

Then he lay down again. His head pained more and more;—it seemed as if the cervical vertebrae were filled with fluid iron. And still his skin remained dry as if tanned. Then the anguish grew so intense as to force a groan with almost every aspiration... Nausea,—and the stinging bitterness of quinine rising in his throat;—dizziness, and a brutal wrenching within his stomach. Everything began to look pink;— the light was rose-colored. It darkened more,—kindled with deepening tint. Something kept sparkling and spinning before his sight, like a firework... Then a burst of blood mixed with chemical bitterness filled his mouth; the light became scarlet as claret... This—this was... not malaria...

VI

... Carmen knew what it was; but the brave little woman was not afraid of it. Many a time before she had met it face to face, in Havanese summers; she knew how to wrestle with it; she had torn Feliu's life away from its yellow clutch, after one of those long struggles that strain even the strength of love. Now she feared mostly for Chita. She had ordered the girl under no circumstances to approach the cabin.

Julien felt that blankets had been heaped upon him,—that some gentle hand was bathing his scorching face with vinegar and water. Vaguely also there came to him the idea that it was night. He saw the shadow-shape of a woman moving against the red light upon the wall;—he saw there was a lamp burning.

Then the delirium seized him: he moaned, sobbed, cried like a child,—talked wildly at intervals in French, in English, in Spanish.

—"Mentira!—you could not be her mother... Still, if you were—And she must not come in here,— jamais!... Carmen, did you know Adele,—Adele Florane? So like her,—so like,—God only knows how like!... Perhaps I think I know;—but I do not—do not know justly, fully—how like!... Si! si!—es el vomito!—yo lo conozco, Carmen!... She must not die twice... I died twice... I am going to die again. She only once. Till the heavens be no more she will not rise... Moi, au contraire, il faut que je me leve toujours! They need me so much;—the slate is always full; the bell will never stop. They will ring that bell for me when I am dead... So will I rise again!—resurgam!... How could I save him?—could not save myself. It was a bad case,—at seventy years!... There! Qui ca?"...

He saw Laroussel again,—reaching out a hand to him through a whirl of red smoke. He tried to grasp it, and could not... "N'importe, mon ami," said Laroussel,—"tu vas la voir bientot." Who was he to see soon?—"qui done, Laroussel?" But Laroussel did not answer. Through the red mist he seemed to smile;—then passed.

For some hours Carmen had trusted she could save her patient,—desperate as the case appeared to be. His was one of those rapid and violent attacks, such as often despatch their victims in a single day. In the Cuban hospitals she had seen many and many terrible examples: strong young men,—soldiers fresh from Spain,—carried panting to the fever wards at sunrise; carried to the cemeteries at sunset. Even troopers riddled with revolutionary bullets had lingered longer... Still, she had believed she might save Julien's life: the burning forehead once began to bead, the burning hands grew moist.

But now the wind was moaning;—the air had become lighter, thinner, cooler. A stone was gathering in the east; and to the fever-stricken man the change meant death... Impossible to bring the priest of the

Caminada now; and there was no other within a day's sail. She could only pray; she had lost all hope in her own power to save. Still the sick man raved; but he talked to himself at longer intervals, and with longer pauses between his words;—his voice was growing more feeble, his speech more incoherent. His thought vacillated and distorted, like flame in a wind.

Weirdly the past became confounded with the present; impressions of sight and of sound interlinked in fastastic affinity,—the face of Chita Viosca, the murmur of the rising storm. Then flickers of spectral lightning passed through his eyes, through his brain, with every throb of the burning arteries; then utter darkness came,—a darkness that surged and moaned, as the circumfluence of a shadowed sea. And through and over the moaning pealed one multitudinous human cry, one hideous interblending of shoutings and shriekings… A woman's hand was locked in his own… "Tighter," he muttered, "tighter still, darling! hold as long as you can!" It was the tenth night of August, eighteen hundred and fifty-six…

—"Cheri!"

Again the mysterious whisper startled him to consciousness,—the dim knowledge of a room filled with ruby colored light,—and the sharp odor of vinegar. The house swung round slowly;—the crimson flame of the lamp lengthened and broadened by turns;—then everything turned dizzily fast,—whirled as if spinning in a vortex… Nausea unutterable; and a frightful anguish as of teeth devouring him within,— tearing more and more furiously at his breast. Then one atrocious wrenching, rending, burning,—and the gush of blood burst from lips and nostrils in a smothering deluge. Again the vision of lightnings, the swaying, and the darkness of long ago. "Quick!—quick!—hold fast to the table, Adele!—never let go!"…

… Up,—up,—up!—what! higher yet? Up to the red sky! Red—black-red… heated iron when its vermilion dies. So, too, the frightful flood! And noiseless. Noiseless because heavy, clammy,—thick, warm, sickening—blood? Well might the land quake for the weight of such a tide!—Why did Adele speak Spanish? Who prayed for him?…

—"Alma de Cristo santisima santificame!

"Sangre de Cristo, embriagame!

"O buen Jesus, oye me!"…

Out of the darkness into—such a light! An azure haze! Ah!—the delicious frost!… All the streets were filled with the sweet blue mist… Voiceless the City and white;—crooked and weed grown its narrow ways!… Old streets of tombs, these… Eh! How odd a custom!—a Night-bell at every door. Yes, of course!—a night-bell!—the Dead are Physicians of Souls: they may be summoned only by night,—called up from the darkness and silence… Yet she?—might he not dare to ring for her even by day?… Strange he had deemed it day!—why, it was black, starless… And it was growing queerly cold… How should he ever find her now? It was so black… so cold!…

—"Cheri!"

All the dwelling quivered with the mighty whisper. Outside, the great oaks were trembling to their roots;—all the shore shook and blanched before the calling of the sea. And Carmen, kneeling at the feet of the dead, cried out, alone in the night:—

—"O Jesus misericordioso!—tened compasion de el!"

Kate Chopin (1850–1904)

"The voice of the sea is seductive; never ceasing, whispering, clamoring, murmuring, inviting the soul to wander for a spell in abysses of solitude; to lose itself in mazes of inward contemplation. The voice of the sea speaks to the soul. The touch of the sea is sensuous, enfolding the body in its soft, close embrace."

The above quote is from Kate Chopin's masterpiece, *The Awakening*. The sea at Grand Isle speaks to Edna Pontellier, the main character in Chopin's turn-of-the-century novel. In fact, the sea at Grand Isle finally enfolds Edna's body in its "soft, close embrace," as she swims far, far out. We learn early on the great role that setting plays in the novel, not just at Grand Isle, but also in nearby New Orleans. Chopin is often categorized as a Naturalist writer, a writer who uses the environment to shape the lives of the characters. She does so also in her short stories, "At the 'Cadian Ball," and "The Storm," two brief narratives about women and desire set in South Louisiana.

Chopin came to writing late in life, after marrying Oscar Chopin and rearing six children. She was born Katherine O'Flaherty on February 8, 1850, in St. Louis, Missouri. At the age of five, she was enrolled in the Academy of the Sacred Heart, which she attended off and on for the next thirteen years. Also that year her father, Thomas O'Flaherty, died in a railroad crash with twenty-nine other prominent St. Louis businessmen. Kate grew up very close to her great grandmother, Madame Victoire Charlesville, who home-schooled her until her death when Kate was only five. Her great grandmother's storytelling seemed to make a lasting impression on little Kate, as did her French, history, and music lessons. In fact, her ease in French surely would have played a role in her relationship with her future husband, Oscar, and her life in New Orleans.

Oscar Chopin was a cotton factor in New Orleans when he and Kate first met. They lived in the city until 1879, but after two consecutive years of failing cotton crops, the Chopins moved to Oscar's family plantation in Cloutierville, Louisiana, in Natchitoches Parish. Unfortunately, only three years after their move to Cloutierville, in 1883, Oscar died of malaria. Kate was left alone to raise six children and with an estate that was seriously in debt. After selling off much of Oscar's property to pay the considerable debt, Kate Chopin decided to continue to run the general store and remain in Cloutierville. Even though she finally did get the family finances in order, in 1884, Kate Chopin moved her family back to St. Louis to be closer to her aging mother, and it is there that she began her writing career, publishing her first works in 1889. She wrote poems, short stories, children's literature, and novels during a career that spanned little more than ten years.

Although almost all critics of the time praised Chopin's skill as a writer, they were not so kind about her subject matter. In fact, *The Awakening* was banned from St. Louis libraries, city wide. In the short stories collected here, she does write about illicit passion and even adultery, topics neither critics nor readers welcomed at the turn of the twentieth century.

The two short stories here, "At the 'Cadian Ball" and "The Storm," are companion pieces. We first meet Calixta and Alcée at a country ball or fais-do-do, in "At the 'Cadian Ball," and Chopin makes much of their disparity in class. Calixta is the earthy, passionate Cajun also of Cuban descent, while Alcée is the local Creole landowner, who is enamored of Calixta for a time, that is until Clarisse, a woman of his own class appears, and he muses: "Calixta was like a myth, now. The one, only, great reality in the world was Clarisse standing before him, telling him that she loved him." Class and family name play a role in both stories.

In 1898, the same year Chopin finished *The Awakening,* she wrote three other short stories, one of which was "The Storm," a sequel to "At the 'Cadian Ball." "The Storm" was yet another work about a married woman giving way to illicit passion, this time with a former lover while a storm rages outside. According to Chopin biographer, Per Seyersted, unlike with *The Awakening,* Chopin was "quite aware of how daring she had been in this tale," and that she never tried to publish it,[1] omitting the work from the manuscript of her third collection of short stories because she was afraid that publishers would reject the entire collection with that story in it.[2] Remarkably, "The

---

1   Per Seyersted, *Kate Chopin: a Critical Biography.* (Baton Rouge: LSUP, 1969), 164. Much of the biographical information included here is taken from Seyersted.

2   Ibid., 223.

Storm," one of Chopin's strongest short stories, was not published until 1969, when Seyersted himself included it in his edition, *The Complete Works of Kate Chopin*.

Kate Chopin was truly a writer ahead of her time. Having to maintain a certain moral standard in literature was so restrictive that after the critical condemnation of *The Awakening* Chopin's literary career all but ended. She did continue writing poetry and short stories, but many of the latter were rejected, further discouraging one of the genuinely great Louisiana writers, whose works were largely ignored for some fifty years after her death in 1904.

At the 'Cadian Ball[1]

Bobinôt, that big, brown, good-natured Bobinôt, had no intention of going to the ball, even though he knew Calixta would be there. For what came of those balls but heartache, and a sickening disinclination for work the whole week through, till Saturday night came again and his tortures began afresh? Why could he not love Ozéina, who would marry him to-morrow; or Fronie, or any one of a dozen others, rather than that little Spanish vixen? Calixta's slender foot had never touched Cuban soil; but her mother's had, and the Spanish was in her blood all the same. For that reason the prairie people forgave her much that they would not have overlooked in their own daughters or sisters.

Her eyes,—Bobinôt thought of her eyes, and weakened,—the bluest, the drowsiest, most tantalizing that ever looked into a man's, he thought of her flaxen hair that kinked worse than a mulatto's close to her head; that broad, smiling mouth and tip-tilted nose, that full figure; that voice like a rich contralto song, with cadences in it that must have been taught by Satan, for there was no one else to teach her tricks on that 'Cadian prairie. Bobinôt thought of them all as he plowed his rows of cane.

There had even been a breath of scandal whispered about her a year ago, when she went to Assumption,— but why talk of it? No one did now. "C'est Espagnol, ça," most of them said with lenient shoulder-shrugs. "Bon chien tient de race," the old men mumbled over their pipes, stirred by recollections. Nothing was made of it, except that Fronie threw it up to Calixta when the two quarreled and fought on the church steps after mass one Sunday, about a lover. Calixta swore roundly in fine 'Cadian French and with true Spanish spirit, and slapped Fronie's face. Fronie had slapped her back; "Tiens, bocotte, va!" "Espèce de lionèse; prends ça, et ça!" till the curé himself was obliged to hasten and make peace between them. Bobinôt thought of it all, and would not go to the ball.

But in the afternoon, over at Friedheimer's store, where he was buying a trace-chain, he heard some one say that Alcée Laballière would be there. Then wild horses could not have kept him away. He knew how it would be—or rather he did not know how it would be—if the handsome young planter came over to the ball as he sometimes did. If Alcée happened to be in a serious mood, he might only go to the card-room and play a round or two; or he might stand out on the galleries talking crops and politics with the old people. But there was no telling. A drink or two could put the devil in his head,—that was what Bobinôt said to himself, as he wiped the sweat from his brow with his red bandanna; a gleam from Calixta's eyes, a flash of her ankle, a twirl of her skirts could do the same. Yes, Bobinôt would go to the ball.

That was the year Alcée Laballière put nine hundred acres in rice. It was putting a good deal of money into the ground, but the returns promised to be glorious. Old Madame Laballière, sailing about the spacious galleries in her white volante, figured it all out in her head. Clarisse, her goddaughter helped her a little, and together they built more air-castles than enough. Alcée worked like a mule that time; and if he did not kill himself, it was because his constitution was an iron one. It was an every-day affair for him to come in from the field well-nigh exhausted, and wet to the waist. He did not mind if there were visitors;

1   From: Kate Chopin. *Two Tales*. (Boston, 1892). Rep. in Per Seyersted, ed., *The Complete Works of Kate Chopin*. (Baton Rouge: LSUP, 1969).

he left them to his mother and Clarisse. There were often guests: young men and women who came up from the city, which was but a few hours away, to visit his beautiful kinswoman. She was worth going a good deal farther than that to see. Dainty as a lily; hardy as a sunflower; slim, tall, graceful, like one of the reeds that grew in the marsh. Cold and kind and cruel by turn, and everything that was aggravating to Alcée.

He would have liked to sweep the place of those visitors, often. Of the men, above all, with their ways and their manners; their swaying of fans like women, and dandling about hammocks. He could have pitched them over the levee into the river, if it hadn't meant murder. That was Alcée. But he must have been crazy the day he came in from the rice-field, and, toil-stained as he was, clasped Clarisse by the arms and panted a volley of hot, blistering love-words into her face. No man had ever spoken love to her like that.

"Monsieur!" she exclaimed, looking him full in the eyes, without a quiver. Alcée's hands dropped and his glance wavered before the chill of her calm, clear eyes.

"Par exemple!" she muttered disdainfully, as she turned from him, deftly adjusting the careful toilet that he had so brutally disarranged.

That happened a day or two before the cyclone came that cut into the rice like fine steel. It was an awful thing, coming so swiftly, without a moment's warning in which to light a holy candle or set a piece of blessed palm burning. Old madame wept openly and said her beads, just as her son Didier, the New Orleans one, would have done. If such a thing had happened to Alphonse, the Laballière planting cotton up in Natchitoches, he would have raved and stormed like a second cyclone, and made his surroundings unbearable for a day or two. But Alcée took the misfortune differently. He looked ill and gray after it, and said nothing. His speechlessness was frightful. Clarisse's heart melted with tenderness; but when she offered her soft, purring words of condolence, he accepted them with mute indifference. Then she and her nénaine wept afresh in each other's arms.

A night or two later, when Clarisse went to her window to kneel there in the moonlight and say her prayers before retiring, she saw that Bruce, Alcée's negro servant, had led his master's saddle-horse noiselessly along the edge of the sward that bordered the gravel-path, and stood holding him near by. Presently, she heard Alcée quit his room, which was beneath her own, and traverse the lower portico. As he emerged from the shadow and crossed the strip of moonlight, she perceived that he carried a pair of well-filled saddle-bags which he at once flung across the animal's back. He then lost no time in mounting, and after a brief exchange of words with Bruce, went cantering away, taking no precaution to avoid the noisy gravel as the negro had done.

Clarisse had never suspected that it might be Alcée's custom to sally forth from the plantation secretly, and at such an hour; for it was nearly midnight. And had it not been for the telltale saddle-bags, she would only have crept to bed, to wonder, to fret and dream unpleasant dreams. But her impatience and anxiety would not be held in check. Hastily unbolting the shutters of her door that opened upon the gallery, she stepped outside and called softly to the old negro.

"Gre't Peter! Miss Clarisse. I was n' sho it was a ghos' o' w'at, stan'in' up dah, plumb in de night, dataway."

He mounted halfway up the long, broad flight of stairs. She was standing at the top.

"Bruce, w'ere has Monsieur Alcée gone?" she asked.

"W'y, he gone 'bout he business, I reckin," replied Bruce, striving to be noncommittal at the outset.

"W'ere has Monsieur Alcée gone?" she reiterated, stamping her bare foot. "I won't stan' any nonsense or any lies; mine, Bruce."

"I don' ric'lic ez I eva tole you lie yit, Miss Clarisse. Mista Alcée, he all broke up, sho."

"W'ere—has—he gone? Ah, Sainte Vierge! faut de la patience! butor, va!"

"W'en I was in he room, a-breshin' off he clo'es to-day," the darkey began, settling himself against the stair-rail, "he look dat speechless an' down, I say, 'You 'pear tu me like some pussun w'at gwine have a spell o' sickness, Mista Alcée.' He say, 'You reckin?' 'I dat he git up, go look hisse'f stiddy in de glass. Den he go to de chimbly an' jerk up de quinine bottle an po' a gre't hoss-dose on to he han'. An' he swalla dat mess in a wink, an' wash hit down wid a big dram o' w'iskey w'at he keep in he room, aginst he come all soppin' wet outen de fiel'.

"He 'lows, 'No, I ain' gwine be sick, Bruce.' Den he square off. He say, 'I kin mak out to stan' up an' gi' an' take wid any man I knows, lessen hit 's John L. Sulvun. But w'en God A'mighty an' a 'omen jines fo'ces agin me, dat 's one too many fur me.' I tell 'im, 'Jis so,' while I 'se makin' out to bresh a spot off w'at ain' dah, on he coat colla. I tell 'im, 'You wants li'le res', suh.' He say, 'No, I wants li'le fling; dat w'at I wants; an I gwine git it. Pitch me a fis'ful o' clo'es in dem 'ar saddle-bags.' Dat w'at he say. Don't you bodda, missy. He jis' gone a-caperin' yonda to de Cajun ball. Uh—uh—de skeeters is fair' a-swarmin' like bees roun' yo' foots!"

The mosquitoes were indeed attacking Clarisse's white feet savagely. She had unconsciously been alternately rubbing one foot over the other during the darkey's recital.

"The 'Cadian ball," she repeated contemptously. "Humph! Par exemple! Nice conduc' for a Laballière. An' he needs a saddle-bag, fill' with clothes, to go to the 'Cadian ball!"

"Oh, Miss Clarisse; you go on to bed, chile; git yo' soun' sleep. He 'low he come back in couple weeks o' so. I kiarn be repeatin' lot o' truck w'at young mans say, out heah face o' a young gal."

Clarisse said no more, but turned and abruptly reentered the house.

"You done talk too much wid yo' mouf already, you ole fool nigga, you," muttered Bruce to himself as he walked away.

Alcée reached the ball very late, of course—too late for the chicken gumbo which had been served at midnight.

The big, low-ceiled room—they called it a hall—was packed with men and women dancing to the music of three fiddles. There were broad galleries all around it. There was a room at one side where sober-faced men were playing cards. Another, in which babies were sleeping, was called le parc aux petits. Any one who is white may go to a 'Cadian ball, but he must pay for his lemonade, his coffee and chicken gumbo. And he must behave himself like a 'Cadian. Grosboeuf was giving this ball. He had been giving them since he was a young man, and he was a middle-aged one, now. In that time he could recall but one disturbance, and that was caused by American railroaders, who were not in touch with their surroundings and had no business there. "Ces maudits gens du raiderode," Grosboeuf called them.

Alcée Laballière's presence at the ball caused a flutter even among the men, who could not but admire his "nerve" after such misfortune befalling him. To be sure, they knew the Laballières were rich—that there were resources East, and more again in the city. But they felt it took a brave homme to stand a blow like that philosophically. One old gentleman, who was in the habit of reading a Paris newspaper and knew things, chuckled gleefully to everybody that Alcée's conduct was altogether chic, mais chic. That he had more panache than Boulanger. Well, perhaps he had.

But what he did not show outwardly was that he was in a mood for ugly things to-night. Poor Bobinôt alone felt it vaguely. He discerned a gleam of it in Alcée's handsome eyes, as the young planter stood in the doorway, looking with rather feverish glance upon the assembly, while he laughed and talked with a 'Cadian farmer who was beside him.

Bobinôt himself was dull-looking and clumsy. Most of the men were. But the young women were very beautiful. The eyes that glanced into Alcée's as they passed him were big, dark, soft as those of the young heifers standing out in the cool prairie grass.

But the belle was Calixta. Her white dress was not nearly so handsome or well made as Fronie's (she and Fronie had quite forgotten the battle on the church steps, and were friends again), nor were her slippers so stylish as those of Ozéina; and she fanned herself with a handkerchief, since she had broken her red fan at the last ball, and her aunts and uncles were not willing to give her another. But all the men agreed she was at her best to-night. Such animation! and abandon! such flashes of wit!

"Hé, Bobinôt! Mais w'at's the matta? W'at you standin' planté là like ole Ma'ame Tina's cow in the bog, you?"

That was good. That was an excellent thrust at Bobinôt, who had forgotten the figure of the dance with his mind bent on other things, and it started a clamor of laughter at his expense. He joined good-naturedly. It was better to receive even such notice as that from Calixta than none at all. But Madame Suzonne, sitting in a corner, whispered to her neighbor that if Ozéina were to conduct herself in a like manner, she should immediately be taken out to the mule-cart and driven home. The women did not always approve of Calixta.

Now and then were short lulls in the dance, when couples flocked out upon the galleries for a brief respite and fresh air. The moon had gone down pale in the west, and in the east was yet no promise of day. After such an interval, when the dancers again assembled to resume the interrupted quadrille, Calixta was not among them.

She was sitting upon a bench out in the shadow, with Alcée beside her. They were acting like fools. He had attempted to take a little gold ring from her finger; just for the fun of it, for there was nothing he could have done with the ring but replace it again. But she clinched her hand tight. He pretended that it was a very difficult matter to open it. Then he kept the hand in his. They seemed to forget about it. He played with her ear-ring, a thin crescent of gold hanging from her small brown ear. He caught a wisp of the kinky hair that had escaped its fastening, and rubbed the ends of it against his shaven cheek.

"You know, last year in Assumption, Calixta?" They belonged to the younger generation, so preferred to speak English.

"Don't come say Assumption to me, M'sieur Alcée. I done yeard Assumption till I 'm plumb sick."

"Yes, I know. The idiots! Because you were in Assumption, and I happened to go to Assumption, they must have it that we went together. But it was nice— hein, Calixta?— in Assumption?"

They saw Bobinôt emerge from the hall and stand a moment outside the lighted doorway, peering uneasily and searchingly into the darkness. He did not see them, and went slowly back.

"There is Bobinôt looking for you. You are going to set poor Bobinôt crazy. You 'll marry him some day; hein, Calixta?"

"I don't say no, me," she replied, striving to withdraw her hand, which he held more firmly for the attempt.

"But come, Calixta; you know you said you would go back to Assumption, just to spite them."

"No, I neva said that, me. You mus' dreamt that."

"Oh, I thought you did. You know I 'm going down to the city."

"W'en?"

"To-night."

"Betta make has'e, then; it 's mos' day."

"Well, to-morrow 'll do."

"W'at you goin' do, yonda?"

"I don't know. Drown myself in the lake, maybe; unless you go down there to visit your uncle."

Calixta's senses were reeling; and they well-nigh left her when she felt Alcée's lips brush her ear like the touch of a rose.

"Mista Alcée! Is dat Mista Alcée?" the thick voice of a negro was asking; he stood on the ground, holding to the banister-rails near which the couple sat.

"W'at do you want now?" cried Alcée impatiently. "Can't I have a moment of peace?"

"I ben huntin' you high an' low, suh," answered the man. "Dey—dey some one in de road, onda de mulbare-tree, want see you a minute."

"I would n't go out to the road to see the Angel Gabriel. And if you come back here with any more talk, I 'll have to break your neck." The negro turned mumbling away.

Alcée and Calixta laughed softly about it. Her boisterousness was all gone. They talked low, and laughed softly, as lovers do.

"Alcée! Alcée Laballière!"

It was not the negro's voice this time; but one that went through Alcée's body like an electric shock, bringing him to his feet.

Clarisse was standing there in her riding-habit, where the negro had stood. For an instant confusion reigned in Alcée's thoughts, as with one who awakes suddenly from a dream. But he felt that something of serious import had brought his cousin to the ball in the dead of night.

"W'at does this mean, Clarisse?" he asked.

"It means something has happen' at home. You mus' come."

"Happened to maman?" he questioned, in alarm.

"No; nénaine is well, and asleep. It is something else. Not to frighten you. But you mus' come. Come with me, Alcée."

There was no need for the imploring note. He would have followed the voice anywhere.

She had now recognized the girl sitting back on the bench.

"Ah, c'est vous, Calixta? Comment ça va, mon enfant?"

"Tcha va b'en; et vous, mam'zélle?"

Alcée swung himself over the low rail and started to follow Clarisse, without a word, without a glance back at the girl. He had forgotten he was leaving her there. But Clarisse whispered something to him, and he turned back to say "Good-night, Calixta," and offer his hand to press through the railing. She pretended not to see it.

                    . . .

"How come that? You settin' yere by yo'se'f, Calixta?" It was Bobinôt who had found her there alone. The dancers had not yet come out. She looked ghastly in the faint, gray light struggling out of the east.

"Yes, that 's me. Go yonda in the parc aux petits an' ask Aunt Olisse fu' my hat. She knows w'ere 't is. I want to go home, me."

"How you came?"

"I come afoot, with the Cateaus. But I 'm goin' now. I ent goin' wait fu' 'em. I 'm plumb wo' out, me."

"Kin I go with you, Calixta?"

"I don' care."

They went together across the open prairie and along the edge of the fields, stumbling in the uncertain light. He told her to lift her dress that was getting wet and bedraggled; for she was pulling at the weeds and grasses with her hands.

"I don' care; it 's got to go in the tub, anyway. You been sayin' all along you want to marry me,

Bobinôt. Well, if you want, yet, I don' care, me."

The glow of a sudden and overwhelming happiness shone out in the brown, rugged face of the young Acadian. He could not speak, for very joy. It choked him.

"Oh well, if you don' want," snapped Calixta, flippantly, pretending to be piqued at his silence.

"Bon Dieu! You know that makes me crazy, w'at you sayin'. You mean that, Calixta? You ent goin' turn roun' agin?"

"I neva tole you that much yet, Bobinôt. I mean that. Tiens," and she held out her hand in the business-like manner of a man who clinches a bargain with a hand-clasp. Bobinôt grew bold with happiness and asked Calixta to kiss him. She turned her face, that was almost ugly after the night's dissipation, and looked steadily into his.

"I don' want to kiss you, Bobinôt," she said, turning away again, "not to-day. Some other time. Bonté divine! ent you satisfy, yet!"

"Oh, I 'm satisfy, Calixta," he said.

…

Riding through a patch of wood, Clarisse's saddle became ungirted, and she and Alcée dismounted to readjust it.

For the twentieth time he asked her what had happened at home.

"But, Clarisse, w'at is it? Is it a misfortune?"

"Ah Dieu sait! It 's only something that happen' to me."

"To you!"

"I saw you go away las night, Alcée, with those saddle-bags," she said, haltingly, striving to arrange something about the saddle, "an' I made Bruce tell me. He said you had gone to the ball, an' wouldn' be home for weeks an' weeks. I thought, Alcée—maybe you were going to—to Assumption. I got wild. An' then I knew if you didn't come back, now, to-night, I could n't stan' it,—again."

She had her face hidden in her arm that she was resting against the saddle when she said that.

He began to wonder if this meant love. But she had to tell him so, before he believed it. And when she told him, he thought the face of the Universe was changed—just like Bobinôt. Was it last week the cyclone had well-nigh ruined him? The cyclone seemed a huge joke, now. It was he, then, who, an hour ago was kissing little Calixta's ear and whispering nonsense into it. Calixta was like a myth, now. The one, only, great reality in the world was Clarisse standing before him, telling him that she loved him.

In the distance they heard the rapid discharge of pistol-shots; but it did not disturb them. They knew it was only the negro musicians who had gone into the yard to fire their pistols into the air, as the custom is, and to announce "le bal est fini."

The Storm[1]

I

The leaves were so still that even Bibi thought it was going to rain. Bobinôt, who was accustomed to converse on terms of perfect equality with his little son, called the child's attention to certain sombre clouds that were rolling with sinister intention from the west, accompanied by a sullen, threatening roar. They were at Friedheimer's store and decided to remain there till the storm had passed. They sat within

---

1 From: Kate Chopin. *Two Tales*. (Boston, 1892). Rep. in Per Seyersted, ed. *The Complete Works of Kate Chopin*. (Baton Rouge: LSUP, 1969).

the door on two empty kegs. Bibi was four years old and looked very wise.

"Mama'll be 'fraid, yes, he suggested with blinking eyes.

"She'll shut the house. Maybe she got Sylvie helpin' her this evenin'," Bobinôt responded reassuringly.

"No; she ent got Sylvie. Sylvie was helpin' her yistiday," piped Bibi.

Bobinôt arose and going across to the counter purchased a can of shrimps, of which Calixta was very fond. Then he returned to his perch on the keg and sat stolidly holding the can of shrimps while the storm burst. It shook the wooden store and seemed to be ripping great furrows in the distant field. Bibi laid his little hand on his father's knee and was not afraid.

II

Calixta, at home, felt no uneasiness for their safety. She sat at a side window sewing furiously on a sewing machine. She was greatly occupied and did not notice the approaching storm. But she felt very warm and often stopped to mop her face on which the perspiration gathered in beads. She unfastened her white sacque at the throat. It began to grow dark, and suddenly realizing the situation she got up hurriedly and went about closing windows and doors.

Out on the small front gallery she had hung Bobinôt's Sunday clothes to dry and she hastened out to gather them before the rain fell. As she stepped outside, Alcée Laballière rode in at the gate. She had not seen him very often since her marriage, and never alone. She stood there with Bobinôt's coat in her hands, and the big rain drops began to fall. Alcée rode his horse under the shelter of a side projection where the chickens had huddled and there were plows and a harrow piled up in the corner.

"May I come and wait on your gallery till the storm is over, Calixta?" he asked.

"Come 'long in, M'sieur Alcée."

His voice and her own startled her as if from a trance, and she seized Bobinôt's vest. Alcée, mounting to the porch, grabbed the trousers and snatched Bibi's braided jacket that was about to be carried away by a sudden gust of wind. He expressed an intention to remain outside, but it was soon apparent that he might as well have been out in the open: the water beat in upon the boards in driving sheets, and he went inside, closing the door after him. It was even necessary to put something beneath the door to keep the water out.

"My! what a rain! It's good two years since it rain' like that," exclaimed Calixta as she rolled up a piece of bagging and Alcée helped her to thrust it beneath the crack.

She was a little fuller of figure than five years before when she married; but she had lost nothing of her vivacity. Her blue eyes still retained their melting quality; and her yellow hair, disheveled by the wind and rain, kinked more stubbornly than ever about her ears and temples.

The rain beat upon the low, shingled roof with a force and clatter that threatened to break an entrance and deluge them there. They were in the dining room—the sitting room—the general utility room. Adjoining was her bed room, with Bibi's couch along side her own. The door stood open, and the room with its white, monumental bed, its closed shutters, looked dim and mysterious.

Alcée flung himself into a rocker and Calixta nervously began to gather up from the floor the lengths of a cotton sheet which she had been sewing.

If this keeps up, Dieu sait if the levees goin' to stan it!" she exclaimed.

"What have you got to do with the levees?"

"I got enough to do! An' there's Bobinôt with Bibi out in that storm—if he only didn' left Friedheimer's!"

"Let us hope, Calixta, that Bobinôt's got sense enough to come in out of a cyclone."

She went and stood at the window with a greatly disturbed look on her face. She wiped the frame that was clouded with moisture. It was stiflingly hot. Alcée got up and joined her at the window, looking over her shoulder. The rain was coming down in sheets obscuring the view of far-off cabins and enveloping the distant wood in a gray mist. The playing of the lightning was incessant. A bolt struck a tall chinaberry tree at the edge of the field. It filled all visible space with a blinding glare and the crash seemed to invade the very boards they stood upon.

Calixta put her hands to her eyes, and with a cry, staggered backward. Alcée's arm encircled her, and for an instant he drew her close and spasmodically to him.

"Bonté!" she cried, releasing herself from his encircling arm and retreating from the window, "the house'll go next! If I only knew where Bibi was!" She would not compose herself; she would not be seated. Alcée clasped her shoulders and looked into her face. The contact of her warm, palpitating body when he had unthinkingly drawn her into his arms, had aroused all the old-time infatuation and desire for her flesh.

"Calixta," he said, "don't be frightened. Nothing can happen. The house is too low to be struck, with so many tall trees standing about. There! aren't you going to be quiet? say, aren't you?" He pushed her hair back from her face that was warm and steaming. Her lips were as red and moist as pomegranate seed. Her white neck and a glimpse of her full, firm bosom disturbed him powerfully. As she glanced up at him the fear in her liquid blue eyes had given place to a drowsy gleam that unconsciously betrayed a sensuous desire. He looked down into her eyes and there was nothing for him to do but to gather her lips in a kiss. It reminded him of Assumption.

"Do you remember—in Assumption, Calixta?" he asked in a low voice broken by passion. Oh! she remembered; for in Assumption he had kissed her and kissed and kissed her; until his senses would well nigh fail, and to save her he would resort to a desperate flight. If she was not an immaculate dove in those days, she was still inviolate; a passionate creature whose very defenselessness had made her defense, against which his honor forbade him to prevail. Now—well, now—her lips seemed in a manner free to be tasted, as well as her round, white throat and her whiter breasts.

They did not heed the crashing torrents, and the roar of the elements made her laugh as she lay in his arms. She was a revelation in that dim, mysterious chamber; as white as the couch she lay upon. Her firm, elastic flesh that was knowing for the first time its birthright, was like a creamy lily that the sun invites to contribute its breath and perfume to the undying life of the world.

The generous abundance of her passion, without guile or trickery, was like a white flame which penetrated and found response in depths of his own sensuous nature that had never yet been reached.

When he touched her breasts they gave themselves up in quivering ecstasy, inviting his lips. Her mouth was a fountain of delight. And when he possessed her, they seemed to swoon together at the very borderland of life's mystery.

He stayed cushioned upon her, breathless, dazed, enervated, with his heart beating like a hammer upon her. With one hand she clasped his head, her lips lightly touching his forehead. The other hand stroked with a soothing rhythm his muscular shoulders.

The growl of the thunder was distant and passing away. The rain beat softly upon the shingles, inviting them to drowsiness and sleep. But they dared not yield

III

The rain was over; and the sun was turning the glistening green world into a palace of gems. Calixta, on the gallery, watched Alcée ride away. He turned and smiled at her with a beaming face; and she lifted her pretty chin in the air and laughed aloud.

Bobinôt and Bibi, trudging home, stopped without at the cistern to make themselves presentable.

"My! Bibi, w'at will yo' mama say! You ought to be ashame'. You oughta' put on those good pants. Look at 'em! An' that mud on yo' collar! How you got that mud on yo' collar, Bibi? I never saw such a boy!" Bibi was the picture of pathetic resignation. Bobinôt was the embodiment of serious solicitude as he strove to remove from his own person and his son's the signs of their tramp over heavy roads and through wet fields. He scraped the mud off Bibi's bare legs and feet with a stick and carefully removed all traces from his heavy brogans. Then, prepared for the worst—the meeting with an over-scrupulous housewife, they entered cautiously at the back door.

Calixta was preparing supper. She had set the table and was dripping coffee at the hearth. She sprang up as they came in.

"Oh, Bobinôt! You back! My! but I was uneasy. W'ere you been during the rain? An' Bibi? he ain't wet? he ain't hurt?" She had clasped Bibi and was kissing him effusively. Bobinôt's explanations and apologies which he had been composing all along the way, died on his lips as Calixta felt him to see if he were dry, and seemed to express nothing but satisfaction at their safe return.

"I brought you some shrimps, Calixta," offered Bobinôt, hauling the can from his ample side pocket and laying it on the table.

"Shrimps! Oh, Bobinôt! you too good fo' anything!" and she gave him a smacking kiss on the cheek that resounded, "J'vous réponds, we'll have a feas' to-night! umph-umph!"

Bobinôt and Bibi began to relax and enjoy themselves, and when the three seated themselves at table they laughed much and so loud that anyone might have heard them as far away as Laballière's.

IV

Alcée Laballière wrote to his wife, Clarisse, that night. It was a loving letter, full of tender solicitude. He told her not to hurry back, but if she and the babies liked it at Biloxi, to stay a month longer. He was getting on nicely; and though he missed them, he was willing to bear the separation a while longer—realizing that their health and pleasure were the first things to be considered.

V

As for Clarisse, she was charmed upon receiving her husband's letter. She and the babies were doing well. The society was agreeable; many of her old friends and acquaintances were at the bay. And the first free breath since her marriage seemed to restore the pleasant liberty of her maiden days. Devoted as she was to her husband, their intimate conjugal life was something which she was more than willing to forego for a while.

So the storm passed and everyone was happy.

Grace King (1852–1932)

Grace King was born in New Orleans, on November 29, 1852, to William Woodson and Sarah Ann Miller King. King's father was born in rural Georgia, but at the age of five, moved to what is now Montevallo, Alabama, where he remained until attending Transylvania College in Lexington, Kentucky. [1] After studying law at the University of Virginia in Charlottesville, William King moved to New Orleans where he became a very successful lawyer. King's mother, Sarah Ann Miller, was William King's second wife. He had married in Montevallo, and had two sons by his first wife. Grace King's mother was born and reared in New Orleans, and although a Presbyterian, she was given the finest Catholic Creole education that most of the prominent young women of New Orleans received. The same sort of education Grace King would receive even after the Civil War.

William King became very wealthy practicing law, and, about five years before war broke out, he and his brother bought a sugar cane plantation, *L'Embarras*, near New Iberia, in southwest Louisiana. William King had no intention of living on this plantation, leaving his brother to manage it; however, that would change during the war when Grace was only ten years old.

The family remained in New Orleans, and had every intention of doing so until the city was occupied by Federal troops in 1862. Rather than sign the requisite loyalty oath, the King family left the city, and their dramatic departure, which Grace King captures in *Memories of a Southern Woman of Letters* (1832), rivals a scene from Margaret Mitchell's *Gone with the Wind*. William King had to flee the city under darkness and send for his family later, but Sarah King needed a passport in order to travel, and they were difficult to come by. Her plan to attain one is reminiscent of Scarlett's visit to Rhett Butler in the Atlanta jailhouse. Sarah, dressed in her finest, went to visit the Union commanding general, and although he denied her request, another general within earshot, who had heard her plea, sympathized with her and sent her travel papers that day. King describes her mother's foray to the enemy camp and the night of their departure:

> The night was dark. In the dimly lighted street two carriages stood before the garden gate, and at a little distance the cart for the trunks. Neighbors and friends thronged about us as we left the house. The sentinel withdrew to a distance.... As we were driving away, someone thrust into my hand a rag doll "for you to play with," and then we were off. The doll, ugly, heavy, and cumbersome, was hideously dressed, but I eagerly clasped it to my bosom, and day and night kept it in my arms, loving it as only little girls love ugly dolls. By the time we reached the plantation, its seams had begun to open, and we found that it was stuffed with Confederate money. [2]

The family boarded a steamboat that night and, under gunfire, left the city on a trip that would last several days and be every bit as eventful as their departure.

The King family lived on the plantation until the war's end in 1865, when they returned to the city. All the children, including Grace King, were eager to return to their formal schooling, and she was sent to *Institut St. Louis,* a school for young creole women which stressed the study of language and history, which would become invaluable to King when she would write her textbook, *A History of Louisiana,* in 1893. King graduated from *Inistitut St. Louis* at the age of sixteen and went on to study at two other local institutes, but more importantly, that year she also met and began to study under Louisiana historian, Charles Gayarré, who was also very influential in her turning to historical writing.

More important here, however, is her work as a fiction writer, which she turned to on a dare from American poet, former Union soldier, and editor in chief of *Century* magazine, Richard Watson Gilder. In *Memories of a Southern Woman of Letters,* King describes the scene as taking place in 1885 at the Pickwick Club, an exclusive social club for wealthy white men of New Orleans that still exists today. After dinner, King was paired with

---

1   For more on Grace King and the source of much of the biographical included here, see Robert Bush, *Grace King, a Southern Destiny* (Baton Rouge: LSUP, 1983).

2   Grace King. *Memories of a Southern Woman of Letters* (New York: McMillan, 1932). Rep. (New Orleans: Pelican Publishing, 2007), 9.

Gilder, who asked why New Orleanians dismissed Cable as a writer, and she responded: "…Cable proclaimed his preference for colored people over white and assumed the inevitable superiority… of the quadroons over the Creoles. He was a native of New Orleans and had been well treated by its people, and yet he stabbed the city in the back, as far as we felt, in a dastardly way to please the Northern press".[1] According to King, Gilder's response was frosty: "if Cable is so false to you, why do not some of you write better?"[2]. It was a very good question and all it took for King to put her pen to paper to create "Monsieur Motte," which she first sent to *Century* anonymously. They rejected it. She did receive $150 for the story, however, when it was published in the *New Princeton Review* in 1888. Her career as a fiction writer had begun, and she would later adapt "Monsieur Motte" into a novel of the same title.

King, aside from writing three novels, also produced two collections of short stories, *Tales of a Time and Place* (1892), and *Balcony Stories* (1893), from which the selections in this anthology were taken. King explains the premise for her collection:

> There is much of life passed on the balcony in a country where the summer unrolls in six moon-lengths, and where the nights have to come with a double endowment of vastness and splendor to compensate for the tedious, sun-parched days.
>
> And in that country the women love to sit and talk together of summer nights, on balconies, in their vague, loose white garments,—men are not balcony sitters,—with their sleeping children within easy hearing, the stars breaking the cool darkness, or the moon making a show of light—oh, such a discreet show of light!—through the vines. And the children inside, waking to go from one sleep into another, hear the low, soft mother-voices on the balcony, talking about this person and that, old times, old friends, old experiences; and it seems to them, hovering a moment in wakefulness, that there is no end of the world or time, or of the mother-knowledge; but, illimitable as it is, the mother-voices and the mother-love and protection fill it all…. Experiences, reminiscences, episodes picked up as only women know how to pick them from other women's lives—or other women's destinies…. and told as only women know how to relate them….[3]

Indeed, the two works included here both concern women of New Orleans. The first story, "La Grande Demoiselle," is a tale of the daughter of the once wealthiest plantation owners in New Orleans, Idalie Sainte Foy Mortemart des Islets. Even though this is a story about Idalie's reversal of fortune after the Civil War, King, by painting a very disagreeable protagonist, does not draw on readers' sympathies as we would expect from such a story. In fact, Idalie is so spoiled and self-absorbed, that we come to despise her before the war ever comes to their plantation, Reine Sainte Foy: "…even in prayer, [she] talked nothing but commands…. And at night, when she came from the balls, tired, tired to death as only balls can render one, she would throw herself down upon her bed in her tulle skirts,—on top, or not, of the exquisite flowers, she did not care,—and make her maid undress her in that position; often having her bodices cut off her, because she was too tired to turn over and have them unlaced." Truly an incredible picture of excess in antebellum New Orleans, so naturally, she must fall, and fall she does, hard. One failure of this story today, however, that King was unable to foresee, is that we don't care. In fact, we want her to suffer. When the Yankee troops overtake Reine Sainte Foy, naturally, King makes them "a colored company." And years later, when Idalie is forced to do the unthinkable—get a job!—she works as the "teacher at the colored public school." The only one who seems to care at all about her reversal of fortune is Old Champigny, who, out of a sense of noblesse oblige, marries Idalie: "It was not an act of charity to himself, no doubt cross and disagreeable, besides being ugly!" Nonetheless, we cannot, as King might want us to do, pity him either.

One of her most sophisticated short stories, "The Little Convent Girl," is a true tale of a "tragic mulatta." The young protagonist is raised in a convent in Cincinnati, seeing her father during vacations, but when he dies, she is sent to her mother downriver in New Orleans. She is excited about meeting her mother, and her trip by steamer

---

1   Ibid., 60.

2   Ibid., 60.

3   Grace Elizabeth King. *Balcony Stories*. (New Orleans, The L. Graham Co., Ltd., 1914), 1-2.

down to New Orleans is her first contact with the outside world. There are many hints in the story that the little convent girl may be of mixed race. King describes her mourning garb naturally as being black, but more telling is her black hair that "had a strong inclination to curl" and her eyes that "seemed blacker than either [her hair or her dress]".[1] By the time they land in New Orleans, the captain has taken her under his wing, but that ends when he sees that her mother is black. Then everyone on board ignores her as she leaves the ship silently with her mother. We know that the story must end tragically, but the tragedy here is that the little convent girl is of mixed race.

King was an accomplished writer and she was right to rise to Gilder's challenge. Today, even though her stories seem dated and sometimes implausible, her works exemplify New Orleans and southern traditions long gone. Over the course of her life, King traveled often to the North and to Europe, particularly France, but she never married. On March 17, 1915, Cable was visiting New Orleans and was asked to address a meeting of the Louisiana Historical Society, of which King was a member. He was given a standing ovation, and the crowd rushed to shake hands with him, King included. Grace King died in New Orleans on January 14, 1932, at the age of 79, and her last book, *Memories of a Southern Lady* was published by MacMillan just months after her death.

La Grande Demoiselle

That was what she was called by everybody as soon as she was seen or described. Her name, besides baptismal titles, was Idalie Sainte Foy Mortemart des Islets. When she came into society, in the brilliant little world of New Orleans, it was the event of the season, and after she came in, whatever she did became also events. Whether she went, or did not go; what she said, or did not say; what she wore, and did not wear—all these became important matters of discussion, quoted as much or more than what the president said, or the governor thought. And in those days, the days of '59, New Orleans was not, as it is now, a one-heiress place, but it may be said that one could find heiresses then as one finds type-writing girls now.

Mademoiselle Idalie received her birth, and what education she had, on her parents' plantation, the famed old Reine Sainte Foy place, and it is no secret that, like the ancient kings of France, her birth exceeded her education.

It was a plantation, the Reine Sainte Foy, the richness and luxury of which are really well described in those perfervid pictures of tropical life, at one time the passion of philanthropic imaginations, excited and exciting over the horrors of slavery. Although these pictures were then often accused of being purposely exaggerated, they seem now to fall short of, instead of surpassing, the truth. Stately walls, acres of roses, miles of oranges, unmeasured fields of cane, colossal sugar-house—they were all there, and all the rest of it, with the slaves, slaves, slaves everywhere, whole villages of negro cabins. And there were also, most noticeable to the natural, as well as to the visionary, eye—there were the ease, idleness, extravagance, self-indulgence, pomp, pride, arrogance, in short the whole enumeration, the moral sine qua non, as some people considered it, of the wealthy slaveholder of aristocratic descent and tastes.

What Mademoiselle Idalie cared to learn she studied, what she did not she ignored; and she followed the same simple rule untrammeled in her eating, drinking, dressing, and comportment generally; and whatever discipline may have been exercised on the place, either in fact or fiction, most assuredly none of it, even so much as in a threat, ever attainted her sacred person. When she was just turned sixteen, Mademoiselle Idalie made up her mind to go into society. Whether she was beautiful or not, it is hard to say. It is almost impossible to appreciate properly the beauty of the rich, the very rich. The unfettered development, the limitless choice of accessories, the confidence, the self-esteem, the sureness of expression, the simplicity of purpose, the ease of execution—all these produce a certain effect of beauty

---

1   Ibid., 144-7.

behind which one really cannot get to measure length of nose, or brilliancy of eye. This much can be said: there was nothing in her that positively contradicted any assumption of beauty on her part, or credit of it on the part of others. She was very tall and very thin with small head, long neck, black eyes, and abundant straight black hair,—for which her hair-dresser deserved more praise than she,—good teeth, of course, and a mouth that, even in prayer, talked nothing but commands; that is about all she had en fait d'ornements, as the modistes say. It may be added that she walked as if the Reine Sainte Foy plantation extended over the whole earth, and the soil of it were too vile for her tread. Of course she did not buy her toilets in New Orleans. Everything was ordered from Paris, and came as regularly through the custom-house as the modes and robes to the milliners. She was furnished by a certain house there, just as one of a royal family would be at the present day. As this had lasted from her layette up to her sixteenth year, it may be imagined what took place when she determined to make her début. Then it was literally, not metaphorically, carte blanche, at least so it got to the ears of society. She took a sheet of note-paper, wrote the date at the top, added, "I make my début in November," signed her name at the extreme end of the sheet, addressed it to her dressmaker in Paris, and sent it.

It was said that in her dresses the very handsomest silks were used for linings, and that real lace was used where others put imitation,—around the bottoms of the skirts, for instance,—and silk ribbons of the best quality served the purposes of ordinary tapes; and sometimes the buttons were of real gold and silver, sometimes set with precious stones. Not that she ordered these particulars, but the dressmakers, when given carte blanche by those who do not condescend to details, so soon exhaust the outside limits of garments that perforce they take to plastering them inside with gold, so to speak, and, when the bill goes in, they depend upon the furnishings to carry out a certain amount of the contract in justifying the price. And it was said that these costly dresses, after being worn once or twice, were cast aside, thrown upon the floor, given to the negroes—anything to get them out of sight. Not an inch of the real lace, not one of the jeweled buttons, not a scrap of ribbon, was ripped off to save. And it was said that if she wanted to romp with her dogs in all her finery, she did it; she was known to have ridden horseback, one moonlight night, all around the plantation in a white silk dinner-dress flounced with Alençon. And at night, when she came from the balls, tired, tired to death as only balls can render one, she would throw herself down upon her bed in her tulle skirts,—on top, or not, of the exquisite flowers, she did not care,—and make her maid undress her in that position; often having her bodices cut off her, because she was too tired to turn over and have them unlaced.

That she was admired, raved about, loved even, goes without saying. After the first month she held the refusal of half the beaux of New Orleans. Men did absurd, undignified, preposterous things for her; and she? Love? Marry? The idea never occurred to her. She treated the most exquisite of her pretenders no better than she treated her Paris gowns, for the matter of that. She could not even bring herself to listen to a proposal patiently; whistling to her dogs, in the middle of the most ardent protestations, or jumping up and walking away with a shrug of the shoulders, and a "Bah!"

Well! Everyone knows what happened after '59. There is no need to repeat. The history of one is the history of all. But there was this difference—for there is every shade of difference in misfortune, as there is every shade of resemblance in happiness. Mortemart des Islets went off to fight. That was natural; his family had been doing that, he thought, or said, ever since Charlemagne. Just as naturally he was killed in the first engagement. They, his family, were always among the first killed; so much so that it began to be considered assassination to fight a duel with any of them. All that was in the ordinary course of events. One difference in their misfortunes lay in that after the city was captured, their plantation, so near, convenient, and rich in all kinds of provisions, was selected to receive a contingent of troops—a colored company. If it had been a colored company raised in Louisiana it might have been different; and these negroes mixed with the negroes in the neighborhood,—and negroes are no better than whites, for the proportion of good and bad among them,—and the officers were always off duty when they should have been on, and on when they should have been off.

One night the dwelling caught fire. There was an immediate rush to save the ladies. Oh, there was no hesitation about that! They were seized in their beds, and carried out in the very arms of their enemies; carried away off to the sugar-house, and deposited there. No danger of their doing anything but keep very quiet and still in their chemises de nuit, and their one sheet apiece, which was about all that was saved from the conflagration that is, for them. But it must be remembered that this is all hearsay. When one has not been present, one knows nothing of one's own knowledge; one can only repeat. It has been repeated, however, that although the house was burned to the ground, and everything in it destroyed, wherever, for a year afterward, a man of that company or of that neighborhood was found, there could have been found also, without search-warrant, property that had belonged to the Des Islets. That is the story; and it is believed or not, exactly according to prejudice.

How the ladies ever got out of the sugar-house, history does not relate; nor what they did. It was not a time for sociability, either personal or epistolary. At one offensive word your letter, and you, very likely, examined; and Ship Island for a hotel, with soldiers for hostesses! Madame Des Islets died very soon after the accident—of rage, they say; and that was about all the public knew.

Indeed, at that time the society of New Orleans had other things to think about than the fate of the Des Islets. As for la grande demoiselle, she had prepared for her own oblivion in the hearts of her female friends. And the gentlemen,—her preux chevaliers,—they were burning with other passions than those which had driven them to her knees, encountering a little more serious response than "bahs" and shrugs. And, after all, a woman seems the quickest thing forgotten when once the important affairs of life come to men for consideration.

It might have been ten years according to some calculations, or ten eternities,—the heart and the almanac never agree about time,—but one morning old Champigny (they used to call him Champignon) was walking along his levee front, calculating how soon the water would come over, and drown him out, as the Louisianians say. It was before a seven-o'clock breakfast, cold, wet, rainy, and discouraging. The road was knee-deep in mud, and so broken up with hauling, that it was like walking upon waves to get over it. A shower poured down. Old Champigny was hurrying in when he saw a figure approaching. He had to stop to look at it, for it was worth while. The head was hidden by a green barege veil, which the showers had plentifully besprinkled with dew; a tall, thin figure. Figure! No; not even could it be called a figure: straight up and down, like a finger or a post; high-shouldered, and a step—a step like a plowman's. No umbrella; no—nothing more, in fact. It does not sound so peculiar as when first related—something must be forgotten. The feet—oh, yes, the feet—they were like waffle-irons, or frying-pans, or anything of that shape.

Old Champigny did not care for women—he never had; they simply did not exist for him in the order of nature. He had been married once, it is true, about a half century before; but that was not reckoned against the existence of his prejudice, because he was célibataire to his finger-tips, as any one could see a mile away. But that woman intrigue'd him.

He had no servant to inquire from. He performed all of his own domestic work in the wretched little cabin that replaced his old home. For Champigny also belonged to the great majority of the nouveaux pauvres.

He went out into the rice-field, where were one or two hands that worked on shares with him, and he asked them. They knew immediately; there is nothing connected with the parish that a field-hand does not know at once. She was the teacher of the colored public school some three or four miles away. "Ah," thought Champigny, "some Northern lady on a mission." He watched to see her return in the evening, which she did, of course; in a blinding rain. Imagine the green barege veil then; for it remained always down over her face.

Old Champigny could not get over it that he had never seen her before. But he must have seen her, and, with his abstraction and old age, not have noticed her, for he found out from the negroes that she had been teaching four or five years there. And he found out also—how, is not important—that she was Idalie Sainte Foy Mortemart des Islets. La grande demoiselle! He had never known her in the old days, owing to his uncomplimentary attitude toward women, but he knew of her, of course, and of her family. It should have been said that his plantation was about fifty miles higher up the river, and on the opposite bank to Reine Sainte Foy. It seemed terrible. The old gentleman had had reverses of his own, which would bear the telling, but nothing was more shocking to him than this—that Idalie Sainte Foy Mortemart des Islets should be teaching a public colored school for—it makes one blush to name it—seven dollars and a half a month. For seven dollars and a half a month to teach a set of—well! He found out where she lived, a little cabin—not so much worse than his own, for that matter—in the corner of a field; no companion, no servant, nothing but food and shelter. Her clothes have been described.

Only the good God himself knows what passed in Champigny's mind on the subject. We know only the results. He went and married la grande demoiselle. How? Only the good God knows that too. Every first of the month, when he goes to the city to buy provisions, he takes her with him—in fact, he takes her everywhere with him.

Passengers on the railroad know them well, and they always have a chance to see her face. When she passes her old plantation la grande demoiselle always lifts her veil for one instant—the inevitable green barege veil. What a face! Thin, long, sallow, petrified! And the neck! If she would only tie something around the neck! And her plain, coarse cottonade gown! The negro women about her were better dressed than she.

Poor old Champignon! It was not an act of charity to himself, no doubt cross and disagreeable, besides being ugly. And as for love, gratitude!

The Little Convent Girl

S he was coming down on the boat from Cincinnati, the little convent girl. Two sisters had brought her aboard. They gave her in charge of the captain, got her a state-room, saw that the new little trunk was put into it, hung the new little satchel up on the wall, showed her how to bolt the door at night, shook hands with her for good-by (good-bys have really no significance for sisters), and left her there. After a while the bells all rang, and the boat, in the awkward elephantine fashion of boats, got into midstream. The chambermaid found her sitting on the chair in the state-room where the sisters had left her, and showed her how to sit on a chair in the saloon. And there she sat until the captain came and hunted her up for supper. She could not do anything of herself; she had to be initiated into everything by someone else.

She was known on the boat only as "the little convent girl." Her name, of course, was registered in the clerk's office, but on a steamboat no one thinks of consulting the clerk's ledger. It is always the little widow, the fat madam, the tall colonel, the parson, etc. The captain, who pronounced by the letter, always called her the little convent girl. She was the beau-ideal of the little convent girl. She never raised her eyes except when spoken to. Of course she never spoke first, even to the chamber maid, and when she did speak it was in the wee, shy, furtive voice one might imagine a just-budding violet to have; and she walked with such soft, easy, carefully calculated steps that one naturally felt the penalties that must have secured them—penalties dictated by a black code of deportment.

She was dressed in deep mourning. Her black straw hat was trimmed with stiff new crape, and her stiff new bombazine dress had crape collar and cuffs. She wore her hair in two long plaits fastened around her head tight and fast. Her hair had a strong inclination to curl, but that had been taken out of it as austerely as the noise out of her footfalls.

Her hair was as black as her dress; her eyes, when one saw them, seemed blacker than either, on account of the bluishness of the white surrounding the pupil. Her eye-lashes were almost as thick as the black veil which the sisters had fastened around her hat with an extra pin the very last thing before leaving. She had a round little face, and a tiny pointed chin; her mouth was slightly protuberant from the teeth, over which she tried to keep her lips well shut, the effort giving them a pathetic little forced expression. Her complexion was sallow, a pale sallow, the complexion of a brunette bleached in darkened rooms. The only color about her was a blue taffeta ribbon from which a large silver medal of the Virgin hung over the place where a breastpin should have been. She was so little, so little, although she was eighteen, as the sisters told the captain; otherwise they would not have permitted her to travel all the way to New Orleans alone.

Unless the captain or the clerk remembered to fetch her out in front, she would sit all day in the cabin, in the same place, crocheting lace, her spool of thread and box of patterns in her lap, on the handkerchief spread to save her new dress. Never leaning back—oh, no! always straight and stiff, as if the conventual back board were there within call. She would eat only convent fare at first, notwithstanding the importunities of the waiters, and the jocularities of the captain, and particularly of the clerk. Every one knows the fund of humor possessed by a steamboat clerk, and what a field for display the table at meal-times affords. On Friday she fasted rigidly, and she never began to eat, or finished, without a little Latin movement of the lips and a sign of the cross. And always at six o'clock of the evening she remembered the angelus, although there was no church bell to remind her of it.

She was in mourning for her father, the sisters told the captain, and she was going to New Orleans to her mother. She had not seen her mother since she was an infant, on account of some disagreement between the parents, in consequence of which the father had brought her to Cincinnati, and placed her in the convent. There she had been for twelve years, only going to her father for vacations and holidays. So long as the father lived he would never let the child have any communication with her mother. Now that he was dead all that was changed, and the first thing that the girl herself wanted to do was to go to her mother.

The mother superior had arranged it all with the mother of the girl, who was to come personally to the boat in New Orleans, and receive her child from the captain, presenting a letter from the mother superior, a facsimile of which the sisters gave the captain.

It is a long voyage from Cincinnati to New Orleans, the rivers doing their best to make it interminable, embroidering themselves *ad libitum* all over the country. Every five miles, and sometimes oftener, the boat would stop to put off or take on freight, if not both. The little convent girl, sitting in the cabin, had her terrible frights at first from the hideous noises attendant on these landings—the whistles, the ringings of the bells, the running to and fro, the shouting. Every time she thought it was shipwreck, death, judgment, purgatory; and her sins! her sins! She would drop her crochet, and clutch her prayer-beads from her pocket, and relax the constraint over her lips, which would go to rattling off prayers with the velocity of a relaxed windlass. That was at first, before the captain took to fetching her out in front to see the boat make a landing.

Then she got to liking it so much that she would stay all day just where the captain put her, going inside only for her meals. She forgot herself at times so much that she would draw her chair a little closer to the railing, and put up her veil, actually, to see better. No one ever usurped her place, quite in front, or intruded upon her either with word or look; for every one learned to know her shyness, and began to feel a personal interest in her, and all wanted the little convent girl to see everything that she possibly could.

And it was worth seeing—the balancing and *chasséeing* and waltzing of the cumbersome old boat to make a landing. It seemed to be always attended with the difficulty and the improbability of a new enterprise; and the relief when it did sidle up anywhere within rope's-throw of the spot aimed at! And the roustabout throwing the rope from the perilous end of the dangling gang-plank! And the dangling roustabouts hanging like drops of water from it—dropping sometimes twenty feet to the land, and not infrequently into the river itself. And then what a rolling of barrels, and shouldering of sacks, and singing of Jim Crow songs, and pacing of Jim Crow steps; and black skins glistening through torn shirts, and white teeth gleaming through red lips, and laughing, and talking and—bewildering! entrancing! Surely the little convent girl in her convent walls never dreamed of so much unpunished noise and movement in the world!

The first time she heard the mate—it must have been like the first time woman ever heard man—curse and swear, she turned pale, and ran quickly, quickly into the saloon, and—came out again? No, indeed! not with all the soul she had to save, and all the other sins on her conscience. She shook her head resolutely, and was not seen in her chair on deck again until the captain not only reassured her, but guaranteed his reassurance. And after that, whenever the boat was about to make a landing, the mate would first glance up to the guards, and if the little convent girl was sitting there he would change his invective to sarcasm, and politely request the colored gentlemen not to hurry themselves—on no account whatever; to take their time about shoving out the plank; to send the rope ashore by post-office—write him when it got there; begging them not to strain their backs; calling them mister, colonel, major, general, prince, and your royal highness, which was vastly amusing. At night, however, or when the little convent girl was not there, language flowed in its natural curve, the mate swearing like a pagan to make up for lost time.

The captain forgot himself one day: it was when the boat ran aground in the most unexpected manner and place, and he went to work to express his opinion, as only steamboat captains can, of the pilot, mate, engineer, crew, boat, river, country, and the world in general, ringing the bell, first to back, then to head, shouting himself hoarser than his own whistle—when he chanced to see the little black figure hurrying through the chaos on the deck; and the captain stuck as fast aground in midstream as the boat had done.

In the evening the little convent girl would be taken on the upper deck, and going up the steep stairs there was such confusion, to keep the black skirts well over the stiff white petticoats; and, coming down, such blushing when suspicion would cross the unprepared face that a rim of white stocking might be visible; and the thin feet, laced so tightly in the glossy new leather boots, would cling to each successive step as if they could never, never make another venture; and then one boot would (there is but that word) hesitate out, and feel and feel around, and have such a pause of helpless agony as if indeed the next step must have been wilfully removed, or was nowhere to be found on the wide, wide earth.

It was a miracle that the pilot ever got her up into the pilot-house; but pilots have a lonely time, and do not hesitate even at miracles when there is a chance for company. He would place a box for her to climb to the tall bench behind the wheel, and he would arrange the cushions, and open a window here to let in air, and shut one there to cut off a draft, as if there could be no tenderer consideration in life for him than her comfort. And he would talk of the river to her, explain the chart, pointing out eddies, whirlpools, shoals, depths, new beds, old beds, cut-offs, caving banks, and making banks, as exquisitely and respectfully as if she had been the River Commission.

It was his opinion that there was as great a river as the Mississippi flowing directly under it—an underself of a river, as much a counterpart of the other as the second story of a house is of the first; in fact, he said they were navigating through the upper story. Whirlpools were holes in the floor of the upper river, so to speak; eddies were rifts and cracks. And deep under the earth, hurrying toward the subterranean stream, were other streams, small and great, but all deep, hurrying to and from that great mother-stream underneath, just as the small and great overground streams hurry to and from their mother Mississippi. It was almost more than the little convent girl could take in: at least such was the expression of her eyes; for they opened as all eyes have to open at pilot stories. And he knew as much of astronomy as he did of hydrology, could call the stars by name, and define the shapes of the constellations; and she, who had studied astronomy at the convent, was charmed to find that what she had learned was all true. It was in the pilot-house, one night, that she forgot herself for the first time in her life, and stayed up until after nine o'clock. Although she appeared almost intoxicated at the wild pleasure, she was immediately overwhelmed at the wickedness of it, and observed much more rigidity of conduct thereafter. The engineer, the boiler-men, the firemen, the stokers, they all knew when the little convent girl was up in the pilot-house: the speaking-tube became so mild and gentle.

With all the delays of river and boat, however, there is an end to the journey from Cincinnati to New Orleans. The latter city, which at one time to the impatient seemed at the terminus of the never, began, all of a sudden, one day to make its nearingness felt; and from that period every other interest paled before the interest in the immanence of arrival into port, and the whole boat was seized with a panic of preparation, the little convent girl with the others. Although so immaculate was she in person and effects that she might have been struck with a landing, as some good people might be struck with death, at any moment without fear of results, her trunk was packed and repacked, her satchel arranged and rearranged, and, the last day, her hair was brushed and plaited and smoothed over and over again until the very last glimmer of a curl disappeared. Her dress was whisked, as if for microscopic inspection; her face was washed; and her finger-nails were scrubbed with the hard convent nailbrush, until the disciplined little tips ached with a pristine soreness. And still there were hours to wait, and still the boat added up delays. But she arrived at last, after all, with not more than the usual and expected difference between the actual and the advertised time of arrival.

There was extra blowing and extra ringing, shouting, commanding, rushing up the gangway and rushing down the gangway. The clerks, sitting behind tables on the first deck, were plied, in the twinkling of an eye, with estimates, receipts, charges, countercharges, claims, reclaims, demands, questions, accusations, threats, all at topmost voices. None but steamboat clerks could have stood it. And there were throngs composed of individuals every one of whom wanted to see the captain first and at once: and those who could not get to him shouted over the heads of the others; and as usual he lost his temper and politeness, and began to do what he termed "hustle."

"Captain! Captain!" a voice called him to where a hand plucked his sleeve, and a letter was thrust toward him. "The cross, and the name of the convent." He recognized the envelop of the mother superior. He read the duplicate of the letter given by the sisters.

He looked at the woman—the mother—casually, then again and again.

The little convent girl saw him coming, leading someone toward her. She rose. The captain took her hand first, before the other greeting, "Good-by, my dear," he said. He tried to add something else, but seemed undetermined what. "Be a good little girl—" It was evidently all he could think of. Nodding to the woman behind him, he turned on his heel, and left.

One of the deck-hands was sent to fetch her trunk. He walked out behind them, through the cabin, and the crowd on deck, down the stairs, and out over the gangway. The little convent girl and her mother went with hands tightly clasped. She did not turn her eyes to the right or left, or once (what all passengers do) look backward at the boat which, however slowly, had carried her surely over dangers that she wot not of. All looked at her as she passed. All wanted to say good-by to the little convent girl, to see the mother who had been deprived of her so long. Some expressed surprise in a whistle; some in other ways. All exclaimed audibly, or to themselves, "Colored!"

It takes about a month to make the round trip from New Orleans to Cincinnati and back, counting five days' stoppage in New Orleans. It was a month to a day when the steamboat came puffing and blowing up to the wharf again, like a stout dowager after too long a walk; and the same scene of confusion was enacted, as it had been enacted twelve times a year, at almost the same wharf for twenty years; and the same calm, a death calmness by contrast, followed as usual the next morning.

The decks were quiet and clean; one cargo had just been delivered, part of another stood ready on the levee to be shipped. The captain was there waiting for his business to begin, the clerk was in his office getting his books ready, the voice of the mate could be heard below, mustering the old crew out and a new crew in; for if steamboat crews have a single principle,—and there are those who deny them any,—it is never to ship twice in succession on the same boat. It was too early yet for any but roustabouts, marketers, and church-goers; so early that even the river was still partly mist-covered; only in places could the swift, dark current be seen rolling swiftly along.

"Captain!" A hand plucked at his elbow, as if not confident that the mere calling would secure attention. The captain turned. The mother of the little convent girl stood there, and she held the little convent girl by the hand. "I have brought her to see you," the woman said. "You were so kind—and she is so quiet, so still, all the time, I thought it would do her a pleasure."

She spoke with an accent, and with embarrassment; otherwise one would have said that she was bold and assured enough.

"She don't go nowhere, she don't do nothing but make her crochet and her prayers, so I thought I would bring her for a little visit of 'How d' ye do' to you."

There was, perhaps, some inflection in the woman's voice that might have made known, or at least awakened, the suspicion of some latent hope or intention, had the captain's ear been fine enough to detect it. There might have been something in the little convent girl's face, had his eye been more sensitive—a trifle paler, may-be, the lips a little tighter drawn, the blue ribbon a shade faded. He may have noticed that, but—And the visit of "How d' ye do" came to an end.

They walked down the stairway, the woman in front, the little convent girl—her hand released to shake hands with the captain—following, across the bared deck, out to the gangway, over to the middle of it. No one was looking, no one saw more than a flutter of white petticoats, a show of white stockings, as the little convent girl went under the water.

The roustabout dived, as the roustabouts always do, after the drowning, even at the risk of their good-for-nothing lives. The mate himself jumped overboard; but she had gone down in a whirlpool. Perhaps, as the pilot had told her whirlpools always did, it may have carried her through to the underground river, to that vast, hidden, dark Mississippi that flows beneath the one we see; for her body was never found.

Mollie Evelyn Moore (M.E.M.) Davis (1852–1909)

Mollie Moore Davis, who is better known by her pen name M.E.M. Davis, was born Mary Evelina Moore to John and Marian Crutchfield Moore on April 12, 1844, in White Plains, Alabama. If you look on such websites as the United Daughters of the Confederacy, Texas Division, you might find that she was born some eight years later and that her father was a successful physician and planter, while in actuality, he struggled throughout his life to support his wife and nine children. Much of the confusion about Davis' biography was of her own making. According to Davis biographer, Patricia Brady, in the 1880s Davis, in *Wide Awake,* a series of sketches published in the *New Orleans Picayune,* "began to reimagine her own past... embroidered on the theme of a prosperous past... [and] loosely connected incidents of life on a plantation during the Civil War [in which] the family is well-to-do, the house is large, and the father has an impressive library of the classics—both a financial and an intellectual status symbol."[1] These popular sketches were also narrated by a young girl of eight, which might account for the confusion over Davis' age, one which she never cleared up.[2] While her readers and even her close friends believed this rather grand version of her family history, Brady calls Davis' childhood in Texas "a hand-to-mouth existence."[3]

Davis' parents met and married in Alabama, where her father had moved from Massachusetts in order to finish training and begin his medical career. According to Wilkinson, he was never a very successful doctor, and, eleven years after Davis was born, the family moved to Tyler, Texas, where Davis began writing poetry. With nine children, little money, and a peripatetic existence, Davis' education was erratic at best, yet still by the age of sixteen she was working as a teaching assistant at Professor Hand's Charnwood School in Tyler, Texas and published her first poem in the local newspaper, the Tyler *Reporter* in 1960.[4] That same year she changed her name from Mary to Mollie and began to write as Mollie E. Moore, a name she would continue to use until her marriage in 1874. But the years leading up to her marriage were difficult ones for Mollie.

During the war years, Davis' patriotic poetry became very popular, and according to Brady, that is also the time that the Tyler newspaper began referring to her as "the song bird of Texas."[5] In the early 1860s her poems began to appear in other Texas newspapers, including the Houston *Telegraph* and the Galveston *News,* so she was better able to support her family financially, especially after her mother's death in 1867.

The owner/editor of the *Telegraph,* F.H. Cushing, took a special interest in Davis and her poetry and invited her for an extended visit to Houston, where she was introduced to an active social life, the likes of which she had never known. Her first collection, *Minding the Gap and Other Poems,* was published in 1867 and helped her land a permanent job with the *News.* Davis' family moved to Galveston, where she met her future husband, successful businessman and former Confederate Major, Thomas E. Davis.

The Davises would not remain in Texas for long. In 1879, after his tobacco business failed and he turned to newspaper writing, Thomas Davis took a position with the New Orleans *Times.* That was a big year for Mollie Moore Davis, as her father and her patron, E.H. Cushing, both died, and according to Brady, she also discovered that she, like her mother and three of her brothers, had contracted tuberculosis.[6] The move to New Orleans, however, was propitious for the Davises, as both found success there writing for local newspapers.

Mollie Moore Davis did become a very popular writer in New Orleans, but she also achieved renown in the city's social scene. Sid S. Johnson, in "Some Biographies of Old Settlers," describes her French Quarter home: "A

---

1   Patricia Brady. "Mollie Moore Davis: A Literary Life," *Louisiana Women Writers: New Essays and Comprehensive Bibliography,* ed. Dorothy H. Brown and Barbara Ewell (Baton Rouge: LSUP, 1992), 99-118. Much of the biographical information comes from Brady's essay and from Clyde W. Wilkinson, "The Broadening Stream: The Life and Literary Career of Mollie E. Moore Davis," (Ph.D. dissertation, University of Illinois, 1947).

2   Ibid., 111.

3   Ibid., 111.

4   *Alabama Authors.* "Davis, Mary Evelina Moore." University of Alabama University Libraries. Accessed May 25, 2012.

5   Brady, op. cit., 100.

6   Ibid., 102.

dark-browed, old brick mansion in Royal Street, with a dusky, tunnel-like entrance terminating in the picturesque bit of court yard common to the houses in the French Quarter of New Orleans—an old house with a legendary past."[1] The Davises lived in this Royal Street house for over twenty years, and here Mollie Moore Davis held her many social functions, including her weekly French class and a woman's club, the Geographics, as well as her Friday "salons."[2]

By the late 1880s, Thomas Davis had become the editor in chief of the New Orleans *Picayune,* and Mollie had turned to writing and publishing prose. The short story included here, "At La Glorieuse," which appeared in her collection, *An Elephant's Track and Other Stories* (1897), is typical of her Louisiana gothic style and is one of the most popular of Davis' short stories today. The story opens in April some twenty years after the Civil War on the Arnault family plantation, La Glorieuse (The Glorious), not far from New Orleans on Bayou L'Eperon (Spur Bayou). Although this is a fictional bayou, in *The Acts Passed at the Second Session of the Fourteenth Legislature of the State of Louisiana* in 1840, Act 82 provides for the removal of the wooded "Eperon" near Donaldsonville, upriver of New Orleans, in order to prevent further flooding in that city.[3] Moore Davis might have been familiar with this area, but both the bayou and the plantation are imagined and provide the murky setting for romance, mystery, betrayal, suicide, and sacrifice.

Like so much gothic fiction, out of an idyllic setting spring horror and intrigue. The grand dame of La Glorieuse, Madame Raymonde-Arnault, or "mere," is watching her granddaughter, Fèlice fall for the dashing Richard Keith, just like her daughter-in-law, Hélène Pallacier Arnault, fell for his father some twenty years earlier. Madame Arnault knows that nothing good can come of the relationship between Fèlice and Richard, so she tries to hurry him on his way back to his home in Maryland. Richard notices, however, that La Glorieuse is haunted by the beautiful spirit of Hélène, and he becomes so obsessed with her that mère gets her wish, and Richard Keith leaves the plantation for good, but not until he hears the story of his father's love for Hélène, the beautiful wife of his best friend, Fèlice's father, Fèlix Arnault. Richard is tormented for three years by this beautiful spirit before he finally realizes that the real object of his affection is Fèlice. Again, typical of gothic fiction, the lovers are star-crossed, and he returns too late to declare his love, only to see Fèlice take her vows as Sister Mary of the Cross.

Davis went on to write short stories, young adult fiction, novels, plays, and poetry up until 1908. And although she and Thomas Davis were unable to have children, they did adopt Pearl in 1886, and Mollie Davis devoted herself to her, sometimes even referring to herself as "Mother of Pearl."[4] Unfortunately, Davis' health issues continued to plague her, and she and Pearl would leave every summer for an extended stay with Mollie Davis' family in Texas. By 1908, she could barely leave the house, yet she still published her last short story collection that year, *The Moons of Balbanca.* M.E.M Davis died on New Year's Day 1909, at the age of 63.

At La Glorieuse[5]

Madame Raymonde-Arnault leaned her head against the back of her garden-chair, and watched the young people furtively from beneath her half-closed eyelids. "He is about to speak," she murmured under her breath; "she, at least, will be happy!" and her heart fluttered violently, as if it had been her own thin, bloodless hand which Richard Keith was holding in his; her dark, sunken eyes, instead of Félice's brown ones, which drooped beneath his tender gaze.

Marcelite, the old *bonné,* who stood erect and stately behind her mistress, permitted herself also to

1   Sid S. Johnson. *Mrs. Mollie E. Moore Davis, "Some Biographies of Old Settlers," Historical, Personal and Reminiscent. Volume I,* (Tyler, Texas: Sid S. Johnson Publisher, 1900), 328-331. USGen Web Archives. Accessed May 26, 2012.

2   Brady, op. cit. 109.

3   *The Acts Passed at the Second Session of the Fourteenth Legislature of the State of Louisiana.* Resolution 82 (New Orleans: Published by Authority of the State of Louisiana, Bullit, Magne & Co., State Printers, 1840), 94.

4   Brady, op, cit. 112.

5   From: M.E.M. Davis, *An Elephant's Track and Other Stories* (New York: Harper and Bros., 1897), 89-125.

regard them for a moment with something like a smile relaxing her sombre, yellow face; then she too turned her turbaned head discreetly in another direction.

The plantation house at La Glorieuse is built in a shining loop of Bayou L'Eperon. A level grassy lawn, shaded by enormous live-oaks, stretches across from the broad stone steps to the sodded levee, where a flotilla of small boats, drawn up among the flags and lily-pads, rise and fall with the lapping waves. On the left of the house the white cabins of the quarter show their low roofs above the shrubbery; to the right the plantations of cane, following the inward curve of the bayou, sweep southward field after field, their billowy, blue-green reaches blending far in the rear with the indistinct purple haze of the swamp. The great square house, raised high on massive stone pillars, dates back to the first quarter of the century; its sloping roof is set with rows of dormer-windows, the big red double chimneys rising oddly from their midst; wide galleries with fluted columns enclose it on three sides; from the fourth is projected a long, narrow wing, two stories in height, which stands somewhat apart from the main building, but is connected with it by a roofed and latticed passageway. The lower rooms of this wing open upon small porticos, with balustrades of wrought iron-work rarely fanciful and delicate. From these you may step into the rose-garden—a tangled pleasance which rambles away through alleys of wild-peach and magnolia to an orange-grove, whose trees are gnarled and knotted with the growth of half a century.

The early shadows were cool and dewy there that morning; the breath of damask-roses was sweet on the air; brown, gold-dusted butterflies were hovering over the sweet-peas abloom in sunny corners; birds shot up now and then from the leafy aisles, singing, into the clear blue sky above; the chorus of the negroes at work among the young cane floated in, mellow and resonant, from the fields. The old mistress of La Glorieuse saw it all behind her drooped eyelids. Was it not April, too, that long-gone, unforgotten morning? And were not the bees busy in the hearts of the roses, and the birds singing, when Richard Keith, the first of the name who came to La Glorieuse, held her hand in his, and whispered his love-story yonder by the ragged thicket of crepe-myrtle? Ah, Félice, my child, thou art young, but I too have had my sixteen years; and yellow as are the curls on the head bent over thine, those of the first Richard were more golden still. And the second Richard, he who—

Marcelite's hand fell heavily on her mistress's shoulder. Madame Arnault opened her eyes and sat up, grasping the arms of her chair. A harsh, grating sound had fallen suddenly into the stillness, and the shutters of one of the upper windows of the wing which overlooked the garden were swinging slowly outward. A ripple of laughter, musical and mocking, rang clearly on the air; at the same moment a woman appeared, framed like a portrait in the narrow casement. She crossed her arms on the iron window-bar and gazed silently down on the startled group below. She was strangely beautiful and young, though an air of soft and subtle maturity pervaded her graceful figure. A glory of yellow hair encircled her pale, oval face, and waved away in fluffy masses to her waist; her full lips were scarlet; her eyes, beneath their straight, dark brows, were gray, with emerald shadows in their luminous depths. Her low-cut gown, of some thin, yellowish-white material, exposed her exquisitely rounded throat and perfect neck; long, flowing sleeves of spidery lace fell away from her shapely arms, leaving them bare to the shoulder; loose strings of pearls were wound around her small wrists, and about her throat was clasped a strand of blood-red coral, from which hung to the hollow of her bosom a single translucent drop of amber. A smile at once daring and derisive parted her lips; an elusive light came and went in her eyes.

Keith had started impatiently from his seat at the unwelcome interruption. He stood regarding the intruder with mute, half-frowning inquiry.

Félice turned a bewildered face to her grandmother. "Who is it, Mère?" she whispered. "Did—did you give her leave?"

Madame Arnault had sunk back in her chair. Her hands trembled convulsively still, and the lace on her bosom rose and fell with the hurried beating of her heart. But she spoke in her ordinary measured, almost formal tones, as she put out a hand and drew the girl to her side. "I do not know, my child. Perhaps Suzette Beauvais has come over with her guests from Grandchamp. I thought I heard but now the sound of boats on the bayou. Suzette is ever ready with her pranks. Or perhaps—"

She stopped abruptly. The stranger was drawing the batten blinds together. Her ivory-white arms gleamed in the sun. For a moment they could see her face shining like a star against the dusky glooms within; then the bolt was shot sharply to its place.

Old Marcelite drew a long breath of relief as she disappeared. A smothered ejaculation had escaped her lips, under the girl's intent gaze; an ashen gray had overspread her dark face. "Mam'selle Suzette, she been an' dress up one o' her young ladies jes fer er trick," she said, slowly, wiping the great drops of perspiration from her wrinkled forehead.

"Suzette?" echoed Félice, incredulously. "She would never dare! Who can it be?"

"It is easy enough to find out," laughed Keith. "Let us go and see for ourselves who is masquerading in my quarters."

He drew her with him as he spoke along the winding violet-bordered walks which led to the house. She looked anxiously back over her shoulder at her grandmother. Madame Arnault half arose, and made an imperious gesture of dissent; but Marcelite forced her gently into her seat, and, leaning forward, whispered a few words rapidly in her ear.

"Thou art right, Marcelite," she acquiesced, with a heavy sigh. "'Tis better so."

They spoke in nègre, that mysterious patois which is so uncouth in itself, so soft and caressing on the lips of women. Madame Arnault signed to the girl to go on. She shivered a little, watching their retreating figures. The old bonne threw a light shawl about her shoulders, and crouched affectionately at her feet. The murmur of their voices as they talked long and earnestly together hardly reached beyond the shadows of the wild-peach tree beneath which they sat.

"How beautiful she was!" Félice said, musingly, as they approached the latticed passageway.

"Well, yes," her companion returned, carelessly. "I confess I do not greatly fancy that style of beauty myself." And he glanced significantly down at her own flower-like face.

She flushed, and her brown eyes drooped, but a bright little smile played about her sensitive mouth. "I cannot see," she declared, "how Suzette could have dared to take her friends into the ball-room!"

"Why?" he asked, smiling at her vehemence.

She stopped short in her surprise. "Do you not know, then?" She sank her voice to a whisper. "The ball-room has never been opened since the night my mother died. I was but a baby then, though sometimes I imagine that I remember it all. There was a grand ball there that night. La Glorieuse was full of guests, and everybody from all the plantations around was here. Mère has never told me how it was, nor Marcelite; but the other servants used to talk to me about my beautiful young mother, and tell me how she died suddenly in her ball dress, while the ball was going on. My father had the whole wing closed at once, and no one was ever allowed to enter it. I used to be afraid to play in its shadow, and if I did stray anywhere near it, my father would always call me away. Her death must have broken his heart. He rarely spoke; I never saw him smile; and his eyes were so sad that I could weep now at remembering them. Then he too died while I was still a little girl, and now I have no one in the world but dear old Mère." Her voice trembled a little, but she flushed, and smiled again beneath his meaning look. "It was many years before even the lower floor was reopened, and I am almost sure that yours is the only room there which has ever been used."

They stepped, as she concluded, into the hall.

"I have never been in here before," she said, looking about her with shy curiosity. A flood of sunlight poured through the wide arched window at the foot of the stair. The door of the room nearest the entrance stood open; the others, ranging along the narrow hall, were all closed.

"This is my room," he said, nodding towards the open door.

She turned her head quickly away, with an impulse of girlish modesty, and ran lightly up the stair. He glanced downward as he followed, and paused, surprised to see the flutter of white garments in a shaded corner of his room. Looking more closely, he saw that it was a glimmer of light from an open window on the dark, polished floor.

The upper hall was filled with sombre shadows; the motionless air was heavy with a musky, choking odor. In the dimness a few tattered hangings were visible on the walls; a rope, with bits of crumbling evergreen clinging to it, trailed from above one of the low windows. The panelled double door of the ball-room was shut; no sound came from behind it.

"The girls have seen us coming," said Félice, picking her way daintily across the dust-covered floor, "and they have hidden themselves inside."

Keith pushed open the heavy valves, which creaked noisily on their rusty hinges. The gloom within was murkier still; the chill dampness, with its smell of mildew and mould, was like that of a funeral vault.

The large, low-ceilinged room ran the entire length of the house. A raised dais, whose faded carpet had half rotted away, occupied an alcove at one end; upon it four or five wooden stools were placed; one of these was overturned; on another a violin in its baggy green-baize cover was lying. Straight high-backed chairs were pushed against the walls on either side; in front of an open fireplace with a low wooden mantel two small cushioned divans were drawn up, with a claw-footed table between them. A silver salver filled with tall glasses was set carelessly on one edge of the table; a half-open fan of sandalwood lay beside it; a man's glove had fallen on the hearth just within the tarnished brass fender. Cobwebs depended from the ceiling, and hung in loose threads from the mantel; dust was upon everything, thick and motionless; a single ghostly ray of light that filtered in through a crevice in one of the shutters was weighted with gray, lustreless motes. The room was empty and silent. The visitors, who had come so stealthily, had as stealthily departed, leaving no trace behind them.

"They have played us a pretty trick," said Keith, gayly. "They must have fled as soon as they saw us start towards the house." He went over to the window from which the girl had looked down into the rose garden, and gave it a shake. The dust flew up in a suffocating cloud, and the spiked nails which secured the upper sash rattled in their places.

"That is like Suzette Beauvais," Félice replied, absently. She was not thinking of Suzette. She had forgotten even the stranger, whose disdainful eyes, fixed upon herself, had moved her sweet nature to something like a rebellious anger. Her thoughts were on the beautiful young mother of alien race, whose name, for some reason, she was forbidden to speak. She saw her glide, gracious and smiling, along the smooth floor; she heard her voice above the call and response of the violins; she breathed the perfume of her laces, backward blown by the swift motion of the dance!

She strayed dreamily about, touching with an almost reverent finger first one worm-eaten object and then another, as if by so doing she could make the imagined scene more real. Her eyes were downcast; the blood beneath her rich dark skin came and went in brilliant flushes on her cheeks; the bronze hair, piled in heavy coils on her small, well-poised head, fell in loose rings on her low forehead and against her white neck; her soft gray gown, following the harmonious lines of her slender figure, seemed to envelop her like a twilight cloud.

"She is adorable," said Richard Keith to himself.

It was the first time that he had been really alone with her, though this was the third week of his stay in the hospitable old mansion where his father and his grandfather before him had been welcome guests. Now that he came to think of it, in that bundle of yellow, time-worn letters from Félix Arnault to Richard Keith, which he had found among his father's papers, was one which described at length a ball in this very ballroom. Was it in celebration of his marriage, or of his home-coming after a tour abroad? Richard could not remember. But he idly recalled portions of other letters, as he stood with his elbow on the mantel watching Félix Arnault's daughter.

"Your son and my daughter," the phrase which had made him smile when he read it yonder in his Maryland home, brought now a warm glow to his heart. The half-spoken avowal, the question that had trembled on his lips a few moments ago in the rose-garden, stirred impetuously within him.

Félice stepped down from the dais where she had been standing, and came swiftly across the room, as if his unspoken thought had called her to him. A tender rapture possessed him to see her thus drawing towards him; he longed to stretch out his arms and fold her to his breast. He moved, and his hand came in contact with a small object on the mantel. He picked it up. It was a ring, a band of dull, worn gold, with a confused tracery graven upon it. He merely glanced at it, slipping it mechanically on his finger. His eyes were full upon hers, which were suffused and shining.

"Did you speak?" she asked, timidly. She had stopped abruptly, and was looking at him with a hesitating, half-bewildered expression.

"No," he replied. His mood had changed. He walked again to the window and examined the clumsy bolt. "Strange!" he muttered. "I have never seen a face like hers," he sighed, dreamily.

"She was very beautiful," Félice returned, quietly. "I think we must be going," she added. "Mère will be growing impatient." The flush had died out of her cheek, her arms hung listlessly at her side. She shuddered as she gave a last look around the desolate room. "They were dancing here when my mother died," she said to herself.

He preceded her slowly down the stair. The remembrance of the woman began vaguely to stir his senses. He had hardly remarked her then, absorbed as he had been in another idea. Now she seemed to swim voluptuously before his vision; her tantalizing laugh rang in his ears; her pale, perfumed hair was blown across his face; he felt its filmy strands upon his lips and eyelids. "Do you think," he asked, turning eagerly on the bottom step, "that they could have gone into any of these rooms?"

She shrank unaccountably from him.

"Oh no!" she cried. "They are in the rose-garden with Mère, or they have gone around to the lawn. Come;" and she hurried out before him.

Madame Arnault looked at them sharply as they came up to where she was sitting. "No one!" she echoed, in response to Keith's report. "Then they really have gone back?"

"Madame knows dat we has hear de boats pass up de bayou whilse m'sieu' an' mam'selle was inside," interposed Marcelite, stooping to pick up her mistress's cane.

"I would not have thought Suzette so-so indiscreet," said Félice. There was a note of weariness in her voice.

Madame Arnault looked anxiously at her and then at Keith. The young man was staring abstractedly at the window, striving to recall the vision that had appeared there, and he felt, rather than saw, his hostess start and change color when her eyes fell upon the ring he was wearing. He lifted his hand covertly, and turned the trinket around in the light, but he tried in vain to decipher the irregular characters traced upon it.

"Let us go in," said the old madame. "Félice, my child, thou art fatigued."

Now when in all her life before was Félice ever fatigued? Félice, whose strong young arms could send a pirogue flying up the bayou for miles; Félice, who was ever ready for a tramp along the rose-hedged lanes to the swamp lakes when the water-lilies were in bloom; to the sugar-house in grinding-time; down the levee road to St. Joseph's, the little brown ivy-grown church, whose solitary spire arose slim and straight above the encircling trees.

Marcelite gave an arm to her mistress, though, in truth, she seemed to walk a little unsteadily herself. Félice followed with Keith, who was silent and self-absorbed.

The day passed slowly, a constraint had somehow fallen upon the little household. Madame Arnault's fine high-bred old face wore its customary look of calm repose, but her eyes now and then sought her guest with an expression which he could not have fathomed if he had observed it. But he saw nothing. A mocking red mouth; a throat made for the kisses of love; white arms strung with pearls—these were ever before him, shutting away even the pure sweet face of Félice Arnault.

"Why did I not look at her more closely when I had the opportunity, fool that I was?" he asked himself, savagely, again and again, revolving in his mind a dozen pretexts for going at once to the Beauvais plantation, a mile or so up the bayou. But he felt an inexplicable shyness at the thought of putting any of these plans into action, and so allowed the day to drift by. He arose gladly when the hour for retiring came—that hour which he had hitherto postponed by every means in his power. He kissed, as usual, the hand of his hostess, and held that of Félice in his for a moment; but he did not feel its trembling, or see the timid trouble in her soft eyes.

His room in the silent and deserted wing was full of fantastic shadows. He threw himself on a chair beside a window without lighting his lamp. The rose-garden outside was steeped in moonlight; the magnolia bells gleamed waxen-white against their glossy green leaves; the vines on the tall trellises threw a soft net-work of dancing shadows on the white-shelled walks below; the night air stealing about was loaded with the perfume of roses and sweet-olive; a mockingbird sang in an orange-tree, his mate responding sleepily from her nest in the old summerhouse.

"To-morrow," he murmured, half aloud, "I will go to Grandchamp and give her the ring she left in the old ball-room."

He looked at it glowing dully in the moonlight; suddenly he lifted his head, listening. Did a door grind somewhere near on its hinges? He got up cautiously and looked out. It was not fancy. She was standing full in view on the small balcony of the room next his own. Her white robes waved to and fro in the breeze; the pearls on her arms glistened. Her face, framed in the pale gold of her hair, was turned towards him; a smile curved her lips; her mysterious eyes seemed to be searching his through the shadow. He drew back, confused and trembling, and when, a second later, he looked again, she was gone.

He sat far into the night, his brain whirling, his blood on fire. Who was she, and what was the mystery hidden in this isolated old plantation house? His thoughts reverted to the scene in the rose-garden, and he went over and over all its details. He remembered Madame Arnault's agitation when the window opened and the girl appeared; her evident discomfiture—of which at the time he had taken no heed, but which came back to him vividly enough now—at his proposal to visit the ball-room; her startled recognition of the ring on his finger; her slurring suggestion of visitors from Grandchamp; the look of terror on Marcelite's face. What did it all mean? Félice, he was sure, knew nothing. But here, in an unused portion of the house, which even the members of the family had never visited, a young and beautiful girl was shut up a prisoner, condemned perhaps to a life-long captivity.

"Good God!" He leaped to his feet at the thought. He would go and thunder at Madame Arnault's door, and demand an explanation. But no; not yet. He calmed himself with an effort. By too great haste he might injure her. "Insane?" He laughed aloud at the idea of madness in connection with that exquisite creature.

It dawned upon him, as he paced restlessly back and forth, that although his father had been here more than once in his youth and manhood, he had never heard him speak of La Glorieuse nor of Félix

Arnault, whose letters he had read after his father's death a few months ago—those old letters whose affectionate warmth, indeed, had determined him, in the first desolation of his loss, to seek the family which seemed to have been so bound to his own. Morose and taciturn as his father had been, surely he would sometimes have spoken of his old friend if—Worn out at last with conjecture; beaten back, bruised and breathless, from an enigma which he could not solve; exhausted by listening with strained attention for some movement in the next room, he threw himself on his bed, dressed as he was, and fell into a heavy sleep, which lasted far into the forenoon of the next day.

When he came out (walking like one in a dream), he found a gay party assembled on the lawn in front of the house. Suzette Beauvais and her guests, a bevy of girls, had come from Grandchamp. They had been joined, as they rowed down the bayou, by the young people from the plantation houses on the way. Half a dozen boats, their long paddles laid across the seats, were added to the home fleet at the landing. Their stalwart black rowers were basking in the sun on the levee, or lounging about the quarter. At the moment of his appearance, Suzette herself was indignantly disclaiming any complicity in the jest of the day before.

"Myself, I was making o'ange-flower conserve," she declared; "an' anyhow I wouldn't go in that ball-room unless madame send me."

"But who was it, then?" insisted Felice.

Mademoiselle Beauvais spread out her fat little hands and lifted her shoulders. "Mo pas connais," she laughed, dropping into patois.

Madame Arnault here interposed. It was but the foolish conceit of some teasing neighbor, she said, and not worth further discussion. Keith's blood boiled in his veins at this calm dismissal of the subject, but he gave no sign.

He saw her glance warily at himself from time to time.

"I will sift the matter to the bottom," he thought, "and I will force her to confess the truth, whatever it may be, before the world."

The noisy chatter and meaningless laughter around him jarred upon his nerves; he longed to be alone with his thoughts; and presently, pleading a headache—indeed his temples throbbed almost to bursting, and his eyes were hot and dry—he quitted the lawn, seeing but not noting until long afterwards, when they smote his memory like a two-edged knife, the pain in Félice's uplifted eyes, and the little sorrowful quiver of her mouth. He strolled around the corner of the house to his apartment. The blinds of the arched window were drawn, and a hazy twilight was diffused about the hall, though it was mid-afternoon outside. As he entered, closing the door behind him, the woman at that moment uppermost in his thoughts came down the dusky silence from the farther end of the hall. She turned her inscrutable eyes upon him in passing, and flitted noiselessly and with languid grace up the stairway, the faint swish of her gown vanishing with her. He hesitated a moment, overpowered by conflicting emotions; then he sprang recklessly after her.

He pushed open the ball-room door, reaching his arms out blindly before him. Once more the great dust-covered room was empty. He strained his eye helplessly into the obscurity. A chill reaction passed over him; he felt himself on the verge of a swoon. He did not this time even try to discover the secret door or exit by which she had disappeared; he looked, with a hopeless sense of discouragement, at the barred windows, and turned to leave the room. As he did so, he saw a handkerchief lying on the threshold of the door. He picked it up eagerly, and pressed it to his lips. A peculiar delicate perfume which thrilled his senses lurked in its gossamer folds. As he was about thrusting it into his breast-pocket, he noticed in one corner a small blood-stain fresh and wet. He had then bitten his lip in his excitement.

"I need no further proof," he said aloud, and his own voice startled him, echoing down the long hall. "She is beyond all question a prisoner in this detached building, which has mysterious exits and entrances. She has been forced to promise that she will not go outside of its walls, or she is afraid to do so. I will bring home this monstrous crime. I will release this lovely young woman who dares not speak, yet so plainly appeals to me." Already he saw in fancy her star-like eyes raised to his in mute gratitude, her white hand laid confidingly on his arm.

The party of visitors remained at La Glorieuse overnight. The negro fiddlers came in, and there was dancing in the old-fashioned double parlors and on the moonlit galleries. Félice was unnaturally gay. Keith looked on gloomily, taking no part in the amusement.

"Il est bien bête, your yellow-haired Marylander," whispered Suzette Beauvais to her friend.

He went early his room, but he watched in vain for some sign from his beautiful neighbor. He grew sick with apprehension. Had Madame Arnault—But no; she would not dare. "I will wait one more day," he finally decided; "and then—"

The next morning, after a late breakfast, someone proposed impromptu charades and tableaux. Madame Arnault good-naturedly sent for the keys to the tall presses built into the walls, which contained the accumulated trash and treasure of several generations. Mounted on a step-ladder, Robert Beauvais explored the recesses and threw down to the laughing crowd embroidered shawls and scarfs yellow with age, soft muslins of antique pattern, stiff big-flowered brocades, scraps of gauze ribbon, gossamer laces. On one topmost shelf he came upon a small wooden box inlaid with mother-of-pearl. Félice reached up for it, and, moved by some undefined impulse, Richard came and stood by her side while she opened it. A perfume which he recognized arose from it as she lifted a fold of tissue-paper. Some strings of Oriental pearls of extraordinary size, and perfect in shape and color, were coiled underneath, with a coral necklace, whose pendant of amber had broken off and rolled into a corner. With them—he hardly restrained an exclamation, and his hand involuntarily sought his breast-pocket at sight of the handkerchief with a drop of fresh blood in one corner! Félice trembled without knowing why. Madame Arnault, who had just entered the room, took the box from her quietly, and closed the lid with a snap. The girl, accustomed to implicit obedience, asked no questions; the others, engaged in turning over the old-time finery, had paid no attention.

"Does she think to disarm me by such puerile tricks?" he thought, turning a look of angry warning on the old madame; and in the steady gaze which she fixed on him he read a haughty defiance.

He forced himself to enter into the sports of the day, and he walked down to the boat-landing a little before sunset to see the guests depart. As the line of boats swept away, the black rowers dipping their oars lightly in the placid waves, he turned, with a sense of release, leaving Madame Arnault and Félice still at the landing, and went down the levee road towards St. Joseph's. The field gang, whose red, blue, and brown blouses splotched the squares of cane with color, was preparing to quit work; loud laughter and noisy jests rang out on the air; high-wheeled plantation wagons creaked along the lanes; negro children, with dip-nets and fishing-poles over their shoulders, ran homeward along the levee, the dogs at their heels barking joyously; a schooner, with white sail outspread, was stealing like a fairy bark around a distant bend of the bayou; the silvery waters were turning to gold under a sunset sky.

It was twilight when he struck across the plantation, and came around by the edge of the swamp to the clump of trees in a corner of the home field which he had often remarked from his window. As he approached, he saw a woman come out of the dense shadow, as if intending to meet him, and then draw back again. His heart throbbed painfully, but he walked steadily forward. It was only Félice. Only Félice! She was sitting on a flat tombstone. The little spot was the Raymonde-Arnault family burying-ground. There were many marble head-stones and shafts, and two broad low tombs side by side and a little apart from the others. A tangle of rose-briars covered the sunken graves, a rank growth of grass choked the narrow paths, the little gate, interlaced and overhung with honeysuckle, sagged away from its posts; the fence itself had lost a picket here and there, and weeds flaunted boldly in the gaps. The girl looked wan and ghostly in the lonely dusk.

"This is my father's grave, and my mother is here," she said, abruptly, as he came up and stood beside her. Her head was drooped upon her breast, and he saw that she had been weeping. "See," she went on, drawing her finger along the mildewed lettering: " 'Félix Marie-Joseph Arnault... âgé de trente-quatre ans.'... 'Hélène Pallacier, épouse de Félix Arnault... décédée a l'âge de dix-neuf ans.' Nineteen years old," she repeated, slowly. "My mother was one year younger than I am when she died—my beautiful mother!"

Her voice sounded like a far-away murmur in his ears. He looked at her, vaguely conscious that she was suffering. But he did not speak, and after a little she got up and went away. Her dress, which brushed in passing, was wet with dew. He watched her slight figure, moving like a spirit along the lane, until a turn in the hedge hid her from sight. Then he turned again towards the swamp, and resumed his restless walk.

Some hours later he crossed the rose-garden. The moon was under a cloud; the trunks of the crepe-myrtles were like pale spectres in the uncertain light. The night wind blew in chill and moist from the swamp. The house was dark and quiet, but he heard the blind of an upper window turned stealthily as he stepped into the latticed arcade.

"The old madame is watching me—and her," he said to himself.

His agitation had now become supreme. The faint familiar perfume that stole about his room filled him with a kind of frenzy. Was this the chivalric devotion of which he had so boasted? this the desire to protect a young and defenceless woman? He no longer dared question himself. He seemed to feel her warm breath against his cheeks. He threw up his arms with a gesture of despair. A sigh stirred the death-like stillness. At last! She was there, just within his doorway; the pale glimmer of the veiled moon fell upon her. Her trailing laces wrapped her about like a silver mist; her arms were folded across her bosom; her eyes—he dared not interpret the meaning which he read in those wonderful eyes. She turned slowly and went down the hall. He followed her, reeling like a drunkard. His feet seemed clogged, the blood ran thick in his veins, a strange roaring was in his ears. His hot eyes strained her as she vanished, just beyond his touch, into the room next his own. He threw himself against the closed door in a transport of rage. It yielded suddenly, as if opened from within. A full blaze of light struck his eyes, blinding him for an instant; then he saw her. A huge four-posted bed with silken hangings occupied a recess in the room. Across its foot a low couch was drawn. She had thrown herself there. Her head was pillowed on crimson gold-embroidered cushions; her diaphanous draperies, billowing foam-like over her, half concealed, half revealed her lovely form; her hair waved away from her brows, and spread like a shower of gold over the cushions. One bare arm hung to the door; something jewel-like gleamed in the half-closed hand; the other lay across her forehead, and from beneath it her eyes were fixed upon him. He sprang forward with a cry....

At first he could remember nothing. The windows were open; the heavy curtains which shaded them moved lazily in the breeze; a shaft of sunlight that came in between them fell upon the polished surface of the marble mantel. He examined with languid curiosity some trifles that stood there—a pair of Dresden figures, a blue Sèvres vase of graceful shape, a bronze clock with gilded rose-wreathed Cupids; and then raised his eyes to the two portraits which hung above. One of these was familiar enough—the dark, melancholy face of Félix Arnault, whose portrait by different hands and at different periods of his life hung in nearly every room at La Glorieuse. The blood surged into his face and receded again at sight of the other. Oh, so strangely like! The yellow hair, the slumberous eyes, the full throat clasped about with a single strand of coral. Yes, it was she! He lifted himself on his elbow. He was in bed. Surely this was the room into which she had drawn him with her eyes. Did he sink on the threshold, all his senses swooning into delicious death? Or had he, indeed, in that last moment thrown himself on his knees by her couch? He could not remember, and he sank back with a sigh.

Instantly Madame Arnault was bending over him. Her cool hands were on his forehead."Dieu merci!" she exclaimed, "thou art thyself once more, mon fils."

He seized her hand imperiously. "Tell me, madame," he demanded—"tell me, for the love of God! What is she? Who is she? Why have you shut her away in this deserted place? Why—"

She was looking down at him with an expression half of pity, half of pain.

"Forgive me," he faltered, involuntarily, all his darker suspicions somehow vanishing; "but—oh, tell me!"

"Calm thyself, Richard," she said, soothingly, seating herself on the side of the bed, and stroking his hand gently. Too agitated to speak, he continued to gaze at her with imploring eyes. "Yes, yes, I will relate the whole story," she added, hastily, for he was panting and struggling for speech. "I heard you fall last night," she continued, relapsing for greater ease into French; "for I was full of anxiety about you, and I lingered long at my window watching for you. I came at once with Marcelite, and found you lying insensible across the threshold of this room. We lifted you to the bed, and bled you after the old fashion, and then I gave you a tisane of my own making, which threw you into a quiet sleep. I have watched beside you until your waking. Now you are but a little weak from fasting and excitement, and when you have rested and eaten—"

"No," he pleaded; "now, at once!"

"Very well," she said, simply. She was silent a moment, as if arranging her thoughts. "Your grandfather, a Richard Keith like yourself," she began, "was a college-mate and friend of my brother, Henri Raymonde, and accompanied him to La Glorieuse during one of their vacations. I was already betrothed to Monsieur Arnault, but I—No matter! I never saw Richard Keith afterwards. But years later he sent your father, who also bore his name, to visit me here. My son, Félix, was but a year or so younger than his boy, and the two lads became at once warm friends. They went abroad, and pursued their studies side by side, like brothers. They came home together, and when Richard's father died, Felix spent nearly a year with him on his Maryland plantation. They exchanged, when apart, almost daily letters. Richard's marriage, which occurred soon after they left college, strengthened rather than weakened this extraordinary bond between them. Then came on the war. They were in the same command, and hardly lost sight of each other during their four years of service.

"When the war was ended, your father went back to his estates. Félix turned his face homeward, but drifted by some strange chance down to Florida, where he met her"—she glanced at the portrait over the mantel. "Hélène Pallacier was Greek by descent, her family having been among those brought over some time during the last century as colonists to Florida from the Greek islands. He married her, barely delaying his marriage long enough to write me that he was bringing home a bride. She was young, hardly more than a child, indeed, and marvellously beautiful"—Keith moved impatiently; he found these family details tedious and uninteresting—"a radiant, soulless creature, whose only law was her own selfish enjoyment, and whose coming brought pain and bitterness to La Glorieuse. These were her rooms. She chose them because of the rose-garden, for she had a sensuous and passionate love of nature. She used to lie for hours on the grass there, with her arms flung over her head, gazing dreamily at the fluttering leaves above her. The pearls—which she always wore—some coral ornaments, and a handful of amber beads were her only dower, but her caprices were the insolent and extravagant caprices of a queen. Félix, who adored her, gratified them at whatever expense; and I think at first she had a careless sort of regard for him. But she hated the little Félice, whose coming gave her the first pang of physical pain she had ever known. She never offered the child a caress. She sometimes looked at her with a suppressed rage which filled me with terror and anxiety.

"When Félice was a little more than a year old, your father came to La Glorieuse to pay us a long-promised visit. His wife had died some months before, and you, a child of six or seven years, were left in charge of relatives in Maryland. Richard was in the full vigor of manhood, broad-shouldered, tall, blue-eyed, and blond-haired, like his father and like you. From the moment of their first meeting Hélène exerted all the power of her fascination to draw him to her. Never had she been so whimsical, so imperious, so bewitching! Loyal to his friend, faithful to his own high sense of honor, he struggled against a growing weakness, and finally fled. I will never forget the night he went away. A ball had been planned by Félix in honor of his friend. The ball-room was decorated under his own supervision. The house was filled with guests from adjoining parishes; everybody, young and old, came from the plantations around. Hélène was dazzling that night. The light of triumph lit her cheeks; her eyes shone with a softness which I had never seen in them before. I watched her walking up and down the room with Richard, or floating with him in the dance. They were like a pair of radiant god-like visitants from another world. My heart ached for them in spite of my indignation and apprehension; for light whispers were beginning to circulate, and I saw more than one meaning smile directed at them. Félix, who was truth itself, was gayly unconscious.

"Towards midnight I heard far up the bayou the shrill whistle of the little packet which passed up and down then, as now, twice a week, and presently she swung up to our landing. Richard was standing with Hélène by the fireplace. They had been talking for some time in low, earnest tones. A sudden look of determination came into his eyes. I saw him draw from his finger a ring which she had one day playfully bade him wear, and offer it to her. His face was white and strained; hers wore a look which I could not fathom. He quitted her side abruptly and walked rapidly across the room, threading his way among the dancers, and disappeared in the press about the door. A few moments later a note was handed me. I heard the boat steam away from the landing as I read it. It was a hurried line from Richard. He said that he had been called away on urgent business, and he begged me to make his adieus to Madame Arnault and Félix. Félix was worried and perplexed by the sudden departure of his guest. Helene said not a word, but very soon I saw her slipping down the stair, and I knew that she had gone to her room. Her absence was not remarked, for the ball was at its height. It was almost daylight when the last dance was concluded, and the guests who were staying in the house had retired to their rooms.

"Félix, having seen to the comfort of all, went at last to join his wife. He burst into my room a second later, almost crazed with horror and grief. I followed him to this room. She was lying on a couch at the foot of the bed. One arm was thrown across her forehead, the other hung to the floor, and in her hand she held a tiny silver bottle with a jewelled stopper. A handkerchief, with a single drop of blood upon it, was lying on her bosom. A faint, curious odor exhaled from her lips and hung about the room, but the poison had left no other trace.

"No one save ourselves and Marcelite ever knew the truth. She had danced too much at the ball that night, and she had died suddenly of heart-disease. We buried her out yonder in the old Raymonde-Arnault burying-ground. I do not know what the letter contained which Félix wrote to Richard. He never uttered his name afterwards. The ball-room—the whole wing, in truth—was at once closed. Everything was left exactly as it was on that fatal night. A few years ago, the house being unexpectedly full, I opened the room in which you have been staying, and it has been used from time to time as a guest-room since. My son lived some years, prematurely old, heart-broken, and desolate. He died with her name on his lips."

Madame Arnault stopped.

A suffocating sensation was creeping over her listener. Only in the last few moments had the signification of the story begun to dawn upon him. "Do you mean," he gasped, "that the girl whom I—

that she is—was—"

"Hélène, dead wife of Félix Arnault," she replied, gravely. "Her restless spirit has walked here before. I have sometimes heard her tantalizing laugh echo through the house, but no one had ever seen her until you came—so like the Richard Keith she loved!"

"When I read your letter," she went on, after a short silence, "which told me that you wished to come to those friends to whom your father had been so dear, all the past arose before me, and I felt that I ought to forbid your coming. But I remembered how Félix and Richard had loved each other before she came between them. I thought of the other Richard Keith whom I—I loved once; and I dreamed of a union at last between the families. I hoped, Richard, that you and Félice—"

But Richard was no longer listening. He wished to believe the whole fantastic story an invention of the keen-eyed old madame herself. Yet something within him confessed to its truth. A tumultuous storm of baffled desire, of impotent anger, swept over him. The ring he wore burned into his flesh. But he had no thought of removing it—the ring which had once belonged to the beautiful golden-haired woman who had come back from the grave to woo him to her!

He turned his face away and groaned.

Her eyes hardened. She arose stiffly. "I will send a servant with your breakfast," she said, with her hand on the door. "The down boat will pass La Glorieuse this afternoon. You will perhaps wish to take advantage of it."

He started. He had not thought of going—of leaving her—her! He looked at the portrait on the wall and laughed bitterly.

Madame Arnault accompanied him with ceremonious politeness to the front steps that afternoon.

"Mademoiselle Félice?" he murmured, inquiringly, glancing back at the windows of the sitting-room.

"Mademoiselle Arnault is occupied," she coldly returned. "I will convey to her your farewell."

He looked back as the boat chugged away. Peaceful shadows enwrapped the house and overspread the lawn. A single window in the wing gleamed like a bale-fire in the rays of the setting sun.

The years that followed were years of restless wandering for Richard Keith. He visited his estate but rarely. He went abroad and returned, hardly having set foot to land; he buried himself in the fastnesses of the Rockies; he made a long, aimless sea-voyage. Her image accompanied him everywhere. Between him and all he saw hovered her faultless face; her red mouth smiled at him; her white arms enticed him. His own face became worn and his step listless. He grew silent and gloomy. "He is madder than the old colonel, his father, was," his friends said, shrugging their shoulders.

One day, more than three years after his visit to La Glorieuse, he found himself on a deserted part of the Florida sea-coast. It was late in November, but the sky was soft and the air warm and balmy. He bared his head as he paced moodily to and fro on the silent beach. The waves rolled languidly to his feet and receded, leaving scattered half-wreaths of opalescent foam on the snowy sands. The wind that fanned his face was filled with the spicy odors of the sea. Seized by a capricious impulse, he threw off his clothes and dashed into the surf. The undulating billows closed around him; a singular lassitude passed into his limbs as he swam; he felt himself slowly sinking, as if drawn downward by an invisible hand. He opened his eyes. The waves lapped musically above his head; a tawny glory was all about him, a luminous expanse, in which he saw strangely formed creatures moving, darting, rising, falling, coiling, uncoiling.

"You was jess on de eedge er drownin', Mars Dick," said Wiley, his black body-servant, spreading his own clothes on the porch of the little fishing-hut to dry. "In de name o' Gawd, whar mek you wanter go in swimmin' dis time o' de yea', anyhow? Ef I hadn'er splurge in an' fotch you out, dey'd er been mo'nin' yander at de plantation, sho!"

His master laughed lazily. "You are right, Wiley," he said; "and you are going to smoke the best tobacco in Maryland as long as you live." He felt buoyant. Youth and elasticity seemed to have come back to him at a bound. He stretched himself on the rough bench, and watched the blue rings of smoke curl lightly away from his cigar. Gradually he was aware of a pair of wistful eyes shining down on him. His heart leaped. They were the eyes of Félice Arnault! "My God, have I been mad!" he muttered. His eyes sought his hand. The ring, from which he had never been parted, was gone. It had been torn from his finger in his wrestle with the sea. " Get my traps together at once, Wiley," he said. "We are going to La Glorieuse."

"Now you talkin', Mars Dick," assented Wiley, cheerfully.

It was night when he reached the city. First of all, he made inquiries concerning the little packet. He was right; the Assumption would leave the next afternoon at five o'clock for Bayou L'Éperon. He went to the same hotel at which he had stopped before when on his way to La Glorieuse. The next morning, too joyous to sleep, he rose early, and went out into the street. A gray, uncertain dawn was just struggling into the sky. A few people on their way to market or to early mass were passing along the narrow banquettes; sleepy-eyed women were unbarring the shutters of their tiny shops; high-wheeled milk-carts were rattling over the granite pavements; in the vine-hung courtyards, visible here and there through iron grilles, parrots were scolding on their perches; children pattered up and down the long, arched corridors; the prolonged cry of an early clothes-pole man echoed, like the note of a winding horn, through the close alleys. Keith sauntered carelessly along.

"In so many hours," he kept repeating to himself, "I shall be on my way to La Glorieuse. The boat will swing into the home landing; the negroes will swarm across the gang-plank, laughing and shouting; Madame Arnault and Félice will come out on the gallery and look, shading their eyes with their hands. Oh, I know quite well that the old madame will greet me coldly at first. Her eyes are like steel when she is angry. But when she knows that I am once more a sane man—And Félice, what if she—But no! Félice is not the kind of woman who loves more than once; and she did love me, God bless her! unworthy as I was."

A carriage, driven rapidly, passed him; his eyes followed it idly, until it turned far away into a side street. He strayed on to the market, where he seated himself on a high stool in *L'Appel du Matin* coffee-stall. But a vague, teasing remembrance was beginning to stir in his brain. The turbaned woman on the front seat of the carriage that had rolled past him yonder, where had he seen that dark, grave, wrinkled face, with the great hoops of gold against either cheek? Marcelite! He left the stall and retraced his steps, quickening his pace almost to a run as he went. Félice herself, then, might be in the city. He hurried to the street into which the carriage had turned, and glanced down between the rows of wide-caved cottages with green doors and batten shutters. It had stopped several squares away; there seemed to be a number of people gathered about it. "I will at least satisfy myself," he thought.

As he came up, a bell in a little cross-crowned tower began to ring slowly. The carriage stood in front of a low red-brick house, set directly on the street; a silent crowd pressed about the entrance. There was a hush within. He pushed his way along the banquette to the steps. A young nun, in a brown serge robe, kept guard at the door. She wore a wreath of white artificial roses above her long coarse veil. Something in his face appealed to her, and she found a place for him in the little convent chapel.

Madame Arnault, supported by Marcelite, was kneeling in front of the altar, which blazed with candles. She had grown frightfully old and frail. Her face was set, and her eyes were fixed with a rigid stare on the priest who was saying mass. Marcelite's dark cheeks were streaming with tears. The chapel, which wore a gala air, with its lights and flowers, was filled with people. On the left of the altar, a bishop, in gorgeous robes, was sitting, attended by priests and acolytes; on the right, the wooden panel behind an iron grating had been removed, and beyond, in the nun's choir, the black-robed sisters of the Carmelite order were gathered. Heavy veils shrouded their faces and fell to their feet. They held in their hands tall wax-candles, whose yellow flames burned steadily in the semi-darkness. Five or six young girls knelt, motionless as statues, in their midst. They also carried tapers, and their rapt faces were turned towards the unseen altar within, of which the outer one is but the visible token. Their eyelids were downcast. Their white veils were thrown back from their calm foreheads, and floated like wings from their shoulders.

He felt no surprise when he saw Félice among them. He seemed to have foreknown always that he should find her thus on the edge of another and mysterious world into which he could not follow her.

Her skin had lost a little of its warm, rich tint; the soft rings of hair were drawn away under her veil; her hands were thin, and as waxen as the taper she held. An unearthly beauty glorified her pale face.

"Is it forever too late?" he asked himself in agony, covering his face with his hands. When he looked again the white veil on her head had been replaced by the sombre one of the order. "If I could but speak to her!" he thought; "if she would but once lift her eyes to mine, she would come to me even now!"

Félice! Did the name break from his lips in a hoarse cry that echoed through the hushed chapel, and silenced the voice of the priest? He never knew. But a faint color swept into her cheeks. Her eyelids trembled. In a flash the rose-garden at La Glorieuse was before him; he saw the turquoise sky, and heard the mellow chorus of the field gang; the smell of damask-roses was in the air; her little hand was in his… he saw her coming swiftly towards him across the dusk of the old ball-room; her limpid, innocent eyes were smiling into his own…. she was standing on the grassy lawn; the shadows of the leaves flickered over her white gown….

At last the quivering eyelids were lifted. She turned her head slowly, and looked steadily at him. He held his breath. A cart rumbled along the cobble-stones outside; the puny wail of a child sounded across the stillness; a handful of rose-leaves from a vase at the foot of the altar dropped on the hem of Madame Arnault's dress. It might have been the gaze of an angel in a world where there is no marrying nor giving in marriage, so pure was it, so passionless, so free of anything like earthly desire.

As she turned her face again towards the altar the bell in the tower above ceased tolling; a triumphant chorus leaped into the air, borne aloft by joyous organ tones. The first rays of the morning sun streamed in through the small windows. Then light penetrated into the nun's choir, and enveloped like a mantle of gold Sister Mary of the Cross, who in the world had been Félicité Arnault.

Alcée Fortier (1856–1914)

Alcée Fortier was the first author to translate and compile Louisiana Black Creole folktales, beginning in 1895. Since then, several Louisiana scholars and folklorists have carried on similar studies, including Calvin Claudel in 1948 and Corinne Saucier, who in 1949 looked at the French fairy tales and numbskull stories, and Elizabeth Brandon, who in 1955 collected popular French jokes and tall tales.[1] Little has been done, however, with Louisiana African American Creole tales since Fortier's collection, which makes it so vital to readers of Louisiana literature today.

Alcée Fortier's father, Florent Fortier, was born into a prominent Louisiana family on a plantation in St. Charles Parish and married his cousin, Edwige, the daughter of the even more prominent Valcour Aime, in 1836. The Fortiers moved into Valcour Aime's renowned Le Petit Versailles, so named, ironically, for its ornate English garden. Upon the death of Edwige's brother, Gabriel, Valcour Aime's only son, in 1855, Aime lost all interest in the lavish family plantation and turned its management over to Florent.

All of the Fortier's ten children were born at Le Petit Versailles, including their youngest, Alcée, whose twin, Florent survived for only one year. In fact, four of the ten Fortier children died in infancy or early childhood, and their eldest son, Louis died at the age of twenty on his way home from serving in the Civil War in 1865, making Alcée the only surviving son.

Like his father before him, Alcée Fortier received the finest education and was enrolled in the University of Virginia when the Civil War broke out. That and a severe illness prompted his return to Louisiana, where for a time he studied law under Judge St. M. Berault.[2] By the end of the war, however, the Aime and Fortier fortunes were lost, so Alcée Fortier took a job in a New Orleans banking house. He continued his studies and finally gave up his clerk position to turn to teaching at the University of Louisiana, now Tulane University. By 1880, Fortier was a professor of French, and subsequently professor of Romance Languages, and finally Dean of the Graduate College of Tulane University.[3]

Fortier was always interested in Louisiana history and culture, especially the state's French heritage. He was the president of *l'Athenee Louisianais,* a literary club founded by Dr. Alfred Mercier, an officer in the New Orleans Academy of Sciences, the American Folklore Society, the American Dialect Society and president of the Modern Language Association of America, and appointed to the Louisiana State Board of Education.[4] In addition, he arguably did more to promote the study of Louisiana folklore than anyone before him simply by collecting and translating the folktales of black Creoles and founding the Louisiana Association of the American Folk-Lore Society in 1892.

Nonetheless, his discussions of these tales are sometimes difficult to abide due to their racist nature, even if acceptable at the time. Fortier, in his introduction to *Louisiana Folk-Tales,* tells the reader that "It is a strange fact that the old negroes do not like to relate those tales with which they enchanted their little masters before the war," and that "one must bear in mind that most of them were related to children by childlike people; this accounts for their naïveté."[5] Fortier admits that like the "little masters" whom he mentions in his introduction, he too was first introduced to these tales by his family slaves on the Aime plantation in Vacherie, Louisiana. Perhaps his most astonishing assertion comes while discussing the origin of these tales: "The Louisiana folk-tales were brought over to this country by Europeans and Africans, and it is interesting to note what changes have been made in some

---

1   For more on the collection of traditional folktales in Louisiana, see Barry Ancelet, Ed. *Cajun and Creole Folktales* (Jackson: University of Mississippi Press, 1994).

2   Alcée Fortier et al, Eds. *Biographical and Historical Memoires of Louisiana,* Vol 1, (Chicago: Goodspeed Publishing Co., 1892), 420-421.

3   Estelle M. Fortier Cochran, *The Fortier Family and Allied Families* (Louisiana: Estelle M.F. Cochran, 1963), 170.

4   Fortier, *Biographical and Historical Memoires of Louisiana,* 420.

5   Alcée Fortier, ed. *Louisiana Folk-Tales in French Dialect and English Translation.* (New York: Houghton, Mifflin and Company, 1895), ix.

well-known tales by a race rude and ignorant, but not devoid of imagination and poetical feeling."[1] Naturally, such prejudice is not conducive to impartial research, and Carl Lindahl, in his foreword to Barry Ancelet's *Cajun and Creole Folktales,* states that these "arbitrary restrictions of traditional scholarly boundaries.... (and) compartmentalizing stereotypes... dominated early research,"[2] and he refers specifically to Fortier.

Fortier focused on black Creole folktales, but moreover on animal tales, several of which featured the wily trickster rabbit, Compair Lapin, and his dimmer and more gullible sidekick, Bouki, the hyena. The most familiar of these tales would be "The Tar Baby," (*"Piti Bonhomme Godron"*). There are, of course, many versions of the tar baby tale, and the one that most readers are familiar with is "Brer Rabbit and the Tar Baby" made famous in Joel Chandler Harris's *Uncle Remus* tales, but the tale originated much earlier and Fortier's version makes its African origins quite apparent.

The tale presented here, "The Marriage of Compair Lapin" (*"Mariage Compair Lapin"*), is another example of Compair Lapin's ability to outwit his adversaries, in this case the rulers of the animal kingdom, elephants and lions, by pitting them against one another. Along the way, we learn a few very interesting facts about the natural world, such as why dogs "smell each other everywhere," and at the end we find a more significant phenomenon explained: how one litter of rabbits can include one white bunny and one black. These are African tales told by slaves explaining racism and the reaction to it to young children using the more palatable animals to convey their often serious messages.

Fortier's life's work was the transcription and translation of Creole and French works—including Isleño dècimas (see below)—into English for the increasingly American population of Louisiana. In 1881, he married Marie Lanauze, and they went on to have eight children, three of whom died in infancy. Two of his sons, Edouard and James, followed in their father's footsteps by working to defend and promote the French culture of the state. Alcée Fortier died in New Orleans on February 14, 1914, at the age of 58.

The Marriage of Compair Lapin[3]

You all must remember, after they had thrown Compair Lapin into the briers, how quickly he had run away, saying that it was in those very thorns that his mother had made him. Now then, I will tell you that on the same day Miss Leonine went to meet him, and they started traveling. They walked a long time, for at least a month; at last they reached the bank of a river which was very deep. The current was strong, too strong for them to swim over. On the other side of the river there was a pretty place: the trees were green and loaded with all kinds of fruits. Under the trees were flowers of every kind that there is in the world. When a person breathed there, it was as if a bottle of essence had been opened in a room.

Miss Leonine said: "Let us go to live there; besides, we cannot return to my father's. There, we shall be happy, and no one will bother us; but how shall we do to cross over to the other side?"

"Stop," said Compair Lapin, "let me think a moment," and then he began to walk and walk, until he saw a large piece of dry wood which had fallen into the water. "That is what I want," said he. He cut a tall pole, and then he mounted on the log and told Leonine to follow him. Poor Miss Leonine mounted also, but she was so much afraid that she was trembling dreadfully.

"Hold on well; you will see how we shall pass;" and he pushed with his stick. The log began to go down the current; they were going like lightning, and Lapin kept on paddling. They sailed for half a day before they were able to reach the other side, for the current was so strong that the log was carried along all the time. At last it passed very near the shore. "Jump, jump,"said Compair Lapin, and hardly had he

---

1   Ibid.

2   Carl Lindahl, Foreword, *Cajun and Creole Folktales,* x.

3   From: *Louisiana Folk-Tales in French Dialect and English Translation,* Collected and Edited by Alcée Fortier (New York: Houghton, Mifflin and Company, 1895).

spoken than he was on shore. Miss Leonine finally jumped also, and they found themselves on the other side of the river. They were very glad, and the first thing they did was to eat as much as they could of the good things they found there. Then they took a good rest.

They found a pretty place to pass the night, and the next day, at dawn, they took a good walk. As everything they saw was so fine, they thought they would remain there to live. When they had run away, they had not been able to take any money with them, so they were without a cent. But God had blessed them, for they had come to a place where they did not need much money. They had already been there a good while, and they were quiet and contented, and they thought that they were alone, when one day, they heard all once, a noise, a tumult, as if thunder was rolling on the ground.

"What is that, my lord? Go to see, Compair Lapin."

"I, no, as if I am foolish to go, and then catch something bad. It is better for me to stay quiet, and, in that way, nothing can happen to me."

The noise kept on increasing, until they saw approaching a procession of elephants. As they were passing quietly without attacking any one, it gave Compair Lapin a little courage. He went to the chief of the elephants and told him that he asked his permission to remain in his country; he said that he came from the country of King Lion, who had wanted to kill him, and he had run away with his wife.

The elephant replied: "That is good; you may remain here as long as you want, but don't you bring here other animals who know how to eat one another. As long as you will behave well, I will protect you, and nobody will come to get you here. Come sometimes to see me, and I will try to do something for you."

Some time after that, Compair Lapin went to see the king of elephants, and the king was so glad when Compair Lapin explained to him how he could make a great deal of money, that he named immediately Compair Lapin captain of his bank and watchman of his property. When Compair Lapin saw all the money of the king it almost turned his head, and as he had taken the habit of drinking since they had dug in his country a well, of which the water made people drunk, he continued his bad habit whenever he had the chance. One evening he came home very drunk, and he began quarreling with his wife. Leonine fell upon him and gave him such a beating that he remained in bed for three weeks.

When he got up, he asked his wife to pardon him; he said that he was drunk, and that he would never do it again, and he kissed her. In his heart, however, he could not forgive Leonine. He swore that he would leave her, but before that he was resolved to give her a terrible beating. One evening when Leonine was sleeping, Compair Lapin took a rope and tied her feet before and behind. In that way he was sure of his business. Then he took a good whip, and he whipped her until she lost consciousness. Then he left her and went on traveling. He wanted to go to a place where they would never hear of him any more, because he was afraid that Leonine would kill him, and he went far.

When Miss Leonine came back to herself, she called, she called; they came to see what was the matter, and they found her well tied up. They cut the ropes, and Leonine started immediately. She left her house, she traveled a long time, until she came to the same river which she had crossed with Compair Lapin upon the log. She did not hesitate, but jumped into the water. The current carried her along, and she managed, after a great many efforts, to cross over to the other side. She was very tired, and she had to take some rest; then she started to return to her father. When her father saw her, he kissed her and caressed her, but his daughter began to cry, and told him how Compair Lapin had treated her. When King Lion heard that, he was so angry that all who were near him began to tremble.

"Come here, Master Fox; you shall go to the king of elephants, and tell him, that if he does not send Compair Lapin to me as soon as he can, I shall go to his country to kill him and all the elephants, and all the other animals, and everything which is in his country. Go quick!"

Master Fox traveled a long time, and arrived at last in the country where Compair Lapin was hidden. But he did not see him; he asked for him, but no one could give him any news of him. Master Fox went to see the king of elephants and told him what King Lion had said. The elephants hate the lions, so the king replied: "Tell your master that if he wishes me to break his jaw-bone, let him come. I shall not send anything or anybody, and first of all, get away from here quick. If you want good advice, I can tell you that you had better remain in your country. If ever Lion tries to come here, I shall receive him in such a manner that no one of you will ever return home."

Master Fox did not wait to hear any more; but he had no great desire to go back to his country, for he thought Lion would kill him if he returned without Compair Lapin. He walked as slowly as he could, and all along the road he saw that they were making preparations for war. He thought that perhaps the elephants were going to attack King Lion. He went on his way, and on arriving at a prairie he saw Compair Lapin, who was running in zigzags, sometimes on one side of the road, sometimes on the other. He stopped whenever he met animals and spoke to them, and then he started again as rapidly as before. At last Master Fox and Compair Lapin met, but the latter did not recognize his old friend.

"Where are you going like that, running all the time?"

"Ah!" replied Compair Lapin, "you don't know the bad news. Lion has declared war against all elephants, and I want to notify all mules, horses, and camels to get out of the way."

"But you, why are you running so? They are surely not going to make a soldier of you?"

"No, you believe that. Ah, well, with all your cunning you know nothing. When the officers of the king will come to get the horses and mules for the cavalry to go to war, they will say: 'That's a fellow with long ears; he is a mule; let us take him.' Even if I protest, and say that I am a rabbit, they will say: 'Oh, no! look at his ears; you see that he is a mule!' and I should be caught, enlisted, and forced to march. It seems to me that I know you, but it is such a long time since I have seen you. May God help me, it is Master Fox, my old friend!"

"Yes, yes, it is I, my good fellow. Well! what do you say about all that bad business?"

"All that is for a woman," said Compair Lapin; "we must try, my friend, to have nothing to do with that war."

"But what shall we do?" said Master Fox. "They will force us into it."

"No, you must be King Lion's adviser, and I will be that of King Elephant, and in that way we shall merely look on and let them fight as much as they want."

"You know," said Master Fox, "Leonine has returned to her father; and as you were not married before the church, I believe that Lion is about to marry her to one of his neighbors. Does it not grieve you, Compair Lapin, to think of that?"

"Oh, no; *qa zit pas oua tcheur pas fait mal* (we feel no sorrow for what we do not see)."

The two cunning fellows conversed a long time, for they were glad to meet after such a long absence. As they were about to part, they saw two dogs, that stood nose to nose, growling fiercely, and then turned around rapidly and began to smell each other everywhere.

"You, Master Fox, who know everything, can you tell me why dogs have the bad habit of smelling each other in that way?"

"I will tell you, Compair Lapin, why they do that. In old, old times, when there was but one god, called Mr. Jupiter, all the dogs considered their lot so hard and unhappy that they sent a delegation to ask Mr. Jupiter to better their condition. When they arrived at the house of the god in heaven, all the dogs were so frightened that they ran away. Only one remained; it was Brisetout, the largest dog of the party. He was not afraid of anything, and he came to Mr. Jupiter, and spoke thus:

"'My nation sent me to see you to ask you whether you think that we are going to watch over our masters all day and all night, bark all the time, and then be kicked right and left and have nothing to eat. We are too unhappy, and we want to know if you will allow us once in a while to eat one of the sheep of our masters. We cannot work like this for nothing. What do you say, Mr. Jupiter?'

"'Wait a moment; I shall give you such a reply that you will never wish to annoy me any more. I am tired of hearing all sorts of complaints. I am tired, do you hear?'

"Then Mr. Jupiter spoke a language that no one could understand, and one of his clerks went out to get something. He told the dog to sit down. Brisetout remained on the last step of the staircase. He thought that Mr. Jupiter was going to give him a good dinner; but the first thing he knew, the clerk returned with another man. They took hold of Brisetout, they tied him well, then they took a tin pan in which they put red pepper and turpentine. They rubbed the dog all over with the mixture; it burnt him so much that he howled and bellowed. When they let him go, Mr. Jupiter told him: 'You will give my reply to your comrades, and each one that will come to complain will be received in the same manner; you hear?'

"Ah, no, Brisetout did not hear; he ran straight ahead without knowing where he was going. At last he arrived at a bayou, fell into it, and was drowned. Some time after that, Mr. Jupiter did not feel well. He thought he would leave heaven and take a little trip to earth. On his way he saw an apple tree which was covered with beautiful apples. He began to eat some; and while he was eating, a troop of dogs came to bark at him. Mr. Jupiter ordered his stick to give them a good drubbing. The stick began to turn to the right and to the left, and beat the dogs so terribly, that they scattered about in a minute. There remained but one poor dog, who was all mangy. He begged the stick to spare him. Then Stick pushed him before Mr. Jupiter, and said: 'Master, that dog was so thin that I did not have the courage to beat him.'

"'It is very well,' said Mr. Jupiter, 'let him go; but if ever any dog comes to bark at me again, I shall destroy them all. I don't want to be bothered by you, I say. You have already sent me a delegation, and I received them so well that I don't think they will like to come back to see me. Have you already forgotten that?'

"The poor lean dog replied: 'What you say is true, but we never saw again the messenger we sent you; we are still waiting for him.'

"Mr. Jupiter then said: 'I will tell you how you can find out the messenger you had sent to me: let all dogs smell one another, and the one which will smell turpentine is the messenger.'

"You see now, Compair Lapin, why dogs smell one another. It was all Mr. Jupiter's doing. Poor old fellow, he has now lost all his clients, since the pope ordered everybody to leave him, and he has had to close his shop. He left the heaven, and no one knows where he went to hide. You understand, Compair Lapin, people get tired of having always the same thing; so they took another religion, and I think that the one we have now is good."

"Thank you, thank you, Master Fox, for your good story; and in order to show you that I am your old friend, I will tell you what we can do. As I told you already, we must remain very quiet. As the elephants want to go to attack King Lion in his own country, they will make a bridge for the army to pass. When the bridge will be finished they will go straight ahead, without stopping anywhere, to attack King Lion, for they want to take him by surprise. Don't you tell that to anybody, you hear."

Compair Lapin and Master Fox then shook hands, and they parted. Master Fox went on his way, and Compair Lapin went to the king of elephants and asked him to give orders to all the carpenters and blacksmiths in the country to obey him. When all the workmen were assembled, Compair Lapin began to make the bridge, and soon finished it. On the side of the river which was in the country of the elephants, he made at the end of the bridge a large park. These were bars of iron planted in the earth; they were at least ten feet high, and so sharp that a fly could not touch one without being pierced through. Compair Lapin then covered the bars of iron with branches and brambles to make it appear like a patch of briers, in order that they might not know that it was a snare. Then he took four cows with their calves, and tied them in the very middle of the pit. Then he put in it red pepper, ashes, and tobacco snuff. Then he placed in the trap a great number of tubs of water, in which there was a drug that made people go to sleep right off. After he had finished all this, Compair Lapin said: "Now let King Lion come to attack us."

Master Fox was still traveling to render an account of his errand to King Lion; but he was so much afraid to return without Compair Lapin, that he concluded that it was better not to return at all. On his way he met a hen; he killed it, and covered an old rag with the blood. He tied his hind paw with the rag, and he began to limp, and jump on three feet. At last he met Bourriquet, to whom he said: "My dear friend, render me a little service; you see how sick I am. I pray you to go to King Lion, to tell him that I cannot come to see him. The elephants broke my leg because I had come to claim Compair Lapin."

"Oh, no!" said Bourriquet; "you were always against me with Compair Lapin. Go yourself."

"That is good,"said Master Fox; "*c'estpasjis einfois la bouche besoin manger* (I shall have my chance again, you will need me again). If you knew what I have seen and what I know, you would listen to me."

"Well, tell me all," said Bourriquet; "and I will go, since you cannot walk."

"That is all right; listen well. The elephants intend to come to attack King Lion in his country. They are making a bridge to cross the river, and as soon as the bridge will be finished they will come immediately to surprise Lion. If the king understood his business, he would hasten to attack the elephants in their own country, before they come to lift him up before he knows it."

As soon as Master Fox had finished speaking, Bourriquet galloped away and went to King Lion, to whom he said what Master Fox had related to him. The king was so glad that he ordered someone to give Bourriquet a little hay to eat. Bourriquet was not very much pleased, and he began grumbling. "Don't you know, Bourriquet,"said the king's servant, "*qué ein choual donnin to doite pas gardé la bride* (that you must not look at the bridle of a horse which was given to you)."

"Well," said Bourriquet, "I had expected a better reward, but I'll take that anyhow, because *ein ti zozo dans la main vaut mit qué plein ti zozos quapé voltigé dans bois* (a bird in the hand is better than two in the bush)."

All at once they heard a dreadful noise. It was King Lion, who was starting for the war with all the animals which he could find: tigers, bears, wolves, all King Lion's subjects were there. As to Master Fox, he had run back to notify Compair Lapin that the enemies were coming.

Miss Leonine was with the army, and her father used to tell her all the time: "I am glad that you came; Compair Lapin will have to pay for all his tricks; you must treat him as he treated you."

King Lion was at the head of the army, and coming near the bridge he saw Master Fox, who was lying in the road with his leg broken. "Oh! oh!" said Lion, "this is the way they treated you! They shall have to pay for all that."

"Make haste,"said Master Fox; "don't wait till they come to attack you; pass the bridge immediately; that will throw them in confusion."

The army went on. They all ran to pass over the bridge, King Lion at the head, with his daughter. As soon as they arrived at the place where was the snare, and they saw the cows and their calves, King Lion and his troops killed them and began to eat them. Then they quarreled among themselves and began to fight. They scattered about the ashes, the red pepper, and the tobacco snuff, and were completely blinded. They fought terribly; they massacred one another; then those that were left drank the water in the tubs. Two hours later they were all sound asleep.

The elephants, which had remained prudently at a distance, hearing no more noise, came to the bridge. They killed all the animals that were left in Lion's army, and threw their bodies in the river. They flayed King Lion; they took his skin and sewed Bourriquet into it; then they tied some straw, covered with pitch, to Bourriquet's tail; they put fire to the straw, and they let him go to announce the news in Lion's country.

When Bourriquet passed on the bridge, he was galloping so fast that one might have thought that it was thunder that was rolling on the bridge, as if it were more than one hundred cart-loads. When Bourriquet arrived in his country his tail was entirely consumed by the fire, but he said that he had lost it in a battle. Although he announced very sad news, no one could help laughing at him: he was so funny without his tail, and so proud of his glorious wound.

As soon as all was over at the bridge, Compair Lapin went to get Master Fox, and took him to the king of the elephants. He presented him to his majesty, and told him that Master Fox was his good friend, and if the king wanted to accept his services, they would both be his very faithful subjects. The king of elephants said to them: "I believe that you are two cunning rascals, and that in my war with King Lion, Master Fox *té galpé avec chévreil et chassé avec chien* (had been on both sides of the fence); but all right, he may remain here, if he wants. As for you, Compair Lapin, I want you to get married. Here is Miss White Rabbit; she is rich, and will be a good match for you. Tomorrow I want to dance at the wedding."

The next day all the people assembled, and celebrated with great splendor the marriage of Compair Lapin with Miss White Rabbit. Master Fox was the first groomsman. Three weeks after the wedding, Mrs. Compair Lapin gave birth to two little ones; one was white and the other as black as soot. Compair Lapin was not pleased, and he went to see the king of elephants.

"Oh! you know nothing," said the king; "you are married before the church, and I will not grant you a divorce. Besides, I must tell you that in the family of Mrs. Compair Lapin it happens very often that the little ones are black. It is when the ladies are afraid in a dark night; so console yourself, and don't be troubled."

Compair Lapin consented to remain with his wife until death should part them, and that is how he married after all his pranks.

As I was there when all that happened, I ran away to relate it to you.

Leona Queyrouze (1861–1938)

In his short story, "'Tite Poulette," George Washington Cable writes about the French Creoles of New Orleans, both black and white, and their disdain for outsiders. The fact that they are Creoles trumps their race. The poets of Les Cenelles write of their strong Creole heritage in a time when their race plays a larger role in their inequality, after the American purchase of the Louisiana Territory. Nonetheless, they remain proud of their French Creole ancestry. Writer and composer, Leona Queyrouze continued that tradition, writing as a proud French Creole, sometimes even when it was to her disadvantage.

Queyrouze was born in New Orleans in 1861, to Leon and Anne Marie Clara Tertrou Queyrouze.[1] Both her parents came to Louisiana from France, and Leona was the first of their two children. She had a younger brother, Jacques Maximé. Her father was a wine merchant and owned and operated Queyrouze Co. wine shop at what is now 523-25 St. Louis Street, where the family also resided. They also owned Leona plantation in St. Martinville, her mother's childhood home. Leona's father, like author Sallie Rhett Roman's husband, Alfred Roman, served under General P.G.T. Beauregard and also like Alfred Roman, was wounded at the Battle of Shiloh.

According to Queyrouze biographer, Donna Meletio, Leona's father wanted his daughter to be well-educated, so she attended school in New Orleans and in France, and by the time she was nineteen, she was fluent in seven languages, naturally in French and English, but also in Italian, German, Spanish, Latin, and Greek; the latter two she learned by studying the classics in school. Meletio also describes the intellectual and artistic salons that the Queyrouze family hosted and where Leona met many artists and thinkers of the time who would remain her lifelong friends, like chess champion Paul Morphy, whose mother was Leona's piano teacher, and writers Alfred Mercier, Charles Gayarré, both of whom appear in this collection.

Leona's father, along with Alfred Mercier, Alcée Fortier, and other prominent New Orleanians, founded *L'Athénée Louisianais,* and Leona was the only female member of this exclusive literary society.[2] She also wrote for many of the local newspapers of the time, in both French and English, and all but one of her poems here originally appeared in the French language paper, *L'Abeille* (The Bee). However, Meletio devotes much of her work on Queyrouze to her relationship with Lafcadio Hearn, which appears to have been more than simply a friendship.

Junko Hagiwara, in his article, "Lafcadio Hearn and Leona Queyrouze," cites their mutual friend, Dr. Rudolph Matas, to whom Hearn dedicated his novel, *Chita,* saying of Hearn and Queyrouze that "their romantic involvement…[was] a given."[3] Evidence of that romance is seen in their correspondence and in Queyrouze's poetry included here. Although there is no sign that they ever met after Hearn left New Orleans, two of Queyrouze's poems to him appeared in *L'Abeille:* "Response to L. H." in 1887, and "Phantom of the West To Lafcadio Hearn" in 1894.

The first poem "Response to L. H." appeared in the newspaper shortly after Hearn and Queyrouze took a trip to the Queyrouze plantation, Leona, in St. Martinville, and, according to Eduoard L. Tinker in *Lafcadio Hearn's American Days,* Hearn later wrote about the run-down plantation as providing the perfect setting for Medea to grow herbs for her charms and potions in order to bewitch men.[4]

Before Euripedes, the most accepted and complete version of Medea's tale was Apollonius's *Argonautica,* and in that and other versions, Medea, although very vindictive and powerful, did not murder her children. In Queyrouze's poem, the speaker is addressing the same cruel and powerful Medea who "sees in the night with cold

---

1   Both the biographical information and the text of the poems included here can be found in Donna M. Meletio, "Leona Queyrouze (1861-1938) Louisiana French Creole Poet, Essayist and Composer," Ph.D. diss., Louisiana State University, 2005, *etd.lsu.edu.* Web. 12 May 2013.

2   For more on *L'Athénée Louisianais* see the chapter on Alfred Mercier, and both the University of New Orleans and Tulane University have *L'Athénée Louisianais* collections in their Special Collections.

3   Junko Hagiwara, "Lafcadio Hearn and Leona Queyrouze," *Lafcadio Hearn Journal,* Vol 1:2. (The Lafcadio Hearn Collection Special Collections Division, Howard Tilton Memorial Library, Tulane University).

4   Edward L. Tinker, *Lafcadio Hearn's American Days,* (New York, 1924), 267.

clarity/ the places of tombs that give rise to hate/ where she will reap her harvest while humanity sleeps." If this is in response to Hearn's reaction to her family plantation, Queyrouze does maintain the metaphor of farming the land, not for growth and sustenance, but in order to harm others.

"Phantom of the West: To Lafcadio Hearn" is a much more obvious and tender tribute to Hearn. Queyrouze uses the "Chrysanthemum," native to Asia, and "slender threads" to evoke Japan, where Hearn settled after leaving New Orleans. But she also goes on to say that "A distant phantom…/ Can never entirely escape the bonds that tie,/ Of azure blooms and white magnolias," suggesting that he will always be connected to the South, to New Orleans, or perhaps to her. Nonetheless, his being a phantom is "tearful" in the end.

In her poem "O France," Queyrouze writes as a "jealous lover" and a "spouse" of her love affair with France. She longs to "find new words in an unknown language/ In accents laid bare," certainly not the American English being spoken in New Orleans by the end of the century. Like champagne made from the "sparkling grapes pressed into wine" their "loving cup" like her love for France, will overflow. She still finds solace in the French Creole culture she worked so hard to uphold.

Finally, "Nocturne," as Meletio points out, was written just weeks before her marriage to widower Pierre Marie Etienne Barel in 1901, when Queyrouze was forty years old. According to the Historic New Orleans Collection website, there are no romantic missives between her and Barel aside from this poem among her papers, and calling this poem romantic is a stretch, as it opens: "We come to this old table together in our ennui/ Before the icy hands pass over us." She does go on to say that they will be joined in "infinite sweetness," but that last line is the most loving and romantic in the poem.

Queyrouze went on to live until 1938, but Barel preceded her in death as did all of her family and friends who had once attended her salons. By the end of her life she was blind, but, according to Meletio, she still rejected conveniences of modern times like the telephone and typewriter, and up to the end, longed for the days when she and other French Creoles set the standard in New Orleans.

Response to L.H.[1]

Medea, you have spoken; and you were right
Hence your name, woman with somber eyes
With a heart proud yet fierce, full of revolt and shadow,
And you hold the hand of a friend named: Betrayal!

Poets make your honey, she poisons it
With curses and countless prayers
Which call from the heavens, when hope grows dim
And risk weakening the prison walls.

She drinks deep the rose's dew from the trembling chalice;
Takes thee the rays that the dawn brings
But leaves the night shining in cold clarity

The graveyards give rise to hate
Where she will reap her harvest while humanity sleeps
And flies quietly like a moth in the night.

---

1   The poems collected here were never published in book form but appeared in the French language periodical, *L'Abeille de la Nouvelle Orleans*, New Orleans, Louisiana. Translations by Nancy Dixon. "Response to L.H." is from *L'Abeille*, March 27, 1887.

Phantom of the West: To Lafcadio Hearn[1]

The golden Chrysanthemum now blooms
Without restraint under the vast night skies
In a place of mystery, and in a strange embrace
The growing slender threads catch the light.

The ghost of the moon appears quietly
Pretending to hide its face in its palms
—A distant phantom, with a vague complaint
All at once it disappears, fainting away.

It comes from this country where the pure yellow Night
Can never escape the bonds that tie,
Or the azure blooms, like a white magnolia.

The moon gives birth to trembling stars,
Each one a tear from crying eyes, or Ophelia's shadow
In a deep river, they cast their veils.   (1894)

O France[2]

O France, I wish, like a jealous lover
To find new words, an unknown language
In accents laid bare
To speak of love.

I pray with the elders forehead on your knees
I want to welcome the night
So in my sleep I can feel upon my flesh
Your embrace like the kiss of a spouse.

While my soul ascends to the light
With ears trembling under the moist eyelid
Waking to the frail, blue morning light

Like violets, and feel the blood in my veins
The sparkling grapes pressed into wine
To fill to overflowing our loving cup.

---

1   From: *L'Abeille*, December 23, 1894.
2   From: *L'Abeille*, 1892.

Nocturne[1]

We come to this old table together in our ennui
Before the icy hands pass over us.
Yes, a tangled golden glow envelops us
And we find serenity here.

Come, reread this book with me. It is the one
That will ease our confusion. Here is the place.
We choose not to believe our lives are passing, but the trace
Of our tears and the echo of our laughter tells us so.

Our stirring will be in harmony
To the radiant lute strings
As our spirits become one in the divine breath.

Like turning these leaves of poetry
So too shall we be joined in the end,
You and I as always, in infinite sweetness.

---

1   Manuscript, 1901.

O. Henry (1862–1910)

Most readers do not associate William Sidney Porter[1], better known as O. Henry, with New Orleans, but his connection to the city is significant. In 1896, he came to New Orleans on the lam rather than face imprisonment for embezzlement in Texas, fled from the city to Trujillo, Honduras, and returned about a year and a half later on his way back to Austin to face the music and see his dying wife, Athol, one last time. It is no surprise that O. Henry turned from banking to writing, as his life is the stuff of fiction.

Porter was born at the height of the Civil War on September 11, 1862, in Greensboro, North Carolina, to Dr. Algernon Sidney and Mary Jane Virginia Swaim Porter. His maternal grandfather, William Swaim, was also a writer and the editor of the Greensboro *Patriot* up until his death in 1835. Porter's father was an esteemed local physician, and Porter grew up working in his uncle's drugstore, becoming a licensed pharmacist at the age of seventeen, an experience that would lead to his running the prison pharmacy at the Ohio Penitentiary in Columbus, Ohio, some two decades later. Porter was educated at his aunt Evelina Maria Porter's (Aunt Lina) elementary school until 1876, when he graduated and attended the local Lindsey Street High School. His mother died of consumption (tuberculosis) when Porter was only three years old, a disease that would later claim his first wife, Athol.

Porter was a frail youth, pale and anemic with a constant cough, so he moved out West to Texas, at the age of twenty, hoping that the climate would improve his health, and he remained there until he fled to New Orleans in 1896. He worked for a time on a sheep ranch where he learned Spanish from the itinerant immigrant farmhands, another skill that would come in handy later when he fled to Honduras. In 1884, Porter settled in Austin, where he held several jobs, as a pharmacist, bank teller, draftsman, and journalist. In Austin, he also began his career as a short story writer, publishing his first pieces in the Detroit *Free Press* in 1887, just months after his marriage to Athol Estes.[2]

Porter and Athol met in 1885, while she was still in high school. He was hardly in a position to consider marriage at the time, working only part time in a cigar store, but two years later he got on with the Texas General Land Office (GLO) earning $100 a month. Still, the wealthy Estes family was against the marriage, primarily because of Athol's consumption, which also took the life of her father and her grandmother, and she would die from it a decade later. Nonetheless, she and Porter eloped and had two children. The first, a son, died at birth, but the second, Margaret, remained the focus of her father's life up to the end.

Will Porter left the GLO and went to work as a teller in the First National Bank of Austin, which he later claimed was in a state of disarray. He also claimed that due to lax practices, the bank was audited and he was made the scapegoat for the Feds who demanded that he be prosecuted for embezzling. In one of his New Orleans stories, "Blind Man's Holiday," Porter addresses his being wrongly accused, when the protagonist, Lorison, says to his intended, Norah, "I am an outcast from honest people; I am wrongly accused of one crime, and am, I believe, guilty of another."

It took the Feds four years to bring Porter to trial, and Athol's wealthy stepfather put up his bond. But in the meantime, he had to find work, naturally having left the bank, so he turned to journalism, buying Brann's *Iconoclast* in 1894, which he would later entitle *The Rolling Stone*. Neither title was successful, and the paper folded only a year later, but his work led him to a more lucrative position with the Houston *Post*. In 1896, however, the summons came from Austin, and his case was finally coming to trial. William Porter purchased a train ticket from Houston to Austin, but he never arrived. Somewhere along the way, he changed direction and ended up in New Orleans.

---

1   For more on O. Henry or William Sidney Porter (He changed the spelling of his middle name to Sydney, and he also fudged on his birth date by five years.), and the source of much of the biographical information included here, see Robert H. Davis and Arthur B. Maurice, *The Caliph of Bagdad: Being Arabian Nights Flashes of the Life, Letters, and Work of O. Henry (William Sydney Porter)* (New York: D. Appleton and Co., 1931).

2   The only evidence of this is a letter from *Free Press* editor A. Mosely asking Porter for his "string" for the month of August, 1887. Davis and Maurice, 63.

There is little documentation about his time in New Orleans, but we do know that he arrived in the city penniless. Unable to apply for a job for which he was qualified due to his outstanding warrant, Porter turned to the backbreaking work of a stevedore.[1] It is difficult to say how long he remained in New Orleans, but just a few months later he took one of Sam Zamurray's banana boats to Trujillo, Honduras, where he met renowned bank robber, Al Jennings and his brother Frank.[2] Porter and Al Jennings would be reunited in the Ohio Penitentiary in 1899.

Although Porter tried to convince Athol and Margaret to join him in Honduras, she was too ill to do so, and January of 1897 found him back in New Orleans on his way back to Austin, where he would be tried and sentenced to five years in jail for embezzlement in March of 1898, eight months after Athol's death. While in Trujillo, Porter wrote his first collection of short stories, *Cabbages and Kings*, published by Doubleday in 1904, which has the first of his eight New Orleans stories, "The Shamrock and the Palm."[3] Also in that book he coined the term "banana republic," a term that is still used today in reference to many third world countries.

Aside from living briefly in the city, Porter has other connections to New Orleans. While serving his time, which ended up being three years and three months, Porter continued to write and publish. The stories took a circuitous route to his New York publishers, first being sent to a woman he would never meet, a sister of a New Orleans banker who, like Porter, was doing time in the Ohio Penitentiary, and she would send them along to various journals and magazines. Likewise, Porter would ask that the checks for the stories be returned to the New Orleans address.

He also claimed that he adopted his pen name in New Orleans. "It was during those days in New Orleans that I adopted my pen name. I said to a friend: 'I am going to send out some stuff. I don't know if it amounts to much, so I want to get a literary alias. Help me pick a good one.'" His friend suggested they take a look at the local society page, where O. Henry said "my eye lighted on Henry.... That'll do for a last name. Now for a first name. I want something short.... O is about the easiest letter written. O it is then."[4]

One of his earliest successes, "Whistling Dick's Christmas Stocking," included here, is set in New Orleans and its rural environs downriver. It was first published in *McClure's Magazine* in 1899, and it is also the first time he would use the pseudonym, O. Henry. The story opens with Dick, a vagrant just off the train looking for a "certain bench in Lafayette Square" in the city he calls the "cold weather paradise of tramps." Dick's attempts to reach that bench are thwarted when the good officer "Fritz," warns him that "'Article 5716' [to] arrest on suspicion" any vagrants was in full effect. Porter was probably well aware of that city ordinance, as he claims to have spent time on many park benches in the city.[5] We learn later on in the story just how irksome the vagrancy problem is not only to New Orleanians but to those wealthy plantation owners downriver as well, like the one in the story who explains the problem further:

> They swarm up and down the river every winter.... They overrun New Orleans, and we catch the surplus, which is generally the worst part... the police catch a dozen or two, and the remaining three or four thousand overflow up and down the levees.... They won't work... and they make friends with my dogs.

Dick is one of those vagrants who refuses to work, but Porter also paints him as the most admirable character in the story, an honest, yet very talented hobo, who can whistle Carl Maria von Weber's Der Freischütz (The Marksman) impeccably.

---

1   For more on Porter's time in New Orleans, see Francis Richardson, "O. Henry and New Orleans," *The Bookman*, May 1914.

2   Jennings writes about his meeting Porter in his book, *Through the Shadows with O. Henry* (New York: H.K. Fly Co., 1921).

3   The other seven are "Phoebe," "Cherchez la Femme," "Blind Man's Holiday," "A Matter of Mean Elevation," "Helping the Other Fellow," "Whistling Dick's Christmas Stocking," and "The Renaissance at Charleoi."

4   George MacAdam, *O. Henry Papers, Containing Some Sketches of his Life Together with an Alphabetical Index of his Complete Works* (New York: Doubleday, Page & Co., 1922), 19.

5   Davis and Maurice, 91.

O. Henry's New Orleans stories often focus on the poor humble characters of the city. Porter does not capitalize on the local color so popular at the time. Readers will not see Mardi Gras, hurricanes, or Twelfth Night celebrations, but rather the honest poor who work hard to improve their lots in life with whom Porter wishes readers to sympathize.

While there is also much conjecture about how Porter spent his time in New Orleans, we do know that after being released from the penitentiary in Ohio, Porter moved to New York City and then to Asheville, North Carolina. In 1907, he married again to Sara Coleman Lindsay, a childhood friend. His daughter Margaret came to live with them in their house on Long Island and again later when her father had moved to Asheville to improve his health that had been compromised from too many years of hard drinking. He suffered a fatal stroke in New York City on June 3, 1910; his funeral was held at the Protestant Episcopal Church of the Transfiguration in New York. He is buried in Asheville.

Whistling Dick's Christmas Stocking

It was with much caution that Whistling Dick slid back the door of the box-car, for Article 5716, City Ordinances, authorized (perhaps unconstitutionally) arrest on suspicion, and he was familiar of old with this ordinance. So, before climbing out, he surveyed the field with all the care of a good general.

He saw no change since his last visit to this big, alms-giving, long-suffering city of the South, the cold weather paradise of the tramps. The levee where his freight-car stood was pimpled with dark bulks of merchandise. The breeze reeked with the well-remembered, sickening smell of the old tarpaulins that covered bales and barrels. The dun river slipped along among the shipping with an oily gurgle. Far down toward Chalmette he could see the great bend in the stream outlined by the row of electric lights. Across the river Algiers lay, a long, irregular blot, made darker by the dawn which lightened the sky beyond. An industrious tug or two, coming for some early sailing ship, gave a few appalling toots, that seemed to be the signal for breaking day. The Italian luggers were creeping nearer their landing, laden with early vegetables and shellfish. A vague roar, subterranean in quality, from dray wheels and street cars, began to make itself heard and felt; and the ferryboats, the Mary Anns of water craft, stirred sullenly to their menial morning tasks.

Whistling Dick's red head popped suddenly back into the car. A sight too imposing and magnificent for his gaze had been added to the scene. A vast, incomparable policeman rounded a pile of rice sacks and stood within twenty yards of the car. The daily miracle of the dawn, now being performed above Algiers, received the flattering attention of this specimen of municipal official splendour. He gazed with unbiased dignity at the faintly glowing colours until, at last, he turned to them his broad back, as if convinced that legal interference was not needed, and the sunrise might proceed unchecked. So he turned his face to the rice bags, and, drawing a flat flask from an inside pocket, he placed it to his lips and regarded the firmament.

Whistling Dick, professional tramp, possessed a half-friendly acquaintance with this officer. They had met several times before on the levee at night, for the officer, himself a lover of music, had been attracted by the exquisite whistling of the shiftless vagabond. Still, he did not care, under the present circumstances, to renew the acquaintance. There is a difference between meeting a policeman on a lonely wharf and whistling a few operatic airs with him, and being caught by him crawling out of a freight-car. So Dick waited, as even a New Orleans policeman must move on some time—perhaps it is a retributive law of nature—and before long "Big Fritz" majestically disappeared between the trains of cars.

Whistling Dick waited as long as his judgment advised, and then slid swiftly to the ground. Assuming as far as possible the air of an honest labourer who seeks his daily toil, he moved across the network of railway lines, with the intention of making his way by quiet Girod Street to a certain bench in Lafayette Square, where, according to appointment, he hoped to rejoin a pal known as "Slick," this adventurous pilgrim having preceded him by one day in a cattle-car into which a loose slat had enticed him.

As Whistling Dick picked his way where night still lingered among the big, reeking, musty warehouses, he gave way to the habit that had won for him his title. Subdued, yet clear, with each note as true and liquid as a bobolink's, his whistle tinkled about the dim, cold mountains of brick like drops of rain falling into a hidden pool. He followed an air, but it swam mistily into a swirling current of improvisation. You could cull out the trill of mountain brooks, the staccato of green rushes shivering above chilly lagoons, the pipe of sleepy birds.

Rounding a corner, the whistler collided with a mountain of blue and brass.

"So," observed the mountain calmly, "You are already pack. Und dere vill not pe frost before two veeks yet! Und you haf forgotten how to vistle. Dere was a valse note in dot last bar."

"Watcher know about it?" said Whistling Dick, with tentative familiarity; "you wit yer little Gherman-band nixcumrous chunes. Watcher know about music? Pick yer ears, and listen agin. Here's de way I whistled it—see?"

He puckered his lips, but the big policeman held up his hand.

"Shtop," he said, "und learn der right way. Und learn also dot arolling shtone can't vistle for a cent."

Big Fritz's heavy moustache rounded into a circle, and from its depths came a sound deep and mellow as that from a flute. He repeated a few bars of the air the tramp had been whistling. The rendition was cold, but correct, and he emphasized the note he had taken exception to.

"Dot p is p natural, und not p vlat. Py der vay, you petter pe glad I meet you. Von hour later, und I vould half to put you in a gage to vistle mit der chail pirds. Der orders are to bull all der pums after sunrise."

"To which?"

"To bull der pums—eferybody mitout fisible means. Dirty days is der price, or fifteen tollars."

"Is dat straight, or a game you givin' me?"

"It's der pest tip you efer had. I gif it to you pecause I pelief you are not so bad as der rest. Und pecause you gan visl 'Der Freisechutz' bezzer dan I myself gan. Don't run against any more bolicemans aroundt der corners, but go away from town a few tays. Good-pye."

So Madame Orleans had at last grown weary of the strange and ruffled brood that came yearly to nestle beneath her charitable pinions.

After the big policeman had departed, Whistling Dick stood for an irresolute minute, feeling all the outraged indignation of a delinquent tenant who is ordered to vacate his premises. He had pictured to himself a day of dreamful ease when he should have joined his pal; a day of lounging on the wharf, munching the bananas and cocoanuts scattered in unloading the fruit steamers; and then a feast along the free-lunch counters from which the easy-going owners were too good-natured or too generous to drive him away, and afterward a pipe in one of the little flowery parks and a snooze in some shady corner of the wharf. But here was a stern order to exile, and one that he knew must be obeyed. So, with a wary eye open from the gleam of brass buttons, he began his retreat toward a rural refuge. A few days in the country need not necessarily prove disastrous. Beyond the possibility of a slight nip of frost, there was no formidable evil to be looked for.

However, it was with a depressed spirit that Whistling Dick passed the old French market on his chosen route down the river. For safety's sake he still presented to the world his portrayal of the part of the worthy artisan on his way to labour. A stall-keeper in the market, undeceived, hailed him by the generic name of his ilk, and "Jack" halted, taken by surprise. The vender, melted by this proof of his own acuteness, bestowed a foot of Frankfurter and half a loaf, and thus the problem of breakfast was solved.

When the streets, from topographical reasons, began to shun the river bank the exile mounted to the top of the levee, and on its well-trodden path pursued his way. The suburban eye regarded him with cold suspicion, individuals reflected the stern spirit of the city's heartless edict. He missed the seclusion of the crowded town and the safety he could always find in the multitude.

At Chalmette, six miles upon his desultory way, there suddenly menaced him a vast and bewildering industry. A new port was being established; the dock was being built, compresses were going up; picks and shovels and barrows struck at him like serpents from every side. An arrogant foreman bore down upon him, estimating his muscles with the eye of a recruiting-sergeant. Brown men and black men all about him were toiling away. He fled in terror.

By noon he had reached the country of the plantations, the great, sad, silent levels bordering the mighty river. He overlooked fields of sugar-cane so vast that their farthest limits melted into the sky. The sugar-making season was well advanced, and the cutters were at work; the wagons creaked drearily after them; the Negro teamsters inspired the mules to greater speed with mellow and sonorous imprecations. Dark-green groves, blurred by the blue of distance, showed where the plantation-houses stood. The tall chimneys of the sugar-mills caught the eye miles distant, like lighthouses at sea.

At a certain point Whistling Dick's unerring nose caught the scent of frying fish. Like a pointer to a quail, he made his way down the levee side straight to the camp of a credulous and ancient fisherman, whom he charmed with song and story, so that he dined like an admiral, and then like a philosopher annihilated the worst three hours of the day by a nap under the trees.

When he awoke and again continued his hegira, a frosty sparkle in the air had succeeded the drowsy warmth of the day, and as this portent of a chilly night translated itself to the brain of Sir Peregrine, he lengthened his stride and bethought him of shelter. He travelled a road that faithfully followed the convolutions of the levee, running along its base, but whither he knew not. Bushes and rank grass crowded it to the wheel ruts, and out of this ambuscade the pests of the lowlands swarmed after him, humming a keen, vicious soprano. And as the night grew nearer, although colder, the whine of the mosquitoes became a greedy, petulant snarl that shut out all other sounds. To his right, against the heavens, he saw a green light moving, and, accompanying it, the masts and funnels of a big incoming steamer, moving as upon a screen at a magic-lantern show. And there were mysterious marshes at his left, out of which came queer gurgling cries and a choked croaking. The whistling vagrant struck up a merry warble to offset these melancholy influences, and it is likely that never before, since Pan himself jigged it on his reeds, had such sounds been heard in those depressing solitudes.

A distant clatter in the rear quickly developed into the swift beat of horses' hoofs, and Whistling Dick stepped aside into the dew-wet grass to clear the track. Turning his head, he saw approaching a fine team of stylish grays drawing a double surrey. A stout man with a white moustache occupied the front seat, giving all his attention to the rigid lines in his hands. Behind him sat a placid, middle-aged lady and a brilliant-looking girl hardly arrived at young ladyhood. The lap-robe had slipped partly from the knees of the gentleman driving, and Whistling Dick saw two stout canvas bags between his feet—bags such as, while loafing in cities, he had seen warily transferred between express waggons and bank doors. The remaining space in the vehicle was filled with parcels of various sizes and shapes.

As the surrey swept even with the sidetracked tramp, the bright-eyed girl, seized by some merry, madcap impulse, leaned out toward him with a sweet, dazzling smile, and cried, "Mer-ry Christ-mas!" in a shrill, plaintive treble.

Such a thing had not often happened to Whistling Dick, and he felt handicapped in devising the correct response. But lacking time for reflection, he let his instinct decide, and snatching off his battered derby, he rapidly extended it at arm's length, and drew it back with a continuous motion, and shouted a loud, but ceremonious, "Ah, there!" after the flying surrey.

The sudden movement of the girl had caused one of the parcels to become unwrapped, and something limp and black fell from it into the road. The tramp picked it up, and found it to be a new black silk stocking, long and fine and slender. It crunched crisply, and yet with a luxurious softness, between his fingers.

"Ther bloomin' little skeezicks!" said Whistling Dick, with a broad grin bisecting his freckled face. "W't d' yer think of dat, now! Mer-ry Chris-mus! Sounded like a cuckoo clock, da'ts what she did. Dem guys is swells, too, bet yer life, an' der old 'un stacks dem sacks of dough down under his trotters like dey was common as dried apples. Been shoppin' for Chrismus, and de kid's lost one of her new socks w'ot she was goin' to hold up Santy wid. De bloomin' little skeezicks! Wit' her 'Mer-ry Chris-mus!' W'ot d' yer t'ink! Same as to say, 'Hello, Jack, how goes it?' and as swell as Fift' Av'noo, and as easy as a blowout in Cincinnat."

Whistling Dick folded the stocking carefully, and stuffed it into his pocket.

It was nearly two hours later when he came upon signs of habitation. The buildings of an extensive plantation were brought into view by a turn in the road. He easily selected the planter's residence in a large square building with two wings, with numerous good-sized, well-lighted windows, and broad verandas running around its full extent. it was set upon a smooth lawn, which was faintly lit by the far-reaching rays of the lamps within. A noble grove surrounded it, and old-fashioned shrubbery grew thickly about the walks and fences. The quarters of the hands and the mill buildings were situated at a distance in the rear.

The road was now enclosed on each side by a fence, and presently, as Whistling Dick drew nearer the house, he suddenly stopped and sniffed the air.

"If dere ain't a hobo stew cookin' somewhere in dis immediate precint," he said to himself, "me nose as quit tellin' de trut'."

Without hesitation he climbed the fence to windward. He found himself in an apparently disused lot, where piles of old bricks were stacked, and rejected, decaying lumber. In a corner he saw the faint glow of a fire that had become little more than a bed of living coals, and he thought he could see some dim human forms sitting or lying about it. He drew nearer, and by the light of a little blaze that suddenly flared up he saw plainly the fat figure of a ragged man in an old brown sweater and cap.

"Dat man," said Whistling Dick to himself softly, "is a dead ringer for Boston Harry. I'll try him wit de high sign."

He whistled one or two bars of a rag-time melody, and the air was immediately taken up, and then quickly ended with a peculiar run. The first whistler walked confidently up to the fire. The fat man looked up, and spake in a loud, asthmatic wheeze:

"Gents, the unexpected but welcome addition to our circle is Mr. Whistling Dick, an old friend of mine for whom I fully vouches. The waiter will lay another cover at once. Mr. W. D. will join us at supper, during which function he will enlighten us in regard to the circumstances that gave us the pleasure of his company."

"Chewin' de stuffin' out 'n de dictionary, as usual, Boston," said Whistling Dick; "but t'anks all de same for de invitashun. I guess I finds meself here about de same way as yous guys. A cop gimme de tip dis mornin'. Yous workin' on dis farm?"

"A guest," said Boston, sternly, "shouldn't never insult his entertainers until he's filled up wid grub. 'Tain't good business sense. Workin'!—but I will restrain myself. We five—me, Deaf Pete, Blinky, Goggles, and Indiana Tom—got put on to this scheme of Noo Orleans to work visiting gentlemen upon her dirty streets, and we hit the road last evening just as the tender hues of twilight had flopped down upon the daisies and things. Blinky, pass the empty oyster-can at your left to the empty gentleman at your right."

For the next ten minutes the gang of roadsters paid their undivided attention to the supper. In an old five-gallon kerosene can they had cooked a stew of potatoes, meat, and onions, which they partook of from smaller cans they had found scattered about the vacant lot.

Whistling Dick had known Boston Harry of old, and knew him to be one of the shrewdest and most successful of his brotherhood. He looked like a prosperous stock-drover or solid merchant from some country village. He was stout and hale, with a ruddy, always smoothly shaven face. His clothes were strong and neat, and he gave special attention to his decent-appearing shoes. During the past ten years he had acquired a reputation for working a larger number of successfully managed confidence games than any of his acquaintants, and he had not a day's work to be counted against him. It was rumoured among his associates that he had saved a considerable amount of money. The four other men were fair specimens of the slinking, ill-clad, noisome genus who carried their labels of "suspicious" in plain view.

After the bottom of the large can had been scraped, and pipes lit at the coals, two of the men called Boston aside and spake with him lowly and mysteriously. He nodded decisively, and then said aloud to Whistling Dick:

"Listen, sonny, to some plain talky-talk. We five are on a lay. I've guaranteed you to be square, and you're to come in on the profits equal with the boys, and you've got to help. Two hundred hands on this plantation are expecting to be paid a week's wages to-morrow morning. To-morrow's Christmas, and they want to lay off. Says the boss: 'Work from five to nine in the morning to get a train load of sugar off, and I'll pay every man cash down for the week and a day extra.' They say: 'Hooray for the boss! It goes.' He drives to Noo Orleans to-day, and fetches back the cold dollars. Two thousand and seventy-four fifty is the amount. I got the figures from a man who talks too much, who got 'em from the bookkeeper. The boss of this plantation thinks he's going to pay this wealth to the hands. He's got it down wrong; he's going to pay it to us. It's going to stay in the leisure class, where it belongs. Now, half of this haul goes to me, and the other half the rest of you may divide. Why the difference? I represent the brains. It's my scheme. Here's the way we're going to get it. There's some company at supper in the house, but they'll leave about nine. They've just happened in for an hour or so. If they don't go pretty soon, we'll work the scheme anyhow. We want all night to get away good with the dollars. They're heavy. About nine o'clock Deaf Pete and Blinky'll go down the road about a quarter beyond the house, and set fire to a big cane-field there that the cutters haven't touched yet. The wind's just right to have it roaring in two minutes. The alarm'll be given, and every man Jack about the place will be down there in ten minutes, fighting fire. That'll leave the money sacks and the women alone in the house for us to handle. You've heard cane burn? Well, there's mighty few women can screech loud enough to be heard above its crackling. The thing's dead safe. The only danger is in being caught before we can get far enough away with the money. Now, if you—"

"Boston," interrupted Whistling Dick, rising to his feet, "T'anks for the grub yous fellers has given me, but I'll be movin' on now."

"What do you mean?" asked Boston, also rising.

"W'y, you can count me outer dis deal. You oughter know that. I'm on de bum all right enough, but dat other t'ing don't go wit' me. Burglary is no good. I'll say good night and many t'anks fer—"

Whistling Dick had moved away a few steps as he spoke, but he stopped very suddenly. Boston had covered him with a short revolver of roomy calibre.

"Take your seat," said the tramp leader. "I'd feel mighty proud of myself if I let you go and spoil the game. You'll stick right in this camp until we finish the job. The end of that brick pile is your limit. You go two inches beyond that, and I'll have to shoot. Better take it easy, now."

"It's my way of doin'," said Whistling Dick. "Easy goes. You can depress de muzzle of dat twelve-incher, and run 'er back on de trucks. I remains, as de newspapers says, 'in yer midst.'"

"All right," said Boston, lowering his piece, as the other returned and took his seat again on a projecting plank in a pile of timber. "Don't try to leave; that's all. I wouldn't miss this chance even if I had to shoot an old acquaintance to make it go. I don't want to hurt anybody specially, but this thousand dollars I'm going to get will fix me for fair. I'm going to drop the road, and start a saloon in a little town I know about. I'm tired of being kicked around."

Boston Harry took from his pocket a cheap silver watch, and held it near the fire.

"It's a quarter to nine," he said. "Pete, you and Blinky start. Go down the road past the house, and fire the cane in a dozen places. Then strike for the levee, and come back on it, instead of the road, so you won't meet anybody. By the time you get back the men will all be striking out for the fire, and we'll break for the house and collar the dollars. Everybody cough up what matches he's got."

The two surly tramps made a collection of all the matches in the party, Whistling Dick contributing his quota with propitiatory alacrity, and then they departed in the dim starlight in the direction of the road.

Of the three remaining vagrants, two, Goggles and Indiana Tom, reclined lazily upon convenient lumber and regarded Whistling Dick with undisguised disfavour. Boston, observing that the dissenting recruit was disposed to remain peaceably, relaxed a little of his vigilance. Whistling Dick arose presently and strolled leisurely up and down keeping carefully within the territory assigned him.

"Dis planter chap," he said, pausing before Boston Harry, "w'ot makes yer t'ink he's got de tin in de house wit' 'im?"

"I'm advised of the facts in the case," said Boston. "He drove to Noo Orleans and got it, I say, to-day. Want to change your mind now and come in?"

"Naw, I was just askin'. Wot kind o' team did de boss drive?"

"Pair of grays."

"Double surrey?"

"Yep."

"Women folks along?"

"Wife and kid. Say, what morning paper are you trying to pump news for?"

"I was just conversin' to pass de time away. I guess dat team passed me in de road dis evenin'. Dat's all."

As Whistling Dick put his hands in his pockets and continued his curtailed beat up and down by the fire, he felt the silk stocking he had picked up in the road.

"Ther bloomin' little skeezicks," he muttered, with a grin.

As he walked up and down he could see, through a sort of natural opening or lane among the trees, the planter's residence some seventy-five yards distant. The side of the house toward him exhibited spacious, well-lighted windows through which a soft radiance streamed, illuminating the broad veranda and some extent of the lawn beneath.

"What's that you said?" asked Boston, sharply.

"Oh, nuttin' 't all," said Whistling Dick, lounging carelessly, and kicking meditatively at a little stone on the ground.

"Just as easy," continued the warbling vagrant softly to himself, "an' sociable an' swell an' sassy, wit' her 'Mer-ry Chris-mus,' Wot d'yer t'ink, now!"

* * *

Dinner, two hours late, was being served in the Bellemeade plantation dining-room.

The dining-room and all its appurtenances spoke of an old regime that was here continued rather than suggested to the memory. The plate was rich to the extent that its age and quaintness alone saved it from being showy; there were interesting names signed in the corners of the pictures on the walls; the viands were of the kind that bring a shine into the eyes of gourmets. The service was swift, silent, lavish, as in the days when the waiters were assets like the plate. The names by which the planter's family and their visitors addressed one another were historic in the annals of two nations. Their manners and conversation had that most difficult kind of ease—the kind that still preserves punctilio. The planter himself seemed to be the dynamo that generated the larger portion of the gaiety and wit. The younger ones at the board found it more than difficult to turn back on him his guns of raillery and banter. It is true, the young men attempted to storm his works repeatedly, incited by the hope of gaining the approbation of their fair companions; but even when they sped a well-aimed shaft, the planter forced them to feel defeat by the tremendous discomfiting thunder of the laughter with which he accompanied his retorts. At the head of the table, serene, matronly, benevolent, reigned the mistress of the house, placing here and there the right smile, the right word, the encouraging glance.

The talk of the party was too desultory, too evanescent to follow, but at last they came to the subject of the tramp nuisance, one that had of late vexed the plantations for many miles around. The planter seized the occasion to direct his good-natured fire of raillery at the mistress, accusing her of encouraging the plague. "They swarm up and down the river every winter," he said. "They overrun New Orleans, and we catch the surplus, which is generally the worst part. And, a day or two ago, Madame New Orleans, suddenly discovering that she can't go shopping without brushing her skirts against great rows of the vagabonds sunning themselves on the banquettes, says to the police: 'Catch 'em all,' and the police catch a dozen or two, and the remaining three or four thousand overflow up and down the levee, and madame there,"—pointing tragically with the carving-knife at her—"feeds them. They won't work; they defy my overseers, and they make friends with my dogs; and you, madame, feed them before my eyes, and intimidate me when I would interfere. Tell us, please, how many to-day did you thus incite to future laziness and depredation?"

"Six, I think," said madame, with a reflective smile; "but you know two of them offered to work, for you heard them yourself."

The planter's disconcerting laugh rang out again.

"Yes, at their own trades. And one was an artificial-flower maker, and the other a glass-blower. Oh, they were looking for work! Not a hand would they consent to lift to labour of any other kind."

"And another one," continued the soft-hearted mistress, "used quite good language. It was really extraordinary for one of his class. And he carried a watch. And had lived in Boston. I don't believe they are all bad. They have always seemed to me to rather lack development. I always look upon them as children with whom wisdom has remained at a standstill while whiskers have continued to grow. We passed one this evening as we were driving home who had a face as good as it was incompetent. He was whistling the intermezzo from 'Cavalleria' and blowing the spirit of Mascagni himself into it."

A bright eyed young girl who sat at the left of the mistress leaned over, and said in a confidential undertone:

"I wonder, mamma, if that tramp we passed on the road found my stocking, and do you think he will hang it up to-night? Now I can hang up but one. Do you know why I wanted a new pair of silk stockings when I have plenty? Well, old Aunt Judy says, if you hang up two that have never been worn, Santa Claus will fill one with good things, and Monsieur Pambe will place in the other payment for all the words you have spoken—good or bad—on the day before Christmas. That's why I've been unusually nice and polite to everyone to-day. Monsieur Pambe, you know, is a witch gentleman; he—"

The words of the young girl were interrupted by a startling thing.

Like the wraith of some burned-out shooting star, a black streak came crashing through the window-pane and upon the table, where it shivered into fragments a dozen pieces of crystal and china ware, and then glanced between the heads of the guests to the wall, imprinting therein a deep, round indentation, at which, to-day, the visitor to Bellemeade marvels as he gazes upon it and listens to this tale as it is told.

The women screamed in many keys, and the men sprang to their feet, and would have laid their hands upon their swords had not the verities of chronology forbidden.

The planter was the first to act; he sprang to the intruding missile, and held it up to view.

"By Jupiter!" he cried. "A meteoric shower of hosiery! Has communication at last been established with Mars?"

"I should say—ahem—Venus," ventured a young-gentleman visitor, looking hopefully for approbation toward the unresponsive young-lady visitors.

The planter held at arm's length the unceremonious visitor—a long dangling black stocking. "It's loaded," he announced.

As he spoke, he reversed the stocking, holding it by the toe, and down from it dropped a roundish stone, wrapped about by a piece of yellowish paper. "Now for the first interstellar message of the century!" he cried; and nodding to the company, who had crowded about him, he adjusted his glasses with provoking deliberation, and examined it closely. When he finished, he had changed from the jolly host to the practical, decisive man of business. He immediately struck a bell, and said to the silent-footed mulatto man who responded: "Go and tell Mr. Wesley to get Reeves and Maurice and about ten stout hands they can rely upon, and come to the hall door at once. Tell him to have the men arm themselves, and bring plenty of ropes and plough lines. Tell him to hurry." And then he read aloud from the paper these words:

> To the Gent of de Hous:
>
> Dere is five tuff hoboes xcept meself in the vaken lot near de road war de old brick piles is.
> Dey got me stuck up wid a gun see and I taken dis means of communication. 2 of der lads
> is gone down to set fire to de cain field below de hous and when yous fellers goes to turn
> de hoes on it de hole gang is goin to rob de hous of de money yoo gotto pay off wit say git
> a move on ye say de kid dropt dis sock on der rode tel her mery crismus de same as she
> told me. Ketch de bums down de rode first and den sen a relefe core to get me out of soke
> youres truly,
>
> Whistlen Dick.

There was some quiet, but rapid, mavoeuvring at Bellemeade during the ensuring half hour, which ended in five disgusted and sullen tramps being captured, and locked securely in an outhouse pending the coming of the morning and retribution. For another result, the visiting young gentlemen had secured the unqualified worship of the visiting young ladies by their distinguished and heroic conduct. For still another, behold Whistling Dick, the hero, seated at the planter's table, feasting upon viands his experience had never before included, and waited upon by admiring femininity in shapes of such beauty and "swellness" that even his ever-full mouth could scarcely prevent him from whistling. He was made to disclose in detail his adventure with the evil gang of Boston Harry, and how he cunningly wrote the note and wrapped it around the stone and placed it at the toe of the stocking, and, watching his chance, sent it silently, with a wonderful centrifugal momentum, like a comet, at one of the big lighted windows of the dining-room.

The planter vowed that the wanderer should wander no more; that his was a goodness and an honesty that should be rewarded, and that a debt of gratitude had been made that must be paid; for had he not saved them from a doubtless imminent loss, and maybe a greater calamity? He assured Whistling Dick that he might consider himself a charge upon the honour of Bellemeade; that a position suited to his powers would be found for him at once, and hinted that the way would be heartily smoothed for him to rise to as high places of emolument and trust as the plantation afforded.

But now, they said, he must be weary, and the immediate thing to consider was rest and sleep. So the mistress spoke to a servant, and Whistling Dick was conducted to a room in the wing of the house occupied by the servants. To this room, in a few minutes, was brought a portable tin bathtub filled with water, which was placed on a piece of oiled cloth upon the floor. There the vagrant was left to pass the night.

By the light of a candle he examined the room. A bed, with the covers neatly turned back, revealed snowy pillows and sheets. A worn, but clean, red carpet covered the floor. There was a dresser with a beveled mirror, a washstand with a flowered bowl and pitcher; the two or three chairs were softly upholstered. A little table held books, papers, and a day-old cluster of roses in a jar. There were towels on a rack and soap in a white dish.

Whistling Dick set his candle on a chair and placed his hat carefully under the table. After satisfying what we must suppose to have been his curiosity by a sober scrutiny, he removed his coat, folded it, and laid it upon the floor, near the wall, as far as possible from the unused bathtub. Taking his coat for a pillow, he stretched himself luxuriously upon the carpet.

When, on Christmas morning, the first streaks of dawn broke above the marshes, Whistling Dick awoke, and reached instinctively for his hat. Then he remembered that the skirts of Fortune had swept him into their folds on the night previous, and he went to the window and raised it, to let the fresh breath of the morning cool his brow and fix the yet dream-like memory of his good luck within his brain.

As he stood there, certain dread and ominous sounds pierced the fearful hollow of his ear.

The force of plantation workers, eager to complete the shortened task allotted to them, were all astir. The mighty din of the ogre Labour shook the earth, and the poor tattered and forever disguised Prince in search of his fortune held tight to the window-sill even in the enchanted castle, and trembled.

Already from the bosom of the mill came the thunder of rolling barrels of sugar, and (prison-like sounds) there was a great rattling of chains as the mules were harried with stimulant imprecations to their places by the waggon-tongues. A little vicious "dummy" engine, with a train of flat cars in tow, stewed and fumed on the plantation tap of the narrow-gauge railroad, and a toiling, hurrying, hallooing stream of workers were dimly seen in the half darkness loading the train with the weekly output of sugar. Here was a poem; an epic—nay, a tragedy—with work, the curse of the world, for its theme.

The December air was frosty, but the sweat broke out upon Whistling Dick's face. He thrust his head out of the window, and looked down. Fifteen feet below him, against the wall of the house, he could make out that a border of flowers grew, and by that token he overhung a bed of soft earth.

Softly as a burglar goes, he clambered out upon the sill, lowered himself until he hung by his hands alone, and then dropped safely. No one seemed to be about upon this side of the house. He dodged low, and skimmed swiftly across the yard to the low fence. It was an easy matter to vault this, for a terror urged him such as lifts the gazelle over the thorn bush when the lion pursues. A crash through the dew-drenched weeds on the roadside, a clutching, slippery rush up the grassy side of the levee to the footpath at the summit, and—he was free!

The east was blushing and brightening. The wind, himself a vagrant rover, saluted his brother upon the cheek. Some wild geese, high above, gave cry. A rabbit skipped along the path before him, free to turn to the right or to the left as his mood should send him. The river slid past, and certainly no one could tell the ultimate abiding place of its waters.

A small, ruffled, brown-breasted bird, sitting upon a dog-wood sapling, began a soft, throaty, tender little piping in praise of the dew which entices foolish worms from their holes; but suddenly he stopped, and sat with his head turned sidewise, listening.

From the path along the levee there burst forth a jubilant, stirring, buoyant, thrilling whistle, loud and keen and clear as the cleanest notes of the piccolo. The soaring sound rippled and trilled and arpeggioed as the songs of wild birds do not; but it had a wild free grace that, in a way, reminded the small, brown bird of something familiar, but exactly what he could not tell. There was in it the bird call, or reveille, that all birds know; but a great waste of lavish, unmeaning things that art had added and arranged, besides, and that were quite puzzling and strange; and the little brown bird sat with his head on one side until the sound died away in the distance.

The little bird did not know that the part of that strange warbling that he understood was just what kept the warbler without his breakfast; but he knew very well that the part he did not understand did not concern him, so he gave a little flutter of his wings and swooped down like a brown bullet upon a big fat worm that was wriggling along the levee path.

Alice Dunbar Nelson (1875–1935)

Alice Dunbar Nelson was born Alice Ruth Moore in New Orleans on July 19, 1875, to Joseph and Patricia Wright Moore. Her mother was born a slave in Opelousas, Louisiana, and her father was a merchant marine. In her essay, "Race and Gender in the Early Works of Alice Dunbar Nelson," Violet Harrington Bryan suggests that Joseph Moore's race was questionable, and Dunbar Nelson often wrote about being "light-skinned," as she does in her essay, "Brass Ankles Speaks," in which she denounces racial prejudice among darker skinned African Americans for those with lighter complexions: "It seems but fair and just now for some of the neglected light skinned colored people, who have not "passed" to rise and speak a word in self-defense."[1] In that same essay Dunbar Nelson tells a story of her youth, describing the way she was bullied as a child and called "yaller." The discrimination she suffered at the hands of other blacks informed her lifelong fight for civil rights and against racism. She knew that it was vital for African Americans to fight together against the white racist establishment and not among themselves. However, Dunbar Nelson began her career writing fiction.

At the age of fifteen, she enrolled in a teacher training program at Straight University—now Dillard—in New Orleans. Upon graduating two years later, she began to teach in the city and published her first collection of short stories, poems, and sketches, *Violets and Other Tales* in 1895. Shortly thereafter, Dunbar Nelson moved to New York to further pursue her literary career. She attended Columbia University and two years later her second book was published, *The Goodness of Saint Rocque,* her strongest and most anthologized work.

Before moving from New Orleans to New York, she began a correspondence with then renowned poet, Paul Lawrence Dunbar, who had read and admired some of her early poetry. Obviously, he also admired her beauty, as he wrote to her on June 25, 1895: "Please let me have your photo as soon as possible and don't consider me selfish for saying that I would rather not send you mine."[2] Their correspondence continued after her move to New York, and they finally married in 1898. Their marriage was not a happy one, and four years later they separated. Paul Dunbar died four years after that, and by this time Alice Dunbar Nelson had taken a teaching job at Howard High School in Wilmington, Delaware, a position she would hold for nearly twenty years, until 1920.

According to Dunbar Nelson biographer, Gloria T. Hull, while at Howard High, Dunbar Nelson secretly married a colleague.[3] Little is known about this secret marriage, and in 1916, she married journalist and political activist, Robert J. Nelson. By the time of her marriage to Nelson, she had received her Ph.D. from Cornell University, writing her dissertation on William Wordsworth, but after her marriage her literary interests took a back seat to her career as a journalist and political activist working for civil and women's rights, a career to which she would devote the rest of her life.

The work included here, "The Goodness of Saint Rocque," is the title story of her second collection. Like Armand Lanusse's "A Marriage of Conscience," this story is about Creoles of color whose race is never mentioned. Of course, in *fin de siècle* New Orleans, Dunbar Nelson was not writing under the same restrictions that Lanusse had been some sixty years earlier, so not divulging the race of the characters was a conscious choice of hers. Most local readers would know that these were Creoles of color; however, readers today might not. Dunbar Nelson departs from her first collection and does address racism in the African American community in this short story, but she does so without mentioning the race of her characters.

The protagonist, Manuela, is angry because her boyfriend, Theophile, has "deserted her for Claralie, blonde and petite." She will not, however, sit idly by while her man dallies with the lighter skinned Claralie. As the story opens, we see Manuela sneaking down Marais Street heading for the voodoo woman's house. Dunbar Nelson also addresses classism in the story when she describes the conjurer's house: "It was a sombre room within, with a bare yellow-washed floor and ragged curtains at the little window..... the room was furnished by a little, wizened

---

1   Much of the biographical information included here comes from Violet Harrington Bryan, "Race and Gender in the Early Works of Alice Dunbar Nelson, *Louisiana Women Writers,* ed. Dorothy H. Brown and Barbara C. Ewell (Baton Rouge: LSUP, 1992), 120-138.

2   Ibid., 123.

3   Gloria T. Hull, *Give Us Each Day: The Diary of Alice Dunbar Nelson* (New York: Norton, 1986), 376.

316 N.O. Lit: 200 Years of New Orleans Literature

yellow woman, who, black-robed, turbaned, and stern, sat before an uncertain table whereon were greasy cards." It is obvious that the voodoo woman is not of Manuela's circle, which is made up of young Creole families who have leisure time to spend at "Milneburg-on-the-lake."

Manuela is successful in the errand, and the voodoo woman, after reading her cards, prescribes "... one lil' charm fo' to ween him back, yaas" along with a "prayer at St. Rocque an' burn can'le." Perhaps the most interesting aspect of this short story is the intermingling of Catholicism and voodoo. Although readers can assume that Manuela is sneaking down the street to the conjurer's house hiding behind her hat and veil because voodoo is not publicly accepted, we nonetheless discover that Claralie too has sought her help. The last line in the story suggests that the Catholic St. Rocque and not voodoo was responsible for Manuela and Theophile's engagement: "But St. Rocque knows, for he is a good saint, and if you believe in him and are true and good, and make your novenas with a clean heart, he will grant your wish." But that line is almost like an insider's "wink-wink," as any readers in the know will realize the power of voodoo and its importance in the New Orleans Creole community.

Even though Dunbar Nelson continued to write fiction, this is the last collection of hers that was published in her lifetime. She and her husband were co-editors and publishers of the *Wilmington Advocate,* a progressive African American newspaper, and she was a popular public speaker for women's and civil rights. In 1932, her husband took a job with the Pennsylvania Athletic Commission, so they moved from Wilmington to Philadelphia, but this would be her last move, as she died of heart disease three years later.

The Goodness of Saint Rocque[1]

Manuela was tall and slender and graceful, and once you knew her the lithe form could never be mistaken. She walked with the easy spring that comes from a perfectly arched foot. To-day she swept swiftly down Marais Street, casting a quick glance here and there from under her heavy veil as if she feared she was being followed. If you had peered under the veil, you would have seen that Manuela's dark eyes were swollen and discoloured about the lids, as though they had known a sleepless, tearful night. There had been a picnic the day before, and as merry a crowd of giddy, chattering Creole girls and boys as ever you could see boarded the ramshackle dummy-train that puffed its way wheezily out wide Elysian Fields Street, around the lily-covered bayous, to Milneburg-on-the-Lake. Now, a picnic at Milneburg is a thing to be remembered for ever. One charters a rickety-looking, weather-beaten dancing-pavilion, built over the water, and after storing the children—for your true Creole never leaves the small folks at home—and the baskets and mothers downstairs, the young folks go up-stairs and dance to the tune of the best band you ever heard. For what can equal the music of a violin, a guitar, a cornet, and a bass viol to trip the quadrille to at a picnic?

Then one can fish in the lake and go bathing under the prim bath-houses, so severely separated sexually, and go rowing on the lake in a trim boat, followed by the shrill warnings of anxious mamans. And in the evening one comes home, hat crowned with cool gray Spanish moss, hands burdened with fantastic latanier baskets woven by the brown bayou boys, hand in hand with your dearest one, tired but happy.

At this particular picnic, however, there had been bitterness of spirit. Theophile was Manuela's own especial property, and Theophile had proven false. He had not danced a single waltz or quadrille with Manuela, but had deserted her for Claralie, blonde and petite. It was Claralie whom Theophile had rowed out on the lake; it was Claralie whom Theophile had gallantly led to dinner; it was Claralie's hat that he wreathed with Spanish moss, and Claralie whom he escorted home after the jolly singing ride in town on the little dummy-train.

---

1   From: Alice Dunbar Nelson, *The Goodness of St. Rocque and Other Stories* (New York: Dodd, 1899; rep. College Park, MD: McGarth, 1969).

Not that Manuela lacked partners or admirers. Dear no! she was too graceful and beautiful for that. There had been more than enough for her. But Manuela loved Theophile, you see, and no one could take his place. Still, she had tossed her head and let her silvery laughter ring out in the dance, as though she were the happiest of mortals, and had tripped home with Henri, leaning on his arm, and looking up into his eyes as though she adored him.

This morning she showed the traces of a sleepless night and an aching heart as she walked down Marais Street. Across wide St. Rocque Avenue she hastened. "Two blocks to the river and one below—" she repeated to herself breathlessly. Then she stood on the corner gazing about her, until with a final summoning of a desperate courage she dived through a small wicket gate into a garden of weed-choked flowers.

There was a hoarse, rusty little bell on the gate that gave querulous tongue as she pushed it open. The house that sat back in the yard was little and old and weather-beaten. Its one-story frame had once been painted, but that was a memory remote and traditional. A straggling morning-glory strove to conceal its time-ravaged face. The little walk of broken bits of brick was reddened carefully, and the one little step was scrupulously yellow-washed, which denoted that the occupants were cleanly as well as religious.

Manuela's timid knock was answered by a harsh "Entrez."

It was a small sombre room within, with a bare yellow-washed floor and ragged curtains at the little window. In a corner was a diminutive altar draped with threadbare lace. The red glow of the taper lighted a cheap print of St. Joseph and a brazen crucifix. The human element in the room was furnished by a little, wizened yellow woman, who, black-robed, turbaned, and stern, sat before an uncertain table whereon were greasy cards.

Manuela paused, her eyes blinking at the semi-obscurity within. The Wizened One called in croaking tones:

"An' fo' w'y you come here? Assiez-la, ma'amzelle."

Timidly Manuela sat at the table facing the owner of the voice.

"I want," she began faintly; but the Mistress of the Cards understood: she had had much experience. The cards were shuffled in her long grimy talons and stacked before Manuela.

"Now you cut dem in t'ree part, so—un, deux, trois, bien! You mek' you' weesh wid all you' heart, bien! Yaas, I see, I see!"

Breathlessly did Manuela learn that her lover was true, but "dat light gal, yaas, she mek' nouvena in St. Rocque fo' hees love."

"I give you one lil' charm, yaas," said the Wizened One when the seance was over, and Manuela, all white and nervous, leaned back in the rickety chair. "I give you one lil' charm fo' to ween him back, yaas. You wear h'it 'roun' you' wais', an' he come back. Den you mek prayer at St. Rocque an' burn can'le. Den you come back an' tell me, yaas. Cinquante sous, ma'amzelle. Merci. Good luck go wid you."

Readjusting her veil, Manuela passed out the little wicket gate, treading on air. Again the sun shone, and the breath of the swamps came as healthful sea-breeze unto her nostrils. She fairly flew in the direction of St. Rocque.

There were quite a number of persons entering the white gates of the cemetery, for this was Friday, when all those who wish good luck pray to the saint, and wash their steps promptly at twelve o'clock with a wondrous mixture to guard the house. Manuela bought a candle from the keeper of the little lodge at the entrance, and pausing one instant by the great sun-dial to see if the heavens and the hour were propitious, glided into the tiny chapel, dim and stifling with heavy air from myriad wish-candles blazing on the wide table before the altar-rail. She said her prayer and lighting her candle placed it with the others.

Mon Dieu! how brightly the sun seemed to shine now, she thought, pausing at the door on her way out. Her small finger-tips, still bedewed with holy water, rested caressingly on a gamin's head. The ivy which enfolds the quaint chapel never seemed so green; the shrines which serve as the Way of the Cross never seemed so artistic; the baby graves, even, seemed cheerful.

Theophile called Sunday. Manuela's heart leaped. He had been spending his Sundays with Claralie. His stay was short and he was plainly bored. But Manuela knelt to thank the good St. Rocque that night, and fondled the charm about her slim waist. There came a box of bonbons during the week, with a decorative card all roses and fringe, from Theophile; but being a Creole, and therefore superstitiously careful, and having been reared by a wise and experienced maman to mistrust the gifts of a recreant lover, Manuela quietly thrust bonbons, box, and card into the kitchen fire, and the Friday following placed the second candle of her nouvena in St. Rocque.

Those of Manuela's friends who had watched with indignation Theophile gallantly leading Claralie home from High Mass on Sundays, gasped with astonishment when the next Sunday, with his usual bow, the young man offered Manuela his arm as the worshippers filed out in step to the organ's march. Claralie tossed her head as she crossed herself with holy water, and the pink in her cheeks was brighter than usual.

Manuela smiled a bright good-morning when she met Claralie in St. Rocque the next Friday. The little blonde blushed furiously, and Manuela rushed post-haste to the Wizened One to confer upon this new issue.

"H'it ees good," said the dame, shaking her turbaned head. "She ees 'fraid, she will work, mais you' charm, h'it weel beat her."

And Manuela departed with radiant eyes.

Theophile was not at Mass Sunday morning, and murderous glances flashed from Claralie to Manuela before the tinkling of the Host-Bell. Nor did Theophile call at either house. Two hearts beat furiously at the sound of every passing footstep, and two minds wondered if the other were enjoying the beloved one's smiles. Two pair of eyes, however, blue and black, smiled on others, and their owners laughed and seemed none the less happy. For your Creole girls are proud, and would die rather than let the world see their sorrows.

Monday evening Theophile, the missing, showed his rather sheepish countenance in Manuela's parlour, and explained that he, with some chosen spirits, had gone for a trip—"over the Lake."

"I did not ask you where you were yesterday," replied the girl, saucily.

Theophile shrugged his shoulders and changed the conversation.

The next week there was a birthday fete in honour of Louise, Theophile's young sister. Everyone was bidden, and no one thought of refusing, for Louise was young, and this would be her first party. So, though the night was hot, the dancing went on as merrily as light young feet could make it go. Claralie fluffed her dainty white skirts, and cast mischievous sparkles in the direction of Theophile, who with the maman and Louise was bravely trying not to look self-conscious. Manuela, tall and calm and proud-looking, in a cool, pale yellow gown was apparently enjoying herself without paying the slightest attention to her young host.

"Have I the pleasure of this dance?" he asked her finally, in a lull of the music.

She bowed assent, and as if moved by a common impulse they strolled out of the dancing-room into the cool, quaint garden, where jessamines gave out an overpowering perfume, and a caged mocking-bird complained melodiously to the full moon in the sky.

It must have been an engrossing tete-a-tete, for the call to supper had sounded twice before they heard and hurried into the house. The march had formed with Louise radiantly leading on the arm of papa. Claralie tripped by with Leon. Of course, nothing remained for Theophile and Manuela to do but to bring up the rear, for which they received much good-natured chaffing.

But when the party reached the dining-room, Theophile proudly led his partner to the head of the table, at the right hand of maman, and smiled benignly about at the delighted assemblage. Now you know, when a Creole young man places a girl at his mother's right hand at his own table, there is but one conclusion to be deduced therefrom.

If you had asked Manuela, after the wedding was over, how it happened, she would have said nothing, but looked wise.

If you had asked Claralie, she would have laughed and said she always preferred Leon.

If you had asked Theophile, he would have wondered that you thought he had ever meant more than to tease Manuela.

If you had asked the Wizened One, she would have offered you a charm.

But St. Rocque knows, for he is a good saint, and if you believe in him and are true and good, and make your nouvenas with a clean heart, he will grant your wish.

Sherwood Anderson (1876–1941)

Sherwood Anderson was not from New Orleans and was a decidedly Midwestern writer. He moved to the city for the first time in January of 1922, after having won the first annual *Dial* Award for his outstanding contribution to literature in December and with it two thousand dollars. According to Anderson biographer Walter B. Rideout, he was also escaping the cold Chicago winter as well as his second wife, and what better place than a city Anderson dubbed in a letter to his older brother Karl, "the most cultural town in America."[1] While in New Orleans, Anderson met such writers as Lyle Saxon, Roark Bradford, Hamilton Basso, and William Faulkner, on whom the character David is based in his short story, "A Meeting South." Anderson biographer Irving Howe claims that, "seldom before and probably never afterward did Anderson feel so radiant and vigorous, so ready to forget for the moment the personal and career troubles," as he did in New Orleans.[2] Sherwood Anderson was 45 when he first moved to New Orleans, and the book for which he is best known, *Winesburg Ohio,* published in 1919, was behind him.

Sherwood Anderson was born to Irwin and Emma Anderson in Camden, Ohio, on September 3, 1876. His father, a Union Army captain, was a harness maker in Camden, and very involved in the community. That would change, however. By the time Sherwood was ten years old, and after the family had moved to Clyde, Ohio, the town on which *Winesburg* is based, his father was working less and drinking more, so his mother had to take in laundry. According to Howe, Sherwood too had several jobs as a teen to supplement the family income: newsboy, errand boy, waterboy, cow-driver, stable groom, and sign painter. His industriousness led to his missing much class and prompted his classmates to nickname him "Jobby."[3] Anderson, although an avid reader, was no stellar student, and the only way he saw to leave Clyde after his mother's death at the age of 43, was to enlist in the Army to fight in the Spanish American War. He had moved briefly to Chicago to work rolling apple barrels in cold storage, and from there he wrote the following to his older brother Karl: "I prefer yellow fever in Cuba to living in cold storage in Chicago."[4] After returning from the war, Anderson attended Wittenburg Academy in Springfield, Ohio, and upon graduation he moved to Chicago to begin his career as an advertising copy editor, a career he would pursue for over a decade in order to make a living, all the while devoted to his passion, creative writing.

In 1904, Anderson married Cornelia Lane in Chicago, and they soon moved to Cleveland, where he took the more prominent position of president of United Factories Company. He and Cornelia had two sons, Robert and John, and in 1907 the family moved to suburban Elyria, forty miles outside of Cleveland. The environment of small-town Elyria must have seemed stifling to Anderson, who was becoming much more interested in the Chicago literary scene, but he now had a family to support. Although Cornelia was skeptical of his desire to be a writer, he never kept his passion for writing secret, and according to Howe, he even had his secretary type early drafts of his first novel, *Windy McPherson's Son.*[5] Finally, Anderson's inability to reconcile the drudgery of his day job with his desire to pursue his creative writing prompted his very public mental breakdown which was chronicled in the *Cleveland Leader* on December 2, 1912:

> Wandering gypsy-like about the countryside after disappearing from his home in Elyria four days ago, walking almost incessantly save for a few hours of sleep snatched in thickets.... Anderson was found by a physician to be suffering from the effects of some severe mental strain.... Anderson is about thirty-seven years old, but looked older, with a several days' growth of beard on his face and haggard lines resulting from his unusual fatigue and exposure.

The following day the *Leader* reported that his "Elyria friends... were of the belief yesterday that Anderson had

---

1   Walter B. Rideout, "'The Most Cultural Town in America': Sherwood Anderson and New Orleans," *Southern Review* 24, no. 1 (Winter 1988), 79.

2   Irving Howe, *Sherwood Anderson* (New York: William Sloane Associates, 1951), 141. Howe is the source of much of the biographical information included here.

3   Ibid., 16.

4   Ibid., 28.

5   Ibid., 44.

broken down under the strain of work on a novel." It is much more likely that the breakdown occurred because he could find neither the time nor the resources necessary to complete his novel without shirking his responsibility of providing for his family. Whatever the cause of his breakdown, it did signal the end of his marriage to Cornelia and the beginning of the end of his career in the advertising business. In 1913, he moved his family to Chicago, the following year he and Cornelia separated, and two years later his first novel was published.

Anderson dove into the Chicago literary scene which included other Midwestern writers, such as Carl Sandburg, Floyd Dell, Ben Hecht, and Edgar Lee Masters. It was a very productive time for Anderson, and before moving to New Orleans in 1921, he would publish three novels, two collections of short stories, and a collection of poetry.

Also while in Chicago, he divorced Cornelia and in 1916, married piano tuner and music teacher, Tennessee Mitchell, who had much more in common with the 19th-century suffragist after whom she was named, Tennessee Claflin, than did Anderson's first wife.[1] Five years later, he would move to New Orleans without Tennessee, and upon his return to Chicago the following year, he would ask her for a divorce which she would not grant until 1924.

Anderson's time in New Orleans was very productive. While there, he completed his fourth novel, *Many Marriages,* which was published in 1923, and he regularly contributed to *The Double Dealer,* edited by his friend, Julius Friend. Rideout writes that "the time in New Orleans was, in sum, a condition of happiness.... [and] the happiness spilled over into his essay, 'New Orleans, *The Double Dealer* and the Modern Movement in America...' a hail and farewell to the city he had come to love."[2] In fact, Anderson did not stay away from New Orleans for long, and in 1924, he returned with his third wife, Elizabeth Sprall.

By all accounts, this too was a happy and productive time for Anderson, and on this stay in New Orleans, Anderson met William Faulkner. Faulkner was not a complete stranger to the Anderson family, as Elizabeth had hired him when she managed the Doubleday bookstore in New York City, where she and Sherwood Anderson met. Obviously, Faulkner made quite an impression on Anderson, as he not only urged his publisher Horace Liverwright to publish Faulkner's first novel *Soldiers' Pay,* saying that he was "the one writer here of promise,"[3] but he also wrote a short story devoted to their meeting in New Orleans.

"A Meeting South" is the narrator's remembrance of meeting David, a young man from Alabama, who, as an aviator for the British, had been injured on a mission in World War I, which has little to do with Faulkner's actual history. He was from Mississippi and had indeed enlisted in the Canadian Royal Air Force, not the British Royal Flying Corps, but by the war's end he had not finished his training in Canada so he never saw action. Anderson believed Faulkner's version of history and based his character David on it. According to Rideout, Anderson later told Ben Wasson, "that he was extremely upset to learn how Faulkner had lied to him about his war service."[4] Such "lies" or exaggeration would become standard procedure for Faulkner, who was fiercely protective of his private life. Perhaps Anderson's reference to P.T. Barnum in the story is proof that he was in fact not hoodwinked by Faulkner's tall tales.

In the end, this short story proves that Anderson did admire Faulkner, not only as a writer, but as a friend. Anderson quietly examines the deep and almost immediate connection between the narrator, "a Northern man," and David "the Southerner," one night out of time in New Orleans, when he takes him to see Aunt Sally, a fellow Midwesterner and former brothel madam. Much like Anderson enjoyed helping Faulkner get his first novel published, the narrator in "A Meeting South" is pleased that he is able to offer David some sort of comfort and notices that "there was no doubt that he... was happy, had been happy ever since [he] had brought him into the presence of Aunt Sally." The story captures the genuine nature of both the city and the characters who are haunted by a past that is often difficult to reconcile with the present.

Anderson spent more time with Faulkner before moving to Virginia, where he and Elizabeth would divorce. Ironically, after leaving the city, Anderson's career was winding down, while Faulkner's, in part thanks to

---

1   Ibid., 81.

2   Rideout, 87.

3   Ibid., 99.

4   Ibid., 98.

Anderson, soared meteorically, and the men's paths seldom crossed. Anderson bought some land in Troutdale, Virginia, where he built his last home and married his last wife, Eleanor Copehnaver. In his later years, under Eleanor's influence, he turned to writing in support of the factory workers throughout the South. He also bought the two local Virginia newspapers near Troutdale which he and his sons ran for a time. In 1941, while sailing on a tour of South America with his wife, Anderson met a rather ignominious end. While eating hors d'oeuvres on board the ship, he swallowed a toothpick, which resulted in peritonitis and finally his death at the age of 65 in March of 1942.[1]

A Meeting South[2]

He told me the story of his ill fortune—a crack-up in an airplane—with a very gentlemanly little smile on his very sensitive, rather thin lips. Such things happened. He might well have been speaking of another. I liked his tone and I liked him.

This happened in New Orleans, where I had gone to live. When he came, my friend, Fred, for whom he was looking, had gone away, but immediately I felt a strong desire to know him better and so suggested we spend the evening together. When we went down the stairs from my apartment I noticed that he was a cripple. The slight limp, the look of pain that occasionally drifted across his face, the little laugh that was intended to be jolly, but did not quite achieve its purpose, all these things began at once to tell me the story I have now set myself to write.

"I shall take him to see Aunt Sally," I thought. One does not take every caller to Aunt Sally. However, when she is in fine feather, when she has taken a fancy to her visitor, there is no one like her. Although she has lived in New Orleans for thirty years, Aunt Sally is Middle Western, born and bred.

However I am plunging a bit too abruptly into my story.

First of all I must speak more of my guest, and for convenience's sake I shall call him David. I felt at once that he would be wanting a drink and, in New Orleans—dear city of Latins and hot nights—even in Prohibition times such things can be managed. We achieved several and my own head became somewhat shaky but I could see that what we had taken had not affected him. Evening was coming, the abrupt waning of the day and the quick smoky soft-footed coming of night, characteristic of the semi-tropic city, when he produced a bottle from his hip pocket. It was so large that I was amazed. How had it happened that the carrying of so large a bottle had not made him look deformed? His body was very small and delicately built. "Perhaps, like the kangaroo, his body has developed some kind of a natural pouch for taking care of supplies," I thought. Really he walked as one might fancy a kangaroo would walk when out for a quiet evening stroll. I went along thinking of Darwin and the marvels of Prohibition. "We are a wonderful people, we Americans," I thought. We were both in fine humor and had begun to like each other immensely.

He explained the bottle. The stuff, he said, was made by a Negro man on his father's plantation somewhere over in Alabama. We sat on the steps of a vacant house deep down in the old French Quarter of New Orleans—the Vieux Carré—while he explained that his father had no intention of breaking the law—that is to say, in so far as the law remained reasonable. "Our nigger just makes whisky for us," he said. "We keep him for that purpose. He doesn't have anything else to do, just makes the family whisky, that's all. If he went selling any, we'd raise hell with him. I dare say Dad would shoot him if he caught him up to any such unlawful trick, and you bet, Jim, our nigger, I'm telling you of, knows it too."

---

1   Howe, 241.

2   From: Sherwood Anderson, *Death in the Woods and Other Stories* (New York: Liveright, inc. 1933). Originally appeared in *The Dial*, April 1925.

"He's a good whisky-maker, though, don't you think?" David added. He talked of Jim in a warm friendly way. "Lord, he's been with us always, was born with us. His wife cooks for us and Jim makes our whisky. It's a race to see which is best at his job, but I think Jim will win. He's getting a little better all the time and all of our family—well, I reckon we just like and need our whisky more than we do our food."

Do you know New Orleans? Have you lived there in the Summer when it is hot, in the Winter when it rains, and through the glorious late Fall days? Some of its own, more progressive, people scorn it now. In New Orleans there is a sense of shame because the city is not more like Chicago or Pittsburgh.

It, however, suited David and me. We walked slowly, on account of his bad leg, through many streets of the Old Town, Negro women laughing all around us in the dusk, shadows playing over old buildings, children with their shrill cries dodging in and out of old hallways. The old city was once almost altogether French, but now it is becoming more and more Italian. It however remains Latin. People live out of doors. Families were sitting down to dinner within full sight of the street—all doors and windows open. A man and his wife quarreled in Italian. In a patio back of an old building a Negress sang a French song.

We came out of the narrow little streets and had a drink in front of the dark cathedral and another in a little square in front. There is a statue of General Jackson, always taking off his hat to Northern tourists who in Winter come down to see the city. At his horse's feet an inscription—"The Union must and will be preserved." We drank solemnly to that declaration and the general seemed to bow a bit lower. "He was sure a proud man," David said, as we went over toward the docks to sit in the darkness and look at the Mississippi. All good New Orleanians go to look at the Mississippi at least once a day. At night it is like creeping into a dark bedroom to look at a sleeping child—something of that sort—gives you the same warm nice feeling, I mean. David is a poet and so in the darkness by the river we spoke of Keats and Shelley, the two English poets all good Southern men love.

All of this, you are to understand, was before I took him to see Aunt Sally.

Both Aunt Sally and myself are Middle Westerners. We are but guests down here, but perhaps we both in some queer way belong to this city. Something of the sort is in the wind. I don't quite know how it has happened.

A great many Northern men and women come down our way and, when they go back North, write things about the South. The trick is to write nigger stories. The North likes them. They are so amusing. One of the best-known writers of nigger stories was down here recently and a man I know, a Southern man, went to call on him. The writer seemed a bit nervous. "I don't know much about the South or Southerners," he said. "But you have your reputation," my friend said. "You are so widely known as a writer about the South and about Negro life."

The writer had a notion he was being made sport of. "Now look here," he said, "I don't claim to be a highbrow. I'm a business man myself. At home, up North, I associate mostly with business men and when I am not at work I go out to the country club. I want you to understand I am not setting myself up as a highbrow."

"I give them what they want," he said. My friend said he appeared angry. "About what now, do you fancy?" he asked innocently.

However, I am not thinking of the Northern writer of Negro stories. I am thinking of the Southern poet, with the bottle clasped firmly in his hands, sitting in the darkness beside me on the docks facing the Mississippi.

He spoke at some length of his gift for drinking. "I didn't always have it. It is a thing built up," he said. The story of how he chanced to be a cripple came out slowly. You are to remember that my own head was a bit unsteady. In the darkness the river, very deep and very powerful off New Orleans, was creeping away to the gulf. The whole river seemed to move away from us and then to slip noiselessly into the darkness like a vast moving sidewalk.

When he had first come to me, in the late afternoon, and when we had started for our walk together I had noticed that one of his legs dragged as we went along and that he kept putting a thin hand to an equally thin cheek.

Sitting over by the river he explained, as a boy would explain when he has stubbed his toe running down a hill.

When the World War broke out he went over to England and managed to get himself enrolled as an aviator, very much, I gathered, in the spirit in which a countryman, in a city for a night, might take in a show.

The English had been glad enough to take him on. He was one more man. They were glad enough to take any one on just then. He was small and delicately built but after he got in he turned out to be a first-rate flyer, serving all through the War with a British flying squadron, but at the last got into a crash and fell.

Both legs were broken, one of them in three places, the scalp was badly torn and some of the bones of the face had been splintered.

They had put him into a field hospital and had patched him up. "It was my fault if the job was rather bungled," he said. "You see it was a field hospital, a hell of a place. Men were torn all to pieces, groaning and dying. Then they moved me back to a base hospital and it wasn't much better. The fellow who had the bed next to mine had shot himself in the foot to avoid going into a battle. A lot of them did that, but why they picked on their own feet that way is beyond me. It's a nasty place, full of small bones. If you're ever going to shoot yourself don't pick on a spot like that. Don't pick on your feet. I tell you it's a bad idea.

"Anyway, the man in the hospital was always making a fuss and I got sick of him and the place too. When I got better I faked, said the nerves of my leg didn't hurt. It was a lie, of course. The nerves of my leg and of my face have never quit hurting. I reckon maybe, if I had told the truth, they might have fixed me up all right."

I got it. No wonder he carried his drinks so well. When I understood, I wanted to keep on drinking with him, wanted to stay with him until he got tired of me as he had of the man who lay beside him in the base hospital over there somewhere in France.

The point was that he never slept, could not sleep, except when he was a little drunk. "I'm a nut," he said smiling.

It was after we got over to Aunt Sally's that he talked most. Aunt Sally had gone to bed when we got there, but she got up when we rang the bell and we all went to sit together in the little patio back of her house. She is a large woman with great arms and rather a paunch, and she had put on nothing but a light flowered dressing-gown over a thin, ridiculously girlish, nightgown. By this time the moon had come up and, outside, in the narrow street of the Vieux Carré, three drunken sailors from a ship in the river were sitting on a curb and singing a song,

> *I've got to get it,*
> *You've got to get it,*
> *We've all got to get it*
> *In our own good time.*

They had rather nice boyish voices and every time they sang a verse and had done the chorus they all laughed together heartily.

In Aunt Sally's patio there are many broad-leafed banana plants and a Chinaberry tree throwing its soft purple shadows on a brick floor.

As for Aunt Sally, she is as strange to me as he was. When we came and when we were all seated at a little table in the patio, she ran into her house and presently came back with a bottle of whisky. She, it seemed, had understood him at once, had understood without unnecessary words that the little Southern man lived always in the black house of pain, that whisky was good to him, that it quieted his throbbing nerves, temporarily at least. "Everything is temporary, when you come to that," I can fancy Aunt Sally saying.

We sat for a time in silence, David having shifted his allegiance and taken two drinks out of Aunt Sally's bottle. Presently he rose and walked up and down the patio floor, crossing and re-crossing the network of delicately outlined shadows on the bricks. "It's really all right, the leg," he said, "something just presses on the nerves, that's all." In me there was a self-satisfied feeling. I had done the right thing. I had brought him to Aunt Sally. "I have brought him to a mother." She has always made me feel that way since I have known her.

And now I shall have to explain her a little. It will not be so easy. That whole neighborhood in New Orleans is alive with tales concerning her.

Aunt Sally came to New Orleans in the old days, when the town was wild, in the wide-open days. What she had been before she came no one knew, but anyway she opened a place. That was very, very long ago when I was myself but a lad, up in Ohio. As I have already said Aunt Sally came from somewhere up in the Middle-Western country. In some obscure subtle way it would flatter me to think she came from my State.

The house she had opened was one of the older places in the French Quarter down here, and when she had got her hands on it, Aunt Sally had a hunch. Instead of making the place modern, cutting it up into small rooms, all that sort of thing, she left it just as it was and spent her money rebuilding falling old walls, mending winding broad old stairways, repairing dim high-ceilinged old rooms, soft-colored old marble mantels. After all, we do seem attached to sin and there are so many people busy making sin unattractive. It is good to find someone who takes the other road. It would have been so very much to Aunt Sally's advantage to have made the place modern, that is to say, in the business she was in at that time. If a few old rooms, wide old stairways, old cooking ovens built into the walls, if all these things did not facilitate the stealing in of couples on dark nights, they at least did something else. She had opened a gambling and drinking house, but one can have no doubt about the ladies stealing in. "I was on the make all right," Aunt Sally told me once.

She ran the place and took in money, and the money she spent on the place itself. A falling wall was made to stand up straight and fine again, the banana plants were made to grow in the patio, the Chinaberry tree got started and was helped through the years of adolescence. On the wall the lovely Rose of Montana bloomed madly. The fragrant Lantana grew in a dense mass at a corner of the wall.

When the Chinaberry tree, planted at the very center of the patio, began to get up into the light it filled the whole neighborhood with fragrance in the Spring.

Fifteen, twenty years of that, with Mississippi River gamblers and race-horse men sitting at tables by windows in the huge rooms upstairs in the house that had once, no doubt, been the town house of some rich planter's family—in the boom days of the Forties. Women stealing in, too, in the dusk of evenings. Drinks being sold. Aunt Sally raking down the kitty from the game, raking in her share, quite ruthlessly.

At night, getting a good price too from the lovers. No questions asked, a good price for drinks. Moll Flanders might have lived with Aunt Sally. What a pair they would have made! The Chinaberry tree beginning to be lusty. The Lantana blossoming—in the Fall the Rose of Montana.

Aunt Sally getting hers. Using the money to keep the old house in fine shape. Salting some away all the time.

A motherly soul, good, sensible Middle-Western woman, eh? Once a race-horse man left twenty-four thousand dollars with her and disappeared. No one knew she had it. There was a report the man was dead. He had killed a gambler in a place down by the French Market and while they were looking for him he managed to slip in to Aunt Sally's and leave his swag. Some time later a body was found floating in the river and it was identified as the horseman but in reality he had been picked up in a wire-tapping haul in New York City and did not get out of his Northern prison for six years.

When he did get out, naturally, he skipped for New Orleans. No doubt he was somewhat shaky. She had him. If he squealed there was a murder charge to be brought up and held over his head. It was night when he arrived and Aunt Sally went at once to an old brick oven built into the wall of the kitchen and took out a bag. "There it is," she said. The whole affair was part of the day's work for her in those days.

Gamblers at the tables in some of the rooms upstairs, lurking couples, from the old patio below the fragrance of growing things.

When she was fifty, Aunt Sally had got enough and had put them all out. She did not stay in the way of sin too long and she never went in too deep, like that Moll Flanders, and so she was all right and sitting pretty. "They wanted to gamble and drink and play with the ladies. The ladies liked it all right. I never saw none of them come in protesting too much. The worst was in the morning when they went away. They looked so sheepish and guilty. If they felt that way, what made them come? If I took a man, you bet I'd want him and no monkey-business or nothing doing.

"I got a little tired of all of them, that's the truth." Aunt Sally laughed. "But that wasn't until I had got what I went after. Oh, pshaw, they took up too much of my time, after I got enough to be safe."

Aunt Sally is now sixty-five. If you like her and she likes you she will let you sit with her in her patio gossiping of the old times, of the old river days. Perhaps—well, you see there is still something of the French influence at work in New Orleans, a sort of matter-of-factness about life—what I started to say is that if you know Aunt Sally and she likes you, and if, by chance, your lady likes the smell of flowers growing in a patio at night—really, I am going a bit too far. I only meant to suggest that Aunt Sally at sixty-five is not harsh. She is a motherly soul.

We sat in the garden talking, the little Southern poet, Aunt Sally and myself—or rather they talked and I listened. The Southerner's great-grandfather was English, a younger son, and he came over here to make his fortune as a planter, and did it. Once he and his sons owned several great plantations with slaves, but now his father had but a few hundred acres left, about one of the old houses—somewhere over in Alabama. The land is heavily mortgaged and most of it has not been under cultivation for years. Negro labor is growing more and more expensive and unsatisfactory since so many Negroes have run off to Chicago, and the poet's father and the one brother at home are not much good at working the land. "We aren't strong enough and we don't know how," the poet said.

The Southerner had come to New Orleans to see Fred, to talk with Fred about poetry, but Fred was out of town. I could only walk about with him, help him drink his home-made whisky. Already I had taken nearly a dozen drinks. In the morning I would have a headache.

I drew within myself, listening while David and Aunt Sally talked. The Chinaberry tree had been so and so many years growing—she spoke of it as she might have spoken of a daughter. "It had a lot of different sicknesses when it was young, but it pulled through." Someone had built a high wall on one side of her patio so that the climbing plants did not get as much sunlight as they needed. The banana plants, however, did very well and now the Chinaberry tree was big and strong enough to take care of itself. She kept giving David drinks of whisky and he talked.

He told her of the place in his leg where something, a bone perhaps, pressed on the nerve, and of the place on his left cheek. A silver plate had been set under the skin. She touched the spot with her fat old fingers. The moonlight fell softly down on the patio floor. "I can't sleep except somewhere out of doors," David said.

He explained how that, at home on his father's plantation, he had to be thinking all day whether or not he would be able to sleep at night.

"I go to bed and then I get up. There is always a bottle of whisky on the table downstairs and I take three or four drinks. Then I go out doors." Often very nice things happened.

"In the Fall it's best," he said. "You see the niggers are making molasses." Every Negro cabin on the place had a little clump of ground back of it where cane grew and in the Fall the Negroes were making their 'lasses. "I take the bottle in my hand and go into the fields, unseen by the niggers. Having the bottle with me, that way, I drink a good deal and then lie down on the ground. The mosquitoes bite me some, but I don't mind much. I reckon I get drunk enough not to mind. The little pain makes a kind of rhythm for the great pain—like poetry.

"In a kind of shed the niggers are making the 'lasses, that is to say, pressing the juice out of the cane and boiling it down. They keep singing as they work. In a few years now I reckon our family won't have any land. The banks could take it now if they wanted it. They don't want it. It would be too much trouble for them to manage, I reckon.

"In the Fall, at night, the niggers are pressing the cane. Our niggers live pretty much on 'lasses and grits.

"They like working at night and I'm glad they do. There is an old mule going round and round in a circle and beside the press a pile of the dry cane. Niggers come, men and women, old and young. They build a fire outside the shed. The old mule goes round and round.

"The niggers sing. They laugh and shout. Sometimes the young niggers with their gals make love on the dry cane pile. I can hear it rattle.

"I have come out of the big house, me and my bottle, and I creep along, low on the ground, 'til I get up close. There I lie. I'm a little drunk. It all makes me happy. I can sleep some, on the ground like that, when the niggers are singing, when no one knows I'm there.

"I could sleep here, on these bricks here," David said, pointing to where the shadows cast by the broad leaves of the banana plants were broadest and deepest.

He got up from his chair and went limping, dragging one foot after the other, across the patio and lay down on the bricks.

For a long time Aunt Sally and I sat looking at each other, saying nothing, and presently she made a sign with her fat finger and we crept away into the house. "I'll let you out at the front door. You let him sleep, right where he is," she said. In spite of her huge bulk and her age she walked across the patio floor as softly as a kitten. Beside her I felt awkward and uncertain. When we had got inside she whispered to me. She had some champagne left from the old days, hidden away somewhere in the old house. "I'm going to send a magnum up to his dad when he goes home," she explained.

She, it seemed, was very happy, having him there, drunk and asleep on the brick floor of the patio. "We used to have some good men come here in the old days too," she said. As we went into the house through the kitchen door I had looked back at David, asleep now in the heavy shadows at a corner of the wall. There was no doubt he also was happy, had been happy ever since I had brought him into the presence of Aunt Sally. What a small huddled figure of a man he looked, lying thus on the brick, under the night sky, in the deep shadows of the banana plants.

I went into the house and out at the front door and into a dark narrow street, thinking. Well, I was, after all, a Northern man. It was possible Aunt Sally had become completely Southern, being down here so long.

I remembered that it was the chief boast of her life that once she had shaken hands with John L. Sullivan and that she had known P. T. Barnum.

"I knew Dave Gears. You mean to tell me you don't know who Dave Gears was? Why, he was one of the biggest gamblers we ever had in this city."

As for David and his poetry—it is in the manner of Shelley. "If I could write like Shelley I would be happy. I wouldn't care what happened to me," he had said during our walk of the early part of the evening.

I went along enjoying my thoughts. The street was dark and occasionally I laughed. A notion had come to me. It kept dancing in my head and I thought it very delicious. It had something to do with aristocrats, with such people as Aunt Sally and David. "Lordy," I thought, "maybe I do understand them a little. I'm from the Middle West myself and it seems we can produce our aristocrats too." I kept thinking of Aunt Sally and of my native State, Ohio. "Lordy, I hope she comes from up there, but I don't think I had better inquire too closely into her past," I said to myself, as I went smiling away into the soft smoky night.

Frances Parkinson Keyes (1885–1970)

Frances Parkinson Keyes was born Frances Parkinson Wheeler at Monroe Hill, the former home of the fifth president of the United States, James Monroe, on the campus of the University of Virginia, where her father, John Henry Wheeler, was the chair of the Greek department. Keyes's parents met on a ship sailing from Baltimore to Bremen, Germany, where John Wheeler was headed to attain his doctorate degree from the University of Bonn. Keyes's mother was Mrs. Louise Johnson Underhill at the time, and John Wheeler would be the second of her three husbands. The Wheelers had been married six years when Frances was born, and they had already lost one child, a young boy, so as Keyes writes in her memoir, *Roses in December,* the day she was born "was one of great rejoicing."[1] That happiness would be short lived, however, for John Wheeler died when Frances was not yet two years old.

Her mother had another child by her previous marriage, ten-year-old James Underhill, so she now had to figure out how to provide for two children. Louise Wheeler's father, Edward Carleton Johnson, was a native of Newbury, Vermont, but Louise had been born and raised in New York City. After living a life of ease and luxury in New York City, she never imagined returning to the Johnson family homestead in rural Vermont to live, but she had little choice, as the remainder of her family fortune would not last long in New York.

Only two years after her father's death, Keyes recalls throwing a tantrum when asked to descend the stairs in her fluffy white dress in order to attend her mother's marriage to Mr. Albert E. Pillsbury, a former Harvard classmate of John Wheeler. Pillsbury had taken care of all the funeral arrangements when John Wheeler died and had been a frequent visitor to the Wheeler house since then, but Keyes was too young to realize that he had been courting her twice widowed mother. The family soon moved to Boston, where Pillsbury had a successful law practice, with his eye on the governor's mansion. Louise Johnson Underhill Wheeler Pillsbury would dash those dreams when she divorced the philandering Pillsbury some six years later.

After an extended stay in Europe, Louise and Frances returned to the house in Newbury which became their main residence. Frances attended school in Boston, either staying with friends and family or in a home that Louise rented, and as much as Frances loved school, she always considered Newbury her home. It is also where she met and married her husband Henry Wilder (Harry) Keyes, twenty-seven years her senior.

When Frances was only thirteen years old, Harry Keyes, who lived in New Hampshire, just across the Connecticut River from Newbury, Vermont, began visiting their home often, much to her chagrin, since she thought that he was courting her now-divorced mother, Louise. Although he was not courting Louise, nor was he courting Frances, they were engaged to be married some four years later, when Frances was only seventeen. According to Frances Keyes, that was not soon enough for Harry:

> He had been "troubled about something for two years." Afterward I learned that the trouble was
> occasioned because he had wanted, for two years, to ask me to marry him before he finally did so;
> obviously, even if he were trying to teach me how a grown-up girl should behave, when I was fifteen,
> that was not an age at which it was proper for me to receive a formal proposal![2]

Pendleton Hogan, in his short biography, *Lunch with Mrs. Keyes,* claims that Frances Keyes's mother objected to the rather remarkable age difference between the two lovers: "Because of 'Harry' Keyes' age, her mother opposed the marriage and after it never offered her daughter an allowance."[3] Keyes herself never mentions this in her own memoirs. In fact, Frances Keyes insists that Mrs. Wheeler (After her divorce, her mother resumed using Frances's father's name.) objected only to the Keyes' refusal to meet with her to discuss the upcoming nuptials. Frances Keyes later discovered that Mrs. Keyes' reluctant acceptance of the marriage lay with her mother and her rather indecorous three marriages: ",,.they so thoroughly disapproved of my mother that they could not countenance the

---

1   Frances Parkinson Keyes, *Roses in December* (New York: Doubleday, 1960), 11.

2   Ibid., 240.

3   Pendleton Hogan, *Lunch with Mrs. Keyes: a Short Biography of Frances Parkinson Keys* (New Orleans: The Keyes Foundation Beauregard-Keyes House, 1989), 13.

idea of any connection with her."[1] Harry insisted, however, and they were married on June 8, 1903.

Harry Keyes served in both houses of the New Hampshire legislature before being elected governor of the state in 1916. He later served as a United States senator from New Hampshire for eighteen years, retiring in 1937, a year before his death. As the wife of a U.S. senator, Frances returned to live in her native Virginia for almost twenty years, where she raised three sons. According to Hogan, she was well-known for her gracious entertaining in the Washington D.C. area, with such notable guests as the wives of Franklin D. Roosevelt, Warren Harding, and Calvin Coolidge, but more importantly, in the 1920s she also began her writing career as a journalist for *Good Housekeeping,* where she first published her *Letters from a Senator's Wife.* Her first novel, *The Old Grey Homestead,* was also published around that time, so her prolific writing career had begun.

A year after Harry's death, a dear friend of Mrs. Keyes whom she'd met in Peking, China, in 1925, Clarence Bussey Hewes, a retired American diplomat from Jeanerette, Louisiana, suggested that she come to New Orleans to see Carnival, which he was certain she would feel compelled to write about. Bussey Hewes was right. Keyes saw Carnival for the first time in 1940, and *Crescent Carnival* was published in 1942. She went on to publish several books about Louisiana, the most well-known being her 1948 novel, *Dinner at Antoine's,* her first romance mystery. Keyes was primarily a novelist; however, she also wrote several biographies, a memoir, and even a cookbook, along with one collection of short stories in 1968, entitled *The Restless Lady.* She writes in the book's forward that each story is "complete in itself, but linked to the others by the spell of Washington (D.C.) which hangs over them all," all except for two of the stories, which are set in New Orleans: "Bayou D'Amour" and "… And She Wore Diamonds,"[2] the latter of which is included here.

Like so much of Keyes's New Orleans fiction, the story swirls around carnival season in New Orleans, and the protagonist, Prue Morton must satisfy her curiosity about the most popular Mardi Gras ball, the Pacifici Ball, by reading about it in the society pages of the New Orleans evening paper. Up until her father's recent death, Prue would have attended that ball, perhaps might have been crowned queen, but she now is consigned to reading about her once dearest friend, Marianne Newton, Queen of Pacifici, while Prue was not even invited.

The sting of her exclusion still smarts so much that Prue feels obligated to lie to her coworker at the Great Blue Fleet cruise lines, Julio Fernandez, by telling him that she attended Pacifici. The irony of trying to impress a man her mother refers to as "a strange man from some mongrel Central American country" is not lost on Prue, but she does want to impress him. Keyes captures the close-knit, wealthy New Orleans families that so many New Orleans writers describe, like Dimitry in "Le Tombeau Blanc" or Cable in "'Tite Poulette." No matter that Prue and her mother must skip a meal or two to entertain the few friends who still deign to visit them, a Latino with a name like Fernandez is still unwelcome in Mrs. Morton's home.

In fact, Mrs. Morton essentially tries to sell her daughter, Prue to the fabulously wealthy and perpetually drunk Rodney Tucker, who is willing to pull strings in order to make Prue Queen of the prestigious Krewe of Helvetians. Prue, having dated Rodney some years ago and having been nearly sexually assaulted by him, knows the price she must pay, but she is initially willing to do so for her family.

By the time Prue sees Julio at work the next day, that willingness fails, and she sacrifices everything for him, even the diamonds worn by the Mardi Gras royalty, or so she thinks. She spends the night in Julio's Pontalba apartment at Jackson Square, but naturally he gives her the bed and sleeps elsewhere. Keyes would have it no other way, as after her conversion to Catholicism, relatively late in life, she believed in chastity until marriage. Like most of Keyes's fiction, this story ends happily and offers plenty of local color which surrounded her while she was writing the short story in the French Quarter.

In 1944, Keyes rented the entire second floor of the former French Quarter home of Confederate General Pierre Gustave Toutant Beauregard from the "Beauregard House Association, a somewhat uncertain but deserving volunteer group of determined, patriotic women."[3] For the next twenty-five years, until her death in 1970, Keyes spent winters there writing and undertaking major restoration projects of the house. Three years before moving

---

1   Keyes, *Roses in December,* 261.

2   "…And She Wore Diamond Earrings" *The Restless Lady* (New York: Signet, 1968), 297-308.

3   Hogan, *Lunch, 10.*

into the Beauregard House, Keyes had restored a twenty-room antebellum plantation, "The Cottage," upriver from New Orleans, in order to write her novel, *The River Road,* but the undertaking proved too much for her and took a toll on her already failing health, so she abandoned the project and moved into the French Quarter. She also bought a house in Crowley, Louisiana, in order to write her novel about the building of a rice empire, *Blue Camellia,* and all the while maintained her family mansion in New Hampshire, a house in Vermont and one in Virginia! Frances Parkinson Keyes died in the Beauregard-Keyes French Quarter home on July 3, 1970, some three weeks shy of her 85th birthday.

...And She Wore Diamond Earrings[1]

P rue Morton picked up the evening paper and shook it open, even before letting herself into the house with her latchkey. Then, without stopping to remove her wraps, she went into the living room and, slumping down in a big shabby chair, spread the paper out on her lap. When she found the society column, she read, with avidity, the description of what had been worn at the Carnival ball the night before.

She knew about the tableau already; there had been an account of that in the morning paper. And she knew about the favors. Marianne Newton had come in the office of the Great Blue Fleet, where Prue was employed, to get literature on the spring cruises, and had stopped long enough to talk to Prue about the favors. The Newton family fortunes had been rising steadily during the last few years and Marianne had been the queen of one of the first balls that season and a maid in the court of several others. The Morton family fortunes, on the other hand, had fallen quite as steadily; there had not been money enough, after Mr. Morton's death, for Prue to make a formal debut, and she had not been invited to the Pacifici Ball— the one which had taken place the night before— though she had been to a few less important ones. The worst of it was, a word from Marianne, in the right quarter, would have meant an invitation. That was what really hurt. Because once Marianne and Prue had been such good friends.

Oh, well, Prue thought. She would read about what had been worn by those whose families had not lost their money and their social standing. Then she would talk about it, with authority, to her fellow clerk, Julio Fernandez, who, as far as she knew, had not been invited anywhere in New Orleans. At least she had never met him at any of the few houses where she was still asked to cocktail parties and *brûlots* and very large buffet suppers. Once she had hinted to her mother that they might invite Julio to their house, and her mother had recoiled as if Prue had made a highly improper suggestion.

"You mean that strange looking boy from somewhere in Central America, who's been sent to the New Orleans' office of the Great Blue Fleet so that he could pick up a little English?"

"I don't think he's so strange looking. I think he's quite nice looking. He wasn't just sent up from 'somewhere,' either. He'd been in the Blue Fleet office at Puerto de Oro and he'd done very well there. When he came to New Orleans, it was a promotion and Mr. Foxworth, the president of the company, gave him a personal letter of recommendation. And Julio speaks beautiful English. He didn't have to come to New Orleans to 'pick it up.' He'd been to school in the United States already."

"Well, I'm not going to have a strange man from some mongrel Central American port coming to this house, no matter where he's been to school or how many languages he speaks. As for Orson Foxworth, he hasn't any background himself, he doesn't even recognize the lack of it in anyone

---

1   From: Frances Parkinson Keyes, *The Restless Lady* (New York: Signet, 1968), 297-308.

else. I'm certainly not going to help some protégé of his to worm his way into good society. I have some pride left."

Prue had never again suggested bringing Julio home to dinner. As a matter of fact, she realized that it *would* have hurt her pride to do so—not because Julio was a social inferior, but because she had gathered he enjoyed good food, and dinner at the Morton mansion was no longer a gourmet's delight, to say the least. Several times he had suggested that, perhaps, Prue would dine with him, at Antoine's or Brennan's, or some other good restaurant; but at her mother's insistence, she had declined—regretfully, because she had a feeling Julio might be quite good company at dinner, and besides, she herself could have done with one that was a gourmet's delight. This was one of the evenings when she had declined a dinner invitation from Julio, not merely because her acceptance would have displeased her mother; but because he expected her to tell him about the Pacifici Ball, and she had not gathered enough, from the morning paper and from Marianne's tittle-tattle, to describe it convincingly. So she devoured the social column instead.

"Among the stunning gowns seen at the Pacifici Ball last night was the one worn by Mrs. Alexandre Brugiere, the mother of the queen," Prue read, holding the limp page close to the inadequate light. "Mrs. Brugiere chose metallic brocade, made in surplice style, and she wore diamond earrings. Her cousin, Mrs. Richard Elves, of Richmond, Virginia, was in lavender satin, the full skirt caught up with bunches of violets. Miss Natica Livingstone, a former Queen of the Pacifici, was in white tulle with pearl trimmings. Mrs. Shirley Townsend was in bouffant changeable taffeta and she wore diamond earrings. Miss Mary Bruse, a maid in last year's court, was in coral-colored crepe and wore an antique necklace of carved coral which blended beautifully with her dress. Mrs. Malcolm Towne was regal in black velvet and she wore long diamond earrings."

Prue thrust the paper away from her and then snatched it up again. No two of the gorgeously gowned women who had arrested the society editor's coveted attention had been dressed alike; every style, every fabric, every color had been different, But three of them had worn diamond earrings—three whom she had read about already, and she had nowhere nearly finished the column. She began it again, and this time she read it through to the end. Apparently, there had been only one gown conspicuous for its "plunging neckline," only one with a "tiered skirt," only one with a "wide crushed band of material across the hips." What was more, only one girl had worn pearls worthy of attention, only one, carved coral. But there had been three fortunate possessors of diamond earrings, the ornament of all others which Prue had longed to own, ever since she could remember . .

Belatedly, she took off her weather-beaten hat and tossed it onto a nearby sofa. She knew she should have taken off her jacket, too; it was bad for tailored clothes to lounge around in them, and this was the only well- cut outfit she had left, At that, it wasn't smart enough, any longer, to wear to a good restaurant. So, on account of it, she was glad she had declined Julio's invitation. She didn't want to tell him about the ball, either. She was tired of pretending—that it didn't matter she and Marianne weren't great friends any more; that it didn't matter whether she was invited to balls or not; that pretty clothes and lovely jewels didn't matter. Such things were important in every girl's life and all the other girls she knew had them..

Her mother came into the room and realized, after one swift glance, how Prue had been occupied since returning from the office. "You've been reading about last night's ball!" she said accusingly.

"Yes, Mother."

"I shouldn't think you'd want to, when you weren't invited. I didn't."

"I know. I found the paper, all wet, on the front gallery."

"I think stop taking the paper, It's a needless expense. The less I learn about all the dreadful things going on in the world, the better it is for my peace of mind. And I certainly don't want to read about the good times my former friends—my false friends—are having without me. I've too much pride."

"I know," Prue said again. "Mother… didn't anyone in our family ever have any diamond earrings?"

"Why, yes, of course. In my mother's day, every lady used to have diamond earrings."

"Well, what happened to them all?"

Mrs. Morton began to look rather vague. "I'm not sure. I think some of them were made over into engagement rings—one pair of earrings made two very nice solitaires. And, of course., in my day, every young lady expected to have a solitaire engagement ring."

"There weren't any long diamond earrings?"

"No, there weren't any long diamond earrings, as far as I know. Why should there have been?"

"No reason why there should have been. I just thought there might have been, And in that case, they couldn't have been used up very fast to make solitaire engagement rings. As a matter of fact, I don't see how they all could have been used up anyway. You just said every lady had a pair, and every pair made two engagement rings, and in Grandmother's family alone, there were seven sisters. Were there fourteen engaged girls in yours that had no other way of getting rings?"

"No-o. I think, perhaps— well, I think, perhaps, some of the earrings were disposed of."

"What do you mean, disposed of?"

"Prue, don't snap at me like that! And don't ask such embarrassing questions! As if it were necessary. As if you didn't know we had to sell them, as we did lots of other things. But if you had any regard for my pride…"

Now she was crying. There was a time when Mrs. Morton's tears had been very moving to Prue. But that was long, long ago. She picked up her hat and turned to leave the room.

"Where are you going?" her mother asked suddenly.

"Just to put my things away. And then to get some cookies, unless you meant to have supper right off. Why?"

"There aren't any cookies in the house. And I didn't mean to have supper right off. I came to tell you something and then you distracted me, talking about diamond earrings."

"I'm sorry, Mother. What was it you came to tell me?"

"Rodney Tucker telephoned me late this morning. He wants to come and see you tomorrow evening."

"Was he sober when he said so?"

"Prue, what makes you ask such a question? Of course, he was sober! He sounded very much in earnest."

"Well, he isn't always—sober, I mean. Or very much in earnest, either, for that matter. Did he tell you what he wanted to see me about?"

"Yes, he did… I wish you wouldn't stand there, by the door, Prue, as if you were trying to run away from me."

Prue sat down silently. Her mother drew a deep breath and went on

"He said he realized you weren't making an official debut, that you were so serious minded you didn't care much for frivolous society. Of course, that was just his nice way of putting it. He knows you couldn't afford to make a debut, But he said a lovely girl like you ought to be in at least one court. He—he said it could be arranged."

"This late in the season! Now I know he wasn't sober!"

"Prue, you're the most uncharitable creature I ever knew! The girl who was to be Queen of the Helvetians is down with scarlet fever. So one of the girls, who was to be a maid, could be queen, instead, and that would leave room for one more girl in the court. Or else, the Helvetians might leave the court as it is and select another queen."

Prue looked at her mother without answering. Again Mrs. Morton drew a deep breath.

"He said you could choose, Prue. If you didn't care to be queen, you could be in the court. He said of course he realized there was less expense connected with being a maid than with being a queen. But he said, since you're earning a good salary, it would be easy for you to get a loan—he could arrange that, too. Oh, Prue, if you only knew what a disappointment it's been to me that you never... I told Mr. Tucker that you'd expect him at six tomorrow. I've been out and bought some Bourbon, so I didn't have any money left for other things. But you won't mind, just for tonight, will you, when tomorrow...."

Probably it was because she was hungry that she couldn't sleep. She lay very still, thinking things over. She had never been especially popular with boys, as a teen-ager. Her gray eyes did not have much snap to them and her soft straight hair did not have much sheen. To be sure, she did have nice skin, but her pleasant smile and manner, which were considered a great asset in the office, went unnoticed in a group where loud laughter and much shouting prevailed. Besides, even in her school days, she had cared more about getting good marks than about having dates. If she had known a boy like Julio, that would have been different. But she never had, until she met Julio himself.

Still, Rodney Tucker, who was a good deal older, had gone out of his way to show her that he liked her. Prue had met him the first time at Marianne's house and he had invited her to a Sugar Bowl Game, All the other girls envied her. But they needn't have. She didn't realize, at first, what the matter was with Rodney Tucker, because, after all, she was just a kid, and this was her first date. But pretty soon she knew he acted the way he did because he had had too much to drink, even before they started for the game. And, on the way home, he not only drove very strangely, he took a very roundabout route; and when Prue called his attention to this, thinking he had made a mistake about the best way to get to her house, he laughed and stopped the car.

She had never told her mother about this, she had never told anyone; but she had never forgotten it, either. Nothing terrible happened. Rodney was not so drunk he did not realize, when she fought him off, that she was really frightened, really revolted. Suddenly sobered, suddenly sorry, he took her home. The next day, he sent her two dozen long-stemmed red roses. After that, he quite frequently sent her roses and, quite frequently, invited her to go out with him. She could not send back the flowers, because they always came anonymously; but she steadfastly refused to go out with him again. And, after she stopped visiting Marianne, because she was working and Marianne was making her debut, she had hardly seen him at all., And now, he had offered to make her queen of a Carnival ball!

Prue knew what this meant. She was sure he knew just how modest her "good salary" was, how impossible it would be for her to pay off a large loan with any degree of promptness. Although it would all be done tactfully and indirectly, Rodney would be underwriting her financially. She would be under obligations to him; and when he asked her to marry him, he would expect her to accept him, because that was what he wanted and he had given her what she wanted, or at any rate, what he had every reason to suppose she wanted. Prue did not believe there was a girl in New Orleans who would not have given her eyeteeth to be Queen of the Helvetians.

If she married Rodney Tucker she could go to all the balls after this. She could stop working in the office of the Great Blue Fleet and take one of those famous spring cruises herself, for a honeymoon. She could have a house on St. Charles Avenue and belong to the Orleans Club. She would have all the beautiful clothes she wanted. She could have diamond earrings.

Mrs. Morton was still asleep when Prue got up the next morning and, as she did not want to run any risk of waking her mother by moving about in the kitchen, she decided that she would go down to the French Market and have a cup of coffee and some doughnuts before she went to the office. It was a lovely mild morning and, as she sat on the open terrace of the Cafe du Monde, looking out on Jackson Square, where the azaleas were already in bloom, she began to feel better. She was just rising to leave when she heard someone calling out her name, in a very welcoming way, and saw that Julio Fernandez was hurrying in her direction,

"Prue! Please stay and have coffee with me." "Thanks, but I've just had some. And I'm afraid I ought to be getting to the office."

"There's no law against having two cups, is there? And it's early yet."

He beckoned to a waiter and sat down at the table she had been about to leave, as if the matter were settled. "I wish I'd asked you to take breakfast with me, here, long before this," he said. "I come here almost every morning. It's very convenient, because I live at the Pontalba."

He lighted a cigarette and leaned back in his chair. "You promised to tell me about the Pacifici Ball," he said. "Why wouldn't this be a good time?"

"It was simply superb," Prue answered, trying to speak glibly. "The official favors were bracelets, copied from one a member of the Krewe brought home from Ceylon, when he took a trip around the world."

"I'm sorry you didn't wear yours this morning, so I could see it,"

"It isn't the sort of thing you'd wear to work. But, Julio, I've got something to tell you I think—I'm almost sure—I can get you an invitation to one of the later balls—one of the best."

"You mean that I'd take you?"

He sounded so happy at the prospect that Prue regretted her impulse to confide in him. She had found it an effort to speak about the Pacifici Ball and the change of subject had seemed like an inspiration. Now she realized it had been a mistake. But there was no help for it, she would have to go on.

"No, I don't mean that. I mean something a lot more wonderful. You mustn't breathe a word, it's a deadly secret. But I'm going to be Queen of the Helvetians, have a limousine with a special police escort. There'll be an awning and a carpet at a private entrance of the Auditorium, on purpose for me and my court. I'll lead the Grand March. I'll sit on a throne with the masked king and everyone will come and bow to us-I mean all the members of the Krewe and all the girls in the call-out section. The other guests—the girls who aren't in the call-out section and all the male guests, except the committeemen—will be in the balcony looking on."

"That's where I'd be—in the balcony looking on?"

"Yes. I'm sorry, but that would be the best I could do for you. It's hard to get any kind of an invitation to the Helvetian Ball."

Julio rose, crushing the stub of his cigarette. "I do not think I would care much about just looking on from a balcony," he said thoughtfully. "Thank you for thinking of me, Prue. Truly my feelings have not been hurt by the lack of invitations to Carnival balls. It would have been wonderful if I could have taken you to one, that's all,—. And now, I am afraid it is time for us to get to the office,"

He was silent as they walked up Chartres Street and across Canal, and there was a strain to the silence. Moreover, the strain seemed to persist all through the day. Julio did not come over to Prue's desk, every now and then; it almost seemed as if he were avoiding her, and this troubled her. Presently, it would be time for her to go home, and Rodney Tucker would be there, drinking Bourbon and waiting to tell her that she was going to be Queen of the Helvetians and that she was not to worry about money or anything else. But she was worrying already. When Rodney Tucker had told her what he had come to say and she had thanked him, he would be on a different footing in the house. He could come there whenever he chose. And pretty soon, she would be there all the time. She would not see Julio any more.

At four o'clock, she heard Mr. Forrestal, the manager, tell Julio that he was leaving for the day, but that there were still some memoranda on his desk that he would like Julio to look after. Julio went into the private office and closed the door. At first, Prue could hear him talking on the telephone and moving about; but after a while, there were no sounds. For some reason, this silence proved unendurable. At last, she could stand it no longer. She knocked on the door and then, without waiting for an answer, she went in.

Julio was sitting at Mr. Forrestal's beautiful big desk, but he did not appear to be doing anything about the memoranda. He appeared to be thinking about something which made him very unhappy. When Prue walked in, he looked up and rose. "What can I do for you?" he asked, rather formally.

"You can listen to what I'm going to say."

"All right, Prue," he said easily. "Shoot!"

"I didn't go to the Pacifici Ball," she said. "I didn't go to any of those other balls I told you about, either. I wasn't invited to them, any more than you were. I was just pretending. Somehow, I couldn't leave without telling you so."

Julio appeared to consider all this, carefully but not critically. Then he remarked, "Well, I'm sure there must have been some good reason for pretending. Were you just pretending about being queen, too?"

"No, that part was true. A man is coming to see me this evening who can make me queen—Who wants to 'make me queen."

"I see. And then you wouldn't pretend any more?"

"No. Because I wouldn't need to."

"I see," Julio said again. "Well, I suppose this man you mention is very much in love with you—of course, that is easy to understand. But I don't understand whether you are very much in love with him."

"No, I'm not. I'm not in love with him at all."

Suddenly, she felt as if she were back in that parked car, suddenly she seemed to hear Rodney Tucker laughing at her and trying to take her in his arms. She had escaped that time, but the next time— the time that was so near now—she would be trapped. And nothing in the world would be worth that—not the fulfillment of her mother's ambition, nor the power of retaliation which would henceforth be hers, nor the preeminence of her future position. She felt humiliated because she had ever thought it would, so humiliated that she was afraid she was going to disgrace herself by crying. She might even fall, her knees were shaking so; in fact she was trembling, uncontrollably, all over. But she didn't fall, because Julio reached forward and put his arms around her; when this happened, she did not try to fight him off, she did not want to. She wanted him to hold her closer and closer and keep on kissing her and repeating what he was saying. She could not understand any of the words, because they were all Spanish words, but their meaning was very clear and it was music to her ears.

At quarter past six, Mrs. Morton, who was very angry, began telephoning the office of the Great Blue Fleet. She kept on doing so, at intervals, after Rodney Tucker, who was very angry, too, left the house. She did not get any answer, because the office had closed, as usual, promptly at five, and

Prue had gone with Julio to his apartment at the Pontalba Building.

It was she who had suggested it. And then he said, well, perhaps he might be forgiven for following her suggestion, though he knew that, even in the United States, a gentleman did not—or at any rate should not —take his *novia* to his apartment, unless another lady were there to receive her. But they would stay only long enough, before they went out to dinner, for him to tell her again how much he loved her and to give her some kind of keepsake, as a souvenir of the day.

Prue was vaguely surprised by the appearance of Julio's apartment. Some of the old paintings on the walls were rather beautiful, and so were various carved chests and silver ornaments. Julio settled her on a big sofa and then excused himself, saying he would be back in a minute. As Prue waited for his return, she realized that everything she had coveted before seemed to have lost its glamour, and mingled with her newfound joy, there was suddenly a sense of thanksgiving.

Julio came back into the drawing room, carrying a small blue velvet box. "I must measure your finger for a ring before we go on to Brennan's," he said. "Unless you prefer something else, I should like to give you an emerald. But meanwhile, as I said, I want you to have a souvenir of today—my great-grandfather's first present to his *novia.*"

"As if I needed a souvenir to help me remember today!"

"But you will accept a gift, won't you, since it is our family custom to make one on such an occasion?"

He put his arms around her again and then handed her the box, still unopened. She turned it over, two or three times, with fingers that trembled slightly. Then she pressed the golden spring and the lid flew open.

Inside, on a bed of white satin that had yellowed with age, lay a pair of long diamond earrings.

🐝

Lyle Saxon (1891–1946)

By all accounts, Lyle Saxon was a charming, likeable, yet troubled man.[1] Much like Mollie Moore Davis, he fictionalized his early years, painting a portrait of romantic plantation life growing up in rural Louisiana. But in fact, he was born in Bellingham, Washington, in 1891, to Hugh Allan and Katherine (Kitty) Chambers Saxon, a fact he seldom, if ever mentioned. The two Saxon biographers, Harvey and Thomas, set forth conflicting accounts of Saxon's birth, especially concerning his parents' marital status. Harvey discovered an Orleans Parish marriage license dated December 10, 1890; however, Thomas maintains that a marriage license does not guarantee a marriage, simply an intent to marry, and that the common belief at the time among their Baton Rouge friends— they met at LSU—is that they were not married. Nonetheless, before the year was out, Katherine Saxon had returned to Baton Rouge with her son, and his father Hugh returned to Los Angeles where he pursued both writing and acting careers and where he remarried and remained until his death in the 1950s. Saxon never mentioned his father, and his mother, according to Harvey, was listed in the 1905-06 Baton Rouge City Directory as "widow of Hugh A."[2]

Lyle Saxon was reared by his mother and her maiden sisters, Maude and Elizabeth Chambers, in his maternal grandfather's house in Baton Rouge. Not only did Saxon not come from a family of planters, but rather, shopkeepers, as his grandfather owned a bookstore in downtown Baton Rouge. Saxon attended LSU, but left just three credits shy of graduating, a fact he later omitted from his résumés.[3] The reason for his early departure from LSU is a matter of debate. Harvey claims that he might have dropped out due to financial reasons; however, Rosan Jordan and Frank De Caro claim that he left due to a sex scandal involving him and his best friend, George Favrot, when the two were discovered drunk and dressed in women's clothing.[4] Nevertheless, like the plantation myth of his youth and being a Louisiana native, he added LSU class of 1912.

Saxon seemed to drift for the next few years, working several odd jobs before settling down to journalism, first selling house paint in Mobile, Alabama, then teaching remedial English in Pensacola, Florida, in a small school house accessible only by boat.[5] By 1917, however, he began his journalism career in earnest as a cub reporter for the *Chicago Daily News,* and the job might have suited him, but the freezing Chicago winters did not, so he returned to Louisiana in less than a year, partly due to his failing health. While in Chicago he underwent a physical examination for the draft but was rejected for having tuberculosis, a charge he denied.[6] By the following year, he was working for the New Orleans *Item.*

Most critics agree that Saxon aspired not to be a journalist, but a fiction writer, like many of the famous writers with whom he became friends in New Orleans in the 1920s, including Sherwood Anderson, William Faulkner, Hamilton Basso, and John Steinbeck, who in 1943 was married in Saxon's Madison Street home.[7] All of whom went on to become successful and some even famous writers. That degree of success and fame always eluded Saxon, and he is still best known today for editing the WPA Federal Writing Project's 1938 *New Orleans City Guide.* That WPA guide was considered to be "the masterpiece of the whole series... a literary gem."[8] Unfortunately, Saxon came to the WPA project late in life, and it took a toll on his already failing health. His

---

1   For more on Lyle Saxon, and the source of much of this biographical information, see Chance Harvey, *The Life and Selected Letters of Lyle Saxon* (Gretna, Louisiana: Pelican Publishing, 2003), and James W. Thomas, *Lyle Saxon: A Critical Biography* (Birmingham: Summa, 1991).

2   Harvey, 28.

3   Ibid., 39.

4   Rosan Augusta Jordan and Frank De Caro, "'In This Folk-Lore Land': Race, Class, Identity, and Folklore Studies in Louisiana," *The Journal of American Folklore* 109, no. 431 (Spring, 1987), 31-59.

5   Harvey, 43.

6   Ibid., 45.

7   Jordan and DeCaro, 48.

8   Lawrence N. Powell, Introduction, *New Orleans City Guide,* 1938 (Washington D.C.: Federal Writers' Project of the Works Progress Administration, 1938), 1A-7A.

editorship also took time away from his fiction writing, which he lamented repeatedly in his nine years on the job, but it was a job, and Saxon needed the money.

When he took on the *New Orleans City Guide,* he was writing his novel, *Children of Strangers,* and most of that book was written at Melrose Plantation up near Natchitoches, Louisiana, even though he was living in the French Quarter at the time. According to Harvey, Saxon met Cammie Garrett Henry, the chatelaine of Melrose, at one of Grace King's Friday literary salons in 1923, when he was writing his "Literature and Less" column for the *Times-Picayune,* which is also when he was dubbed "Mr. New Orleans" by his adoring readers.[1] Saxon would continue to visit Melrose for decades, and that is where he completed the story included here, "The Centaur Plays Croquet."

First published in the short story collection, *The American Caravan,* in 1927, "The Centaur Plays Croquet" is a wild and sexy story of a married woman swept off her feet by a handsome centaur. Saxon often wrote of the fantastic, and Harvey speculates that the inspiration for this short story is Edward J. Trelawny's *Recollections of the Last Days of Shelley and Byron* (1858), a copy of which Saxon owned and annotated, especially noting that perhaps Byron was a satyr.[2] Also like many of Saxon's works of fiction, this one is set on a plantation, in this case located in fictional Mimosa, Louisiana. Like Saxon, the protagonist, Ada, is fatherless, and also like him, she is thrilled by Mardi Gras when she visits New Orleans on her honeymoon with her much older husband John Calander. Shortly after the couple's return to Mimosa, the centaur, Horace, appears and their lives are forever changed.

Saxon's use of reportage to substantiate the fantastic tale that ensues seems almost ironic, especially in scenes like the one in which Ada and Horace attend the opera (*Faust,* naturally), as recounted by Miss Amélie Boudousquié, whom Ada met while honeymooning in New Orleans. In fact, the entire tale is retold by different characters involved in the lives of Ada and John, and Saxon claims that each account is "taken down from sworn testimony of competent eye witnesses." Until Horace appears, we have little reason to suspect otherwise.

Much like his heroine, Ada, Saxon remained lonely and unfulfilled, leading to a sense of alienation and real depression which he tried to relieve with alcohol. He was thrilled that this story was selected by the editors of *The American Caravan,* but his literary success remained elusive. By the end of his life, "Mr. New Orleans" joked that he was "internationally famous locally,"[3] a fact that was unfortunately true. Saxon's last public appearance was during Mardi Gras, which he so loved. He delivered a live broadcast of the Rex Parade from the balcony of St. Charles Hotel where he spent the last decade of his life.

The Centaur Plays Croquet

THE STRANGE CASE OF MRS. JOHN DAVID CALANDER OF MIMOSA, LOUISIANA, AND THE FABULOUS
MONSTER WHICH SHE KEPT AS A PET, THEREBY CAUSING GREAT SCANDAL IN THE COMMUNITY.

A COMPLETE HISTORY OF THE UNFORTUNATE AFFAIR, TAKEN DOWN FROM SWORN
TESTIMONY OF COMPETENT EYE WITNESSES.

*Testimony of Matthew A. Fleming, MA., Ph.D., Member of the American Association of
Sciences, and head of the Department of Ancient Languages at the University of Mimosa.*

I hesitate, for various reasons, to enter into any discussion whatever relative to the strange case of Mrs. Ada Weatherford Calander of Mimosa, Louisiana, as so much nonsense has been written on the subject; and, in this state, the story (odd and unnatural enough as it appears even in its truthful aspect) has attained something of the fanciful and miraculous quality of a heathen legend, where fairies, gnomes

---

1   Harvey, 80-81.

2   Ibid., 93.

3   Thomas, ix.

and elves are taken for granted. In addition to this, the religious and pagan elements entering into it have been so distorted in various versions (spread by fanatics as propaganda for their respective creeds, and colored by their spites and prejudices, no doubt) as to cause indecision in the mind of any sane and serious student. Such a maze of mental cobwebs surrounds the whole unfortunate affair, that there is a tendency to doubt the story in toto. However, as numerous witnesses were available in various parts of the Pelican State, I have taken their testimony exactly as they have given it to me (in most cases having the parties appear before a convenient Notary Public and affix their signatures to same) and I offer these testimonials here, after giving to my readers a brief synopsis of the principal facts.

Little is known of the true origin of Ada Weatherford, save that she was an orphan in a Catholic Orphan Asylum, and was adopted, when approximately six years old, by Mr. Alphonse Adams Weatherford, of Mimosa. She was educated for some years by a governess, one Sarah Jingles, who has been lost sight of, and who came, rather mysteriously, to the Weatherford home in the early Spring of 1870, the year of Ada's adoption by her foster parents. The little girl was taught the elements of education: viz., reading, writing and number work, and, in addition, the arts of the home, which the Weatherfords considered Woman's True Sphere; in other words, fine cookery, sewing and those things pertaining to the house management. It is said that the little one never really learned to use her needle properly, and had small aptitude for homemaking, but preferred spending her time in the woods and fields. Those who remember her as a child, tell of her strange likes and dislikes: her preference for moonlight, for example, to God's sunlight; and they also tell of her habit of talking constantly to unseen companions whom she imagined real. Miss Jingles, sad to relate, rather spoiled her pupil by giving way to her whims; and, it is said, that frequently the two would absent themselves from the plantation house for a whole day at a time, going deep into the quagmires and swamps to "study nature." What really went on in the woods, no one knows, and no one can safely conjecture; but there are stories afloat of the child riding upon the back of a white goat, through glade and grove; and once she was nearly shot by a hunter who mistook her for a large hare.

Miss Jingles was in sole charge of the child after the death of Mrs. Weatherford in 1875, when Ada was 11 years old; and, in the years following, the intimacy between teacher and pupil progressed rapidly. The humbler studies were abandoned for the quadrivium: arithmetic, music, geometry and astronomy. There were lessons in French and in Mythology. Mr. Weatherford humored his adopted daughter to a great extent, giving her expensive presents, among others a fine piano, upon which the girl played eerie melodies which sounded, say those who listened, like nothing they had ever heard before. In so far as is known, Miss Jingles was her only teacher in music, but the young girl soon out-stripped her instructress in the art of keyboard manipulation.

Ada grew to womanhood in that lonely plantation house of the Weatherfords, with few friends but with many books. Her favorite copy of Burton's "Anatomy of Melancholy" is before me as I write, the margin covered with hieroglyphs that I am unable to decipher. Upon the flyleaf, there is a creditable drawing of a Centaur, possessing a handsome man's head with pointed beard and wild eyes. The lower portion of the figure is that of a horse, with four well-shaped legs and flowing tail. Oddly enough, in the drawing, the Centaur is shown holding a lady's high-heeled slipper in one hand. Whether this is the work of Ada 'Weatherford or of Miss Jingles, it is impossible to say. It is highly probable, however, that Ada drew the picture, having seen similar things in the books of pagan mythology which had been allowed to fall into her hands.

When Ada was 18 years old, she was married to Mr. John David Calander of Mimosa, a fine, upstanding man of many good qualities. He was a member of the Baptist Church, a large landholder, and in addition, a lawyer of considerable local reputation. He was, at the time of his marriage, a bachelor of 38 years of age, and, it is said, he idolized his wife, so many years his junior. They were married, according to the church records of Mimosa, on February 24th, 1882, in the home of the bride's father, and went afterward to New Orleans for the Mardi Gras festivities, staying at the St. Charles Hotel, as is proved by the register of that year, which was, fortunately, saved from the fire which destroyed that hostelry a few years later.

A miniature of the young Mrs. Calander, painted in New Orleans at that time, shows her a slim, dark-eyed young woman with a highbred, oval-shaped face, wearing her hair parted madonna fashion. The eyes of the portrait are limpid and beautiful, and the full lips are richly red. There is one peculiarity about this portrait: although the face is unsmiling, almost grave in expression, it is, at the same time, full of secret laughter. The longer one studies the likeness, the more puzzled one becomes. Those who remember her best, say that the resemblance of the painting to the original is indeed striking.

During the brief honeymoon, the new Mrs. Calander met many friends of her husband's; among them Miss Amélie Boudousquié, whose sworn testimony is appended to these notes. Miss Boudousquié, a member of a fine old Creole family, is quick to praise Mrs. Calander's beauty and wit, but hesitates to comment upon the moral quality of her conversation, which she found "advanced" (to use her own phraseology) for that time. She (Ada Calander, as we must now call her) appeared distrait and dreamy, Miss Boudousquié testifies, but enjoyed the Mardi Gras parades and balls in the French Opera House, appearing to enjoy particularly the mythological quality of the festivities. Among the nymphs, mermaids, satyrs and fauns of the Carnival land of make-believe, she was radiantly happy, and even had her husband allow her to purchase costumes and disguises, including gilded horses' heads of papier mâché and, winged slippers, from the shop of one Madame Alabau in Bourbon Street. What became of these gaudy trifles afterward can only be conjectured, but, according to the proprietor of the shop, they were shipped to the plantation at Mimosa.

The news of the death of Mr. Weatherford cut short their gaiety in New Orleans, and they returned home before their allotted time. Miss Boudousquié says that she found Ada Calander in tears in her room at the St. Charles Hotel one afternoon when she called, and was told of Mr. Weatherford's sudden demise (caused by a fall from a horse). The Calanders left that night for Mimosa and Miss Boudousquić did not see Mrs. Calander again for three years—and then it was at the performance of "Faust" at the French Opera, all of which is given in detail in Miss Boudousquié's sworn testimony.

When Mr. Weatherford's will was read, it was found that Ada Calander was sole heir; she received the plantation, and various and sundry monies and other properties. She turned the management of the land over to her husband, giving him free rein, but keeping as her own a considerable quantity of ready gold which was locked in a large safe in the library of the country house. Mr. Calander, it is said, never questioned his wife's actions, loving her devotedly and passionately, and only accepting her properties because he knew her incapable of handling them for advantage to herself. Throughout this history, one never doubts the devotion of this sterling man for his wife, but one is often amazed at the strange tests to which she put his affection.

So they lived, these two, in that lonely place, seeing few people and entertaining visitors but rarely. True, he drove into the town of Mimosa daily, to his office in the old brick building on Mandolin Street, but she remained at home, deep in her studies.

According to the testimony of "Aunt" Charity Jimmeson, a Negress (long a cook in the Weatherford household), Ada resumed her life in the woods, frequently remaining absent for eight hours at a time, strolling, it is supposed, through dell and glade of the wooded estate. It was at this time that she published (in *Harper's Magazine*) her first poem, "The Were-Wolf," which has become so widely known for its mysterious quality and for its pagan note of unbelief in the Divine Mercy of God.

Other poems followed shortly: "Pan" in 1883; "Phantom Lovers" and "Europa" in the same year.

In 1884, she published "Leda," in January, followed almost immediately by "Una and the Lion" and "The Bride of the Faun." These poems, it was considered, were too realistic for the taste of the period, and Harper's refused to publish her later effusions, which are said to show respect for neither God nor man. One of these unpublished "prose-poems" (as she called them) will be quoted in its proper place, as it throws considerable light upon her ultimate downfall. She did not write at all after November, 1884.

One shudders to think of the humiliation of Mr. Calander at this trying period; but despite the busy tongues of Mimosa, he remained loyal to his wife, worshiping her devotedly, and passing the neighbor's comments of his wife's writings, with a smile and a shrug. Ada could do no wrong, and, like Caesar's wife, she was above suspicion—although, to be quite accurate, the Bard of Avon says that "Caesar's wife should be above suspicion," if I remember Shakespeare correctly.

In June, 1884, when Ada Calander was 20 years old, she brought a strange pet home with her—a Centaur, according to the testimony of Charity Jimmeson, who declares that Horace (for thus Ada called him) was a very handsome fellow, half-man, half-beast. It is impossible to shake her testimony, as this aged Negress declared that she helped take care of "Mr. Horace" and knew him well; she refused absolutely to believe the theory (advanced by Mrs. James Branch in her statement) that the Centaur was nothing more than an unusually intelligent horse which the perverse and unhappy woman had disguised in some way to resemble a man.

At any rate, this horse, or Centaur, was very timid about entering the house; but by careful coaxing, Mrs. Calander induced him to enter the drawing room, where he stood, restless and wild-eyed and switching his tail, while she played for him upon the piano.

Perhaps it is as well to introduce here the "prose poem" called "The Centaur Plays Croquet," which was written by Ada Calander at this time (approximately). Needless to say, this effusion was never printed, but was found among her papers, after her death:

"Come, my Centaur, let us have a game of croquet! The colored balls lie like painted flowers on the lawn and the wickets stand in order as do the events of my life. It amuses me to have you play so prim a game—you who remember Pan and who have cavorted with nymphs. Sadly you stand, slowly swaying your tail, and holding the mallet poised; while I, with tiny black lace parasol tilted against the sun, lift mincingly my skirt and strike the ball with an affected scream of excitement—strike daintily, for fear of splitting my polonaise of striped silk.

"Your body, tanned by the sun, is like creamy ivory, and the texture of your flesh has the humid quality of a magnolia petal. You stand before me, my simple, sinewy fellow, with shoulders drooping — shoulders strong and hairless like those of the men of Castile. Your black curls shine sleekly; your teeth are of snowy whiteness and your lips are vivid beneath your beard. At the loins, where your man's body melts into that of the stallion, you become wholly animal; there your hide has the sheen of satin and is mottled like moonlight under trees.

"What a Godlike brute you are, my Centaur! Still, you gaze at me with wistful eyes. Is it a soul you seek? Perhaps, who knows? For you have no soul, you fabulous man, you glorious beast, born two thousand years too late… Or is it I who have mislaid my era?

"If it is a soul you long for, you may have mine. See, I will tear it from my breast and offer it to you, glowing, in my pink-tipped fingers! (But the striped silk is stronger than I thought, and my stays resist my tugging.)

"As I fail, then, to give you what you ask, let us try to find another road to happiness. Take me upon your back and let us fly to the countries of your youth; let us return through the ages to your brothers who whinny upon Thessalian hillsides, while the old Gods whisper in the twilight beside trickling fountains. Laughter lies waiting for us there, lingering in those Pagan times before the Babe of Bethlehem was born, and the old Gods sighed and died. But before I mount to begin our riotous journey against the years, let me twine crimson pomegranate blossoms for your hair, and let me put the first purple violet of Spring into your curling beard.

"Ah no! I am cruel, my Centaur… Come, let us have a game of croquet!"

While it is not incumbent upon me to make any criticism of this remarkable document, I must say that I consider it an extremely indiscreet paper. That a Southern lady should write such a thing at all is unheard of, and that a Southern lady did write so brazenly in 1884, is unthinkable. Especially so to a student of mythology. For the behaviour of Centaurs, even in antiquity, was not always all that it should have been, as is amply borne out in many works of ancient art. (I am thinking, particularly, of the central part of the western pediment of the temple of Zeus at Olympia.)

But to return to the day of his appearance, and to take up again the statement of Charity Jimmeson:

Mr. Calander, upon his return that night, gave an amazed cry at seeing the Centaur in the parlor, but, behind closed doors, he was presented and seemed to welcome the animal even as his wife had done. At any rate, Horace remained and soon became an exacting charge upon the household.

His diet consisted, for the greater part, of green things: vegetables from the garden, which he ate raw; oats and other grain; and he quaffed great quantities of wine. Shortly after his arrival, in order to please him, Mrs. Calander became a vegetarian. And in all things she deferred to the brute's tastes. Of all this, Mr. Calander was pleasantly indulgent, and ordered that Charity and the other servants should obey his wife's wishes to the letter. He (deluded man) also harkened to her whim for secrecy. Ada was afraid that, if the presence of Horace upon the plantation became known, crowds of strangers would come there to see him; and she dreaded this more than any one other thing, as her devotion was touching. Never did mortal woman lavish such tender affection upon an animal as did Mrs. Calander upon that beast. According to Charity Jimmeson, she had met him nearly a year before in the deepest part of the swamp behind the house, and had, with infinite tenderness, formed a friendship with him, taming him from his wild state. She even taught him to talk, but as French was the language they used, and as he seldom spoke except in that language, which Charity did not understand, she can offer but few direct quotations.

He mooned all day before Mrs. Calander, nuzzling her shoulder, or eating sugar from her fingers. Together they would go into the woods, leaving the house in the early morning, taking a picnic lunch under the trees in distant parts of the estate; and together they would return at twilight. Sometimes she rode upon his back, sitting sideways, her arm around his neck.

On one such occasion, Charity Jimmeson says, she saw Mr. Calander, who was watching from the dining-room window, turn away and cover his face with his hand.

In the following year, Mrs. Calander's dreaminess increased and she seemed to suffer from melancholy. She hardly allowed her husband to touch her hand, nowadays, and aside from playing upon the piano, she did little. She never read or studied now—save to read French poems to Horace, who did not appear to understand. Sometimes they played at croquet upon the lawn, or tossed quoits; or, reclining under a tree, played at chess or at cards—"Pope Joan" being their favorite game. All visitors were rigidly excluded from the grounds. Signs were posted, "Trespassers will be Prosecuted" (a very unusual thing in Louisiana in those days of fox hunting). When a caller came, Horace was hidden away. The old Negress tells of one such occasion, when the Centaur pranced about the polished floor of the guest bed-chamber where he had been concealed, until the visitor (Mrs. James Branch, of Mimosa) asked what animal was parading in the house, and demanded to see for herself. In her testimony, which is appended to these notes, she tells of Mrs. Calander's fear and rage, and of the summary dismissal of the guest from the plantation house, which Mrs. Branch says she felt very keenly.

A tension of ever-increasing nervousness seemed to invade the hitherto peaceful spot. All the servants felt it, and this sense of brooding tragedy worried poor Charity Jimmeson so, that she became cross and irritable, and upon one summer's night, lost her temper and gave notice, despite the fact that she had been with the Weatherford family for more than twenty years.

It was eight o'clock, and the family was assembled at the long table, dining by candlelight. Mr. Calander, who appeared on the verge of a nervous breakdown, spoke sharply to Charity for the first time in his life: "Do as you please," he said, "But for the love of God, be quiet now!" Nothing more than that, and the words hardly louder than a whisper. Mrs. Calander, showing only the slightest interest in the affair, continued calmly eating white grapes, and sipping, now and then, from her glass of wine. Opposite her, Horace pawed the floor at intervals, quivering with impatience to have done and begone into the moonlit woods. He took his meals with the family now, eating at one end of the long candlelighted table, using his finger to convey the greens and grain to his mouth, but handling his thin wine glass with the greatest delicacy. In order to cover his nakedness, Ada Calander had designed a silken shirt which covered his torso, a shirt ending just where his man's anatomy joined the body of the horse. Sometimes she even dressed him in her husband's shirts, vests, collars and ties, and at these times, if one saw the upper part of Horace, one would have considered him the very handsomest man ever seen, were it not for his dilating nostrils, the nervous movements of his shoulders, and the wild, sidelong glance of those black eyes, when someone walked behind him.

But, upon the occasions of Horace donning masculine attire, Mr. Calander became so melancholy that he could hardly hold up his head; great sighs shook his frame, and tears were seen to stand in his eyes. But, according to Charity Jimmeson, he never reproved his wife for her adoration of this beast, but bore all her foibles with a true Christian fortitude. Charity believes that the man realized that he had married a mad woman, but even knowing this terrible fact, still loved her. Horace was the plaything of his wife, and that was enough for David Calander.

Charity was thinking of all this, she says, as she stood there, defiantly, on that hot August night, looking at the strange trio about the table. There was moonlight outside the windows, but there was thunder in the air, and the atmosphere was humid and heavy. The candle flames did not flicker, but rose straight up to prodigious heights. Mr. Calander, wearing an old-fashioned black stock about his neck, leaned forward, head on hand, gazing at the cloth, trying to control the quinching that seemed to shake him from head to foot. Horace, or that part of Horace that showed above the table's edge, was, like the master, in a strange state of agitation; his eyes roved toward the windows. Young Mrs. Calander, dressed in a pomegranate colored gown, cut like a riding habit—(a style she wore almost always, now) sat leaning white arms upon the damask, a grape against her lips; her eyes looked dreamily into the candle flames. In the doorway stood Charity, the gaunt old Negress, sullen and baffled.

With an effort, the master broke the long silence with a bit of trivial conversation: "I saw a beautiful mare in the lane as I came in tonight, Ada," he said. "Never have I seen a more beautiful animal—white, graceful, almost like a creature from another world…" His eyes moved toward Horace, who was listening intently and whose nervousness seemed to have vanished under the even flow of words. "An exquisite, slim white mare, grazing in the moonlight," David Calander continued.

His eyes went back to his wife, who had paused with another grape half-way to her lips and with a look of horror in her eyes. For Horace, with a terrible deliberation, was divesting himself of his silken shirt. Slowly he slipped it from his shoulders, and it fell to the floor; his creamy flesh was seen gleaming in the candleshine.

Ada Calander rose from her place, her chair falling over with a loud noise on the polished floor: "Horace!" she cried. But the Centaur, with one bound of his muscled body, was gone through a window, out into the moonlit world beyond. They heard the clattering of hoofs as he crossed a bridge over the bayou which divided the flower garden from the lane. She stood like a woman stricken, her arms outstretched.

That according to Charity, was the real beginning of Ada Calander's insanity, for she shrieked like a woman possessed. She fell fainting to the floor, pulling with her the damask cloth, and upsetting the candles, so that the only light was of the moon which shone in at the long windows, Her husband was near madness himself, with the excitement and sorrow for what his wife had come to; and through a remark of his, made in all idleness. But, upon recovering her wits, she would not have it so. He had done it on purpose, she declared, and she moaned for Horace to return to her; and her moans turned to screams when she realized that he was away from her side, traipsing after a strange white mare.

All night long she mourned and cried, and finally fell into so deep a swoon that her life was despaired of, and old Charity Jimmeson was sent, riding a mule, to fetch a doctor from Mimosa. The man of medicine arrived at sunrise, and found the lady asleep, worn out from hysteria; and he found her good, kind husband verging on madness, too, He prescribed sleeping draughts and soothing medicines, and went away, shaking his head, but promising to return late in the afternoon.

Along about midday, the lady began to call again for her pet Centaur, and Charity, relenting a little, and despairing for her mistress's reason otherwise, went in search of the animal, but could find no trace of him. She did find hoof-prints—of two horses, so she swears—in a flower bed, and followed the tracks a ways, but lost them again, a little further along, where the garden joined the woodland.

The madness of the lady progressed, it seemed, by leaps and bounds. Now she clung to her husband, sobbing and begging him to save her from imaginary terrors; now she pushed him aside, crying for her brute; again she shrieked her hate, and cursed her spouse for deliberately winning her pet away from her, swearing that her husband was a scheming hypocrite and a vile villain. At other times they clung together like frightened children. And so they were at twilight when the physician returned. And again the doctor departed, shaking his head.

At midnight the lady's moans became so piteous that her husband put aside all thought of self and went forth into the darkness in search of the Centaur; but though he searched until sunrise, neither hide nor hair of the rascal did he discover, save a few glossy strands from his tail, caught in a yellow rosebush.

But, on the second day, in the depths of the wildwood, the master found him, lying as snug as you please, under a tree, the Centaur's arm around the throat of the white mare. David Calander promised Horace anything if the beast would only return to the house again, even going so far as to say that the mistress would die if he refused. But Horace was proud and coquettish, and would come only on condition that the mare come too. And so it was arranged. For, after all, the master reasoned, there was no surer way of curing his fair wife's infatuation than by letting her see the true nature of the beast.

So the mare was put into the pasture and Horace came back into the drawing room once more; but he was vague and distant. In the midst of Ada's fondest protestations of affection, he would turn deliberately and gaze from the window to where the white mare was feeding contentedly in the field; and he spent hours in making chains of flowers which he strung about the mare's neck, chiding her playfully when she did but devour them.

Within the house Ada pined, miserably sick for her fabulous companion, but too proud, now, to enter into contest with Alice, the mare, (for so Horace called her).

And so the thing continued, week in, week out. And so great was John David Calander's love for his wife, that he pined with her, feeling, no doubt, that Horace had played a scurvy trick upon her, in so treating the love and affection that she lavished upon him. In vain, however, did the master use all his logic and oratory to reconcile his spouse to the perfidy of the Centaur. She did but moan in reply, and kept to her bed.

In the late Fall (November 22, to be exact), she arose and began to go about the house and grounds as usual. But, according to the old Negress's story, there burned an unholy light in her eyes. She became friendly with the mare, bringing her sugar and oats, and even offering her nosegays of flowers from the garden; all of which the mare received with scant appreciation; for she was a thankless wench, coming from God knows where, and thinking nothing of all the love and affection that the Centaur lavished upon her. She seemed unutterably bored, and would not lift her head when Horace came whinnying toward her, but seemed to prefer the porringer of oats that Ada brought, to all his love-making.

It was in November, as I have said, that Ada Calander rose from her bed. It was the day before Thanksgiving that she prepared a silver bowl of grain for the mare. Although Charity Jimmeson suspects that poison was added to the oats, she has no direct means of knowing; but certain she is that shortly after this, the mare fell sick and died, miserably and in great pain. So it was, that Horace came hack to live in the house once more.

News of these strange doings, however, had filtered somehow into the town of Mimosa, and it came to pass that a mass-meeting was held, and a body of citizens, headed by the Mayor and the Baptist minister, came a-riding to the plantation one sunny winter afternoon, to see for themselves what strange thing this was. But a Negro servant, meeting them in the lane, had made a short cut through the fields, and arriving at the house before them, had given the alarm. When the men arrived, expecting they knew not what, they found only an empty house. Both mistress and Centaur were missing.

Great was the agony of John David Calander when he returned home at dusk to find the house deserted, and the iron safe in the library standing open. For, in her flight upon the Centaur's back, Ada Calander had seen fit to take a bag of gold with her—and was gone without leaving a trace. Although dogs were brought out by the master of the house, the trail was lost in the quagmires which lay some miles back of the plantation house.

Ten days later, Mr. Calander was found dead upon his bed, a pistol clasped in his hand; and the red hole in his breast told that his aim had been true. When his will was opened, it was found that he had left his entire estate to his wife, should she see fit to claim it at any time.

There were rumors that Ada Colander and the Centaur were seen in New Orleans, and elsewhere, but they were only vague reports; upon investigation, I have been unable to find one person, save Miss Amaie Boudousquié (and her mother) who saw them. And even Miss Boudousquié's testimony is a trifle disappointing in its incompleteness.

Now Ada Calander fled from the plantation on February 14th, 1885, but on May 24th, she returned to Mimosa just at dusk, bringing with her a large packing case which she had transported immediately to the country estate. Aside from her hurried passage (heavily veiled) through Mimosa, she has not been seen by the townspeople from that day to this. A few who dared call were dismissed at the door with the news that the lady was indisposed. And some boys of the town, inspired by curiosity, who crept to the garden after nightfall, saw the mistress weeping over a new-made grave under a magnolia tree. She lived and died alone, it is understood, with only a few servants around her; and I believe that I was the only guest admitted to the parlor of the house prior to her death.

Becoming interested in the strange stories which seemed to grow as the years passed, I decided, in the interest of my scientific work, to brave the lady in her home, and try to set these wild rumors at rest. I thought by careful explanation, I could convince the unhappy woman of my impersonal interest in her story. So, in the Spring of 1905, I made a pilgrimage to the Weatherford plantation.

I had considerable difficulty in getting there, for in the two decades which had passed since she had taken refuge, the foliage had grown densely in the lane which formed an avenue from the public road to the edge of the flower garden. I took with me on this visit, my daughter, Mildred-Virginia Fleming, who was most anxious to see the quaint old place of which she had heard so many romantic stories. My daughter was at that time, a young lady of 19 summers, a scholar and student as well, and as interested as I in the pathological features of the unfortunate woman's history.

I regret to say that the visit was without scientific import, aside from one chance remark which the lady let fall at the close of the conversation— But I progress too rapidly with my story.

We approached the house, I repeat, with some difficulty, owing to the heavy underbrush which had grown up in the roads leading to it. For some time I debated taking the less arduous road, which ran around the garden and ended at the quarters of the Negroes in the rear; but finally I discarded this idea as undignified and unsportsmanlike. My daughter and I left the surrey in the lane, being unable to pass a large clump of canes which had grown across the driveway, and proceeded on foot. After a walk of half an hour or more, we reached the garden gate, now overgrown with ivy, and made our way inside. The garden had been allowed to run wild; roses were drowned in masses of weeds; a tangle of vines festooned themselves from tree to tree; and the two magnolias beside the entrance were covered with scarlet trumpet vines, the flowers vivid against the gray of the trailing Spanish moss. The steps had rotted away, and we were forced to climb upon the front porch with some difficulty. A startled man-servant, an aged Negro, met us at the door, with uplifted arm and scowling face; but finally, after a generous bribe and a long explanation, he consented to inform his mistress that we were at the door. I can hardly explain the strange trepidation that I felt as we waited there upon that mouldering veranda, listening to the shuffling feet of the old man as he departed to some distant wing of the house. After a long time he returned, telling us that his mistress would see us.

Now, as Ada Weatherford Calander was born in 1864, and this was the year of Our Lord 1905, I knew that the lady could not be more than 41 years old, and was profoundly shocked to see a woman old and bent, a woman so weakened and debilitated that she seemed unable to rise from her chair as we entered. From her appearance I should have judged her to be 70 years of age. She was seated in a tattered armchair in a corner of a vast and almost empty room at the back of the house, a study or library, I surmised, by the bookcases which reached from floor to ceiling; a room once lovely, doubtless, but now fallen into a dirty and slovenly state, owing, most likely, to the increasing sluttishness of its mistress.

The old blue-stocking was surrounded with open books, large volumes of scientific works, it appeared, and, at her elbow beside the open window, stood a large telescope. Skymaps were hanging on the walls, and I noticed that one of them, just behind her chair, had the constellation Sagittarius outlined in red chalk or crayon. There were spider webs everywhere and the floor was deep in dust, the dust being particularly noticeable, as the boards were scarred deep, as though by the prancing of a horse, or other animal.

She was civil, but distant, and the haughty demeanor that I had heard described so many times, had fallen from her. She asked me, briefly, to state my business and be gone; and, I regret to say, she offered us neither chairs nor refreshment after our wearisome journey.

With some hesitation, I asked her if she had once possessed a pet Centaur, and awaited her answer with eagerness. I expected either vehement denial, or polite acquiescence, but I was totally unprepared for the answer: "Ah, I do not remember..." which drifted like a mere thread of sound from her lips. So astounded was I, that I motioned to my daughter Mildred-Virginia to divert her with polite conversation while I prepared for further questioning. But my daughter's pleasant chit chat seemed to fall upon deaf ears. The old lady sat peering forward with her short-sighted eyes, and seemed to hear nothing. Only once did she make a response to a girlish statement from my daughter, relative to her own lack of interest in men (which Mildred-Virginia meant well enough, I am sure, but in which I detected a curious mental connection with the subject uppermost in our thoughts). My daughter said, if I remember correctly: "Men have but little interest for me; I do not believe I shall ever marry!" or a similar, sweeping statement, such as young girls are prone to utter. And Mrs. Calander, seeming to rouse from a reverie, said then in a faraway voice: "Ali, my dear, wait until the right horse comes along!"

At my daughter's surprised shriek: "What did you say, madam?" the old lady, suddenly becoming infuriated, ordered our instant departure from the premises, screaming in a raucous voice for the servants to eject us without further ado.

We left hastily, through the same corridor as we entered, descended from the rotting porch, and began our passage down the overgrown walk. However, my eye alighting upon a grave under a tree, I signalled my daughter to read the inscription upon the headstone, which stood clear of the grass. She read the following: "In Memory of My Beloved Horace," and below, the year of his death, 1885, but no further date was given, nor the place of his death. But lower still, was this inscription in Gothic script: "His soul goes whinnying down the wind." (My daughter is quite positive that she read it correctly.)

She had no more than finished reading, when two fierce dogs were upon us, and my daughter was severely bitten upon the thigh—a wound which, despite the good cause in which it was received, gave her considerable pain and annoyance afterward. The graceless behavior of Mrs. Calander so injured our dignity that we left immediately, hastening back to the surrey in the lane.

I intended to make a report of the vicious dogs to the town authorities at Mimosa, but my daughter dissuaded me, saying that, after all, we had been told to leave, and that we had no proof that the dogs had been set upon us at the old lady's order. All of which was right and proper.

This brings my report to a close, except to add that Ada Weatherford Calander died the following Autumn, September 4, 1905; and her property reverted to some distant cousinry of her husband's in Virginia, relatives who subsequently sold the property to an organization of business men. The Mimosa Country Club stands today upon the site of the Weatherford plantation house. The grave of Horace, unfortunately, has been leveled and the stone lost or thrown away. However, appended to this testimonial, is the report of the old stone cutter of the town, which bears out my statement as to the inscription.

In this chronicle, I have done my best to point out the facts as I found them and to steer away from any hint of the religious intolerance with which the Calander case is wrapped in Louisiana, and which will be made clear by the affirmations and disavowals in the sworn statements appended to this paper.

(Signed) Matthew A. Fleming, M.A., Ph.D.

Testimony of Mother St. Abraham, Superior of nuns of the Meaer Dolorosa Convent, Mimosa, Louisiana.

Inasmuch as I feel it my duty to our Holy Order and to our Divine Savior, to set at rest persistent rumors pertaining to Ada Weatherford (afterward Ada Weatherford Calander), and her nativity, I will state, here in the presence of Judge James G. Blount and other witnesses, that the rumor that this child was the daughter of a nun, is a most outrageous falsehood, spread no doubt, by those Black Protestants who are so eager to cast a blot upon the fair name of Catholicism. As a matter of fact, the child was found in a basket, perfectly nude and quite cold, in the doorway of the Convent on June 3, 1864, evidently abandoned there by some poor lost soul, who knew that our Holy Order could not refuse such a sacred charge. I was a very young nun at that time, and it was my duty to wash and dress the baby. I remember distinctly that the child appeared to be about three months old. She was a beautiful baby, always strong and well. Despite the fact that there was no clew as to her parentage, she was treated exactly as all of our orphans are treated, with love and kindness. She was baptised, of course, into the Roman Catholic Church. She was unusually intelligent. At the age of six, she knew the Catechism by heart and was fitted to make her First Communion, but was not allowed to do so, because of her youth. A prettier child I have never seen, always light-hearted and gay, and full of love and affection. So she was when adopted by Mr.

Alphonse Adams Weatherford, who came to our Convent in 1870, with the avowed intention of adopting a child for his wife, she being childless. Because of her winsomeness, they chose Ada—for so we called her, having christened her in honor of Saint Adaline of the Messed Palms.

I never saw her again after her adoption, nor did any of the Sisters of our Order, and it is ridiculous to suppose that her early training had anything to do with her behavior afterward—if bad it was. Is it not more likely that, living as she did, in a worldly household, she forgot her early teachings, and therefore wandered away from the righteousness of her upbringing? Mr. Weatherford, I have been informed, was an Episcopalian, and David Calander, the man she married, was a Baptist.

(Signed) Mother St. Abraham.

Testimony of Mrs. James Branch, of Mimosa, pertaining to the peculiar behavior of Mrs. Calander on July 14, 1881.

I had known David Calander all of my life. We were childhood friends, you might say, and it was perfectly natural that I should try to be nice to his wife, although I had never known Ada Weatherford in her unmarried days. People said she was very odd and studious, and did not care to mingle with the people of Mimosa, and I for one, have never cared for those who hold themselves better than others. Nevertheless, I deemed it my duty to visit her after her marriage, and so I did. I found her pleasant enough, and very pretty, but she certainly was an affected woman, if there ever was one. For instance, she would say something perfectly extraordinary, in a perfectly serious manner, and then, just as you got your breath to answer her, you would see that she had gone off into a sort of day dream—yes, a regular trance, right in the middle of the conversation. In addition to the things about her that I didn't like, she refused point-blank to join the Ladies-Aid, and so I left, rather irritated, and declared to my husband that night that I would never set foot in her house again. However, later on, during her so-called "indisposition," I felt it my duty as a Christian to forgive and forget, and so I went, on July 14, 1884, to the Weatherford plantation, driving out in my phaeton in the afternoon. I found her in a highly nervous state, and she hardly listened to my polite inquiries relative to her health. She appeared to be listening to strange sounds that came from an adjoining room, a stamping and pawing—exactly as though a horse was there in the guest bedroom. As I had heard some mighty funny stories about that woman, I thought I would just ask her straight out what sort of pet she had in the house— and so I did. She did not answer immediately, and so I repeated the question, adding in a friendly tone: "Oh, do let me see!" rising as I spoke, and making a movement toward the closet door. At this, she flew into a rage, and ordered me out of the house. Naturally I never returned to it. I've always told my husband that if he had been any kind of a man at all he would have had it out with David Calander; but he refused to take any part in the controversy. This was one of the things that led to our divorce, later on, but that is aside from the story of Ada Calander. I have said, and said repeatedly, that I knew she kept a horse in her bedroom, but I never said I saw a Centaur there—for, as a matter of fact, I do not believe that they exist, save in the diseased imaginations of insane and heathen peoples. It is my opinion that the story is all rot, and that Ada Calander was merely a crazy woman who took delight in driving her poor husband to suicide by her manias for animals. And that's all I've got to say about her!

(Signed) Jessie Mayo Branch (Mrs. James Branch).

Testimony of Miss Amélie Boudousquié, of New Orleans, with particular reference to the Centaur's one appearance in the city.

I first met Mrs. Calander in February, 1882, when she came to New Orleans on her honeymoon.

Her husband was an old friend of my mother's family, the Beaumonts. I called to see her at the St. Charles Hotel, taking my mother with me, of course; and later on, we had them to dinner at our house on Esplanade Avenue. I found her a very pretty woman, and quite witty, speaking French almost flawlessly, which pleased my mother very much. One afternoon, when calling at the hotel to take her for a drive in our carriage, I found her in a passion of tears, *pauvre enfant*, because she had just received the news of her foster-father's death. Despite the fact that she was his sole heir, she was deeply grieved, I am sure, and so I told Mama when I went home. I took her and her husband to the steamboat landing in our family barouche, instead of taking them upon the pleasant drive that we had anticipated.

Imagine my surprise, then, three years later, to see her in a box at the French Opera, where I had gone with Mama to witness a performance of "Faust," the favorite opera of all my family. I had been chatting with some friends in one of the proscenium boxes, when I gave a cry of surprise, recognizing Mrs. Calander and a gentleman in a box nearby. Accordingly, as is our free and easy custom in Nouvelle Orleans, I rapped lightly with my knuckles upon the door of the box, and walked in. Almost immediately, I regretted taking the liberty, for I saw at once that the gentleman with her was not her husband, but a total stranger to me! He was standing in the back of the box, partly behind her chair, and he only bowed deeply when I spoke to him and offered my hand. As he was a very handsome man, I was somewhat chagrined because he did not say something complimentary to me, and I looked at him very closely. I tell you there was something funny about that man! He was dressed in evening clothes, but the lower part of him was covered with a big black curtain! This apron struck me as odd, but being a true Creole lady, I did not mention it. She, poor thing, appeared so distrait, so nervous, so worried by my entrance into the box, that I felt I had committed a faux pas in coming in at all. And it dawned upon me, suddenly, that there was more in this visit to the opera than appeared on the surface. "Aha!" I thought, "what is this? A liaison? A rendezvous? Perhaps, who can tell?"

Upon my return to our box, just at the beginning of the last act, I communicated my impression to Mama, who shared my curiosity. Accordingly, we decided to watch them leave the theater. Ah yes, we planned it all out together, so that our actions should not appear indiscreet. At the final curtain, we hastened from our places and took our stand at one of the exits quite near their box, knowing that they would have to pass by us on the way out. Minutes went by and they did not come. "Now that is odd!" said Mama. The theater emptied gradually, and a man began to turn out the gas lights in the chandeliers, when I saw Ada Calander peeping out from between the curtains of the box. As she had seen us, no doubt, as we were the only ones left in the theater, I felt I could stand there no longer with any sort of propriety. So Mama and I went outside and took our places under a darkened arcade in Toulouse Street. Gradually, the street emptied, and just as I thought that the guilty couple had given us the slip, I saw her emerge from the door, wearing a purple dolman. She was alone, and she stood there, looking to the right and left; then she motioned someone within, and presently a strange figure appeared. Outlined in the door, I saw plainly, a tall man with a high silk hat, wearing, to my amazement, a long, trailing cloak which fell to the ground all around, and, dragging behind him a body, an appendage resembling the hindquarters of a quadruped. "What horror!" I said to Mama, "She is taking some deformed relative to the Opera and is ashamed of being seen!" But just as I was about to run across the street and offer her a seat in our carriage, a preposterous thing happened. The gentleman, who had been descending the steps with extreme difficulty, suddenly whisked off the cloak, and revealed that he was not a man at all, but a horse! Without a word, Mrs. Calander vaulted lightly upon his back, and he started at a gallop out Toulouse Street, toward Lake Pontchartrain. I could not believe my eyes, and my hysterical screams attracted a policeman, who, I regret to say, did not believe my story and refused to give chase.

(Signed) Amélie Boudousquié.

Testimony of the Reverend J. J. McBryde, of Mimosa.

I never saw Mrs. Calander but twice in my life, once when I married her to her husband, and again when I made it my business to go to the Weatherford home to remonstrate with her for her alleged outrageous behavior; for, as I said to myself: "Where there's smoke, there's bound to be fire!" And there were many scandalous stories afloat in Mimosa concerning her—stories that blackened her name, and besmirched the honor of her husband, who, prior to his marriage, had been a member of my church. Of her marriage day, it is unnecessary to speak; but of the call I made on February 2nd, 1885, I have a very distinct and unpleasant impression, even after all these years.

After the long drive in my buggy, I was very angry when the servant who had admitted me to the parlor, returned and said that his mistress begged to be excused, as she was very busy. Now, as I sat waiting, I had been profoundly shocked by an obscene picture on the wall[1] and at a bronze statue[2] of a half-man, half-beast, called a Centaur, I understand, who carried a naked woman upon his back. So, I walked right past that impudent nigger, and entered the library which was in the back part of the house. There she sat, all alone at a table, reading a book! Reading! Wasting her time with some vile trash, doubtless, and refusing the Minister when he came to call!

"Madam!" I said, "what is the meaning of that dirty picture in your drawing room? And that indecent statue? What is your husband thinking of to allow you to have such vile things in his house?"

"I haven't an idea what you mean," she drawled at me, looking at me with those mocking, hypocritical, Catholic eyes of hers. And so I told her how depraved her taste appeared to a respectable person like myself. Especially that statue of the man with a beast's body.

"But what is your objection to my Centaur?" she asked.

I then pointed out that the thing was impossible, abnormal, and perverse. Such things never existed at any time, I told her.

She caught at the word "abnormal."

"For that matter," she said, "even Angels cannot be said to be wholly normal, you know, according to your standards, Mr. McBryde, as they are always pictured as having both the bodies of men and the wings of birds. Do you know," she continued in her slow drawling voice, "the problem of their comfort when sleeping has often stirred my wonder. Do they, do you suppose, lie down to rest, as human beings do, or do Angels roost, like chickens, in the trees?"

"Blasphemer!" I shouted. "You'll burn in hell for this!" And turning upon my heel, I quitted the room and the house.

When I returned, white and shaken, to Mimosa, I took the matter up with the Mayor, who agreed with me that such a woman was a menace to the morals of the community. Accordingly a secret meeting was held, and a group of men went to the plantation one afternoon, in the absence of her husband (for he was not a party to her outrageous behavior). We had no intention of doing her bodily harm, but we intended to throw the fear of God into her heart. A nigger servant gave her the warning of our approach, however, and she escaped on horseback. But our little group destroyed the sinful picture and the statue, and gave that nigger a good whipping to teach him not to interfere with Southern justice.

I feel that I have done my duty, and I am not ashamed of it. If more men would take the stand that I do, there would be less laxity in Louisiana.

(Signed) Rev. J. J. McBryde.

---

1   Author's note: A reproduction of the painting by Paul Veronese of "Europa." The original is in the Doges' Palace at Venice, Italy.

2   Author's note: By Clodion.

Testimony of Adolph Wunsch, an aged stone-cutter of Mimosa, relative to the tombstones ordered in advance by John David Calander.

I, Adolph Wunsch, being in a sane state of mind, do appear and solemnly swear that the following is true:

Sometime in the early Spring of 1885, Mr. J. D. Calander came into my shop and said that he would like to order two tombstones for the family lot in Mimosa Cemetery; one for himself and one for his wife; something neat but costly, he said, with a simple design, and a place for a short epitaph. I wondered what was up, as both he and his wife were well at that time, for all I knew; but as he paid cash down, and I was in need of money just then, I only thanked God for his foolishness, and wished that more men would order their tombstones in advance.

Well, sir, he picked out two headstones, exactly alike, and had me carve on them. His name on one, and his wife's name on the other. On his, he ordered the date of his birth, and had a place left for the date of his death. The same on hers, he said. But in the empty space at the bottom, he ordered, on his: "He did his best to understand, and failing, died." But on hers, he had a more flighty inscription, if you will excuse my way of speaking. On hers he had carved: "She was carried away by her hobby; but for all her strangeness, she was a charming woman." And so I cut it on the stone. You'll find them both in the Mimosa Cemetery, if you care to look for them.

(Signed) Adolph Wunsch.

Elma Godchaux (1896–1941)

Elma Godchaux was born into one of the wealthiest and well-known families in Louisiana on November 30, 1896.[1] She was the second of three children born to Edward and Ophelia Gumbel Godchaux and was named after the plantation on which she was born in Napoleonville, Elm Hall. Her father was the second son of Lion Godchot, who arrived in New Orleans from Alsace in 1837 at the age of thirteen and soon thereafter changed his name to the more French, Leon Godchaux. Like many Jewish merchants in the region, Leon Godchaux turned to peddling his wares along the Mississippi in the rural areas surrounding the city. From this humble beginning, he grew to be the largest sugar magnate in the state and opened one of the first retail clothing stores, Godchaux's, in downtown New Orleans.

Elma Godchaux grew up in the family mansion at 5726 St. Charles Avenue, right down the street from Edward's younger brother Charles, but like her father before her, she spent weekends, holidays, and any other free time at the family's Reserve Plantation, upriver from New Orleans in Reserve, Louisiana.[2] Elma Godchaux later drew on the time she spent in Reserve for her fiction, much of which was set on or near the Mississippi River in sugar cane country. Also like her father, Elma was interested in and learned all aspects of the sugar cane industry which Leon Godchaux had expanded to all parts of South Louisiana, including Raceland, Diamond, Bell Point, Star, and of course Reserve.[3] He even built his own railroad to service all the Godchaux sugar plantations in the region. Well into adulthood, Elma would take her visiting friends and family to Reserve Plantation, and according to Laura Renée Westbrook, "She felt that, if her friends were to understand her, they must know Reserve."[4]

When Elma was two years old, her younger sister, Lucille was born, and they were always very close. When they were just nine and seven years old, respectively, they both contracted malaria and were treated with quinine, which led to hearing loss in both girls. Elma attended private school in New Orleans and graduated from Sophie Newcomb High School in 1912. She had already shown a flare for writing; however, she did not publish her first short stories until her own daughter Charlotte was grown. After graduating, Elma Godchaux went to Wellesley College just outside of Boston, where she met her future husband, Walter Kahn who attended Harvard. When their relationship became more serious, Godchaux transferred to Radcliffe to be closer to him.[5] Elma and Walter married in New Orleans in 1916 after he graduated and moved to Cambridge where he took a position as a lecturer. Elma never did complete her studies at Radcliffe and instead turned to working for the war effort.

Leon Godchaux instilled in all his children the need to give back to the community, and Elma, like her father, carried on that tradition; however, her family at times thought her activism went too far. At one point in the late 1930s, she went so far as to take a stand against the Godchaux Sugar Company in Reserve and fight on the side of the workers for a unionized workforce, a move which led to her estrangement from many of her family members, naturally, but not from her sister Lucille.[6] It is apparent that she drew on her experience championing the less fortunate and disenfranchised in her fiction, especially in "Chains," the story included here.

Elma's marriage was less successful. She and Walter Kahn had one child, Charlotte, who was raised in New York, where Walter worked as an investment banker, but the New York social scene never really appealed to Elma, and she and Walter grew apart. They separated in 1933, and Elma and Charlotte moved to New Orleans, where Charlotte attended her last year of high school before leaving for Radcliffe.[7] Godchaux was glad to be back home among family and friends, and once Charlotte left for college, Elma began her own writing career. She was

---

1   For more on Elma Godchaux and from where most of the biographical information included here is taken, see Laura Renée Westbrook, "The Godchaux Family in Louisiana History, Literature, and Public Folklore," (Ph.D. dissertation, University of Louisiana at Lafayette, 2001).

2   Westbrook, 79.

3   Ibid., 53.

4   Ibid., 139.

5   Ibid., 104.

6   Ibid. 147.

7   Ibid., 118.

especially glad to be reunited with Lucille who was a "liberated woman... (and) widely known as a gracious, witty, and inventive hostess."[1] According to William Holditch, Lucille hosted many prominent writers of the time, including Gertrude Stein, Thomas Wolfe, Tennessee Williams, and Carl Sandburg.[2] Westbrook writes that "in 1926 William Faulkner and Bill Spratling took up residence in the attic apartment of Lucille's and Marc's (Antony) home at the corner of St. Peter Street and Cabildo Alley,"[3] so Elma Godchaux was surrounded by some of the foremost writers of her time.

Sherwood Anderson and his third wife, Elizabeth, were living in that building at the time as well, and she claims in her memoir that the yacht trip described in Faulkner's *Mosquitoes* was based on an actual outing that included some of those very prominent writers, and even though the guest of honor, Anita Loos, was a no-show: "the party was set to go and so it did. Ham Basso came, with a giddy young girl. Bill Faulkner, Bill Spratling, Lillian Marcus Friend, Marc and Lucille Antony were all on board, as were several young girls Sherwood had casually asked along."[4] Although Elma Godchaux was not comfortable with the social whirl of Manhattan, she fit right in with the bohemian crowd in New Orleans. Although she never did remarry, she did seem to enjoy the company of such men as Enrique Alférez, whose sculptures grace the lakefront, City Park, and several buildings throughout the city, and Disciples of Christ preacher, Gerald L.K. Smith.[5]

"Chains" is a haunting story about a Cajun, Lurie Webre, who lives on a swamp in the shadow of "the nigger prison at Angola." It is not odd that Lurie lives on a swamp in South Louisiana, but it is odd that his swamp is surrounded on all sides by sugarcane farms, and for that he is ridiculed: "'It ain't natural or right living on stilts up here in the cane country like you was a fisherman down on the Lake front. No good's ever going to come of it.'"[6] But it costs money to drain his swamp, so Lurie feels that his father, in leaving him this land, chained him to it. He dreams of holding his beautiful neighbor, Dena Larue, or of floating off down the Mississippi. Finally, he gets a chance to prove himself to the men who belittle him constantly, by capturing one of the escaped prisoners, and in the end he discovers that "he was as free as any of them (the men in the town)."[7] Godchaux proves the maxim that there are always those less fortunate, and that reaching out to them is a way to achieve personal empowerment.

The protagonists in many of her stories lead fairly miserable lives, chained to land that is unable to support them in the manner they once knew. Though Godchaux's relationship to her family's land on their several plantations could not be more dissimilar, she is still able to create complicated characters that linger long after the story is finished.

Unfortunately, just a few years after Godchaux returned to New Orleans, she contracted diabetes which made her life much more difficult both physically and emotionally. According to Westbrook, "in her altered psychological state, Elma neglected to treat her diabetes, or to provide herself with adequate sustenance,"[8] and she died at the age of 45 on April 3, 1941.

---

1   Ibid., 128.

2   Kenneth W. Holditch. "The Brooding Air of the Past," Literary New Orleans: *Essays and Meditations,* Ed. Richard S. Kennedy (Baton Rouge: LSUP, 1992), 62-71.

3   Westbrook, 130.

4   Elizabeth Anderson, *Miss Elizabeth: A Memoir* (Boston: Little Brown, 1969), 118.

5   Westbrook, 136.

6   Ibid., 278.

7   Ibid., 297.

8   Westbrook, 149.

Chains[1]

Lurie Webre often walked along the *batture*. Sometimes he spent more than two hours there weaving in and out among the willows or sometimes just standing still looking at the river. The grass on the levee was burned the color of dry pin-oak leaves. Skinny cows and mules bunched under the shade of the trees, motionless except for their tails swinging at the bugs and horseflies. The willows and cypresses crowded together making good places to hide from the sun. Sometimes Lurie sat on a stump and kicked the pieces of dead wood at his feet to powder and watched the black ants run; the ants were fat as if they all carried eggs. Sometimes Lurie just sat and watched the river. He could see how fast it had fallen since the June rise and it was still falling. He could see the old water line and the grass above it dried and stiff as though water had never covered it. He could see across the river just as easy, the trees strung out along that *batture*. He could see the sugarhouse across the river. Seemed as if the heat brought everything close. The smokestacks and houses and trees across the river looked close enough to touch. Everything was still, like a painted picture. Nothing ever happened. Up above near where the river curved he could see the heavy brick stacks of the nigger prison at Angola. A man could get across easy swimming, Lurie thought; he knew a man could if he let himself go with the current. For a minute he imagined himself runaway. Today there was a cool and gentle mercy in the river. He could feel the water at his armpits and rifling between his toes. He felt the movement of her slow swells against his body. Under her brown skin dove-like palpitations moved. He got up grinning sheepishly. Some summer, God knows, she might tempt him. He was a fool. He turned his back. And picked his way over the trash of roots and dead leaves and rotted wood. He was very thin; his body seemed shriveled under his shirt and overall. He climbed the levee and stood for a minute on the summit picked out against the hazy blue sky. For the minute he stood there he seemed to stand against the sky. He could see the store gallery filled with men. They were chewing tobacco and jabbering. Every evening after their work was done they sat like that, chewing and jabbering. Lurie raised his head suddenly and marched towards the store. He was thinking fiercely to himself that he wasn't chained. He was as free as any of them. He had as much right as any of them to sit there chewing and jabbering. With his head high and his face flushed the least bit he marched straight to the store.

He walked up and sat on the gallery's lowest step. The talk hushed. He hated the talk hushing like that. But he pushed himself in securely and swept his eyes over the men. He wished the talk would go on. But everybody was quiet. The buzz of insects suddenly rose. A nigger in the store laughed and his laugh came out the door and seemed to poise for a long time on the dull air. The men looked at Lurie and chewed their tobacco hunks slowly and spat out to the road.

Then John Boudreaux cleared his throat and his voice breaking the stillness was like the sudden sound of something solid splashing into dead- quiet water. "Why you don't drain your swamp, Lurie, and raise cane on shares like we all do?"

Lurie answered flushing, "One of these days I'm going to drain it." His voice was heavy and rough.

"You been saying that a long time," Maxie Webre, Lurie's cousin, drawled, "you ought to be doing it soon, Lurie. It ain't natural or right living on stilts up here in the cane country like you was a fisherman down on the Lakefront."

"No good's ever going to come of it," Boudreaux put in angrily.

---

1   Elma Godchaux, "Chains," *Louisiana in the Short Story*, Ed. Lizzie Carter McVoy (Baton Rouge: LSUP, 1940), 277. Originally appeared in *Southern Review,* vol. I #4, Spring 1936, 782-98.

"Sho' ain't," another man echoed.

"You never do nothing," Maxie continued, "you're sho' one lazy Cajin, Lurie."

The men laughed. Lurie sat forward watching some dust from the road run through his fingers. The laughs hit against his face like slaps, making it burn.

"Lurie's pretty busy on the *batture* most of the time," Paul Morelle joked. "What you got on the *batture,* Lurie? You got a woman hid in the willows down there?"

The men laughed again. "Bet he has," somebody laughed.

"Come on, Lurie, ain't you?'

"The *batture* ain't nothing to visit alone and you ain't after driftwood for kindling these days."

Lurie tried to laugh too. He ducked his head and giggled. He stood up at last and looked down the road. "I reckon I better be getting home." He hesitated. "Well, so long."

He turned away. The men's eyes followed him. He tried to pretend he didn't feel those eyes on him. He spat in the dust and climbed the levee. It was nobody's business what he did on the *batture.* He spat again. He wished he could sit and jabber.

In front of him the sun was swollen and red. The waters of the river seemed to burn. The cane leaves glinted brazenly. A couple of cows passed waddling with their bags full and they shone under the heavy red hand of the sun. Niggers too slouching along. Not a breath stirred the suspended glow. Children dribbled from the houses along the way onto the steps and the yards. Lurie wiped the sweat from his face and opposite his own house turned and went slantways down the levee with his body stiffened, holding back against the stiff run of the slope. He could see all about him the spread of Mr. Labidet's cane. He stepped on to the raised plank walk that led to his door. Beneath him and all about the house was an island of swamp ground covered with wild hyacinths. The swamp seemed to take the little man and swallow him. The hyacinths bunched tightly and made what looked like solid ground of green. Here and there the sharp points of iris leaves pierced. Walking above it Lurie could see the earth between the leaves was caking in the dry heat. Bad weather for sugarcane, Lurie thought; summers ought to be hot but wet. A couple of turkey-buzzards and then more dropped down behind Lurie's house. Lurie could hear them flop down on to the ground after something dead in the leaves, a rabbit or a field rat. He looked about him. His sunken ground was always the first thing to fall away into darkness. A black hand seemed to press down on the swamp and on him too. The heaviness clamped down on his heart. It made a wall round him smooth and black. He couldn't see the house next door where Dena Larue lived; he lost the stretch of cane; he couldn't see nothing. He moved impatiently hurrying along the walk. The swamp wasn't nothing to chain a man down. He went on into the house and over the uncovered passageway to the shed where he did his cooking. He sat down at the table with a plate of cold grits and bacon. He never took much time cooking. He bent low over his plate, but not paying attention to the food, thinking. He imagined how his swamp would look covered with cane. His cane would spread evenly, continuing the rows of the other men. Nobody but himself and Hypolite Larue and Mr. Labidet would know where his fields ended and where Larue's and Mr. Labidet's took up. But he felt the iron chain of the swamp round his neck was unbreakable. He ate quickly, shoveling up the grits in big spoonfuls. A mosquito-hawk flew into the room and was whirring and bumping against the window sill. The heat hugged the shed, filling the room with a motionless pressure. Sweat dyed the shirt Lurie wore and ran down his cheeks. When he was finished eating he moved over to the sink and washed his plate and a couple of pots. Then he took up the bucket of kitchen slop and walked out the door with it, going across the swamp.

The big moon was faint in a sky still lit by the sunken sun. Lurie saw two niggers standing on the levee. They disappeared suddenly going down the slope to the *batture.* At night the niggers hid among the trees on the *batture* and made love. White folks too. Lurie's heart swung heavily. He threw the slop from his bucket into the pen for Tony Cascio's pigs. The pigs came running and grunted, gobbling the stuff. Lurie moved away, returning the way he had come across the swamp. His feet rattled the dry leaves and raised the dust. Darkness was like a contagion spreading from the swamp. But the moon had brightened and taken firmness and shape. It seemed to swing very low just above Dena's gate. And as Lurie looked, Dena was standing there lit from head to foot. He could see the lines of her body emphasized by the light from the moon. He stopped. And put his bucket down. She stood there enormous and spotlighted as if she were raised on a stage with the world about her falling away in darkness. Lurie's mouth hung open. Silence humming with insects suspended between them. Then while he stood she turned and saw him.

Her full voice swung out to him across the swamp. "Hello, Lurie. I come out, me, to see if I can't get a breath of air." He stood stupidly catching the sound of her voice and watching her. "You ain't bogged in the hyacinths, are you," she laughed.

He moved towards her, dragging his feet and wiping his hands off inside his pockets.

"Our sheet-iron roof makes our house hot as a oven," she continued.

He could see her firm breasts move as she breathed and her breath pushed against his cheeks. He stood before her, not speaking.

He made her feel uncomfortable, not saying a word, "Well, Lurie." She cleared her throat. "Ain't you begun draining yet?" She was always teasing him.

He looked at her earnestly. "No, but it's easy enough to drain. All you have to do is fill in a little and cut quarter drains the same as you do sugar land."

"Whyn't you do it?"

"I'm going to do it."

"I reckon it costs money."

"Oh not much," he assured her in his masculine voice.

"You're always talking about draining," she said, "but you never do nothing."

"After this grinding," he interrupted quickly, "I'm going to do something." His thin serious face thrust towards her, very white, washed with sweat. But her head was raised. He couldn't see her eyes. She looked at something beyond him. He wanted to reach her.

Then above his head her voice suddenly belled, "Oh hello."

Lurie jumped. A hand fell on his shoulder and Maxie's voice sounded close to his ear. "Well, if it ain't little Lurie." The blood burned Lurie's face. "What you all jabbering about?"

"Lurie's swamp," Dena explained.

Lurie coughed.

"Speaking of draining, hunh," Maxie asked with laughs in his voice. "I'm going to drain," Lurie cried.

"You got to fill in plenty," Maxie observed. "Well," he broke off, "come on, Dena."

They moved off together quickly, the darkness mingling their two figures.

Then Dena called back, "So long, Lurie."

Lurie swallowed. "So long."

He heard them in the dry grass going up the levee. He felt hollow, like an old man. He licked his thin lips. Maxie thought he knew everything. He made Dena think it too. Lurie knew there were lots of secret things nobody knew, neither Maxie or Boudreaux. Lurie's feet dragged along the walk. He couldn't make headway against the darkness. It was like Dena's presence, so full of life it pushed aside his own. He felt helpless. There was something everlasting about these things, as everlasting as this swamp that had always been, a dark interruption in the even sweep of the cane. When the hyacinths bloomed, the pale flowers did not erase the desolation that hovered over the sunken ground. When Lurie was a child he used to give the place a wide berth. But now it had caught him. The swamp was his. His father had left it to him. Sometimes he got to thinking he was the swamp's. He ducked his head entering his doorway. A big deer's antler was nailed above it. He wished folks could have heard the strong bang of his gun that had dropped the deer. Sometimes little men did big things. Dena and Maxie were on the *batture*. Maxie carried Dena off easy. Maxie was always doing something, talking at the store or making grinding at Labidet's sugarhouse or working his own fields, plowing or planting or laying by. He kept busy all the time. Lurie pouted and thought of himself and his father, who had bought this swamp off a nigger and was going to plant the low ground in rice and hadn't ever done it.

Lurie didn't light the lamp on the table. He dragged his cot from the hot wall between the two doors where there might be a draft. He got into bed naked and drew the sheet over him. He squashed a mosquito on his forehead. The voice of Tony Cascio's wife came to him faintly. It was far away. He closed his eyes. He held Dena's hand. A pulse beat in her hand; it beat like a bird's excited heart. Big blobs of sweat stood up on his pale forehead and his body lying irreguarly on the bed with the sheet thrown back looked as if it had been hurled down furiously. But he slept with his lips spread in a smile.

In summers Lurie never had anything much to do. The sugarhouse was closed and Lurie had plenty of time to think. He fed Tony Cascio's shoats and did odd jobs for the dago. But he had plenty of time on his hands. He walked along the top of the levee now with his hands in his pockets, thinking. It was after midday and a hard glare was settled down on the land. The fat sides of the levee looked white. Dust mingled with the bright haze and covered everything, houses, fence rails, cane leaves. The dust's hot dry taste was always in Lurie's mouth. He could feel the sweat running down inside his loose shirt and trousers. Tony Cascio was in his yard hitching his horse. His littlest kid sat on the step hugging a coon. The Cascios kept all kinds of animals. Their yard was all cluttered up with chickens and a couple of goats and pigs. Lurie passed a couple of niggers sitting below him on the fence beside the road doing nothing. They looked calm and comfortable. Niggers were like that; they didn't like to worry. Lurie liked niggers. Before he came to the store he ducked down the levee. He wound in and out among the trees until he stood beside the river. He stood with his legs spread watching it. He watched steadfastly. His eyes went up and down it. It lapped lazily at his feet, winding slowly past the solid walls of Angola prison and past all the places Lurie knew. He sat down at last on a cypress stump, took out his pocket knife, and began whittling a stick. He wished he could do something. He didn't like to whittle all day. He looked at the river seeking something; he didn't know what. Sometimes he shook his head. Sometimes he spat as if getting ready to say something. One night, he thought, he ought to come out and take a bath in the river naked. It would be heathen to do that he knew. But he bet it would be nice, the heavy cool water wrapping round him. He stopped whittling and with his elbows on his knees squinted out over the river. He wished it would take him away. When he heard somebody walking on the levee he lifted his head and listened. He didn't want anybody to see him. He ought not to be sitting by himself like this doing nothing but whittling and studying. He kept thinking he had to have considerable money to drain his swamp. He knew he was a good man in the sugarhouse grinding; he was worth some money to Mr. Labidet. But Mr. Labidet said money didn't grow on the trees. That was exactly what Mr. Labidet had said. Lurie remembered every word. Mr. Labidet was painting his mule stable and Lurie found him in the mule yard. Some niggers were on ladders and with their arms spread painting the wall they looked as if they were stretched on crosses. Lurie remembered the manure pile in the yard and the flies swarming above it. Lurie had coughed and wiped the sweat off his face and watched Mr. Labidet and not known how to begin. He coughed again and stumbled over his words. He wanted to raise cane on shares like the other men did. If his wages were a little higher he could drain his swamp. Could Mr. Labidet raise him? He was a good man at the centrifugals. Would Mr. Labidet raise him? "But, Lurie," Mr. Labidet said, "money don't grow on trees. Don't you know we don't need any more land in cane? Raising cane in Louisiana is too expensive. You men don't use your heads. That's why you all never get on. Money don't grow on the trees." That's why Lurie didn't get on. Money didn't grow on trees. The river lapped at Lurie's feet. Money don't grow on trees. Leaves are on the trees. Not money, Lurie. God, he wished the river would hush. When he had left Labidet's mule stable he had passed Boudreaux's house where by the gate a white rag was tied on a pole stuck into the roadside. Zillah Boudreaux was going to have a baby and the white rag was the signal for the doctor. That flag, Lurie felt, was the sign of John Boudreaux's manhood. It would never fly for him. He couldn't do nothing. He hung round all summer and fed the dago's pigs and sat whittling by the river like a nigger. He felt hollow, emptied of manhood. His heart swung in the empty cavity of his body. No, the flag would never fly for him. But it would for Dena. And in the hot weather Dena would sit in the open doorway nursing her baby. When the baby was full she would spread her knees and lay it across her lap. When it fretted she would pat it and nestle it at her breast again, and Lurie would hear the little thing sucking. It finished and Dena bent over the child before her dress was hooked and her full white breast hung loose for the minute she bent and tended to it. Lurie felt filled with his feelings. Blood throbbed in his head and cheeks. He was a good man at the centrifugals; he knew he was. Mr. Labidet forgot. He only remembered money didn't grow on.... Oh shut up about that. A man at the centrifugals had to be strong to shove the door against the heavy flow of the sugar., Lurie didn't look strong. But he was. Nobody could see his strength. The hot sugar was browner than the river and moved faster. The river moved so slowly you had to watch it before you noticed its motion. Then you saw it sliding away. Lurie felt himself going with it, slipping by all the things he knew surrounded by the broad sheet of its protection. He sat for a long time leaning on his elbows, holding the knife and the whittled stick and feeling the water's cool stroking. He didn't know what time it was. The mosquitoes were right bad. Cows were moving by him up the levee. He felt his empty stomach. But he wasn't lonesome. He grinned; he was lazy as a nigger. Then he heard noises, a horse galloping and some men's voices calling out. He got up. And listened. Then wove his way quickly through the litter of leaves and wood and dung to the levee top. He saw a commotion of horses and people before the store. He hurried down the levee and along the road.

Niggers were standing on the edges of the crowd staring and listening. A nigger on the gallery was leaning on a broom with his eyes big. John Boudreaux stood on the top step. Lurie saw Maxie and men from a good distance away in the crowd. Little Lurie pushed himself among them and got as near the gallery as he could. Nobody noticed him. Folks looked over his head gesturing and talking.

Boudreaux spat a swift jet of tobacco juice past Lurie to the road and wiped his mouth. "You all with horses get started now," he called; "I'll meet you later on with what dogs I can get."

"I thought you said the prison man brought down dogs," Maxie called from the road.

"I did say so," Boudreaux answered, "but it ain't going to hurt how many dogs we got."

The niggers' eyes were spreading; they were white; they looked like big marbles. Lurie listened.

"Sho' it ain't going to hurt," Maxie shot back to Boudreaux. "Sho' not," men echoed. Lurie cleared his throat to speak. But Boudreaux's voice drowned out everything. "The prison man said he was going to lay back on the edge of the woods near the drainage machine. He's there now I reckon waiting for what men he can get. The nigger's bound to come out the woods sooner or later likely near the drainage machine where he might think he could get in touch with some other nigger."

"Huh-hunh."

"What," stammered Lurie, "what's wrong?"

Maxie grabbed his gaze away.

Lurie tried a nigger standing near him. "What, what's the matter?" The nigger made as if he didn't hear the question; he listened to the talk swinging back and forth.

"They sho' he's in the woods back yonder," somebody asked. "Sho'. The dogs smelled him."

"If we all know how to hunt," explained Boudreaux, "we can round him out at the drainage machine where the guard is waiting."

"It'll be easy."

Lurie pushed up the gallery steps to the nigger with the broom; he knew the nigger. "What's the matter? What's wrong," he pressed.

"Nigger murderer run off from Angola," the nigger whispered, "he in the woods back yonder." The big white eyes slid away to Maxie who was talking.

"Dust'll muffle the horses' hoofs. That nigger ain't going to know nothing until we got the handcuffs on him."

"Sho' ain't."

Laughs broke out. The men moved.

"How much'd you say the reward was?"

"Twenty-five dollars. Twenty-five dollars is plenty enough for a nigger."

"Sho'. That's enough." Lurie's eyes were big. A couple of horses started from the crowd and the men turned in their saddles. "So long."

"So long."

Dust flew up making a thick screen for the riders.

"I'm getting on home so I can get ready," Maxie announced, "I wouldn't miss it, me, for nothing, hunting a nigger with dogs. I don't care so much for the reward as hunting the nigger."

"I reckon be there," Lurie said suddenly. The words choked him. But he had to say them. This was his chance. He had to go. Maybe he'd catch the nigger.

Maxie who was moving off stopped and grinned. Chuckles rippled over the gallery and on to the road. Lurie dipped his head. "Whyn't you look for the nigger in your own swamp, Lurie?"

"Oh Lord," sputtered somebody.

"Yes, why don't you?"

Even the niggers grinned.

"I've hunted before this," Lurie announced in that stubborn voice of his, "none of you all ain't hunted more than me."

"You ought to know that hunting bear and deer or rabbit is different from hunting nigger," asserted Maxie.

"Sho'," everybody agreed, "that's so."

"Reckon, me, I can make out with a nigger same as the rest," Lurie argued.

"Oh you ain't got no horse, Lurie."

"No. How you going without a horse?"

"Sho'. You can't go."

Lurie seemed to wilt. His head hung. He wiped his face.

"Well," Boudreaux began, "we all better be getting started. The nigger ain't going to sit round waiting."

The crowd began to spread out and thin. A few of the men made new groups and huddled together talking. A man on horseback turned and laughed towards Lurie.

Lurie walked off. He could hear the talk going on behind his back. He wished he could catch the nigger. God, he wished he could. Twenty-five dollars was a good lot of money. He'd start right off draining. He'd march the nigger to the store. He reckoned they would run a column about it in the parish paper. "Lurie Webre Catches Nigger Murderer," it would say, and in smaller letters, "without a horse Lurie brings in big buck nigger that murdered several nigger field hands." God. If he only could. But nobody could get back behind to the drainage machine without a horse. He could see the men standing round listening to the way he had caught the nigger; Maxie and Boudreaux were there. Little men could do big things. Maybe he could borrow Tony's horse. The dago never bothered much with what was going on. Lurie hurried. He didn't intend to meet the other men. He was going off alone. A whole bunch of horses would be bound to make some noise. He stopped at Tony's gate. He put his hand on the latch. He stopped dead staring. Tony was under a chinaberry tree settling the saddle on his horse. The scene etched itself sharply on Lurie's sight. He would never forget it. It burned into him like a sharp tragedy, a killing being enacted before his eyes, Tony's kids standing round watching, the littlest one still hugging the coon, and Tony himself reaching for the saddle girth under the horse's belly and tightening it so that he jerked the horse up with the strap. Tony swung himself to the horse's back and came towards Lurie. Lurie didn't move. He stood watching the horse and rider, spellbound, as if he expected something extraordinary to happen. But nothing did. Cascio called out as he went by. Lurie licked his dry lips and sank down on the side of the levee.

A group of horsemen loped by him, a strong army of horses and men. He didn't raise his head; he stared between his legs at the grass. He wasn't thinking. He was just sitting there lost. Sometimes he raised his hand and slapped at the mosquitoes and a horsefly that kept buzzing about his head. When he looked up he saw the dust settled like a thick scum on the hyacinth leaves. He didn't move. He was chained. Then Dena came out and stood in her yard looking at him. So he got up and started home.

She called to him. "Hello, Lurie. Ain't you going on the hunt?"

"I don't reckon so," he answered, "I been away on business and I ain't ate all day."

He could hardly see her. A mist swung between his eyes and her. A wagon jolted by and the wagon's noise got between him and Dena. He kept fighting to hold her and his senses kept losing her. "I wonder who's going to catch the nigger," she was saying, "I reckon Maxie will."

Bright strips of color stretched across the sky where the sun was sinking.

"I'm right scared of the nigger," Dena went on; "a nigger murderer, you can't tell what they'll do."

"He ain't going to do nothing," Lurie said in his slow rough voice; "there ain't nothing to be scared of."

"Well, it's sho' scary," Dena insisted, "with all the men away." Lurie cleared his throat. "It ain't a bit. Likely the nigger ain't as bad as he sounds."

"Anyway I don't feel safe," she asserted, "with him around. I sho' hope Maxie catches him." She paused and swung at the mosquitoes. "The mosquitoes are eating me up and I reckon you're tired and hongry if you been away all day so say goodnight. Goodnight."

"Goodnight."

He moved away. Then stopped and called. "You don't have to be scared of nothing, Dena."
She was gone into the house.

He kept on across the swamp. Beyond the gloomy hollow of his ground there were house lights, Tony Cascio's chickens settled in the chinaberry trees making dark lumps along the branches. A dog barked and a couple of the chicken lumps moved, spreading their wings. Then everything settled again into quietness and that steady buzzing that seemed only the voice of quietness. A big moon was swinging over the levee. Lurie felt the heat coming out of the ground. He was dead-tired.

He lit the lamp and pulled out the bed, went to the kitchen shed and drank a glass of milk. He brought a loaf of bread back to the bedroom and chewed on it while he undressed. Moths and bugs flew about the light. Sometimes a creature landed on the strip of fly-paper hanging from the ceiling. Lurie sat down on the bed, took off his shoes and scratched his toes. He stopped. Listened. His toes stiffened. He stood up listening. Something rustled the hyacinth leaves. He moved to the door. Darkness stretched everywhere and silence. He tried to puncture the darkness and the stillness. Lightning-bugs kept rising and falling and things kept humming. Lurie pushed his head into the darkness. Then he turned from the door, thinking some animal had been hunting in the leaves. He blew out the light and got into bed. He closed his eyes. He might as well sleep. He couldn't do nothing. He kept his eyes shut. He wished his world would slide away. He wished the river would carry him off. God, he wished he could skim away. He wished he wasn't chained. Wished he was sitting at the store, spitting and swapping talk. Wished he could bring the nigger back. God, he wished he could. His closed eyes saw Dena's light go out. He moved. He hoped she wasn't scared. He wished he could shoot the nigger. He heard his gun go off. He wished the men could hear. He wished he could scream so they could hear. He screamed. He screamed again. He felt the agony of the scream constricting his throat. Then the pain eased off him and he was dropping into the nothingness of dreamless sleep. A fly landed on his face. But he didn't know it. Then suddenly he felt himself swing plummet on the string of a noise. The next minute he was awake. He sat up. He was icy cold. He stared and listened. He couldn't hear a thing, just the frogs and crickets singing. His sweat was cold. He heard the noise. It sounded like feet thumping on to the ground from the height of, say, a fence. It came, faint, from Tony Cascio's pig pen. Lurie heard it just there. Then it dropped away into stillness. He slipped out of bed. Put his pants on. No lights showed anywhere. He got his gun from the shelf; he had to stand on a chair to reach it. He stuffed the cartridges into his pocket and crept out the doorway.

The moon had slid down behind the levee. Lurie cut through the swamp towards Cascio's pig pen, picking his steps so they wouldn't rattle the leaves and loading his gun. He made for the big hackberry tree standing on the edge of the swamp. He peeped round it at the pen. Everywhere quiet. The stillness stretched over the pen where the two old sows were lying against the fence asleep and the boar was nosing some slop. Lurie kept staring into the thin darkness. Earth was quiet as the broad dim arch of sky. Lurie could hear himself breathing. Then he lowered his gun and grinned. He was glad nobody saw him like this, foolishly searching the darkness. He tried to hide his gun behind him as he tiptoed away. He spat, a little sick. He was a fool.

Night was passing into day. The moon was fading out. An old white mule was standing on the levee. It took no notice of Lurie. Lurie went on down the levee to the *batture.* He went slowly with his head hanging thinking he was a fool. He reckoned he'd been dreaming about a noise and there wasn't no noise really. He was nearly to his stump when he knew somebody was watching him. The nigger was sitting with his knees drawn up and his back against the stump. He must have just waked. Lurie raised the gun. And the nigger's eyes were big looking right into the barrel. His mouth hung down.

Whispers came from him. "Don't shoot, don't shoot, boss."

Lurie kept the gun pointing and his heart kept beating, choking him with thanks. Moss and twigs were stuck in the nigger's wool and his face was marked with welts and clotted blood.

"Get up," commanded Lurie, "and you make a try to escape, I'll shoot you where you stand."

"Yes sir." The nigger got up stiffly.

He was a big nigger. His hands hanging by his sides looked swollen. He was almost naked. But Lurie could see part of his pants clinging to him were convict-striped. Lurie trembled. He coughed, choking a little. "How'd you get here, nigger?"

"On the river, boss."

Lurie stared at the nigger unbelieving. Then his eyes went to the river and his heart kept praising Jesus. The river was unchaining him like he knew it could. It was as if it were taking him away. Its gentle touch pushed him on. He caught himself up. He was the same old fool. He was arresting the nigger murderer; he ought to remember that. Folks would be stirring soon. He wanted to wait until folks were in their yards feeding their animals and the men began to straggle back from the woods. He was going to keep the nigger just in front of the gun when he marched him to the store. But nobody was stirring yet. He had to kill time.

"How'd you get here on the *batture*, nigger? I thought you was back yonder in the woods." God, Lurie thought, he was a big nigger. Folks wouldn't know how Lurie had caught such a big one.

"I ain't never been in the woods," the nigger was saying, "I know the woods is the first place they hunts a man. I been in that swamp yonder. I knows folks steers clear of a big old swamp like that one yonder." The nigger pouted. He watched the gun. "I was hunting something to eat and resting up," he went on mournfully, "before I took to the river again."

"Wasn't you scared of that swamp," Lurie asked, killing time.

"No, boss," the nigger answered, "I ain't scared of no swamp. I ain't scared of nothing 'cept a gun."

Lurie steadied the gun.

"It was sho' nice on the river," the nigger went on in his slow mournful voice, remembering. "I floated down on sticks and truck. Reckon I was going to be in New Orleans soon. But I got hongry." His voice fell and died. Then he began again, "the river sho' was nice lifting me up by the arms and legs. I felt safe like I was in my mamma's lap. It was cool too. When my head got hot I dove it under the water and the river kept toting me away from trouble."

The nigger's voice was low. Lurie could hardly hear it. But he bet he knew how nice the river felt. Seemed as if he instead of the nigger was floating away. He felt the water soft against him. It had touched the nigger like that. Lurie knew he would kill the man who recalled him from so cool an escape. He felt how his heart would swing a dead weight in his chest while he shot to kill. But the nigger didn't try to harm him. The nigger's heart must be heavy. He stood there studying the river, thinking yesterday he had floated down. He looked like he was about to cry. It was getting late. Lurie had to march him to the store.

"Come on, nigger," ordered Lurie, "time to get started. March straight ahead."

The nigger turned in front of Lurie. They started off. The nigger went slowly dragging his feet. Lurie kept close to the nigger pointing his gun. They twisted round the trees. A horse loped by on the levee. It struck its hoofs sharply on the path. Lurie looked up. The man on its back was a heavy lump joggled by the horse's motion. Lurie stared. The lump looked sodden, without feelings. Lurie knew he wasn't jerked up and down without will. He was different from that thing on horseback. He moved by himself. He was free. He did what he wanted. He didn't have to listen to every black lump on horseback. He had a mind of his own. That lump was Boudreaux or Maxie. Lurie felt choked. He was full of a burning assurance.

"Wait a minute, nigger." The nigger turned. Lurie looked at him. The nigger was his nigger. Nobody couldn't tell him what to do with his nigger. He was a big nigger too.

"Go on," Lurie cried suddenly, "go on, nigger, get in the river." The nigger stared.

"Go on," Lurie repeated, "get in." He was going to unchain the big nigger. The nigger was going to float away. After the dry yard of Angola prison the river felt cool, Lurie bet. Lurie did what he wanted to do. He was a free man, thank God.

"Don't you hear me, nigger," he cried; "get in the river."

The nigger didn't move. He stared. His eyes bulged; they looked like beads sewed in a doll's head.

"You ain't deaf, are you, nigger? Go on."

The nigger dropped on his knees. "Lord Jesus, Lord Jesus, boss, you going to kill me. You going to kill me when my head is bobbing on the water. Lord Jesus, boss. Please."

"Get in." Lurie shoved the nigger with the gun. "Get in the water, you. Make haste. Folks going to see you. Get in, I tell you. Get in."

The nigger fell on the ground. Lurie pushed him with the muzzle of the gun. The nigger rolled over, over leaves and twigs and dung, bruising himself against stumps. The gun kept nudging him. Over and over. He splashed into the water. He kept his head under.

Lurie could see the waves running above the nigger's body where he was swimming under water. When he came up for air he was far out, nearly in the middle of the stream. Lurie waved. He watched until he couldn't see the nigger any longer. He turned away slowly—he was smiling—and hunted in the bushes for a place to hide his gun. He stuck it under some branches and covered it with leaves. He didn't want folks joking him for carrying a gun. He patted the branches into place over it. When he walked up the levee he was still smiling and his heart kept beating thanks. He went slowly, a little man looking shriveled under his loose clothes. He carried his head hanging in his usual way. But he didn't feel the same. When men on horseback passed him he raised his head. He was as free as any of them.

William Faulkner (1897–1962)

Like many Mississippians even today, William Faulkner had come down to New Orleans on road trips with his friends to enjoy the many pleasures that the city has to offer, but he also had another connection to the city. He was greatly intrigued by the literary scene in New Orleans, and according to Faulkner biographer, Joseph Blotner, Faulkner went to New Orleans "to be with people that have the same problems and the same interests as him, that won't laugh at what he says no matter how foolish it might sound to the Philistine."[1] In 1922, his second published poem, "Portrait," appeared in *The Double Dealer*. His only other work published outside of the Ole Miss newspaper, *The Mississippian*, was the poem "L'Apres-Midi d'un Faune" which appeared in *The New Republic* in 1922. After his brief stay in New Orleans in 1924, Sherwood Anderson would persuade him to turn his hand to writing prose.

By all accounts, by the time Faulkner did come to New Orleans to write, his friends and family were concerned that he was aimlessly drifting, drinking too much, and wasting his talent. So his trip to the city and to meet Sherwood Anderson was fortuitous, and Faulkner's writing career took off in earnest, even if the excessive drinking, which the city is known to encourage, did not stop. Faulkner's father, with whom he had long had a strained relationship, wrote of his eldest son that "William is in New Orleans & doing well... has had a book of Poems published—expects to go abroad this year—"[2] after Faulkner's first book, *The Marble Faun*, was published by The Four Seas Company in 1921.

William Faulkner was born to Murry Cuthbert and Maud Butler Faulkner on September 25, 1897, in New Albany, Mississippi. He was the oldest of four boys and his mother's favorite. When Faulkner was five years old, the family moved to Oxford, Mississippi, a town made famous by his having lived there. Faulkner was admittedly not a very diligent student and by high school was more interested in sports than academics, so he dropped out in the 11th grade. Nonetheless, he would further develop his love for literature that his mother Maude instilled in him and forge lifelong friendships in school that would shape both his writing career and private life. While in school, he met Estelle Oldham, who would later become his wife, and Faulkner also met Phil Stone, who attended Ole Miss and who shared his love for literature. Stone would later be instrumental in getting Faulkner's *Marble Faun* published.

Some of Faulkner's most difficult years came after he dropped out of school. For one thing, Estelle Oldham was engaged and finally married the wealthy and dashing Cornell Franklin, as per her family's wishes, and the couple then moved to Hawaii, leaving Faulkner devastated. Phil Stone, who had moved on to Yale law school, knew that Faulkner was depressed and had ramped up his drinking, so he invited him up to New Haven for a visit. There they hatched a plan for Faulkner to enlist in the Canadian Royal Air Force (CRAF), since the United States Army's Signal Corps had rejected him "as too short and too light."[3]

Even though Faulkner served only about six months with the CRAF, never saw any action, and probably never even flew a plane, that is not the experience he described to others. In fact, by the time he got to New Orleans in 1924, he was using a cane and walking with a limp, which he attributed to a plane wreck on a mission for the RAF in France, a myth that Sherwood Anderson fictionalized in his story "A Meeting South."

After his experience with the CRAF, Faulkner returned to Oxford, entered Ole Miss for a time, but other than publishing some of his writing in the school newspaper, *The Mississippian*, he did little better academically than he had in high school. In 1924, he decided to sail to Europe, but first he wanted to go to New Orleans to meet Sherwood Anderson, whom he greatly admired and whose wife had once hired him in New York, when she managed Doubleday Books.

Once in New Orleans, Faulkner not only met Anderson, but many of the city's literary set, including Basil Thompson, Albert Goldstein, and Julius Friend, founding editors of *The Double Dealer*, and John McClure,

---

1   Most of the biographical information here is from Joseph Blotner, *Faulkner, A Biography, One-Volume Edition* (New York: Random House, 1984).

2   Ibid., 122.

3   Ibid., 60.

literary editor of the *Times-Picayune*. In 1925, Faulkner began contributing to both rags regularly. *The Double Dealer* published his piece, "New Orleans," which was comprised of eleven short character sketches, some of which he expanded for his longer "The Mirrors of Chartres Street" series published that same year in the *Times-Picayune*, whose title is a play on the "Mirrors of Washington" column which also appeared in the *Times-Picayune*, and Harold Begbie's *Mirrors of Downing Street*, a popular work that described the goings on in British politics.[1] All Faulkner's pieces were collected in *New Orleans Sketches* (1958), edited and with an introduction by Carvel Collins, the man whom Eudora Welty met in New Orleans and who is reportedly the inspiration for her short story "No Place for You, My Love."[2]

Three brief "New Orleans" character sketches are included here, "The Cobbler," "The Kid Learns" and "Out of Nazareth." In his introduction, Collins states that Faulkner spent the thirty years after penning these pieces "developing many of the themes, techniques, thoughts, and feelings which appeared in these apprentice sketches,"[3] which is most apparent in both "The Cobbler" and "The Kid learns."

The short "New Orleans" character sketches focus on local New Orleanians, like "The Cop" or "The Longshoreman," but he opens with "Wealthy Jew" and ends with "The Tourist." So he is concerned with several "types" that make up the city, from priest to prostitute, immigrant to beggar, but most often the disenfranchised.

The four-paragraph piece, "The Cobbler," describes one of those "types," a poor old Tuscan cobbler who pines for the young love he lost long ago. We learn that the poor cobbler lost his love to "a grand signor in velvet with rings of pure gold—like a lord... with his dark, proud look, line a thin sword in a velvet sheath." While this now humble cobbler was a young goatherd in Tuscany, his lover chided him on his "backwardness in the dance" and on the way he "labored and saved," instead of learning to dance. So when the dashing stranger came to town, the young lover watched helplessly as they "danced as none of that village had ever danced," and that night the goatherd fled to foreign shores.

In "The Kid Learns," a "young tough" falls instantly for a young, blonde beauty who he is unable to resist, even to his own peril. Even more striking is Faulkner's use of internal monologue, which he later perfects in the form of stream of consciousness in his novels *The Sound and the Fury* and *As I Lay Dying*.

Of the other "Mirrors of Chartres Street" sketches, again Faulkner often turns to the disenfranchised as he does in the title story about a crippled beggar who gets arrested for vagrancy in "Out of Nazareth." The protagonist, David, is "hungry, but there was nothing of the beggar in him." In fact, this is a vagrant who refuses to take money from the two men who offer it, and in this case the two men are Faulkner and Bill Spratling, Faulkner's artist friend whom he names in this story.

Faulkner left with Spratling for Europe in July of 1925, and the last of the sketches appeared in the newspaper in the fall of that year while Faulkner was living in Paris, and that is where he learned that his novel *Mayday* would be published under the new title, *Soldiers' Pay*. While in New Orleans, Sherwood Anderson said he would convince his own publisher, Horace Liveright, to publish *Soldiers' Pay*, "so long as I don't have to read his damn manuscript."[4] Of course, Faulkner went on to eclipse Anderson in the literary world, and though he did return to New Orleans for a time, he moved to Oxford, Mississippi, married his long time love, Estelle Oldham Franklin after her divorce, and they set up house in Rowan Oak, where he died in 1962.

The Cobbler[5]

Y ou wan' getta thees shoe today? Si, si. Yes, I coma from-tella in my tongue? Buono signor.

Yes, I come from Tuscany, from the mountains, where the plain is gold and brown in the barren

---

1   Carvel Collins, Introduction to William Faulkner, *New Orleans Sketches* (New Brunswick, NJ: Rutgers University Press, 1958).

2   Faulkner's *New Orleans Sketches* was reprinted in 2002 by the University Press of Mississippi.

3   Collins, 34.

4   Blotner, 146.

5   All three of the sketches collected here are from: William Faulkner, *New Orleans Sketches* (New Brunswick, NJ:

sun, and the ancient hills brood bluely above the green and dreaming valleys. How long? Ah, who knows? I am very old: I have forgotten much.

When I was young I lived much in the sun, tending goats. The people of my village labored among the vineyards sprawled upon the slopes drinking up the sun; as I followed my flocks I could see them, the bright colors, and hear the faint, sweet singing like the broken flight of golden birds. I munched my bread and cheese at noon, and drowsed among the sun-swelled rocks until the air and heat and silence sent me to swim in warm slumber. And always at sunset an ancient father of goats roused me with his cold nose.

And she was young also. Almost daily we met among the hills, I with my goats and she having slipped away from her set tasks, to idle in the sweet sun. How like a little goat she was, leaping chasms at which I paused, taking what pleasure the day offered, knowing that punishment awaited her for slipping away, knowing that she could slip away again on the morrow. And so it was.

And ah, how she bloomed; how, when we both become older, how the eyes of the young men did follow her. But I had not been idle: I had labored, I had goats of my own; and so we were promised: it was all arranged. She no longer climbed the morning hill with me now. She must remain at home, baking and making cheeses of goats' milk, treading out the grapes in the autumn, staining her sweet white feet with the sunned purple juice, as though the dear Christ Himself had bathed her feet in His own dear blood, as I would gladly have done.

And on the feast days, in her scarlet kerchief, how she shone among the others! Her tossing hair in the dance, her sweet wild breasts arbored amid her hair! It is no wonder, signor, that the young men panted and wept for her, for where in our valley, in all the world, was her equal? But we were promised: it was all arranged.

After the fiddles were silent and the sun had dropped beyond the dreaming purple hills and the bells chimed across the dusk like the last golden ray of the sun broken and fallen echoed among the rocks, we often walked. The belled flocks were stilled and candles guttered gold about the supper tables, and we walked hand in hand while the stars came out so big, so near—it is not like that in your America, signor.

She often chided me on my backwardness in the dance or with the girls-how I labored and saved, and at the dancing looked but diffidently on while others danced and wooed her in their colored shirts and copper flashing rings. And she often teased me, saying that one of her beauty deserved better than I. With which I agreed, for where in our valley was her equal? But we were promised. Am I married? No, signor. The saints had willed otherwise. She?... (I am old: I forget easily.) Ah. There was one came to our village; a grand signor in velvet and with rings of pure gold—like a lord he was, with his dark, proud look, like a thin sword in a velvet sheath. He, too, saw her upon the green, saw her like a sweet music one has forgot, and he, too, became as the other young men. And she, when she saw that grand one with eyes for none save her, she danced as none of that village had ever danced. They who watched were hushed as though they had looked briefly into heaven, for she was like the music of a hundred fiddles become one white and scarlet flame, she was like to make the sleeping saints in heaven wake sad, and know not why. But what would you? He wore velvet, and his rings were of pure gold. But then, we were promised.

That night, amid the hills where I walked, the great stars were loud as bells in the black sky, loud as great golden-belled sheep cropping the hill of heaven, like the great old ones among goats who had seen much sorrow, and still browsed on. But soon the night was gone away, and the stars were gone, and the hills were azure and gold in the morning. And there, in the dust beneath her window, where I was wont to pause briefly of a morning, was this yellow rose. It was not then as it is now: now it is old and black and twisted, as I am; but then it was green and fresh and young. Yes, I have kept it. When she returns she will doubtless desire me to have kept it; had I not kept it, she will be sad. And it has well repaid me: yearly it

Rutgers University Press, 1958).

renews itself-like this. The saints are very good.

What? Was I sad? I do not know. I have known joy and sorrow, but now I do not remember. I am very old: I have forgotten much. You getta thees shoe today. Si, si.

The Kid Learns

Competition is everywhere: competition makes the world go round. Not love, as some say. Who would want a woman nobody else wanted? Not me. And not you. And not Johnny. Same way about money. If nobody wanted the stuff, it wouldn't be worth fighting for. But more than this is being good in your own line, whether it is selling aluminum or ladies' underwear or running whiskey, or what. Be good, or die.

"Listen," said Johnny, tilted back against the wall in his chair, "a man ain't only good in our business because he'd get his otherwise, he's good because he wants to be a little better than the best, see?"

"Sure," said his friend Otto, sitting beside him, not moving.

"Anybody can keep from getting bumped off. All you gotta do is get took on a street gang or as a soda squirt. What counts is being good as you can—being good as any of 'em. Getting yours or not getting yours just shows how good you are or how good you ought to of been."

"Sure," agreed his friend Otto, tilting forward his brief derby and spitting.

"Listen, I ain't got nothing against the Wop, see; but he sets hisself up as being good and I sets myself up as being good, and some day we got to prove between us which is the best."

"Yeh," said Otto, rolling a slender cigarette and flicking a match on his thumb nail, "but take your time. You're young, see; and he's an old head at this. Take your time. Get some age onto you and I'm playing you on the nose at any odds. They wasn't no one ever done a better job in town than the way you taken that stuff away from him last week, but get some age onto you before you brace him, see? I'm for you: you know damn well."

"Sure," said Johnny in his turn, "I ain't no fool. Gimme five years, though, and it'll be Johnny Gray, with not even the bulls to remember the Wop. Five years, see?"

"That's the kid. They ain't nothing to complain, the way we done lately. Let her ride as she lays, and when the time comes we'll clean 'em all."

"And he's right," thought Johnny, walking down the street. "Take time, and get yourself good. They ain't nobody good from the jump; you got to learn to be good. I ain't no fool, I got sense enough to lay off the Wop until the time comes. And when it does—good night."

He looked up and his entrails became briefly cold—not with fear, but with the passionate knowledge of what was some day to be. Here was the Wop in an identical belted coat and Johnny felt a sharp envy in spite of himself. They passed; Johnny nodded, but the other only jerked a casual, patronizing finger at him. Too proud to look back, he could see in his mind the swagger of the other's revealed shoulders and the suggestion of a bulge over his hip. Some day! Johnny swore beneath his breath, and he ached for that day.

Then he saw her.

Down the street she came, swinging her flat young body with all the awkward grace of youth, swinging her thin young arms; beneath her hat he saw hair neither brown nor gold, and gray eyes. Clean as a colt she swung past him, and turning to follow her with his eyes and all the vague longing of his own youth, he saw the Wop step gracefully out and accost her.

Saw her recoil, and saw the Wop put his hand on her arm. And Johnny knew that that thing he had wanted to wait for until his goodness was better had already come. The Wop had prisoned both her arms when he thrust between them, but he released his grasp in sheer surprise on recognizing Johnny.

"Beat it," commanded Johnny coldly.

"Why, you poor fish, whatayou mean? You talking to me?"

"Beat it, I said," Johnny repeated.

"You little ——," and the older man's eyes grew suddenly red, like a rat's. "Don't you know who I am?" He thrust Johnny suddenly aside and again grasped the girl's arm. The back of her hand was pressed against her mouth and she was immovable with fear. When he touched her she screamed, Johnny leaped and struck the Wop on his unguarded jaw, and she fled down the street, wailing. Johnny's pistol was out and he stood over the felled man as Otto ran up.

"My God!" Otto shouted, "you've done it now!" He dragged a weighted bit of leather from his pocket. "I don't dast croak him here. I'll put him out good, and you beat it, get out of town, quick!" He tapped the still groggy man lightly and ran. "Beat it quick, for God's sake!" he cried over his shoulder. But Johnny had already gone after the girl, and a policeman, running heavily, appeared.

Before a darkened alleyway he overtook her. She had stopped, leaning against the wall with her face in the crook of her arm, gasping and crying. When he touched her she screamed again, whirling and falling. He caught and supported her.

"It ain't him, it's me," he told her obscurely. "There, there; it's all right. I laid him out." She clung to him, sobbing; and poor Johnny gazed about him, trapped. Cheest, what did you do with a weeping girl?

"Now, now, baby," he repeated, patting her back awkwardly, as you would a dog's, "it's all right. He won't bother you. Tell me where you live, and I'll take-you home."

"O-o-o-oh, he sc-scared me s-o," she wailed, clinging to him. Poor kid, she didn't know that he was the one to be scared, that his was the life that was about to take a dark and unknown corner, for better or worse, only the gods knew. There is still time to get out of town, though, caution told him. Otto is right; he knows best. Leave her and beat it, you fool! Leave her, and him back yonder? Youth replied. Not by your grandmother's false teeth, I won't.

He felt her pliant young body shudder with fear and her choked weeping.

"There, there, kid," he repeated inanely. He didn't know what to say to 'em, even. But he must get her away from here. The Wop would be about recovering now, and he'd be looking for him. He held her closer and her trembling gradually died away; and looking about him he almost shouted with relief. Here was old Ryan the cop's house, that had known him boy and lad for fifteen years. The very place.

"Why, say, here's the very place. Mrs. Ryan knows me, she'll look after you until I come back for you."

She clasped him sharply in her thin arms. "No, no, don't leave me! I'm so scared!"

"Why, just for a minute, honey," he reassured her, "just until I find where he went, see? We don't wanta stumble on him again."

"No, no, no, he'll hurt you!" Her wet salty face was against his. "You mustn't! You mustn't!"

"Sure, justa while, baby. I won't be no time." She moaned against Johnny's face and he kissed her cold mouth, and it was as though dawn had come among the trees where the birds were singing. They looked at each other a moment.

"Must you?" she said in a changed voice, and she allowed herself to be led to the dark door; and they clung to each other until footsteps came along the passage within the house. She put her arms around Johnny's neck again.

"Hurry back," she whispered, "and oh, be careful. I'm so afraid!"

"Baby!"

"Sweetheart!"

The door opened upon Mrs. Ryan, there was a brief explanation, and with her damp kiss yet on his face, Johnny ducked quickly from the alleyway.

Here were flying remote stars above, but below were flashing lights and paved streets, and all the city smells that he loved. He could go away for a while, and then come back, and things—lights and streets and smells—would be the same. "No!" he swore. "I've got a girl now. I ruther be bumped off than have her know I run." But ah, if this could have been put off a while! How sweet she is! Is this love, I wonder? he thought, or is it being afraid, makes me want to run back to her and risk letting things work themselves out instead of doing it myself? Anyway, I done it for her: I wasn't doublecrossing the boys. I had to do it: anyone can see that.

"Well, I ain't as good as I wanted, but I can be as good as I can." He looked again at the flying stars, his pistol loose in his pocket, and smelled again the smells of food and gasoline that he loved; and one stepped quickly from out a doorway.

Why, say, here she was again beside him, with her young body all shining and her hair that wasn't brown and wasn't gold, and her eyes the color of sleep; but she was somehow different at the same time.

"Mary?" said Johnny, tentatively. "Little sister Death," corrected the shining one, taking his hand.

Out of Nazareth

Beneath the immaculate shapes of lamps we passed, between ancient softly greenish gates, and here was Jackson park. Sparrows were upon Andrew Jackson's head as, childishly conceived, he bestrode his curly horse in terrific arrested motion. Beneath his remote stare people gaped and a voice was saying: "Greatest piece of statuary in the world: made entirely of bronze, weighing two and a half tons, and balanced on its hind feet." And, thinking of how our great men have suffered at the hands of the municipal governments which they strove to make possible, pondering on how green the trees were, and the grass, and the narcissi and hyacinths like poised dancers; blessing that genius who conceived a park without any forbidden signs, where tramps could lie in the sun and children and dogs could pleasure themselves in the grass without reprimand; I remarked to Spratling how no one since Cezanne had really dipped his brush in light. Spratling, whose hand has been shaped to a brush as mine has (alas!) not, here became discursive on the subject of transferring light to canvas; but not listening to him I looked at the faces of old men sitting patiently on iron benches as we slowly paced-men who had learned that living is not only not passionate or joyous, but is not even especially sorrowful. One, in a worn frock coat and a new pair of tennis shoes, explained to me the virtue of tennis shoes and borrowed pipe tobacco from me. And then, beneath sparrows delirious in a mimosa, and a vague Diana in tortuous escape from marble draperies in the background, we saw him.

Hatless, his young face brooded upon the spire of the Cathedral, or perhaps it was something in the sky he was watching. Beside him was a small pack; leaning against his leg was a staff. Spratling saw him first. "My God," he said, clutching me, "look at that face."

And one could imagine young David looking like that. One could imagine Jonathan getting that look from David, and, serving that highest function of which sorry man is capable, being the two of them beautiful in similar peace and simplicity—beautiful as gods, as no woman can ever be. And to think of speaking to him, of entering that dream, was like a desecration.

His gray gaze returned to earth and he replied easily to our greeting. "Hello," he said. His voice, his speech was Middle Western: one thought of wheat slumbrous beneath a blue sky and a haze of dust, along the land; of long, peaceful lands where the compulsions of labor and food and sleep filled men's lives. But he could have come from anywhere, and he probably had. He was eternal, of the earth itself.

"Going far?" he asked him.

"I dunno: just looking around."

He was hungry, but there was nothing of the beggar in him. He reminded one of a pregnant woman in his calm belief that nature, the earth which had spawned him, would care for him, that he was serving his appointed ends, had served his appointed end and now need only wait. For what? He had probably never thought of it. As all the simple children of earth know, he knew that even poverty would take care of its own.

He had worked (always with his hands) and liked it—liked to feel a worn hoe or rake handle in his palm, or a pick handle. "It's like holding a new shoe in your hands," he explained to us, "and when you are tired and your arms kind of ache, but you have a few dollars in your pocket." He liked to sleep in hay better than in a bed, he told us, especially when the cattle stand there after dark, making "night sounds" and you can smell milk, sort of, and the ground, too.

This developed over lunch at Victor's. He ate frankly, like an animal and though he employed his cutlery as one should not, there was nothing offensive about it—it was exactly what he should have done.

No, he told Spratling, he hadn't seen many pictures. But some he liked, when there were people like you see every day in them, or trees. Especially trees. Trees were nicer than flowers, he thought.

"So you are a writer?" he asked me shyly. "Do you write like this book?" From his sorry jacket he drew a battered "Shropshire Lad" and as he handed it to me he quoted the one beginning, "Into my heart an air that kills—" telling us he kind of thought it was the best he had seen.

"Why don't you go home?" I asked him.

"I will, some day. But that ain't why I liked that one. I like it because the man that wrote it felt that way, and didn't care who knew it."

"Is that so unusual?" I asked.

"Sir?"

"I mean, to feel something, and then write it exactly as you feel?"

Spratling here asked him if he had read Elizabeth Browning or Robert Frost. He had not—never heard of them. It seems that in Kentucky he had been given a meal in payment for which he had sawed wood; and, on leaving, a woman had asked him to throwaway some old books and magazines. And among them he had found his "Shropshire Lad."

Again upon the street we had that feeling of imminence, of departure and a sundering of the cords of contact.

"But you will need money," I remarked.

Spratling interposed. "Come to me tomorrow at three. I can use you for a model."

"But I may not be here tomorrow," he objected.

"Then take some money," Spratling suggested.

"Thank you, sir," he replied. "I'll get along all right. Thank you both, mister, for the dinner."

"Don't be a fool," Spratling rejoined.

"No, sir, I'll be all right."

Mankind is never as complex as we would like to believe ourselves to be. And so I said: "We will give you a dollar, and tomorrow you come to this address."

"But mister, I am not begging; I don't need your money. I will have a job by night."

"No, no; take the money, and call on us tomorrow."

"Why, I can get a job any time."

"Surely," Spratling replied, "but I want you to come to me tomorrow afternoon."

"But, mister, I may not be here."

"But won't you come, as a favor?"

His gaze brooded down Chartres street. "I guess I can. But I had rather give you something for the money." He turned to me. "Here, you are a writing man. I will give you this, and if I ain't there, you can have this for the dollar." And this is what he gave me. There is bad punctuation here, and misspelling: there is one word I have never deciphered. But to correct it would ruin it.

An open road stretching into the distance. Long lines of fences heming it in. Back of the fields, low hills in the distance. Not big hills but rolling formations overhung by a blue haze.

Cars whizz by. Cars filled with touring families. Cars with a single occupant. Dilapidated Fords in which farmers drive to town. Cars filled with family parties bound to visit relatives in some nearby town.

With a pack on my back (consisting of necessary articles rolled in two blankets) I trudge along. The smell of farm house fires drifts down the wind to me. Pure air fills my lungs and gives an exhilaration unlike any other that I know. The morning sun casts long shadows accross the fields. The dew of early morning glitters and the tall grass overhanging the side of the road is heavy with it. I am at peace with the world. Nothing matters.

I have eaten at a little restaurant. I have slept well on dried corn stalks between long rows of corn. I need not travel. I have no destination. I am at peace with the world.

I have my thoughts as a companion. Days spent alone have given me the habit of talking aloud to myself. Roosters crow, birds sing, a crow slowly wings his way from one distant wood clump to another. I seem to be in true communion with nature.

As the sun creeps higher the glare of summer is reflected from long rows of yellow corn. The road glistens and is a white streak which has no definite end at the horrizon. I sweat. Great drops roll down my face and settle in my open collar. The heat is good. It loosens the legs and warms the ground for the night's sleep.

Miles slide behind me. Now and again a car stops and I am given a ride. I do not ask for it. Why should I ask for rides when all around me is content? Those who wish to help me may do so, others may go on their way. I have no destination. Why should I hurry?

Noon comes and I lunch frugally on soup and milk. The hills that were before me this morning now surround me. The road no longer runs straight, but winds and dips among them. Trees overhang it and give a welcome shade from the noonday sun. Nature seems to plan my protection.

All afternoon I loll on the back seat of a speeding car (who's owner had invited me to ride). There is a dog in the back seat with me and we converse together as best we may. I scratch his ears and he cocks his head to one side and wags his tail. I stop for a minute to watch the changing form of some hill and he gently nudges me with his nose. My hand returns to his head and we resume our camradie.

The sun sinks lower and is hidden beyond the hill. There is still plenty of time to find a camp.

We come to a busy hill town and my heaviest meal is eaten. The food tastes as only food can taste to an appetite sharpened by a day spent in constant motion in the open air.

A slow tramp through the main street of the town and through the residential district brings me to the city camp. As I walk I look at the people resting on the porches, reading, talking and basking in the pleasant thought of a full day gone. Farther out I come to a region of stoops. Here shoeless laborers sit against buildings, one foot propped on a knee, smoking and talking shop, sports and politics. I catch words, sentences, fragments as I swing along.

Now and again a party sitting on a stoop stops its conversation to look at me. Perhaps a voice calls, "Where you from, kid?" and another, "Where you going?"

At the camp I find a place as far as possible from the rows of tents and spread my blankets. I wash my socks, which have become caked with sweat and the dust from the road. I brush my teeth and bathe as best I can.

I would ordinarily prefer to sleep in an open field or in a sheltering wood away from people. But tonight I desire the society of my own kind, so I stroll through the camp exchanging road gossip, stories, experiences, with motherly fat women washing dishes, wandering workers, business men out for a change, or a group of young men off for somewhere. Perhaps I help one of the women with her dishes and am rewarded with breakfast the next morning.

As it grows dark the fires stand out. The whitewalls of the tents reflect the light through, some music starts up and a party of young people start a dance on the porch of the small general store which serves the wants of the campers.

At the dance no introductions are necessary. We are all brothers and sisters. We are members of the fraternity of the open road, some for a short time, others forever.

Friendships develop quickly. Here is a German doctor (sic), a curious twisted little person with his hat on one side, playing some card game with a young Swede from the Dakotas who, it is evident, has lived in this country but a short time. The actor is going to the West to try the movies, the Swede is out to see the country. When he uses up his money he will sell his car and go to work.

A thin-faced, gangling Arkansan is discurrsing to several silent Westerners his difficulties in the Northwest. His youngest son, a boy of nine years, says to a playmate, "We pritt' nigh been all ova the country. We was in Vancouvar through California. We air headin' for the East now, and we'll get there prit' soon if Pop don't haf' to stop and get a job carpentering to buy us gas and food."

I have given his story word for word, as he wrote it. The spelling I have not changed, nor the punctuation. Some of the words mean nothing, as far as I know (and words are my meat and bread and drink), but to change them would be to destroy David himself. And so I have given it as it was given to me: blundering and childish and "arty," and yet with something back of it, some impulse which caused him to want to write it out on paper. And who knows? Give him time. He confided to Spratling and me, blushing, that he is seventeen.

But seeing him in his sorry clothes, with his clean young face and his beautiful faith that life, the world, the race, is somewhere good and sound and beautiful, is good to see.

He would not promise to call upon us. "You see, I wrote this, and I liked it. Of course it ain't as good as I wisht it was. But you are welcome to it." His young face stared into an ineffable sky, and the sun was like a benediction upon him.

"You see," he told us, "I can always write another one."

Hamilton Basso (1904–1964)

Hamilton Basso published over ten novels, two of which were made into Hollywood films, *Days Before Lent* (1939) and *The View From Pompey's Head* (1954); the latter was on the *New York Times* best-seller list for weeks, a Literary Guild selection, and translated into over seven languages.[1] Now, however, one of the most popular writers of the mid-twentieth century is all but forgotten. Nonetheless, he is still an important literary figure in New Orleans, where he began his writing career.

Basso was born to Dominick and Louise Calamari Basso on September 5, 1904, in his parents' and grandparents' home in the French Quarter. His grandfather had moved to New Orleans from Genoa, Italy, in the 1880s and opened a shoe repair shop which he later expanded into a shoe factory. Basso describes his grandfather's "small industry" in his essay "A New Orleans Childhood, the House on Decatur Street":

> Somewhere around 1890, he bought a few machines and set up a shoe factory behind the store. It was
> a modest operation during my childhood, employing no more than six men, two of them cobblers
> who made shoes to order, but when the workmen were bustling amidst a complicated arrangement
> of whirring belts and spinning wheels, I found the factory just as impressive as many years later as I
> was to find Willow Run (Ford manufacturing plant in Michigan for military aircraft).

His grandfather's shoe factory obviously made a life-long impression on Basso, so his disappointment in his father comes as no surprise when, after inheriting the factory, he sold it almost immediately. Even more disappointing to Basso was the fact that his father remained in the shoe business, no longer as a factory owner, but as a mere salesman.[2] Basso was again disappointed when, also after his grandfather's death, his father moved the family out of the French Quarter to the other side of Canal Street, what was at the time considered a suburb.

Basso attended Easton High School on Canal Street and then Tulane University studying pre-law; however, he dropped out four months shy of graduating, later explaining that "New Orleans is a very social place. Something like the law is apt to get in the way."[3] While at Tulane, he began his journalism career as editor-in-chief of the school newspaper, *Jambalaya*, but also writing for three local papers, the *Tribune*, *Item*, and *Times-Picayune*, a fitting job for an aspiring writer.[4] Probably more influential than his college writing classes or his newspaper experience was the crowd of writers who had sprung up around the *Double Dealer*, many of whose works are included in this collection, such as Sherwood Anderson, Lyle Saxon, and William Faulkner. In fact, Basso and Faulkner would remain life-long friends, and upon Faulkner's death in 1962, Basso wrote a eulogy for him in the *Saturday Review* praising his "vision of the South."[5]

For a time, Basso moved to New York, where he thought a young writer should live and where he held a number of jobs not necessarily advantageous for a young writer, working in a print shop, for a truck freighter, and in a department store as a salesman, and in a little over a year, he was back in New Orleans working again for the newspaper.[6] The next few years were big for Basso. In 1929, he published his first novel, *Relics and Angels*, and the following year he married Etolia (Toto) Simmons, whom he had met at Tulane. According to Lake, Etolia's parents were not pleased that their daughter was to marry a struggling writer, who by this time was working as a copy editor for a local advertising firm.[7] But the marriage by all accounts was successful, and the Bassos went

---

1   For more on Basso, and from where much of the biographical information comes, see Joseph R. Millichap, *Hamilton Basso* (Boston: Twayne Publishers, 1979), and Inez Hollander Lake, *The Road from Pompey's Head* (Baton Rouge: LSUP, 1999).

2   Lake, 5.

3   Hamilton Basso, "Some Important Fall Authors Speak for Themselves," *New York Herald Tribune Book Review,* October 24, 1954, 4.

4   Lake, 13.

5   Basso, "Faulkner," 13.

6   Millichap, 15.

7   Lake, 54.

on to have one son, Keith.

Although Basso always had a fondness for his hometown, he chose not to live there, and in 1932, he and Etolia moved from the city for good, living for a time in North Carolina, South Carolina, southern France, Virginia, New York, and finally Connecticut. His first published short story, "I Can't Dance," (1929) is one of the few set in New Orleans. The story is biographical, to some extent. The young protagonist, Malcolm, like Basso at the time, works nights writing for a local newspaper for very little money. Unlike Basso, however, he does not drink and did not think that the local speakeasies were "wild wicked places." Basso was known to be a big drinker and was very fond of dancing and the French Quarter night life.

"A New Orleans Childhood, the House on Decatur Street" (1954), included here, is a nonfiction essay written almost thirty years after his first short story and his departure from New Orleans. Basso reminisces about his charming life in the French Quarter as a ten-year-old boy, but he also bemoans the loss of the Quarter as a real neighborhood, especially focusing on Bourbon Street, which to him had become little more than a tourist mecca full of bars blaring bad jazz music and cheap dancing girls. Ironically, it had become just the sort of place Malcolm in "I Can't Dance" was in search of. Also remarkable about this essay is the fact that it could be written now. Bourbon Street is no longer peppered with bad jazz clubs, but inundated with cheap karaoke bars, daiquiri and t-shirt shops, and condos. However, as Basso notes, "the Quarter was not yet lost," and that is still true today.

Basso also wrote poetry early on, but he spent most of his career writing novels and publishing nonfiction in such powerhouses as *Time*, *New Yorker*, and *Saturday Review*. In 1957, he was elected Vice President of National Institute of Arts and Letters. His masterpiece, *The View from Pompey's Head* was the first in a trilogy, but he only lived long enough to complete the second in the series, *The Light Infantry Ball*. His last novel, *A Touch of the Dragon*, was not well-received, and Lake believes that it may contribute to Basso's current obscurity. It was written while he was suffering from lung cancer (He had been a long-time smoker.), to which he succumbed in New Haven, Connecticut, on May 13, 1964.

A New Orleans Childhood, the House on Decatur Street[1]

Finding myself in New Orleans recently—a pleasant place to be and one that I get to as often as I can—I decided to have another look at the French Quarter. I say "another look" because I have been looking at the French Quarter, off and on, for well over forty years. It is where I come from. I was born in the Quarter and spent the first ten years of my life there. Then my family moved to another part of New Orleans, but I continued to spend a good deal of time in the section, because my father's parents still lived there. They had always lived in the Quarter, and it never occurred to them to live anywhere else. Certainly it never occurred to them or to me that the Quarter would some day become one of the principal tourist attractions in the United States, or that one of its main thoroughfares, Bourbon Street, would turn into as noisy a stretch of pavement as can be found this side of Hong Kong. The last trip to New Orleans was my first in several years, and I had not paid much attention to the Quarter on my two or three previous stopovers, so this time, largely because of what I had been reading about my old neighborhood in the magazines, I was curious to see for myself just what had happened to it. A lot had happened, I found, and the most unattractive part of it had happened to Bourbon Street. What they say about that particular bit of Dixie, it saddens me to report, is mostly true.

Bourbon Street runs the length of the Quarter, which is fourteen blocks long and seven blocks wide, and once was all there was to New Orleans When French was generally spoken in the city, it used to be known as Le Vieux Carré. This translates into English as the Old Quadrangle. Nowadays, some local-color enthusiasts in New Orleans go rather out of their way to refer to the section as Le Vieux Carré—a tendency especially noticeable among those whose Gallic tradition has its roots in Kansas or South

---

1   From: *New Yorker*, October 9, 1954, 89-101.

Dakota—but I think we can let that pass. We can also let pass the street signs that have been put up since my day—signs that read "Rue de Chartres" and "Rue Royale," for instance. There was never that kind of self-conscious Gallicizing in the Quarter when I lived there. Some of the older members of the French-speaking households might call a thoroughfare a rue in the bosom of the family, but in public a street was always called a street. My suspicion is that if any of these worthies had walked forth one morning in their alpaca coats and bombazine dresses and seen their streets labeled rues they would have concluded, not without testiness, that those American late-comers in the city administration were trying to have some ill-mannered fun at their expense.

Many tourists think it is amusing that a convivial street like Bourbon, should have the same name as a whiskey (I must say I have managed to keep from being bowled over by the coincidence), and a lot of them appear to be under the impression that the street was named after the beverage. The facts are otherwise. The street arrived first. The whiskey made its appearance in Bourbon County, Kentucky—a state that I wouldn't want to offend, God knows, but the truth of the matter is that hardly anybody ventured into it before 1750, and the whiskey really didn't start flowing until a couple of decades later. Bourbon Street was in business long before that. It was one of the first streets laid out in New Orleans, back around 1718, and it was christened in honor of the royal house of France.

The street we lived on during my childhood was Decatur Street—named after Stephen Decatur, the naval hero—which is parallel to Bourbon, and three blocks from it. We lived between Barracks Street, which was called that because it was where the French troops had had their barracks, and Hospital Street (now Governor Nicholls Street), on which the first hospital in New Orleans had stood. We were only two blocks from the Mississippi River, which was half a mile wide here, and we were even closer to the United States Mint. There was, naturally, a kind of wonder attached to the river, where ships from all over the world mingled with our little ferryboats, and old men fished for catfish in the sun. The austere, grey Mint was still in operation during my childhood, and as soon as I was able to take in the fact that money was coined there, I regarded it with awe. Pennies were the coins I knew most about in those days—they bore the very Grecian profile of an Indian in a war bonnet, on the band of which was inscribed the word "LIBERTY"—and in the matter of wealth my imagination never went further than them. I used to have a dream in which I would light upon a small cache of pennies, blazing like the sun, and though the dream frequently repeated itself, I was always too overcome by my find to count up how much it amounted to—about twenty cents, I would guess. I stopped having that dream before we moved away from the Quarter, but even now when I am given pennies in change I go through them, hoping for an Indian-head.

Bourbon Street had nothing that could compete with the river or the Mint, and my immediate neighborhood was much more entertaining in my eyes. Besides, Bourbon Street was then pretty much a residential street—not that streets in the Quarter were completely residential then or ever—while Decatur Street was given over to shopkeepers. My father's father was one of these—at least, to begin with. He had opened a shoe store on Decatur Street in the early eighteen-eighties, and in time he prospered sufficiently to branch out into what would nowadays be called a small industry. Somewhere around 1890, he bought a few machines and set up a shoe factory behind the store. It was a modest operation during my childhood, employing no more than six men, two of them cobblers who made shoes to order, but when the workmen were bustling amidst a complicated arrangement of whirring belts and spinning wheels, I found the factory just as impressive as many years later I was to find Willow Run.

The building was quite large—large enough to house the store, the factory, and all of us besides. Built during the Spanish occupation of New Orleans, or shortly thereafter, it was L-shaped, consisted of three stories and an attic, and had the customary wrought-iron balconies—extremely simple ones compared to some of the others in the Quarter—and the customary courtyard in the rear. My grandparents lived on the floor above the store and the factory, and my parents and I lived on the floor above that. There were six rooms on each floor, and the living quarters were reached by a stairway spiraling up from a door that gave onto the street. The ascending curves were contained in a high, shadowy well whose walls, I remember, were always damp. I have forgotten how many steps there were, but our quarters seemed a long way up.

While I was still quite young, my grandfather roofed the courtyard over with a glass skylight, to provide more space for the factory, but I can recall how the courtyard looked before then, with my grandmother's flower garden, a pair of scraggly banana trees, and a jagged line of broken bottles cemented onto the top of the rear wall, which was about fifteen feet high. This was the Quarter's way of burglar-proofing, and there were few courtyards that were not similarly protected. The glass fragments on our wall always seemed rather ominous to me, telling of the danger that lurked in the outside world, but when the sun shone on them and brought out their colors—brown and green and garnet and blue—I thought they were beautiful. The impression they made must have gone deep, for I have never since seen a stained-glass window—even in Notre Dame—without being reminded of them.

Apart from the broken bottles, what I remember best about the courtyard is one of its tenants—an alligator who lived in it for a time. We always had rather curious pets in our family, and the alligator was one of them. He was a present. My grandfather had a close friend who grew rice in the lower part of Louisiana, not far from the Gulf of Mexico, and he used to keep us supplied with the bounty of that part of the country—sacks of fresh oysters, braces of wild duck, rail birds, an occasional sea turtle, and, somewhere along the line, the alligator. A kind man, he thought the creature might amuse me. I thought so too, when I first heard he was coming, but that was pure ignorance. I had a lot to learn about alligators.

My mother tells me that ours was a relatively small specimen, only three feet long, but to me he seemed enormous. I didn't like his looks much, either, and, for me, he took on the role of the enemy in our midst. We had four other pets at the time: a parrot, who was a splendid conversationalist and could sing part of a march; two canaries; and a bright South American bird, given us by a sea captain we knew. I had heard tales about the cruel appetite of alligators, and I began to fear for the birds—particularly the parrot, a special friend of mine. The other birds were caged, but he had the run of the courtyard, and he thought he owned the place. I had visions of him tangling with the intruder, briefly asserting his rights, and then disappearing, with one last squawk, into the darkness of the alligator's maw. Feeling the need of outside help, I began to mention the parrot in my prayers.

I soon found that I need not have bothered. The alligator, as lazy and torpid as most of his kind, lay motionless for days at a time. The parrot, strutting around about the courtyard and eating sunflower seeds within an inch of his ugly head, never gave him a thought, and neither, after a time, did I, except to reflect occasionally on what a big disappointment he was. He became simply another object in the courtyard. Then he vanished, leaving not a trace. One evening he was in the courtyard, and the next morning he wasn't. There weren't any holes or crevices he could have crawled through, and all the doors had been locked and barred for the night. We had a fine mystery on our hands. I didn't care two cents about that large lizard, and in my heart I knew it, but I wasn't going to miss the chance of making a scene, so I insisted that everybody look for him. Work was held up that morning while my grandfather led an alligator hunt, delivering commands in English, French, and Italian, and my mother, who has never been able to stand the thought of any creature in distress, wandered about the courtyard calling "Here, alligator! Here, alligator!" in a troubled, anxious way that moved even me. I was enjoying the excitement, and, to prolong it, I suggested that we call in the police, but my grandfather and my father were cool to the idea. We never did find out what happened to the alligator; our best guess was that some pilferer had managed to scale the rear wall of the courtyard, braving the wicked barrier of glass, and had carried him off. If that was the case, the fellow must have wanted an alligator pretty badly.

All the other families in our block lived, as we did, over their places of business. Many of them had pets, too—mockingbirds, Brazilian finches, cardinals, macaws. Nor was my alligator the only unusual one. There were also a monkey and a squirrel, and—no less unusual in New Orleans, where the thermometer often hovers around a hundred during the summer—a huge St. Bernard. He belonged to a widow, Mrs. Wallansbach (whose name, like the names of all the other people mentioned in this chronicle, I have changed). A number of German families moved to Louisiana in the early seventeen-hundreds, and Mrs. Wallansbach's husband, a restaurateur, was a descendant of one of them. After his death, which occurred before I had a chance to know him, Mrs. Wallansbach sold the restaurant, but she continued to live above it. I can remember her only vaguely—a pair of steel-rimmed spectacles and a bun of reddish hair—and I doubt whether I would remember her at all if it were not for the St. Bernard, which accompanied her everywhere and was one of the attractions of our neighborhood. The French Market—the largest market in New Orleans, and very much like Les Halles, in Paris—was a few blocks away from us on Decatur Street, and whenever Mrs. Wallansbach went shopping there, the business of the day came to a standstill as everybody stopped to admire the St. Bernard. I felt privileged to be on intimate terms with such a spectacular animal. It was his size that appealed to me, not his personality. I knew that our parrot was more talented and more affectionate—he liked to perch on my shoulder and nibble my ear, whereas the St. Bernard resisted all my attempts at playfulness—but the sheer bulk of the dog made up for his lack of other qualities. Mrs. Wallansbach often let me lead him, or, rather, be led by him—on his evening stroll around the Mint, and I enjoyed nothing better, for then I was at the very center of attention.

Mrs. Wallansbach was a good friend of my grandparents, and I often dropped in to visit her. I was generally accompanied on these calls by my closest friend, a recently arrived little French girl named Hélène Rouillard. Hélène's mother and father had died of yellow fever shortly after they reached New Orleans, and Hélène, an only child, had been adopted by the Wilsons, who kept a bookstore across the street from us. Since Hélène and I were the only small children on the block, we were much in each other's company. Hélène knew hardly any English at first, but we managed to get along. What entranced me most about her was her wooden shoes, the first sabots I had ever seen. Hélène could do anything in them—run, jump, even skip rope—and their hollow clack soon became one of the accustomed sounds of our street. My mother recalls that she could usually tell where Hélène and I were, and even what we were up to, by the clatter of those shoes. After a while, the process of Americanization set in, and Hélène put aside her sabots. For me, she was never again quite the same girl.

We were great droppers-in, we two. We had both houses to roam about in, along with our courtyard and the luxuriant walled garden that lay behind the Wilson's bookstore, but more often than not we went visiting. We were greatly spoiled, and I am afraid we sometimes mad nuisances of ourselves. One of our favorite ports of call was the blacksmith shop around the corner on Hospital Street, facing the Mint. It could not have been as smoky and cavernous as I know remember it, or the sparks as dazzling, or the horses as spirited, or the smith as grimy and gigantic, but about the rings that he used to make for us from horseshoe nails, I am altogether sure: They were masterpieces. After leaving the smithy, Hélène and I would often descend upon the two maiden Valvan sisters, who were milliners. We could count on a bonbon from them, since they both had a passion for sweets, and they thought Hélène was so chic that they let her model hats. We would then drop in on Mr. Gallardo, the baker; visit Peter, the gunsmith; admire the wares in Mr. Mayer's jewelry store; and pass the time of day with Mr. and Mrs. Scheidemann, who owned a crockery shop.

Mr. Scheidmann, a grave, slow-spoken man with heavy shoulders and a bald head, seemed to me to be slightly more than mortal. I had learned from family conversation that it was his habit to spend the late-afternoon hours in his courtyard writing poetry, and even though all I knew about poetry was Mother Goose, and perhaps the first few lines of "Paul Revere's Ride," this dedication of Mr. Scheidemann's set him apart in my eyes. I had only to listen to my grandfather or Mr. Wilson to know that it was no mean thing to be a poet. There was something, I gathered, called "the life of the mind." It interested me, this life of the mind, and I felt a great curiosity to see it close up. What did a poet do when he was writing poetry? How did he look? Did he speak his lines out loud, or what? There came a time when I simply had to find out. Late one afternoon, I left the Wilson's garden, where Hélène and I had been catching dragonflies, and instead of going straight home as I had told her I would, I went down the street and stole into the passage that led to the Sheidemann's courtyard. The long corridor was shadowy, with crates of china piled against the walls, and since this was no conventional visit but deliberate espionage, I was thrilled by my own recklessness. Tiptoeing to the end of the corridor, I peered into the courtyard. Mr. Scheidemann was sitting in a wicker chair, in his suspenders. He was smoking a cigar and had a small writing pad on his knee. I spied on him for what seemed like an hour, and nothing happened. Mr. Scheidemann just sat there, smoking his cigar. It was a disappointing experience, but it had its value. It taught me that poetry can't be hurried, and that a poet may well be a bald-headed man in suspenders, smoking a cigar.

Among the few events that really shook me in those days was the death of an animal with whom I was acquainted, and I was particularly sobered when Mrs. Wallansbach's St. Bernard gave up the ghost. He had been so large and was not so humbled, and my world, as it always did when somebody or something was removed from it, seemed smaller and emptier than before. Then, too, when it came to animals, I felt that there was a great unfairness about the mystery beyond the grave. I knew where dead people went—to Heaven—and it troubled me that no such harbor had been provided for dead animals. I trusted my elders, and hoped they were right when they said that even the smallest creature was sure to be looked after, but since they could not tell me how, or guarantee that there were angelic presences in the shapes of horses, dogs, cats, and parrots, the notion of unfairness persisted. I never brooded for very long, of course. I was as resilient as most children, and anyway I knew how risky it was to question the wisdom of Our Merciful Father. When somebody presently gave Hélène a mallard duckling, it expanded my universe, just as the death of the St. Bernard had contracted it. I quickly recovered from the loss of my towering friend.

Mrs. Wallansbach had a harder time of it. Though I was too young to know it then, I can see now that she gave the St. Bernard all of her affection, except that part of it which in her kindliness she saved for Hélène and me. Unable to bear the thought of losing him completely, she called in a taxidermist and commissioned him to stuff the animal. Needless to say, I wanted to know all the details of the procedure, which sounded fascinating, and I was puzzled by the strange expression that crossed the faces of my parents and grandparents when I brought the matter up. Eventually, it became clear to me that they had certain reservations about the propriety of stuffing a household pet, but I still thought it was a fine thing for Mrs. Wallansbach to do, and so did Hélène. The mallard duckling was beginning to pall a little, for it didn't seem to comprehend that it was supposed to follow us wherever we went, and we were impatient for the day when we would see the St. Bernard again.

The day came about a month later. Hélène was in bed with the measles, and I had gone on a shopping expedition with my mother. On the way home, we ran into Mrs. Wallansbach. She invited me to stop in and visit with her, and I immediately knew the reason for the invitation. The St. Bernard had come back. I followed Mrs. Wallansbach up the stairs and into her parlor. The slatted blinds of the long windows that opened on her balcony had been drawn against the sun, and there in a corner, where the shadows were deepest, stood the St. Bernard. Looming even larger than in life, he stood motionless on his stiff legs, staring at me with blank, dismaying eyes. Mrs. Wallansbach asked me if I didn't want to pat him, and I felt I had to, but I declined the glass of lemonade that she offered me. I stopped dropping in on Mrs. Wallansbach after that, and there has been something of a barrier between St. Bernards and me ever since.

Compared to this street and these people, Bourbon Street didn't amount to much. My grandfather owned a building on it, which he used as a warehouse, and sometimes I would go there with him. This building was thought to have been a barracks when New Orleans and the rest of the Louisiana Territory were ruled by Spain, and some of the windows had iron bars. Our family doctor was on Bourbon Street, too—a small, lively Creole gentleman who kept goldfish and always smelled of snuff—and I would have to go and see him every now and then, usually in connection with my tonsils. But the only real interest Bourbon Street had for me, and that only indirectly, was the French Opera House. The two cobblers who worked for my grandfather, Mr. Fisher and Mr. Auchin, used to make the shoes for the troupes that appeared there.

New Orleans naturally went for opera—first light opera and then grand opera, too. As early as 1810, there were three theatres in the Quarter given over to musical dramas of one kind or the other, and long before I knew the date of the Louisiana Purchase or the fact that General P.G.T. Beauregard, another French Quarter resident, had ordered the firing on Fort Sumter and had thus started the Civil War, I was aware that Jenny Lind and Adelina Patti had sung in New Orleans in the eighteen-fifties. It was sometimes hard for me to be sure where the past ended and the present began, so great was their overlapping. There were a number of things relatively remote from me in which I felt I had a personal stake—the great yellow-fever epidemics, for instance, since my grandfather and my grandmother had lived through several of them. Because of my grandfather's shoe factory I felt that I had a personal stake in everything that had ever happened in the French Opera House.

The building, which was one of the handsomest in the Quarter, was erected in 1859, but it did not come into its full glory until the years between 1890 and 1910. My father always insisted that the opera heard there was better than any ever presented by the Metropolitan in New York. I cannot vouch for his opinion, since my few visits to the French Opera House took place before I reached the age of appreciation. I do know that my father was a man of great local pride, and he tended to view anything—even people, I'm afraid—that came out of New Orleans as automatically superior. In this, I might add, he resembled a substantial portion of the population.

The Opera House was still going strong when I lived in the Quarter. My grandparents sometimes attended performances, and my father was a true devotee. My own link with the opera, however, came through Mr. Fisher and Mr. Auchin. Because of an arrangement my grandfather had with the management, he could always get them a pass to the upper gallery. Mr. Fisher did not go very often, but Mr. Auchin, like my father, rarely missed a performance. Though I find it hard to recall what Mr. Fisher looked like— all I am sure of is that he had a goatee and blue eyes—Mr. Auchin appears plainly before me whenever I come across a picture of Gustave Flaubert. Most of what I know about opera, which isn't much, I learned from Mr. Fisher and Mr. Auchin. I hung round them often, but never so steadily as when they were working on the shoes for the opera company. Their workbenches assumed a gala look then. The shoes were made with satin uppers, and bright squares of satin, of every imaginable hue, would be scattered about like small, dazzling flags; there was one particular shade of scarlet that burns in my memory as the most beautiful color I have ever seen.

It was something of a disappointment to my father, especially after he acquired a phonograph, that I did not appreciate the music of the operas as much as I might have. But I partly made up for that deficiency by my enjoyment of the plots, nearly all of which Mr. Fisher and Mr. Auchin, between them, knew to the last incident. Mr. Auchin was a superb storyteller. To be sure, he had the habit of lapsing into French at the most exciting moments, but he was very patient when I lost the drift, as I soon did, and he had to repeat himself in English. One year, he made the shoes for "Faust," and over his workbench he told me, bit by bit, what happens when you make a pact with the Devil. Mr. Auchin never called Mephistopheles Mephistopheles. He knew the scoundrel for what he was, and was not going to get fancy. In those days, the Devil was much in my thoughts. My grandfather took a scornful view of him, as did my father, but Mr. Auchin, who attended early Mass every Sunday at the St. Louis Cathedral and was considerably more conservative, saw the Devil exactly as my friend Hélène had told me she did—horned, cloven-hoofed, and pitchforked, chalking up the black marks and coldly awaiting the day when he could settle his accounts. I was caught in the middle. I was eager to side with my father and grandfather, since the Devil was the last person I wanted hovering in the background, and I listened very hard when they said that the Devil merely stood for evil, which lurked in every crack and crevice of the world, and particularly in the heart of man. Mr. Auchin and Hélène, though, had Authority on their side. Pulled first one way and then the other, I took a long time to make up my mind. Though I hoped that my father and grandfather were right, and though they seemed quite able to look out for themselves, no matter what, I decided to take no chances. Hélène and Mr. Auchin, plus Authority, won out.

Mr. Auchin told the story of "Faust" so vividly that I asked my father to take me to it. Since I had never asked to go to the opera before, he was pleased to detect in me what he regarded as the first stirrings of a musical turn of mind. The truth of the matter was, however, that I was spurred by the same impulses that had caused me to sneak into Mr. Scheidermann's courtyard. I wanted to see the Devil at his deviltry, just as I had wanted to see a poet at his poetry. The evening was not a success. I had never been so disappointed in anybody as I was in that Devil. Compared to the fellow introduced into my mythology by Mr. Auchin and Hélène, he couldn't have frightened a sick cat. When he first appeared in a puff of smoke, I thought he was sensational and expected great things of him, but he never came through; he was even less convincing than the maskers who paraded in his guise on Mardi Gras. As far as I was concerned, Mr. Auchin's shoes were the best part of the show. My father had to shush me throughout the first act, and for the rest of the evening I had a hard time keeping awake.

I never went to the opera with my father again. As he later admitted, he was driven to the conclusion that the vaudeville bills at the Orpheum Theatre were more in my line. They were, too. My father and I did not get together on the subject of music until I awoke to the appeal of jazz. He was able to appreciate jazz as much as he appreciated opera, and, of course, it had the further advantage of being a native New Orleans product. Here I do not think that patriotism led him astray. Jazz was then first making itself unmistakably heard—in street parades, on marches back from the cemeteries after Negro funerals, on trucks that used to drive through the streets advertising some coming event—usually a prizefight—and the sound of creation filled the air. New Orleans jazz needs no testimonial from me, but those, I swear, were the days.

The French Opera House was destroyed by fire in 1919. My father had moved us from Decatur Street several years before—my sister Mary had arrived, and we needed more room—and when my grandfather died, in 1917, we sold the factory and the old house, and my last family tie with the Quarter was broken. Our new house was in a middle-class neighborhood on the "uptown" side of Canal Street— New Orleans' main thoroughfare, which divides the city in two—and although I eventually got more or less used to our new surroundings, especially after I entered high school and began to make a new set of friends, I don't think I ever felt really at home there. I'm sure my father never did. He had grown up in the French Quarter, and in spirit he never left it. The day after the fire at the French Opera House, my father came home early and took me down to see the charred ruins of the building in which I had spoiled his enjoyment of "Faust." He was silent and subdued, and I was then old enough to understand that he was thinking of the past and all that was in the past, and of how it could never be again.

I understood my father's feelings even better on my recent trip to New Orleans. Around eight o'clock one evening, I walked over to Decatur Street. It was the first time I had been there in more than twenty-five years. All my former friends were gone, I knew—Hélène, the Wilsons, Misses Valvan, Mr. and Mrs. Scheidermann, Mrs. Wallansbach, Peter the gunsmith, and Mr. Gallardo the baker. Our old house was still standing, and as large as I remembered it, but it was barred and shuttered and empty, falling into ruin, and the whole block had a similarly derelict appearance. The only lighted buildings were several of those mean, shabby bars to be found in waterfront districts all over the world. One bar had taken the place of the Wilson's bookstore. As I stood before it, I found myself shaking my head.

At that, though, I liked what has happened to Decatur Street better than I liked what has happened to Bourbon Street. It is lined with one cabaret after another, and apparently the tourists find them attractive, for there are always throngs of them on the street. I don't want to give the impression that I have anything against tourists, because I haven't, and it is perhaps foolish of me, simply because I used to have my tonsils looked at on Bourbon Street and because it was a part of my childhood in other ways, to object to its bars and striptease emporiums, and to its silly pretense of old-world romanticism. I do object, though—strongly. I don't like to see all the walls come tumbling down.

After leaving Decatur Street, I had a cup of coffee in the French Market and then a drink in a non-tourist bar, and at about nine o'clock, I strolled over to Bourbon Street. Even at that early hour, business was thriving. A line of more than a hundred people was waiting to witness the performance of a lady who calls herself the Cat Girl, and I noticed that the Wildcat Girl, the Cupcake Girl, the Tassle Girl, and twenty or so more were also getting play. These, of course, were only the featured performers, with star billing. I have no idea of the number of uncapitalized girls who were less conspicuously stashed away. Each of the divinities who grace Bourbon Street has a barker in her retinue. These attendants stand at the doors of the temples, and it is evidently one of their duties, when they sight a likely customer, to open the doors for an instant, permitting a glimpse of the rites within.

All of this activity—the tourists touring, the barkers barking, the doors opening, the ladies exposing more pink and powdered flesh than ever Reubens got around to painting in his whole industrious lifetime—takes place to the accompaniment of jazz. On the whole, I did not think that it was good jazz, and some of it sounded terrible, but I am getting to be cross and irritable, and after my visit to Decatur Street, I was perhaps not in a very responsive mood. I went by the parking lot where the French Opera House used to stand, and then, a block or so farther on, a whole series of doors began opening as I passed. Through one, I saw a lady standing on a bar, who appeared to be in danger of losing her skirt. A moment later, I came upon two small, white-haired gentlemen talking on the curb. One look at them—their sober clothes, their coloring, the general hang of their appearance—and I knew that they were not far from their homes. They could have been two of our neighbors on Decatur Street. Paying not the slightest attention to their surroundings or to the blare of noise that welled up all about them, they were talking most earnestly. Their speech had an unmistakable French Quarter accent—a way of pronunciation greatly tempered by the several foreign languages that have long been used there, though less today than formerly—and I was able to catch a few sentences as I strolled past. They were talking about the Holy Name Society's picnic the following Sunday. Suddenly, I felt much better about everything. The Quarter was not yet lost. It was being defended, and at its center it still held fast.

⚜

Los Isleños Décimas

A ll historical research on the Canary Islanders or *Isleños*[1] of Louisiana begins with a discussion of the mysterious *Guanches,* the ancient natives of the islands, or of Tenerife in particular. These were a primitive people whose language was never written and whose origin remains uncertain. According to Gilbert Din, the first inhabitants arrived in the Canary Islands between 2500 and 1000 B.C. These inhabitants remained there undisturbed for centuries primarily due to the isolated nature of the islands. The seven Canary Islands, Tenerife, Gran Canaria, Gomera, La Palma, Hierro, Fuerteventura, and Lanzarote, are situated off the west coast of northern Africa, and according to Din there is no evidence that any explorers visited the islands until the time of the Roman Empire. After that, the visits to—or invasions of—the islands occurred with more regularity; explorers and conquerors came from Spain, North Africa, Italy and Portugal, until conquest was finally achieved by the Spanish at the end of the fifteenth century. The islands are still a part of Spain today.

Between 1778 and 1783, almost ten years after the French Louisianians rebelled against Spanish rule under Ulloa—the subject of Thomas Wharton Collens' play *The Martyr Patriots, or Louisiana in 1769*—nearly 2000 Canary Islanders arrived in Louisiana. The Louisiana colony, still under Spanish rule, needed recruits in order to populate the territory and defend it against the British during the American Revolution. It was no accident that the Spanish government turned to the Canary Islands to find them. Matías de Galvez was the Spanish royal lieutenant to the Canaries, and his son, Bernardo, the governor of the Louisiana Territory. The Spanish were looking for soldiers and their families; according to Din, "[m]ulattoes, gypsies, executioners, and butchers" were not eligible![2] Five ships left the Canaries between 1778 and 1779, and arrived in Louisiana, the first via Havana, Cuba, but as Din states, there is no way to determine an exact number of *Isleños* aboard. We do know that there were four original *Isleño* settlements in South Louisiana: Galveztown on Bayou Manchac, Valenzuela on Bayou Lafourche, St. Bernard and Barataria. Ironically, Galveztown, the first, largest and most well-documented settlement, did not survive. There are still *Isleño* families living near Bayou Lafourche south of Donaldsonville, Louisiana, and the *Isleños* of Barataria eventually moved across the Mississippi River joining those in St. Bernard Parish, originally Bayou Terre-aux-Boeufs (Land of Oxen) abutting Orleans Parish. This enclave still exists today and is the one that concerns us here.

In the Canary Islands, most of the inhabitants were farmers, raising crops and livestock, so when they moved to Louisiana, they continued that tradition of living off the land, but in St. Bernard Parish—particularly Delacroix Island, the center of the *Isleño* settlement—that grew to include fishing and trapping as well. In the nineteenth century, *Isleño* soldiers fought in both the War of 1812 and the Civil War. In fact, the Battle of New Orleans was fought in St. Bernard Parish on January 8, 1815, two weeks after the Treaty of Ghent had been signed. After fighting in both of these wars, however, the soldiers returned to St. Bernard to their trapping, fishing, and crabbing. Although they lived only a few miles from New Orleans, the *Isleños* were geographically and socially isolated. Most historians cite the industrialization of the modern world and the two World Wars of the twentieth century as the initial causes of their becoming more Americanized, as some of the men went away to fight and did not return, or returned only to move away to more lucrative and less demanding jobs.

In 1909, Standard Oil moved into St. Bernard Parish and became one of the principal players in the erosion of the wetlands and *Isleño* culture, but that would take over a century. And in 1965—the same year that Hurricane Betsy hit—the Army Corps of Engineers completed the Mississippi River Gulf Outlet (MRGO or "Mr. Go") which, according to historian Samantha Perez, resulted in a loss of "...3,400 acres of fresh/intermediate marsh, more than 10,300 acres of brackish marsh, [and] 4,200 acres of saline marsh..."[3]. And the role that the MRGO played during Hurricane Katrina, channeling the storm surge into the heart of the city, is well-known.

Any *Isleño* will tell you that Hurricane Katrina did more to disperse their community than any other

---

1   For more on the *Isleños,* see Gilbert C. Din, *The Canary Islanders of Louisiana* (Baton Rouge: LSUP, 1988).

2   Din, 16.

3   Samantha Perez, *The Isleños of Louisiana: On the Water's Edge* (Charleston: History Press, 2011).

single event. St. Bernard Parish is still not completely rebuilt, and many have moved away only to return for special occasions, weddings and funerals. Luckily, we have the *décimas* as a way to record the adversity that this community has faced since its arrival here in Louisiana over 200 years ago.[1]

The Spanish *décima* was made fashionable by the very popular sixteenth-century writer Lope de Vega and thought to have been originated by his mentor, Vicente Espinel, in 1591.[2] Originally, the *décima* was a poem consisting of ten octosyllabic verses, and although it fell out of favor in Spain after the Baroque period, it is still popular in Latino or Hispanic-American literature, in forms such as the Mexican *corridor* or the Nuyorican *décima*.[3] The *Isleño décima* no longer consists of ten verses, nor is it often octosyllabic, and since the *Isleño* language was never written, it is sung in a dialect that has nearly disappeared.

According to Samuel G. Armistead, "these songs embody four types of subject matter: events pertaining to local history; humorous commentary on the rigors and hazards of local occupations;…satirical poems about the foibles and misadventures of local individuals, and tall tales concerning fabulous fishing exploits, gigantic crabs…catfish…shrimp."[4] He goes on to say that the only *décimas* that can be dated were all written in the twentieth century. In 1891, however, writer and cultural historian Alcée Fortier transcribed many of the early *décimas,* one of which, sung by Pepe Martín, is included here, *"Una décima de amor"* "A Love Song."[5] This is one of the earliest transcribed *décimas,* and it is a love song, but it also includes the satire and exaggeration that Armistead mentions.

Today, anyone in St. Bernard will tell you that the man most responsible for keeping the *Isleño* culture and the tradition of the *décima* alive is the late Irvan Pérez, who learned to sing these folksongs from his father as a teen. Pérez went on to receive the prestigious National Endowment for the Arts National Heritage Fellowship in 1991, was inducted into the Louisiana Hall of Master Folk Artists and even sang his *décimas* at Carnegie Hall. He was one of the few who wrote original *décimas,* and one of them is included here, *"Setecientos setentaisiete,"* "Seventeen Seventy-Seven," a historical song about the *Isleños'* emigration to the United States and becoming American citizens, fighting in every war to defend this country, while still maintaining their Spanish heritage. Pérez wrote this song after returning from the Canary Islands where the Spanish government had invited him to sing his *décimas,* so it is a tribute to Spain and his Spanish cultural heritage. Another original *décima* by Pérez, which he wrote in both English and *Isleño* Spanish, is "The Father's Prayer," also about the importance of Spanish culture and passing down the pride in that culture and in one's name from one generation to the next.

Two more *décimas* included here are *"La vida de un jaibero,"* "The Crab Fisherman's Lament," and *"La Guerra de los tejanos,"* "The Trappers' War" both sung by Pérez, but neither a Pérez original. The first, is a rather humorous account of the often bleak life of the crabber, especially in the harsh month of February. The second, "The Trappers' War," is an account of the *Isleño* muskrat trappers' uprising in 1926. The Spanish title literally translates "The War of the Texans," because up to that time, the waters and land in and around St. Bernard had been worked by the *Isleños* without deeds or property rights, but once a few, led by long-time parish leader, Leander Pérez, realized that they could make money off the land that these trappers and fishermen worked, they brought in some Texans to help take it by force. However, as we see in the song, the *Isleños* successfully defended the land against the Texans, only to be betrayed again by one of their own, Manuel Molero. Moreover, this song laments the fact that the parish was never the same. Little did they know what the twenty-first century would bring.

The widespread flooding following Hurricane Katrina in 2005, did more damage to the Parish of St. Bernard than any storm or flood before it. Thousands of residents of *Isleño* descent fled the parish for good, and Irvan Pérez, so devastated by the flood, wrote no more *décimas* and died in 2008. Now the parish is still reeling from the

---

1   For more on the *Isleños décimas* see Samuel G. Armistead, *The Spanish Tradition in Louisiana* (Newark, Delaware: Juan de la Cuesta, 1992).

2   Patricia Manning Lestrade, "The Last of the Louisiana *Décimas,*" *Hispania* 87, No. 3, (2004), 447-452.

3   Pamela Gray, *"Décima* Poem Lesson," *NCTE American Collection* (2000), accessed May 25, 2011.

4   Armistead, 13.

5   Armistead, 18.

2010 BP oil spill that put hundreds of fishers, crabbers, oystermen and shrimpers out of work. Although neither of these events has inspired any new *décimas* as of yet, they seem to be too significant not to do so at some time in the future.

A Love Song[1]

If you wish to sell your love
There will be a fierce battle;
I shall be a thunderbolt with wings
Until I can win you, my love.
If any one with false exploits
Will speak of your beauty,
In truth, in your defence,
I shall be a faithful lion in battle.
It is by struggling that love is found
And the crown is gained;
Therefore, tell him to depart.
I shall do what you desire
Because I shall put him to death;
It will be a fierce battle.
The avenging saints of God
Will teach me how to love.
They say that I shall see myself
Resting in your arms.
Here you hold me at your feet;
Tell me indeed that I am your faithful lover.
In defence of your heaven
I shall be a thunderbolt with wings.'

Seventeen Seventy-Seven[2]

In seventeen seventy-seven,
some families left the Canary Islands,
for the shores of Cuba
and Southern Louisiana.
In Southern Louisiana
and on land that was given to them,
they became farmers
to maintain their families.
Some became soldiers;
they fought for their freedom.

---

1   Anon. Translated by Alcée Fortier. From: Alcée Fortier, *Louisiana Studies* (New Orleans: F.F. Hansel & Bro., 1894), 209. Fortier records that he transcribed this song from the dictation of Pepe Martin.

2   Written by Irvan Perez. Translated by Samuel G. Armistead. From: Armistead, *The Spanish Tradition*, 37-8.

They were also victorious
fighting against England.
Long live Spain and her flag!
For with all my heart,
I know we're Americans,
but our blood is Spanish!
When times got tough for them
and they couldn't hold out,
they left their land,
and with other Spaniards,
they became fishermen.
What with ducks and muskrats,
with the water and the marsh,
with the help of the women,
they earned their living.
With sorrow and trouble,
and by the will of God,
that's how they settled
the towns of St. Bernard.
Long live Spain and her flag!
For with all my heart,
I know we're Americans,
but our blood is Spanish.

The Father's Prayer[1]

Oh, it came from your father
That is all he had to give
It is yours for you to cherish
Just as long as you may live

If you lose the watch he gave you
It can always be replaced,
But a black mark on your name, son
Can never be erased.

It was clean the day he gave it
What a worthy name to bear
When you received it from your father
There was no dishonor there

And when your time is over
And everything is said and done,

---

1   Composed in both Spanish and English by Irvan Perez. From: Lestrade, "*Décimas*," 451.

You'll be glad you kept it clean
When you hand it to your son.

The Crab Fisherman's Lament[1]

I went up close to shore
just looking for shelter.
I heard a voice saying:
"Here I am all frozen."
The poor crabber says to himself:
"Damned be the month of February!"
I strike one pole against another
and I struck a crab fisherman.
He went on shore to cut straw
and a bees' nest fell on him.
The poor crabber says to himself:
 "Damned be the month of February!"
It was like he'd gone mad;
he got down on all fours.
His partner, when he saw that,
hit him with a pole from behind.
The poor crabber says to himself:
"Damned be the month of February!"
And his hair was all long
and it got tangled in the mangroves
and he couldn't go out
to check on his lines.
The poor crabber says to himself:
"Damned be the month of February!"
When a crab fisherman dies,
let no one mourn for him,
'cause that poor deceased fellow
is just going to his rest.
The poor crabber says to himself:
"Damned be the month of February!"

The Trappers' War[2]

Now pay attention
What I'm going to sing to you
Each time I remember that day

---

1   Sung by Irvan Perez at Reggio, March 27, 1976. Translated by Samuel G. Armistead. From: Armistead, *The Spanish Tradition*, 37-8.

2   Anon. From: Lestrade, "*Décimas*," 448-9.

I feel like crying.
Of the war of the Texans
When they came to fight
To the island of St. Bernard
Many have forgotten
But I haven't forgotten.

The one who was to blame for all
Of this were Perez and Mero.
We won the marshland,
We gave it over to Manuel Molero
But he didn't keep his promise to the people
He put many foreigners
He has ruined everything that was.
Because of Manuel Molero
The little that remained
To Adam Sardín
He gave it to the foreigners.

And poor John, Paul's son
They took him off the map
They sent him to Shallow Bayou
Where his contract called [for him].
He wandered up and down
All he had left was to cry
"So many dollars that I've paid
And I don't have anywhere to trap."

And José collects on the island
In Point LaHache, Adam,
And Juanillo, the [son] of Uncle Caco,
[Is] the one who collects in Oak River.
And poor Toni Molero
They gave him [the area] from school to here
But he doesn't go to your house
As long as you don't send for him.

And with this I won't sing anymore
About the war of the Texans.
If the thing doesn't change
Good-bye Island of St. Bernard.

Eudora Welty (1909–2001)

In Eudora Welty's autobiographical work, *One Writer's Beginnings,* she writes: "When I wrote stories, atmosphere took its influential role from the start. Commotion in the weather and the inner feelings aroused by such a hovering disturbance connected in dramatic form."[1] And that is precisely what occurs in her New Orleans short story, "No Place for You, My Love." The two characters from up North take a ride from New Orleans to Venice, Louisiana, a fishing village on the Gulf of Mexico—"the end of the road," through the dank, dark swamp land where "the heat came… and wrapped them still, and the mosquitoes had begun to coat their arms and even their eyelids." They were not simply "down here in the South," but "south of the South, below it." This short story does not have the side-splitting humor that we so often associate with Welty. "Why I Live at the P. O." comes to mind. Rather like the tangled, threatening jungle her characters drive through on their way south, their inner turmoil and loneliness are reflected in their fecund and sometimes frightening surroundings.

Welty, of course, is known as a Mississippi writer, but in much of her fiction, her characters go to New Orleans or think about going to New Orleans, like so many Mississippians actually do, as it is the closest big city to Louisiana's neighboring state. The two protagonists, who remain unnamed, are not from Mississippi. He's from Syracuse, New York, and she is from Toledo, Ohio. Even though these are northern tourists to the city, the story is based on a trip Welty herself took to New Orleans from her home in Jackson, Mississippi, in August of 1951. In a letter to Irish novelist and short story writer, Elizabeth Bowen, Welty describes her New Orleans adventure; while lunching at Galatoire's restaurant, like her characters in the story, Welty met Faulkner scholar Carvel Collins and accepted his invitation to drive to Venice, Louisiana.

Her letter to Bowen, like the story itself, includes a ferry ride across the Mississippi River at "Pointe a la Hatche" (sic), a "priest's house with his cassock hung out on the clothesline to air… mosquitoes… so thick, everybody on the road carried a branch of a palm to keep flailing around," and even the juke box, slot machines and Shrimp Dance.[2] According to Welty biographer Suzanne Marrs, even though Welty does not mention it in her letter to Bowen, Carvel Collins, in a conversation with Welty scholar Albert Devlin, claims that on their ride back to New Orleans from Venice he did indeed stop the car and kiss Welty. She was not the type to kiss and tell, but Marrs is certain that "this is the source of the kiss that Eudora put into her story" and that "the Welty/Collins relationship was as fleeting as the one in her story."[3]

Welty had several relationships with men, most notably with fellow Mississippian John Frasier Robinson, a lifelong friend with whom she also had a short romantic relationship. According to Marrs, she at one time hoped to marry Robinson, but he fell in love with and remained in a relationship with his Italian partner, Enzo Rocchigiani. Welty had longed for a fulfilling romantic, sexual relationship and marriage, but it was never realized. She also knew the sometimes stifling nature of loneliness, whether in a relationship or not, and this feeling is the driving force behind her characters in this story.

The story opens at Galatoire's, still a very popular New Orleans restaurant on Bourbon Street, where the "strangers to each other…(and) fairly well strangers to the place (were) now seated side by side at a luncheon… (on) a Sunday in summer—those hours of afternoon that seem 'Time Out' in New Orleans." In fact, what ensues is a "Time Out" in their lives, when they take off for Venice in his rented convertible.

Not only do we not know the characters' names, but we discover very little about them, and much of the information is based on speculation. For instance, we do not know why they are in New Orleans, only that they are lunching with friends, but we do know that "he was long married" and that his wife wishes him to stay on an extra day while she entertains some "old, unmarried college friends without him underfoot." We know even less about her. He assumes that she is having an affair with a married man, but there is no proof of that. She is wearing a large hat that he feels does not suit her but that he nonetheless must retrieve for her when it blows off

1   Eudora Welty, *One Writer's Beginnings* (Cambridge, Massachusetts: Warner Books, 1983), 4.

2   Suzanne Marrs, *Eudora Welty* (New York: Harcourt, inc., 2005), 204-205.

3   Ibid., 206.

on the ferry ride across the Mississippi. Not until the end do we discover that she is wearing the hat at least partly out of necessity to hide the bruise at her temple. We do not know how the bruise got there. We also learn that the *"degrading heat"* of Louisiana in August is as oppressive as their isolation, so they reach out to each other, "two Northerners keeping each other company."

One of the most striking aspects of the story is Welty's ability to capture the sweltering yet exotic landscape of South Louisiana. As they drive further south, they become submerged in the "primeval mud" of the swamp land. The further they are from the city, the closer they cling to each other, until "their arms encircling each other, their bodies circling the odorous, just-nailed down floor, they were, at last, imperviousness in motion.... They were what their separate hearts desired that day, for themselves and each other." But here is where the "Time Out" ends. They return to the city, and he drops her at her hotel. Welty sends them on a trip to the end of the road, a trip brought on by their dissatisfaction with their lives, each other, the unbearable summer heat, only to return to those very lives, which is the very crux of her story; their journey is an internal one.

"No Place for You, My Love" was published in Welty's last collection of short fiction, *The Bride of the Innisfallen,* some ten years after the publication of her first novel, *Delta Wedding,* in 1946. In 1969, when Welty was sixty years old, she won the Pulitzer Prize for her novel *The Optimist's Daughter,* a book in which New Orleans also figures prominently. In both works the city provides not only a rich setting but also a catalyst for action which reflects the characters' inner turmoil. Eudora Welty died in Jackson, Mississippi, on July 22, 2001 at the age of 92.

No Place for You, My Love[1]

They were strangers to each other, both fairly well strangers to the place, now seated side by side at luncheon— a party combined in a free-and-easy way when the friends he and she were with recognized each other across Galatoire's. The time was a Sunday in summer—those hours of afternoon that seem Time Out in New Orleans.

The moment he saw her little blunt, fair face, he thought that here was a woman who was having an affair. It was one of those odd meetings when such an impact is felt that it has to be translated at once into some sort of speculation.

With a married man, most likely, he supposed, slipping quickly into a groove—he was long married—and feeling more conventional, then, in his curiosity as she sat there, leaning her cheek on her hand, looking no further before her than the flowers on the table, and wearing that hat.

He did not like her hat, any more than he liked tropical flowers. It was the wrong hat for her, thought this Eastern businessman who had no interest whatever in women's clothes and no eye for them; he thought the unaccustomed thing crossly.

It must stick out all over me, she thought, so people think they can love me or hate me just by looking at me. How did it leave us—the old, safe, slow way people used to know of learning how one another feels, and the privilege that went with it of shying away if it seemed best? People in love like me, I suppose, give away the short cuts to everybody's secrets.

Something, though, he decided, had been settled about her predicament—for the time being, anyway; the parties to it were all still alive, no doubt. Nevertheless, her predicament was the only one he felt so sure of here, like the only recognizable shadow in that restaurant, where mirrors and fans were busy agitating the light, as the very local talk drawled across and agitated the peace. The shadow lay between

---

her fingers, between her little square hand and her cheek, like something always best carried about the person. Then suddenly, as she took her hand down, the secret fact was still there—it lighted her. It was a bold and full light, shot up under the brim of that hat, as close to them all as the flowers in the center of the table.

Did he dream of making her disloyal to that hopelessness that he saw very well she'd been cultivating down here? He knew very well that he did not. What they amounted to was two Northerners keeping each other company. She glanced up at the big gold clock on the wall and smiled. He didn't smile back. She had that naive face that he associated, for no good reason, with the Middle West—because it said "Show me," perhaps. It was a serious, now-watch-out-everybody face, which orphaned her entirely in the company of these Southerners. He guessed her age, as he could not guess theirs: thirty-two. He himself was further along.

Of all human moods, deliberate imperviousness may be the most quickly communicated—it may be the most successful, most fatal signal of all. And two people can indulge in imperviousness as well as in anything else. "You're not very hungry either," he said.

The blades of fan shadows came down over their two heads, as he saw inadvertently in the mirror, with himself smiling at her now like a villain. His remark sounded dominant and rude enough for everybody present to listen back a moment; it even sounded like an answer to a question she might have just asked him. The other women glanced at him. The Southern look—Southern mask—of life-is-a-dream irony, which could turn to pure challenge at the drop of a hat, he could wish well away. He liked naïveté better.

"I find the heat down here depressing," she said, with the heart of Ohio in her voice.

"Well—I'm in somewhat of a temper about it, too," he said.

They looked with grateful dignity at each other.

"I have a car here, just down the street," he said to her as the luncheon party was rising to leave, all the others wanting to get back to their houses and sleep. "If it's all right with— Have you ever driven down south of here?"

Out on Bourbon Street, in the bath of July, she asked at his shoulder, "South of New Orleans? I didn't know there was any south to here. Does it just go on and on?" She laughed, and adjusted the exasperating hat to her head in a different way. It was more than frivolous, it was conspicuous, with some sort of glitter or flitter tied in a band around the straw and hanging down.

"That's what I'm going to show you."

"Oh—you've been there?"

"No!"

His voice rang out over the uneven, narrow sidewalk and dropped back from the walls. The flaked-off, colored houses were spotted like the hides of beasts faded and shy, and were hot as a wall of growth that seemed to breathe flower-like down onto them as they walked to the car parked there.

"It's just that it couldn't be any worse—we'll see." "All right, then," she said. "We will."

So, their actions reduced to amiability, they settled into the car—a faded-red Ford convertible with a rather threadbare canvas top, which had been standing in the sun for all those lunch hours.

"It's rented," he explained. "I asked to have the top put down, and was told I'd lost my mind."

"It's out of this world. Degrading heat," she said and added, "Doesn't matter."

The stranger in New Orleans always sets out to leave it as though following the clue in a maze. They were threading through the narrow and one-way streets, past the pale-violet bloom of tired squares, the brown steeples and statues, the balcony with the live and probably famous black monkey dipping along the railing as over a ballroom floor, past the grillwork and the lattice-work to all the iron swans painted flesh color on the front steps of bungalows outlying.

Driving, he spread his new map and put his finger down on it. At the intersection marked Arabi, where their road led out of the tangle and he took it, a small Negro seated beneath a black umbrella astride a box chalked "Shou Shine" lifted his pink-and-black hand and waved them languidly good-by. She didn't miss it, and waved back.

Below New Orleans there was a raging of insects from both sides of the concrete highway, not quite together, like the playing of separated marching bands. The river and the levee were still on her side, waste and jungle and some occasional settlements on his—poor houses. Families bigger than housefuls thronged the yards. His nodding, driving head would veer from side to side, looking and almost lowering. As time passed and the distance from New Orleans grew, girls ever darker and younger were disposing themselves over the porches and the porch steps, with jet-black hair pulled high, and ragged palm-leaf fans rising and falling like rafts of butterflies. The children running forth were nearly always naked ones.

She watched the road. Crayfish constantly crossed in front of the wheels, looking grim and bonneted, in a great hurry.

"How the Old Woman Got Home," she murmured to herself.

He pointed, as it flew by, at a saucepan full of cut zinnias which stood waiting on the open lid of a mailbox at the roadside, with a little note tied onto the handle.

They rode mostly in silence. The sun bore down. They met fishermen and other men bent on some local pursuits, some in sulphur-colored pants, walking and riding; met wagons, trucks, boats in trucks, autos, boats on top of autos—all coming to meet them, as though something of high moment were doing back where the car came from, and he and she were determined to miss it. There was nearly always a man lying with his shoes off in the bed of any truck otherwise empty—with the raw, red look of a man sleeping in the daytime, being jolted about as he slept. Then there was a sort of dead man's land, where nobody came. He loosened his collar and tie. By rushing through the heat at high speed, they brought themselves the effect of fans turned onto their cheeks. Clearing alternated with jungle and canebrake like something tried, tried again. Little shell roads led off on both sides; now and then a road of planks led into the yellow-green.

"Like a dance floor in there." She pointed.

He informed her, "In there's your oil, I think."

There were thousands, millions of mosquitoes and gnats—a universe of them, and on the increase.

A family of eight or nine people on foot strung along the road in the same direction the car was going, beating themselves with the wild palmettos. Heels, shoulders, knees, breasts, back of the heads, elbows, hands, were touched in turn—like some game, each playing it with himself.

He struck himself on the forehead, and increased their speed. (His wife would not be at her most charitable if he came bringing malaria home to the family.)

More and more crayfish and other shell creatures littered their path, scuttling or dragging. These little samples, little jokes of creation, persisted and sometimes perished. the more of them the deeper down the road went. Terrapins and turtles came up steadily over the horizons of the ditches.

Back there in the margins were worse—crawling hides you could not penetrate with bullets or quite believe, grins that had come down from the primeval mud.

"Wake up." Her Northern nudge was very timely on his arm. They had veered toward the side of the road. Still driving fast, he spread his map.

Like a misplaced sunrise, the light of the river flowed up; they were mounting the levee on a little shell road.

"Shall we cross here?" he asked politely.

He might have been keeping track over years and miles of how long they could keep that tiny ferry waiting. Now skidding down the levee's flank, they were the last-minute car, the last possible car that could squeeze on. Under the sparse shade of one willow tree, the small, amateurish-looking boat slapped the water, as, expertly, he wedged on board.

"Tell him we put him on hub cap!" shouted one of the numerous olive-skinned, dark-eyed young boys standing dressed up in bright shirts at the railing, hugging each other with delight that that last straw was on board. Another boy drew his affectionate initials in the dust of the door on her side.

She opened the door and stepped out, and, after only a moment's standing at bay, started up a little iron stairway. She appeared above the car, on the tiny bridge beneath the captain's window and the whistle.

From there, while the boat still delayed in what seemed a trance— as if it were too full to attempt the start—she could see the panlike deck below, separated by its rusty rim from the tilting, polished water.

The passengers walking and jostling about there appeared oddly amateurish, too—amateur travelers. They were having such a good time. They all knew each other. Beer was being passed around in cans, bets were being loudly settled and new bets made, about local and special subjects on which they all doted. One red-haired man in a burst of wildness even tried to give away his truckload of shrimp to a man on the other side of the boat—nearly all the trucks were full of shrimp—causing taunts and then protests of "They good! They good!" from the giver. The young boys leaned on each other thinking of what next, rolling their eyes absently.

A radio pricked the air behind her. Looking like a great tomcat just above her head, the captain was digesting the news of a fine stolen automobile.

At last a tremendous explosion burst—the whistle.

Everything shuddered in outline from the sound, everybody said something—everybody else.

They started with no perceptible motion, but her hat blew off. It went spiraling to the deck below, where he, thank heaven, sprang out of the car and picked it up. Everybody looked frankly up at her now, holding her hands to her head.

The little willow tree receded as its shade was taken away. The heat was like something falling on her head. She held the hot rail before her. It was like riding a stove. Her shoulders dropping, her hair flying, her skirt buffeted by the sudden strong wind, she stood there, thinking they all must see that with her entire self all she did was wait. Her set hands, with the bag that hung from her wrist and rocked back and forth—all three seemed objects bleaching there, belonging to no one; she could not feel a thing in the skin of her face; perhaps she was crying, and not knowing it. She could look down and see him just below her, his black shadow, her hat, and his black hair. His hair in the wind looked unreasonably long and rippling. Little did he know that from here it had a red underglearn like an animal's. When she looked up and outward, a vortex of light drove through and over the brown waves like a star in the water.

He did after all bring the retrieved hat up the stairs to her. She took it back—useless—and held it to her skirt. What they were saying below was more polite than their searchlight faces.

"Where you think he come from, that man?" "I bet he come from Lafitte."

"Lafitte? What you bet, eh?"—all crouched in the shade of trucks, squatting and laughing.

Now his shadow fell partly across her; the boat had jolted into some other strand of current. Her shaded arm and shaded hand felt pulled out from the blaze of light and water, and she hoped humbly for more shade for her head. It had seemed so natural to climb up and stand in the sun.

The boys had a surprise—an alligator on board. One of them pulled it by a chain around the deck, between the cars and trucks, like a toy—a hide that could walk. He thought, Well they had to catch one sometime. It's Sunday afternoon. So they have him on board now, riding him across the Mississippi

River....The playfulness of it beset everybody on the ferry. The hoarseness of the boat whistle, commenting briefly, seemed part of the general appreciation.

"Who want to rassle him? Who want to, eh?" two boys cried, looking up. A boy with shrimp-colored arms capered from side to side, pretending to have been bitten.

What was there so hilarious about jaws that could bite? And what danger was there once in this repulsiveness— so that the last worldly evidence of some old heroic horror of the dragon had to be paraded in capture before the eyes of country clowns?

He noticed that she looked at the alligator without flinching at all. Her distance was set—the number of feet and inches between herself and it mattered to her.

Perhaps her measuring coolness was to him what his bodily shade was to her, while they stood pat up there riding the river, which felt like the sea and looked like the earth under them—full of the red-brown earth, charged with it. Ahead of the boat it was like an exposed vein of ore. The river seemed to swell in the vast middle with the curve of the earth. The sun rolled under them. As if in memory of the size of things, uprooted trees were drawn across their path, sawing at the air and tumbling one over the other.

When they reached the other side, they felt that they had been racing around an arena in their chariot, among lions. The whistle took and shook the stairs as they went down. The young boys, looking taller, had taken out colored combs and were combing their wet hair back in solemn pompadour above their radiant foreheads. They had been bathing in the river themselves not long before.

The cars and trucks, then the foot passengers and the alligator, waddling like a child to school, all disembarked and wound up the weed-sprung levee.

Both respectable and merciful, their hides, she thought, forcing herself to dwell on the alligator as she looked back. Deliver us all from the naked in heart. (As she had been told.)

When they regained their paved road, he heard her give a little sigh and saw her turn her straw-colored head to look back once more. Now that she rode with her hat in her lap, her earrings were conspicuous too. A little metal ball set with small pale stones danced beside each square, faintly downy cheek.

Had she felt a wish for someone else to be riding with them? He thought it was more likely that she would wish for her husband if she had one (his wife's voice) than for the lover in whom he believed. Whatever people liked to think, situations (if not scenes) were usually three-way—there was somebody else always. The one who didn't—couldn't—understand the two made the formidable third.

He glanced down at the map flapping on the seat between them, up at his wristwatch, out at the road. Out there was the incredible brightness of four o'clock.

On this side of the river, the road ran beneath the brow of the levee and followed it. Here was a heat that ran deeper and brighter and more intense than all the rest—its nerve. The road grew one with the heat as it was one with the unseen river. Dead snakes stretched across the concrete like markers—inlaid mosaic bands, dry as feathers, which their tires licked at intervals that began to seem clocklike.

No, the heat faced them—it was ahead. They could see it waving at them, shaken in the air above the white of the road, always at a certain distance ahead, shimmering finely as a cloth, with running edges of green and gold, fire and azure.

"It's never anything like this in Syracuse," he said.

"Or in Toledo, either," she replied with dry lips.

They were driving through greater waste down here, through fewer and even more insignificant towns. There was water under everything. Even where a screen of jungle had been left to stand, splashes could be heard from under the trees. In the vast open, sometimes boats moved inch by inch through what appeared endless meadows of rubbery flowers.

Her eyes overcome with brightness and size, she felt a panic rise, as sudden as nausea. Just how far below questions and answers, concealment and revelation, they were running now—that was still a new question, with a power of its own, waiting. How dear—how costly—could this ride be?

"It looks to me like your road can't go much further," she remarked cheerfully. "Just over there, it's all water."

"Time out," he said, and with that he turned the car into a sudden road of white shells that rushed at them narrowly out of the left.

They bolted over a cattle guard, where some rayed and crested purple flowers burst out of the vines in the ditch, and rolled onto a long, narrow, green, mowed clearing: a churchyard. A paved track ran between two short rows of raised tombs, all neatly white-washed and now brilliant as faces against the vast flushed sky.

The track was the width of the car with a few inches to spare. He passed between the tombs slowly but in the manner of a feat. Names took their places on the walls slowly at a level with the eye, names as near as the eyes of a person stopping in conversation, and as far away in origin, and in all their music and dead longing, as Spain. At intervals were set packed bouquets of zinnias, oleanders, and some kind of purple flowers, all quite fresh, in fruit jars, like nice welcomes on bureaus.

They moved on into an open plot beyond, of violent- green grass, spread before the green-and-white frame church with worked flower beds around it, flowerless poinsettias growing up to the windowsills. Beyond was a house, and left on the doorstep of the house a fresh-caught catfish the size of a baby—a fish wearing whiskers and bleeding. On a clothesline in the yard, a priest's black gown on a hanger hung airing, swaying at man's height, in a vague, trainlike, lady-like sweep along an evening breath that might otherwise have seemed imaginary from the unseen, felt river.

With the motor cut off, with the raging of the insects about them, they sat looking out at the green and white and black and red and pink as they leaned against the sides of the car.

"What is your wife like?" she asked. His right hand came up and spread—iron, wooden, manicured. She lifted her eyes to his face. He looked at her like that hand.

Then he lit a cigarette, and the portrait, and the right- hand testimonial it made, were blown away. She smiled, herself as unaffected as by some stage performance; and he was annoyed in the cemetery. They did not risk going on to her husband—if she had one.

Under the supporting posts of the priest's house, where a boat was, solid ground ended and palmettos and water hyacinths could not wait to begin; suddenly the rays of the sun, from behind the car, reached that lowness and struck the flowers. The priest came out onto the porch in his underwear, stared at the car a moment as if he wondered what time it was, then collected his robe off the line and his fish off the doorstep and returned inside. Vespers was next, for him.

After backing out between the tombs he drove on still south, in the sunset. They caught up with an old man walking in a sprightly way in their direction, all by himself, wearing a clean bright shirt printed with a pair of palm trees fanning green over his chest. It might better be a big colored woman's shirt, but she didn't have it. He flagged the car with gestures like hoops.

"You're coming to the end of the road," the old man told them. He pointed ahead, tipped his hat to the lady, and pointed again. "End of the road." They didn't understand that he meant, "Take me."

They drove on. "If we do go any further, it'll have to be by water—is that it?" he asked her, hesitating at this odd point.

"You know better than I do," she replied politely.

The road had for some time ceased to be paved; it was made of shells. It was leading into a small, sparse settlement like the others a few miles back, but with even more of the camp about it. On the lip of the clearing, directly before a green willow blaze with the sunset gone behind it, the row of houses and shacks faced out on broad, colored, moving water that stretched to reach the horizon and looked like an arm of the sea. The houses on their shaggy posts, patchily built, some with plank runways instead of steps, were flimsy and alike, and not much bigger than the boats tied up at the landing.

"Venice," she heard him announce, and he dropped the crackling map in her lap.

They coasted down the brief remainder. The end of the road—she could not remember ever seeing a road simply end—was a spoon shape, with a tree stump in the bowl to turn around by.

Around it, he stopped the car, and they stepped out, feeling put down in the midst of a sudden vast pause or subduement that was like a yawn. They made their way on foot toward the water, where at an idle-looking landing men in twos and threes stood with their backs to them.

The nearness of darkness, the still uncut trees, bright water partly under a sheet of flowers, shacks, silence, dark shapes of boats tied up, then the first sounds of people just on the other side of thin walls— all this reached them. Mounds of shells like day-old snow, pink-tinted, lay around a central shack with a beer sign on it. An old man up on the porch there sat holding an open newspaper, with a fat white goose sitting opposite him on the floor. Below, in the now shadowless and sunless open, another old man, with a colored pencil bright under his hat brim, was late mending a sail.

When she looked clear around, thinking they had a fire burning somewhere now, out of the heat had risen the full moon. Just beyond the trees, enormous, tangerine-colored, it was going solidly up. Other lights just striking into view, looking farther distant, showed moss shapes hanging, or slipped and broke matchlike on the water that so encroached upon the rim of ground they were standing on.

There was a touch at her arm—his, accidental.

"We're at the jumping-off place," he said.

She laughed, having thought his hand was a bat, while her eyes rushed downward toward a great pale drift of water hyacinths—still partly open, flushed and yet moonlit, level with her feet—through which paths of water for the boats had been hacked. She drew her hands up to her face under the brim of her hat; her own cheeks felt like the hyacinths to her, all her skin still full of too much light and sky, exposed. The harsh vesper bell was ringing.

"I believe there must be something wrong with me, that I came on this excursion to begin with," she said, as if he had already said this and she were merely in hopeful, willing, maddening agreement with him.

He took hold of her arm, and said, "Oh, come on—I see we can get something to drink here, at least."

But there was a beating, muffled sound from over the darkening water. One more boat was coming in, making its way through the tenacious, tough, dark flower traps, by the shaken light of what first appeared to be torches. He and she waited for the boat, as if on each other's patience. As if borne in on a mist of twilight or a breath, a horde of mosquitoes and gnats came singing and striking at them first. The boat bumped, men laughed. Somebody was offering somebody else some shrimp.

Then he might have cocked his dark city head down at her; she did not look up at him, only turned when he did. Now the shell mounds, like the shacks and trees, were solid purple. Lights had appeared in the not-quite-true window squares. A narrow neon sign, the lone sign, had come out in bright blush on the beer shack's roof: "Baba's Place." A light was on on the porch.

The barnlike interior was brightly lit and unpainted, looking not quite finished, with a partition dividing this room from what lay behind. One of the four cardplayers at a table in the middle of the floor was the newspaper reader; the paper was in his pants pocket. Midway along the partition was a bar, in the form of a pass-through to the other room, with a varnished, second-hand fretwork overhang. They crossed the floor and sat, alone there, on wooden stools. An eruption of humorous signs, newspaper cutouts and cartoons, razor-blade cards, and personal messages of significance to the owner or his friends decorated the overhang, framing where Baba should have been but wasn't.

Through there came a smell of garlic and cloves and red pepper, a blast of hot cloud escaped from a cauldron they could see now on a stove at the back of the other room. A massive back, presumably female, with a twist of gray hair on top, stood with a ladle akimbo. A young man joined her and with his fingers stole something out of the pot and ate it. At Baba's they were boiling shrimp.

When he got ready to wait on them, Baba strolled out to the counter, young, black-headed, and in very good humor.

"Coldest beer you've got. And food— What will you have?"

"Nothing for me, thank you," she said. "I'm not sure I could eat, after all."

"Well, I could," he said, shoving his jaw out. Baba smiled. "I want a good solid ham sandwich."

"I could have asked him for some water," she said, after he had gone.

While they sat waiting, it seemed very quiet. The bubbling of the shrimp, the distant laughing of Baba, and the slap of cards, like the beating of moths on the screens, seemed to come in fits and starts. The steady breathing they heard came from a big rough dog asleep in the corner. But it was bright. Electric lights were strung riotously over the room from a kind of spider web of old wires in the rafters. One of the written messages tacked before them read, "Joe! At the boy !!" It looked very yellow, older than Baba's Place. Outside, the world was pure dark.

Two little boys, almost alike, almost the same size, and just cleaned up, dived into the room with a double bang of the screen door, and circled around the card game. They ran their hands into the men's pockets.

"Nickel for some pop!"

"Nickel for some pop!"

"Go 'way and let me play, you!"

They circled around and shrieked at the dog, ran under the lid of the counter and raced through the kitchen and back, and hung over the stools at the bar. One child had a live lizard on his shirt, clinging like a breast pin— like lapis lazuli.

Bringing in a strong odor of geranium talcum, some men had come in now—all in bright shirts. They drew near the counter, or stood and watched the game.

When Baba came out bringing the beer and sandwich, "Could I have some water?" she greeted him.

Baba laughed at everybody. She decided the woman back there must be Baba's mother.

Beside her, he was drinking his beer and eating his sandwich—ham, cheese, tomato, pickle, and mustard. Before he finished, one of the men who had come in beckoned from across the room. It was the old man in the palm- tree shirt.

She lifted her head to watch him leave her, and was looked at, from all over the room. As a minute passed, no cards were laid down. In a far-off way, like accepting the light from Arcturus, she accepted it that she was more beautiful or perhaps more fragile than the women they saw every day of their lives. It was just this thought coming into a woman's face, and at this hour, that seemed familiar to them.

Baba was smiling. He had set an opened, frosted brown bottle before her on the counter, and a thick sandwich, and stood looking at her. Baba made her eat some supper, for what she was.

"What the old fellow wanted," said he when he came back at last, "was to have a friend of his apologize. Seems church is just out. Seems the friend made a remark coming in just now. His pals told him there was a lady present."

"I see you bought him a beer," she said.

"Well, the old man looked like he wanted something."

All at once the juke box interrupted from back in the corner, with the same old song as anywhere. The half- dozen slot machines along the wall were suddenly all run to like Maypoles, and thrown into action—taken over by further battalions of little boys.

There were three little boys to each slot machine. The local custom appeared to be that one pulled the lever for the friend he was holding up to put the nickel in, while the third covered the pictures with the flat of his hand as they fell into place, so as to surprise them all if anything happened.

The dog lay sleeping on in front of the raging juke box, his ribs working fast as a concertina's. At the side of the room a man with a cap on his white thatch was trying his best to open a side screen door, but it was stuck fast. It was he who had come in with the remark considered ribald; now he was trying to get out the other way. Moths as thick as ingots were trying to get in. The card players broke into shouts of derision, then joy, then tired derision among themselves; they might have been here all afternoon—they were the only ones not cleaned up and shaved. The original pair of little boys ran in once more, with the hyphenated bang. They got nickels this time, then were brushed away from the table like mosquitoes, and they rushed under the counter and on to the cauldron behind, clinging to Baba's mother there. The evening was at the threshold.

They were quite unnoticed now. He was eating another sandwich, and she, having finished part of hers, was fanning her face with her hat. Baba had lifted the flap of the counter and come out into the room. Behind his head there was a sign lettered in orange crayon: "Shrimp Dance Sun. PM." That was tonight, still to be.

And suddenly she made a move to slide down from her stool, maybe wishing to walk out into that nowhere down the front steps to be cool a moment. But he had hold of her hand. He got down from his stool, and, patiently, reversing her hand in his own—just as she had had the look of being about to give up, faint—began moving her, leading her. They were dancing.

"I get to thinking this is what we get—what you and I deserve," she whispered, looking past his shoulder into the room. "And all the time, it's real. It's a real place— away off down here...."

They danced gratefully, formally, to some song carried on in what must be the local patois, while no one paid any attention as long as they were together, and the children poured the family nickels steadily into the slot machines, walloping the handles down with regular crashes and troubling nobody with winning.

She said rapidly, as they began moving together too well, "One of those clippings was an account of a shooting right here. I guess they're proud of it. And that awful knife Baba was carrying...I wonder what he called me," she whispered in his ear.

"Who?"

"The one who apologized to you."

If they had ever been going to overstep themselves, it would be now as he held her closer and turned her, when she became aware that he could not help but see the bruise at her temple. It would not be six inches from his eyes. She felt it come out like an evil star. (Let it pay him back, then, for the hand he had stuck in her face when she'd tried once to be sympathetic, when she'd asked about his wife.) They danced on still as the record changed, after standing wordless and motionless, linked together in the middle of the room, for the moment between.

Then, they were like a matched team—like professional, Spanish dancers wearing masks—while the slow piece was playing.

Surely even those immune from the world, for the time being, need the touch of one another, or all is lost. Their arms encircling each other, their bodies circling the odorous, just-nailed-down floor, they were, at last, imperviousness in motion. They had found it, and had almost missed it: they had had to dance. They were what their separate hearts desired that day, for themselves and each other.

They were so good together that once she looked up and half smiled. "For whose benefit did we have to show off?"

Like people in love, they had a superstition about themselves almost as soon as they came out on the floor, and dared not think the words "happy" or "unhappy," which might strike them, one or the other, like lightning.

In the thickening heat they danced on while Baba himself sang with the mosquito-voiced singer in the chorus of *"Mai pas l'airaez fa,"* enumerating the *fa's* with a hot shrimp between his fingers. He was counting over the platters the old woman now set out on the counter, each heaped with shrimp in their shells boiled to iridescence, like mounds of honeysuckle flowers.

The goose wandered in from the back room under the lid of the counter and hitched itself around the floor among the table legs and people's legs, never seeing that it was neatly avoided by two dancers—who nevertheless vaguely thought of this goose as learned, having earlier heard an old man read to it. The children called it Mimi, and lured it away. The old thatched man was again drunkenly trying to get out by the stuck side door; now he gave it a kick, but was prevailed on to remain. The sleeping dog shuddered and snored.

It was left up to the dancers to provide nickels for the juke box; Baba kept a drawerful for every use. They had grown fond of all the selections by now. This was the music you heard out of the distance at night—out of the roadside taverns you fled past, around the late corners in cities half asleep, drifting up from the carnival over the hill, with one odd little strain always managing to repeat itself. This seemed a homey place.

Bathed in sweat, and feeling the false coolness that brings, they stood finally on the porch in the lapping night air for a moment before leaving. The first arrivals of the girls were coming up the steps under the porch light—all flowered fronts, their black pompadours giving out breathlike feelers from sheer abundance. Where they'd resprinkled it since church, the talcum shone like mica on their downy arms. Smelling solidly of geranium, they filed across the porch with short steps and fingers joined, just timed to turn their smiles loose inside the room. He held the door open for them.

"Ready to go?" he asked her.

Going back, the ride was wordless, quiet except for the motor and the insects driving themselves against the car. The windshield was soon blinded. The headlights pulled in two other spinning storms, cones of flying things that, it seemed, might ignite at the last minute. He stopped the car and got out to clean the windshield thoroughly with his brisk, angry motions of driving. Dust lay thick and cratered on the roadside scrub. Under the now ash-white moon, the world traveled through very faint stars—very many slow stars, very high, very low.

It was a strange land, amphibious—and whether water- covered or grown with jungle or robbed entirely of water and trees, as now, it had the same loneliness. He regarded the great sweep—like steppes, like moors, like deserts (all of which were imaginary to him); but more than it was like any likeness, it was South. The vast, thin, wide- thrown, pale, unfocused star-sky, with its veils of lightning adrift, hung over this land as it hung over the open sea. Standing out in the night alone, he was struck as powerfully with recognition of the extremity of this place as if all other bearings had vanished—as if snow had suddenly started to fall.

He climbed back inside and drove. When he moved to slap furiously at his shirtsleeves, she shivered in the hot, licking night wind that their speed was making. Once the car lights picked out two people—a Negro couple, sitting on two facing chairs in the yard outside their lonely cabin —half undressed, each battling for self against the hot night, with long white rags in endless, scarflike motions.

In peopleless open places there were lakes of dust, smudge fires burning at their hearts. Cows stood in untended rings around them, motionless in the heat, in the night—their horns standing up sharp against that glow.

At length, he stopped the car again, and this time he put his arm under her shoulder and kissed her— not knowing ever whether gently or harshly. It was the loss of that distinction that told him this was now. Then their faces touched unkissing, unmoving, dark, for a length of time. The heat came inside the car and wrapped them still, and the mosquitoes had begun to coat their arms and even their eyelids.

Later, crossing a large open distance, he saw at the same time two fires. He had the feeling that they had been riding for a long time across a face—great, wide, and upturned. In its eyes and open mouth were those fires they had had glimpses of, where the cattle had drawn together: a face, a head, far down here in the South—south of South, below it. A whole giant body sprawled downward then, on and on, always, constant as a constellation or an angel. Flaming and perhaps falling, he thought.

She appeared to be sound asleep, lying back flat as a child, with her hat in her lap. He drove on with her profile beside his, behind his, for he bent forward to drive faster. The earrings she wore twinkled with their rushing motion in an almost regular beat. They might have spoken like tongues. He looked straight before him and drove on, at a speed that, for the rented, overheated, not at all new Ford car, was demoniac.

It seemed often now that a barnlike shape flashed by, roof and all outlined in lonely neon—a movie house at a cross roads. The long white flat road itself, since they had followed it to the end and turned around to come back, seemed able, this far up, to pull them home.

A thing is incredible, if ever, only after it is told—returned to the world it came out of. For their different reasons, he thought, neither of them would tell this (unless something was dragged out of them): that, strangers, they had ridden down into a strange land together and were getting safely back—by a slight margin, perhaps, but margin enough. Over the levee wall now, like an aurora borealis, the sky of New Orleans, across the river, was flickering gently. This time they crossed by bridge, high above everything, merging into a long light-stream of cars turned cityward.

For a time afterward he was lost in the streets, turning almost at random with the noisy traffic until he found his bearings. When he stopped the car at the next sign and leaned forward frowning to make it out, she sat up straight on her side. It was Arabi. He turned the car right around.

"We're all right now," he muttered, allowing himself a cigarette.

Something that must have been with them all along suddenly, then, was not. In a moment, tall as panic, it rose, cried like a human, and dropped back.

"I never got my water," she said.

She gave him the name of her hotel, he drove her there, and he said good night on the sidewalk. They shook hands.

"Forgive...." For, just in time, he saw she expected it of him.

And that was just what she did, forgive him. Indeed, had she waked in time from a deep sleep, she would have told him her story. She disappeared through the revolving door, with a gesture of smoothing her hair, and he thought a figure in the lobby strolled to meet her. He got back in the car and sat there.

He was not leaving for Syracuse until early in the morning. At length, he recalled the reason; his wife had recommended that he stay where he was this extra day so that she could entertain some old, unmarried college friends without him underfoot.

As he started up the car, he recognized in the smell of exhausted, body-warm air in the streets, in which the flow of drink was an inextricable part, the signal that the New Orleans evening was just beginning. In Dickie Grogan's, as he passed, the well-known Josefina at her organ was charging up and down with *"Clair de Lune."* As he drove the little Ford safely to its garage, he remembered for the first time in years when he was young and brash, a student in New York, and the shriek and horror and unholy smother of the subway had its original meaning for him as the lilt and expectation of love.

Tennessee Williams (1911–1983)

Tennessee Williams, born Thomas Lanier Williams to Cornelius and Edwina Dakin Williams in Columbia, Mississippi, on March 26, 1911, had his first big success with his 1944 play, *The Glass Menagerie.* He called it a "memory play," looking back to his time in St. Louis after his father had left and he was living with his mother and his sister Rose (His younger brother Dakin also lived there, but his character does not appear in the play.). Some thirty years later, Williams wrote another "memory play," *Vieux Carré,* which picks up where *The Glass Menagerie* leaves off, with Tom's arrival in the French Quarter—or Vieux Carré—of New Orleans.

Williams often wrote short stories that would later become the basis for plays, and *Vieux Carré* was no exception. He wrote "The Angel in the Alcove" in 1943, not long after having left New Orleans, while he was living in Santa Monica, California. Yet, he did not write the play until 1977. His brother Dakin claims that the "'angel' part is about the only thing that didn't happen" in the short story, and likewise in the play, which is very faithful to it.[1] In the short story, the young protagonist lives in a dive on world-famous Bourbon Street. In the play and in actuality, the young writer—presumably Williams—lives in a dive of a rooming house on Toulouse Street. The defeated and suspicious landlady appears in both the short story and the play, as does the consumptive artist, whose vicious scene with the landlady prompts the young writer to leave the French Quarter.

In Tom's final monologue in *The Glass Menagerie,* he states, "I didn't go to the moon, I went much further—for time is the longest distance between two places.... I left Saint Louis." And as his brother states, "he 'came out'—the gay way of saying that he had decided on his way of sex and no longer wanted to suppress it."[2] In his own memoir, simply entitled *Memoirs,* Williams discusses how he first "came out" in New Orleans, and he mentions an artist, named Antoine, who "was not a brilliant painter," who sounds much like the dying artist, Nightingale, in *Vieux Carré.*[3]

In both the play and the short story, the young protagonist has a homosexual experience with Nightingale, and in the play, afterwards, the "angel in the alcove" again appears "in the form of an elderly female saint, of course. She materialized soundlessly. Her eyes fixed on me with a gentle questioning look which I came to remember as having belonged to my grandmother." Dakin claims that this is not only a vision of their grandmother, Grand, but also Tennessee's own conscience. She certainly does not condemn this act: "She...seemed to lift one hand very, very slightly before my eyes closed with sleep. An almost invisible gesture of...forgiveness?... through understanding?" In his memoir, Williams celebrates coming out and embracing his homosexuality, and homosexuality is a theme of this and several of Williams' major plays, including *A Streetcar Named Desire, Cat on a Hot Tin Roof,* and *Kingdom of Earth,* to name a few.

Some critics object to the fact that Williams includes themes, characters and motifs in *Vieux Carré*—aside from homosexuality—that we see in other Williams' plays, but that's primarily because they did occur and did shape his life. Sky, the character with whom the young writer leaves New Orleans, certainly resembles Xavier Valentine from Williams' 1957 play, *Orpheus Descending.* In *Vieux Carré,* the landlady, Mrs. Wire, does pour boiling water through the cracks in the floorboards onto the raucous party below in order to quiet them up. Likewise, in *A Streetcar Named Desire,* Eunice does the same thing from her upstairs apartment in an attempt to break up Stanley's rowdy poker game. Dakin claims that did indeed happen, but more importantly, young Tennessee met playwright Roark Bradford and New Orleans writer Lyle Saxon at that very party.[4]

Also reminiscent of *Streetcar,* and more specifically of Blanche Dubois, are the faded southern belles struggling to hold on, Mary Maude and Miss Carrie. We can also see Blanche in Jane, the dying socialite who runs away from New York and turns to sex or desire which she finds with Tye, a coarse but completely sexual character, much like Stanley Kowalski. As one of his last major plays, *Vieux Carré* may inevitably suffer from some recycling, yet there is a haunting dreaminess about this play that makes it important in its own right.

---

1   Dakin Williams and Shepherd Mead, *Tennessee Williams: An Intimate Biography* (New York: Arbor House. 1983), 71.

2   Ibid., 73.

3   Tennessee Williams, *Memoirs* (Garden City, New York: Doubleday, 1975), 50.

4   Williams and Mead, *Intimate Biography,* 75.

By this time Williams' friends were aware of his depression and drug use. Williams was also a heavy drinker and that probably played a role in his death in New York City in 1983, which was finally classified as "acute seconal intolerance."[1]

Nonetheless, Williams never wrote a play that relied more on the setting and characters of New Orleans than *Vieux Carré*. There are very few New Orleanians who have not met crazy landladies like Mrs. Wire, or strung-out strip club barkers like Tye, characters whom Williams in his essay "Amor Perdido" calls "Quarter Rats," who "huddle together for some dim, communal effort… for the companionship of one's own kind." In this play, like in the French Quarter itself, we can see "life getting bigger and plainer and uglier and more beautiful all the time."[2] It is high time lovers of Williams' plays and of New Orleans literature get a glimpse of another play set in the city besides the very worthy but perhaps too familiar *Streetcar*.

Vieux Carré[3]

TIME: The period between winter 1938 and spring 1939.

PLACE: A rooming house, No. 722 Toulouse Street, in the French Quarter of New Orleans.

SETTING: The stage seems bare. Various playing areas may be distinguished by sketchy partitions and doorframes. In the barrenness there should be a poetic evocation of all the cheap rooming houses of the world. This one is in the Vieux Carré of New Orleans, where it remains standing, at 722 Toulouse Street, now converted to an art gallery. I will describe the building as it was when I rented an attic room in the late thirties, not as it will be designed, or realized for the stage.

It is a three-story building. There are a pair of alcoves, facing Toulouse Street. These alcove cubicles are separated by plywood, which provides a minimal separation (spatially) between the writer (myself, those many years ago) and an older painter, a terribly wasted man, dying of tuberculosis, but fiercely denying this circumstance to himself.

A curved staircase ascends from the rear of a dark narrow passageway from the street entrance to the kitchen area. From there it ascends to the third floor, or gabled attic with its mansard roof.

A narrow hall separates the gabled cubicles from the studio (with skylight) which is occupied by Jane and Tye.

Obviously the elevations of these acting areas can be only suggested by a few shallow steps: a realistic setting is impossible, and the solution lies mainly in very skillful lighting and minimal furnishings.

PART ONE
Scene One

WRITER [*spotlighted downstage*]: Once this house was alive, it was occupied once. In my recollection it still is but by shadowy occupants like ghosts. Now they enter the lighter areas of my memory.

[*Fade in dimly visible characters of the play, turning about in a stylized manner. The spotlight fades on the writer and is brought up on Mrs. Wire, who assumes her active character in the play.*]

MRS. WIRE: Nursie! Nursie—where's my pillows?

[*Nursie is spotlighted on a slightly higher level, looking up fearfully at something. She screams.*]

Hey, what the hell is going on in there!

---

1   Austin Smith, "Tennessee Williams' Death Myth," *NYPost: Page Six* (http://pagesix.com/2010/02/15/tennessee-williams-death-myth/).

2   Tennessee Williams, "Amor Perdido," in *New Selected Essays: Where I Live* (New York: New Directions, 2009), 3-7.

3   By Tennessee Williams, from *Vieux Carré*, copyright © 1977 by The University of the South. Reprinted by permission of New Directions Publishing Corp.

NURSIE [*running down in a sort of football crouch*]: A bat, a bat's in the kitchen!

MRS. WIRE: Bat? I never seen a bat nowhere on these premises, Nursie.

NURSIE: Why, Mizz Wire, I swear it was a bull bat up there in the kitchen. You tell me no bats, why, they's a pack of bats that hang upside down from that ole banana tree in the courtyard from dark till daybreak, when they all scream at once and fly up like a—explosion of—damned souls out of a graveyard.

MRS. WIRE: If such a thing was true—

NURSIE: As God's word is true!

MRS. WIRE: I repeat, if such a thing was true—which it isn't— an' you go tawkin' about it with you big black mouth, why it could ruin the reputation of this rooming house which is the only respectable rooming house in the Quarter. Now where's my pillows, Nursie?

NURSIE [sotto voce *as she arranges the pallet*]: Shit…

MRS. WIRE: What you say?

NURSIE: I said shoot… faw shit. You'd see they're on the cot if you had a light bulb in this hall. [*She is making up the cot.*] What you got against light? First thing God said on the first day of creation was, "Let there be light."

MRS. WIRE: You hear him say that?

NURSIE: You never read the scriptures.

MRS. WIRE: Why should I bother to read 'em with you quotin' 'em to me like a female preacher. Book say this, say that, makes me sick of the book. Where's my flashlight, Nursie?

NURSIE: 'Sunder the pillows. [*She stumbles on a heavy knapsack.*] Lawd! What that there?

MRS. WIRE: Some crazy young man come here wantin' a room, I told him I had no vacancies for Bourbon Street bums. He dropped that sack on the floor and said he'd pick it up tomorrow, which he won't unless he pays fifty cents for storage…

NURSIE: It's got something written on it that shines in the dark.

MRS. WIRE: "Sky" —say that's his name. Carry it on upstairs with you, Nursie.

NURSIE: Mizz Wire, I cain't hardly get myself up them steps no more, you know that.

MRS. WIRE: Shoot.

NURSIE: Mizz Wire, I think I oughta inform you I'm thinkin' of retirin'.

MRS. WIRE: *Retirin'* to what, Nursie? The banana tree in the courtyard with the bats you got in your head?

NURSIE: They's lots of folks my age, black and white, that's called bag people. They just wander round with paper bags that hold ev'rything they possess or they can collect. Nights they sleep on doorsteps: spend days on boxes on corners of Canal Street with a tin cup. They get along; they live—long as intended to by the Lord.

MRS. WIRE: Your place is with me, Nursie.

NURSIE: I can't please you no more. You keep callin' Nursie, Nursie, do this, do that, with all these stairs in the house and my failin' eyesight. No Ma'am, it's time for me to retire.

[*She crosses upstage. The kitchen area is dimly lighted. Nursie is at the table with a cup of chicory coffee, eyes large and ominously dark as the continent of her race.*

[A *spot of light picks up the writer dimly at the entrance to the hall.*]

MRS. WIRE: Who? Who?

WRITER: It's—

MRS. WIRE: *You…*

WRITER: Mrs. Wire, you're blinding me with that light [*He shields his left eye with a hand.*]

MRS. WIRE [*switching off the light*]: Git upstairs, boy. We'll talk in the mawnin' about your future plans.

WRITER: I have no plans for the future, Mrs. Wire.

MRS. WIRE: That's a situation you'd better correct right quick.

[*The writer, too, collides with the bizarre, colorfully decorated knapsack.*]

WRITER: What's—?

MRS. WIRE: Carry that Sack upstairs with you. Nursie refused to.

[*With an effort the writer shoulders the sack and mounts a step or two to the kitchen level.*]

WRITER: Mrs. Wire told me to carry this sack up here.

NURSIE: Just put it somewhere it won't trip me.

WRITER: Sky? Sky?

NURSIE: She say that's his *name.* Whose name? I think her mind is goin' on her again. Lately she calls out, "Timmy, Timmy," or she carries on conversations *with* her dead husband, Horace…

WRITER: A *name—Sky? [To himself]* Shines like a prediction.

[*He drops the knapsack at the edge of the kitchen light and wanders musingly back to the table. Nursie automatically pours him a cup of chicory.*]

[*Again the area serving as the entrance passage is lighted, and the sound of a key scraping at a resistant lock is heard.*]

MRS. WIRE [*starting up from her cot*]: Who? Who? [*Jane enters exhaustedly.*]

JANE: Why, Mrs. Wire, you scared me! [*She has an elegance about her and a vulnerability.*]

MRS. WIRE: Miss Sparks, what're you doin' out so late on the streets of the Quarter?

JANE: Mrs. Wire, according to the luminous dial on *my* watch, it is only ten after twelve.

MRS. WIRE: When I give you a room here

JANE: Gave me? I thought *rented…*

MRS. WIRE [*cutting through*]: I told you a single girl was expected in at midnight.

JANE: I'm afraid I didn't take that too seriously. Not since I lived with my parents in New Rochelle, New York, before I went to college, have I been told to be in at a certain hour, and even then I had my own key and disregarded the order more often than not. However, I am going to tell you why and where I've gone tonight. I have gone to the all-night drugstore, Waterbury's, on Canal Street, to buy a spray can of Black Flag, which is an insect repellent. I took a cab there tonight and made this purchase because, Mrs. Wire, when I opened the window without a screen in my room, a cockroach, a *flying* cockroach, flew right into my face and was followed by a squadron of others. *Well!* I do *not* have an Oriental, a Buddhistic tolerance for certain insects, least of all a cockroach and even less a flying one. Oh, I've learned to live reluctantly with the ordinary pedestrian kind of cockroach, but to have one fly directly into my face almost gave me convulsions! Now as for the window without a screen, if a screen has not been put in that window by tomorrow, I will buy one for it myself and deduct the cost from next month's rent. [*She goes past Mrs. Wire toward the steps.*]

MRS. WIRE: Hold on a minute, young lady. When you took your room here, you gave your name as Miss Sparks. Now is that young fellow that's living up there with you Mr. Sparks, and if so why did you register as Miss instead of Mrs.?

JANE: I'm sure you've known for some time that I'm sharing my room with a young man, whose name is not Mr. Sparks, whose name is Tye McCool. And if that offends your moral scruples—well—sometimes it offends mine, too.

MRS. WIRE: If I had not been a young lady myself once! Oh yes, once, yaiss! I'd have evicted both so fast you'd think that…

JANE: No, I've stopped thinking. Just let things happen to me.

[*Jane is now at the stairs and starts up them weakly. Mrs. Wire grunts despairingly and falls back to her cot. Jane enters the kitchen.*]

NURSIE: Why, hello, Miss Sparks.

JANE: Good evening, Nursie—why is Mrs. Wire sleeping in the entrance hall?

NURSIE: Lawd, that woman, she got the idea that 722 Toulouse Street is the address of a jailhouse. And she's the keeper— have some hot chicory with me?

JANE: Do you know I still don't know what chicory is? A beverage of some kind?

NURSIE: Why chicory's South'n style coffee.

JANE: Oh, well, thank you, maybe I could try a bit of it to get me up that flight of stairs .

[*She sits at the table. Below, the door has opened a third time. The painter called Nightingale stands in the doorway with a pickup.*]

MRS. WIRE: Who? Ah!

NIGHTINGALE [*voice rising*]: Well, cousin, uh, Jake...

PICKUP [*uneasily*]: Blake.

NIGHTINGALE: Yes, we do have a lot of family news to exchange. Come on in. We'll talk a bit more in my room.

MRS. WIRE: In a pig's snout you will!

NIGHTINGALE: Why, Mrs. Wire! [*He chuckles, coughs.*] Are you sleeping in the hall now?

MRS. WIRE: I'm keeping watch on the comings and goings at night of tenants in my house.

NIGHTINGALE: Oh, yes, I know your aversion to visitors at night, but this is my first cousin. I just bumped into him at Gray Goose bus station. He is here for one day only, so I have taken the license of inviting him in for a little family talk since we'll have no other chance.

MRS. WIRE: If you had half the cousins you claim to have, you'd belong to the biggest family since Adam's.

PICKUP: Thanks, but T got to move on. Been nice seeing you— cousin...

NIGHTINGALE: Wait—here—take this five. Go to the America Hotel on Exchange Alley just off Canal Street, and I will drop in at noon tomorrow—cousin. [*He starts to cough.*]

PICKUP: Thanks, see ya, cousin.

MRS. WIRE: Hah, cousin.

[*Nightingale coughs and spits near her cot.*] Don't you spit by my *bed!*

NIGHTINGALE: Fuck off, you old witch!

MRS. WIRE: What did you say to me?

NIGHTINGALE: Nothing not said to and about you before! [*He mounts the steps.*]

MRS. WIRE: Nursie! Nursie! [*Receiving no response she lowers herself with a groan onto the cot.*]

NIGHTINGALE: [*starting up the stairs*]: Midnight staircase—still in—your [*coughs*] fatal position... [*He climbs slowly up.*]

[*The writer, Jane, and Nursie are in the kitchen. The crones enter, wild-eyed and panting with greasy paper bags. The kitchen area is lighted.*]

MARY MAUDE: Nursie? Miss Carrie and I ordered a little more dinner this evening than we could eat, so we had the waiter put the remains of the, the—

MISS CARRIE [*her wild eyes very wild*]: The steak "Diane," I had the steak Diane and Mary Maude had the chicken "bonne femme." But our eyes were a little bigger than our stomachs.

MARY MAUDE: The sight of too much on a table can kill your appetite! But this food is too good to waste.

MISS CARRIE: And we don't have ice to preserve it in our room, so would you kindly put it in Mrs.

Wire's icebox, Nursie.

NURSIE: The last time I done that Miss Wire raised Cain about it, had me throw it right out. She said it didn' smell good.

JANE: I have an icebox in which I'd be glad to keep it for you ladies.

MARY MAUDE: Oh, that's very kind of you!

WRITER [*rising from the kitchen table*]: Let me carry it up.

[*He picks up the greasy bags and starts upstairs. Miss Carrie's asthmatic respiration has steadily increased. She staggers with a breathless laugh.*]

MARY MAUDE: Oh, Miss Carrie, you better get right to bed— She's having another attack of her awful asthma. Our room gets no sun, and the walls are so damp, so— dark…

[*They totter out of the light together.*]

NURSIE [*averting her face from the bag with a sniff of repugnance*]: They didn't go to no restaurant. They been to the garbage pail on the walk outside, don't bother with it, it's spoiled [*pointing upstage*] just put it over there. I'll throw it out.

JANE: I wonder if they'd be offended if I bought them a sack of groceries at Solari's tomorrow.

NURSIE: Offend 'em did you say?

JANE: I meant their pride.

NURSIE: Honey, they gone as far past pride as they gone past mistaking a buzzard for a bluebird.

[*She chuckles. Tye appears. Jane pretends not to notice.*]

JANE: I'm afraid pride's an easy thing to go past sometimes. I am living—I am sharing my studio with a, an addicted—delinquent, a barker at a—stripshow joint. [*She has pretended to ignore Tye's disheveled, drugged, but vulnerably boyish appearance at the edge of the light.*]

TYE [*in a slurred voice*]: You wouldn't be tawkin' about—nobody—present…

JANE: Why, hello, Tye. How'd you get back so early? How'd you get back at all, in this—condition?

TYE: Honey! If I didn't have my arms full of—packages.

JANE: The less you say out loud about the hot merchandise you've been accumulating here…

TYE: Babe, you're asking for *a*— [*He doubles his fist.*]

JANE: Which I'd return with a kick in the balls! [*She gasps.*] My Lord, did I say that?

MRS. WIRE: What's that shoutin' about?

[*Jane breaks into tears. She falls back into the chair and buries her head in her arms.*]

TYE: Hey, love, come here, I knocked off work early to be with you—do you think I'd really hit you?

JANE: I don't know…

TYE: Come to—bed…

JANE: Don't lean on me.

[*They cross out of the light. The writer looks after them wistfully as the light dims out.*]

Scene Two

The writer has undressed and is in bed, Nightingale coughs—a fiendish, racking cough. he is hacking and spitting up bloody phlegm. He enters his cubicle.

Then across the makeshift partition in the writer's cubicle, unlighted except by a faint glow in its alcove window, another sound commences—a sound of dry and desperate sobbing which sounds as though nothing in the world could ever appease the wound from which it comes: loneliness, inborn and inbred to the bone.

Slowly, as his coughing fit subsides. Nightingale, the quick-sketch artist, turns his head in profile to the sound of the sobbing. Then the writer, across the partition, is dimly lighted, too. He is also sitting up on his cot, staring at the partition between his cell and Nightingale's.

Nightingale clears his throat loudly and sings hoarsely and softly a pop song of the era such as "If I Didn't Care" or "Paper Doll." Slowly the audience of one whom he is serenading succeeds in completely stifling the dry sobbing with a pillow. Nightingale's voice rises a bit as be gets up and lights a cigarette; then he goes toward the upstage limit of the dim stage lighting and makes the gesture of opening a door.

He moves into the other gable room of the attic and stands, silent, for several beats of the song as the writer slowly, reluctantly, turns on his cot to face him.

NIGHTINGALE: I want to ask you something.

WRITER: Huh?

NIGHTINGALE: The word "landlady" as applied to Mrs. Wire and to all landladies that I've encountered in my life—isn't it the biggest one-word contradiction in the English language? [*The writer is embarrassed by Nightingale's intrusion and steady scrutiny.*] She owns the land, yes, but is the witch a lady? Mind if I switch on your light?

WRITER: The bulb's burned out.

NIGHTINGALE [*chuckles and coughs*]: She hasn't replaced a burnt-out light bulb in this attic since I moved here last spring. I have to provide my own light bulbs by unscrewing them from the gentleman's lavatory at the City of the Two Parrots, where I ply my trade. Temporarily, you know. Doing portraits in pastel of the tourist clientele. [*His voice is curiously soft and intimate, more as if he were speaking of personal matters.*] Of course I... [*He coughs and clears his throat.*]...have no shame about it, no guilt at all, since what I do there is a travesty of my talent, I mean a prostitution of it, I mean, painting these tourists at the Two Parrots, which are actually two very noisy macaws. Oh, they have a nice patio there, you know, palm trees and azaleas when in season, but the cuisine and the service... abominable. The menu sometimes includes cockroaches... [There are a lot of great eating places in New Orleans, like Galatoire's, Antoine's, Arnaud's in the Vieux Carré and... Commander's Palace and Plantation House in the Garden District... lovely old mansions, you know, converted to restaurants with a gracious style... haunted by dead residents, of course, but with charm...]

[*This monologue is like a soothing incantation, interspersed with hoarseness and coughing.*]
Like many writers, I know you're a writer, you're a young man of very few spoken words, compared to my garrulity.

WRITER: Yes, I...

NIGHTINGALE: So far, kid, you're practically... monosyllabic.

WRITER: I... don't feel well... tonight.

NIGHTINGALE: That's why I intruded. You have a candle on that box beside your cot.

WRITER: Yes, but no matches.

NIGHTINGALE: I have matches, light it. Talk is easier...[*He strikes the match and advances to the writer's bedside.*] between two people visible to each other, if not too sharply... [*He lights the candle.*] Once I put up for a night in a flophouse without doors, and a gentleman entered my cubicle without invitation, came straight to my cot and struck a match, leaned over me peering directly into my face... and then said, "No," and walked out... as if he assumed that I would have said, "Yes." [*He laughs and coughs.*]

[*Pause*]

You're not a man of few words but a boy of no words. I'll just sit on the cot if you don't object.

WRITER: I, uh, do need sleep.

NIGHTINGALE: You need some company first. I know the sound of loneliness, heard it through the partition. [*He has sat on the cot. The writer huddles away to the wall, acutely embarrassed.*]

Trying not to, but crying... why try not to? Think it's unmanly? Crying is a release for man or woman...

WRITER: I was taught not to cry because it's... humiliating...

NIGHTINGALE: You're a victim of conventional teaching, which you'd better forget. What were you crying about? Some particular sorrow or... for the human condition.

WRITER: Some... particular sorrow. My closest relative died last month.

NIGHTINGALE: Your mother?

WRITER: The mother of my mother, Grand. She died after a long illness just before I left home, and at night I remember...

NIGHTINGALE [*giving a comforting pat*]: Well, losses must be accepted and survived. How strange it is that we've occupied these adjoining rooms for about three weeks now and have just barely said hello to each other when passing on the stairs. You have interesting eyes.

WRITER: In what way do you mean?

NIGHTINGALE: Isn't the pupil of the left one a little bit lighter?

WRITER: I'm afraid I'm developing a—cataract in that eye.

NIGHTINGALE: That's not possible for a kid.

WRITER: I am twenty-eight.

NIGHTINGALE: What I meant is your face is still youthful as your vulnerable nature, they go—together. Of course, I'd see an oculist if you suspect there's a cataract.

WRITER: I plan to when I... if I... can ever afford to... the vision in that eye's getting cloudy.

NIGHTINGALE: Don't wait till you can afford to. Go straight away and don't receive the bill.

WRITER: I couldn't do that.

NIGHTINGALE: Don't be so honest in this dishonest world. [*He pauses and coughs*] Shit, the witch don't sleep in her bedroom you know.

WRITER: Yes, I noticed she is sleeping on a cot in the hall now.

NIGHTINGALE: When I came in now she sprang up and hollered out, "Who?" And I answered her with a hoot owl imitation, "Hoo, hooo, hooooooo." Why, the lady is all three furies in one. A single man needs visitors at night. Necessary as bread, as blood in the body. Why, there's a saying, "Better to live with your worst enemy than to live alone."

WRITER: Yes, loneliness is an—affliction.

NIGHTINGALE: Well, now you have a friend here.

WRITER [*dryly*]: Thanks.

NIGHTINGALE: Of course we're in a madhouse. I wouldn't tolerate the conditions here if the season wasn't so slow that—my financial condition is difficult right now. I don't like insults and *la vie solitaire*—with bedbugs bleeding me like leeches... but now we know each other, the plywood partition between us has been dissolved, no more just hellos. So tonight you were crying in here alone. What of it? Don't we all? Have a cigarette.

WRITER: Thanks. [*Nightingale holds the candle out.*] I won't smoke it now, I'll save it till morning. I like a cigarette when I sit down to work. [*Nightingale's steady scrutiny embarrasses him. They fall silent. After several beats, the writer resumes.*] There's—a lot of human material—in the Quarter for a writer...

NIGHTINGALE: I used to hear you typing. Where's your typewriter?

WRITER: I, uh, hocked it.

NIGHTINGALE: That's what I figured. Wha'd you get for it?

WRITER: Ten dollars. It was a secondhand Underwood portable. I'm worried about just how I'll redeem it. [*He is increasingly embarrassed.*]

NIGHTINGALE: Excuse my curiosity, I mean concern. It's sympathetic... smoke a cigarette now and have another for 'mawnin'. You're not managing right. Need advice and company in this sad ole house—I'm happy to give both if accepted.

WRITER: ...I appreciate... both.

NIGHTINGALE: You don't seem experienced yet... kid, are you... excuse my blunt approach... but are you...? [*He completes the question by placing a shaky band on the writer's crumpled, sheet-covered body.*]

WRITER [*in a stifled voice*]: Oh I'm not sure I know...

NIGHTINGALE: Ain't come out completely, as we put it?

WRITER: Completely, no, just one—experience.

NIGHTINGALE: Tell me about that one experience.

WRITER: I'm not sure I want to discuss it.

NIGHTINGALE: That's no way to begin a confidential friendship.

WRITER: Well, New Year's Eve, I was entertained by a married couple I had a letter of introduction to when I came down here, the... man's a painter, does popular bayou pictures displayed in shop windows in the Quarter, his name is...

NIGHTINGALE: Oh, I know him. He's got a good thing going, commercially speaking, tourists buy them calendar illustrations in dreamy rainbow colors that never existed but in the head of a hack like him.

WRITER: ...The, uh, atmosphere is... effective.

NIGHTINGALE: Oh, they sell to people that don't know paint from art. Maybe you've never seen artistic paintings. [*His voice shakes with feverish pride.*] I could do it, in fact I've done good painting, serious work. But I got to live, and you can't live on good painting until you're dead, or nearly. So, I make it, temporarily, as a quick sketch artist. I flatter old bitches by makin em ten pounds lighter and ten years younger and with some touches of—decent humanity in their eyes that God forgot to put there, or they've decided to dispense with, not always easy. But what is? So—you had an experience with the bayou painter? I didn't know he was, oh, inclined to boys, this is killing.

WRITER [*slowly with embarrassment*]: It wasn't with Mr. Block, it was with a... paratrooper.

NIGHTINGALE: Aha, a paratrooper dropped out of the sky for you, huh? You have such nice smooth skin... Would you like a bit of white port? I keep a half pint by my bed to wash down my sandman special when this touch of flu and the bedbugs keep me awake. Just a mo', I'll fetch it, we'll have a nightcap—now that we're acquainted! [*He goes out rapidly, coughing, then rushes back in with the bottle.*] The witch has removed the glass, we'll have to drink from the bottle. I'll wash my pill down now, the rest is yours. [*He pops a capsule into his mouth and gulps from the bottle, immediately coughing and gagging. He extends the bottle to the writer.*

[*Pause. The writer half extends his hand toward the bottle, then draws it back and shakes his head.*] Oh yes, flu is contagious, how stupid of me, I'm sorry.

WRITER: Never mind, I don't care much for liquor.

NIGHTINGALE: Where you from?

WRITER: St. Louis.

NIGHTINGALE: Christ, do people live there?

WRITER: It has a good art museum and a fine symphony orchestra and....

NIGHTINGALE: No decent gay life at all?

WRITER: You mean...

NIGHTINGALE: You know what I mean, I mean like the... paratrooper.

WRITER: Oh. No. There could be but... living at home....

NIGHTINGALE: Tell me, how did it go with the paratrooper who descended on you at Block's?

WRITER: Well at midnight we went out on the gallery and he, the paratrooper, was out on the lower gallery with a party of older men, antique dealers, they were all singing "Auld Lang Syne."

NIGHTINGALE: How imaginative and *appropriate* to them.

WRITER: —I noticed him down there and he noticed me.

NIGHTINGALE: Noticing him?

WRITER: ...Yes. He grinned, and hollered to come down; he took me into the lower apartment. It was vacant, the others still on the gallery, you see I... couldn't understand his presence among the...

NIGHTINGALE: Screaming old faggots at that antique dealer's. Well, they're rich and they buy boys, but that's a scene that you haven't learned yet. So. What happened downstairs?

WRITER: He took me into a bedroom; he told me I looked pale and wouldn't I like a sunlamp treatment. I thought he meant my face so I—agreed—

NIGHTINGALE: Jesus, you've got to be joking.

WRITER: I was shaking violently like I was a victim of—St. Vitus's Dance, you know, when he said, "Undress"!

NIGHTINGALE: But you did.

WRITER: Yes. He helped me. And I stretched out on the bed under the sunlamp and suddenly he—

NIGHTINGALE: ...turned it off and did you?

WRITER: Yes, that's what happened. I think that he was shocked by my reaction.

NIGHTINGALE: You did *him* or—?

WRITER: ...I told him that I... loved... him. I'd been drinking.

NIGHTINGALE: Love can happen like that. For one night only.

WRITER: He said, he laughed and said, "Forget it. I'm flying out tomorrow for training base."

NIGHTINGALE: He said to you, "Forget it," but you didn't forget it,

WRITER: No... I don't even have his address and I've forgotten his name.

NIGHTINGALE: Still, I think you loved him.

WRITER: ...Yes. I... I'd like to see some of your serious paintings sometime.

NIGHTINGALE: Yeah. You will. Soon. When I get them canvases shipped down from Baton Rouge next week. But meanwhile... [*His hand is sliding down the sheet.*] How about this?

WRITER [*with gathering panic*]:... I think I'd better get some sleep now. I didn't mean to tell you all that. Goodnight, I'm going to sleep.

NIGHTINGALE [*urgently*]: This would help you.

WRITER: I need to sleep nights—to work.

NIGHTINGALE: You are alone in the world, and I am too. Listen. Rain!

[*They are silent. The sound of rain is heard on the roof.*]

Look. I'll give you two things for sleep. First, this. [*He draws back the sheet. The light dims.*] And then one of these pills I call my sandman special.

WRITER: I don't...

NIGHTINGALE: Shh, walls have ears! Lie back and imagine the paratrooper.

[*The dim light goes completely out. A passage of blues piano is heard. It is an hour later. There is a spotlight on the writer as narrator, smoking at the foot of the cot, the sheet drawn about him like a toga.*]

WRITER: When I was alone in the room, the visitor having retreated beyond the plywood partition between his cubicle and mine, which was chalk white that turned ash-gray at night, not just he but everything visible was gone except for the lighter gray of the alcove with its window over Toulouse

Street. An apparition came to me with the hypnotic effect of the painter's sandman special. It was in the form of an elderly female saint, of course. She materialized soundlessly. Her eyes fixed on me with a gentle questioning look which I came to remember as having belonged to my grandmother during her sieges of illness, when I used to go to her room and sit by her bed and want, so much, to say something or to put my hand over hers, but could do neither, knowing that if I did, I'd betray my feelings with tears that would trouble her more than her illness... Now it was she who stood next to my bed for a while. And as I drifted toward sleep, I wondered if she'd witnessed the encounter between the painter and me and what her attitude was toward such—perversions? Of longing?

[*The sound of stifled coughing is heard across the plywood partition.*]

Nothing about her gave me any sign. The weightless hands clasping each other so loosely, the cool and believing gray eyes in the faint pearly face were as immobile as statuary. I felt that she neither blamed nor approved the encounter. No. Wait. She... seemed to lift one hand very, very slightly before my eyes closed with sleep. An almost invisible gesture of... forgiveness?... through understanding?... before she dissolved into sleep...

Scene Three

Tye is in a semi-narcotized state on the bed in Jane's room. Jane is in the hall burdened with paper sacks of groceries; the writer appears behind her.

Jane [*brightly*]: Good morning.

Writer [*shyly*]: Oh, good morning.

Jane: Such a difficult operation, opening a purse with one hand.

Writer: Let me hold the sacks for you.

Jane: Oh, thanks; now then, come in, put the sacks on one of those chairs. Over the weekend we run out of everything. Ice isn't delivered on Sundays, milk spoils. Everything of a perishable kind has got to be replaced. Oh, don't go out. Have you had a coffee?

Writer [*looking at Tye*]: I was about to but...

Jane: Stay and have some with me. Sorry it's instant, can you stand instant coffee?

Writer: I beg your pardon?

Jane: Don't mind him, when his eyes are half open it doesn't mean he is conscious.

Tye: Bullshit, you picked up a kid on the street?

Jane [*suppressing anger*]: This is the young man from across the hall— I'm Jane Sparks, my friend is Tye McCool, and you are—

Writer [*pretending to observe a chess board to cover his em*barrassment]: What a beautiful chess board!

Jane: Oh, that, yes!

Writer: Ivory and ebony? Figures?

Jane: The white squares are mother-of-pearl. Do you play chess?

Writer: Used to. You play together, you and Mr.—McCool?

Tye: Aw, yeh, we play together but not chess. [*He rubs his crotch. Jane and the writer nervously study the chess board.*]

Jane: I play alone, a solitary game, to keep in practice in case I meet a partner.

Writer: Look. Black is in check.

Jane: My imaginary opponent. I choose sides you see, although I play for both.

Writer: I'd be happy to—I mean sometimes when you—

TYE [*touching the saucepan on the burner*]: OW!

JANE: I set it to boil before I went to the store. [*Jane sets a cup and doughnuts on the table.*]

TYE: Hey, kid, why don't you take your cup across the hall to your own room?

JANE: Because I've just now—you heard me—invited him to have it here in this room with me.

TYE: I didn't invite him in, and I want you to git something straight: I live here. And if I live in a place I got equal rights in this place, and it just so happens I don't entertain no stranger to look at me undressed.

WRITER [*gulping down his coffee*]: Please. Uh, please, I think I'd rather go in my room because I, I've got some work to do there. I always work immediately after my coffee.

JANE: I will not have this young grifter who has established squatter's rights here telling me that I can't enjoy a little society in a place where—frankly I am frantic with loneliness!

[*The writer does not know what to do. Tye suddenly grins. He pulls out a chair for the writer at the table as if it were for a lady.*]

TYE: Have a seat kid, you like one lump or two? Where's the cat? Can I invite the goddam cat to breakfast?

JANE: Tye, you said you were pleased with the robe I gave you for your birthday, but you never wear it.

TYE: I don't dress for breakfast.

JANE: Putting on a silk robe isn't dressing.

[*She removes the robe from a hook and throws it about Tye's shoulders. Automatically he circles her hips with an arm.*]

TYE: Mmm. Good. Feels good.

JANE [*shyly disengaging herself from his embrace*]: It ought to. Shantung silk.

TYE: I didn't mean the robe, babe.

JANE: Tye, behave yourself. [*She turns to the writer.*] I've cherished the hope that by introducing Tye to certain little improvements in wearing apparel and language, I may gradually, despite his resistance—

TYE: Ain't that lovely? That classy langwidge she uses?

JANE: Inspire him to—seek out some higher level of employment. [*Ignoring Tye, she speaks*] I heard that you are a writer?

WRITER: I, uh—write, but—

JANE: What form of writing? I mean fiction or poetry or...

TYE: Faggots, they all do something artistic, all of 'em.

JANE [*quickly*]: Do you know, I find myself drinking twice as much coffee here as I did in New York. For me the climate here is debilitating. Perhaps because of the dampness and the, and the—very low altitude, really there's no altitude at all, it's slightly under sea level. Have another cup with me?

[*The writer doesn't answer. Jane prepares two more cups of the instant coffee. Tye is staring steadily, challengingly at the writer, who appears to be hypnotized.*]

Of course, Manhattan hasn't much altitude either. But I grew up in the Adirondacks really. We lived on high ground, good elevation.

TYE: I met one of 'em once by accident on the street. You see, I was out of a job, and he came up to me on a corner in the Quarter an' invited me to his place for supper with him. I seen right off what he was an' what he wanted, but I didn't have the price of a poor boy sandwich so I accepted, I went. The place was all Japanese-like, everything very artistic. He said to me, "Cross over that little bridge that crosses my little lake which I made myself and sit on the bench under my willow tree while I make supper for us and bathe an' change my clo'se. I won't be long." So I crossed over the bridge over the lake, and I stretched out under the weepin' willow tree: fell right asleep. I was woke up by what looked like a female but was him in drag. "Supper ready," he—she—said. Then this freak, put her hand on my—I said, "It's gonna cost you more than supper…"

JANE: Tye.

TYE: Huh, baby?

JANE: You will not continue that story.

TYE: It's a damn good story. What's your objection to it? I ain't got to the part that's really funny. [*He speaks to the writer, who is crossing out of the light.*] Don't you like the story?

[*The writer exits.*]

JANE: Why did you do that?

TYE: Do what?

JANE: You know what, and the boy knew what you meant by it. Why did you want to hurt him with the implication that he was in a class with a common, a predatory transvestite?

TYE: Look Jane… You say you was brought up on high ground, good elevation, but you come in here, you bring in here and expose me to a little queer, and…

JANE: Does everyone with civilized behavior, good manners, seem to be a queer to you?

TYE: …Was it good manners the way he looked at me, Babe?

JANE [*voice rising*]: Was it good manners for you to stand in front of him rubbing your—groin the way you did?

TYE: I wanted you to notice his reaction.

JANE: He was just embarrassed.

TYE: You got a lot to learn about life in the Quarter.

JANE: I think that he's a serious person that I can talk to and I need someone to talk to!

[*Pause*]

TYE: You can't talk to *me* huh?

JANE: With you working all night at a Bourbon Street strip-joint and sleeping nearly all day? Involving yourself with all the underworld elements of this corrupt city…

TYE: 'Sthat all I do? Just that? I never pleasure you, Babe?

[*Fade in piano blues. She draws a breath and moves as if half asleep behind Tye's chair.*]

JANE: Yes, you—pleasure me, Tye.

TYE: I try to do my best to, Babe. Sometimes I wonder why a girl—

JANE: Not a girl, Tye. A woman.

TYE: —How did— why did—you get yourself mixed up with me?

JANE: A sudden change of circumstances removed me from— how shall I put it so you'd understand?

TYE: Just—say.

JANE: What I'd thought was myself. So I quit my former connections, I came down here to—[She *stops short.*] Well, to make an adjustment to—[*Pause.*] We met by chance on Royal Street when a deluge of rain backed me into a doorway. Didn't know you were behind me until you put your hand on my hip and I turned to say, "Stop that!" but didn't because you were something I'd never encountered before— faintly innocent—boy's eyes. Smiling. Said to myself, "Why not, with nothing to lose!" Of course you pleasure me, Tye!—I'd been alone so long .

[*She touches his throat with trembling fingers. He leans sensually back against her. She runs her hand down his chest.*]

Silk on silk is—lovely… regardless of the danger.

[*As the light on this area dims, typing begins offstage. The dim-out is completed.*]

Scene Four

A lighted area represents Mrs. Wire's kitchen, in which she is preparing a big pot of gumbo despite the hour, which is midnight. She could be mistaken for a witch from Macbeth in vaguely modern but not new costume.

The writer's footsteps catch her attention. He appears at the edge of the light in all that remains of his wardrobe: riding boots and britches, a faded red flannel shirt.

MRS. WIRE: Who, who?—Aw, you, dressed up like a jockey in a donkey race!

WRITER: —My, uh, clothes are at the cleaners.

MRS. WIRE: Do they clean clothes at the pawnshop, yeah, I reckon they do clean clothes not redeemed. Oh. Don't go upstairs. Your room is forfeited, too.

WRITER: …You mean I'm…

MRS. WIRE: A loser, boy. Possibly you could git a cot at the Salvation Army,

WRITER [*averting his eyes*]: May I sit down a moment?

MRS. WIRE: Why, for what?

WRITER: Eviction presents… a problem.

MRS. WIRE: I thought you was gittin' on the WPA Writers' Project? That's what you tole me when I inquired about your prospects for employment, you said, "Oh, I've applied for work on the WPA for writers."

WRITER: I couldn't prove that my father was destitute, and the fact he contributes nothing to my support seemed—immaterial to them.

MRS. WIRE: Why're you shifty-eyed? I never seen a more shifty-eyed boy.

WRITER: I, uh, have had a little eye trouble, lately.

MRS. WIRE: You're gettin' a cataract on your left eye, boy, face it!—Catatacts don't usually hit at your age.

WRITER: I've noticed a lot of things have hit me—prematurely…

MRS. WIRE [*stirring gumbo*]: Hungry? I bet. I eat at irregular hours. I suddenly got a notion to cook up a gumbo, and when I do, the smell of it is an attraction, draws company in the kitchen. Oh ho—footsteps fast. Here come the ladies,

WRITER: Mrs. Wire, those old ladies are starving, dying of malnutrition.

[*Miss Carrie and Mary Maude appear at the edge of the lighted area with queer, high-pitched laughter or some bizarre relation to laughter.*]

MRS. WIRE: Set back down there, boy. [*Pause.*] Why, Mizz Wayne an' Miss Carrie, you girls still up at this hour!

MISS CARRIE: We heard you moving about and wondered if we could…

MARY MAUDE: Be of some assistance.

MRS. WIRE: Shoot, Mrs. Wayne, do you imagine that rusty ole saucepan of yours is invisible to me? Why, I know when I put this gumbo on the stove and lit the fire, it would smoke you ladies out of your locked room. What do you all do in that locked room so much?

MARY MAUDE: We keep ourselves occupied.

MISS CARRIE: We are compiling a cookbook which we hope to have published. A Creole cookbook, recipes we remember from our childhood.

MRS. WIRE: A recipe is a poor substitute for food.

MARY MAUDE [*with a slight breathless pause*]: We ought to go out more regularly for meals but our… our light bulbs have burned out, so we can't distinguish night from day anymore. Only shadows come in.

MISS CARRIE.: Sshh! [*Pause.*] Y'know, I turned down an invitation to dinner this evening at my cousin Mathilde Devereau Pathet's in the Garden District.

MRS. WIRE: Objected to the menu?

MISS CARRIE: No, but you know, very rich people are so inconsiderate sometimes. With four limousines and drivers at their constant disposal, they wouldn't send one to fetch me.

MRS. WIRE: Four? Limousines? Four drivers?

[*A delicate, evanescent music steals in as the scene acquires a touch of the bizarre. At moments the players seem bewildered as if caught in a dream.*]

MISS CARRIE: Oh, yes, four, four... spanking new Cadillacs with uniformed chauffeurs!

MRS. WIRE: Now, that's very impressive.

MISS CARRIE: They call Mr. Pathet the "Southern Planter."

MRS. WIRE: Has a plantation, in the Garden District?

MISS CARRIE [*gasping*]: Oh, no, no, no, no. He's a mortician, most prominent mortician, buries all the best families in the parish.

MRS. WIRE: And poor relations, too? I hope.

MARY MAUDE: Miss Carrie goes into a family vault when she goes.

MRS. WIRE: When?

MARY MAUDE: Yes, above ground, has a vault reserved in...

MISS CARRIE: Let's not speak of that... now.

MRS. WIRE: Why not speak of that? You got to consider the advantage of this connection. Because of the expenses of "The Inevitable" someday soon, 'specially with your asthma? No light? And bad nutrition?

MISS CARRIE: The dampness of the old walls in the Quarter— you know how they hold damp. This city is actually eight feet below sea level. Niggers are buried under the ground, and their caskets fill immediately with water.

MRS. WIRE: But I reckon your family vault is above this nigger water level?

MISS CARRIE: Oh, yes, above water level, in fact, I'll be on top of my great-great-uncle, Jean Pierre Devereau, the third.

[*The writer laughs a bit, involuntarily. The ladies glare at him.*]

Mrs. Wire, who is this... transient? Young man?

MARY MAUDE: We did understand that this was a guesthouse, not a... refuge for delinquents.

MISS CARRIE [*turning her back on the writer*]: They do set an exquisite table at the Pathets, with excellent food, but it's not appetizing, you know, to be conducted on a tour of inspection of the business display room, you know, the latest model of caskets on display, and that's what Rene Pathet does, invariably escorts me, proud as a peacock, through the coffin display rooms before... we sit down to dinner. And all through dinner, he discusses his latest clients and... those expected shortly.

MRS. WIRE: Maybe he wants you to pick out your casket cause he's noticed your asthma from damp walls in the Quarter,

MISS CARRIE: I do, of course, understand that business is business with him, a night and day occupation.

MRS. WIRE: You know, I always spit in a pot of gumbo to give it special flavor, like a bootblack spits on a shoe. [*She pretends to spit in the* pot. *The crones try to laugh.*] Now help yourself, fill your saucepan full, and I'll loan you a couple of spoons, but let it cool a while, don't blister your gums... [*She hands them spoons.*] ...and Mrs. Wayne, I'll be watching the mailbox for Buster's army paycheck.

MARY MAUDE: That boy has never let me down, he's the most devoted son a mother could hope for.

Mrs. Wire: Yais, if she had no hope.

Mary Maude: I got a postcard from him...

Mrs. Wire: A postcard can't be cashed.

Mary Maude [*diverting Mrs. Wire's attention, she hopes, as Miss* Carrie *ladles out gumbo*]: Of course, I wasn't prepared for the circumstance that struck me when I discovered that Mr. Wayne had not kept up his insurance payments, *that* I was not prepared for, that it was *lapsed.*

Mrs. Wire [*amused*]: I bet you wasn't prepared for a little surprise like that.

Mary Maude: No, not for that nor for the discovery that secretly for years he'd been providing cash and real estate to that little redheaded doxy he'd kept in Bay St. Louie.

Miss Carrie: Owwwww!

[*Mrs. Wire whirls about, and Miss Carrie is forced to swallow the scalding mouthful.*]

Mrs. Wire: I bet that mouthful scorched your throat, Miss Carrie. Didn't I tell you to wait?

Mary Maude: Carrie, give me that saucepan before you spill it, your hand's so shaky. Thank you, Mrs. Wire. Carrie, thank Mrs. Wire for her being so concerned always about our— circumstances here. Now let's go and see what can be done for that throat. [*They move toward the stairs but do not exit.*]

Mrs. Wire: Cut it, if all else fails.

[*Something crashes on the stairs. All turn that* way. *Tye appears dimly, bearing two heavy cartons; he speaks to the* writer, *who is nearest to him.*]

Tye: Hey, you boy?

Writer: —Me?

Tye: Yeh, yeh, you, I dropped one of these packages on the steps, so goddamn dark I dropped it. And I'd appreciate it if you'd pick it up fo' me an' help me git it upstairs.

Writer: I'll be—glad to try to...

[*Tye focuses dimly on Miss Carrie. He blinks several times in disbelief.*]

Tye: Am I... in the right place?

Mrs. Wire [*shouting*]: Not in your present condition. Go on back out. Sleep it off in the gutter.

Miss Carrie [*to Mrs. Wire*]: Tragic for such a nice-looking young man to return to his wife in that condition at night.

Mrs. Wire: Practically every night. [*Miss Carrie and Mary Maude exit.*]

[*Tye has almost miraculously managed to collect his dropped packages, and he staggers to stage right where the lower steps to the attic are dimly seen. The writer follows.*]

Tye [*stumbling back against the writer*]: Can you make it? Can you make *it,* kid?

[*They slowly mount the steps. The lighted kitchen is dimmed out. There is a brief pause; soft light is east on the attic hall.*]

Tye: Now, kid, can you locate my room key in my pocket?

Writer: Which, uh—pocket?

Tye: Pan's pocket.

Writer: Left pocket or—

Tye: —Head—spinnin'—money in hip pocket, key in—right— lef' side. Shit—key befo' I—fall...

[*The writer's hand starts to enter a pocket when Tye collapses, spilling the boxes on the floor and sprawling across them.*]

Writer: You're right outside my cubbyhole. I suggest you rest in there before you—wake up your wife...

Tye: M'ole lady, she chews my ass off if I come home this ways . [*He struggles heroically to near standing position as the writer guides him into his cubicle.*]... This—bed?

[*There is a soft, ghostly laugh from the adjoining cubicle. A match strikes briefly.*]

Writer: Swing your legs the other way, that way's the pillow—would you, uh, like your wet shoes off?

Tye: Shoes? Yes, but nothin' else. Once I—passed out on— Bourbon Street—late nighr—in a dark doorway—woke up—this guy, was takin' liberties with me and I don't go for that stuff—

Writer: I don't take advantages of that kind, I am—going back downstairs, if you're comfortable now.

Tye: I said to this guy, "Okay, if you want to blow me, you can pay me one hunnerd dollars—before, not after."

[*Tye's voice dies out. Nightingale becomes visible, rising stealthily in his cubicle and slipping on a robe, as Tye begins to snore.*

[*The attic lights dim out. The lights on the kitchen come up as the writer re-enters.*]

Mrs. Wire: Got that bum to bed? Set down, son. Ha! I called you, son. Where do you go nights?

Writer: Oh, I walk, I take long solitary walks. Sometimes I... I...

Mrs. Wire: Sometimes you what? You can say it's none of my business, but I, well, I have a sort of a, well you could say I have a sort of a—maternal—concern. You see, I do have a son that I never see no more, but I worry about him so I reckon it's natural for me to worry about you a little. And get things straight in my head about you—you've changed since you've been in this house. You know that?

Writer: Yes, I know that.

Mrs. Wire: This I'll tell you, when you first come to my door. I swear I seen and I recognized a young gentleman in you—shy. Shaky, but...

Writer: Panicky! Yes! Gentleman? My folks say so. I wonder.

[*The light narrows and focuses on the writer alone; the speech becomes an interior reflection.*]

I've noticed I do have some troublesome little scruples in my nature that may cause difficulties in my... [*He rises and rests his foot on the chair.*] ...negotiated—truce with—life. Oh—there's a price for things, that's something I've learned in the Vieux Carré. For everything that you purchase in this marketplace you pay out of *here!* [*He thumps his chest.*] And the cash which is the stuff you use in your work can be overdrawn, depleted, like a reservoir going dry in a long season of drought...

[*The scene is resumed on a realistic level with a change in the lighting.*]

Mrs. Wire [*passing a bowl of gumbo to the writer*]: Here, son, have some gumbo. Let it cool a while. I just pretended to spit in it, you know.

Writer: I know.

Mrs. Wire: I make the best gumbo. I do the best Creole cookin' in Louisiana. It's God's truth, and now I'll tell you what I'm plannin' to do while your gumbo's coolin'. I'll tell you because it involves a way you could pay your room and board here.

Writer: Oh?

Mrs. Wire: Uh huh, I'm plannin' to open a lunchroom.

Writer: On the premises? Here?

Mrs. Wire: On the premises, in my bedroom, which I'm gonna convert into a small dinin' room. So I'm gonna git printed up some bus'ness cards. At twelve noon ev'ry day except Sundays you can hit the streets with these little bus'ness cards announcin' that lunch is bein' served for twenty-five cents, a cheaper lunch than you could git in a greasy spoon on Chartres... and no better cooking in the Garden District or the Vieux Carré.

Writer: Meals for a quarter in the Quarter.

Mrs. Wire: Hey! That's the slogan! I'll print it on those cards that you'll pass out.

WRITER [*dreamily*]: Wonderful gumbo.

MRS. WIRE: Why this "Meals for a quarter in the Quarter" is going to put me back in the black, yeah! Boy!... [*She throws him the key to his attic room. The lights dim out briefly.*]

TYE'S VOICE: Hey! Whatcha doin'? Git yuh fuckin hands off me.

[*The writer appears dimly in the attic hall outside his room. He stops.*]

NIGHTINGALE'S VOICE: I thought that I was visiting a friend.

TYE'S VOICE: 'Sthat how you visit a friend, unzippin' his pants pullin' out his dick?

NIGHTINGALE'S VOICE: I assure you it was a mistake of—identity...

TYE [*becoming visible on the side* of *the bed in the writer's cubicle*]: This ain't my room. Where is my ole lady? Hey, *hey, Jane!*

WRITER: You collapsed in the hall outside your door so I helped you in here.

TYE: Both of you git this straight No goddam faggot messes with me, never! For less'n a hundred dollars!

[*Jane becomes visible in the hall before this line.*]

A hunnerd dollars, yes, maybe, but nor a dime less—

NIGHTINGALE [*emerging from the cubicle in his robe*]: I am afraid that you have priced yourself out of the market.

JANE: Tye, come out of there.

TYE: I been interfered with 'cause you'd locked me out

WRITER: Miss, uh, Sparks, I didn't touch your friend except to offer him my bed till you let him in.

JANE: Tye, stand up—if you can stand! Stand. Walk.

[*Tye stumbles against her, and she cries out as she is pushed against the wall.*]

TYE'S VOICE: Locked out, bolted outa my room, to be— molested.

JANE: I heard you name a price, with you everything has a price. Thanks, good night.

[*During this exchange Nightingale in his purple robe has leaned, smoking with a somewhat sardonic look, against the partition between the two cubicles. The writer reappears.*]

NIGHTINGALE: Back so quick? —*Tant pis...*

WRITER: I think if I were you, I'd go in your own room and get to bed.

[*The writer enters his cubicle. Nightingale's face slowly turns to a mask of sorrow past expression. There is music. Nightingale puts out his cigarette and enters his cubicle.*

[*Jane undresses Tye. The writer undresses. Nightingale sits on his cot. Tye and Jane begin to make love. Downstairs, Nursie mops the floor, singing to herself. The writer moves slowly to his bed and places his hand on the warm sheets that Tye has left. The light dims.*

[*There is a passage of time.*]

Scene Five

The attic rooms are dimly lit, Nightingale is adjusting a neckerchief about his wasted throat. He enters the writer's cubicle without knocking.

NIGHTINGALE: May I intrude once more? It's embarrassing— this incident. Not of any importance, nothing worth a second thought. [*He coughs.*] Oh Christ. You know my mattress is full of bedbugs. Last night I smashed one at least the size of my thumbnail; it left a big blood spot on the pillow. [*He coughs and gasps* for *breath.*] I showed it to the colored woman that the witch calls Nursie, and Nursie told her about it, and she came charging up here and demanded that I exhibit the bug, which I naturally... [*A note of uncertainty and fear enters his voice.*]

WRITER: ...removed from the pillow.

NIGHTINGALE: Who in hell wouldn't remove the remains of a squashed bedbug from his pillow? Nobody I'd want social or any acquaintance with... she even... intimated that I coughed up the blood, as if I had... [*coughs*] consumption.

WRITER [*stripped to his shorts and about to go to bed*]: I think with that persistent cough of yours you should get more rest.

NIGHTINGALE: Restlessness. Insomnia. I can't imagine a worse affliction, and I've suffered from it nearly all my life. I consulted a doctor about it once, and he said, "You don't sleep because it reminds you of death," A ludicrous assumption—the only true regret I'd have over leaving this world is that I'd leave so much of my serious work unfinished.

WRITER [*holding the bed-sheet up to his chin*]: Do show me your serious work.

NIGHTINGALE: I know why you're taking this tone.

WRITER: I am not taking any tone.

NIGHTINGALE: Oh yes you are, you're very annoyed with me because my restlessness, my loneliness, made me so indiscreet as to—offer my attentions to that stupid but—physically appealing young man you'd put on that cot with the idea of reserving him for yourself. And so I do think your tone is a bit hypocritical, don't you?

WRITER: All right, I do admit I find him attractive, too, but I did *not* make a pass at him,

NIGHTINGALE: I heard him warn you.

WRITER: I simply removed his wet shoes.

NIGHTINGALE: Little man, you are sensual, but I, I—am rapacious.

WRITER: And I am tired.

NIGHTINGALE: Too tired to return my visits? Not very appreciative of you, but lack of appreciation is something I've come to expect and almost to accept as if God—the alleged—had stamped on me a sign at birth— "This man will offer himself and not be accepted, not by anyone ever!"

WRITER: Please don't light that candle.

NIGHTINGALE: I shall, the candle is lit.

WRITER: I do wish that you'd return to your side of the wall— well, now I am taking a tone, but it's... justified. Now do *please* get out, get out, I mean it, when I blow out the candle I want to be alone.

NIGHTINGALE: You know, you're going to grow into a selfish, callous man. Returning no visits, reciprocating no... caring.

WRITER: ...Why do you predict that?

NIGHTINGALE: That little opacity on your left eye pupil could mean a like thing happening to your heart. [*He sits on the cot.*]

WRITER: You have to protect your heart.

NIGHTINGALE: With a shell of *calcium?* Would that improve your work?

WRITER: You talk like you have a fever, I...

NIGHTINGALE: I have a fever you'd be lucky to catch, a fever to hold and be held! [*He throws off his tattered silk robe.*] Hold me! Please, please hold me.

WRITER: I'm afraid I'm tired, I need to sleep and... I don't want to catch your cold.

[*Slowly with dignity, Nightingale rises from the cot and puts his silk robe on.*]

NIGHTINGALE: And I don't want to catch yours, which is a cold in the heart, that's a hell of a lot more fatal to a boy with literary pretensions.

[*This releases in the writer a cold rage which he has never felt before. He springs up and glares at Nightingale, who is coughing.*]

WRITER [*in a voice quick and hard as a knife*]: I think there has been some deterioration in your condition and you ought to face it! A man has got to face everything sometime and call it by its true name, not to try to escape it by—cowardly!—evasion—go have your lungs x-rayed and don't receive the doctor's bill when it's sent! But go there quick, have the disease stated clearly! Don't, don't call it a cold anymore or a touch of the flu!

NIGHTINGALE [*turning with a gasp*]: You've gone mad, you've gone out of your mind here, you little one-eyed bitch! [*He coughs again and staggers out of the light.*]

MRS. WIRE'S VOICE: I heard you from the kitchen, boy! Was he molesting you in here? I heard him. Was he molesting you in here? Speak up! [*Her tone loses its note of concern as she shouts* to *Nightingale.*] You watch out, I'll get the goods on you yet!

NIGHTINGALE'S VOICE: The persecution continues.

Scene Six

Daylight appears in the alcove window—daylight tinged with rain. The room of Jane and Tye is lighted. Tye is sprawled, apparently sleeping, in shorts on the studio bed. Jane has just completed a fashion design. She stares at it with disgust, then crumples it and throws it to the floor with a sob of frustration.

JANE: Yes? Who's there?

WRITER: Uh, me, from across the hall, I brought in a letter for you—it was getting rained on.

JANE: Oh, one moment, please. [*She throws a robe over her panties and bra and opens the door.*] A letter for me?

WRITER: The mail gets wet when it rains since the lid's come off the mailbox.

[*His look irresistibly takes in the figure of Tye. Jane tears the letter open and gasps softly. She looks slowly up, with a stunned expression, at the young writer.*]

JANE: Would you care for some coffee?

WRITER: Thanks, no, I just take it in the morning.

JANE: Then please have a drink with me. I need a drink. Please, please come *in*. [*Jane is speaking hysterically but abruptly controls it.*] Excuse me—would you pour the drinks—I can't. I…

WRITER [*crossing to the cabinet*]: Will you have…

JANE: Bourbon. Three fingers.

WRITER: With?

JANE: Nothing, nothing.

[*The writer glances again at Tye as he pours the bourbon.*]

Nothing… [*The writer crosses to her with the drink.*] Nothing. And—you?

WRITER: Nothing, thanks. I have to retype the manuscripts soaked in the rain.

JANE: *Manuscript,* you said? Oh, yes, you're a writer. I knew, it just slipped my mind. The manuscripts were returned? Does that mean rejection? —Rejection is always so painful.

WRITER [*with shy pride*]: This time instead of a printed slip there was this personal signed note…

JANE: Encouraging—that. Oh, my glass is weeping—an Italian expression. Would you play barman again? Please? [*She doesn't know where to put the letter, which he keeps glancing at.*]

WRITER: Yes, I am encouraged. He says, "This one doesn't quite make it but try us again." *Story* magazine—they print William Saroyan, you know!

JANE: It takes a good while to get established in a creative field.

WRITER: And meanwhile you've got to survive.

JANE: I was lucky, but the luck didn't hold. [*She is taking little sips of the straight bourbon.*]

WRITER: You're—upset by that—letter? I noticed it came from— isn't Ochsner's a clinic?

JANE: Yes, actually. I am, I was. It concerns a relative rather— critically ill there.

WRITER: Someone close to you?

JANE: Yes. Quite close, although lately I hardly recognize the lady at all anymore.

[*Tye stirs on the bed; the writer irresistibly glances at him.*]

Pull the sheet over him. I think he unconsciously displays himself like that as if posing for a painter of sensual inclinations. Wasted on me. I just illustrate fashions for ladies.

TYE [*stirring*]: Beret? Beret?

[*The writer starts off, pausing at the edge of the light.*]

WRITER: Jane, what was the letter, wasn't it about you?

JANE: Let's just say it was a sort of a personal, signed rejection slip, too.

[*The writer exits with a backward glance.*]

TYE: Where's Beret, where's the goddam cat?

[*Jane is fiercely tearing the letter to bits. The lights dim out.*]

Scene Seven

Dim light comes up on the writer, stage front, as narrator.

WRITER: The basement of the building had been leased by Mrs. Wire to a fashionable youngish photographer, one T. Hamilton Biggs, a very effete man he was, who had somehow acquired a perfect Oxford accent in Baton Rouge, Louisiana. He made a good living in New Orleans out of artfully lighted photos of debutantes and society matrons in the Garden District, but for his personal amusement—he also photographed, more realistically, some of the many young drifters to be found along the streets of the Vieux Carré.

[*The lights go up on the kitchen. Mrs. Wire is seen at the stove, which bears steaming pots of water.*]

MRS. WIRE [*to the writer*]: Aw, it's you sneakin' in at two a.m. like a thief.

WRITER: Yes, uh, good night.

MRS. WIRE: Hold on, don't go up yet. He's at it again down there, he's throwin' one of his orgies, and this'll be the last one he throws down there. By God an' by Jesus, the society folk in this city may tolerate vice but not me. Take one of them pots off the stove,

WRITER: You're uh… cooking at this hour?

MRS. WIRE: Not cooking… I'm boiling water! I take this pot and you take the other one, we'll pour this water through the hole in this kitchen floor, which is directly over that studio of his!

WRITER: Mrs. Wire, I can't be involved in…

MRS. WIRE: Boy, you're employed by me, you're fed and housed here, and you do like I tell you or you'll go on the street. [*She lifts a great kettle off the stove.*] Take that pot off the stove! [*She empties the steaming water on the floor. Almost instant screams are heard below.*] Hahh, down there, what's the disturbance over?!

WRITER: Mrs. Wire, that man has taken out a peace warrant against you, you know that.

MRS. WIRE: Git out of my way, you shifty-eyed little— [*With demonical energy she seizes the other pot and empties it onto the floor, and the screams continue. She looks and runs to the proscenium as if peering out a window.*] Two of 'em run out naked. Got two of you, I'm not done with you yet!… you perverts!

WRITER: Mrs. Wire, he'll call the police.

MRS. WIRE: Let him, just let him, my nephew is a lieutenant on the police force! But these Quarter police, why anybody can buy 'em, and that Biggs, he's got big money. Best we be quiet, sit tight. Act real casual-like. If they git in that door, you seen a, you seen a—

WRITER: What?

MRS. WIRE: A drunk spillin' water in here.

WRITER: …that much water?

MRS. WIRE: Hush up. One contradictory word out of you and I'll brain you with this saucepan here. [*Nightingale enters in his robe.*]

NIGHTINGALE: May I inquire what this bedlam is about? [*He pants for breath.*] I had just finally managed to… [*He gasps.*] This hellish disturbance…

MRS. WIRE: May you inquire, yeah, you may inquire. Look. Here's the story! You're in a doped-up condition. Drunk and doped-up— you staggered against the stove and accidentally knocked a kettle of boiling water off it. Now that's the story you'll tell in payment of back rent and your habits!… disgracing my house!'

NIGHTINGALE [*to writer*]: What is she talking about?

MRS. WIRE: And you… one eye! [*She turns to the writer.*] You say you witnessed it, you back up the story, you heah?

WRITER [*grinning*]: Mrs. Wire, the story wouldn't… hold water.

MRS. WIRE: I said accidental. In his condition who'd doubt it?

NIGHTINGALE: Hoo, hoo, hoo!

MRS. WIRE: That night court buzzard on the bench, he'd throw the book at me for no reason but the fight that I've put up against the corruption and evil that this Quarter is built on! All I'm asking is…

[*Abruptly Miss Carrie and Mary Maude in outrageous negligees burst into the kitchen. At the sight of them, Mrs. Wire starts to scream wordlessly as a peacock at a pitch that stuns the writer but not Nightingale and the crones. Just as abruptly she falls silent and flops into a chair.*]

MISS CARRIE: Oh, Mrs. Wire!

MARY MAUDE: We thought the house had caught fire!

NIGHTINGALE [*loftily*]: …What a remarkable… *tableau vivant.* The paddy wagon's approaching. Means night court, you know.

WRITER: …I think I'll… go to bed now .

MRS. WIRE: Like shoot you will!

[*Jane appears, stage right, in a robe. She speaks to the writer, who is nearest to her.*]

JANE: Can you tell me what is going on down here?

WRITER: Miss Sparks, why don't you stay in your room right now?

JANE: Why?

WRITER: There's been a terrible incident down here I think the police are coming.

[*Mary Maude screams, wringing her bands.*]

MARY MAUDE: Police!

MISS CARRIE: Oh, Mary Maude, this is not time for hysterics. You're not involved, nor am I! We simply came in to see what the disturbance was about.

JANE [*to the writer*]: Was Tye here? Was Tye involved in this…

WRITER [*in a low voice to Jane*]: Nobody was involved but Mrs. Wire. She poured boiling water through a hole in the floor.

MRS. WIRE [*like a field marshal*]: Everybody in here stay here and sit tight till the facts are reported.

[*Nursie enters with black majesty. She is humming a church hymn softly, "He walks with me and he talks with me." She remains at the edge of the action, calm as if unaware.*]

I meant ev'ry goddam one of you except Nursie. Nursie! Don't stand there singin' gospel, barefoot, in that old dirty nightgown!

Writer [*to Jane*]: She wants us to support a totally false story.

Mrs. Wire: I tell you—the Vieux Carré is the new Babylon destroyed by evil in Scriptures!!

Jane: It's like a dream…

Nightingale: The photographer downstairs belongs to the Chateau family, one of the finest and most important families in the Garden District.

Mrs. Wire: Oh, do you write the social register now?

Nightingale: I know he is New Orleans's most prominent society photographer!

Mrs. Wire: I know he's the city's most notorious pervert and occupying space in *my* building!

Miss Carrie: Mary Maude and I can't afford the notoriety of a thing like this.

[*Mary Maude cries out and leans against the table.*]

Mary Maude: Mrs. Wire, Miss Carrie and I have—positions to maintain!

Jane: Mrs. Wire, surely there's no need for these ladies to be involved in this.

Mrs. Wire: Deadbeats, all, all! Will stay right here and—

Jane: Do what?

Mrs. Wire: —testify to what happened!

Nightingale: She wishes you all to corroborate her lie! That I, that I! Oh, yes, I'm appointed to assume responsibility for—

Photographer [*off stage*]: Right up there! Burns like this could disfigure me for life!

[*Mrs. Wire rushes to slam and bolt the door.*]

Miss Carrie [to *Mary Maude*]: Honey? Can you move now?

Mrs. Wire: No, she caint, she stays—which applies to you all!

Photographer: The fact that she is insane and allowed to remain at large… doesn't excuse it.

[*A patrolman bangs at the door.*]

Mrs. Wire: Shh! Nobody make a sound!

Photographer: Not only she but her tenants; why, the place is a psycho ward.

[*More banging is heard.*]

Mrs. Wire: What's this banging about?

Patrolman: Open this door.

Photographer: One of my guests was the nephew of the District Attorney!

Patrolman: Open or I'll force it.

Photographer: Break it in! Kick it open!

Mrs. Wire [*galvanized*]: You ain't comm' in here, you got no warrant to enter, you filthy—morphodite, you!

Writer: Mrs. Wire you said not to make a sound.

Mrs. Wire: Make no sound when they're breaking in my house, you one-eyed Jack? [*The banging continues.*] What's the meaning of this, wakin' me up at two a.m. in the mawnin'?

Photographer: Scalded! Five guests, including two art models!

Mrs. Wire [*overlapping*]: You broken the terms of your lease, and it's now broke. Rented you that downstair space for legitimate business, you turned it into a—continual awgy!

Patrolman: Open that door, ma'am, people have been seriously injured.

Mrs. Wire: That's no concern of mine! I open no door till I phone my nephew, a lieutenant on the police force, Bill Flynn, who knows the situation I've put up with here, and then we'll see who calls the law on who!

WRITER: I hear more police sirens comin'.

[*The pounding and shouting continue. A patrolman forces entry, followed by another. All during the bit just preceding, Miss Carrie and Mary Maude have clung together, their terrified whispers maintaining a low-pitched threnody to the shouting and banging. Now as the two patrolmen enter, their hysteria erupts in shrill screams. The screams are so intense that the patrolmen's attention is directed upon them.*]

PATROLMAN 1: Christ! Is this a fuckin' madhouse?

[*Still clinging together, the emaciated crones sink to their knees as if at the feet of an implacable deity.*]

MRS. WIRE [*inspired*]: Officers, remove these demented, old horrors. Why, you know what they done? Poured water on the floor of my kitchen, boiling water!

NIGHTINGALE: She's lying. These unfortunate old ladies just came in, they thought the house was on fire.

Photographer: This woman is the notorious Mrs. Wire, and it was she who screamed out the window. Why, these old women should be hospitalized, naturally, but it's her, her! [*He points at Mrs. Wire from the door.*] that poured the scalding water into my studio, and screamed with delight when my art models and guests ran naked into the street!

MRS. WIRE: There, now, AWGY CONFESSED!!

PATROLMAN 2: All out to the wagon!

[*The scene is dimmed out fast. A spot comes up on the writer in the witness box at night court.*]

OLD JUDGE'S VOICE: Let's not have no more beatin' aroun' the bush in this court, young fellow. The question is plain. You're under oath to give an honest answer. Now for the last time, at risk of being held in contempt of court, "Did you or did you not see the proprietor of the rooming house…"

MRS. WIRE'S VOICE [*shrilly*]: Restaurant *and* roomin' house respectfully run!

[*The judge pounds his gavel.*]

OLD JUDGE'S VOICE: Defendant will keep silent during the witness testimony. To repeat the question: "Did you or did you not see this lady here pour boiling water through the floor of her kitchen down into the studio of Mr. T. Hamilton Biggs?"

WRITER [*swallows, then in a low voice*]: I, uh… think it's unlikely… a lady would do such a thing.

OLD JUDGE'S VOICE: Speak up so I can heah you! What's that you said?

WRITER: I said I thought it *very* unlikely a lady would do such a thing.

[*Laughter is heard in the night court. The judge gavels, then pronounces the verdict.*]

OLD JUDGE'S VOICE: This court finds the defendant, Mrs. Hortense Wire, guilty as charged and imposes a fine of fifty dollars plus damages and releases her on probation in the custody of her nephew, Police Lieutenant James Flynn of New Orleans Parish, for a period of…

[*His voice fades out as does the scene. A spotlight comes up on Mrs. Wire in a flannel robe, drinking at the kitchen table. The writer appears hesitantly at the edge of the kitchen light.*]

MRS. WIRE [*without turning*]: I know you're standing there, but I don't wanta see you. It sure does surprise me that you'd dare to enter this house again after double-crossing me in court tonight.

WRITER: —I—just came back to pick up my things.

MRS. WIRE: You ain't gonna remove nothing from this place till you paid off what you owe me.

WRITER: You know I'm—destitute.

MRS. WIRE: You get tips from the customers.

WRITER: Nickels and dimes. [*Pause. The sound of rain is heard.*] —Mrs. Wire? [*She turns slowly to look at him.*] Do you think I really intended to lose you that case? Other witnesses had testified I was in the kitchen when you poured those kettles of water through the floor. And the judge knew I could see with at least one eye. I was on the witness stand under oath, couldn't perjure myself. I did try not to answer directly. I *didn't* answer directly. All I said was—

Mrs. Wire: You said what lost me the case, goddam it! Did you expect that old buzzard on the bench to mistake me for a lady, my hair in curlers, me wearin' the late, long ago Mr. Wire's old ragged bathrobe. Shoot! All of you witnesses betrayed me in night court because you live off me an' can't forgive me for it.

Writer: —I guess you want me to go…

Mrs. Wire: To where would you go? How far could you get on your nickels and dimes? You're shiverin' like a wet dog. Set down. Have a drink with me befo' you go up to bed.

Writer: You mean I can stay? [*She nods slightly. He sits down at the kitchen table; she pours him a drink.*] I don't think I ever saw you drink before, Mrs. Wire.

Mrs. Wire: I only touch this bottle, which also belonged to the late Mr. Wire before he descended to hell between two crooked lawyers, I touch it only when forced to by such a shocking experience as I had tonight, the discovery that I was completely alone in the world, a solitary ole woman cared for by no one. You know, I heard some doctor say on the radio that people die of loneliness, specially at my age. They do. Die of it, it kills 'em. Oh, that's not the cause that's put on the death warrant, but that's the *true* cause. I tell you, there's so much loneliness in this house that you can hear it. Set still and you can hear it: a sort of awful—soft—groaning in all the walls.

Writer: All I hear is rain on the roof.

Mrs. Wire: You're still too young to hear it, but I hear it and I feel it, too, like a—ache in ev'ry bone of my body. It makes me want to scream, but I got to keep still. A landlady ain't permitted to scream. It would disturb the tenants. But some time I will, scream, I'll scream loud enough to bring the roof down on us all.

Writer: This house is full of people.

Mrs. Wire: People I let rooms to. Less than strangers to me.

Writer: There's—Me. I'm not.

Mrs. Wire: You—just endure my company 'cause you're employed here, boy.

Writer: Miss Sparks isn't employed here.

Mrs. Wire: That woman is close to no one but the bum she keeps here, show you. [*She rises and knocks her chair over, then bawls out as if to Tye.*] More boxes! Take 'em out an' stay out with 'em, sleep it off on the streets!

[*Jane rises in her dim spot of light. She crosses to the door.*]

Jane [Off Stage]: Tye! Tye! I thought I heard Tye down there.

Mrs. Wire: Miss Sparks—don't you know that bum don't quit work till daybreak and rarely shows here before noon?

Jane: Sorry. Excuse me.

Writer [*his speech slurred by drink*]: God, but I was ignorant when I came here! This place has been a—I ought to pay you— tuition…

Mrs. Wire: One drink has made you drunk, boy. Go up to bed. We're goin' on tomorrow like nothing happened. [*He rises and crosses unsteadily from the kitchen light.*] Be careful on the steps.

Writer [*pausing to look back at her*]: Good night, Mrs. Wire. [*He disappears.*]

Mrs. Wire: —It's true, people die of it .

[*On the hall stairs the writer meets Nightingale, who speaks before the writer enters his own cubicle.*]

Nightingale [*imitating the writer's testimony in night court*]: "I, uh, think it's unlikely a lady would do such a thing." [*He coughs.*] —A statement belonging in a glossary of deathless quotations. [*He coughs again.*] —Completely convinced me you really do have a future in the—literary—profession.

[*The light builds on Mrs. Wire, and she rises from the kitchen table and utters a piercing cry. Nursie appears.*]

NURSIE: Mizz Wire, what on earth is it? A bat?

MRS. WIRE: I just felt like screaming, and so I screamed! That's all…

[*The lights dim out.*]

Interval

PART TWO
Scene Eight

A spotlight focuses on the writer working at his dilapidated typewriter in his gabled room in the attic.

WRITER: Instinct, it must have been [*He starts typing.*] directed me here, to the Vieux Carré of New Orleans, down country as a—river flows no plan. I couldn't have consciously, deliberately, selected a better place than here to discover—to encounter—my true nature. *Exposition! Shit!*

[*He springs up and kicks at the worn, wobbly table. A lean, gangling young man, whose charming but irresponsible nature is apparent in his genial grin, appears at the entrance of the writer's cubicle.*]

SKY: Having trouble?

WRITER: Even the typewriter objected to those goddamn lines. The ribbon's stuck, won't reverse.

SKY: Let me look at it. [*He enters the cubicle.*] Oh, my name is Schuyler but they call me Sky.

WRITER: The owner of the knapsack with "SKY" printed on it, that was—that was deposited here last winter sometime?

SKY [*working on the typewriter*]: Right. Landlady won't surrender it to me for less than twenty-five bucks, which is more than I can pay. Yeah, you see—I'm a fugitive from—from legal wedlock in Tampa, Florida, with the prettiest little bitsy piece of it you ever did see. There, now the ribbon's reversing, it slipped out of the slots like I slipped out of matrimony in Tampa—couldn't you see that?

WRITER: I don't think there's a room in this building where you could be certain it was night or day, and I've…

SKY: Something wrong with that eye.

WRITER: Operation. For a cataract. Just waiting till it heals.— Are you staying here?

SKY: Just for a day or two while I look into spots for a jazz musician in the Quarter.

WRITER: There's several jazz combos just around the corner on Bourbon Street.

SKY: Yeah, I know, but they're black and not anxious to work with a honky. So, I'll probably drive on West.

WRITER: How far West?

SKY: The Coast. Is there a toilet up here? I gotta piss. Downstairs john's occupied.

WRITER: I know a girl across the hall with a bathroom, but she's probably sleeping,

SKY: With the angels wetting the roof, would it matter if I did, too?

WRITER: Go ahead.

[*Sky leaps onto the alcove and pisses upstage out of the window.*]

Why'd you decide not to marry?

SKY: Suddenly realized I wasn't ready to settle. The girl, she had a passion for pink, but she extended it out of bounds in the love nest she'd picked out for us. Pink, pink, pink. So I cut out before daybreak.

WRITER: Without a word to the girl?

SKY: A note, "Not ready. Be back." Wonder if she believed it, or if I did. That was Christmas week.

I asked permission to leave my knapsack here with the landlady, overnight. She said, "For fifty cents." Extortionary, but I accepted the deal. However was unavoidably detained like they say. Returned last night for my gear and goddam, this landlady here refuses to surrender it to me except for twenty-five bucks. Crazy witch!

[*Mrs. Wire is at the cubicle entrance.*]

Mrs. Wire: What's he doin' up there?

Sky: Admiring the view.

Mrs. Wire: You was urinating out of the window! Jailbird! You ain't been in a hospital four months, you been in the House of Detention for resistin' arrest and assaultin' an officer of the law. I know. You admire the view in the bathroom. I don't allow no trashy behavior here. [*She turns to the writer.*] Why ain't you on the streets with those business cards?

Writer: Because I'm at the last paragraph of a story.

Mrs. Wire: Knock it off this minute! Why, the streets are swarming this Sunday with the Azalea Festival trade.

Writer: The time I give to "Meals for a Quarter in the Quarter" has begun to exceed the time originally agreed on, Mrs. Wire.

Mrs. Wire: It's decent, healthy work that can keep you off bad habits, bad company that I know you been drifting into.

Writer: How would you know anything outside of this moldy, old—

Mrs. Wire: Don't talk that way about this—historical old building. Why, 722 Toulouse Street is one of the oldest buildings in the Vieux Carré, and the courtyard, why, that courtyard out there is on the tourist list of attractions!

Writer: The tourists don't hear you shoutin' orders and insults to your, your—prisoners here!

Mrs. Wire: Two worthless dependents on me, that pair of scavenger crones that creep about after dark.

[*Nightingale coughs in his cubicle. Mrs. Wire raises her voice.*]

And I got that TB case spitting contagion wherever he goes, leaves a track of blood behind him like a chicken that's had its head chopped off.

Nightingale: 'sa goddam libelous lie!

Mrs. Wire [*crossing to the entrance of the adjoining cubicle*]: Been discharged from the Two Parrots, they told you to fold up your easel and git out!

Nightingale [*hoarsely*]: I'm making notes on these lies, and my friend, the writer, is witness to them!

Mrs. Wire: You is been discharged from the Two Parrots. It's God's truth, I got it from the cashier!

[*Sky chuckles, fascinated. He sits on the edge of the table or cot, taking a cigarette and offering one to the writer. Their casual friendly talk is contrapuntal to the violent altercation in progress outside.*]

She told me they had to scrub the pavement around your easel with a bucket of lye each night, that customers had left without payin' because you'd hawked an' spit by their tables!

Nightingale: Bucket of lies, not lye, that's what she told you!

Mrs. Wire: They only kept you there out of human pity!

Nightingale: Pity!

Mrs. Wire: Yais, pity! But finally pity and patience was exhausted, it run out there and it's run out here! Unlock that door! NURSIE!

Nursie [*off stage*]: Now what?

Mrs. Wire: Bring up my keys! Mr. Nightingale's locked himself in! You're gonna find you'self mighty quicker than you expected in a charity ward on your way to a pauper's grave!

WRITER: Mrs. Wire, be easy on him…

MRS. WIRE: You ain't heard what he calls me? Why, things he's said to me I hate to repeat. He's called me a fuckin' ole witch, yes, because I stop him from bringin' pickups in here at midnight that might stick a knife in the heart of anyone in the buildin' after they done it to him.

NIGHTINGALE [*in a wheezing voice as he drops onto the cot in his cubicle*]: It's you that'll get a knife stuck in you, between your—dried up old—dugs…

WRITER [sotto voce, *near tears*]: Be easy on him; he's dying.

MRS. WIRE: Not here. He's defamed this place as infested with bedbugs to try to explain away the blood he coughs on his pillow.

WRITER: That's—his last defense against—

MRS. WIRE: The truth, there's no defense against truth. Ev'rything in that room is contaminated, has got to be removed to the incinerator an' burned. Start with the mattress, Nursie!

[*Nursie has entered the lighted area with a bunch of rusty keys.*]

NIGHTINGALE: I warn you, if you attempt to enter my room, I'll strike you down with this easel!

MRS. WIRE: You do that, just try, the effort of the exertion would finish you right here! Oh, shoot, here's the master key, opens all doors!

NIGHTINGALE: At your own risk—I'll brain you, you bitch.

MRS. WIRE: Go on in there, Nursie!

NURSIE: Aw, no, not me! I told you I would never go in that room.

MRS. WIRE: We're coming in!

NIGHTINGALE: WATCH OUT!

[*He is backed into the alcove, the easel held over his head like a crucifix to exorcise a demon. A spasm of coughing wracks him. He bends double, dropping the easel, collapses to his knees, and then falls flat upon the floor.*]

NURSIE [*awed*]: Is he daid, Mizz Wire?

MRS. WIRE: Don't touch him. Leave him there until the coroner gets here.

NIGHTINGALE [*gasping*]: Coroner, your ass— I'll outlive you.

MRS. WIRE: If I dropped dead this second! Nursie, haul out that filthy mattress of his, pour kerosene on it.

NURSIE: Wouldn't touch that mattress with a pole…

MRS. WIRE: And burn it. Git a nigger to help you haul everything in here out, it's all contaminated. Why, this whole place could be quarantined!

NURSIE: Furniture?

MRS. WIRE: All! Then wash off your hands in alcohol to prevent infection, Nursie.

NURSIE: Mizz Wire, the courtyard is full of them Azalea Festival ladies that paid admission to enter! You want me to smoke 'em out?

MRS. WIRE: Collect the stuff you can move.

NURSIE: Move where?

MRS. WIRE: Pile it under the banana tree in the courtyard, cover it with tarpaulin, we can burn it later.

NIGHTINGALE: If anyone lays a hand on my personal effects, I'll [*His voice chokes with sobs.*] —I will be back in the Two Parrots tonight. I wasn't fired. I was given a leave of absence till I recovered from… asthma.

MRS. WIRE [*with an abrupt compassion*]: Mr. Nightingale.

NIGHTINGALE: Rossignol—of the Baton Rouge Rossignols, as any dog could tell you…

MRS. WIRE: I won't consult a dawg on this subject. However, the place for you is not here but in the charity ward at St. Vincent's. Rest there till I've made arrangements to remove you.

SKY: The altercation's subsided.

WRITER [*to Sky, who has begun to play his clarinet*]: What kind of horn is that?

[*Mrs. Wire appears at the entrance to the writer's cubicle. Sky plays entrance music— "Ta-ta-taaa!"*]

SKY: It's not a horn, kid, horns are brass. A clarinet's a woodwind instrument, not a horn.

MRS. WIRE: Yais, now about you all.

SKY: Never mind about us. We're leaving for the West Coast.

[*Mrs. Wire and the writer are equally stunned in opposite ways.*]

MRS. WIRE: —What's he mean, son? You're leavin' with this jailbird?

WRITER: —I—

MRS. WIRE: You won't if I can prevent it and I know how. In my register book, when you signed in here, you wrote St. Louis. We got your home address, street and number. I'm gonna inform your folks of the vicious ways and companions you been slipping into. They's a shockin' diff'rence between your looks an' manners since when you arrived here an' now, mockin' me with that grin an' that shifty-eyed indifference, evidence you're setting out on a future life of corruption. Address and phone number, I'll write, I'll phone! —You're not leavin' here with a piece of trash like that that pissed out the window! —Son, son, don't do it! [*She covers her face unraveled with emotion. Exchanging a look with Sky, the writer places an arm gingerly about her shoulder.*] You know I've sort of adopted you like the son took away from me by the late Mr. Wire and a—and a crooked lawyer, they got me declared to be—mentally incompetent.

WRITER: Mrs. Wire, I didn't escape from one mother to look for another.

[*Nursie returns, huffing, to the lighted area.*]

NURSIE: Mizz Wire, those tourists ladies, I can't control them, they're pickin' the azaleas off the bushes, and—

MRS. WIRE: That's what I told you to stay in the courtyard to stop.

NURSIE: Oh, I try, but one of 'em jus' called me a impudent ole nigger, and I won't take it. I come here to tell you I QUIT!

MRS. WIRE: AGAIN! COME BACK OUT THERE WITH ME! [*She turns to the writer.*] We'll continue this later. [*She exits with Nursie.*]

WRITER [*to Sky*]: —Were you serious about the West Coast offer?

SKY: You're welcome to come along with me. I don't like to travel a long distance like that by myself.

WRITER: How do you travel?

SKY: I've got a beat-up old '32 Ford across the street with a little oil and about half a tank of gas in it. If you want to go, we could share the expense. Have you got any cash?

WRITER: I guess I've accumulated a capital of about thirty-five dollars.

SKY: We'll siphon gas on the way.

WRITER: Siphon?

SKY: I travel with a little rubber tube, and at night I unscrew the top of somebody's gas tank and suck the gas out through the tube and spit it into a bucket and empty it into my car. Is it a deal?

WRITER [*with suppressed excitement*]: How would we live on the road?

SKY [*rolling a cigarette with obvious practice*]: We'd have to exercise our wits. And our personal charm. And, well, if that don't suffice, I have a blanket in the car, and there's plenty of wide open spaces between here and the Coast. [*He pauses for a beat.*] Scared? Of the undertaking?

WRITER [*smiling slowly*]: No—the Coast—starting when?

SKY: Why not this evening? The landlady won't admit me to the house again, but I'll call you, just keep your window open. I'll blow my clarinet in the courtyard. Let's say about six.

[*The conversation may continue in undertones as the area is dimmed out.*]

Scene Nine

The lights come up on Jane's studio area. The shuttered doors to the windows overlooking the courtyard below are ajar. Jane is trying to rouse Tye from an unnaturally deep sleep. It is evident that she has been engaged in packing her effects and his.

JANE: Tye, Tye, oh—Christ.

[*He drops a bare arm off the disordered bed and moans slightly. She bends over to examine a needle mark on his arm.*]

TYE: —Wh—?

[*Jane crosses to the sink and wets a towel then returns to slap Tye's face with it. He begins to wake slowly.*]

Some men would beat a chick up for lessin that, y'know.

JANE: All right, get out of bed and beat me up, but get up.

TYE [*stroking a promontory beneath the bed sheet*]: —Can't you see I am up?

JANE: I don't mean that kind of up, and don't bring stripshow lewdness in here this—Sunday afternoon.

TYE: Babe, don't mention the show to me t'day.

JANE: I'd like to remind you that when we first stumbled into this—crazy—co-habitation, you promised me you'd quit the show in a week.

TYE: For what? Tight as work is for a dude with five grades of school and no skill training from the Mississippi sticks?

JANE: You could find something less—publicly embarrassing, like a—filling station attendant.

TYE: Ha!

JANE: But of course your choice of employment is no concern of mine now.

TYE: Why not, Babe?

JANE: I'm not "Babe" and not "Chick"!

TYE: You say you're not my chick?

JANE: I say I'm nobody's chick.

TYE: Any chick who shacks with me's my chick.

JANE: This is my place. You just—moved in and stayed.

TYE: I paid the rent this month.

JANE: Half of it, for the first time, my savings being as close to exhaustion as me.

[*There is the sound of a funky piano and a voice on the Bourbon Street corner: "I've stayed around and played around this old town too long." Jane's mood softens under its influence.*]

Lord, I don't know how I managed to haul you to bed.

TYE: Hey, you put me to bed last night?

JANE: It was much too much exertion for someone in my condition.

TYE [*focusing on her more closely*]: —Honey, are you pregnant?

JANE: No, Lord, now who'd be fool enough to get pregnant by a Bourbon Street stripshow barker?

TYE: When a chick talks about her condition, don't it mean she's pregnant?

JANE: All female conditions are not pregnancy, Tye. [*She staggers, then finishes her coffee.*] Mine is that of a desperate young woman living with a young bum employed by gangsters and using her place as a depository for hot merchandise. Well, they're all packed. You're packed too.

Tye: —Come to bed.

Jane: No, thank you. Your face is smeared with lipstick; also other parts of you. I didn't know lip rouge ever covered so much—territory.

Tye: I honestly don't remember a fuckin' thing after midnight.

Jane: That I do believe. Now have some coffee. I've warmed it. It isn't instant, it's percolated.

Tye: Whose birthday is it?

Jane: It's percolated in honor of our day of parting.

Tye: Aw, be sweet, Babe; please come back to bed. I need comfort, not coffee.

Jane: You broke a promise to me.

Tye: Which?

Jane: Among the many? You used a needle last night. I saw the mark of it on you.

Tye: No shit. Where?

Jane [returning to the bedside]: There, right there on your— [He circles her with his arm and pulls her onto the bed] I've been betrayed by a—sensual streak in my nature. Susceptibility to touch. And you have skin like a child. I'd gladly support you if I believed you'd—if I had the means to and the time to. Time. Means. Luck. Things that expire, run out. And all at once you're stranded.

Tye: Jane you—lie down with me and hold me.

Jane: I'm afraid, Tye, we'll just have to hold each other in our memories from now on.

Tye [childishly]: Don't talk that way. I never had a rougher night in my life. Do I have to think and remember?

Jane: Tye, we've had a long spell of dreaming, but now we suddenly have to.

Tye: Got any aspirin, Babe?

Jane: You're past aspirin, Tye. I think you've gone past all legal—analgesics.

Tye: You say words to me I've never heard before.

Jane: Tye, I've been forced to make an urgent phone call to someone I never wanted to call.

Tye: Call?

Jane: And then I packed your personal belongings and all that loot you've been holding here. Exertion of packing nearly blacked me out. Trembling, sweating—had to bathe and change.

Tye: Babe?

Jane: You're vacating the premises, "Babe." It's afternoon.

Tye: Look, if you're knocked up, have the kid. I'm against abortion.

Jane: On moral principles?

Tye: Have the kid, Babe. I'd pull myself together for a kid.

Jane: You didn't for me.

Tye: A baby would be a livin' thing between us, with both our blood.

Jane: Never mind.

[Voices in the courtyard are heard.]

Nursie: Any donations t'keep the cou'tyard up, just drop it in my apron as you go out, ladies!…

Jane: Those tourists down there in the courtyard! If I'd known when I took this room it was over a tourist attraction—

Tye: It's the Festival, Babe. It ain't always Festival… gimme my cigarettes, ought to be some left in a pocket.

Jane [throwing his pants and a fancy sport shirt on the bed]: Here, your clothes, get in them.

TYE [*putting on his shorts*]: Not yet. It's Sunday, Babe... Where's Beret? I like Beret to be here when I wake up.

JANE: Not even a cat will wait ten, twelve hours for you to sleep off whatever you shot last night. How did a girl well-educated and reasonably well brought up get involved in this... Oh, I'm talking to myelf.

TYE: I hear you, Babe, and I see you.

JANE: Then... get up and dressed.

TYE: It's not dark yet, Babe. Y'know I never get dressed till after dark on Sundays.

JANE: Today has to be an exception.... expecting a caller, very important to me.

TYE: Fashion designer?

JANE: No. Buyer... to look at my illustrations. They're no good, I'm no good. I just had a flair, not a talent, and the flair flared out. I'm... finished. These sketches are evidence of it! [*She starts tearing fashion sketches off the wall.*] Look at me! Bangles, jangles! All taste gone! [*She tears off her costume jewelry.*]

TYE: Babe, you're in no shape to meet a buyer.

JANE [*slowly and bitterly*]: He's no buyer of anything but me.

TYE: —Buyer of *you?* Look, You said that you were expecting a buyer to look at your drawin's here.

JANE: I know what I said, I said a buyer to look at my illustrations, but what I said was a lie. Among other things, many other undreamed of before, you've taught me to practice deception.

VOICES OFFSTAGE: Edwina, Edwina, come see this dream of a little courtyard. Oh, my, yaiss, like a dream.

JANE: I know what I said, but let's say, Tye, that I experienced last week a somewhat less than triumphant encounter with the buyer of fashion illustrations *at Vogue Moderne.* In fact, it left me too shattered to carry my portfolio home without a shot of Metaxas brandy at the Blue Lantern, which was on the street level of the building. It was there that I met a gentleman from Brazil. He had observed my entrance, the Brazilian, and apparently took me for a hooker, sprang up with surprising agility for a gentleman of his corpulence, hauled me to his table, and introduced me to his *camaradas,* "Senorita, this is Señor and Señor and Señor," declared me, *"Bonita, muy, muy, bonita"*— tried to press a hundred-dollar bill in my hand. Well, some atavistic bit of propriety surfaced and I, like a fool, rejected it— but did accept his business card, just in case. This morning, Tye, I called him. "Senorita Bonita of the Blue Lantern awaits you, top floor of seven-two-two Toulouse," that was the invitation that I phoned in to the message desk. He must have received it by now at the Hotel Royal Orleans, where the Presidential Suite somehow contains him.

TYE: Who're you talkin' about?

JANE: My expected caller, a responsible businessman from Brazil. Sincerely interested in my bankrupt state...

TYE: Forget it, come back to bed and I'll undress you, Babe, you need rest.

JANE: The bed bit is finished between us. You're moving out today,

[*He slowly stumbles up, crosses to the table, and gulps coffee, then grasps her arm and draws her to bed.*]

No no, no, no, no, no!

TYE: Yes, yes, yes, yes, yes!

[*He throws her onto the bed and starts to strip her; she resists; he prevails. As the lights very gradually dim, a Negro singer-pianist at a nearby bar fades in, "Fly a-way! Sweet Kentucky baby-bay, fly, away..."*]

Mrs. Wire [*from a few steps below the writer*]: What's paralyzed you there? Son?

Writer: Miss Sparks is crying,

[*Mrs. Wire appears behind the writer in the lighted spot.*]

Mrs. Wire: That woman's moanin' in there don't mean she's in pain. Son, I got a suspicion you never had close relations with wimmen in your life.

Jane: Ohhh!

Writer: I never heard sounds like that.

[*Jane utters a wild cry. It impresses even Mrs. Wire.*]

Tye's Voice: Babe, I don't wanna force you...

Jane's Voice: Plee-ase! I'm not a thing, I'm not—a—thing!

Mrs. Wire [*shouting*]: You all quit that loud fornication in there!

Tye's Voice [*shouting back*]: Get the fuck downstairs, goddam ole witch!

Mrs. Wire: Howlin' insults at me in my own house, won't tolerate it! [*She bursts into the room.*] Never seen such a disgustin' exhibition!

[*Tye starts to rise from the bed. Jane clings desperately to him.*]

Jane: As! You sce!—Mrs. Wire!—Everything is!—packed, he's —moving—today...

Tye: The rent is paid in full! So get the fuck outa here!

Jane: Tye, please.

Mrs. Wire: What's in them boxes?

Tye: None of your—

Jane: Our personal—belongings, Mrs. Wire.

Mrs. Wire: That I doubt! The contents of these boxes will be inspected before removed from this place and in the presence of my nephew on the police force!

[*Tye charges toward Mrs. Wire.*]

Don't you expose yourself naykid in my presence! Nursie!

Jane: Mrs. Wire, for once I do agree with you! can you get him out, please, please get him out!

Mrs. Wire [*averting her face with an air of shocked propriety*] Dress at once and—

Nursie: Mizz Wire, I got the hospital on the phone.

Mrs. Wire: They sendin' an ambulance for Nightingale?

Nursie: Soon's they got a bed for him, but they want you to call 'em back and—

Mrs. Wire: St. Vincent's is run by taxpayers' money, remind 'em of that. [*She crosses off stage. Tye slams the door. Jane is sobbing on the bed.*]

Tye: Now, Babe.

Jane: If you approach this bed—

Tye: Just want to comfort you, honey. Can't we just rest together? Can't we? Rest and comfort each other?

[*The area dims as the black pianist sings "Kentucky Baby."*]

Mrs. Wire: Cut out that obscene talking up there. I'm on the phone. Emergency call is from here at 722 Toulouse. Christ Almighty, you drive me to profane language. You mean to admit you don't know the location of the most historical street in the Vieux Carré? You're not talking to no... no nobody, but a personage. Responsible. Reputable. Known to the authorities on the list of attractions. God damn it, you twist my tongue up with your... Nursie! Nursie! Will you talk to this in*competent*... Nursie! Nursie!

[*Nursie appears.*]

Got some idiot on the phone at the hospital. Will you inform this idiot who I am in the Quarter. Phone. Talk.

[*Nursie takes the phone.*]

NURSIE: Stairs... took my breath...

MRS. WIRE [*snatching back the phone*]: Now I want you to know, this here Nightingale case... I don't lack sympathy for the dying or the hopelessly inflicted... [*She kicks at Nursie beside her.*] Git! But I've got responsibilities to my tenants. Valuable paying tenants, distinguished society ladies, will quit my premises this day, I swear they will, if this Nightingale remains. Why, the State Board of Health will clap a suit on me unless... at once... ambulance. When? At what time? Don't say approximate to me. Emergency means immediate. Not when you drag your arse around to it. And just you remember I'm a taxpayer... No, no, you not me. I pay, you collect. Now get the ambulance here immediately, 722 Toulouse, with a stretcher with straps, the Nightingale is violent with fever. [*She slams down the phone.*] Shit!

NURSIE: My guess is they're going to remove you, too. [*Mrs. Wire leans on Nursie.*]

Scene Ten

There is a spotlight on the writer, stage front, as narrator.

WRITER: That Sunday I served my last meal for a quarter in the Quarters then I returned to the attic. From Nightingale's cage there was silence so complete I thought, "He's dead." Then he cried out softly—

NIGHTINGALE: Christ, how long do I have to go on like this?

WRITER: Then, for the first time, I returned his visits. [*He makes the gesture of knocking at Nightingale's door.*]—Mr. Rossignol...

[*There is a sound of staggering and wheezing. Nightingale opens the door; the writer catches him as he nearly falls and assists him back to his cot.*]

—You shouldn't try to dress.

NIGHTINGALE: Got to—escape! She wants to commit me to a charnal house on false charges.

WRITER: It's raining out.

NIGHTINGALE: A Rossignol will not be hauled away to a charity hospital.

WRITER: Let me call a private doctor. He wouldn't allow them to move you in your—condition.

NIGHTINGALE: My faith's in Christ—not doctors...

WRITER: Lie down.

NIGHTINGALE: Can't breathe lying—down...

WRITER: I've brought you this pillow. I'll put it back of your head. [*He places the pillow gently in back of Nightingale.*] Two pillows help you breathe.

NIGHTINGALE [*leaning weakly back*]: Ah—thanks—better... Sit down.

[*A dim light comes up on the studio area as Tye, sitting on the table, lights a joint.*]

WRITER: Theren' nowhere to sit.

NIGHTINGALE: You mean nowhere not contaminated? [*The writer sits.*] —God's got to give me time for serious work! Even God has moral obligations, don't He? —Well, *don't* He?

WRITER: I think that morals are a human invention that He ignores as successfully as we do.

NIGHTINGALE: Christ, that's evil, that is infidel talk. [*He crosses himself.*] I'm a Cathi'lic believer. A priest would say that you have fallen from Grace, boy

WRITER: What's that you're holding?

NIGHTINGALE: Articles left me by my sainted mother. Her tortoise-shell comb with a mother-of-pearl handle and her silver framed mirror.

[*He sits up with difficulty and starts combing his hair before the mirror as if preparing for a social appearance.*]

Precious heirlooms, been in the Rossignol family three generations. I look pale from confinement with asthma. Bottom of box is—toiletries, cosmetics—please!

WRITER: You're planning to make a public appearance, intending to go on the streets with this— advanced case of asthma?

NIGHTINGALE: Would you kindly hand me my Max Factor, my makeup kit?!

WRITER: I have a friend who wears cosmetics at night—they dissolve in the rain.

NIGHTINGALE: If necessary, I'll go into *Sanctuary!*

[*The writer utters a startled, helpless laugh; he shakes with it and leans against the stippled wall.*]

Joke, is it, is it a joke?! Foxes have holes, but the Son of Man hath nowhere to hide His head!

WRITER: Don't you know you're delirious with fever?

NIGHTINGALE: You used to be kind—gentle. In less than four months you've turned your back on that side of your nature, turned rock-hard as the world.

WRITER: I had to survive in the world. Now where's your pills for sleep, you need to rest.

NIGHTINGALE: On the chair by the bed.

[*Pause.*]

WRITER [*softly*]: Maybe this time you ought to take more than one.

NIGHTINGALE: Why, you're suggesting suicide to me which is a cardinal sin, would put me in unhallowed ground in—potter's field. I believe in God the Father, God the Son, and God the Holy Ghost... you've turned into a killer?

WRITER [*compulsively, with difficulty*]: Stop calling it asthma —the flu, a bad cold. Face the facts, deal with them. [*He opens the pillbox.*] Press tab to open, push down, unscrew the top. Here it is where you can reach it,

NIGHTINGALE: —Boy with soft skin and stone heart...

[*Pause. The writer blows the candle out and takes Nightingale's hand.*]

WRITER: Hear the rain, let the rain talk to you, I can't.

NIGHTINGALE: Light the candle.

WRITER: The candle's not necessary. You've got an alcove, too, with a window and bench. Keep your eyes on it, she might come in here before you fall asleep.

[*A strain of music is heard. The angel enters from her dark passage and seats herself, just visible faintly, on Nightingale's alcove bench.*]

Do you see her in the alcove?

NIGHTINGALE: Who?

WRITER: Do you feel a comforting presence?

NIGHTINGALE: None.

WRITER: Remember my mother's mother? Grand?

NIGHTINGALE: I don't receive apparitions. They're only seen by the mad.

[*The writer returns to his cubicle and continues as narrator.*]

WRITER: In my own cubicle, I wasn't sure if Grand had entered with me or not. I couldn't distinguish her from a—diffusion of light through the low running clouds. I thought I saw her, but her image was much fainter than it had ever been before, and I suspected that it would fade more and more as the storm of my father's blood obliterated the tenderness of Grand's. I began to pack my belongings. I was about to make a panicky departure to nowhere I could imagine... The West Coast? With Sky?

[*He is throwing things into a cardboard suitcase. Nursie appears at the edge of his light with a coffee tray.*]

NURSIE: Mrs. Wire knows you're packin' to leave an' she tole me to bring you up this hot coffee and cold biscuits.

WRITER: Thank her. Thank you both.

NURSIE: She says don't make no mistakes.

WRITER [*harshly*]: None, never?

NURSIE: None if you can help, and I agree with her about that. She's phoned your folks about you. They're coming down here tomorrow.

WRITER: If she's not bluffing...

NURSIE: She ain't bluffin', I heard her on the phone myself. Mizz Wire is gettin' you confused with her son Timmy. Her mind is slippin' again. Been through that before. Can't do it again.

WRITER: We all have our confusions... [*He gulps down the coffee as Nursie crosses out of the light*]

NURSIE [*singing softly*]: "My home is on Jordan."

WRITER: Then I started to write. I worked the longest I'd ever worked in my life, nearly all that Sunday. I wrote about Jane and Tye, I could hear them across the narrow hall. —Writers are shameless spies...

Scene Eleven

The studio light builds. Jane is sobbing on the bed, Tye is rolling a joint, seated on the table. The clearing sky has faded toward early blue dusk. Tye regards Jane with a puzzled look. Faintly we hear the black singer-pianist, "Bye, bye, blues. Don't cry blues," etc.

TYE: Want a hit, Babe? [*She ignores the question.*] How long *have* I been asleep? Christ, what are you crying about. Didn't I just give you one helluva Sunday afternoon ball, and you're cryin' about it like your mother died.

JANE: You forced me, you little pig, you did, you forced me.

TYE: You wanted it.

JANE: I didn't.

TYE: Sure you did. [*Jane is dressing again.*] Honey, you got shadows under your eyes.

JANE: Blackbirds kissed me last night. Isn't that what they say about shadows under the eyes, that blackbirds kissed her last night. The Brazilian must have been blind drunk when he took a fancy to me in the Blue Lantern, mistook me for hundred-dollar girl. —Tye, I'm not a whore! I'm the Northern equivalent of a lady, fallen, yes, but a lady, not a whore.

TYE: Whores get paid for it, Babe. I never had to.

JANE: You little—prick! Now I'm talkin' your jive, how do you like it? Does she talk like that when she's smearing you with lipstick, when you ball her, which I know you do, repeatedly, between shows.

TYE: —Who're you talkin' about?

JANE: That headliner at the strip show, the Champagne Girl.

TYE [*gravely*]: She's—not with the show no more.

JANE: The headliner's quit the show?

TYE: Yeah, honey, the Champagne Girl is dead an' so she's not in the show.

JANE: You mean—not such a hot attraction any more?

TYE: Don't be funny about it; it ain't funny.

JANE: You mean she's actually—

TYE: Yes. Ackshally. Dead. Real dead, about as dead as dead, which is totally dead— So now you know why I needed a needle to get me through last night.

Jane: —Well, of course that's—

Tye: You was jealous of her. [*Jane looks away.*] I never touched the Champagne Girl. She was strictly the property of the Man. Nobody else dared t' touch her.

Jane: The Man—what man?

Tye: The Man—no other name known by. —Well—he wasted her.

Jane: —Killed her? —Why?

Tye: 'Cause she quit sleeping with him. She was offered a deal on the West Coast!, Babe. The Man said, "No," The Champagne Girl said, "Yes." So the Man… you don't say no to the Man— if she's going to the West Coast it'll be packed in ice—

[*Voices are heard from the courtyard.*]

Tourist 1: My slippers are wet through. [*Piano music is heard.*]

Tourist 2: What's next on the tour, or is it nearly finished?

Tye: When the Man is annoyed by something, he piles his lupos in the back seat of his bulletproof limo and he let's 'em loose on the source of his annoyance.

Jane: —Lupos?

Tye: Lupos are those big black dawgs that're used for attack. The Man has three of 'em, and when he patrols his territory at night, they sit in the back seat of his Lincoln, set up there, mouths wide open on their dagger teeth and their black eyes rollin' like dice in a nigger crapshooter's hands. And night before last, Jesus! he let 'em into the Champagne Girl's apartment, and they—well, they ate her. Gnawed her tits off her ribs, gnawed her sweet little ass off. Of course the story is that the Champagne Girl entertained a pervert who killed her and ate her like that, but it's pretty well known it was them lupos that devoured that girl, under those ceiling mirrors and crystal chandeliers in her all white satin bedroom. —Yep—gone— the headliner— Y'know what you say when the Man wastes somebody? You got to say that he or she has "Gone to Spain." So they tole me last night, when people ask you where's the Champagne Girl, answer 'em that the Champagne Girl's gone to Spain. —Sweet kid from Pascagoula.

Jane: Please don't—continue—the story.

Tye: All champagne colored without face or body makeup on her, light gold like pale champagne and not a line, not a pore to be seen on her body! Was she meant for dawg food? I said, was she meant for dawg food? Those lupos ate that kid like she was their—last—supper .

Jane [*who has now managed to get round the table*]: Tye, Tye, open the shutters!

Tye: Why? You goin' out naked?

Jane: I'm going to vomit and die—in clean air… [*She has moved slowly upstage to the gallery with its closed shutters, moving from one piece of furniture to another for support. Now she opens the shutter doors and staggers out onto the gallery, and the tourist ladies' voices are raised in thrilled shock and dismay.*]

Tourist 1: Look at that!

Tourist 2: What at?

Tourist 1: There's a whore at the gallery window! Practically naked!

[*All gallery speeches should overlap.*]

Jane [*wildly*]: Out, out, out, out, out!

Nursie: Miss, Miss Sparks! These are Festival ladies who've paid admission.

Jane: Can't endure any more! Please, please, I'm sick!

Tye: Fawgit it, Babe, come back in.

Jane: It isn't real, it couldn't be—

[*The writer shakes his head with a sad smile.*]

But it was—it *is*... like a dream.

TYE: What did you say, Babe?

JANE: Close the gallery door—please?

TYE: Sure, Babe. [*He shuts the door on the voices below.*]

JANE: And—the hall door—bolt it. Why do you bring home nightmare stories to me?!

TYE [*gently*]: Babe, you brought up the subject, you asked me about the Champagne Girl. I wasn't planning to tell you. Chair?

JANE: Bed.

TYE: Weed?

JANE: —Coffee.

TYE: Cold.

JANE: —Cold—coffee.

[*Tye pours her a cup and puts it in her trembling hand. He holds the hand and lifts the cup to her lips, standing behind her. He lets his hand fall to her breasts; she sobs and removes the hand.*

[*The singer-pianist is heard again.*]

JANE: ...Why do you want to stay on here?

TYE: Here's where you are, Babe.

JANE [*shaking her head*]: No more. I... have to dress... [*She dresses awkwardly, frantically. He watches in silence.*] You have to get dressed, too, I told you I was expecting a very important visitor. Tye, the situation's turned impossible on us, face it.

TYE: You're not walkin' out on me.

JANE: Who have I got to appeal to except God, whose phone's disconnected, or this... providential... protector.

TYE: From the banana republic, a greaseball. And you'd quit me for that?

JANE: You've got to be mature and understanding. At least for once, now dress. The Brazilian is past due... I realized your defects, but you touched me like nobody else in my life had ever before or ever could again. But—Tye, I counted on you to grow up, and you refused to. I took you for someone gentle caught in violence and degradation that he'd escape from...

TYE: Whatever you took me for, I took you for honest, for decent, for...

JANE: Don't be so... "Decent"? You ridiculous little... sorry, no. Let's not go into... abuse... Tye? When we went into this it wasn't with any long-term thing in mind. That's him on the steps. Go in the bathroom quiet!

TYE: You go in the bathroom quiet. I'll explain without words.

[*She thrusts his clothes at him. He throws them savagely about the stage.*]

...Well?

[*There is a sound on the stairs.*]

Sounds like the footsteps of a responsible man.

[*Tye opens the door. We see hospital interns with a stretcher. Jane stares out. The interns pass again with Nightingale's dying body on the stretcher. The writer is with them. Jane gasps and covers her face with her arm. The writer turns to her.*]

WRITER: It's just—they're removing the painter.

JANE: —*Just!*

TYE: No Brazilian, no buyer?

JANE: No. No sale.

WRITER [*standing in the open doorway, as narrator*]: It was getting dim in the room.

Tye: It's almost getting dark.

Writer: They didn't talk. He smoked his reefer. He looked at her steady in the room getting dark and said...

Tye: I See you clear.

Writer: She turned her face away. He walked around that way and looked at her from that side. She turned her face the other way. She was crying without a sound, and a black man was playing piano at the Four Deuces round the corner, an oldie, right for the atmosphere... something like [*The piano fades in, "Seem Like Old Times." Tye begins to sing softly with the piano.*]

Jane: Don't.

[*Tye stops the soft singing but continues to stare at Jane.*]

DON'T

[*Pause.*]

Tye: Jane. You've gotten sort of—skinny. How much weight you lost?

Jane: I... don't know...

Tye: Sometimes you walk a block and can't go no further. [*Pause.*]

Jane: I guess I'm a yellow-cab girl. With limousine aspirations.

Tye: Cut the smart talk, Babe. Let's level. [*Pause. She extends her hand.*]

Want a drag? Well?

[*Jane nods and takes a drag off his cigarette.*] Huh?

Jane: Well, after all, why not, if you're interested in it. It hasn't been just lately I've lost weight and energy but for more than a year in New York. Some—blood thing—progressing rather fast at my age... I think I had a remission when I met you.

A definite remission... here... like the world stopped and turned backward, or like it entered another universe—*months!* [*She moves convulsively; Tye grips her shoulders.*] ...Then... it... I...

Tye: Us?

Jane: No, no, that unnatural tiredness started in again. I went to Ochsners. Don't you remember when the doctor's letter was delivered? No, I guess you don't, being half conscious all the rime. It was from Ochsners. It informed me that my blood count had changed for the worse. It was close to... collapse... [*Pause.*]...Those are the clinical details. Are you satisfied with them? Have you any more questions to ask?

[*She stares at him; he averts his face. She moves around him to look at his face; he averts it again. She claps it between her hands and compels him to look at her. He looks down. A scratching sound is heard at the shutter doors.*]

Jane: That's Beret, let her in. Isn't it nice how cats go away and come back and—you don't have to worry about them. So unlike human beings.

[*Tye opens the door. He opens a can of cat food and sets it on the floor, then crosses to his clothes, collecting them from the floor.*]

Tye [*gently*]: Jane, it's getting dark and I—I better get dressed now.

Jane [*with a touch of harshness*]: Yes, dress—dress... [*But he is lost in reflection, lighting a joint. She snatches it from his lips.*]

And leave me alone as always in a room that smells, that reeks of marijuana!

Scene Twelve

WRITER [*as narrator*]: She was watching him with an unspoken question in her eyes, a little resentful now.

MRS. WIRE'S VOICE [*from off stage, curiously altered*]: Why are those stairs so dark?

[*The light in the studio area is dimmed to half during the brief scene that follows. The writer rises and stands apprehensively alert as Mrs. Wire becomes visible* in *a yellowed silk robe with torn lace, a reliquary garment. Her hair is loose, her steps unsteady, her eyes hallucinated.*]

WRITER [*crossing from the studio, dismayed*]: Is that you, Mrs. Wire?

MRS. WIRE: Now, Timmy, Timmy, you mustn't cry every time Daddy gets home from the road and naturally wants to be in bed just with Mommy. It's Daddy's privilege, Mummy's— obligation. You'll understand when you're older—you see, Daddy finds Mommy attractive.

WRITER [*backing away from the cubicle entrance*]: Mrs. Wire, you're dreaming.

MRS. WIRE: Things between grownups in love and marriage can't be told to a child. [*She sits on the writer's cot.*] Now lie down and Mommy will sing you a little sleepy-time song. [*She is staring into space. He moves to the cubicle entrance; the candle is turned over and snuffed out.*]

MRS. WIRE: "Rock-a-bye, baby, in a tree top. If the wind blows, the cradle will rock…"

WRITER: Mrs. Wire, I'm not Timothy, I'm not *Tim,* I'm not Timmy. [*He touches her.*]

MRS. WIRE: Dear child given to me of love…

WRITER: Mrs. Wire, I'm not your child. I am nobody's child. Was maybe, but not now. I've grown into a man, about to take his first step out of this waiting station into the world.

MRS. WIRE: Mummy knows you're scared sleeping alone in the dark. But the Lord gave us dark for sleep, and Daddy don't like to find you took his rightful place…

WRITER: Mrs. Wire, I'm no relation to you, none but a tenant that earned his keep a while… Nursie!Nursie!

NURSIE [*approaching*]: She gone up there? [*Nursie appears.*] She gets these spells, goes back in time. I think it musta been all that Azalea Festival excitement done it.

MRS. WIRE: "If the bough breaks, the cradle will *fall…*"

NURSIE [*at the cubicle entrance*]: Mizz Wire, it's Nursie. I'll take you back downstairs.

MRS. WIRE [*rousing a bit*]: It all seemed so real. —I even remember lovemaking…

NURSIE: Get up, Mizz Wire, come down with Nursie.

MRS. WIRE [*accepting Nursie's support*]: Now I'm—old. [*They withdraw from the light.*]

MRS. WIRE'S VOICE: Ahhhhhhhh… Ahhhhhhhh… Ahhhh… Ahhhhh…

[*This expression of despair is lost in the murmur of the wind. The writer sinks onto his cot; the anger of the alcove appears in the dusk.*]

WRITER: Grand! [*She lifts her hand in a valedictory gesture.*] I guess angels warn you to leave a place by leaving before you.

[*The light dims in the cubicle as the writer begins to pack and builds back up in the studio. The writer returns to the edge of the studio light.*]

JANE: You said you were going to get dressed and go back to your place of employment and resume the pitch for the ladies.

TYE: What did you say, Babe?

[*He has finished dressing and is now at the mirror, absorbed in combing his hair. Jane utters a soft, involuntary laugh.*]

JANE: A hundred dollars, the price, and worth it, certainly worth it. I must be much in your debt, way over my means to pay off!

TYE: Well, I ain't paid to make a bad appearance at work. [*He puts on a sport shirt with girls in grass skirts printed on it.*]

JANE: I *hate* that shirt.

TYE: I know you think it's tacky. Well, I'm tacky., and it's the only clean one I got.

JANE: It isn't clean, not really. And does it express much grief over the Champagne Girl's violent departure to Spain?

TYE: Do you have to hit me with that? What reason...?

JANE: I've really got no reason to hit a goddamn soul but myself that lacked pride to keep my secrets. You know I shouldn't have told you about my—intentions, I should have just slipped away. The Brazilian was far from attractive but—my circumstances required some drastic—compromises.

TYE [*crouching beside her*]: You're talking no sense, Jane. The Brazilian's out of the picture; those steps on the stairs were steps of hospital workers coming to take a—pick a dying fruit outa the place.

JANE: *Do you think I expect you back here again?* You'll say yes, assure me now as if forever—but— reconsider—the moment of impulse....

TYE: Cut some slack for me, Babe. We all gotta cut some slack for each other in this fucking world. Lissen. You don't have to sweat it.

JANE: Give me another remission; one that lasts!

TYE: Gotta go now, it's late, after dark and I'm dressed.

JANE: Well, zip your fly up unless you're now in the show. [*She rises and zips up his fly, touches his face and throat with trembling fingers.*]

TYE: Jane, we got love between us! Don't ya know that?

JANE [*not harshly*]: Lovely old word, love, it's traveled a long way, Tye.

TYE: And still's a long way to go. Hate to leave you alone but—

JANE: I'm not alone. I've got Beret. An animal is a comforting presence sometimes. I wonder if they'd admit her to St. Vincent's?

TYE: St Vincent's?

JANE: That charity hospital where they took the painter called Nightingale.

TYE: You ain't going there, honey.

JANE: It strikes me as being a likely destination.

TYE: Why?

JANE: I watched you dress. I didn't exist for you. Nothing existed for you but your image in the mirror. Understandably so. [*With her last strength she draws herself up.*]

TYE: What's understandable, Jane? —You got a fever? [*He rises, too, and stretches out a hand to touch her forehead. She knocks it away.*]

JANE: What's understandable is that your present convenience is about to become an encumbrance. An invalid, of no use, financial or sexual. Sickness is repellent, Tye, demands more care and gives less and less in return. The person you loved—assuming that you *did* love when she was still useful—is now, is now as absorbed in preparing herself for oblivion as you were absorbed, in your—your image in the—mirror!

TYE [*frightened by her vehemence*]: Hey, Jane! [*Again she strikes away his extended hand.*]

JANE: Readies herself for it as you do for the street! [*She continues as to herself.*] —Withdraws into another dimension. Is indifferent to you except as—caretaker! Is less aware of you than of—[*Panting, she looks up slowly through the skylight.*]— sky that's visible to her from her bed under the skylight—at night, these—filmy white clouds, they move, they drift over the roofs of the Vieux Carré so close that if you have fever you feel as if you could touch them, and bits would come off on your fingers, soft as—cotton candy—

TYE: Rest, Babe. I'll be back early. I'll get Smokey to take over for me at midnight, and come back with tamales and a bottle of vino! [*He crosses out of the light. She rushes to the door.*]

JANE: No, no, not before daybreak and with a new needle mark on your arm. Beret? Beret!

[*She staggers wildly out of the light, calling the cat again and again.*]

WRITER: I lifted her from the floor where she'd fallen.

[*Various voices are heard exclaiming around the house.*

[*The writer reappears in the studio area supporting Jane, who appears half conscious.*]

Jane? Jane?

JANE: —My cat, I scared it away .

NURSIE [*offstage*]: What is goin' on up there?

WRITER: She was frightened by something.

JANE: I lost my cat, that's all. —They don't understand. [*The writer places her on the bed.*] Alone. I'm alone.

WRITER: She'll be back. [*He continues as narrator.*] Jane didn't seem to hear me. She was looking up at the skylight.

JANE: It isn't blue any more, it's suddenly turned quite dark.

WRITER: It was dark as the question in her eyes. [*The blues piano fades in.*]

JANE: It's black as the piano man playing around the corner.

WRITER [*to Jane*]: It must be after six. What's the time now?

JANE: Time? What? Oh. Time. My sight is blurred. [*She shows him her wristwatch.*] Can't make out the luminous dial, can you?

WRITER: It says five of twelve.

JANE: An improbable hour. Must have run down.

WRITER: I'll rake it off. To wind it. [*He puts the watch to his ear.*] I'm afraid it's broken.

JANE [*vaguely*]: I hadn't noticed. — Lately— I tell time by the sky.

WRITER: His name was Sky.

JANE: Tye.

WRITER: No, not Tye. Sky was the name of someone who offered me a ride West.

JANE: —I've had fever all day. Did you ask me a question?

WRITER: I said I'd planned a trip to the West Coast with this young vagrant, a musician.

JANE: Young vagrants are irresponsible. I'm not at all surprised—he let you down? Well. I have travel plans, too.

WRITER: With Tye?

JANE: No, I was going alone, not with Tye. What are you doing there?

WRITER: Setting up the chess board. Want to play?

JANE: Oh, yes, you said you play. I'd have a partner for once! But my concentration's—I warn you— it's likely to be—impaired.

WRITER: Want to play white or black?

JANE: You choose. [*The piano fades in. Jane looks about in a confused way.*]

WRITER: Black. In honor of the musician around the corner.

JANE: —He's playing something appropriate to the occasion as if I'd phoned in a request. How's it go, so familiar?

WRITER: "Makes no difference how things break,

still get by somehow

I'm not sorry, cause it makes no difference now."

JANE: Each of us abandoned to the other. You know this is almost our first private conversation. [*She nearly falls to the floor. He catches her and supports her to the chair at the upstage side of the table.*] Shall we play, let's do. With no distractions at all. [*She seems unable to move; she has a frozen attitude.*]

[*There is a distant sustained high note from Sky's clarinet. They both hear it. Jane tries to distract the writer's attention from the sound and continues quickly with feverish animation. The sound of the clarinet becomes more urgent.*]

Vagrants, I can tell you about them. From experience. Incorrigibly delinquent. Purposeless. Addictive. Grab at you for support when support's what you need—gone? Whistling down the last flight, such a lively popular tune. Well, I have travel plans, but in the company of no charming young vagrant. Love Mediterranean countries but somehow missed Spain. I plan to go. Now! Madrid, to visit the Prado, most celebrated museum of all. Admire the Goyas, El Grecos. Hire a car to cross the—gold plains of Toledo.

WRITER: Jane, you don't have to make up stories, I heard your talk with Tye—all of it.

JANE: Then you must have heard his leaving. How his steps picked up speed on the second flight down—started whistling.

WRITER: He always whistles down stairs—it's habitual to him— you mustn't attach a special meaning to it.

[*The clarinet music is closer; the sound penetrates the shut window.*]

JANE: At night the Quarter's so full of jazz music, so many entertainers. Isn't it now your move?

WRITER [*embarrassed*]: It's your move, Jane.

JANE [*relinquishing her game*]: No yours—your vagrant musician is late but you're not forgotten.

WRITER: I'll call down, ask him to wait till midnight when Tye said he'll be back.

JANE: With tamales and vino to celebrate—[*She staggers to the window, shatters a pane of glass, and shouts.*] —Your friend's coming right down, just picking up his luggage!

[*She leans against the wall, panting, her bleeding hand behind her*]

Now go, quick. He might not wait, you'd regret it.

WRITER: Can't I do something for you?

JANE: Pour me three fingers of bourbon.

[*She has returned to the table. He pours the shot.*]

Now hurry, hurry. I know that Tye will be back early tonight.

WRITER: Yes, of course he will... [*He crosses from the studio light.*]

JANE [*smiling somewhat bitterly*]: Naturally, yes, how could I possibly doubt it. With tamales and vino... [*She uncloses her fist; the blood is running from palm to wrist. The writer picks up a cardboard laundry box and the typewriter case.*]

WRITER: As I left, I glanced in Jane's door. She seemed to be or was pretending to be—absorbed in her solitary chess game. I went down the second flight and on the cot in the dark passageway was—[*He calls out.*] Beret?

[*For the first time the cat is visible, white and fluffy as a piece of cloud. Nursie looms dimly behind him, a dark solemn fact, lamplit.*]

NURSIE: It's the cat Miss Sparks come runnins after.

WRITER Take it to her, Nursie. She's alone up there.

MRS. WIRE: Now watch out, boy. Be careful of the future. It's a long ways for the young. Some makes it and others git lost.

WRITER: I know... [*He turns to the audience.*] I stood by the door uncertainly for a moment or two.

I must have been frightened of it…

 Mrs. Wire: Can you see the door?

 Writer: Yes—but to open it is a desperate undertaking…

 [*He does, hesitantly. Transparencies close from either wing. Dim spots of light touch each character of the play in a characteristic position.*

 [*As he first draws the door open, he is forced back a few steps by a cacophony of sound: the waiting storm of his future—mechanical racking cries of pain and pleasure, snatches of song. It fades out. Again there is the urgent call of the clarinet. He crosses to the open door.*]

 They're disappearing behind me. Going. People you've known in places do that: they go when you go. The earth seems to swallow them up, the walls absorb them like moisture, remain with you only as ghosts; their voices are echoes, fading but remembered.

 [*The clarinet calls again. He turns for a moment at the door.*] This house is empty now.

Truman Capote (1924–1984)

Truman Capote was born Truman Streckfus Persons in New Orleans on September 30, 1924. His mother, Lillie Mae Faulk, was seventeen years old when she married Archulus (Arch) Persons and had Truman. Both his parents were from small towns in Alabama, and when only four years old, Truman was sent to live with his mother's relatives in Monroeville, Alabama, the setting of much of his fiction. In Monroeville, he also met lifelong friend, Harper Lee, who based her character, Dill in *To Kill a Mockingbird* on young Truman. By the early 1930s, however, his mother divorced Arch Persons, moved to New York, never to return to the South, changed her name to Nina, and got remarried to Cuban-born businessman, Joseph Garcia Capote, who legally adopted Truman changing his name to Truman Capote, which he would remain until his death. Capote was soon sent off to several boarding schools in the Northeast, including St. John's Prep and Trinity School in New York City, and later Greenwich High School in fashionable Millbrook, Connecticut, before moving back to New York City into a swanky Park Avenue apartment in 1942. Their lives would abruptly change when his stepfather was convicted of embezzlement ten years later. His mother, unable to cope with such ignominy, committed suicide two years later, and his stepfather was sentenced to one year in Sing Sing Prison.[1]

Capote admits in his 1969 essay, "A Voice from a Cloud" that he made a conscious decision not to attend college:

> I was determined never to set a studious foot inside a college classroom. I felt that either one was
> or wasn't a writer, and no combination of professors could influence the outcome. I still think I was
> correct, at least in my own case; however, I now realize that most young writers have more to gain
> than not by attending college, if only because their teachers and classroom comrades provide a
> captive audience for their work; nothing is lonelier than to be an aspiring artist....

In fact, Capote often was a lonely artist and had abandonment issues that lasted well into his adult life, much of which he spent moving around the globe, though he always maintained an apartment in New York City.

He never did live in New Orleans; however, he did make much of his exotic birthplace and from time to time came to the city, early on visiting his father, and in 1943, by Greyhound bus in order to finish his first published novel, *Other Voices, Other Rooms* in the French Quarter. He goes on to describe his time here in "A Voice from a Cloud":

> I rented a bedroom in the crowded apartment of a Creole family who lived.... on Royal Street. It
> was a small hot bedroom almost entirely occupied by a brass bed, and it was noisy as a steel mill.
> Streetcars racketed under the window and the carousings of sightseers touring the Quarter, the
> boisterous whiskey brawlings of soldiers and sailors made for continuous pandemonium.

Capote would expound on the exuberant life of the French Quarter in his 1980 essay, "Hidden Gardens," which ends with Capote being propositioned by a prostitute in Jackson Square, whom he politely turns down.

Capote's short story included here, "A Tree of Night," takes place entirely on a train to New Orleans. In much of Capote's writing about the city, New Orleans is not the "big easy" as it is so often portrayed, but rather a place of foreboding, or one to which characters escape, like Walter in "Shut a Final Door," or even Capote himself when he went there to finish his novel. In this short story, Kay, a young college student from New Orleans, is not escaping the city but rather returning to college in Atlanta, after having attended an uncle's funeral in rural Alabama. The only thing this uncle left her was a very conspicuous, green Western guitar, which later serves her well as a place to dispose of the gin forced upon her by a drunken street performer/con artist across from whom she is sitting. Kay becomes trapped not only on the train but also in the seat next to the older woman and her companion, a deaf mute with "eyes like a pair of clouded milky-blue marbles...thickly lashed and oddly beautiful" at which Kay cannot help but gawk. When the older woman hears that Kay is from New Orleans, she describes the macabre street show

---

1   Much of this information can be found in Truman Capote's own 1969 essay, "A Voice from a Cloud" and on the *Encyclopedia of Alabama* website, "Truman Capote" by Norman McMillan, at http://www.encyclopediaofalabama.org.

that she and her companion put on in the French Quarter. In the end, Kay, like so many in the Quarter, is conned by these two, reminiscent of the current scam, "I bet I know where you got dem shoes…".

Probably Capote's most well known short story set in New Orleans is "One Christmas," but it is also his last, and he was clearly capitalizing on the very popular, "A Christmas Memory" and "The Thanksgiving Visitor." In a way it is a retelling of the former with the setting moved from rural Alabama to New Orleans.

By the late 1970s, near the end of his life, Capote was in and out of rehab for alcohol and drug dependency. He had become almost as famous for his extravagant persona as he was for his writing. And after the tell-all, "Le Côte Basque 1965," the first chapter of his unfinished novel *Answered Prayers*, appeared in *Esquire* in 1976, he was shunned by the elite New York set, the same ones who clamored for an invitation to his still legendary Black and White Ball held in the Plaza Hotel's Grand Ballroom in 1966. He died from liver cancer on August 25, 1984, at the home of Joanne Carson, late night host Johnny Carson's ex-wife. He was survived by his long-time companion, writer Jack Dunphy, and together their ashes were spread off of Long Island.

A Tree of Night[1]

It was winter. A string of naked light bulbs, from which it seemed all warmth had been drained, illuminated the little depot's cold, windy platform. Earlier in the evening it had rained, and now icicles hung along the station-house eaves like some crystal monster's vicious teeth. Except for a girl, young and rather tall, the platform was deserted, The girl wore a gray flannel suit, a raincoat, and a plaid scarf. Her hair, parted in the middle and rolled up neatly on the sides, was rich blondish-brown; and, while her face tended to be too thin and narrow, she was, though not extraordinarily so, attractive. In addition to an assortment of magazines and a gray suede purse on which elaborate brass letters spelled Kay, she carried conspicuously a green Western guitar.

When the train, spouting steam and glaring with light, came out of the darkness and rumbled to a halt, Kay assembled her paraphernalia and climbed up into the last coach.

The coach was a relic with a decaying interior of ancient red-plush seats, bald in spots, and peeling iodine-colored woodwork, An old-time copper lamp, attached to the ceiling, looked romantic and out of place. Gloomy dead smoke sailed the air; and the car's heated closeness accentuated the stale odor of discarded sandwiches, apple cores, and orange hulls; this garbage, including Lily cups, soda-pop baffles, and mangled newspapers, littered the long aisle. From a water cooler, embedded in the wall, a steady stream trickled to the floor. The passengers, who glanced up wearily when Kay entered, were not, it seemed, at all conscious of any discomfort.

Kay resisted a temptation to hold her nose and threaded her way carefully down the aisle, tripping once, without disaster, over a dozing fat man's protruding leg. Two nondescript men turned an interested eye as she passed; and a kid stood up in his seat squalling, "Hey, Mama, look at de banjo! Hey, lady, lemme play ya banjo!" till a slap from Mama quelled him.

There was only one empty place. She found it at the end of the car in an isolated alcove occupied already by a man and woman who were sitting with their feet settled lazily on the vacant seat opposite. Kay hesitated a second then said, "Would you mind if I sat here?"

The woman's head snapped up as if she had not been asked a simple question, but stabbed with a needle, too. Nevertheless, she managed a smile. "Can't say as I see what's to stop you, honey," she said, taking her feet down and also, with a curious impersonality, removing the feet of the man who was staring out the window, paying no attention whatsoever.

Thanking the woman, Kay took off her coat, sat down, and arranged herself with purse and guitar at her side, magazines in her lap: comfortable enough, though she wished she had a pillow for her back.

The train lurched; a ghost of steam hissed against the window; slowly the dingy lights of the lonesome depot faded past.

"Boy, what a jerkwater dump," said the woman. "No town, no nothin'."

Kay said, "The town's a few miles away."

"That so? Live there?"

No. Kay explained she had been at the Funeral of an uncle. An uncle who, though she did not of course mention it, had left her nothing in his will but the green guitar. Where was she going? Oh, back to college.

After mulling this over, the woman concluded, "What'll you ever learn in a place like that? Let me tell you, honey, I'm plenty educated and I never saw the inside of no college."

"You didn't?" murmured Kay politely and dismissed the matter by opening one of her magazines. The light was dim for reading and none of the stories looked in the least compelling. However, not wanting to became involved in a conversational marathon, she continued gazing at it stupidly till she felt a furtive rap on her knee.

"Don't read," said the woman. "I need somebody to talk to. Naturally, it's no fun talking to him." She jerked a thumb toward the silent man. "He's afflicted: deaf and dumb, know what I mean?"

Kay closed the magazine and looked at her more or less for the first time. She was short; her feet barely scraped the floor. And like many undersized people she had a freak of structure, in her case an enormous, really huge head. Rouge so brightened her sagging, flesh-featured face it was difficult even to guess at her age: perhaps fifty, fifty-five. Her big sheep eyes squinted, as if distrustful of what they saw. Her hair was an obviously dyed red, and twisted into parched, fat corkscrew curls. A once-elegant lavender hat of impressive size flopped crazily on the side of her head, and she was kept busy brushing back a drooping cluster of celluloid cherries sewed to the brim. She wore a plain, somewhat shabby blue dress. Her breath had a vividly sweetish gin smell.

"You do wanna talk to me, don't you honey?"

"Sure," said Kay, moderately amused.

"Course you do. You bet you do. That's what I like about a train. Bus people are a close-mouthed buncha dopes. But a train's the place for putting your cards on the table, that's what I always say." Her voice was cheerful and booming, husky as a man's, "But on accounta him, I always try to get us this here seat; it's more private, like a swell compartment, see?"

"It's very pleasant," Kay agreed. "Thanks for letting me join you." "Only too glad to. We don't have much company; it makes some folks nervous to be around him."

As if to deny it, the man made a queer, furry sound deep in his throat and plucked the woman's sleeve. "Leave me alone, dearheart," she said, as if she were talking to an inattentive child. "I'm O.K. We're just having us a nice little ol' talk. Now behave yourself or this pretty girl will go away. She's very rich; she goes to college." And winking, she added, "He thinks I'm drunk."

The man slumped in the seat, swung his head sideways, and studied Kay intently from the corners of his eyes. These eyes, like a pair of clouded milky-blue marbles, were thickly lashed and oddly beautiful. Now, except for a certain remoteness, his wide, hairless face had no real expression. It was as if he were incapable of experiencing or reflecting the slightest emotion. His gray hair was clipped close and combed forward into uneven bangs. He looked like a child aged abruptly by some uncanny method. He wore a frayed blue serge suit, and he had anointed himself with a cheap, vile perfume. Around his wrist was strapped a Mickey Mouse watch.

"He thinks I'm drunk," the woman repeated. "And the real funny part is, I am. Oh shoot—you gotta do something, ain't that right?" She bent closer. "Say, ain't it?"

Kay was still gawking at the man; the way he was looking at her made her squeamish, but she could not take her eyes off him. "I guess so," she said.

"Then let's us have us a drink," suggested the woman, She plunged her hand into an oilcloth satchel and pulled out a partially filled gin bottle. She began to unscrew the cap, but, seeming to think better of this, handed the bottle to Kay. "Gee, I forgot about you being company," she said. "I'll go get us some nice paper cups."

So, before Kay could protest that she did nor want a drink, the woman had risen and started none too steadily down the aisle toward the water cooler.

Kay yawned and rested her forehead against the windowpane, her fingers idly strumming the guitar: the strings sang a hollow, lulling tune, as monotonously soothing as the Southern landscape, smudged in darkness, flowing past the window. An icy winter moon rolled above the train across the night sky like a thin white wheel.

And then, without warning, a strange thing happened: the man reached out and gently stroked Kay's cheek. Despite the breathtaking delicacy of this movement, it was such a bold gesture Kay was at first too startled to know what to make of it: her thoughts shot in three or four fantastic directions. He leaned forward till his queer eyes were very near her own; the reek of his perfume was sickening. The guitar was silent while they exchanged a searching gaze. Suddenly, from some spring of compassion, she felt for him a keen sense of pity; but also and this she could not suppress, an overpowering disgust, an absolute loathing: something about him, an elusive quality she could not quite put a finger on, reminded her of—of what?

After a little, he lowered his hand solemnly and sank back in the seat, an asinine grin transfiguring his face, as if he had performed a clever stunt for which he wished applause.

"Giddyup! Giddyup! my little bucker-ROOS…" shouted the woman. And she sat down, loudly proclaiming to be, "Dizzy as a witch! Dog tired! Whew!" From a handful of Lily cups she separated two and casually thrust the rest down her blouse, "Keep 'em safe and dry, ha ha ha.…" A coughing spasm seized her, but when it was over she appeared calmer. "Has my boy friend been entertaining?" she asked, patting her bosom reverently, "Ah, he's so sweet." She looked as if she might pass out. Kay rather wished she would.

"I don't want a drink," Kay said, returning the bottle. "I never drink! I hate the taste."

"Mustn't be a kill-joy," said the woman firmly. "Here now, hold your cup like a good girl."

"No, please…"

"Formercysake, hold it still. Imagine, nerves at your age! Me, I can shake like a leaf; I've got reasons. Oh, Lardy, have I got 'em."

"But…

A dangerous smile tipped the woman's face hideously awry. "What's the matter? Don't you think I'm good enough to drink with?"

"Please, don't misunderstand," said Kay, a tremor in her voice, "It's just that I don't like being forced to do something I don't want to. So look, couldn't I give this to the gentleman?"

"Him? No sirree: he needs what little sense he's got. Come on honey, down the hatch."

Kay, seeing it was useless, decided to succumb and avoid a possible scene. She sipped and shuddered. It was terrible gin. It burned her throat till her eyes watered. Quickly, when the woman was not watching, she emptied the cup out into the sound hole of the guitar. It happened, however, that the man saw; and

Kay, realizing it, recklessly signaled to him with her eyes a plea not to give her away. But she could not tell from his clear-blank expression how much he understood.

"Where you from, kid?" resumed the woman presently.

For a bewildered moment, Kay was unable to provide an answer. The names of several cities came to her all at once. Finally, from this confusion, she extracted: "New Orleans. My home is in New Orleans."

The woman beamed. "N.O.'s where I wanna go when I kick off. One time, oh, say 1923, I ran me a sweet little fortune-teller parlor there. Let's see, that was on St. Peter Street." Pausing, she stooped and set the empty gin bottle on the floor. It rolled into the aisle and rocked back and forth with a drowsy sound. "I was raised in Texas— on a big ranch—my papa was rich. Us kids always had the best; even Paris, France, clothes. I'll bet you've got a big swell house, too. Do you have a garden? Do you grow flowers?"

"Just lilacs."

A conductor entered the coach, preceded by a cold gust of wind that rattled the trash in the aisle and briefly livened the dull air. He lumbered along, stopping now and then to punch a ticket or talk with a passenger. It was after midnight. Someone was expertly playing a harmonica. Someone else was arguing the merits of a certain politician. A child cried out in his sleep.

"Maybe you wouldn't be so snotty if you knew who we was," said the woman, bobbing her tremendous head. "We ain't nobodies, not by a long shot."

Embarrassed, Kay nervously opened a pack of cigarettes and lighted one. She wondered if there might not be a seat in a car up ahead. She could not bear the woman, or, for that matter, the man, another minute. But she had never before been in a remotely comparable situation. "If you'll excuse me now," she said, "I have to be leaving. It's been very pleasant, but I promised to meet a friend on the

With almost invisible swiftness the woman grasped the girl's wrist. "Didn't your mama ever tell you it was sinful to lie?" she stage. whispered. The lavender hat tumbled off her head but she made no effort to retrieve it. Her tongue flicked out and wetted her lips. And, as Kay stood up, she increased the pressure of her grip. "Sit down, dear... there ain't any friend.... Why, we're your only friends and we wouldn't have you leave us for the world."

"Honestly, I wouldn't lie."

"Sit down, dear."

Kay dropped her cigarette and the man picked it up. He slouched in the corner and became absorbed in blowing a chain of lush smoke rings that mounted upward like hollow eyes and expanded into nothing.

"Why, you wouldn't want to hurt his feelings by leaving us, now, would you, dear?" crooned the woman softly. "Sit down—down—now, that's a good girl. My, what a pretty guitar. What a pretty, pretty guitar..." Her voice faded before the sudden whooshing, static noise of a second train. And for an instant the lights in the coach went off; in the darkness the passing train's golden windows winked black-yellow-black-yellow-black-yellow. The man's cigarette pulsed like the glow of a firefly, and his smoke rings continued rising Eranquilly. Outside, a bell pealed wildly.

When the lights came on again, Kay was massaging her wrist where the woman's strong fingers had left a painful bracelet mark. She was more puzzled than angry. She determined to ask the conductor if he would find her a different seat. But when he arrived to take her ticket, the request stuttered on her lips incoherently.

"Yes, miss?"

"Nothing," she said.

And he was gone.

The trio in the alcove regarded one another in mysterious silence till the woman said, "I've got something here I wanna show you, honey." She rummaged once more in the oilcloth satchel, "You won't be so snotty after you get a gander at this."

What she passed to Kay was a handbill, published on such yellowed, antique paper it looked as if it must be centuries old. In fragile, overly fancy lettering, it read:

LAZARUS

The Man Who Is Buried Alive

A Miracle

See For Yourself

Adults, 15¢—Children, 10¢

"I always sing a hymn and read a sermon," said the woman. "It's awful sad: some folks cry, especially the old ones. And I've got me a perfectly elegant costume: a black veil and a black dress, oh, very becoming. He wears a gorgeous made-to-order bridegroom suit and a turban and lotsa talcum on his face. See, we try to make it as much like a bonafide funeral as we can. But shoot, nowadays you're likely to get just a buncha smart alecks come for laughs—so sometimes I'm real glad he's afflicted like he is on accounta otherwise his feelings would be hurt, maybe."

Kay said, "You mean you're with a circus or a side-show or something like that?"

"Nope, us alone," said the woman as she reclaimed the fallen hat. "We've been doing it for years and years—played every tank town in the South: Singasong, Mississippi—Spunky, Louisiana—Eureka, Alabama…" These and other names rolled off her tongue musically, running together like rain. "After the hymn, after the sermon, we bury him."

"In a coffin?"

"Sort of. It's gorgeous, it's got silver stars painted all over the lid." "I should think he would suffocate," said Kay, amazed. "How long does he stay buried?"

"All told it takes maybe an hour—course that's not counting the lure."

"The lure?"

"Uh huh. It's what we do the night before the show. See, we hunt up a store, any ol' store with a big glass window'll do, and get the owner to let him sit inside this window, and, well, hypnotize himself. Stays there all night stiff as a poker and people come and look: scares the hell out of 'em…." While she talked she jiggled a finger in her ear, withdrawing it occasionally to examine her find. "And one time this ol' bindle-stiff Mississippi sheriff tried to…"

The tale that followed was baffling and pointless: Kay did not bother to listen. Nevertheless, what she had heard already inspired a reverie, a vague recapitulation of her uncle's funeral; an event which, to tell the truth, had not much affected her since she had scarcely known him. And so, while gazing abstractedly at the man, an image of her uncle's face, white next to the pale silk casket pillow, appeared in her mind's eye. Observing their faces simultaneously, both the man's and uncle's, as it were, she thought she recognized an odd parallel: there was about the man's face the same kind of shocking, embalmed, secret stillness, as though, in a sense, he were truly an exhibit in a glass cage, complacent to be seen, uninterested in seeing.

"I'm sorry, what did you say?"

"I said: I sure wish they'd lend us the use of a regular cemetery. Like it is now we have to put on the show wherever we can mostly in empty lots that are nine times outa ten smack up against some smelly fillin' station, which ain't exactly a big help. But like I say, we got us a swell act, the best. You oughta come see it if you get a chance."

"Oh, I should love to," Kay said, absently.

"Oh, I should love to," mimicked the woman. "Well, who asked you? Anybody ask you?" She hoisted up her skirt and enthusiastically blew her nose on the ragged hem of a petticoat. "Bu-leeve me, it's a hard way to turn a dollar. Know what our rake was last month? Fifty-three bucks! Honey, you try living on that sometime." She sniffed and rearranged her skirt with considerable primness. "Well, one of these days my sweet boy's sure enough going to die down there; and even then somebody'll say it was a gyp."

At this point the man took from his pocket what seemed to be a finely shellacked peach seed and balanced it on the palm of his hand. He looked across at Kay and, certain of her attention, opened his eyelids wide and began to squeeze and caress the seed in an undefinably obscene manner.

Kay frowned, "What does he want?"

"He wants you to buy it."

"But what is it?"

"A charm," said the woman. "A love charm."

Whoever was playing the harmonica stopped. Other sounds, less unique, became at once prominent; someone snoring, the gin bottle seesaw rolling, voices in sleepy argument, the train wheels' distant hum.

"Where could you get love cheaper, honey?"

"It's nice. I mean it's cute...." Kay said, stalling for time. The man rubbed and polished the seed on his trouser leg. His head was lowered at a supplicating, mournful angle, and presently he stuck the seed between his teeth and bit it, as if it were a suspicious piece of silver, "Charms always bring me bad luck. And besides please, can't you make him stop acting that way?"

"Don't look so scared," said the woman, more flat-voiced than ever. "He ain't gonna hurt you,"

"Make him stop, damn it!"

"What can I do?" asked the woman, shrugging her shoulders. "You're the one that's got money. You're rich. All he wants is a dollar, one dollar."

Kay tucked her purse under her arm. "I have just enough to get back to school," she lied, quickly rising and stepping out into the aisle. She stood there a moment, expecting trouble. But nothing happened.

The woman, with rather deliberate indifference, heaved a sigh and closed her eyes; gradually the man subsided and stuck the charm back in his pocket. Then his hand crawled across the seat to join the woman's in a lax embrace.

Kay shut the door and moved to the front of the observation platform. It was bitterly cold in the open air, and she had left her raincoat in the alcove. She loosened her scarf and draped it over her head.

Although she had never made this trip before, the train was traveling through an area strangely familiar: tall trees, misty, painted pale by malicious moonshine, towered steep on either side without a break or clearing. Above, the sky was a stark, unexplorable blue thronged with stars that faded here and there. She could see streamers of smoke trailing from the train's engine like long clouds of ectoplasm. In one corner of the platform a red kerosene lantern cast a colorful shadow.

She found a cigarette and tried to light it: the wind snuffed match after match till only one was left. She walked to the corner where the lantern burned and cupped her hands to protect the last match: the flame caught, sputtered, died. Angrily she tossed away the cigarette and empty folder; all the tension in her tightened to an exasperating pitch and she slammed the wall with her fist and began to whimper softly, like an irritable child.

The intense cold made her head ache, and she longed to go back inside the warm coach and fall asleep. But she couldn't, at least not yet; and there was no sense in wondering why, for she knew the answer very well. Aloud, partly to keep her teeth from chattering and partly because she needed the reassurance of her own voice, she said: "We're in Alabama now, I think, and tomorrow we'll be in Atlanta and I'm nineteen and I'll be twenty in August and I'm a sophomore...." She glanced around at the darkness, hoping to see a sign of dawn, and finding the same endless wall of trees, the same frosty moon. "I hate him, he's horrible and I hate him...." She stopped, ashamed of her foolishness and too tired to evade the truth: she was afraid.

Suddenly she felt an eerie compulsion to kneel down and touch the lantern. Its graceful glass funnel was warm, and the red glow seeped through her hands, making them luminous. The heat thawed her fingers and tingled along her arms.

She was so preoccupied she did not hear the door open. The train wheels roaring clickety-clack-clackety-click hushed the sound of the man's footsteps.

It was a subtle zero sensation that warned her finally; but some seconds passed before she dared look behind.

He was standing there with mute detachment, his head tilted, his arms dangling at his sides. Staring up into his harmless, vapid face, flushed brilliant by the lantern light, Kay knew of what she was afraid: it was a memory, a childish memory of terrors that once, long ago, had hovered above her like haunted limbs on a tree of night. Aunts, cooks, strangers—each eager to spin a tale or teach a rhyme of spooks and death, omens, spirits, demons. And always there had been the unfailing threat of the wizard man: stay close to the house, child, else a wizard man'll snatch you and eat you alive? He lived everywhere, the wizard man, and everywhere was danger. At night, in bed, hear him tapping at the window? Listen!

Holding onto the railing, she inched upward till she was standing erect. The man nodded and waved his hand toward the door. Kay took a deep breath and stepped forward. Together they went inside.

The air in the coach was numb with sleep: a solitary light now illuminated the car, creating a kind of artificial dusk. There was no motion but the train's sluggish sway, and the stealthy rattle of discarded newspapers.

The woman alone was wide awake. You could see she was greatly excited: she fidgeted with her curls and celluloid cherries, and her plump little legs, crossed at the ankles, swung agitatedly back and forth. She paid no attention when Kay sat down. The man settled in the seat with one leg tucked beneath him and his arms folded across his chest.

In an effort to be casual, Kay picked up a magazine. She realized the man was watching her, not removing his gaze an instant: she knew this though she was afraid to confirm it, and she wanted to cry out and waken everyone in the coach. But suppose they did not hear? What if they were not really asleep? Tears started in her eyes, magnifying and distorting the print on a page till it became a hazy blur. She shut the magazine with fierce abruptness and looked at the woman.

"I'll buy it," she said. "The charm, I mean. I'll buy it, if that's all— just all you want."

The woman made no response. She smiled apathetically as she turned toward the man.

As Kay watched, the man's face seemed to change form and recede before her like a moon-shaped rock sliding downward under a surface of water. A warm laziness relaxed her. She was dimly conscious of it when the woman took away her purse, and when she gently pulled the raincoat like a shroud above her head.

Shirley Ann Grau (1929–)

Shirley Ann Grau was born in New Orleans in 1929, to Adolph and Katherine Onions Grau. She grew up in New Orleans and at the age of nine moved to Montgomery, Alabama, until her senior year of high school. She reutrned to New Orleans, graduated from Ursuline Academy and then attended Tulane University, where she received her bachelor's degree, with honors, in English. Nearly all of Grau's fiction is set in the South, and her first book, the short story collection, *The Black Prince and Other Stories* (1954), is no exception. Grau was twenty-five when that book was published, and the following year she married James K. Phiebleman, a philosophy professor at Tulane. They soon moved to the New Orleans suburb of Metairie, where they raised their family of five children.[1] *The Black Prince* received much acclaim, with critics calling it honest and unsentimental and even comparing it to J. D. Salinger's 1954 collection, *Nine Stories.* Ten years later Grau would win the Pulitzer Prize for her 1964 novel, *The Keepers of the House,* which she set in rural Alabama. For over 60 years, Grau has written five novels and four short story collections, the latest in 2003.

Critics were right; the book is honest and unsentimental. But more significant is the fact that it is an honest and unsentimental book about African Americans in the South written by a white woman in 1954, a very uncommon undertaking for white writers even now. Grau's characters in this collection are not the maids, hotel workers, and chauffeurs that readers were accustomed to seeing in fiction by white writers of the time. Instead her characters are fully realized protagonists, like Joshua in the coming-of-age story of the same title or like Celia, the young narrator in the story included here, "Miss Yellow Eyes," which is set in New Orleans in 1953. Many white writers avoided the unavoidable topic of racism in New Orleans, but in this short story, Grau tackles the complex issue from the point of view of the fourteen-year-old, Celia.

The first aspect of racism we see in the story concerns skin color. When Celia's older brother, Pete comes home with his handsome friend Chris, Celia first thinks, "...that's a white man" and wonders "what a white man would do coming here." Once she realizes that Chris is not white, she still notes that "[l]ots of white men were darker." In fact, Pete has brought Chris home to meet his beautiful, light-skinned sister, Lena (Magdalena), knowing that they'll hit it off. And he's right, but they seem to do so initially, simply because they are both light-skinned and good looking. In fact, Lena, "Miss Yellow Eyes," is constantly besieged by the young men in her high school and despised by her female classmates: "The boys in high school all followed her around until the other girls hated her.... She really didn't seem to care." And she doesn't care, until she meets Chris, the handsome, light-skinned friend of her brother Pete.

Pete is the man of the house, as their father, who once worked "as a steward on a United Fruit Lines ship, a real handsome man....[had] gone ashore at Antigua one day and forgot to come back," so Celia had never even met him. Their mother, like so many black women of the time, worked as a maid "in one of the big houses on St. Charles Avenue." All of this seemed to rankle Pete, who, over the course of the story, becomes a more angry, bitter, and militant young black man. He was a founding member of the "Better Days Club," which met in a small room above Lefty's Restaurant and Café on Tulane Avenue, and the sign over the entrance read, "*White* Entrance to *Rear.*"

Chris worked with Pete in the railroad yard, but Chris has joined the Army in order to escape the racist South, and once he meets Lena, whom he names "Miss Yellow Eyes", he convinces her to come with him to Oregon where they can both pass for white, which angers the darker-skinned Pete. Celia notes when admiring Chris and Lena that "they look like a white couple," and she goes on to say that "unless you had sharp trained eyes, like the people down here do, you would have thought they were a white couple." Race and gradations of skin color have long been an issue in New Orleans, as the men of Les Cenelles noted back before the Civil War. Skin color still accounts for racism among both blacks and whites and for the longstanding tradition of "passing" or, as many still say in the city, "passé blanc."

---

1   Much of this biographical information on Grau is taken from Courtney George, "Shirley Ann Grau," *Encyclopedia of Alabama,* encyclopediaofalabama.org. Accessed June 10, 2011.

However, not only is this short story about racism and passing, but about women and gender roles. Celia's father abandons his family; Chris enlists, gets wounded in the Korean War, and finally dies, and it appears that Pete suffers from a self-inflicted wound in order to avoid the draft. The real strength in this family is found in the women, from young Celia telling the story, to beautiful Lena and her mother who both finally stand up to Pete.

Grau tackles subjects in this story and in this collection that very few white writers of the time dared to do. Five of the nine stories in *The Black Prince* are told from the point of view of black characters, almost unheard of for a white woman writer of the 1950s. Throughout her career, she has continued to write honestly and unsentimentally about both white and black characters, poor and wealthy, from the urban and rural South.

Miss Yellow Eyes[1]

Pete brought Chris home one evening after supper. I remember it was early spring, because the Talisman rosebush by the kitchen steps had begun to blossom out. For that time of year it was cool; there was a good stiff wind off the river that shook the old bush and creaked it, knocked the biggest flowers to bits, and blew their petals into a little heap against the side of the wood steps. The Johnsons, who lived in the house next door, had put their bedspread out to air and forgot to take it in. So it was hanging out there on the porch railing, a pink spread with a fan-tailed yellow peacock in the middle. I could hear it flapping—loud when the wind was up, and very soft when it fell. And from out on the river there were the soft low tones of the ships' whistles. And I could hear a mockingbird too, perched up on top the house, singing away, forgetting that it was nighttime. And in all this, Pete's steps in the side alley, coming to the kitchen door.

"Hi, kid," Pete held open the door with one arm stretched behind him. Chris came in.

I thought at first: that's a white man. And I wondered what a white man would do coming here. I got a second look and saw the difference, saw I'd made a mistake. His skin wasn't dark at all, but only sun-tanned. (Lots of white men were darker.) His eyes were a pale blue, the color of the china Ma got with the Octagon soap coupons. He had brown hair—no, it was closer to red, and only slightly wavy. He looked like a white man, almost. But I saw the difference. Maybe it was just his way of carrying himself—that was like a Negro.

But he was the handsomest man I'd ever seen, excepting none. I could feel the bottom of my stomach roll up into a hard ball.

"This here's Celia," Pete said.

Chris grinned and his blue eyes crinkled up into almost closed slits. He sat down at the table opposite me, flipping shut the book I'd been reading. "Evening's no time to be busy, kid."

Pete picked up the coffeepot from where it always stood on the back of the stove and shook it gently. "There's some here all right," he said to Chris as he reached up to the shelf for a couple of cups. "You want anything in yours? I reckon there'd be a can of milk in the icebox."

"No," Chris said. "I like it black."

Pete lit the fire under the speckled enamel coffeepot "Where's Ma?"

"They having a dinner tonight… she said she'll be real late." Ma worked as a cook in one of the big houses on St. Charles Avenue. When there was a dinner, it meant she'd have to stay around and clean up afterwards and wouldn't get home till eleven or twelve maybe.

"She'll get tomorrow off, though," I told Chris.

"Good enough." He grinned and his teeth were very square and bright.

They sat down at the table with me and stretched out their legs. Holding the coffee cup to his mouth,

---

1   "Miss Yellow Eyes" reprinted by permission of G Agency LLC, copyright © 1953 by Shirley Ann Grau.

Chris reached out one finger and rubbed the petals of the big yellow rose in the drinking glass in the center of the table. "That's real pretty."

"Lena's been putting them there," Pete said.

"That's sure the one I want to meet," Chris said, and grinned over at Pete, and I knew that he'd been talking about Lena.

She was the sort of girl you talk about, she was that beautiful—with light-brown hair that was shoulder-length and perfectly straight and ivory skin and eyes that were light brown with flecks of yellow in them. She was all gold- colored. Sometimes when she stood in the sun you could almost think the light was shining right through her.

She was near seventeen then, three years older than I was. The boys in high school all followed her around until the other girls hated her. Every chance they got they would play some mean trick on her, kicking dust in her lunch, or roughing her up playing basketball, or tearing pages out of her books. Lena hardly ever lost her temper; she didn't really seem to care. "I reckon I know who the boys are looking at," she told me. She was right. There was always a bunch of them trying to sit next to her in class or walk next to her down the hall. And when school was through, there was always a bunch of them waiting around the door, wanting to take her home, or for rides if they had cars. And when she finally came sauntering out, with her books tucked up under one arm, she wouldn't pay them much attention; she'd just give them a kind of little smile (to keep them from going to the other girls) and walk home by herself, with maybe a few of them trailing along behind. I used to wait and watch her leave and then I'd go home a different way. I didn't want to interfere.

But, for all that, she didn't go out very much. And never with the same boy for very long. Once Hoyt Carmichael came around and stood in the kitchen door, asking for her, just begging to see her. She wouldn't even come out to talk to him. Ma asked her later if there was something wrong and Lena just nodded and shrugged her shoulders all at once. Ma hugged her then and you could see the relief in her face; she worried so about Lena, about her being so very pretty.

Pete said: "You sure got to meet her, Chris, man."

And I said to Chris: "She's over by the Johnsons'." I got up and opened the door and yelled out into the alley: "Lena!"

She came in a few minutes. We could hear her steps on the alley bricks, slow. She never did hurry. Finally she opened the screen and stood there, looking from one to the other.

I said: "This is my sister, Magdalena."

"And this here is Chris Watkin," Pete said.

Chris had got up and bowed real solemnly. "I'm pleased to meet you."

Lena brushed the hair back from her forehead. She had long fingers, and hands so thin that the veins stood out blue on the backs. "Nobody calls me Magdalena," she said, "except Celia, now and then. Just Lena.'

Chris's eyes crinkled up out of sight the way they had before. "I might could just call you Miss Yellow Eyes. Old Miss Yellow Eyes."

Lena just wrinkled her nose at him. In that light her eyes did look yellow, but usually if a man said something like that she'd walk out. Not this time. She just poured herself a cup of coffee, and when Chris pulled out a chair for her, she sat down, next to him.

I looked at them and I thought: they look like a white couple. And they did. Unless you had sharp trained eyes, like the people down here do, you would have thought they were white and you would have thought they made a handsome couple.

Chris looked over at me and lifted an eyebrow. Just one, the left one; it reached up high and arched in his forehead. "What you looking so solemn for, Celia?"

"Nothing."

And Lena asked: "You work with Pete at the railroad?"

"Sure," he said, and smiled at her. Only, more than his mouth was smiling "We go swinging on and off those old tenders like hell afire. Jumping on and off those cars."

"I reckon that's hard work."

He laughed this time out loud. "I ain't exactly little." He bent forward and hunched his shoulders up a little so she could see the way the muscles swelled against the cloth of his shirt.

"You got fine shoulders, Mr. Watkin," she said. "I reckon they're even better than Pete there."

Pete grunted and finished his coffee. But she was right. Pete's shoulders were almost square out from his neck. Chris's weren't. They looked almost sloped and hunched the way flat bands of muscles reached up into his neck.

Chris shrugged and stood up. "Do you reckon you would like to walk around the corner for a couple of beers?"

"Okay," Pete said.

Lena lifted one eyebrow, just the way he had done. "Mr. Watkin, you do look like you celebrating something." "I sure am," he said.

"What?" I asked.

"I plain tell you later, kid."

They must have been gone near two hours because Ma came home before they did. I'd fallen asleep. I'd just bent my head over for a minute to rest my eyes, and my forehead touched the soft pages of the book—*Treasure Island.* I'd got it from the library at school; it was dog-eared and smelled faintly of peanuts.

Ma was saying: "Lord, honey, why ain't you gone to bed?"

I lifted my head and rubbed my face until I could see Ma's figure in the doorway. "I'm waiting for them," I said.

Ma took off her coat and hung it up on the hook behind the door. "Who them?"

"Lena," I said, "and Pete. And Chris." I knew what she was going to say, so I answered first. "He's a friend of Pete, and Lena likes him."

Ma was frowning very slightly. "I plain wonder iffen he belong to that club."

"I don't know."

It was called the Better Days Club and the clubroom was the second floor of a little restaurant on Tulane Avenue. I'd never gone inside, though I had passed the place: a small wood building that had once been a house but now had a sign saying Lefty's Restaurant and Café in green letters on a square piece of board that hung out over the sidewalk and creaked in the wind. And I'd seen something else too when I passed: another sign, a small one tucked into the right center corner of the screen door, a sign that said 'White Entrance to Rear." If the police ever saw that they'd have found an excuse to raid the place and break up everything in it.

Ma kept asking Pete what they did there. Most time he didn't bother to answer. Once when she'd just insisted, he'd said, "We're fixing to have better times come." And sometimes he'd bring home little papers, not much more than book-size, with names like *New Day* and *Daily Sentinel* and *Watcher.*

Ma would burn the papers if she got hold of them. But she couldn't really stop Pete from going to the meetings. She didn't try too hard because he was *so* good to her and gave her part of his pay check every week. With that money and what she made we always had enough. We didn't have to worry about eating, way some of our neighbors did.

Pete was a strange fellow—moody and restless and not happy. Sometimes—when he was sitting quiet, thinking or resting—there'd be a funny sort of look on his face (he was the darkest of us all): not hurt, not fear, not determination, but a mixture of all three.

Ma was still standing looking at me with a kind of puzzled expression on her face when we heard them, the three of them, coming home. They'd had a few beers and, what with the cold air outside, they all felt fine. They were singing too; I recognized the tune; it was the one from the jukebox around the corner in that bar.

Ma said: "They got no cause to be making a racket like that. Somebody might could call the police." Ma was terribly afraid of the police. She'd never had anything to do with them, but she was still afraid. Every time a police car passed in the street outside, she'd duck behind the curtain and peep out. And she'd walk clear around a block so she wouldn't come near one of the blue uniforms.

The three came in the kitchen door, Pete first and then Lena and Chris.

Pete had his arms full of beer cans; he let them all fall out on the table, "Man, I like to drop them sure." "We brought some for you, Ma," Lena said.

"And Celia too," Chris added.

"It's plenty late," Ma said, looking hard at Chris. "You don't have to work tomorrow," I said.

So we stayed up late. I don't know how late. Because the beer made me feel fine and sick all at once. First everything was swinging around inside my head and then the room too. Finally I figured how to handle it. I caught hold and let myself ride around on the big whooshing circles. There were times when I'd forget there was anybody else in the room, I'd swing so far away.

"Why, just you look at Celia there," Ma said, and everybody turned and watched me.

"You sure high, kid," Chris said.

"No, I'm not." I was careful to space the words, because I could tell by the way Ma had run hers together that she was feeling the beer too.

Pete had his guitar in his lap, flicking his fingers across the strings. "You an easy drunk." He was smiling, the way he seldom did. "Leastways you ain't gonna cost some man a lotta money getting you high."

"That absolutely and completely right." Ma bent forward, with her hands one on each knee, and the elbows sticking out, like a skinny football-player. "You plain got to watch that when boys come to take you out."

"They ain't gonna want to take me out."

"Why not, kid?" Chris had folded his arms on the tabletop and was leaning his chin on them. His face was flushed so that his eyes only looked bluer.

"Not after they see Lena." I lifted my eyes up from his and let them drop over where I knew Lena was sitting. I just had time to notice the way the electric light made her skin gold and her eyes gold and her hair too, so that she seemed all one blurry color. And then the whole world tipped over and I went skidding off—but feeling extra fine because Chris was sitting just a little bit away next to Lena and she was looking at him like she'd never looked at anybody else before.

Next thing I knew, somebody was saying: "Celia, look." There was a photograph in front of me. A photograph of a young man, in a suit and tie, leaning back against a post, with his legs crossed, grinning at the camera.

I looked up. Ma was holding the photograph in front of me. It was in a wide silver-colored frame, with openwork, roses or flowers of some sort.

Pete began laughing. "just you look at her," he said; "she don't even know her own daddy."

"I never seen that picture before," I said, loud as I could.

I'd never seen my daddy either. He was a steward on a United Fruit Lines ship, a real handsome man. He'd gone ashore at Antigua one day and forgot to come back.

"He looks mighty much like Chris," Ma said as she cleared a space on the shelf over between the windows. She put the picture there. And I knew then that she'd got it out from the bottom of a drawer somewhere, because this was a special occasion for her too.

"Chris," I said, remembering, "you never did tell us what you celebrating."

He had twisted sideways in his chair and had his arms wrapped around the back. "I going in the army."

Out of the corner of my eye I saw Pete staring at him, his mouth twisting and his face darkening.

Ma clucked her tongue against her teeth. "That a shame."

Chris grinned, his head cocked aside a little. "I got to leave tomorrow."

Pete swung back and forth on the two legs of his tilted chair. "Ain't good enough for nothing around here, but we good enough to put in the army and send off."

"Man"—Chris winked at him—"there ain't nothing you can do. And I plain reckon you gonna go next."

"No." Pete spoke the word so that it was almost a whistle.

"I'm a man, me," Chris said. "Can't run out on what I got to do." He tipped his head back and whistled a snatch of a little tune.

"I wouldn't like to go in the army," Lena said.

Chris went on whistling. Now we could recognize the song:

Yellow, yellow, yellow, yellow, yellow gal, Yellow, yellow, yellow, yellow, yellow gal, She's pretty and fine

Is the yellow gal....

Lena tossed her head. "I wouldn't like to none."

Chris stopped whistling and laughed. "You plain sound like Pete here."

Pete's face all crinkled up with anger. I thought: he looks more like a Negro when he loses his temper; it makes his skin darker somehow.

"Nothing to laugh about," he said "can't do nothing around here without people yelling nigger at you."

"Don't stay around here, man. You plain crazy to stay around here." Chris tilted back his chair and stared at the ceiling. "You plain crazy to stay a nigger. I done told you that"

Pete scowled at him and didn't answer.

Lena asked quickly: "Where you got to go?"

"Oregon." Chris was still staring at the ceiling and still smiling. "That where you cross over."

"You sure?"

Chris looked at her and smiled confidently. "Sure I'm sure."

Pete mumbled something under his breath that we didn't hear.

"I got a friend done it," Chris said, Two years ago. He working out of Portland there, for the railroad. And he turn white."

Lena was resting her chin on her folded hands. 'They don't look at you so close. Or anything?"

"No," Chris said. "I heard all about it. You can cross over if you want to."

"You going?" I asked.

"When I get done with the stretch in the army." He lowered his chair back to its four legs and stared out the little window, still smiling. "There's lots of jobs there for a railroad man."

Pete slammed the flat of his hand down against the table. Ma's eyes flew open like a door that's been kicked wide back. "I don't want to pretend I'm white," he said. "I ain't and I don't want to be. I reckon I want to be same as white and stay right here.'

Ma murmured something under her breath and we all turned to look at her. Her eyes had dropped half-closed again and she had her hands folded across her stomach. Her mouth opened very slowly and this time she spoke loud enough for us all to hear. "Talking like that—you gonna do nothing but break you neck that way."

I got so sleepy then and so tired, all of a sudden, that I slipped sideways out of my chair. It was funny. I didn't notice I was slipping or moving until I was on the floor. Ma got hold of my arm and took me off to bed with her. And I didn't think to object. The last thing I saw was Lena staring at Chris with her long light-colored eyes. Chris with his handsome face and his reddish hair and his movements so quick they almost seemed jerky.

I thought it would be all right with them.

I was sick the whole next day from the beer; so sick I couldn't go to school. Ma shook her head and Pete laughed and Lena just smiled a little.

And Chris went off to the army, all right. It wasn't long before Lena had a picture from him. He'd written across the back: "Here I am a soldier." She stuck the picture in the frame of the mirror over her dresser.

That was the week Lena quit school. She came looking for me during lunch time. "I'm going home," she said. "You can't do that."

She shook her head. "I had enough."

So she walked out of school and didn't ever go back. (She was old enough to do that.) She bought a paper on her way home and sat down and went through the classified ads very carefully, looking for a job. It was three days before she found one she wanted: with some people who were going across the lake to Covington for the summer. Their regular city maid wouldn't go.

They took her on right away because they wanted to leave. She came back with a ten-dollar bill in her purse. "We got to leave in the morning," she said.

Ma didn't like it, her quitting school and leaving home, but she couldn't really stop her.

And Lena did want to go. She was practically jumping with excitement after she came back from the interview. "They got the most beautiful house," she said to Ma. "A lot prettier than where you work." And she told me: "They say the place over the lake is even prettier—even prettier."

I knew what she meant. I sometimes went to meet Ma at the house where she worked. I liked to. It was nice to be in the middle of fine things, even if they weren't yours.

"It'll be real nice working there," Lena said.

That next morning, when she had got her things together and closed the lid of the suitcase, she told me to go down to the grocery at the corner, where there was a phone, and call a taxi. They were going to pay for it, she said.

I reckon I was excited; so excited that I called the wrong cab. I just looked at the back cover of the phone book where there was a picture of a long orange-color cab and a number in big orange letters. I gave them the address, then went back to the house and sat down on the porch with Lena.

The orange cab turned at the corner and came down our street. The driver was hanging out the window looking for house numbers; there weren't any except for the Stevenses' across the way. Bill Stevens had painted his number with big whitewash letters on his front door. The cab hit a rut in the street and the driver's head smacked the window edge. He jerked his head back inside and jammed the gears into second. Then he saw us: Lena and me and the suitcase on the edge of the porch.

He let the car move along slow in second with that heavy pulling sound and he watched us. As he got closer you could see that he was chewing on the corner of his lip. Still watching us, he went on slowly— right past the house. He said something once, but we were too far away to hear. Then he was down at the other corner, turning, and gone.

Lena stood and looked at me. She had on her best dress: a light-blue one with round pockets in front. Both her hands were stuffed into the pockets. There was a handkerchief in the left one; you could see her fingers twisting it.

White cabs didn't pick up colored people: I knew that. But I'd forgot and called the first number, a white number, a wrong number. Lena didn't say anything, just kept looking at me, with her hand holding the handkerchief inside her pocket. I turned and ran all the way down to the corner and called the right number, and a colored cab that was painted black with gold stripes across the hood came and Lena was gone for the next four months, the four months of the summer.

It could have been the same cab brought her back that had come for her: black with gold stripes. She had on the same dress too, the blue one with round pockets; the same suitcase too, but this time in it was a letter of recommendation and a roll of bills she'd saved, all hidden in the fancy organdy aprons they'd given her.

She said "He wanted me to stay on through the winter, but she got scared for their boy." And she held her chin stiff and straight when she said that.

I understood why that woman wanted my sister Lena out of the house. There wasn't any boy or man either that wouldn't look at her twice. White or colored it didn't seem to make a difference, they all looked at her in the same way.

That was the only job Lena ever took. Because she hadn't been home more than a few days when Chris came back for her.

I remember how it was—early September and real foggy. It would close down every evening around seven and wouldn't lift until ten or ten thirty in the morning. All night long you could hear the foghorns and the whistles of the boats out on the river; and in the morning there'd be even more confusion when everybody tried to rush away from anchor. That Saturday morning Lena had taken a walk up to the levee to watch. Pete was just getting up. I could hear him in his room. Ma had left for work early. And me, I was scrubbing out the kitchen, the way I did every Saturday morning. That was when Chris came back.

He came around to the kitchen. I heard his steps in the alley—quickly coming, almost running. He came bursting in the door and almost slipped on the soapy floor. "Hi, kid," he said, took off his cap, and rubbed his hand over his reddish hair. "You working?"

"Looks like," I said.

He'd grown a mustache, a thin line. He stood for a moment chewing on his lip and the little hairs he had brushed so carefully into a line. Finally he said: "Where's everybody?"

"Lena went up on the levee to have a look at the river boats."

He grinned at me, flipped his cap back on, gave a kind of salute, and jumped down the two steps into the yard.

I sat back on my heels, picturing him and Lena in my mind and thinking what a fine couple they made. And the little picture of my father grinned down at me from the shelf by the window.

Pete called: "Seems like I heard Chris in there." "He went off to look for Lena."

Pete came to the door; he was only half dressed and he was still holding up his pants with his one hand. He liked to sleep late Saturdays. "He might could have stayed to say hello."

"He wanted to see Lena, I reckon."

Pete grinned briefly and the grin faded into a yawn. "You ought to have let him look for her."

"Nuh-uh." I picked up the bar of soap and the scrubbing brush again. "I wanted them to get together, I reckon."

"Okay, kid," Pete said shortly, and turned back to his room. "You helped them out."

Chris and Lena came back after a while. They didn't say anything, but I noticed that Lena was kind of smiling like she was cuddling something to herself. And her eyes were so bright they looked light yellow, almost transparent.

Chris hung his army cap on the back of a chair and then sprawled down at the table. "You fixing to offer me anything to eat?"

"You can't be hungry this early in the morning," Lena said.

"Men are always hungry," I said. They both turned. "You tell 'em, kid," Chris said. "You tell 'em for me." "Let's us go to the beach," Lena said suddenly. "Sure, honey," Chris said softly.

She wrinkled her nose at him and pretended she hadn't heard. "It's the last night before they close down everything for the winter."

"Okay—we gonna leave right now?"

"Crazy thing," Lena smiled. "Not in the morning. Let's us go right after supper."

"I got to stay here till then?"

"Not less you want to."

"Reckon I do," Chris said.

"You want to come, Celia?" Lena asked.

"Me?" I glanced over at Chris quickly. "Nuh-uh." "Sure you do," Lena said. "You just come along." And Chris lifted one eyebrow at me. "Come along," he said. "Iffen you don't mind going out with people old as me."

"Oh, no," I said. "Oh, no."

I never did figure out quite why Lena wanted me along that time. Maybe she didn't want to be alone with Chris because she didn't quite trust him yet. Or maybe she just wanted to be nice to me. I don't know. But I did go. I liked the beach. I liked to stare off across the lake and imagine I could see the shore on the other side, which of course I couldn't

So I went with them, that evening after supper. It took us nearly an hour to get there—three changes of busses because it was exactly across town: the north end of the city. All the way, all along in the bus, Chris kept talking, telling stories.

"Man," he said, "that army sure is something—big—I never seen anything so big. Just in our little old camp there ain't a space of ground big enough to hold all the men, if they called them all out together...."

We reached the end of one bus line. He put one hand on Lena's arm and the other on mine and helped us out the door. His hand was broad and hard on the palm and almost cool to the touch.

In the other bus we headed straight for the long seat across the back, so we could sit all three together. He sat in the middle and, leaning forward a little, rested both hands on his knees. Looking at him out the corner of my eye, I could see the flat broad strips of muscle in his neck, reaching up to under his chin. And once I caught Lena's eye, and I knew that on the other side she was watching too.

"All together like that," he said. "It gives you the funniest feeling—when you all marching together, so that you can't see away on either side, just men all together—it gives you a funny sort of feeling."

He turned to Lena and grinned; his bright square teeth flashed in the evening dusk. "I reckon you think that silly."

"No," she said quickly, and then corrected herself: "of course I never been in the army."

"Look there," I said. We were passing the white beach. Even as far away as the road where we were, we could smell the popcorn and the sweat and the faint salt tingle from the wind off the lake.

"It almost cool tonight," Lena said.

"You ain't gonna be cold?"

"You don't got to worry about me."

"I reckon I do," he said.

Lena shook her head, and her eyes had a soft holding look in them. And I wished I could take Chris aside and tell him that he'd said just the right thing.

Out on the concrete walks of the white beach, people were jammed so close that there was hardly any space between. You could hear all the voices and the talking, murmuring at this distance. Then we were past the beach (the driver was going fast, grumbling under his breath that he was behind schedule), and the Ferris wheel was the only thing you could see, a circle of lights like a big star behind us. And on each side, open ground, low weeds, and no trees.

"There it is," Chris said, and pointed up through the window. I turned and looked and, sure enough, there it was; he was right: the lights, smaller maybe and dimmer, of Lincoln Beach, the colored beach.

"Lord," Lena said, "I haven't been out here in I don't know when. It's been that long."

We got off the bus; he dropped my arm but kept hold of Lena's. "You got to make this one night last all winter." She didn't answer.

We had a fine time. I forgot that I was just tagging along and enjoyed myself much as any.

When we passed over by the shooting gallery Chris winked at Lena and me. "Which one of them dolls do you want?"

Lena wrinkled her nose. "I reckon you plain better see about getting 'em first."

He just shrugged. "You think I can do it, Celia?" "Sure," I said. "Sure, sure you can."

"That's the girl for you," the man behind the counter said. "Thinks you can do anything."

"That my girl there all right." Chris reached in his pocket to pay the man. I could feel my ears getting red.

He picked up the rifle and slowly knocked down the whole row of green and brown painted ducks. He kept right on until Lena and I each had a doll in a bright pink feather skirt and he had a purple wreath of flowers hung around his neck. By this time the man was scowling at him and a few people were standing around watching.

"That's enough, soldier," the man said. "This here is just for amateurs."

Chris shrugged. We all turned and walked away. "You did that mighty well," Lena said, turning her baby doll around and around in her hands, staring at it. "I see lots of fellows better."

"Where'd you learn to shoot like that?" I tugged on his sleeve.

"I didn't learn—"

"Fibber!" Lena tossed her head.

"You got to let me finish. Up in Calcasieu parish, my daddy, he put a shotgun in my hand and give me a pocket of shells…. I just keep shooting till I hit something or other."

It was hard to think of Chris having a father. "Where's he now?"

"My daddy? He been dead."

"You got a family?"

"No," Chris said. "Just me."

We walked out along the strip of sand, and the wind began pulling the feathers out of the dolls' skirts. I got out my handkerchief and tied it around my doll, but Lena just lifted hers up high in the air to see what the wind would do. Soon she just had a naked baby doll that was pink celluloid smeared with glue.

Lena and Chris found an old log and sat down. I went wading. I didn't want to go back to where they were, because I knew that Chris wanted Lena alone. So I kept walking up and down in the water that came just a little over my ankles.

It was almost too cold for swimmers. I saw just one, about thirty yards out, swimming up and down slowly. I couldn't really see him, just the regular white splashes from his arms. I looked out across the lake, the way I liked to do. It was all dark now; there was no telling where the lower part of the sky stopped and the water began. It was all the one color, all of it, out beyond the swimmer and the breakwater on the left where the waves hit a shallow spot and turned white and foamy. Except for that, it was all the same dark until you lifted your eyes high up in the sky and saw the stars.

I don't know how long I stood there, with my head bent back far as it would go, looking at the stars, trying to remember the names for them that I had learned in school: names like Bear and Archer. I couldn't tell which was which. All I could see were stars, bright like they always were at the end of the summer and close; and every now and then one of them would fall.

I stood watching them, feeling the water move gently around my legs and curling my toes in the soft lake sand that was rippled by the waves. And trying to think up ways to stay away from those two who were sitting back up the beach, on a piece of driftwood, talking together.

Once the wind shifted a little suddenly or Chris spoke too loud, because I heard one word: "Oregon."

All of a sudden I knew that Lena was going to marry him. Just for that she was going to marry him; because she wanted so much to be white.

And I wanted to tell Chris again, the way I had wanted to in the bus, that he'd said just the right thing.

After a while Lena stood up and called to me, saying it was late; so we went home. By the time we got there, Ma had come. On the table was a bag of food she had brought. And so we all sat around and ate the remains of the party: little cakes, thin and crispy and spicy and in fancy shapes; and little patties full of oysters that Ma ran in the oven to heat up; and little crackers spread with fishy-tasting stuff, like sugar grains only bigger, that Ma called caviar; and all sorts of little sandwiches.

It was one nice thing about the place Ma worked. They never did check the food. And it was fun for us, tasting the strange things.

All of a sudden Lena turned to me and said: "I reckon I want to see where Oregon is." She gave Chris a long look out of the corner of her eyes.

My mouth was full and for a moment I couldn't answer. "You plain got to have a map in your schoolbooks."

I finally managed to swallow. "Sure I got one—if you want to see it."

I got my history book and unfolded the map of the whole country and put my finger down on the spot that said Oregon in pink letters. "There," I said; "that's Portland there."

Lena came and leaned over my shoulder; Pete didn't move; he sat with his chin in his hand and his elbows propped on the table.

"I want to stay here and be the same as white," he said, but we weren't listening to him.

Chris got out of the icebox the bottles of beer he had brought.

"Don't you want to see?" Lena asked him.

He grinned and took out his key chain, which had an opener on it, and began popping the caps off the bottles. "I looked at a map once. I know where it's at."

Ma was peering over my other shoulder. "It looks like it mighty far away."

"It ain't close," Chris said.

"You plain want to go there—" Ma was frowning at the map, straining to see without her glasses.

"Yes," Chris said, still popping the tops off bottles. "And be white," Lena added very softly.

"Sure," Chris said. "No trouble at all to cross over." "And you going there," Ma said again. She couldn't quite believe that anybody she was looking at right now could ever go that far away.

"Yea," Chris said, and put the last opened bottle with the others in a row on the table. "When I get out the army, we sure as hell going there."

"Who's we?" I asked.

"Lena and me."

Ma looked up at him so quickly that a hairpin tumbled out of her head and clicked down on the table.

"When we get married," he said.

Lena was looking at him, chewing her lower lip. "We going to do that?"

"Yea," he said. "Leastways if that what you want to do."

And Lena dropped her eyes down to the map again, though I'd swear this time she didn't know what she was seeing. Or maybe everywhere she'd look she was seeing Chris. Maybe that was it. She was smiling very slightly to herself, with just the corners of her lips, and they were trembling.

They got married that week in St. Michers Church. It was in the morning—nine thirty, I remember— so the church was cold: biting empty cold. Even the two candles burning on the altar didn't look like they'd be warm.

Though it only took a couple of minutes, my teeth were chattering so that I could hardly talk. Ma cried and Pete scowled and grinned by turns and Lena and Chris didn't seem to notice anything much.

The cold and the damp had made a bright strip of flush across Lena's cheeks. Old Mrs. Roberts, who lived next door, bent forward—she was sitting in the pew behind us —and tapped Ma on the shoulder. "I never seen her look prettier."

Lena had bought herself a new suit, with the money she'd earned over the summer: a cream-colored suit, with small black braiding on the cuffs and collar. She'd got a hat too, of the same color velvet. Cream was a good color for her; it was lighter than her skin somehow, so that it made her face stand out.

("She ought to always have clothes like that," Mayme Roberts said later, back at our house. She was old Mrs. Roberts's daughter, and seven kids had broken her up so that she wasn't even jealous of pretty girls any more. "Maybe Chris'll make enough money to let her have pretty clothes like that.")

Lena and Chris went away because he had to get back to camp. And for the first time since I could remember, I had a room all to myself. So I made Lena's bed all nice and careful and put the fancy spread that Ma had crocheted on it—the one we hardly ever used. And put the little pink celluloid doll in the middle.

Sometime after the wedding, I don't remember exactly when, Pete had an accident. He'd been out on a long run, all the way up to Abiline. It was a long hard job and by the time he got back to town he was dead tired, and so he got a little careless. In the switch yards he got his hand caught in a loose coupling.

He was in the hospital for two weeks or so, in the colored surgical ward on the second floor of a huge cement building that said Charity Hospital in carved letters over the big front door. Ma went to see him on Tuesdays and Saturdays and I just went on Saturdays. Walking over from the bus, we'd pass Lefty's Restaurant and Café. Ma would turn her head away so that she wouldn't see it.

One time the first Saturday I went with Ma, we brought Pete a letter, his induction notice. He read it and started laughing and crying all at once—until the ward nurse got worried and called an intern and together they gave him a shot. Right up till he passed out, he kept laughing.

And I began to wonder if it had been an accident. .

After two weeks he came home. We hadn't expected him; we hadn't thought he was well enough to leave. Late one afternoon we heard steps in the side alley; Ma looked at me, quick and funny, and rushed over to open the door: it was Pete. He had come home alone on the streetcar and walked the three blocks from the car stop. By the time he got to the house he was ready to pass out: he had to sit down and rest his head on the table right there in the kitchen. But he'd held his arm careful so that it didn't start to bleed again. He'd always been afraid of blood.

Accidents like that happened a lot on the road. Maybe that was why the pay was so good. The fellows who sat around the grocery all day or the bar all had pensions because they'd lost an arm or a hand or a leg. It happened a lot; we knew that, but it didn't seem to make any difference.

Ma cried very softly to herself when she saw him so dizzy and weak he couldn't stand up. And I went out in the back yard, where he couldn't see, and was sick to my stomach.

He stayed in the house until he got some strength back and then he was out all day long. He left every morning just like he was working and he came back for dinner at night. Ma asked him once where he went, but he wouldn't say; and there was never any trouble about it. A check came from the railroad every month, regular; and he still gave Ma part of it.

Pete talked about his accident, though. It was all he'd talk about. "I seen my hand," he'd tell anybody who'd listen. "After they got it free, with the blood running down it, I seen it. And it wasn't cut off. My fingers was moving. I seen 'em. Was no call for them to go cut the hand off. There wasn't any call for them to do that, not even with all it hurting." (And it had hurt so bad that he'd passed out. They'd told us he just tumbled down all of a sudden —so that the cinders along the tracks cut in his cheek.)

He'd say: "Iffen it wasn't a man my color they wouldn't done it. They wouldn't go cut off a white man's hand."

He'd say: "It was only just one finger that was caught, they didn't have cause to take off the whole hand."

And when I heard him I couldn't help wondering. Wondering if maybe Pete hadn't tried to get one finger caught. The army wouldn't take a man with one finger missing. But just one finger gone wouldn't hamper a man much. The way Pete was acting wasn't like a man that had an accident he wasn't expecting. But like a man who'd got double-crossed somehow.

And looking at Ma, I could see that she was thinking the same thing.

Lena came home after a couple of months—Chris had been sent overseas.

She used to spend most of her days lying on the bed in our room, reading a magazine maybe, or writing to Chris, or just staring at the ceiling. When the winter sun came in through the window and fell on her, her skin turned gold and burning.

Since she slept so much during the days, often in the night she'd wake up and be lonesome. Then she'd call me. "Celia," she'd call real soft so that the sound wouldn't carry through the paperboard walls. "Celia, you awake?" And I'd tell her yes and wake up quick as I could.

Then she'd snap on the little lamp that Chris had given her for a wedding present. And she'd climb out of bed, wrapping one of the blankets around her because it was cold. And she'd sit on the cane-bottomed old chair and rock it slowly back and forth while she told me just what it would be like when Chris came back for her.

Sometimes Pete would hear us talking and would call: "Shut up in there." And Lena would only toss her head and say that he was an old grouch and not to pay any attention to him.

Pete had been in a terrible temper for weeks, the cold made his arm hurt so. He scarcely spoke any more. And he didn't bother going out after supper; instead he stayed in his room, sitting in a chair with his feet propped up on the windowsill, looking out where there wasn't anything to see. Once I'd peeped in through the half-opened door. He was standing in the middle of the room, at the foot of the bed, and he was looking at his stub arm, which was still bright-red-colored. His lips were drawn back tight against his teeth, and his eyes were almost closed, they were so squinted.

Things went on this way right through the first part of the winter. Chris was in Japan. He sent Lena a silk kimono —green, with a red dragon embroidered across the back. He didn't write much, and then it was just a line saying that he was fine. Along toward the middle of January. I think it was, one of the letters mentioned fighting. It wasn't so bad, he said; and it wasn't noisy at all. That's what he noticed most, it seemed: the quietness. From the other letters we could tell that he was at the front all the rest of the winter.

It was March by this time. And in New Orleans March is just rain, icy splashing rain. One afternoon I ran the dozen or so blocks home from school and all I wanted to do was sit down by the stove. I found Ma and Pete in the kitchen. Ma was standing by the table, looking down at the two yellow pieces of paper like she expected them to move.

The telegram was in the middle of the table—the folded paper and the folded yellow envelope. There wasn't anything else, not even the big salt-shaker which usually stood there.

Ma said: "Chris got himself hurt."

Pete was sitting across the room with his chair propped against the wall, tilting himself back and forth. "Ain't good enough for nothing around here," he said, and rubbed his stump arm with his good hand. "Ain't good enough for white people, but sure good enough to get killed."

"He ain't killed," Lena said from the next room. The walls were so thin she could hear every word. "He ain't got killed."

"Sure, Lena, honey," Ma said, and her voice was soft and comforting. "He going to be all right, him. Sure."

"Quit that," Ma told Pete in a fierce whisper. "You just quit that." She glanced over her shoulder toward Lena's room. "She got enough trouble without that you add to it."

Pete glared but didn't answer.

"You want me to get you something, Lena?" I started into our room. But her voice stopped me.

"No call for you to come in," she said.

Maybe she was crying, I don't know. Her voice didn't sound like it. Maybe she was though, crying for Chris. Nobody saw her.

Chris didn't send word to us. It was almost like he forgot. There was one letter from a friend of his in Japan, saying that he had seen him in a hospital there and that the nurses were a swell set of people and so were the doctors.

Lena left the letter open on the table for us all to see. That night she picked it up and put it in the drawer of her dresser with the yellow paper of the telegram.

And there wasn't anything else to do but wait.

No, there were two things, two things that Lena could do. The day after the telegram came, she asked me to come with her.

"Where?"

"St. Michers." She was drying the dishes, putting them away in the cupboard, so I couldn't see her face, but I could tell from her voice how important this was.

"Sure," I said. "Sure, come. Right away."

St. Michel's was a small church. I'd counted the pews once: there were just exactly twenty; and the side aisles were so narrow two people could hardly pass. The confessional was a single little recess on the right side in the back, behind the baptismal font. There was a light burning —Father Graziano would be back there.

"You wait for me," Lena said. And I sat down in the last pew while she walked over toward the light. I kept my head turned so that she wouldn't think I was watching her as she went up to the confessional and knocked very softly on the wood frame. Father Graziano stuck his gray old head out between the dark curtains. I didn't have to listen; I knew what Lena was asking him. She was asking him to pray for Chris. It only took her a minute; then she walked quickly up to the front, by the altar rail. I could hear her heels against the bare boards, each one a little explosion. There were three or four candles burning already. She lit another one—I saw the circle of light get bigger as she put hers on the black iron rack.

"Let's go," she said. "Let's go."

Father Graziano had come out of the confessional and was standing watching us. He was a small man, but heavy, with a big square head and a thick neck. He must have been a powerful man when he was young. Chris had a neck like that, muscled like that.

For a minute I thought he was going to come over and talk to us. He took one step, then stopped and rubbed his hand through his curly gray hair.

Lena didn't say anything until we reached the corner where we turned to go home. Without thinking, I turned.

"Not that way." She caught hold of my arm. "This way here." She went in the opposite direction.

I walked along with her, trying to see her face. But it was too dark and she had pulled the scarf high over her head.

"We got to go to Maam's," she said and her voice was muffled in the collar of her coat.

"To what?" not believing I'd heard her right.

"To Maam's."

Maam was a grisgris woman, so old nobody could remember when she'd been young or middle-aged even. Old as the river and wrinkled like it too, when the wind blows across.

She had a house on the *batture*, behind a clump of old thick hackberries. There was the story I'd heard: she had wanted a new house after a high water on the river had carried her old one away. (All this was fifty years ago, maybe.) So she'd walked down the levee to the nearest house, which was nearly a mile away: people didn't want to live close to her. She'd stood outside, looking out at the river and calling out: "I want a house. A fine new house. A nice new house. For me." She didn't say anything else, just turned and walked away. But the people inside had heard her and spread the word. Before they even began to fix the damage the flood had done to their own houses, the men worked on her house. In less than a week it was finished. They picked up their tools and left, and the next day they sent a kid down to spy and, sure enough, there was smoke coming out of the chimney. Maam had moved in: she must have been watching from somewhere close. Nobody knew where she had spent the week that she didn't have a house. And everybody was really too scared to find out.

She was still living in that house. It was built on good big solid pilings so that flood waters didn't touch it. I'd seen it once; Pete had taken me up on the levee there and pointed it out: a two-room house that the air and the river damp had turned black, on top a flat tin roof that shone in the sun. At the beginning of the dirt path that led down to the house I saw a little pile of food people had left for her: some white pieces of slab bacon, some tin cans. Pete wouldn't let me get close. "No sense fooling with things you don't understand," he said.

Maam didn't leave her house often. But when she did, when she came walking down the streets or along the levee, people got out of her way. Either they slipped down into the *batture* bushes and waited until she passed by on the top of the levee, or, in town, they got off the banquette and into the street when she came by—an old woman with black skin that was nearly gray and eyes hidden in the folds of wrinkles, an old woman wearing a black dress, and a red shawl over her head and shoulders, a bright red shawl with silver and black signs sewed onto it. And always she'd be staring at the girls; what she liked best was to be able to touch them, on the arm or the hand, or catch hold of a little piece of their clothes. That didn't happen often, everybody was so careful of her.

And still Lena had said: "We going to Maam's."

"Lord," I said, "why?"

"For Chris."

There wasn't anything I could answer to that.

It was still early, seven thirty or eight, but nights don't seem to have time. The moon wasn't up yet; the sky was clear, with hard flecks of stars. Out on the river one ship was moving out—slipping between the riding lights of the other anchored ships that were waiting their turn at the docks below the point. You could hear the steady sound of the engines.

On top the levee the river wind was strong and cold and heavy-wet. I shivered even with a coat and scarf. There was a heavy frost like mold on the riverside slant of the levee. I stopped and pulled a clover and touched it to my lips and felt the sting of ice.

There was a light in Maam's house. We saw that as we came down the narrow little path through the hackberry bushes, the way that Pete wouldn't let me go when I was little. She must have heard us coming—walking is noisy on a quiet night—because without our knocking Maam opened the door.

I never did see her face. She had the red scarf tied high around her head so that it stuck out far on the sides. She mightn't have had a face, for all I could tell. The house was warm, very warm; I could feel the heat rush out all around her. She was wearing a black dress without sleeves, of some light material with a sheen like satin. She had tied a green cord tight around her middle. Under it her stomach stuck out like a pregnant woman's.

"I came to fetch something," Lena said. Her voice was tight and hard.

Inside the house a round spot was shining on the far wall. I stared at it hard: a tray, a round tin tray, nailed to the wall. I couldn't see more than that because there wasn't much light; just a single kerosene lamp standing in the middle of the room, on the floor. Being low like that, it made the shadows go upward on the walls so that even familiar things looked strange.

"I came to fetch something," Lena said. "For somebody that's sick."

Maam didn't move.

"To make him well," Lena added.

Maam turned around, made a circle back through her cabin, ending up behind her half-open door, where we couldn't see. I suppose we could have stepped inside and watched her—but we didn't. And in a couple of seconds she was back at the doorway. She was holding both arms straight down against her sides, the hands clenched. And she kept looking from Lena to me and back again.

Lena took her left hand out of her coat pocket and I could see that she was holding a bill and a couple of coins. She moved them slowly back and forth; Maam's eyes followed but she did not move.

"You got to give it to me," Lena said. Her voice was high-pitched and rasping. I hadn't known it could be as rough as that.

Maam held out her hand: a thin black arm, all the muscles and tendons showing along the bone. She held out her arm, palm down, fist clenched. Then slowly, so that the old muscles under the thin skin moved in twisting lines, she turned the arm and opened the fingers. And in the palm there was a small bundle of cloth, white cloth. As we stared at it the three edges of the cloth, which had been pressed down in her hand popped up slowly until they stuck straight up.

Lena reached out her right hand and took the three pointed edges of the cloth while her other hand dropped the money in its place. I could see how careful she was being not to touch the old woman.

Then we turned and almost ran back up the path to the top of the levee. I turned once near the top and looked back. Maaan was *still* standing in the door, in her thin black sleeveless dress. She seemed to be singing something; I couldn't make out the words, just the sound. As she stood there, the lamplight all yellow behind her, I could feel her eyes reach out after us.

Lena had done all she could. She'd gone to the church and she'd prayed and lit a candle and asked the priest for special prayers. And she'd gone to the voodoo woman. She'd done all she could. Now there wasn't anything to do but wait.

You could see how hard waiting was for her. Her face was always thin, a little long, with fine features. And now you could almost see the strain lines run down her cheeks. The skin under her eyes turned blue; she wasn't sleeping. I knew that. She always lay very quiet in her bed, never tossing or turning. And that was just how I knew she was awake. Nobody lies stiff and still like that if they're really asleep; and their breathing isn't so shallow and quick.

I'd lie awake and listen to her pretending that she was asleep. And I'd want to get up and go over there and comfort her somehow. Only, some people you can't comfort. You can only go along with their pretending and pretend yourself.

That's what I did. I made out I didn't notice anything. Not the circles under her eyes; not the way she had of blinking rapidly (her eyes were so dry they burned); not the little zigzag vein that stood out blue on her left forehead.

One night we had left the shade up. There was a full moon, so bright that I woke up. Lena was really asleep then. I looked over at her: the light hadn't reached more than the side of her bed; it only reached her hand that was dangling over the edge of the bed, the fingers limp and curled a little. A hand so thin that the moonlight was like an X-ray, showing the bones.

And I wanted to cry for her if she couldn't cry for herself. But I only got up and pulled down the shade, and made the room all dark so I couldn't see any more.

Chris died. The word came one Thursday late afternoon. Ma was out sweeping off the front steps and she took the telegram from the boy and brought it to Lena. Her hand was trembling when she held it out. Lena's thin hand didn't move even a little bit.

Lena opened the envelope with her fingernail, read it, cleared the kitchen table, and put it out there. (We didn't need to read it.)

She didn't make a sound. She didn't even catch her breath. Her face didn't change, her thin, tired face, with the deep circles under the eyes and the strain lines down the cheeks. Only there was a little pulse began to beat in the vein on her forehead—and her eyes changed, the light eyes with flecks of gold in them. They turned one color: dark, dull brown.

She put the telegram in the middle of the table. Her fingers let loose of it very slowly. Their tips brushed back and forth on the edges of the paper a couple of times before she dropped her arm to her side and very slowly turned and walked into the bedroom, her heels sounding on the floor, slow and steady. The bed creaked as she sat down on it.

Ma had been backing away from the telegram, the corner of her mouth twitching. She bumped into a chair and she looked down—surprised at its being there, even. Then, like a wall that's all of a sudden collapsing, she sat down and bent her head in her lap. She began to cry, not making a sound, her shoulders moving up and down.

Pete was balancing himself on his heels, teetering back and forth, grinning at the telegram like it was a person. I never saw his face look like that before; I was almost afraid of him. And he was Pete, my brother.

He reached down and flicked the paper edge with his fingers. "Good enough to die," he said. "We good enough to die."

There was a prickling all over me, even in my hair. I reckon I was shivering.

I tried to think of Chris dead. Chris shot. Chris in the hospital. Lying on a bed, and dead. Not moving. Chris, who was always moving. Chris, who was so handsome.

I stood and looked at the yellow telegram and tried to think what it would be like. Now, for Chris. I thought of things I had seen dead: dogs and mice and cats. They were born dead, or they died because they were old. Or they died because they were killed. I had seen them with their heads pulled aside and their insides spilled out red on the ground. It wouldn't be so different for a man.

But Chris...

"Even if you black," Pete was saying, "you good enough to get sent off to die."

And Ma said: "You shut you mouth!" She'd lifted her head up from her lap, and the creases on her cheeks were quivering and her brown eyes stared—cotton eyes, the kids used to call them.

"You shut you mouth!" Ma shouted. She'd never talked that way before. Not to Pete. Her voice was hoarser even, because she had been crying without tears.

And Pete yelled right back, the way he'd never done before: "Sweet Jesus, I ain't gonna shut up for nobody when I'm talking the truth."

I made a wide circle around him and went in the bedroom. Lena was sitting there, on the bed, with the pillows propped behind her. Her face was quiet and dull. There wasn't anything moving on it, not a line. There was no way of telling if she even heard the voices over in the kitchen.

I stood at the foot of the bed and put both hands on the cold iron railing. "Lena," I said, "you all right?"

She heard me. She shifted her eyes slowly over to me until they were looking directly at me. But she didn't answer. Her eyes, brown now and dark, stared straight into mine without shifting or moving or blinking or lightening. I stepped aside. The eyes didn't move with me. They stayed where they were, caught up in the air.

From the kitchen I could hear Pete and Ma shouting back and forth at each other until Ma finally gave way in deep dry sobbings that slowed and finally stopped. For a second or so everything was perfectly still. Then Ma said what had been in the back of our minds for months, only I didn't ever expect to hear her say it, not to her only boy.

"You no son of mine." She paused for a minute and I could hear the deep catching breath she took. "You no man even." Her voice was level and steady. Only, after every couple of words she'd have to stop for breath. "You a coward. A god-damn coward. And you made youself a cripple for all you life.'

All of a sudden Pete began to laugh—high and thin and ragged. 'Maybe—maybe. But me, I'm breathing. And he ain't....Chris was fine and he ain't breathing."

Lena didn't give any sign that she'd heard. I went around to the side of the bed and took her hand: it was cold and heavy.

Pete was giggling; you could hardly understand what he was saying. "He want to cross over, him."

Ma wasn't interrupting him now. He went right ahead, choking on the words. "Chris boy, you fine and you brave and you ain't run out on what you got to do. And you ain't breathing neither. But you a man...."

Lena's hand moved ever so slightly.

"Lena," I said, "you all right?"

"Chris boy... you want to cross over... and you sure enough cross over... why, man, you sure cross over… but good, you cross over."

"Lena," I said, "don't you pay any mind to him. He's sort of crazy."

In the kitchen Pete was saying: "Chris, you a man, sure… sure… you sure cross over…but ain't you gonna come back for Lena? Ain't you corning back to get her?"

I looked down and saw that my hand was shaking. My whole body was. It had started at my legs and come upward. I couldn't see clearly either. Edges of things blurred together. Only one thing I saw clear: Chris lying still and dead.

"It didn't get you nowhere, Chris boy," Pete was giggling. "Being white and fine, where it got you? Where it got you? Dead and rotten."

And Lena said: "Stop him, Chris."

She said; "Stop him, Chris, please."

I heard her voice, soft and low and pleading, the way she wouldn't speak to anyone else, but only her husband.

Chris, dead on the other side of the world, covered with ground.

Tom Dent (1932–1998)

Tom Dent knew when he wrote the play, *Ritual Murder* in 1967, that understanding why young black men were killing young black men was key to stopping the bloodshed. Today, forty-five years since the play was written, New Orleans has one of the highest per capita murder rates in the United States, and Louisiana has the highest rate of incarceration in the world! Dent recognized decades ago that the city is coming at the problem in the wrong way. The threat of incarceration is not working now any more than it did for the play's protagonist, Joe Brown, Jr. Getting to the root of "ritual murders" is at the heart of this play.

Thomas Covington Dent was born in New Orleans on March 20, 1932, to Albert Walter and Ernestine Jessie Covington Dent.[1] When Dent was nine years old, his father was named the president of Dillard University, a position he would hold for twenty-eight years. His mother, Jessie, was a classically trained pianist originally from Houston. As a prominent black family in New Orleans, their home was often open to many renowned leaders of the civil rights era, so Dent's interest in the movement was formed at a young age, and his work for civil rights for African Americans would last his lifetime.

Dent graduated from Morehouse College in Atlanta in 1952, with a degree in political science. While there, he also began his writing career as the editor of the Morehouse *Maroon Tiger* while also writing for *The Houston Informer*, the oldest black newspaper west of the Mississippi. After going on to graduate school at Syracuse University from 1952 to 1956, Dent served in the Army for two years, all the while continuing to pursue writing by taking a *Reader's Digest* correspondence course in short story writing. He did not return to Syracuse to finish his graduate studies, but instead moved to New York City where he wrote for *New York Age*, an African American newspaper founded by former slave Timothy Thomas Fortune in 1884, and where W.E.B. Dubois also once worked.

In New York, Dent became even more involved in the political scene, and Justice Thurgood Marshall appointed him press liaison for the NAACP Legal Defense Fund, taking Dent back into the deep South to help with getting James Meredith admitted to Ole Miss. He and Amiri Baraka created the Umbra Writers' Workshop on the Lower East Side in 1962, setting the stage for the Black Arts Movement. Dent returned to New Orleans three years later where he began to work with John O'Neal and Gilbert Moses in the Free Southern Theater (FST), and where he wrote the one-act play *Ritual Murder* in 1967.[2] Soon afterward, the core members of the FST left for New York, but Dent remained in New Orleans, dedicated to developing an artistic group in the black community. The result, BLKARTSOUTH creative writing and acting workshops and the accompanying literary journal, *Nkombo*, the Bantu word for gumbo.

Funding for the journal was often a problem, and while living in New Orleans, Dent also taught at Mary Holmes Junior College in West Point, Mississippi, from 1968 to 1970, and at the University of New Orleans from 1979 to 1981, and was a community organizer for the city's Social Welfare Planning Council and Total Community Action. Dent also attained a masters degree in poetry and African American literature at Goddard College in 1974, the same year he married Roberta "Bobbi" Yancy, a marriage that would last only six years. Two years later, his first book of poetry was published, *Magnolia Street*, a book poet David Henderson called "a heavy trip through New Orleans."[3]

In 1969, Dent, along with Jerry Ward and Charles Rowell, founded the black literary journal, *Callaloo* where *Ritual Murder* was first published. The play opens with a narrator telling the audience that "Last Summer, Joe Brown, Jr., black youth of New Orleans, La., committed murder." Dent, who had long been a music aficionado, infuses his play with songs by such notable greats as Gil Evans and Otis Redding. The song "Summertime" is playing behind the narrator's opening remarks and whenever Joe Brown, Jr. and his victim and best friend, James

---

1   For more on Dent see Tom Dent Papers, Amistad Research Center, Tulane University Campus, New Orleans, from which comes much of the biographical information included here.

2   Although Dent wrote the play in 1967, it did not debut until almost ten years later, in 1976 at the Ethiopian Theater in New Orleans, directed by Chakula Cha Jua. It was first published in *Callaloo*, February 1978, 67-81.

3   *Berkley Barb*, March 4-10, 1977, 8.

Roberts are on the stage.

The first character to appear on the stage after the narrator is Joe Brown's wife, Bertha, saying "Joe just didn't have any sense," but she also admits that "he is smart, oh yes, has a good brain." And Dent depicts an exceptionally intelligent character in Joe Brown Jr., but we see that little is done in his community to encourage that intelligence. His elementary school teacher, Mrs. Williams, says that "Joe was like all the others from the Ninth Ward, not interested in doing anything for themselves," but that is not the man that Dent portrays in this play. Mrs. Williams is more worried about "irritating her gas" and buying a new Oldsmobile than she is about teaching her students, a commentary on the state of education for black children in New Orleans.

The play centers around trying to get to the bottom of this murder: just why did Joe Brown, Jr. murder his best friend James Roberts? His wife Bertha believes that "Joe knifed that boy because he was foolish, wouldn't settle down and accept things as they are." Mrs. Williams says it was "because he was headed that way in the beginning." His white employer states that "it has to do with nigras and the way they get wild on the weekend." Joe's mother, Mrs. Brown agrees: "It's just one of those things that happens on Saturday night in a colored bar; like a disease." What we do discover over the course of the play is that Joe Brown, Jr. was neglected in school, a brilliant young man who received a poor education; neglected at home by a father who had abandoned him to start another family; and is a young man unable to find any decent representation of young black men like him or like the man he should become anywhere in his home, community, society, or the media. Even his best friend reinforces his sense of hopelessness, telling him, "You a black mother-fucker and you may as well learn to make the best of it." But that's not good enough for Joe Brown, Jr., and it shouldn't be.

Finally, the black court-appointed psychologist, Dr. Brayboy gets to the root of the problem, a problem that still exists in New Orleans today:

> When murder occurs for no apparent reason but happens all the time as in our race on Saturday nights, it is ritual murder. That is, no apparent reason. There are reasons. The reasons are both personal and common. When a people who have no method of letting off steam against the source of their oppression explode against each other, homicide, under these conditions, is a form of group suicide.

Dr. Brayboy says no more than that and does not point to the explicit reasons, but throughout the play Dent suggests that these ritual murders are a result of oppression, lack of a decent home life, a decent education, decent employment opportunities, decent role models, both public and private, and until these issues are addressed, ritual murders in the New Orleans black community will continue.

Before Tom Dent died in 1998, he was witness to New Orleans becoming the murder capital of the nation, but the fact that he addressed the ritual murders of young black men in the city thirty five years before his death is astounding. He would be saddened to know that little has been done since then to stem this ritual violence. Dent spent his life writing literature, working in the black community, and in the end documenting the stories of his people and their struggles, hopefully to offer some opportunity to young black men like those he portrays in this play.

Ritual Murder

CHARACTERS: Narrator, Joe Brown Jr., Bertha (Joe's wife), Mrs. Williams (Joe's teacher), Dr. Brayboy (a black psychiatrist), Mr. Andrews (Joe's boss), Mrs. Brown (Joe's mother), Mr. Brown (Joe's father), James Roberts (Joe's friend), Mr. Spaulding (anti-poverty program administrator), Chief of Police.

SETTING: New Orleans, La.

TIME: Now. It is important that the actors make their speeches in rhythm to the background music.

NARRATOR: Last Summer, Joe Brown Jr., black youth of New Orleans, La., committed murder. Play a special *Summertime* for him and play the same *Summertime* for his friend James Roberts who he knifed to death. [*We hear* Summertime *under the narrator's voice.*] In every black community of America; in the ghettos and neighborhood clubs where we gather to hear our music, we play *Summertime;* and in each community the bands play it differently. In no community does it sound like the *Summertime* of George Gershwin. It is bluesier, darker, with its own beat and logic, its joys unknown to the white world. It is day now. The routine events of life have passed under the bridge. Joe Brown Jr. has been arrested, indicted, and formally charged with murder. It happened…. it happened in a Ninth Ward bar—we need not name it for the purposes of this presentation. The stabbing was the culmination of an argument Joe Brown had with his friend. We have learned this, but the *Louisiana Weekly* only reported, "James Roberts is said to have made insulting remarks to Joe Brown, whereupon Brown pulled out a switchblade knife and stabbed Roberts three times in the chest before he could be subdued." The story received front page play in the *Louisiana Weekly,* and a lead in the crime-of-the-day section in the white *Times-Picayune.* After that, it received only minor news play, since there are other crimes to report in New Orleans. Play *Summertime* for Joe Brown Jr., and play the same *Summertime* for his friend James Roberts who he knifed to death. [*The music dies out.*] Why did this murder happen? No one really knows. The people who know Joe Brown best have ideas.

[*We see Bertha looking at TV. The sound is off, only the picture shows. Bertha is young, about 20. She is Joe's wife. She is ironing while looking at the set-ironing baby things.*]

BERTHA: Joe just didn't have any sense. He is smart, oh yes, has a good brain, but didn't have good sense. The important thing was to settle down, get a good job, and take care of his three children. We been in the Florida Ave. project now for almost a year, and we never have enough money. Look at the people on T.V., they make out okay. They fight, but they never let their fights destroy them. Joe didn't have control of his temper. He was a dreamer, he wanted things. But he wouldn't work to get them. Oh, he would take jobs in oyster houses, and he'd worked on boats ever since he was a kid. But he wouldn't come in at night, and sometimes he wouldn't get up in the morning to go to work. Sometimes he would come in and snap off the T.V. and say it was driving him crazy. It's not his T.V.—my father bought it, and besides, I like it, it's the only thing I have. This is just a 17 inch set, but I want a 21 inch set. Now I'll never get one because he had to go out and do something foolish. You ask me why he killed that boy? I don't know. But I think he killed him because he had a bad temper and wouldn't settle down. Joe was a mild person, but he carried knives and guns—that's the way his family is. I used to tell him about it all the time. Once I asked him, "When are you gonna get a better job and make more money?" He said, "When I get rid of you and those snotty kids." He could have done something if he had tried, if he had only tried; but instead, he wanted to take it out on us. I'll go see him, but now look; I have to do everything in this house myself: Iron the clothes, cook the meals, buy the food, apply for relief and get some help from my parents-and my father ain't working right now. Joe didn't want to have our last baby, Cynthia, but we couldn't murder her before she was even born and now I got to take care of her too. Joe knifed that boy because he was foolish, wouldn't settle down and accept things as they are, and because he didn't have common sense.

NARRATOR: Mrs. Williams, could you comment on your former student, Joe Brown Jr.?

MRS. WILLIAMS: I don't remember Joe Brown Jr very well. I have so many children to try to remember. I had him three or four years ago just before he dropped out of school. I was his homeroom teacher. Joe was like all the others from the Ninth Ward, not interested in doing anything for themselves. You can't teach them anything. They don't want to learn, they *never* study, they won't sit still and pay attention in class. It's no surprise to me that he's in trouble. I try to do my best here, but I have only so much patience. I tell you you don't know the things a teacher goes through with these kids. They come to class improperly dressed, from homes where they don't get any home training, which is why they are so ill-mannered. We try to teach them about America-about the opportunities America has to offer. We try to prepare them to get the best jobs they can-and you know a Negro child has to work harder. I teach History, Arithmetic, English, and Civics every day, and it goes in one ear and comes out the other. It gives me a terrible gas pain to have to go through it every day, and the noise these kids make is too, too hard on my ears. I've worked for ten years in this school, and I don't get paid much at all. But next month my husband and I will have saved enough money to buy a new Oldsmobile, which I'm happy to say will be the smartest, slickest, smoothest thing McDonough No. 81 has ever seen. Two boys got into a fight in the yard the other day and it was horrible. It pains me to hear the names they call each other-irritates my gas. Some of them even bring knives and guns to school. It's just terrible. I'm only relieved when I get home, turn on my T.V., take my hair down and face off, drink a nice strong cup of coffee, look out at my lawn in Pontchartrain Park, and forget the day. You ask me why Joe Brown murdered his friend in a Negro bar on a Saturday night and I tell you it is because he was headed that way in the beginning. These kids just won't listen, and don't want to learn, and that's all there is to it.

[*Lights on Joe Brown Jr. He is wearing blue jeans and a tee shirt. He is seated. He faces the audience. There is a table in front of him. On the table is a small transistor radio, but the music we hear is Gil Evans'* Barbara Song.]

NARRATOR: Here is Joe Brown Jr..

JOE BROWN JR.: Once I saw a feature about surfing on T.V. Surfing on beautiful waves on a beach in Hawaii, or somewhere…

[*The lights shift to another man who is seated on the opposite side of the stage. He is a much older man, dressed in a business suit. He is a negro. He is Dr. Brayboy, a psychiatrist. His chair does not face the audience; it faces Joe Brown Jr.*]

NARRATOR: A black psychiatrist, Dr. Thomas L. Brayboy.

DR. BRAYBOY: At the core of Joe Brown's personality is a history of frustrations. Psychological, sociological, economic…

JOE BROWN JR.: … and I wanted to do that… surf. It was a dream I kept to myself. Because it would have been foolish to say it aloud. Nobody wants to be laughed at. And then I thought, I never see black people surfing…

DR. BRAYBOY: We might call Joe Brown's homocidal act an act of ritual murder. When murder occurs for no apparant reason but happens all the time, as in our race on Saturday nights, it is ritual murder. When I worked in Harlem Hospital in the emergency ward, I saw us coming in bleeding, blood seeping from the doors of the taxicabs,… icepicks and knives…

[*These speeches must be slow, to the rhythm of music.*]

NARRATOR: Play *Summertime* for Joe Brown Jr., and a very funky *Summertime* for his friend James Roberts, who he knifed to death.

JOE BROWN JR.: … And then I thought, I don't see any black folks on T.V., ever. Not any real black folks, anyway. There are those so called black shows like *Good Times* and the *Jeffersons,* but they are so far removed from the kind of folks I know that they may as well be white too. I see us playing football, basketball, and baseball, and half the time I miss that because they be on in the afternoon, and I'm usually shelling oysters. "Where am I?", I asked my wife, and she answered, "In the Florida Avenue project where you are doing a poor job of taking care of your wife and children." My boss answered, "On the job, if you would keep your mind on what you are doing… count the oysters."

DR. BRAYBOY: … Ice picks and knives and frustration. My tests indicate that Joe Brown Jr. is considerably above average in intelligence. Above average in intelligence. *Above* average. Vocabulary and reading comprehension extraordinary…

NARRATOR: [*To Audience*] Our purpose here is to discover why.

Dr. Brayboy: … But school achievement extremely low. Dropped out at 18 in the eleventh grade.

Joe Brown Jr.: I began watching all the T.V. sets I could, looking for my image on every channel, looking for someone who looked like me. I knew I existed, but I didn't see myself in the world of television or movies. Even the black characters were not me. All the black characters were either weak and stupid, or some kind of superman who doesn't really exist in my world. I couldn't define myself, and didn't know where to begin. When I listened to soul music on the radio I understood that, and I knew that was part of me, but that didn't help me much. Something was not right, and it was like… like I was the only cat in the whole world who knew it. Something began to come loose in me, like my mind would float away from my body and lay suspended on a shelf for hours at a time watching me open oysters. No one ever suspected, but my mind was trying to define me, to tell me who I was the way other people see me, only it couldn't because it didn't know where to begin.

[*The scene shifts to the desk of The Chief Of Police. He may be played by a white actor, or a black actor in white face.*]

Narrator: The Chief of Police.

Chief of Police: The rate of crime in the streets in New Orleans has risen sharply. We know that most of our colored citizens are wholesome, law abiding, decent citizens. But the fact remains that the crime wave we are witnessing now across the nation is mostly nigger crime. Stop niggers and you will stop crime. The police must have more protection, more rights, and more weapons of all types to deal with the crime wave. We need guns, machine guns, multi-machine guns, gas bombs and reinforced nightsticks. Otherwise America is going to become a nightmare of black crime in the streets.

[*Lights up on Mr. Andrews, Joe's boss. He is sitting behind a terribly messy desk with papers stuck in desk holders. His feet are on the desk. He is eating a large muffuletta sandwich. His image must be one of a relaxed, informal interview at his office during lunch time. If there are no white actors, the part can be played by a black actor in whiteface, but instead of eating lunch, he should be smoking a huge cigar.*]

Narrator: Joe Brown's employer, Mr. Andrews.

Mr. Andrews: I have trouble with several of my nigra boys, but I likes 'em. [*He almost chokes on his sandwich.*] Joe was a little different from the rest… what would you say… dreamier… more absent minded. Joe was always quitting, but he must have liked it here 'cause he always came back. You can't tell me anything about those people. One time, during lunch hour, they were singing and dancing outside to the radio and I snuck up to watch. If they had seen me they would've stopped. It was amazing. The way them boys danced is fantastic. They shore got rhythm and a sense of style about them. Yes sir… and guess who got the most style… ole Joe. [*Bites and eats.*] That boy sure can dance. I loves to watch him. [*Bites*] Recently, he been going to the bathroom a lot and staying a long time. I ask the other boys, "where's that doggone Joe?" They tell me. So one day I go to the john and there he is, sitting on the stool… readin'. I say, "Boy, I pay you to read or shell oysters?" He comes out all sulky. [*Smiling*] He could be kind of sensitive at times, you know. I been knowing him since he was a kid… born around here… kind of touchy. [*Andrews has finished his sandwich. He takes his feet off the desk, throws the wrapper into the trash, and wipes his hands. A serious look comes over his face.*] As for why he killed that boy, I can't give you any answers. I think it has to do with nigras and the way they get wild on the weekend. Sometimes the good times get a little rough. And them [*Pause*] you don't know what a boy like Joe can get mixed up in, or any of them out there. [*Waves toward the door*] I don't understand it, and I know and likes 'em all, like they was my own family. My job is to keep 'em straight here… any trouble out of any of 'em and out the door they go.

[*The scene shifts to another white man. He is well dressed with his tie loosened, sitting behind an extremely disordered desk. Black actor can play in white face. He must, throughout his speech wear a public relations smile. He must speak with a winning air.*]

Narrator: Mr. Richard Spaulding, Director of the Poverty Program in New Orleans.

Mr. Spaulding: Last year we spent 3.5 million in five culturally deprived areas of New Orleans. This money has made a tremendous difference in the lives of our fine colored citizens. We have provided jobs, jobs, and more jobs. By creating, for the first time, indigenous community organizations controlled and operated by the people of the five target areas, we have, for the first time, provided a way to close the cultural and economic gap. Social Service Centers are going up in all these areas. We will develop a level of competency on par with American society as a whole. In the Desire area alone, 750 mothers go to our medical center each day. We have, in short, provided hope. Of course, there are still problems.

Narrator: Any insights into the murder of James Roberts last Summer by Joe Brown Jr.?

Mr. Spaulding: We are building community centers, baseball diamonds, basketball courts, little leagues, golden agers facilities, barbecue pits, swimming pools, badminton nets, and… if our dreams come true… well supervised and policed bowling alleys. It is our firm hope that sociology will stay out of neighborhood bars.

Narrator: Thank you, Mr. Spaulding. [*The scene shifts to a middle aged woman sitting on a well worn couch. She is wearing a plain dress. There is a small table with a lamp and bible on it next to the couch. She is Mrs. Brown, Joe's mother. Across the stage, sitting in a big easy chair is a middle aged man in work clothes. He is Mr. Brown, Joe's father. He is drinking a large can of beer which, from time to time, he will place on the floor. He listens to what Mrs. Brown says intently, but there must be an air of distance in his attitude toward her and what she says, never affection. The audience must be made to believe they are in different places.*]

Narrator: [*Solemnly*] This is Joe Brown's mother. [*A spot focuses on Mrs. Brown. There is enough light however to see Mr. Brown.*]

Mrs. Brown: Joe was always a sweet kind boy, but Joe's problem is that he… stopped… going… to… church. I told him about that but it didn't make any difference. When we climb out of Christ chariot we liable to run into trouble. I tell the truth about my own children, like I tell it on anyone else. Once, before Joe got married he came home in a temper about his boss and his job. Talking bad about the white folks. Said he wished something from another planet would destroy them all. Said he didn't like the way his boss talked to him, that he should be paid more, and like that. We all get mad at the white people, but there is no point in it. So many colored folks ain't even got a job. I told him, "If you think you can do better, go back and finish school." But no, he didn't finish school, he just complained. "Stay in church," I told him, but he started hanging around with bad friends. Bad friends lead to a bad end. Talking bad about white people is like busting your head against a brick wall.

Narrator: Mrs. Brown, do you feel your son would kill for no reason? There must have been a reason.

Mrs. Brown: When you hang around a bad crowd on Saturday nights, troubles are always gonna come. I told him to stay out of those bars. I don't know what happened or why. A friend told me the other boy was teasing Joe and Joe got mad. He was sensitive, you know, very serious and sensitive. He didn't like to be rubbed the wrong way.

Narrator: Mrs. Brown. the purpose of this program is to discover why your son knifed his friend. No one seems to have answers. We are using the scientific approach. Do *you* have any answers?

Mrs. Brown: [*Despairingly*] I don't know why. I don't understand. You try to protect your children as best you can. It's just one of those things that happens on Saturday nights in a colored bar; like a disease. You hope you and nobody you know catches it. The Lord is the only protection.

Narrator: And your husband? Would he have any information, any ideas?

Mrs. Brown: [*Sharply*] I haven't seen that man in four years.

[*Both Mrs. Brown and narrator look at Mr. Brown.*]

MR. BROWN: I plan to go see the boy… I just haven't had a chance yet. I have another family now and I can't find any work. I help him out when I can, but… [*Pause*]… I can't understand why he would do a thing like that.

NARRATOR: If we could hear what James Roberts has to say. [*We return to the summertime theme and the scene of the crime, the barroom where the play began with Joe Brown Jr standing over James Roberts' body and all other actors frozen in their original positions as in the opening scene. After the narrator speaks the body of James Roberts begins to slowly arise from the floor aided by Joe Brown. It is important that Brown helps Roberts get up.*]

JAMES ROBERTS: [*Begins to laugh…*] It was all a joke. Nothing happened that hasn't happened between us before. Joe is still my best friend…if I were alive I would tell anyone that. That Saturday was a terrible one… not just because the lights went out for me. I heard a ringing in my ears when I woke up that morning. When I went to work at the hotel the first thing I had to do was take out the garbage. Have you ever smelled the stink of shrimp and oyster shells first thing in the morning? I hate that. The sounds of the street and the moan of the cook's voice; that's enough to drive anyone crazy, and I heard it every day. That day I decided to leave my job for real… one more week at the most.

JOE BROWN JR.: [*Getting up from the bunk into a sitting position*] Damn. The same thing happened to me that day. I decided I was going to leave my job.

JAMES ROBERTS: [*Looking at Joe with disgust.*] Man, you are disgusting. You all the time talking about leaving your job.

NARRATOR: [*To Roberts, then to Joe.*] Get to what happened at the cafe please. We don't have all night.

JAMES ROBERTS: We were both very uptight… mad at our jobs-everybody… everything around us.

JOE BROWN JR.: [*Excitedly*] I know I was… I was ready to shoot somebody.

JAMES ROBERTS: Shut up. This is my scene.

JOE BROWN JR.: You won't even let anybody *agree* with you.

NARRATOR: Please.

JAMES ROBERTS: Joe went on and on all evening and all night. We were getting higher and higher, going from bar to bar. We went to Scotties, then to Shadowland, to the Havana… we had my sister's car… Joe getting mad and frustrated and talking 'bout what he was gonna do. By the time we got to the Ninth Ward Cafe, we was both stoned out of our minds. Joe getting dreamier and dreamier. He was talking about all his problems, his wife, his job, his children. I could understand that.

JOE BROWN JR.: You really couldn't because you don't have those problems.

[*We hear Otis Redding's "Satisfaction" from the album,* Otis Redding Live.]

JAMES ROBERTS: Joe was screaming about the white man. He said he was $1500 in debt… working like hell for the white man, then turning right around and giving it back to him. He said he couldn't laugh no more.

[*From this point on there must be little connection between Joe's thoughts and those of James Roberts. The Otis Redding recording continues, but must not drown out the speeches.*]

JOE BROWN JR.: I had a dream… I had a dream… I dreamed I had 66 million dollars left to me by an unknown relative…

JAMES ROBERTS: [*Slow, to the music. As much pantomime as possible, as though he is re-enacting the scene.*] We were in the Ninth Ward Cafe sitting in a booth by ourselves. There was something on the juke box, I believe it was Otis Redding. It was a hot night. Joe was talking about how there was nowhere he could go to relax anymore. Then suddenly, his mind would go off into outer space somewhere and I had to jerk him back. I would ask him what he was thinking about, and he would say he wasn't happy with himself. He didn't know himself or where he was headed to anymore.

Joe Brown Jr.: ... I always get screwed up when I try to figure out the *first* thing I'm going to buy... a new car... maybe... Mark IV... a new house... a brick one with wood paneling... a new suit... a tailor made three piece... new shoes... some high steppers... a new transistor radio... a big Sony that plays loud with big sound... Then I'd give everybody a bill... but I can't figure out what I'm going to buy *first*.

James Roberts: I said, man what are you talking about. I don't understand all this blues over what happens everyday. He said he wanted to believe there is hope. I told him there is no hope. You a black mother-fucker and you may as well learn to make the best of it.

Joe Brown Jr.: ... People always tell me I can't make up my mind what I want, or I want things that don't make sense, or I want too much instead of being satisfied with just a little. People always tell me I ask too many questions... especially questions that no one can answer... and I am just frustrating myself because I can never find the answers. The way I figure it you may as well dream 66 million as 66 thousand. The way I figure it, you may as well ask questions you *don't* have answers to; what's the point in asking questions everyone knows the answers to. Life is just a little thing anyway... doesn't really amount to much when you think about time and place.

James Roberts: [*Intensely and quicker*] Then he just blew. Screamed nobody calls him a black mother fucker. I just laughed. Everybody calls him that cause that's just what he is. There nothing wrong with calling anyone a black mother fucker. We been doing it to each other all our lives, and we did it all evening while we were drinking. I just laughed. He jumps up, pulls out his blade and goes for my heart. I could outfight Joe any day but...

Joe Brown Jr.: High steppers...

James Roberts: ... He got the jump on me and I couldn't get to my blade. It was ridiculous. He was like a crazy man... a wild man... turning on me for no reason when I done nothing to him at all... and shouting, "there is no hope."

Joe Brown Jr.: High steppers...

James Roberts: Before I knew it I was stunned and weak and there was blood all over the chest of my yellow polo shirt... I felt the lights darken, and my whole body turned to rubber...

Joe Brown Jr.: High steppers on a Saturday night...

James Roberts: ... But I couldn't move anything [*Pause*] Last thing I heard was Booker T. and the M. G.s playing *Groovin'*... Joe ... his eyes blazing... everything turned red.

Narrator: [*To Roberts after pause*] You mean this caused such a brutal act? You called him a name?

James Roberts: That's all it takes sometimes.

Narrator: And you think this makes sense? To lose your life at nineteen over such an insignificant thing?

James Roberts: It happens all the time. I accept it. Joe is still my friend. Friends kill each other all the time... unless you have an enemy you can both kill.

Narrator: And you Joe?

Joe Brown Jr.: What is there to say? It happened. It happens all the time. One thing I learned; when you pull a knife or gun don't fool around, use it, or you might not have a chance to. Better him dead than me. He would say the same thing if it was the other way around.

Narrator: [*To Joe Brown Jr.*] What did you mean when you said there is no hope?

Joe Brown Jr.: [*Evenly*] I don't know. *There is no hope.* Here in this jail, with my fate, I might be better off dead.

Narrator: One more question. [*To James Roberts*] Do you feel you died for anything? Is there any meaning in it?

James Roberts: Yes, I died for something. But I don't know what it means.

Narrator: [*To Joe Brown Jr.*] And did your act mean anything?

JOE BROWN JR.: [*Softly*] I suppose so. But I can't imagine what. [*The music of a bluesy* Summertime. *The narrator comes out to downstage center, as in the beginning of the play. He addresses the audience directly in even tones.*]

NARRATOR: Play *Summertime* for Joe Brown Jr. and play a very funky *Summertime* for his friend James Roberts who he knifed to death.

[Summertime *theme continues as narrator slowly scrutinizes the people he has just interviewed.*]

Our purpose here is to discover why. No one seems to have answers. Do you have any?

[*Narrator moves to actors who plays Bertha, Mrs. Williams, Mrs. Brown, Joe Brown Sr., and Dr. Brayboy asking the question "Do you have answers?" To which they respond:*]

BERTHA: Joe knifed that boy because he was foolish, wouldn't settle down and accept things as they are, and because he didn't have common sense.

MRS. WILLIAMS: You ask me why Joe Brown murdered his friend in a Negro bar on a Saturday night and I tell you it is because he was headed that way in the beginning. These kids just won't listen, and don't want to learn, and that's all there is to it.

MR. BROWN: I plan to go see the boy… I just haven't had a chance yet. I help him out when I can but [*Pause*] I can't understand why he would do a thing like that.

MRS. BROWN: It's just one of those things that happens on a Saturday night in a colored bar… like a disease. You hope you and nobody you know catches it. The Lord is the only protection.

DR. BRAYBOY: When murder occurs for no apparent reason but happens all the time as in our race on Saturday nights, it is ritual murder. That is, no apparent reason. There are reasons. The reasons are both personal and common. When a people who have no method of letting off steam against the source of their oppression exploit against each other, homicide, under these conditions, is a form of group suicide. When personal chemistries don't mix just a little spark can bring about the explosion. Icepicks and knives and whatever happens to be lying around.

NARRATOR: When murder occurs for no apparent reason, but happens all the time, as in our race on a Saturday night, it is ritual murder.

[*The following lines should be distributed among the actors and delivered to the audience directly.*]

That is, no apparent reason. There are reasons. The reasons are both personal and common. When a people who have no method of letting off steam against the source of their oppression explode against each other, homicide, under these conditions, is a form of group suicide. When personal chemistries don't mix just a little spark can bring about the explosion. Icepicks, knives and whatever happens to be lying around.

NARRATOR: [*Moving downstage facing audience directly.*] We have seen something unpleasant, but the play is over. Yes, we see this thing [*Gesturing to stage behind him*] night after night, weekend after weekend. Only you have the power to stop it. It has to do with something in our minds. [*Pause.* Summertime *music gradually increases in volume.*] Play *Summertime* for Joe Brown Jr., and play a very funky *Summertime* for his friend James Roberts who he knifed to death. [*Narrator walks over to Dr. Brayboy and shakes his hand as lights fade to black.*]

Everette Maddox (1944–1989)

In the introduction to the 2009 *I hope it's not over, and goodby: Selected Poems of Everette Maddox,* editor and friend of Everette Maddox, Ralph Adamo writes that Maddox's brother Bill gave up tenure "to move to New Orleans, drink, and write."[1] The same could be said of Everette Maddox, who initially came to New Orleans from Tuscaloosa, Alabama, in 1976 as Poet in Residence at Xavier University, a position that lasted only one year. Luckily his writing—and unfortunately his drinking—lasted the rest of his short lifetime. Perhaps poet Andrei Codrescu captures Maddox best when he writes on the Xavier Review Press website that "the South, New Orleans, decay, poetry, wit, crippling nostalgia, and carpe diem—all of these things wafted off Everette like the smell of whiskey and cigarettes...."

When Everette Maddox arrived in New Orleans, he and his then wife Celia rented an apartment at 2900 Prytania where F. Scott Fitzgerald and Zelda had lived when they were in New Orleans, a fact that was not lost on Maddox, who admired not only Fitzgerald's writing but the life that he and Zelda led. After Maddox's job at Xavier ended, he went on to teach at the University of New Orleans, but he lost that gig too, then he and Celia split, and by the end of his time in New Orleans, he was homeless.

After spending four months in Alabama and returning to the city in 1979, Maddox wrote about New Orleans in a letter to his friend, Bob Woolf: "They'll have to pry me up to get me out of this town again.... Every day I'm gladder I came back: 7-11's advertising not merely Ice Beer Liquor but also Racing Forms.... 'Where yat' and 'Yeah you right' ringing in the air... King Cakes... an old favorite, the Hit and Run Package Store.... Zo far zo good."[2] In his letters to his friend, Maddox is able to capture the city using the same combination of humor and poetic language found in so much of his writing. After his return in 1979, Maddox began the Sunday afternoon Maple Leaf poetry reading series, one of the longest in the nation, and still ongoing thanks to the dedication of poet Nancy Harris. Much, if not most, of his poetry was read there, and many New Orleans poets are still devoted to Maddox and continue to publish his work.

While here, he wrote several books published by local small presses. The first, his chapbook *The Thirteen Original Poems,* was published in 1976 by Xavier University Press. That collection was followed by *The Everette Maddox Songbook* in 1982, published by Maxine Cassin's New Orleans Poetry Journal Press, then *Bar Scotch* the year before his death in 1988, published by Pirogue Publishing. The last three collections were published posthumously: *Rette's Last Stand,* Tensaw Press, 2004; *Umpteen Ways of Looking at a Possum,* Xavier University Press, 2006; and finally, *I hope it's not over, and good-by: Selected Poems of Everette Maddox,* UNO Press, 2009. He was notorious for scribbling poems on scraps of paper and bar napkins, and many of his published poems first appeared in these forms. He also had his poem, "Shades Mountain," published in the *New Yorker* in 1971.

The first of the poems included here is one of Maddox's best, "Moon Fragment." Adamo writes of Maddox's poetry that it "moved and changed... over time from a somewhat detached and humorous posture to a profoundly entangled and humorous posture, while his concerns remained pretty constant."[3] Many of those concerns appear in this poem: love, writing, work, and how all are fleeting. Adamo also states that Maddox's poetry "bears the distinction of being almost entirely about himself and the life he was living."[4] In the melancholy "Moon Fragment" he talks about holding office hours at night so that he is not disturbed by students and is free to write, drink, and smoke. The poem opens with a beautiful image of a "Moon-eater," perhaps a poet, "A man squats by the railroad tracks tonight/ eating a moon fragment: not cheese/ at all, but a honeydew melon...." The poem evolves into a love poem, or one of love lost, and the speaker knows that what he has to offer his love—a tethered moon—is not what she wants. It finally ends with the conundrum, "...It means, whatever this is between/ you and me, I hope it's not

1   Ralph Adamo, ed., *"I hope it's not over, and good-by": Selected Poems of Everette Maddox* (New Orleans: UNO Press, 2009), 11.

2   "Letters of Everette Maddox To Robert Woolf: A Selection From 1976 to 1982," *New Orleans Review,* Vol. 20 (1994), 99-100.

3   Adamo, 13.

4   Ibid., 12.

over, and good-by," a heartbreaking riddle.

"How I Got In" is a shorter, more humorous, "night in the life" poem. He begins by dedicating the poem, "For Wade," and continues that pun throughout. The speaker is drowning in grief outside "the Muddy Waters," a popular 1980s music club across from Maddox's hangout, the Maple Leaf, that was "flooded with friends." He wants to enter and tells the doorman, "I know Wade" and the doorman responds, "Well Wade on in." So much of his later poetry is centered around that one block of Maple Street.

"Flowing on the Bench" describes a dream the speaker had while sleeping on the "iron bench/in the back of the bar," the Maple Leaf. The speaker feels a part of something, "...like one river joining another," and the poem ends with Maddox paying tribute to Twain's *Huckleberry Finn*. In a 1978 letter to Bob Woolf, Maddox writes, "Whenever I go back to Twain, I wonder why I ever read anybody else. He's life-giving."[1]

Maddox's "Thirteen Ways of Being Looked at by a Possum," is another funny poem, a riff on Wallace Stevens' "Thirteen Ways of Looking at a Blackbird." Maddox, while discussing poetry in a letter to Woolf, writes, "I DON'T CARE if it's academic, I just want it to be funy" (sic).[2] Possums are funny, and so is this poem. Maddox was a fan of Stevens. In a letter to Woolf comparing Stevens' poetry to Kurt Vonnegut's prose he writes, "I can't identify with [Vonnegut's] tone as I can w/Wallie's.... But there are novelists of a talent equivalent to Stevens' & Kurt he never wert."[3]

Every few years a new collection of Maddox's poetry is published for a reason. His sometimes cynical but more often romantic view of New Orleans is difficult to resist, even if one is not a fan of the man. I first met him when I tended bar at Tyler's, an Uptown jazz club. He was drunk and rifling through the dirty ashtrays searching for the largest butt he could find. In fact, I never saw him sober. In 1979, he wrote about what mattered in life, and booze was one of those things: "O.K. I think (know) now the most important things in my life are, in order: 1) love, being loved, 2) literature, and 3) booze."[4] Unfortunately, his life ended too soon. In 1989, at the age of 44, Maddox died of esophageal cancer in Charity Hospital.

Moon Fragment[5]

> A man squats by the railroad tracks tonight
> eating a moon fragment: not cheese
> at all, but a honeydew melon. His hands
> are fuzzy. A train roars past. In the
> lighted windows men and women stand
> with pewter cups raised. Tea slops out.
> Then it is dark again. Moon-eaters have
> no time for such foolishness. The silence
> is not absolute, though, because the world's
> longest accordion, the world's longest
> musical expansion bridge, is playing
> somewhere. I am up in my office
> watching the glitter of my last cigar sail
> out the window, over the shrubbery, down
> into the darkness where summer is

---

1   "Letters of Everette Maddox," 87.

2   Ibid., 79.

3   Ibid., 72-73.

4   Ibid., 92.

5   All the poems reprinted here are from Ralph Adamo, ed., *"I hope it's not over, and good-by": Selected Poems of Everette Maddox*. (New Orleans: UNO Press, 2009). Rep. by permission.

ending. I keep office hours at night so
nobody comes around to bother me. Not even
you. The moon comes around, though. I want to
drag it down and hand it to you and say, "Here,
this is lovely and useless and it cost me
a lot of trouble. You can tie it up on
the river behind your house, and go down to
look at it whenever you like." The trouble is,
you don't want it tied up, and you are
right. This is no new problem. Eight hundred
years ago a man heads home from the
Fair, pushing a wheelbarrow full of real
moon pies. For ten years he has been
stealing wheelbarrows, and nobody even
suspects. Well, what is all this? you
want to know. Right again. I could
say I don't know myself because the evidence
is not all in, never will be. I could say it's
the unfinished moon poem I've always wanted
to almost write. Well, what is it all about? you
ask. What does it mean? You have me
there. It means, whatever this is between
you and me, I hope it's not over, and good-by.

Thirteen Ways of Being Looked at by a Possum

1

I awake, three in the morning, sweating
from a dream of possums.
I put my head under the fuzzy swamp of cover.
At the foot of darkness two small eyes glitter.

2

Rain falls all day: I remain indoors.
For comfort I take down a favorite volume.
Inside, something slimy, like a tail, wraps around my finger.

3

Hear the bells clang at the fire station:
not hoses, but the damp noses of possums issue forth.

4

Passing the graveyard at night
I wish the dead would remain dead,
but there is something queer and shaggy about these mounds.

5

From the grey pouch of a cloud
the moon hangs by its tail.

6

At the cafeteria they tell me they are out of persimmons.
I am furious. Who is that grey delegation
munching yellow fruit at the long table?

7

I reach deep into my warm pocket
to scratch my balls; but I find, instead,
another pocket there; and inside, a small possum.

8

My friend's false teeth clatter in the darkness
on a glass shelf;
around them a ghostly possum forms.

9

At an art gallery the portraits seem to threaten me;
tails droop down out of the frames.

10

I screech to a stop at the red light.
Three o'clock, school's out:
eight or ten juvenile possums fill the crosswalk.

11

Midnight at Pasquale's. I lift my fork,
and the hard tails looped there
look curiously unlike spaghetti.

12

When I go to the closet to hang my shirt on the rack,
I have to persuade several possums to move over.

13

Drunk, crawling across a country road tonight,
I hear a shriek, look up, and am paralyzed
by fierce headlights and a grinning grill.
I am as good as gone!

How I Got In

For Wade

Well
I was hanging
up to my belt buckle in grief
outside the Muddy Waters
I had my dirty hands all over a
lamp post
It looked so flooded with
friends in there
that I didn't see how
I was going to gain access—
Then somebody said
"Know anybody?"
I thought & said
"I know Wade"
& they said
"Well Wade on in"
& so I lit my torch
& shook a leg
& waded on in
& had a hell of a time

Flowing on the Bench

As I was going to sleep
on the iron bench
in the back of the bar
I felt all right
I felt I was joining something
Not the Kiwanis Club
No
I felt like one river joining another
I felt like the Mississippi
flowing into the Ohio
Right where Jim & I
passed Cairo in the fog
Right where the book got good

Richard Ford (1944–)

Richard Ford resists being categorized as a regional writer and particularly bristles at being labeled a southern writer. In fact, relatively few of his works are set in the South; however, he was born there. Ford was the only child of Parker Carol and Edna Akin Ford, born in Jackson, Mississippi in 1944. He was named after his maternal grandmother's second husband, Ben Shelley, who boxed under the name "Kid Richard."[1] When Ford was born, his father worked as a salesman for the Faultless Company, still the biggest spray starch company in the country, and Jackson was the center of his territory. He and his mother would often travel with Parker Ford to nearby Arkansas, where Richard Ford's mother was born. When Ford was sixteen, his father suffered a fatal heart attack, and the following year Ford moved to Little Rock, Arkansas, to work as a fireman then switchman for the Missouri Pacific Railroad.[2]

Like so many in this collection, Ford did not initially set out to be a writer. According to biographer Elinor Ann Walker, he first aspired to become a hotel manager like his maternal grandfather who worked at the renowned Arlington Hotel in Hot Springs, Arkansas. Once he enrolled in Michigan State University in 1962, however, he switched his major and received his BA in English in 1966. He still pursued several careers before settling down to writing.

He first joined the Marines but was discharged in 1965 after a bout of hepatitis. He then taught junior high in Flint, Michigan before moving to New York to work as assistant science editor for *American Druggist.* He tried law school at Washington University in St. Louis for one semester before dropping out and moving back to Arkansas to work as a substitute teacher for a time. Not long after marrying Kristina Hensley, whom he met at Michigan State, he turned his hand to writing and enrolled in the creative writing program at the University of California, Irvine. Ford admits, "deciding to be a writer was something I did purely on instinct and whimsy…a gesture against the practical life…."[3] After receiving his MFA in 1970, Ford was elected to the University of Michigan's Society of Fellows, a program that allowed him to devote much of his time to writing, and while there he completed his first novel, *A Piece of My Heart,* which garnered less than rave reviews, but it is the last of Ford's novels to do so.

Like many novelists, Ford began as a short story writer, and he returns to that form often. In his 2003 collection, *A Multitude of Sins,* as *The Observer* critic, Tim Adams notes, he addresses only one sin, adultery, the subject of the story included here, "Calling," one of the few short stories that Ford sets in New Orleans. Like Frances Parkinson Keyes's "…And She Wore Diamond Earrings," and so many other New Orleans short stories, Ford depicts a wealthy, uptown New Orleans family perhaps longing for its former grandeur, or at best learning how to cope with its new "calling."

The story's title is packed with meaning and more than a little symbolic. The story opens with the protagonist, Boatwright McKendall, "Buck" remembering a phone call from his father, Boatwright McKendall Sr. who at the time lived in St. Louis with "his great love, Dr. Carter." After Buck's father left his mother for his male lover, his mother embarked on a singing career and moved her African American lover, William Dubinion, into the house, who was "passing himself off to the neighborhood as the yard man."

Buck's parents are both dead by the time of the story's telling, but he fondly recalls the fine figure his father cut as a young man and that of many young men in the city: "New Orleans produces men like my father…clubmen, racquets players, deft, balmy-day sailors, soft-handed Episcopalians with progressive attitudes, good educations, effortless manners, but with secrets." And here again, Ford evokes the story's title: "These men, when you meet them…seem like the very best damn old guys you could ever know. You want to call them up the very next day and set some plans going." We learn over the course of the story that this is simply the kindness of memory. When Buck's father does call to take him duck hunting, a rite of passage for any New Orleans boy who can afford it, their

---

1   For more information on Ford, and from where much of this biographical information comes, see Elinor Ann Walker, *Richard Ford* (New York: Twayne Publishers, 2000).

2   Ibid., 3.

3   Richard Ford, quoted in Don Lee, "About Richard Ford," *Ploughshares* 22, nos. 2-3 (August 1996): 227-28.

trip ends up being their last. As much as Buck looked forward to duck hunting in the "fabled Grand Lake marsh," he reluctantly agrees, as this will be their first meeting since his father ran off with Dr. Carter after a New Year's party at the Boston Club. Buck has reason to dread the trip.

His father does not arrive to pick him up in a taxi before dawn but sends a driver instead to drive him to Reggio in St. Bernard Parish, not far from his Garden District home on McKendall St. When Buck does see his father in the bow of the skiff, he is drunk, in his top coat and tuxedo from the night before with a "pink shirt, a bright red bow tie and a pink carnation....also wearing white and black spectator shoes," hardly dressed for this sport. He is accompanied by Mr. Renard Theriot, Junior, "Fabrice....a duck caller of surprising subtlety," and again, calling comes into play. The duck hunt and the relationship between the three men in the boat and in the duck blind is fraught with anxiety.

The drunk homosexual father going duck hunting in a pink tuxedo shirt, and the mother taking up with a black lover masquerading as the yard man might seem zany to readers outside of New Orleans, but these characters are not that farfetched. Ford captures some of the idiosyncrasies of the city while addressing universal conflicts. Buck is angry at both of his parents for their divorce, but he is also a teen embarrassed by them while trying to come to terms with his life as it is now. His rite of passage is made all the more difficult because his parents are breaking all boundaries established by the wealthy Garden District set into which he was born. Buck later admits, "Life had already changed. That morning represented just the first working out of particulars I would evermore observe."

After Ford's first novel was published, he received a Guggenheim and a National Endowment for the Arts fellowship, the first of a litany of awards that he would earn for his writing, culminating with the Pulitzer Prize for Fiction for his 1995 novel, *Independence Day.* His latest novel, *Canada* (2012) came out to much acclaim. Ford and his wife lived in the French Quarter and later in the Garden District, and they now have homes in Maine, Montana, and Mississippi, but will always have a connection to New Orleans.

Calling

A year after my father departed, moved to St. Louis, and left my mother and me behind in New Orleans to look after ourselves in whatever manner we could, he called on the telephone one afternoon and asked to speak to me. This was before Christmas, 1961. I was home from military school in Florida. My mother had begun her new singing career, which meant taking voice lessons at a local academy, and also letting a tall black man who was her accompanist move into our house and into her bedroom, while passing himself off to the neighborhood as the yard man. William Dubinion was his name, and together he and my mother drank far too much and filled up the ashtrays and played jazz recordings too loud and made unwelcome noise until late, which had not been how things were done when my father was there. However, it was done because he was not there, and because he had gone off to St. Louis with another man, an ophthalmologist named Francis Carter, never to come back. I think it seemed to my mother that in view of these facts it didn't matter what she did or how she lived, and that doing the worst was finally not much different from doing the best.

They're all dead now. My father. My mother. Dr. Carter. The black accompanist, Dubinion. Though occasionally I still see a man on St. Charles Avenue, in the business district, a man entering one of the new office buildings they've built—a tall, handsome, long-strided, flaxen-haired, youthful, slightly ironic-looking man in a seersucker suit, bow tie and white shoes, who will remind me of my father, or how he looked, at least, when these events occurred. He must've looked that way, in fact, all of his years, into his sixties. New Orleans produces men like my father, or once did: clubmen, racquets players, deft, balmy-day sailors, soft-handed Episcopalians with progressive attitudes, good educations, effortless manners, but with secrets. These men, when you meet them on the sidewalk or at some uptown dinner, seem like the very best damn old guys you could ever know. You want to call them up the very next day and set some plans going. It seems you always knew about them, that they were present in the city but you just hadn't seen a lot of them—a glimpse here and there. They seem exotic, and your heart expands with the thought of a long friendship's commencement and your mundane life taking a new and better turn. So you do call, and you do see them. You go spec fishing off Pointe a la Hache. You stage a dinner and meet their pretty wives. You take a long lunch together at Antoine's or Commander's and decide to do this every week from now on to never. Yet someplace along late in the lunch you hit a flat spot. A silent moment occurs, and your eyes meet in a way that could signal a deep human understanding you'd never ever have to speak about. But what you see is, suddenly—and it is sudden and fleeting—you see this man is far, far away from you, so far in fact as not even to realize it. A smile could be playing on his face. He may just have said something charming or incisive or flatteringly personal to you. But then the far, far away awareness dawns, and you know you're nothing to him and will probably never even see him again, never take the trouble. Or, if you do chance to see him, you'll cross streets midblock, cast around for exits in crowded dining rooms, sit longer than you need to in the front seat of your car to let such a man go around a corner or disappear into the very building I mentioned. You avoid him. And it is nothing unsavory not that there is anything so wrong with him, or misaligned. Nothing sexual. You just know he's not for you. And that is an end to it. It's simple really. Though of course it's more complicated when the man in question is your father.

When I came to the telephone and my father's call—my mother had answered, and they had spoken some terse words—my father began right away to talk. "Well, let's see, is it Van album, or Mickey Mantle?" These were two heroes of the time whom I had gone on and on about and alternately wanted to be when my father was still in our lives. I had already forgotten them.

"Neither one," I said. I was in the big front hall, where the telephone alcove was. I could see outside through the glass door to where William Dubinion was on his knees in the monkey grass that bordered my mother's camellias. It was a fine situation, I thought—staring at my mother's colored boyfriend while talking to my father in his far-off city, living as he did. "Oh, of course," my father said. "Those were our last year's fascinations."

"It was longer ago," I said. My mother made a noise in the next room. I breathed her cigarette smoke, heard the newspaper crackle. She was listening to everything, and I didn't want to seem friendly to my father, which I did not in any case feel. I felt he was a bastard.

"Well now, see here, ole Buck Rogers," my father continued. "I'm calling up about an important matter to the future of mankind. I'd like to know if you'd care to go duck hunting in the fabled Grand Lake marsh. With me, that is. I have to come to town in two days to settle some legal business. My ancient father had a trusted family retainer named Renard Theriot, a disreputable old *yat*. But Renard could unquestionably blow a duck call. So, I've arranged for his son, Mr. Renard, Jr., to put us both in a blind and call in several thousand ducks for our pleasure." My father cleared his throat in the stagy way he always did when he talked like this—high-falutin'. "I mean if you're not over-booked, of course," he said, and cleared his throat again.

"I might be," I said, and felt strange even to be talking to him. He occasionally called me at military school, where I had to converse with him in the orderly room. Naturally, he paid all my school bills, sent an allowance, and saw to my mother's expenses. He no doubt paid for William Dubinion's services, too, and wouldn't have cared what their true nature was. He had also conceded us the big white Greek Revival raised cottage on McKendall Street in uptown. (McKendall is our family name—*my* name. It is such a family as that.) But still it was very odd to think that your father was living with another man in a distant city, and was calling up to ask you to go duck hunting. And then to have my mother listening, sitting and smoking and reading the *States Item*, in the very next room and thinking whatever she must've been thinking. It was nearly too much for me.

And yet, I *wanted* to go duck hunting, to go by boat out into the marsh that makes up the vast, brackish tidal land south and east of our city. I had always imagined I'd go with my father when I was old enough. And I *was* old enough now, and had been taught to fire a rifle—though not a shotgun— in my school. Also, when we spoke that day, he didn't sound to me like some man who was living with another man in St. Louis. He sounded much as he always had in our normal life when I had gone to Jesuit and he had practiced law in the Hibernia Bank building, and we were a family. Something I think about my father— whose name was Boatwright McKendall and who was only forty-one years old at the time—something about him must've wanted things to be as they had been before he met his great love, Dr. Carter. Though you could also say that my father just wanted not to have it be that he couldn't do whatever he wanted; wouldn't credit that anything he did might be deemed wrong, or be the cause of hard feeling or divorce or terrible scandal such as 'what sees you expelled from the law firm your family started a hundred years ago and that bears your name; or that you conceivably caused the early death of your own mother from sheer disappointment. And in fact if anything he did had caused someone difficulty, or ruined a life, or set someone on a downward course—well, then he just largely ignored it, or agreed to pay money about it, and afterward tried his level best to go on as if the world was a smashingly great place for everyone and we could all be wonderful friends. It was the absence I mentioned before, the skill he had to not be where he exactly was, but yet to seem to be present to any but the most practiced observer. A son, for instance.

"Well, now look-it here, Mr. Buck-a-roo," my father said over the telephone from—I guessed—St. Louis. Buck is what I was called and still am, to distinguish me from him (our name is the same). And I remember becoming nervous, as if by agreeing to go with him, and to see him for the first time since he'd left from a New Year's party at the Boston Club and gone away with Dr. Carter—as if by doing these altogether natural things (going hunting) I was crossing a line, putting myself at risk. And not the risk you might think, based on low instinct, but some risk you don't know exists until you feel it in your belly, the way you'd feel running down a steep hill and at the bottom there's a deep river or a canyon, and you realize you can't stop. Disappointment was what I risked, I know now. But I wanted what I wanted and would not let such a feeling stop me.

"I want you to know," my father said, "that I've cleared all this with your mother. She thinks it's a wonderful idea."

I pictured his yellow hair, his handsome, youthful, unlined face talking animatedly into the receiver in some elegant, sunny, high-ceilinged room, beside an expensive French table with some fancy art objects on top, which he would be picking up and inspecting as he talked. In my picture he was wearing a purple smoking jacket and was happy to be doing what he was doing. "Is somebody else going?" I said.

"Oh, God no," my father said and laughed. "Like who? Francis is too refined to go duck hunting. He'd be afraid of getting his beautiful blue eyes put out. Wouldn't you, Francis?"

It shocked me to think Dr, Carter was right there in the room with him, listening. My mother, of course, was still listening to me.

"It'll just be you and me and Renard Junior," my father said, his voice going away from the receiver. I heard a second voice then, a soft, cultured voice, say something there where my father was, some possibly ironic comment about our plans. "Oh Christ," my father said in an irritated voice, a voice I didn't know any better than I knew Dr. Carter's. "Just don't say that. This is not that kind of conversation. This is Buck here." The voice said something else, and in my mind I suddenly saw Dr. Carter in a very unkind light, one I will not even describe. "Now you raise your bones at four a.m. on Thursday, Commander Rogers," my father said in his high-falutin' style. "Ducks are early risers. I'll collect you at your house.

Wear your boots and your Dr. Dentons and nothing bright-colored. I'll supply our artillery."

It seemed odd to think that my father thought of the great house where we had all lived, and that his own father and grandfather had lived in since after the Civil War, as my house. It was not my house, I felt. The most it was was my mother's house, because she had married him in it and then taken it in their hasty divorce.

"How's school, by the way," my father said distractedly.

"How's what?" I was so surprised to be asked that. My father sounded confused, as if he'd been reading something and lost his place on a page.

"School. You know? Grades? Did you get all A's? You should. You're smart. At least you have a smart mouth."

"I hate school," I said. I had liked Jesuit where I'd had friends. But my mother had made me go away to Sandhearst because of all the upset with my father's leaving. There I wore a khaki uniform with a blue stripe down the side of my pants leg, and a stiff blue doorman's hat. I felt a fool at all times.

"Oh well, who cares," my father said. "You'll get into Harvard the same way I did."

"What way," I asked, because even at fifteen I wanted to go to Harvard.

"On looks," my father said. "That's how southerners get along. That's the great intelligence. Once you know that, the rest is pretty simple. The world *wants* to operate on looks. It only uses brains if looks aren't available. Ask your mother. It's why she married me when she shouldn't have. She'll admit it now."

"I think she's sorry about it," I said. I thought about my mother listening to half our conversation.

"Oh yes. I'm sure she is, Buck. We're all a little sorry now. I'll testify to that." The other voice in the room where he was spoke something then, again in an ironic tone. "Oh you shut up," my father said. "You just shut up that talk and stay out of this. See you Thursday morning, son," my father said, and hung up before I could answer.

This conversation with my father occurred on Monday, the eighteenth of December, three days before we were supposed to go duck hunting. And for the days in between then and Thursday, my mother more or less avoided me, staying in her room upstairs with the door closed, often with William Dubinion, or going away in the car to her singing lessons with him driving and acting as her chauffeur (though she rode in the front seat). It was still the race times then, and colored people were being lynched and trampled on and burnt out all over the southern states. And yet it was just as likely to cause no uproar if a proper white woman appeared in public with a Negro man in our city. There was no rule or logic to any of it. It was New Orleans, and if you could carry it off you did. Plus Dubinion didn't mind working in the camellia beds in front of our house, just for the record. In truth, I don't think he minded anything very much. He had grown up in the cotton patch in Pointe Coupee Parish, between the rivers, had somehow made it to music school at Wilberforce in Ohio, been to Korea, and had played in the Army band. Later he barged around playing the clubs and juke joints in the city for a decade before he somehow met my mother at a society party where he was the paid entertainment, and she was putting herself into the public eye to make the case that when your husband abandons you for a rich queer, life will go on.

Mr. Dubinion never addressed a great deal to me. He had arrived in my mother's life after I had gone away to military school, and was simply a fait accompli when I came home for Thanksgiving. He was a tall, skinny, solemnly long yellow- faced Negro with sallow, moist eyes, a soft lisp and enormous, bony, pink-nailed hands he could stretch up and down a piano keyboard. I don't think my mother could have thought he was handsome, but possibly that didn't matter. He often parked himself in our living room, drinking scotch whiskey, smoking cigarettes and playing tunes he made up right on my grandfather's Steinway concert grand. He would hum under his breath and grunt and sway up and back like the jazzman

Erroll Garner. He usually looked at me only out of the corner of his yellow Oriental-looking eye, as if neither of us really belonged in such a dignified place as my family's house. He knew, I suppose, he wouldn't be there forever and was happy for a reprieve from his usual life, and to have my mother as his temporary girlfriend. He also seemed to think I would not be there much longer either, and that we had this in common.

The one thing I remember him saying to me was during the days before I went with my father to the marsh that Christmas—Dubinion's only Christmas with us, as it turned out. I came into the great shadowy living room where the piano sat beside the front window and where my mother had established a large Christmas tree with blinking lights and a gold star on top. I had a copy of *The Inferno*, which I'd decided I would read over the holidays because the next year I hoped to leave Sandhearst and be admitted to Lawrenceville, where my father had gone before Harvard. William Dubinion was again in his place at the piano, smoking and drinking. My mother had been singing "You've Changed" in her thin, pretty soprano and had left to take a rest because singing made her fatigued. When he saw the red jacket on my book he frowned and turned sideways on the bench and crossed one long thin leg over the other so his pale hairless skin showed above his black patent leather shoes. He was wearing black trousers with a white shirt, but no socks, which was his normal dress around the house.

"That's a pretty good book," he said in his soft lisping voice, and stared right at me in a way that felt accusatory.

"It's written in Italian," I said. "It's a poem about going to hell."

"So is that where you expect to go?"

"No," I said. "I don't."

"'*Per me si va nella citta dolente. Per me si va nell'eterno dolore.*' That's all I remember," he said, and he played a chord in the bass clef, a spooky, rumbling chord like the scary part in a movie.

I assumed he was making this up, though of course he wasn't "What's that supposed to mean?" I said.

"Same ole," he said, his cigarette still dangling in his mouth. "Watch your step when you take a guided tour of hell. Nothing new."

"When did you read this book?" I said, standing between the two partly closed pocket doors. This man was my mother's boyfriend, her Svengali, her impresario, her seducer and corrupter (as it turned out). He was a strange, powerful man who had seen life I would never see. And I'm sure I was both afraid of him and equally afraid he would detect it, which probably made me appear superior and insolent and made him dislike me.

Dubinion looked above the keyboard at an arrangement of red pyracanthas my mother had placed there. "Well, I could say something nasty. But I won't." He took a breath and let it out heavily. "You just go ahead on with your readin'. I'll go on with my playin'." He nodded but did not look at me again. We didn't have too many more conversations after that. My mother sent him away in the winter. Once or twice he returned but, at some point, he disappeared. Though by then her life had changed in the bad way it probably had been bound to change.

The only time I remember my mother speaking directly to me during these three days, other than to inform me dinner was ready or that she was leaving at night to go out to some booking Dubinion had arranged, which I'm sure she paid him to arrange (and paid for the chance to sing as well), was on Wednesday afternoon, when I was sitting on the back porch poring over the entrance requirement information I'd had sent from Lawrenceville. I had never seen Lawrenceville, or been to New Jersey, never been farther away from New Orleans than to Yankeetown, Florida, where my military school was located in the buildings of a former Catholic hospital for sick and crazy priests. But I thought that Lawrenceville—just the word itself—could save me from the impossible situation I deemed myself to be in. To go to Lawrenceville, to travel the many train miles, and to enter whatever strange, complex place New Jersey was—all that coupled to the fact that my father had gone there and my name and background meant something—all that seemed to offer escape and relief and a future better than the one I had at home in New Orleans.

My mother had come out onto the back porch, which was glassed in and gave a prospect down onto the back-yard grass. On the manicured lawn was an arrangement of four wooden Adirondack chairs and a wooden picnic table, all painted pink. The yard was completely walled in and no one but our neighbors could see—if they chose to—that William Dubinion was lying on top of the pink picnic table with his shirt off, smoking a cigarette and staring sternly up at the warm blue sky.

My mother stood for a while watching him. She was wearing a pair of men's white silk pajamas, and her voice was husky. I'm sure she was already taking the drugs that would eventually disrupt her reasoning. She was holding a glass of milk, which was probably not just milk but milk with gin or scotch or something in it to ease whatever she felt terrible about.

"What a splendid idea to go hunting with your father," she said sarcastically, as if we were continuing a conversation we'd been having earlier, though in fact we had said nothing about it, despite my wanting to talk about it, and despite thinking I ought to not go and hoping she wouldn't permit it. "Do you even own a gun?" she asked, though she knew I didn't. She knew what I did and didn't own. I was fifteen.

"He's going to give me one," I said.

She glanced at me where I was sitting, but her expression didn't change. "I just wonder what it's like to take up with another man of your own social standing," my mother said as she ran her hand through her hair, which was newly colored ash blond and done in a very neat bob, which had been Dubinion's idea. My mother's father had been a pharmacist on Prytania Street and had done well catering to the needs of rich families like the McKendalls. She had gone to Newcombe, married up and come to be at ease with the society my father introduced her into (though I have never thought she really cared about New Orleans society one way or the other—unlike my father, who cared about it enough to spit in its face).

"I always assume," she said, "that these escapades usually involve someone on a lower rung. A stevedore, or a towel attendant at your club." She was watching Dubinion. He must've qualified in her mind as a lower-rung personage. She and my father had been married twenty years, and at age thirty-nine she had taken Dubinion into her life to wipe out any trace of the way she had previously conducted her affairs. I realize now, as I tell this, that she and Dubinion had just been in bed together, and he was enjoying the dreamy aftermath by lying half-naked out on our picnic table while she roamed around the house in her pajamas alone and had to end up talking to me. It's sad to think that in a little more than a year, when I was just getting properly adjusted at Lawrenceville, she would be gone. Thinking of her now is like hearing the dead speak.

"But I don't hold it against your father. The *man* part anyway," my mother said. "Other things, of course, I do." She turned, then stepped over and took a seat on the striped cushion wicker chair beside mine. She set her milk down and took my hand in her cool hands, and held it in her lap against her silky leg. "What if I became a very good singer and had to go on the road and play in Chicago and New York and possibly Paris? Would that be all right? You could come and see me perform. You could wear your school uniform." She pursed her lips and looked back at the yard, where William Dubinion was laid out on the picnic table like a pharaoh.

"I wouldn't enjoy that," I said. I didn't lie to her. She was going out at night and humiliating herself and making me embarrassed and afraid. I wasn't going to say I thought this was all fine. It was a disaster and soon would be proved so.

"No?" she said. "You wouldn't come see me perform in the *Quartier Latin*?"

"No," I said. "I never would."

"Well." She let go of my hand, crossed her legs and propped her chin on her fist. "I'll have to live with that. Maybe you're right." She looked around at her glass of milk as if she'd forgotten where she'd left it.

"What other things do you hold against him?" I asked, referring to my father. The *man* part seemed enough to me.

"Oh," my mother said, "are we back to him now? Well, let's just say I hold his entire self against him. And not for my sake, certainly, but for yours. He could've kept things together here. Other men do. Its perfectly all right to have a lover of whatever category. So, he's no worse than a lot of other men. But that's what I hold against him. I hadn't really thought about it before. He fails to be any better than most men would be. That's a capital offense in marriage. You'll have to grow up some more before you understand that. But you will."

She picked up her glass of milk, rose, pulled her loose white pajamas up around her scant waist and walked back inside the house. In a while I heard a door slam, then her voice and Dubinion's, and I went back to preparing myself for Lawrenceville and saving my life. Though I think I knew what she meant. She meant my father did only what pleased him, and believed that doing so permitted others the equal freedom to do what they wanted. Only that isn't how the world works, as my mother's life and mine were living proof. Other people affect you. It's really no more complicated than that.

My father sat slumped in the bow of the empty skiff at the end of the plank dock. It was the hour before light. He was facing the silent, barely moving surface of Bayou Baptiste, beyond which (though I couldn't see it) was the vacant marshland that stretched as far as the Mississippi River itself, west of us and miles away. My father was bareheaded and seemed to be wearing a tan raincoat. I had not seen him in a year.

The place we were was called Reggio dock, and it was only a rough little boat camp from which fishermen took their charters out in the summer months, and duck hunters like us departed into the marsh by way of the bayou, and where a few shrimpers stored their big boats and nets when their season was off. I had never been to it, but I knew about it from boys at Jesuit who came here with their fathers, who leased parts of the marsh and had built wooden blinds and stayed in flimsy shacks and stilt-houses along the single-lane road down from Violet, Louisiana. It was a famous place to me in the way that hunting camps can be famously mysterious and have a danger about them, and represent the good and the unknown that so rarely combine in life.

My father had not come to get me as he'd said he would. Instead a yellow taxi with a light on top had stopped in front of our house and a driver came to the door and rang and told me that Mr. McKendall had sent him to drive me to Reggio—which was in St. Bernard Parish, and for all its wildness not really very far from the Garden District.

"And is that really you?" my father said from in the boat, turning around, after I had stood on the end of the dock for a minute waiting for him to notice me. A small stunted- looking man with a large square head and wavy black hair and wearing coveralls was hauling canvas bags full of duck decoys down to the boat. Around the camp there was activity. Cars were arriving out of the darkness, their taillights brightening. Men's voices were heard laughing. Someone had brought a dog that barked. And it was not cold, in spite of being the week before Christmas. The morning air felt heavy and velvety, and a light fog had risen off the bayou, which smelled as if oil or gasoline had been let into it. The mist clung to my hands and face, and made my hair under my cap feel soiled. "I'm sorry about the taxi ride," my father said from the bow of the aluminum skiff. He was smiling in an exaggerated way. His teeth were very white, though he looked thin. His pale, fine hair was cut shorter and seemed yellower than I remembered it, and had a wider part on the side. It was odd, but I remember thinking—standing looking down at my father—that if he'd had an older brother, this would be what that brother would look like. Not good. Not happy or wholesome. And of course I realized he was drinking, even at that hour. The man in the coveralls brought down three shotgun cases and laid them in the boat. "This little yat rascal is Mr. Reynard Theriot, Junior," my father said, motioning at the small, wavy-haired man. "There're some people, in New Orleans, who know him as Fabriee, or the Fox. Or Fabree-chay. Take your pick."

I didn't know what all this meant. But Renard Junior paused after setting the guns in the boat and looked at my father in an unfriendly way. He had a heavy, nicked brow, and even in the poor light his dark complexion made his eyes seem small and penetrating. Under his coveralls he was wearing a red shin with tiny gold stars on it.

"Fabree-chay is a duck caller of surprising subtlety," my father said too loudly. "Among, that is to say, his other talents. Isn't that right, Mr. Fabrice? Did you say hello to my son, Buck, who's a very fine boy?" My father flashed his big white-toothed smile around at me, and I could tell he was taunting Renard Junior, who did not speak to me but continued his job to load the boat. I wondered how much he knew about my father, and what he thought if he knew everything.

"I couldn't locate my proper hunting attire," my father said, and looked down at the open front of his topcoat. He pulled it apart, and I could see he was wearing a tuxedo with a pink shirt, a bright-red bow tie and a pink carnation. He was also wearing white-and-black spectator shoes which were wrong for the Christmas season and in any case would be ruined once we were in the marsh. "I had them stored in the garage at mother's," he said, as if talking to himself. "This morning quite early I found I'd lost the key." He looked at me, still smiling. "You have on very good brown things," he said. I had just worn my khaki pants and shirt from school— minus the brass insignias—and black tennis shoes and an old canvas jacket and cap I found in a closet. This was not exactly duck hunting in the way I'd heard about from my school friends. My father had not even been to bed, and had been up drinking and having a good time. Probably he would've preferred staying wherever he'd been, with people who were his friends now.

"What important books have you been reading?" my father asked for some reason, from down in the skiff. He looked around as a boat full of hunters and the big black Labrador dog I'd heard barking motored slowly past us down Bayou Baptiste. Their guide had a sealed-beam light he was shining out on the water's misted surface. They were going to shoot ducks. Though I couldn't see where, since beyond the opposite bank of the bayou was only a flat black treeless expanse that ended in darkness. I couldn't tell where ducks might be, or which way the city lay, or even which way east was.

"I'm reading *The Inferno*," I said, and felt self-conscious for saying "Inferno" on a boat dock.

"Oh, that," my father said. "I believe that's Mr. Fabrice's favorite book. Canto Five: those who've lost the power of restraint. I think you should read Yeats's autobiography, though. I've been reading it in St. Louis. Yeats says in a letter to his friend the great John Synge that we should unite stoicism, asceticism and ecstasy. I think that would be good, don't you?" My father seemed to be assured and challenging, as if he expected me to know what he meant by these things, and who Yeats was, and Synge. But I didn't know. And I didn't care to pretend I did to a drunk wearing a tuxedo and a pink carnation, sitting in a duck boat.

"I don't know them. I don't know what those things are," I said and felt terrible to have to admit it.

"They're the perfect balance for life. All I've been able to arrange are two, however. Maybe one and a half. And how's your mother?" My father began buttoning his overcoat.

"She's fine," I lied.

"I understand she's taken on new household help." He didn't look up, just kept fiddling with his buttons.

"She's learning to sing," I said, leaving Dubinion out of it.

"Oh well," my father said, getting the last button done and brushing off the front of his coat. "She always had a nice little voice. A sweet church voice." He looked up at me and smiled as if he knew I didn't like what he was saying and didn't care.

"She's gotten much better now." I thought about going home right then, though of course there was no way to get home.

"I'm sure she has. Now get us going here, Fabree-chay," my father said suddenly.

Renard was behind me on the dock. Other boats full of hunters had already departed. I could see their lights flicking this way and that over the water, heading away from where we were still tied up, the soft putt-putts of their outboards muffled by the mist. I stepped down into the boat and sat on the middle thwart. But when Renard scooted into the stern, the boat tilted dramatically to one side just as my father was taking a long, uninterrupted drink out of a pint bottle he'd had stationed between his feet, out of sight.

"Don't go Ellin' in, baby," Renard said to my father from the rear of the boat as he was giving the motor cord a strong pull. He had a deep, mellow voice, tinged with sarcasm. "I don't think nobody'll pull ya'll out."

My father, I think, didn't hear him. But I heard him. And I thought he was certainly right.

I cannot tell you how we went in Renard Junior's boat that morning, only that it was out into the dark marshy terrain that is the Grand Lake and is in Plaquemines Parish and seems the very end of the earth. Later, when the sun rose and the mist was extinguished, what I saw was a great surface of gray-brown water broken by low, yellow-grass islands where it smelled like tar and vegetation decomposing, and where the mud was blue-black and adhesive and rank-smelling. Though on the horizon, illuminated by the morning light, were the visible buildings of the city—the Hibernia Bank where my father's office had been—nudged just above the earth's curve. It was strange to feel so outside of civilization, and yet to see it so clearly.

Of course at the beginning it was dark. Renard Junior, being small, could stand up in the rear of the skimming boat, and shine his own light over me in the middle and my father hunched in the boat's bow. My father's blond hair shone brightly and stayed back off his face in the breeze. We went for a ways down the bayou, then turned and went slowly under a wooden bridge and then out along a wide canal bordered by swamp hummocks where white herons were roosting and the first ducks of those we hoped to shoot went swimming away from the boat out of the light, suddenly springing up into the shadows and disappearing. My father pointed at these startled ducks, made a gun out of his fingers and jerked one-two-three silent shots as the skiff hurtled along through the marsh.

Naturally, I was thrilled to be there—even in my hated military school clothes, with my drunk father dressed in his tuxedo and the little monkey that Renard was, operating our boat. I believed, though, that this had to be some version of what the real thing felt like—hunting ducks with your father and a guide—and that anytime you went, even under the most perfect circumstances, there would always be something imperfect that would leave you feeling not exactly good. The trick was to get used to that feeling, or risk missing what little happiness there really was.

At a certain point when we were buzzing along the dark slick surface of the lake, Renard Junior abruptly backed off on the motor, cut his beam light, turned the motor hard left, and let the wake carry us straight into an island of marsh grass I hadn't made out. Though I immediately saw it wasn't simply an island but was also a grass-fronted blind built of wood palings driven into the mud, with peach crates lined up inside where hunters would sit and not be seen by flying ducks. As the boat nosed into the grass bank, Renard, now in a pair of hip waders, was out heeling us farther up onto the solider mud. "It's duck heaven out here," my father said, then densely coughed, his young man's smooth face becoming stymied by a gasp, so that he had to shake his head and turn away.

"He means it's the place where ducks go to heaven," Renard said. It was the first thing he'd said to me, and I noticed now how much his voice didn't sound much like the yat voices I'd heard and that supposedly sound like citizens of New York or Boston—cities of the North. Renard's voice was cultivated and mellow and inflected, I thought, like some uptown funeral director's, or a florist. It seemed to be a voice better suited to a different body than the muscular, gnarly little man up to his thighs just then in filmy, strong-smelling water, and wearing a long wavy white-trash hairstyle.

"When do the ducks come?" I said, only to have something to say back to him. My father was recovering himself, spitting in the water and taking another drink off his bottle.

Renard laughed a little private laugh he must've thought my father would hear. "When they ready to come. Just like you and me," he said, then began dragging out the big canvas decoy sacks and seemed to quit noticing me entirely.

* * *

Renard had a wooden pirogue hidden back in the thick grass, and when he had covered our skiff with a blanket made of straw mats, he used the pirogue to set out decoys as the sky lightened, though where we were was still dark. My father and I sat side by side on the peach boxes and watched him tossing out the weighted duck bodies to make two groups in front of our blind with a space of open water in between. I could begin to see now that what I'd imagined the marsh to look like was different from how it was. For one thing, the expanse of water around us was smaller than I had thought. Other grass islands gradually came into view a quarter mile off, and a line of green trees appeared in the distance, closer than I'd expected. I heard a siren, and then music that must've come from a car at the Reggio dock, and eventually there was the sun, a white disk burning behind the mist, and from a part of the marsh opposite from where I expected it. In truth, though, all of these things—these confusing and disorienting and reversing features of where I was—seemed good, since they made me feel placed, so that in time I forgot the ways I was feeling about the day and about life and about my future, none of which had seemed so good.

Inside the blind, which was only ten feet long and four feet wide and had spent shells and candy wrappers and cigarette butts on the planks, my father displayed the pint bottle of whiskey, which was three-quarters empty. He sat for a time, once we were arranged on our crates, and said nothing to me or to Renard when he had finished distributing the decoys and had climbed into the blind to await the ducks. Something seemed to have come over my father, a great fatigue or ill feeling or a preoccupying thought that removed him from the moment and from what we were supposed to be doing there. Renard unsheathed the guns from their cases. Mine was the old A. H. Fox twenty-gauge double gun, that was heavy as lead and that I had seen in my grandmother's house many times and had handled enough to know the particulars of without ever shooting it. My grandmother had called it her "ladies gun," and she had shot it when she was young and had gone hunting with my father's father. Renard gave me six cartridges, and I loaded the chambers and kept the gun muzzle pointed up from between my knees as we watched the silver sky and waited for the ducks to try our decoys.

My father did not load up, but sat slumped against the wooden laths, with his shotgun leaned on the matted front of the blind. After a while of sitting and watching the sky and seeing only a pair of ducks operating far out of range, we heard the other hunters on the marsh begin to take their shots, sometimes several at a terrible burst. I could then see that two other blinds were across the pond we were set down on—three hundred yards from us, but visible when my eyes adjusted to the light and the distinguishing irregularities of the horizon. A single duck I'd watched fly across the sky, at first flared when the other hunters shot, but then abruptly collapsed and fell straight down, and I heard a dog bark and a man's voice, high-pitched and laughing through the soft air. "Hoo, boo, hoo, lawd oooh lawdy," the man's voice said very distinctly in spite of the distance. "Dat mutha-scootcha was all the way to Terre Bonne Parish when I popped him." Another man laughed. It all seemed very close to us, even though we hadn't shot and were merely scanning the milky sides.

"Coon-ass bastards," my father said. "Jumpin' the shooting time. They have to do that. It's genetic." He seemed to be addressing no one, just sitting leaned against the blind's sides, waiting.

"Already been shootin' time," Renard Junior said, his gaze fixed upwards. He was wearing two wooden duck calls looped to his neck on leather thongs. He had yet to blow one of the calls, but I wanted him to, wanted to see a V of ducks turn and veer and come into our decoy-set, the way I felt they were supposed to.

"Now is that so, Mr. Grease-Fabrice, Mr. Fabree-chay" My father wiped the back of his hand across his nose and up into his blond hair, then closed his eyes and opened them wide, as if he was trying to fasten his attention to what we were doing, but did not find it easy. The blind smelled sour but also smelled of his whiskey, and of whatever ointment Renard Junior used on his thick hair. My father had already gotten his black-and-white shoes muddy and scratched, and mud on his tuxedo pants and his pink shirt and even onto his forehead. He was an unusual-looking figure to be where he was. He seemed to have been dropped out of an airplane on the way to a party.

Renard Junior did not answer back to my father calling him "Grease-Fabrice," but it was clear he couldn't have liked a name like that. I wondered why he would even be here to be talked to that way. Though of course there was a reason. Few things in the world are actually mysterious. Most things have disappointing explanations somewhere behind them, no matter how strange they seem at first.

After a while, Renard produced a package of cigarettes, put one in his mouth, but did not light it—just held it between his damp lips, which were big and sensuous. He was already an odd-looking man, with his star shirt, his head too big for his body—a man who was probably in his forties and had just missed being a dwarf.

"Now there's the true sign of the *yat*," my father said. He was leaning on his shotgun, concentrating on Renard Junior. "Notice the unlit cigarette poached out the front of the too expressive mouth. If you drive the streets of Chalmette, Louisiana, sonny, you'll see men and women and children who're all actually blood-related to Mr. Fabrice, standing in their little postage-stamp yards wearing hip boots with unlighted Picayunes in their mouths just like you see now. *Ecce Homo*."

Renard Junior unexpectedly opened his mouth with his cigarette somehow stuck to the top of his big ugly purple tongue. He cast an eye at my father, leaning forward against his shotgun, smirking, then flicked the cigarette backward into his mouth and swallowed it without changing his expression. Then he looked at me, sitting between him and my father, and smiled. His teeth were big and brown-stained. It was a lewd act. I didn't know how it was lewd, but I was sure that it was.

"Pay no attention to him," my father said. "These are people we have to deal with. French acts, carny types, brutes. Now I want you to tell me about yourself, Buck. Are there any impossible situations you find yourself in these days? I've become expert in impossible situations lately." My father shifted his spectator shoes on the muddy floor boards, so that suddenly his shotgun, which was a beautiful Beretta over- under with silver inlays, slipped and fell right across my feet with a loud clatter—the barrels ending up pointed right at Renard Junior's ankles. My father did not even try to grab the gun as it fell.

"Pick that up right now," he said to me in an angry voice, as if I'd dropped his gun. But I did. I picked the gun up and handed it back to him, and he pinned it to the side of the blind with his knee. Something about this almost violent act of putting his gun where he wanted it reminded me of my father before a year ago. He had always been a man for abrupt moves and changes of attitude, unexpected laughter and strong emotion. I had not always liked it, but I'd decided that was what men did and accepted it.

"Do you ever hope to travel?" my father said, ignoring his other question, looking up at the sky as if he'd just realized he was in a duck blind and for a second at least was involved in the things we were doing. His topcoat had sagged open again, and his tuxedo front was visible, smudged with mud. "You should," he said before I could answer.

Renard Junior began to blow on his duck call then, and crouched forward in front of his peach crate. And because he did, I crouched in front of mine, and my father—noticing us—squatted on his knees too and averted his face downwards. And after a few moments of Renard calling, I peered over the top of the straw wall and could see two black- colored ducks flying right in front of OUT blind, low and over our decoys. Renard Junior changed his calling sound to a broken-up cackle, and when he did the ducks swerved to the side and began winging hard away from us, almost as if they could fly backwards.

"You let 'em see you," Renard said in a hoarse whisper. "They seen that white face."

Crouched beside him, I could smell his breath—a smell of cigarettes and sour meat that must've tasted terrible in his mouth.

"Call, goddamn it, Fabrice," my father said then— shouted, really. I twisted around to see him, and he was right up on his two feet, his gun to his shoulder, his topcoat lying on the floor so that he was just in his tuxedo. I looked out at our decoys and saw four small ducks just cupping their wings and gliding toward the water where Renard had left it open. Their wings made a pinging sound.

Renard Junior immediately started his cackle call again, still crouched, his face down, in front of his peach crate. "Shoot 'em, Buck, shoot 'em," my father shouted, and I stood up and got my heavy gun to my shoulder and, without meaning to, fired both barrels, pulled both triggers at once, just as my father (who at some moment had loaded his gun) also fired one then the other of his barrels at the ducks, which had briefly touched the water but were already heading off, climbing up and up as the others had, going backwards away from us, their necks outstretched, their eyes—or so it seemed to me who had never shot at a duck—wide and frightened.

My two barrels, fired together, had hit one of Renard's decoys and shattered it to several pieces. My father's two shots had hit, it seemed, nothing at all, though one of the gray paper wads drifted back toward the water while the four ducks grew small in the distance until they were shot at by the other hunters across the pond and two of them dropped. "That was completely terrible," my father said, standing at the end of the blind in his tuxedo, his blond hair slicked close down on his head in a way to make him resemble a child. He instantly broke his gun open and replaced the spent shells with new ones out of his tuxedo-coat pocket. He seemed no longer drunk, but completely engaged and sharp-minded, except for having missed everything.

"Y'all shot like a coupla 'ole grandmas," Renard said, disgusted, shaking his head.

"Fuck you," my father said calmly, and snapped his beautiful Italian gun shut in a menacing way. His blue eyes widened, then narrowed, and I believed he might point his gun at Renard Junior. White spit had collected in the corners of his mouth, and his face had gone quickly from looking engaged to looking pale and damp and outraged. "If I need your services for other than calling, I'll speak to your owner," he said.

"Speak to yo' own owner, snooky," Renard Junior said, and when he said this he looked at me, raised his eyebrows and smiled in a way that pushed his heavy lips forward in a cruel, simian way.

"That's *enough*," my father said loudly. "That is absolutely enough." I thought he might reach past me and strike Renard in the mouth he was smiling through. But he didn't. He just slumped back on his peach crate, faced forward and held his newly reloaded shotgun between his knees. His white-and-black shoes were on top of his overcoat and ruined. His little pink carnation lay smudged in the greasy mud.

I could hear my father's hard breathing. Something had happened that wasn't good, but I didn't know what. Something had risen up in him, some force of sudden rebellion, but it had been defeated before it could come out and act. Or so it seemed to me. Silent events, of course, always occur between our urges and our actions. But I didn't know what event had occurred, only that one had, and I could feel it. My father seemed tired now, and to be considering something. Renard Junior was no longer calling ducks, but was just sitting at his end staring at the misty sky, which was turning a dense, warm luminous red at the horizon, as if a fare was burning at the far edge of the marsh. Shooting in the other blinds had stopped. A small plane inched across the sky. I heard a dog bark. I saw a fish roll in the water in front of the blind. I thought I saw an alligator. Mosquitoes appeared, which is never unusual in Louisiana.

"What do you do in St. Louis," I said to my father. It was the thing I wanted to know.

"Well," my father said thoughtfully. He sniffed, "Golf. I play quite a bit of golf. Francis has a big house across from a wonderful park. I've taken it up." He felt his forehead, where a mosquito had landed on a black mud stain that was there. He rubbed it and looked at his fingertips.

"Will you practice law up there?"

"Oh lord no," he said and shook his head and sniffed again. "They requested me to leave the firm here. You know that."

"Yes," I said. His breathing was easier. His face seemed calm. He looked handsome and youthful. Whatever silent event that had occurred had passed off of him, and he seemed settled about it. I thought I might talk about going to Lawrenceville. Duck blinds were where people had such conversations. Though it would've been better, I thought, if we'd been alone, and didn't have Renard Junior to overhear us. "I'd like to ask you…" I began.

"Tell me about your girlfriend situation," my father interrupted me. "Tell me the whole story there."

I knew what he meant by that, but there wasn't a story. I was in military school, and there were only other boys present, which was not a story to me. If I went to Lawrenceville, I knew there could be a story. Girls would be nearby. "There isn't any story…" I started to say, and he interrupted me again.

"Let me give you some advice." He was rubbing his index finger around the muzzle of his Italian shotgun. "Always try to imagine how you're going to feel *after* you fuck somebody *before* you fuck somebody. *Comprendes*? There's the key to everything. History. Morality. Philosophy. You'll save yourself a lot of misery." He nodded as if this wisdom had just become clear to him all over again. "Maybe you already know that," he said. He looked above the front of the blind where the sky had turned to fire, then looked at me in a way to seem honest and to say (so I thought)that he liked me. "Do you ever find yourself saying things in conversations that you absolutely don't believe?" He reached with his two fingers and plucked a mosquito off my cheek. "Do you?" he said distractedly. "Do ya, do ya?"

I thought of conversations I'd had with Dubinion, and some I'd had with my mother. They were that kind of conversation—memorable if only for the things I didn't say. But what I said to my father was "no."

"Convenience must not matter to you much then," he said in a friendly way.

"I don't know if it does or not," I said because I didn't know what convenience meant. It was a word I'd never had a cause to use.

"Well, convenience matters to me very much. Too much, I think," my father said. I, of course, thought of my mother's assessment of him—that he was not better than most men. I assumed that caring too much for convenience led you there, and that my fault in later life could turn out to be the same one because he was my father. But I decided, at that moment, to see to it that my fault in life would not be his.

"There's one ducky duck," my father said. He was watching the sky and seemed bemused. "Fabrice, would you let me apologize for acting ugly to you, and ask you to call? How generous that would be of you. How nice." My father smiled strangely at Renard Junior, who I'd believed to be brooding.

And Renard Junior did call. I didn't see a duck, but when my father squatted down on the dirty planking where his topcoat was smeared and our empty shell casings were littered, I did too, and turned my face toward the floor. I could hear my father's breathing, could smell the whiskey on his breath, could see his pale wet knuckles supporting him unsteadily on the boards, could even smell his hair, which was warm and musty smelling. It was as close as I would come to him. And I understood that it would have to do, might even be the best there could be.

"Wait now, wait on 'im," my father said, hunkered on the wet planks, but looking up out of the tops of his eyes. He put his fingers on my hand to make me be still. I still had not seen anything. Renard Junior was blowing the long, high-pitched rasping call, followed by short bursts that made him grunt heavily down in his throat, and then the long highball call again. "Not quite yet," my father whispered. "Not yet. Wait on him." I turned my face sideways to see up, my eyes cut to the side to find *something*. "No," my father said, close to my ear. "Don't look up." I inhaled deeply and breathed in all the smells again that came off my father. And then Renard Junior said loudly, "Go on, Jesus! Go on! Shoot 'im. Shoot now. Whatchyouwaitin on?"

I just stood up, then, without knowing what I would see, and brought my shotgun up to my shoulder before I really looked. And what I saw, coming low over the decoys, its head turning to the side and peering down at the brown water, was one lone duck. I could distinguish its green head and dark bullet eyes in the haze-burnt morning light and could hear its wings pinging. I didn't think it saw me or heard my father and Renard Junior shouting, "Shoot, shoot, oh Jesus, shoot 'im Buck." Because when my face and gun barrel appeared above the front of the blind, it didn't change its course or begin the backward-upward maneuvering I'd already seen, which was its way to save itself. It just kept looking down and flying slowly and making its noise in the reddened air above the water and all of us.

And as I found the duck over my barrel tops, my eyes opened wide in the manner I knew was the way you shot such a gun, and yet I thought: it's only one duck. There may not be any others. What's the good of one duck shot down? In my dreams there'd been hundreds of ducks, and my father and I shot them so that they fell out of the sky like rain, and how many there were would not have mattered because we were doing it together. But I was doing this alone, and one duck seemed wrong, and to matter in a way a hundred ducks wouldn't have, at least if I was going to be the one to shoot. So that what I did was not shoot and lowered my gun.

"What's wrong?" my father said from the floor just below me, still on all fours in his wrecked tuxedo, his face turned down expecting a gun's report. The lone duck was past us now and out of range.

I looked at Renard Junior, who was seated on his peach crate, small enough not to need to hunker. He looked at me, and made a strange face, a face I'd never seen but will never forget. He smiled and began to bat his eyelids in fast succession, and then he raised his two hands, palms up to the level of his eyes, as if he expected something to fall down into them. I don't know what that gesture meant, though I have thought of it often—sometimes in the middle of a night when my sleep is disturbed. Derision, I think; or possibly it meant he merely didn't know why I hadn't shot the duck and was awaiting my answer. Or possibly it was something else, some sign whose significance I would never know. Fabrice was a strange man. No one would've doubted it.

My father had gotten up onto his muddy feet by then, although with difficulty. He had his shotgun to his shoulder, and he shot once at the duck that was then only a speck in the sky. And of course it did not fall. He stared for a time with his gun to his shoulder until the speck of wings disappeared.

"What the hell happened?" he said, his face red from kneeling and bending. "Why didn't you shoot that duck?" His mouth was opened into a frown. I could see his white teeth, and one hand was gripping the sides of the blind. He seemed in jeopardy of falling down. He was, after all, still drunk. His blond hair shone in the misty light.

"I wasn't close enough," I said.

My father looked around again at the decoys as if they could prove something. "Wasn't close enough?" he said. "I heard the damn duck's wings. How close do you need it? You've got a gun there."

"You couldn't hear it," I said.

"Couldn't hear it?" he said. His eyes rose off my face and found Renard Junior behind me. His mouth took on an odd expression. The scowl left his features, and he suddenly looked amused, the damp corners of his mouth revealing a small, flickering smile I was sure was derision, and represented his view that I had balked at a crucial moment, made a mistake, and therefore didn't have to be treated so seriously. This from a man who had left my mother and me to fend for ourselves while he disported without dignity or shame out of sight of those who knew him.

"You don't know anything," I suddenly said. "You're only…" And I don't know what I was about to say. Something terrible and hurtful. Something to strike out at him and that I would've regretted forever. So I didn't say any more, didn't finish it. Though I did that for myself, I think now, and not for him, and in order that I not have to regret more than I already regretted. I didn't really care what happened to him, to be truthful. Didn't and don't.

And then my father said, the insinuating smile still on his handsome lips, "Come on, sonny boy. You've still got some growing up to do, I see." He reached for me and put his hand behind my neck, which was rigid in anger and loathing. And without seeming to notice, he pulled me to him and kissed me on my forehead, and put his arms around me and held me until whatever he was thinking had passed and it was time for us to go back to the dock.

My father lived thirty years after that morning in December, on the Grand Lake, in 1961. By any accounting he lived a whole life after that. And I am not interested in the whys and why nots of what he did and didn't do, or in causing that day to seem life-changing for me, because it surely wasn't. Life had already changed. That morning represented just the first working out of particulars I would evermore observe. Like my father, I am a lawyer. And the law is a calling which teaches you that most of life is about adjustments, the seatings and reseatings we perform to accommodate events occurring outside our control and over which we might not have sought control in the first place. So that when we are tempted, as I was for an instant in the duck blind, or as I was through all those thirty years, to let myself become preoccupied and angry with my father, or when I even see a man who reminds me of him, stepping into some building in a seersucker suit and a bright bow tie, I try to realize again that it is best just to offer myself release and to realize I am feeling anger all alone, and that there is no redress. We want it. Life can be seen to be about almost nothing else sometimes than our wish for redress. As a lawyer who was the son of a lawyer and the grandson of another, I know this. And I also know not to expect it.

For the record—because I never saw him again—my father went back to St. Louis and back to the influence of Dr. Carter, who I believe was as strong a character as my father was weak. They lived on there for a time until (I was told) Dr. Carter quit the practice of medicine entirely. Then they left America and traveled first to Paris and after that to a bright white stucco house near Antibes, which I in fact once saw, completely by accident, on a side tow of a business trip, and somehow knew to be his abode the instant I came to it, as though I had dreamed it—but then couldn't get away from it fast enough, though they were both dead and buried by then.

Once, in our newspaper, early in the nineteen-seventies, I saw my father pictured in the society section amid a group of smiling, handsome crew-cut men, once again wearing tuxedos and red sashes of some foolish kind, and holding champagne glasses. They were men in their fifties, all of whom seemed, by their smiles, to want very badly to be younger.

Seeing this picture reminded me that in the days after my father had taken me to the marsh, and events had ended not altogether happily, I had prayed for one of the few times, but also for the last time, in my life. And I prayed quite fervently for a while and in spite of all, that he would come back to us and that our life would begin to be as it had been. And then I prayed that he would die, and die in a way I would never know about, and his memory would cease to be a memory, and all would be erased. My mother died a rather sudden, pointless and unhappy death not long afterward, and many people including myself attributed her death to him. In time, my father came and went in and out of New Orleans, just as if neither of us had ever known each other.

And so the memory was not erased. Yet because I can tell this now, I believe that I have gone beyond it, and on to a life better than one might've imagined for me. Of course, I think of life—mine—as being part of their aftermath, part of the residue of all they risked and squandered and ignored. Such a sense of life's connectedness can certainly occur, and conceivably it occurs in some places more than in others. But it is survivable. I am the proof, inasmuch as since that time, I have never imagined my life in any way other than as it is.

Andrei Codrescu (1946–)

The title of the first poem included here, "my name is andrei codrescu," is ironic in that the poet was not born Andrei Codrescu, but Andrei Perlmutter in Sibiu, Romania, in 1946. Andrei Codrescu, however, was not the first pen name he chose, or was forced to choose in anti-Semitic, post-war Romania. He wrote his first poems in Romanian under the name Andrei Steiu, a name he selected from "the most outrageously sincere rustic words from the anti-Semitic vocabulary."[1] It ends up that in cursive his nom-de-plume read more like Stein than Stieu, and he was not interested in trading one Jewish name for another. He writes: "it wasn't until I found 'Codrescu' that I hit the deepest chord of nationalist gore...."[2] He later discusses how he came to be Codrescu in a podcast interview at the United States Holocaust Museum's 2009 *Voices on Anti-Semitism, Podcast Series:*

> When I left Romania, I sent back some poems to a literary journal in Romania and I signed it out
> of a whim "Codrescu," which is a very Romanian name, which means "son of woods" or "wood-
> son," anyway something very not-Jewish. I wasn't aware at the time that I was committing an act
> of unconscious antisemitism, because the name Codrescu is very close to the name Codreanu,
> which is almost the same name. Codreanu is the name of the founder of the Iron Guard, the famous
> antisemitic murderous Iron Guard of Romania. And so in a funny way, weirdly enough and
> unconsciously, I was naming myself after a Jew-hater.[3]

Typical of Codrescu, this is the third or fourth version I have found explaining the origin of his pen name. He has told this story and others of his life repeatedly over his long and prolific writing career, but like his poetry, he can create the story he wants to tell his readers. In his essays, fiction, poetry, we see him alternately as impish, angry, humorous, genius, political, sexy, at times even sentimental, but he remains one of the most important voices of the late 20th and early 21st centuries, and much of that time he spent in New Orleans.

In *Bibliodeath*, Codrescu claims that a single line in one of his poems, "the red cow has ceased giving milk," set in motion his emigration to the United States from Communist Romania in 1965. He and his mother first went to a refugee camp in Rome, Italy, then to Detroit in 1966, where his former high school math teacher "sponsored" their immigration. Once in Detroit, he met poet and activist John Sinclair before moving to New York City where he met Allen Ginsberg, Anne Waldman, and Ted Berrigan and also published his first poetry in English. Until then he had written in Romanian and even Italian, but in 1970 his first book, *License to Carry a Gun,* won the Big Table Award. That same year he moved to San Francisco and after several years on the west coast, he landed a teaching gig at Johns Hopkins in Baltimore and finally at LSU in Baton Rouge, where he began writing poetry about both that city and New Orleans.

He opens "my name is andrei codrescu," talking about his first book of poems, *License to Carry a Gun,* which was written in "1968... the year when guns took down/ Martin Luther King and Robert Kennedy". He goes on to talk about the political role guns play in American society and the role they have played over the years in his own life, finally ending with his son telling him, "You made enough art/ out of guns already./ Let this one pass." We see him move from a low point in this nation's history to a touching yet humorous personal moment in his life as poet and father, a sort of leap that he accomplishes seamlessly in his poetry and one that also reminds us that gun violence is not some remote problem; it's personal.

"our gang" is a day in the life—rather a night in the life—of the post-poetry reading French Quarter scene. He moves from sex to Freud, or rather the current sentiment that Freud is no longer relevant, to missile deployment in Cyprus, snorting heroin, writing a "corpse," a type of communal poem, to too many topics to list here, almost

---

1   This and most of the biographical information included here is from Andrei Codrescu, *Bibliodeath: My Archives (with life in footnotes)*, (antibookclub, 2012).

2   Codrescu, *Bibliodeath,* 11.

3   Andrei Codrescu, Interview, *Voices on Anti-Semitism, Podcast Series*, 2009. United States Holocaust Memorial Museum, 2013, May 22, 2013, Web.

http://www.ushmm.org/museum/exhibit/focus/antisemitism/voices/transcript/?content=20090827 all of them political and again moving into the personal when discussing his conversation with Laura, his wife. Throughout the poem he examines the public and political role of the poet and poetry, which culminates in him and his friends taking up a collection for a stripper who just quit her job after a customer said to her, "'I want to lick your ass!'" He so often reminds us not to take ourselves too seriously.

He again, very humorously but seriously, broaches the subject of art for profit in his poem, "new orleans art for wall street" by opening the poem telling the reader about his epic hangover; he is "the most hungover man in the world". Ironically, he even promotes his "phenomenal new book," his novel, *Wakefield*, and goes on to say that "Wall Streeters consume/ no poems," while ending the poem with the line "Pay up first". He recognizes that art is commodified, but artists should be paid for their work.

Codrescu is a two-time Pushcart Prize winner and in 1995, he won the Peabody for the film *Road Scholar*. He has published essays in *Harper's, New York Times, Chicago Tribune* and too many other publications to mention here. His column, *Penny Post* was a weekly feature in the New Orleans *Gambit*, and he was a regular contributor to NPR's *All Things Considered* for over two decades. After retiring from LSU in 2009, he and his wife Laura Cole moved to Arkansas near the Buffalo River some fifteen miles from the nearest store. And although he is no longer teaching and no longer a regular contributor to NPR, he has not stopped writing, and his latest book, *Bibliodeath: My Archives (with life in footnotes)*, is innovative, smart, funny, and as pertinent as all his books.

my name is andrei codrescu[1]

My first book of poetry was called *License to Carry a Gun*.
It was written in 1968.
1968 was the year when guns took down
Martin Luther King and Robert Kennedy.
The title of my book meant that in a crazy time
one had to be crazier
and that meant not just having a gun
but BEING a gun.
Later that year at a poetry reading
a group of us "shot" some boring poets
with fake guns while shouting
"Death to Bourgeois Poetry!"
and after the poetry reading
I was busted by two plainclothes policemen
who said I had just robbed a store
with my fake gun
and later that year
I got held up at gunpoint.
And later yet
in August of 1996
Jonathan Ferrara handed me a twisted machine-pistol
at a poetry reading
(there were only a few boring bourgeois poets there)
and told me to make art out of it

---

1   All three of the poems reprinted here are copyright © 2003 by Andrei Codrescu. From: Andrei Codrescu, *it was today* (Minneapolis: Coffee House Press, 2003). Rep. by permission.

and I gave the gun to my son to hold
without telling him that I was supposed to make
art out of it
and he put it in his backpack
and later yet
he dropped it in a garbage can
on his way home.
This is why there is no gun here
only a poem.
And when I said to my son: shit,
what and I gonna do with no gun?
he said: You made enough art
out of guns already.
Let this one pass.

our gang

Is it nice
to throw out the window
a man in whose house
you had sex
& in whom you once
invested a sentimental bundle?
was the question I asked when Leigh
wearing a black angora sweater
proudly announced that she had
just lectured to Oschner doctors
on the subject of self-
mutilation from a post-
modern perspective
& in the process she had
thrown "Freud out the window"
to make room I suppose
for Lacan and Saussure
& I thought this most un-
grateful, nay, a form of self-
mutilation given the place
Freud once held in her heart
& in her husband Richard's
fiction
& then Ricard & Gwen & I had
an animated discussion about
formality & informality
European & American
& what public & private means

in history & in the consuming
classes created by advertising
& we concluded as we always do
that New Orleans where masking
is both serious & ironic is as usual
the best place & Gwen said something about self-discipline & I'm
not sure what she meant
because I think that just wearing
clothes takes a lot of self-
discipline as Jeffrey once
said much better
& then Anthony the Cypriot prince
who now lives in Boston
spoke to me about a vast non-
profit corporation dedicated
to world peace of which he was
the president & I congratulated
him on Cyprus' refusal to deploy
long-range missiles
& on behalf of Cyprus Anthony
thanked me sincerely
& then Daniel tripped by & whispered
in my ear: "And now
for something different!"
so I followed him into the men's room
where he proceeded to take out a tiny
tinfoil packet inside of which lay
a fine powder he proclaimed to be
heroin & he warned me & himself
of its dangers before plunging
the tip of his penknife in the powder
& holding it under my nose for me
to partake which I did
& when I returned the poets were
passing around the second corpse
of the night, this one on a theme
I suggested, namely, What Useful Things
Might Poets Do If They Were Not
Poets? and Dave & Vincent & Gwen
& Bill & Richard & Leigh & Daniel
& some others applied themselves
to the topic not at all but produced
nonetheless a gorgeous corpse full
of sexual & mystical imagery just

like the first one which I'd read out
loud nary an hour before
& then Michelle showed up
& announced that she had quit
the stripshow business & henceforth
she would no longer disrobe
for the plebes & when we pressed
her on the reason she said:
A man not really bad looking
nor particularly drunk said to me
"I want to lick your ass!"
& this is why you quit we asked
in amazement, the same
thought having occurred to us many
times & I said, "Maybe you should
have a talk with your ass! It's eating
you out of house & home!"
"Literally," burst Michelle, "I have
no money for rent & I have no job!"
& so a collection was taken on
the spot & Anthony the Cypriot
prince & I drew our ATM cards & got
enough cash to pay $250 out of $275
Michelle's rent & I said I hoped that
she wouldn't go to great lengths
for the remainging $25 but I think
that she might have because at the very
decent hour of one A.M. I left them all
in the bar while I went home to call
Laura who was pissed off at me like
always when I stay out past nine
& that was another night at Molly's
& another $200 out the window
like Freud & many other things
happened, like the pretty boy Michelle
knew who said he was working on
inventing a seven-breasted
seven-wingèd woman & I said
When you're done, give me her phone
number! and he said solemnly, OK.

new orleans art for wall street

I was the most hungover man in the world
when I first attempted to make this work

in praise of New Orleans
for the consumption of Wall Street
I was to put it mildly hungover
but by no means either the most hungover now
or the most hungover in the past
in fact one cannot compare the hangovers of today
with the epic hangovers of yesterday
that in their splendid massiveness rivaled
all the hangovers of the ancient world
from Babylon to Sodom
given such hangovers it's a wonder
a true wonder that this city rose from the swamp
and held up under tropical storms
only less violent than the guts of the lyric citizens
I humbly admit to having but a midget hangover
compared to those colossi
and when I say that I attempted to make a work
I mean only that I thought of making a work
without actually putting pen to paper until later
which is now
and when I say in praise of New Orleans
I must qualify that praise with the deep wariness
of one who has praised before & felt quite insincere
on account of it & suffered guilt
which is a form of hangover
therefore I have resolved never to praise
except accidentally when carried away by emotions
too great to deconstruct
for instance this thing last Mardi Gras
with the dancer and the nurse and Laura
and the gnostics & the brand-new manuscript
of my phenomenal new book with all the feathers
floating around and the whole street on X dancing
in front of Café Brasil
I hate crowds if you must know
but that was praiseworthy so here it is
And when I say that I wrote this
for the consumption of Wall Street
I am fully aware that Wall Streeters consume
no poems no matter how titillating or praiseworthy
and that this whole exercise is art
which is to say something you'll forget
as soon as I say so & I say so
Pay up first

Valerie Martin (1948–)

Author Valerie Martin was born in Sedalia, Missouri, in 1948. At the age of three, her family moved to her mother's hometown, New Orleans, where she grew up and which she still considers her hometown. Martin lived in the Lakeview section of the city and recalls spending much time in the Robert E. Smith branch library reading New Orleans history, which still fascinates her today. She enjoyed reading historical accounts of voodoo, pirates, and slavery which, along with her school fieldtrips to the French Quarter, brought the city to life for her as a young girl.

After graduating from Mt. Carmel high school in New Orleans, Martin began her college career at the University of New Orleans (UNO), then housed in a former U.S. Navy base on the shores of Lake Pontchartrain. There she began reading the works that would inspire her for years to come. She cites Flaubert's *Madame Bovary* as "the most important influence" on her writing, but also mentions French writer Albert Camus and naturalist writer Stephen Crane.[1] She began writing at this time as well.

After receiving her BA from UNO in 1970, Martin moved to Amherst, Massachusetts, where she received her MFA degree in creative writing in 1974. She then returned to New Orleans and began working at the Louisiana State Welfare Office. She also published her first novel, *Set in Motion,* in 1978. The book, set firmly in the often mysterious New Orleans cityscape, features the protagonist, Helene, who works at the State Welfare Office in New Orleans and whose own life becomes as desperate and tenuous as those of the poor welfare recipients she assists in her dreary office.

This novel was followed by two others, *Alexandra* (1979), and *A Recent Martyr* (1987), and her most commercially successful novel, *Mary Reilly,* appeared three years later, in 1990. The ingenious premise of this novel is certainly one of the reasons for its popularity. It is a retelling of Robert Louis Stevenson's 1886 novella *Strange Case of Dr. Jekyll and Mr. Hyde* from the point of view of Dr. Jekyll's maidservant, *Mary Reilly.* In 1996, Columbia TriStar Pictures released the film *Mary Reilly,* based on Martin's novel and directed by Stephen Frears, starring John Malkovich as Dr. Jekyll/Mr. Hyde and Julia Roberts as Mary Reilly. Unfortunately, the film did not do well at the box office, and both Roberts and Frears were nominated for *Razzies* that year. Before the movie came out, Martin had published her fifth novel, *The Great Divorce,* in 1993.

Having a movie based on her novel was certainly financially advantageous for Martin, who up until this time had taught writing at various colleges and universities throughout the nation, including UNO, University of Alabama, University of New Mexico Las Cruces, Mt. Holyoke, UMASS Amherst, and Sarah Lawrence. From 1994 to 1997, Martin lived in Italy, which was the setting for her next two books, the novel *Italian Fever* (1999) and the nonfiction *Salvation: Scenes from the Life of St. Francis* (2001). Her next novel, *Property,* set in 19th-century Louisiana, was the winner of the Britain's prestigious *Orange Prize* in 2003, and since then Martin has published two more novels, *Trespass* (2007) and *The Confessions of Edward Day* (2009). She has also written three collections of short stories, and the first story included here, "The Freeze," is from her second short story collection, *The Consolation of Nature* (1988).

In that collection Martin emphasizes the importance of the relationship between humans and animals. Martin often uses animals in her fiction, and when asked about it in a 2010 interview, she states that we have a "weird relationship [with animals] because we're all animals, yet we can't communicate with them and they can't really communicate with us....it's the sort of intimacy with animals that I'm fascinated by."[2] In "The Freeze," Anne, a single mother on the verge of middle age, has returned from a party where she was spurned by a much younger prospective lover. Later that night while trying to sleep, she hears this nagging *"clink, clink, clink"* which she finds difficult to ignore, but she is finally successful. Upon awakening, she notices the sound had stopped. However, hours later, when she walks out the back door toward the laundry room, she sees the frozen dead cat whose head was stuck in an empty salmon can she had tossed some days earlier, forcing her to think of her own

---

1   "Biography," Valerie Martin, accessed 10 June 2010, http://valeriemartinonline.com/biography/.

2   Valerie Martin, interview with the author, June 2010.

proximity to death.

Animals still figure prominently in Martin's fiction, and she is currently working on a series of short stories set in 19th-century Cajun Louisiana, about transformations, or more specifically, people transforming into animals. She currently lives in Upstate New York, and after a twenty-year absence, she once again teaches at Mt. Holyoke College but returns to New Orleans as often as possible. In 2010, she received the Louisiana Writer of the Year award.

The Freeze[1]

That night, as Anne was dressing in the bathroom, she took a long dreamy look at herself in the mirror. She had finished her make-up. This was the look she always gave herself, critical yet sympathetic; it was intended as a look at the make-up. She was forty years old, twice divorced, a woman who, half a century ago, would have been a statistical failure. But she didn't feel, really, as if she had failed at anything. She looked as good as she ever had. She was strong and healthy and she supported herself and her daughter all alone. She liked being alone, for the most part; she especially liked waking up alone, and she had no intention of changing this, yet she was so pleased by her own reflection in the mirror, it was as if she thought someone else saw her, as if someone were in love with her. And yes, she told herself, pulling the blue silk dress carefully over her head, perhaps someone was in love with her and perhaps she would find out about it tonight.

These were not the vague fancies of middle age. She had a lover in mind and there was a good chance that he would be at this party. But it was absurd, she told herself, joking with herself, because it would have been absurd to anyone else. He was nearly twenty years younger than she. Aaron, she thought, invoking his presence with his name. A rich, charming college student who could certainly find better things to do with his time than make love to a woman twice his age.

She had seen him five times. First, at a friend's, the same friend who was giving this party. He had come in with Jack, the son of the house, a bright, ugly boy who reminded Anne of her high school students. They passed through the kitchen; they were going to play tennis, but Jack paused long enough to introduce his new friend, Aaron Fischer. Anne's first impression of him was indifferent. He was clearly Jewish, his curly hair was blond, his complexion was clear and a little flushed. He looked intelligent. Anne was accustomed to searching for signs of intelligence in the young; it was her profession. He met her eyes as he shook her hand, a firm, self-assured handshake, with a look to match it. She didn't think he really saw her. Jack exchanged a few words with his mother and they went out, but as he turned away from her, Aaron nodded curtly and said, "Peace." They were gone.

"He's an interesting boy," her friend observed.

"I haven't heard anyone say 'Peace' since 1962," Anne replied.

"I hear he has principles too." The two women raised their eyebrows at each other.

"He must be some kind of throwback," Anne concluded.

She saw him again, a week later, as she was coming out of the university library. To her surprise he recognized her. "Anne," he said. "What are you doing here?"

She stammered. She had learned that Yukio Mishima had written a play about the wife of the Marquis de Sade, and, not finding it at the local bookstore, she had come to the library on purpose to read it. It had proved amusing and entirely unshocking, but the title alone was not something she thought this young man would appreciate. "I was just doing a little research," she said. "I'm a teacher, you know."

---

1   From: Valerie Martin, *The Consolation of Nature and Other Stories* (New York: Vintage, 1989), 107-28. Rep. by permission.

"You teach here?" He looked surprised, impressed.

"No. I teach at the arts high school."

"Oh," he said, "I've heard of that." Now, she thought, they would part. But he was interested and appeared to have nothing more important to do than stand on the library stairs chatting with a stranger. After a few more exchanges he suggested coffee, which, he said, was what he was out for, and she agreed.

They went to the bright, noisy university cafeteria, had three cups of coffee each, then proceeded to the dark cavernous university tavern, where they shared a pitcher of beer. Aaron talked with such ease and his range of interests was so wide that Anne, who had expected nervous chatter about his classes, found herself completely charmed. He was idealistic, almost militant in his adherence to a code, though precisely what code Anne couldn't make out. He was a political science major, this was his last year, and then he was going to medical school. By the time they parted, when Anne explained that she must pick up her daughter, who was visiting a friend, Aaron had her phone number scribbled in his small leather notebook. He promised to call. The med school applications were voluminous; he had not, in his expensive education, been taught to use a typewriter; and Anne had offered, had insisted on helping him.

Then followed two long evenings in her living room. The applications were more tedious and time-consuming than she had imagined. Aaron exclaimed over the stupidity of the personal questions. Anne moaned every time she saw the printed grid that meant she had to retype his entire undergraduate transcript. The first night, they finished off a bottle of red wine and when they were done, sat talking comfortably for another hour before Aaron noted the time and hurried off, apologizing for having stayed so late and for having drunk all of her wine.

The next night he arrived with a bottle of champagne. They shared it sparingly as they worked over his applications, and at the end of a few pleasant hours, half of them were ready to be mailed. Aaron was thorough; he was applying to sixty schools.

She was charmed by him, by his youth, by his confidences, by his manner, which was so preternaturally social that she couldn't be sure how much of the pleasure he appeared to take in her company was simply the pleasure he took in any company. He lounged on her couch and looked about her apartment with an appreciative eye, and when he observed that it was time to go (he had a chemistry test at eight in the morning and he hadn't opened a book yet), he added that he did not want to go.

Was he asking to stay?

Anne was cautious. She discussed the matter with her friend, who assured her that it did sound as if the boy was more than superficially interested. And he was a delightful boy; in only a few years he would be, they agreed, a remarkable man. He might be shy; he might fear, as she did, that the attraction he felt for her was something he should not explore. He might think she thought of him as a child and be uncertain or unable to make the first move. Anne might have to make this move, whatever it was, herself. She should be careful. The timing in such matters was extremely delicate; on this the two women were in complete agreement. Anne would see him one more time, to finish the applications, but she might have to wait longer.

Their last meeting was a short one. He had everything completed; it was a matter of a few minutes' typing. He was in a hurry and he complained bitterly of the cause for it. "I have a date," he said. "This ugly girl called me and now I have to go to this stupid party. Why can't I say no? Why didn't I say no?"

"Perhaps she'll be intelligent," Anne suggested.

"No, she won't. She isn't. She's in my eco class and she's failing."

"Do girls call you a lot?" she inquired, pulling the last page out of the typewriter to indicate that the question didn't really interest her.

"Only ugly girls." He gave her a perplexed frown, designed to make her smile.

In a few minutes he was gone.

For two weeks Anne agitated herself with various fantasies. She lay in her bed at night, clutching her pillow, telling herself how it would be, how it would surely be. Their lovemaking would be dizzying; in fact, the first time would be such a relief for them both that they would collapse into each other's arms with the breathless passion of some long-frustrated, star-crossed Victorians. Then afterward she would laugh and tell him how hard it had been, because of their age difference and because they were so many worlds apart, to admit to herself that she was in love with him. For she was in love, she thought with a growing sense of wonder. Was it possible? She was in love as she had not been since she was a girl, only this was harder to bear and more intense, because she knew exactly what it was she wanted. And it wasn't a home, a family, his money, a ride in his Porsche. She would be content if they never left her apartment and she knew none of his friends. She only wanted him to make love to her; that was all.

And now she stood, dressed, perfumed, made up, before her bathroom mirror, and she assured herself that it would be tonight. He would be there as he had promised her friend, and he would be there just for her. She would look different, so elegant that he would be taken by surprise. The dress was perfect; her dark hair, swept back and up in a fashion he had not seen, gleamed with health and life. He would see at a glance that she was perfect for him.

She stepped into her shoes, threw her reflection a last affectionate look, turned out the overhead light, and went into the hall. Hannah stood in the doorway of her daughter's room. "Anne," she said, "you look so nice. What a beautiful dress."

Anne blushed at the admiration she saw in the girl's eyes. "Do you like it?" she said, turning before her.

"It's lovely," the girl said.

Anne's heart swelled with pleasure. As they walked together to the living room it struck her that she was extraordinarily lucky. She wrote her friend's phone number on the phone pad and promised Hannah that she would call if she went anywhere else.

"Don't worry about it," Hannah replied. "Nell's already asleep."

As she walked to the car Anne looked back and saw Hannah standing on the porch. She was waving with one hand as she pulled the screen in tightly with the other. "Good night," Anne called out impetuously, but the girl didn't hear her. She got into her car, fishing in her purse for the keys.

The party was halfway across town. Anne concentrated on driving and on sitting a little stiffly so that she wouldn't wrinkle her dress. When she arrived her friend greeted her at the door. "He's here," she said. "You look terrific."

"Is he alone?" Anne asked.

"Yes. He's in the back, by the bar. I'll take you there."

"That's a good sign, don't you think?" Anne asked. They "passed through the bright rooms filled with glittering crystal, hothouse flowers, silver trays of food, and chatting groups of people., "Your house looks great," she added.

"That he's by the bar?" her friend inquired.

"No, that he's alone," Anne replied.

"Of course it's a good sign." They had come to the last room and as Anne stepped inside she saw Aaron leaning against the far wall. He was talking to an elderly man and he did not see her. "It's a very good sign," her friend agreed. "Get yourself a drink."

Yes, Anne thought. A drink would help. Her knees were decidedly weak. She felt like some wolf waiting for a choice lamb to separate from the fold, and the idea of herself as hungry, as looking hungry to others in the room, struck her with enough force to make her lower her eyes. She told the bartender what she wanted in a voice she scarcely recognized, it was so oily, so sly, the voice of the inveterate predator. When she took the drink he caught her eye and smiled. "This is a party," he said.

"I beg your pardon?" she asked.

"It's a party," he repeated. "You're supposed to be having a good time."

Then she understood him and was annoyed by him. "I just got here," she said, turning away. "Give me a minute."

Aaron was looking at her, had been looking at her, she understood, for some moments, and now he detached himself from the elderly man and made his way toward her. She thought he would say something about her appearance, in which she still had some confidence, and she drew herself up a little to receive a compliment, but when he was near enough to speak, he said, "Christ, that's my chemistry teacher. I didn't expect to find *him* here."

"Did you think he spent his evenings over a hot test tube?" she asked lightly.

He smiled, and his smile was so ingenuous, so charming, that she moved closer to him as if to move into the warm influence of that smile. "I did," he said. "And he might as well, for all he's got to say."

So their conversation began and they continued it for some time. Anne introduced him to some of the people she knew, and several times he went to the bar to refresh their drinks. He seemed content to be near her, to be with her, in fact, and she felt all her nervousness and foreboding melt away. The rooms filled with more and more people, until one had fairly to raise one's voice to be heard. A few couples drifted out onto the patio; it was unseasonably warm and the night air was inviting. Anne and Aaron stood in the doorway, looking out for a few minutes. "Let's go out," Aaron said. "The smoke in here is getting to me."

Anne followed him down the steps of the house and out into the darkness. As she did she watched him and endured such a seizure of desire that her vision clouded. She was not, she realized, drunk; though she could scarcely see, her head was clear. She passed one hand before her eyes and gripped the stair rail tightly with the other, not to steady herself but to hold down a surge of energy. I feel like dynamite, she thought; that was her secret thought behind her hand, and then she looked out. What a sweet thing it was to be alive at that moment, with all the eager force of life throbbing through her, the sensation of being stunning with the force of it so that if anyone looked at her they must stop and admire her beauty, which was only the fleeting surrender of pure energy that sometimes falls to us, without any effort of our own.

But no one saw her and the moment passed. The patio was deep; one side was a high vine-covered wall, along which ran a ledge. People sat in little groups along the ledge and on the scattered iron chairs, and they stood about in groups among the plantains and the palmetto palms, talking. Anne discovered as she passed among them, about the weather. The weatherman had predicted a cold front, a drop in temperature of 30 degrees, with rain and wind by midnight. And here it was, eleven-thirty and 65 degrees. The sky was clear, black, and fathomless overhead.

She followed Aaron, who didn't look back until he had reached the far end of the patio. When he turned she came up to him slowly. "Is this far enough, do you think?" she asked, teasing.

"No," he said. "But there's a wall here."

She stood near him and they looked back at the house. It was so brightly lit that it seemed to be ablaze, and the noise of voices and music poured out the windows and doors like a liquid. Anne detected a melody she knew. "Oh, I like that record," she said.

"Who is that?" Aaron listened, then smiled. "Oh, that's Gato Barbieri. Do you like him?"

"I like that record," she said dreamily, for the music, even at this distance, was languorous and exotic. "It's pretty romantic though."

She met his eyes but he looked away. He had his hand on a branch of a crepe myrtle tree and his arm was so raised that Anne stood in the shadow of it. "I'm going to have to leave soon," he said, shaking the ice in his glass. "As soon as I finish this drink."

"I'm a little tired too," Anne lied.

Then he didn't move, nor did he speak. She stood looking down into her drink. She could feel his eyes on her hair and on her shoulders and she thought that he would touch her, but he didn't. She looked back toward the house, taking in the whole patio of people, none of whom, she saw, was looking in their direction. Say something, she told herself, but she couldn't think of anything. Aaron lifted his drink and sipped it; she heard the clinking sound of the ice, but she didn't look at him. The music was growing more emotional; it exacerbated her desire. She put her drink down at her feet and turned so that she faced the young man, so that she was very close to him, but she didn't meet his eyes because, she thought later, she didn't think it was necessary. Instead she placed her hands lightly on his shoulders and raised up on her toes, for he was several inches taller than she. She had barely touched his lips with her own when he pulled away. "No," he said. "No, thank you."

She dropped back on her heels.

"I'm really flattered," he said. "I really am."

She shook her head, hoping that this moment would pass quickly, that she could shake it away, but time seemed to seep out slowly in all directions like blood from a wound.

"Now I've hurt your feelings," he said.

She looked at the wall past his shoulder, at the bricks between her own feet. She could not look at him, but she moved out of his path. "Please go," she said and he agreed. Yes, he would go. He apologized again; he had no wish to hurt her feelings; he was really so flattered.... She cast him a quick look, enough to be sure that he was as uncomfortable as she. "It's all right," she said. "I'm all right. But please leave now."

"Yes," he replied. "I'll go." And he walked away. She didn't watch him cross the patio. She waited for what seemed a long time, without looking at anything or thinking of anything, as if she were stone. Then she was aware of being cold. The temperature had plummeted in a few minutes, and the other people on the patio were moving indoors, looking about, as they went in, at the trees and the empty air, as if they could see the difference they felt. Anne followed them, but no one spoke to her. Inside, her friend caught her by the arm and pulled her into the kitchen. "What happened?" she asked. "Aaron just left in a hurry. Are you meeting him somewhere?"

Anne smiled; she could feel the bitter tension of her own smile. "I made a pass at him and he turned me down." "He did what?" Her friend was outraged.

"He said, 'No, thank you.'"

"That little prick!"

"I've never made a mistake like this." Anne paused, then added, "I was so sure of myself."

"God, what a jerk. Don't think about it."

Anne was suddenly very tired. "No," she said, "I won't." "Stay a while," her friend urged. "Stay till everyone is gone. Then we can talk."

"I want to go home," Anne replied. "I want to drink some hot milk and wear my flannel pajamas and socks to bed."

"It's so cold," her friend agreed.

By the time she got to her car the temperature had dropped another five degrees. The wind whipped the tree tops and riffled the foliage. Overhead the sky took on a sheen, as if it had received a coat of wax. Anne was oblivious of everything save her own humiliation, which she did not ponder. Rather, she held it close to her and wrapped her senses around it. It was a trick she knew for postponing tears, a kind of physical brooding that kept the consciousness of pain at bay. She steered the car mindlessly around corners, waited at lights, turned up the long entrance to the expressway. There was hardly any traffic; she could drive as rapidly as she liked; but she only accelerated to forty-five. She looked down upon the quiet, sleepy city as she passed over it, and it seemed to her mysterious, like a sleeping animal, breathing quietly beneath her. This must be what death is like, she thought. Coming into some place alien yet familiar.

That was stupid; that was the way people hoped it would be. But what would it be like? She asked herself this question as personally as she could, speaking to herself, who, after all, would miss her more than anyone. What, she asked, will your death be like?

Death was, perhaps, far away, but at that moment, because of her solitude, it seemed that he drew incautiously near, and she imagined his arms closing about her like a lover's. She shrugged. He was so promiscuous. Who could be flattered by such affection when, sooner or later, he would open his arms to all? Yet, she thought, it must be quite thrilling, really, to know oneself at last held in his cold, hollow eyes. Who else can love as death loves; who craves as death craves?

At home she found Hannah awake, surprised at being relieved so early.

"It's getting ugly out there," Anne told her. "You'd better go while you still can." She stood on the porch and watched the girl safely to her car. Now, she thought. Now, let's see how I am.

She closed the porch door and sat down on the couch, flicking off the lamp and plunging the room into welcome darkness. Tears rose to her eyes, but they didn't overflow. Only her vision was blurred and a pleasant numbness welled up, so that she didn't care even to rub the tears away.

Surely this was not important, she thought. It was not an important event. Not worth considering. He was too young; that was all. She had misread him. It wasn't serious. He was flattered, he had said, and that word pricked her. If only he had not said that.

She covered her face with her hands and moaned. Never had she felt such shame; never had she been so thoroughly humiliated. The clear, distinct, precise memory of the failed kiss developed like a strip of film in her memory —his stiffening and drawing away, her own inability to comprehend it so that she had left her hands on his shoulders for many moments when it should have been clear to her that she should release him. He had so immediately withdrawn his lips from her own that she had found her mouth pressed briefly against the corner of his mouth, then his cheek, then thin air. She had staggered away, she knew now, though she had not known it then, staggered to the tree, which had the courtesy to remain solid and hold her up. There she had remained, devoid of feeling, while he beat his retreat, but now the bitterness came flooding in, and it was so pure and thick that she could scarcely swallow.

Ah, she hated him. He had known all along; he had teased her and smiled at her, confided his sophomoric fears and absurd ambitions to her, laughed at her weak jokes, observed her growing affection for him, encouraged her at every turn, all so that he might say "No, thank you," and leave her standing alone, blinded by the shame of having wanted him.

"Well, I wouldn't have him now," she said aloud, "if he paid me." She laughed; it wasn't true. I suppose, she thought, I should be grateful. This sort of thing was bound to happen. Now it's over and I won't ever make the same mistake again.

But she sat for a while, brooding, resigning herself to having played a major part in a dreary business. She was so tired that even the mild activity of preparing for bed seemed more bother than it was worth. But it would shock her daughter to find her asleep on the couch in her dress, and she would be ashamed of herself, more ashamed than she was already. At last, she roused herself.

The wind lashed the house with the same bitter fury she had quelled in her heart, and it suited her, as she walked through the dark rooms, to hear it rattling the doors and windows, blasting bits of branches and leaves against the glass so that they seemed held there by a magical power. She could see through the bamboo shades in her bedroom, and after changing into pajamas she sat for a few moments watching the big plantain tree straining against the force of the wind, its wide leaves plastered helplessly open along the spines like broken hands. The room was getting colder by the minute. She pulled on her warmest socks and, thrusting her legs under the covers, lay down wearily, feeling, as her cheek touched the pillow, a welcome sensation of relief and release. She threw her arms about her pillow and wept into it, amused through her tears at the comfort it gave her. Then she wept her way into sleep.

The sound woke her gradually. She was aware of it, in a state between sleep and consciousness, before she opened her eyes. It was a repeated sound. Her first thought was that it was coming from the wall.

Clink. Clink, clink.

She reached out and touched the wall, then turned and pressed her ear against it.

Clink. Clink, clink.

It wasn't in the wall.

She looked out into the darkness of her room. She could hear many sounds. It was raining, and she could hear the water rushing along the house gutters, pouring out over the porch where the gutters were weak. The wind was still fierce, and it whistled around the house, tearing at the awning (that was the dull flapping sound) and straining the ropes that held it in place. But above all these sounds there was the other sound, the one she couldn't place.

Clink. Clink, clink.

A metallic sound, metal against wood or concrete.

Yes, she thought, it's on the patio. The sound was irregular, but so continuous that it disturbed her. She got up and looked out the window, but all she could see was the plantain tree and the child's swimming pool, which was overflowing with icy water. The weatherman had predicted a freeze, and she did not doubt him now. In the morning the plantains would be tattered and in a day or two the long leaves would be thoroughly brown.

Clink. Clink, clink.

Perhaps a dog had gotten into the yard. Maybe it was the gate. She went into Nell's room and looked out the window. The gate was bolted; she could see it from that window. The rest of the yard looked cold but empty. There was a small corner, the edge of the concrete slab, that she couldn't see from any window.

Clink. Clink, clink.

She diverted herself by contemplating her sleeping daughter. Nell lay on her back with her arms spread wide. Her long hair was sleep-tousled and her mouth was slightly open. She breathed shallowly. Anne arranged the blanket over her, kissed her cool forehead. My darling, she thought, touched by the sweetness of her daughter's innocent sleep. My beautiful girl.

Clink. Clink, clink, clink.

She might go out and see what it was. But it was so cold, so wet; the wind blew against the back door, and as soon as she opened it she would be soaked.

The sound stopped.

It was nothing. Some trash caught in a bush, blown free now.

She looked at the clock as she went back to bed. It was 3:00 A.M. She curled down under the blankets and pulled her pillow down next to her. It was a bad habit, she thought, clutching this pillow like the mate she didn't have. She thought of Aaron.

Clink. Clink, clink.

It was nothing, she thought. Some trash caught in a bush. She would throw it away in the morning. Now it was important not to think, not about the sound and not about the party, or her foolish infatuation, or the engaging smile of a young man who cared nothing for her. These things didn't bear thinking upon. It didn't matter, she told herself, and she knew why it didn't matter, but somehow, as she lay in the darkness, her consciousness drifting into the less palpable darkness of sleep, she couldn't remember why it didn't matter. Exactly why.

Clink. Clink, clink.

She woke up several times that night. Each time she heard the sound, but she would not listen to it. Later she was to recall that, though it was a small, innocuous sound, there had been in it something so disturbing that she shuddered each time she woke and realized that, whatever it was, it was still going on.

Eventually she woke and it was morning. Her daughter stood next to the bed, looking down at her anxiously. "It's too early," Anne complained.

"It's cold in my room. Can I get in bed with you?"

Anne pushed back against the wall and motioned the child in under the blankets.

Clink, clink.

Nell put her arms about her mother's neck. "It's warm in here," she said, curling down gratefully.

"Go to sleep," Anne replied. They fell asleep.

An hour later, when Anne woke and understood that she was awake for the day, she found herself straining to hear the sound. It had stopped. She didn't think of it again, not while she made pancakes for Nell, nor when she browsed leisurely through the morning paper, nor when she stood amidst a week's worth of laundry, sorting the colors and textures for the machine. She collected a pile of clothes in her arms and balanced the soap box on top. Opening the back door to get to the laundry room was always a problem. She worked one hand free beneath the clothes and turned the knob. The door was opened but it had cost her two socks and an undershirt, which lay in the doorway at her feet. Bending down to get them would only mean losing more. Leaving the door open would let the heat out. She bent her knees, reaching down without bending over, like an airline stewardess in bad weather. She retrieved the strayed garments, but the soap powder took the opportunity to fall open, and a thin stream of white fell where the socks had been. "Shit," she said, stepping out onto the patio. In that moment she saw the dead cat.

His body lay in the corner of the patio. In her first glance she knew so much about him, so much about his death, that she closed her eyes as if she could close out what she knew. He lay on his side, his legs stretched out unnaturally. His fur was wet and covered with bits of leaves and dirt. She couldn't see his face, for it was hidden by a tin can, a one-pound salmon can. Anne remembered having thrown it away a few days earlier. The can completely covered the animal's face, up to his ears, and even from a distance she could see that it was wedged on tightly.

"Oh, Jesus," she said. "Oh, Christ."

Anne put the laundry in the washing machine and went back to the yard for a close look. She crouched over the dead animal, pulling her sweater in tightly against the cold. He was a large cat; his fur was white with patches of gray and black. Anne recognized him as one of several neighborhood cats. Someone might feed him regularly and might look for him; she had no way of knowing. The can over his face made him look ludicrous. It would have been funny had she not listened for so many hours to his struggles to free himself. If I'd gone out, she thought, I could have pulled it off. Now she had to deal with the corpse.

When she went inside she found Nell stretched out on her bed with her favorite comic books arranged all about her. "There's a dead cat in the yard," Anne said

The child looked up. "There is?"

"He got his face stuck in a salmon can."

Nell sat up and strained to look out the window.

"You can't see him from here. He's in the corner. I don't think you want to see him."

"I want to see him," she said, getting out of bed. "Where is he? Come show me."

"Put your robe on, put your slippers on," Anne said. "It's freezing out there."

Nell pulled on her slippers, hurriedly wrapped herself in her robe, and went to the door, Anne followed her disconsolately. They went out and stood side by side, looking down at the dead cat.

"What a way to go," Anne remarked.

Nell was quiet a moment; then she said in a voice filled with pity, "Mama, can't you take that can off his face?"

Anne hesitated. She was not anxious to see the expression such a death might leave on its victim's face. But she understood the justice of the request. She grasped the can, thinking it would fall away easily, but instead she found she had lifted the animal's head and shoulders from the concrete. The stiffness that was communicated to her fingertips shocked her; it was like lifting a board, and she laid the can back down gingerly. "It's stuck," she said. "It won't come off."

They stood quietly a few moments more. "Should we bury him?" Nell asked.

"No. Dogs would come and dig him up."

"What can we do then?"

"I'll call the city. They have a special number. They'll come pick him up."

"The city?" the child said.

"Well, the Sanitation Department."

They went inside. "That's like the garbage men,' the child observed. "You're not going to put him in the garbage can?"

"No. I'll put him in a plastic bag."

Nell considered this. "That will be good," she said. "Then some baby won't come along and see him and be upset."

Later Anne called the Sanitation Department. The man she spoke with was courteous. "Just get it to the curb," he said, "and have someone pick it up. But he won't be there till this afternoon." He paused, consulting a schedule, Anne imagined. "He won't be there until after three."

Anne appreciated the man's precision, and, as it was still drizzling, she left the cat where he was until afternoon. Nell would be off visiting her father. Anne wanted to spare her the sight of the impersonal bagging of the creature, though she had noticed with some satisfaction that the child was neither squeamish nor overimaginative when it came to death. She understood it already as in the nature of things.

At noon the rain stopped and the sun appeared, but it was still bitterly cold and windy. Anne drove her daughter to her ex-husband's and stayed to fill in the parts of the dead cat story that the child neglected. It was hard not to make a joke of the absurdity of the accident. Even Nell saw the humor of it when her father observed that the salmon can would be a new object for dread and suicide threats.

"I can't take it anymore," Anne suggested. "I'm going to get the salmon can."

They laughed over it and then she went home. She didn't take off her coat and stopped only in the kitchen to pick up a plastic trash bag. She proceeded directly to the patio. Now when she opened the door there was no shock in the sight. She went straight to the body as if it had beckoned her.

She knelt down beside the cat. The pavement nearby was dry— the sun had taken care of that —but the corpse was outlined by a ring of moisture like a shadow. She slipped the bag over the animal's back feet and carefully, without touching him, pulled it up to his hips. But there it stuck, and she knew that she would have to lift him to get him into the bag.

She had a sensation of repugnance mixed with confidence. It wouldn't be pleasant, but she didn't doubt that she could do it. Five years ago she would have called on a man to do it and stayed in the house until the corpse was gone, but now there was no one to call and, she thought, no need to call anyone, for she could certainly put this dead body in a bag and transfer it to the curb. She was different now and better now. As a young woman she had been in constant fear, but that fear was gone. It was true that her loneliness was hard to bear; it made her foolish and because of it she imagined that rich, idle young men might be in love with her. It was time to face it, she told herself. Her own youth was gone; it was permanently, irretrievably gone. But it was worth that confession to be rid of the fear that had been, for her, the byproduct of dependence. She shrugged against the dreariness of this revelation and bent her will to the task before her.

She touched the cat's side, brushing away some bits of wood that were stuck there. Beneath the wet, soft, dead fur was a wall of flesh as hard as stone. This unpromising rigidity was the cruelest of death's jokes on the living. She imagined that rough treatment might snap the corpse in half, like a thin tube of glass. She lifted the back a little and pulled the bag up to the animal's middle. As she did this she became aware of her own voice in the cold air, addressing the dead cat. "Well, my friend," she was saying, "I wish I'd known; I could have saved you this."

He was a pathetic sight, with his stiff, wet limbs, half in a plastic bag, the red and black label with a great surging silver fish across it all that distinguished his head. It was sad, she thought, such a silly, useless death, though he was certainly not the first creature ever to lose his life in an effort to avoid starvation. She touched his hard, cold side at the place where she thought his heart might be; she patted him softly there. "Poor cat," she said. "While I was tossing around in there worrying about my little heartbreak, you were out here with this."

And she thought of the wall of her bedroom and how she had fretted on one side of it while death stalked on the other side. Tomorrow his prey might be something big; it might be a man or a child. That night it had just been a cat, But he had stalked all the same and waited and watched. It had taken the cat hours to die, with death cold and patient nearby, waiting for what he could claim, man or beast, it was the same to him.

But that was absurd, she thought. The unyielding flesh beneath her hand told her it was not so. The great fluidity, the sinuousness that was in the nature of these animals, had simply gone out of this one. Death had come from the inside and life had gone out. So that's it, she thought. She lifted her hand, held it before her, and gazed down into her own palm. "It comes from the inside," she said.

Anne pushed the bag aside and lifted the dead cat in her arms. She held him in her arms like a dead child and then she laid him in the bag and pulled the sides up over him. She carried him through the yard to the street. Later two men came by in a truck and took the bag away. The cat was gone. It began to rain again and grow colder still. That night, in that city, there was the hardest freeze in fifty years. Pipes burst, houses flooded, and the water pressure was so low that several buildings burned to the ground while the firemen stood about, cursing the empty hoses they held in their cold and helpless hands.

John Biguenet (1949–)

John Biguenet did not set out to be a writer. In fact, while attending Cor Jesu High School (now Brother Martin) in New Orleans, he was much more interested in playing on the high school basketball team, of which he was captain. Bored one day in class, he wrote a poem, but his teacher thought he was passing notes, so he sent him to the principal's office along with his poem. He was reprimanded; however, the principal could not ignore his poetic prowess and sent the poem off to the University of New Orleans poetry contest, where it took first place. That win helped earn him a full scholarship to Loyola University, New Orleans, where he gave up basketball for literature. While at Loyola, he wrote a movie review of Peter Fonda and Dennis Hopper's *Easy Rider,* which won another contest and another full scholarship, this time to the University of Arkansas.[1]

Biguenet admits that he had little to do with his early career, that he was simply propelled by circumstance, but that is certainly no longer true. While growing up just blocks from where he now lives in the Lakeshore neighborhood of New Orleans near the shores of Lake Ponchartrain, he says he "lived in the local library as a kid,"[2] so his career trajectory is not entirely accidental.

In 2002, Biguenet published his first short story collection, *The Torturer's Apprentice* to national and international acclaim. It was praised by *The Telegraph* (U.K.) as having "the hallmarks of the best short stories: economy, pregnancy, nothing wasted…. They (the stories) are linked above all by a sense of moments when the world turns uncanny, under the pressure of desire, or grief, or emergency." His 2003 debut novel, *Oyster,* likewise was touted as "remarkable…captivating from start to finish" by the *Library Journal.* Indeed his writing is captivating, especially when he speaks to "the pressure of desire" mentioned above, as he does in his 2001 short story, "A Work of Art."

Biguenet includes an epigraph from Rilke, which captures the theme of the story: "For beauty is nothing/ but the beginning of terror, which we just barely can still endure." For the protagonist, Peter Lagarde, it is difficult to determine which is more difficult to endure, the beauty of "a work of art" or the terror that ensues, once he happens upon it by accident.

Lagarde is a young New Orleans lawyer visiting a downtown office building in search of a ship chandler to whom he must deliver contracts. Instead, he happens upon J. Greun, a retired art dealer from Philadelphia who moved to New Orleans after his wife died and still keeps his hand in the business from a shabby office in the Effinger Building.

Biguenet quietly establishes Lagarde's vulnerability early on in the short story, when Greun first asks him if he "collects." Of course he does not, but instead he answers, "I've been thinking about expanding my art collection." That fib is his undoing, for he is easily seduced by the Degas maquette, an unfinished sculpture, in this case an 1889 wax Degas, *The Tub.* Immediately, "his breath caught in his throat. A small, exquisite woman gazed up at him from her bath." After that, both men personify the woman of *The Tub,* saying "she's charming," and Lagarde even "felt a kind of jealousy" when Greun asks, "Lovely, no?" In short, Lagarde becomes obsessed with this sculpture and sells the farm, so to speak, in order to acquire it.

He can think of little else while trying to liquidate all his assets in order to pay Greun before the first of the year, when the price rises steeply. He borrows money from his kindhearted and wealthy grandmother, sells his car, his stocks, his house and most of his furniture and moves with the Degas sculpture into a small, empty apartment. He sacrifices everything.

To complicate matters, Biguenet has Lagarde's romance with the woman in the tub coincide with his first real romance with Lauren, a young lawyer from Baton Rouge. He tells his grandmother about his love for both "women," and he even manages to confuse the two, which Biguenet shows us in a hilarious exchange: His generous grandmother asks, "'When am I going to get to see this beautiful woman of yours?' 'Well, I've got her in a crate

---

[1]   John Biguenet, interview by author, New Orleans, LA, March 20, 2012. Most of the biographical information comes from this interview.

[2]   Ibid.

right now,' Lagarde said....'In a crate?' Nana repeated horrified. 'The poor girl. You should be ashamed.' Lagarde suddenly realized what his grandmother was talking about. 'Oh, you mean Lauren.'" In fact, it is difficult to tell who Lagarde cares for more, and he hesitates "introducing" the two.

On New Year's Eve, Lagarde drives to attend Lauren's parents' annual New Year's Eve party, but the next morning, he cannot bear to be away from the sculpture and leaves early, even after Lauren pleads with him to stay. He is actively two-timing these women, and Biguenet leaves it to the reader to sort it out. Like much of the story, Biguenet uses humor in the end, when Lagarde states, "So this is love." By juxtaposing Lagarde's infatuation with both women, it is difficult to decipher which love he is referring to.

Since his award-winning short story collection in which "A Work of Art" appeared, *The Torturer's Apprentice,* Biguenet has also turned to play writing. After his own and the collective experience of the flood following Hurricane Katrina, he has written a dramatic trilogy, the first of which is *Rising Water,* followed by *Shotgun* and *Mold.* All three plays look at the effects of the flood itself and its aftermath on people's lives in New Orleans. His short stories, novels, and plays have all won numerous awards, and Biguenet, currently the Robert Hunter Distinguished University Professor at Loyola University in New Orleans, received the Louisiana Writer Award in 2012. Since Katrina, he has renovated and moved back into his own flooded house, just blocks from where he grew up near the shores of Lake Ponchartrain.

A Work of Art[1]

Denn das Schöne ist nichts
als des Schrecklichen Anfang, den wir noch grade ertragen…
For Beauty is nothing
but the beginning of terror, which we just barely can still endure…
—Rainer Maria Rilke

The young man, lost in the warren of dingy dentist offices, import companies, and commercial insurance agencies on the eighth floor of the old Effinger Building, was attempting to deliver contracts to a ship chandler. He was sure that the directory beside the florid bronze elevator doors downstairs had listed the chandler in 817. But the last door on the dim hall was 815. He tried the knob. It was locked. He tapped on the milky glass pane with his law school ring just below an arc of golden letters that spelled J. GRUEN.

A thin voice answered his knock. Though the door opened only slightly, the overheated air of the office swarmed over him in the chilly hallway. "I'm looking for Hugo Fernandez, the ship supplier," he explained. "I'm Peter Lagarde. An attorney." He passed his business card to the old man peering at him from behind the door.

"Not on this floor. No Fernandez."

Lagarde looked past the old man into the office. Its walls were covered with paintings.

The thin voice strengthened. "You collect?"

"Collect art? A bit." Lagarde had learned in his four years as an associate at Daigle, Johnson to present a version of himself in matters of taste that might win the confidence of the clients and, especially, of the partners of the firm. He could be quite convincing; as an undergraduate, he had taken a minor in art history. But the small house he had bought and the stocks in which he had invested the proceeds of his trust fund left no capital for speculation in the art market. "Actually," Lagarde continued, "I've been thinking about expanding my collection."

"Perhaps I have something that might interest you." The door swung open.

Lagarde entered the small office, crowded with nineteenth-century portraits and religious works. It had been designed for a secretary; another door opened on a larger second room, where he glimpsed an ornately framed landscape. "Ah, the Impressionists." He was on safe ground; he remembered the movement because he had found its works so painfully absent of interest and so resistant to study for examinations.

"Actually, they're Postimpressionists." The old man pushed farther open the door into the other room. "Here, take a closer look."

Lagarde was surprised: the names of the artists were familiar. "I didn't know there were any galleries in this building," he said.

"Gallery? You call this a gallery? In Philadelphia for thirty years, there I had a gallery. But Hedda dies, God rest her, and my daughter makes me move here to New Orleans. I'm too old to live alone, she says. But I'm not going to retire, am I?"

The young man, half listening, surveyed a group of charcoals above a file cabinet.

"No, I sell what I can get a decent price for, the rest I take with me. Now I peddle masterpieces by phone to cowboys in Oklahoma. But it makes my Sarah happy to have me here, so what can I do?" Even as he talked, he urged his guest toward the drawings with a gentle push. "She makes me crazy, though, that girl. The door I have to keep locked, she says. What kind of business keeps its door locked? Bookies, they keep their door locked."

Lagarde recognized a Degas. He flipped the tag dangling at the bottom of the frame and gasped.

"Don't worry, that was just for the insurance during shipping. I can take ten percent off the top. No problem."

"No, I don't think so. And I've got to find Fernandez. He's expecting these papers."

"Wait. I have something for you." The old man was trying to lift a large, shallow box. Lagarde took the crate from him and put it down on a desk full of magazines. "You like Degas. I can tell. Here is something special. I got it cheap, just before I left Philadelphia."

Gruen had trouble flicking open the rusty latch that fastened the plywood top. "Wait a minute." He took a small hammer from a file cabinet and tapped open the hook. The top creaked back on dry hinges. "This is something a young man would like."

As Lagarde looked down, his breath caught in his throat. A small, exquisite woman gazed up at him from her bath.

"A Degas maquette. It's called *The Tub*. 1889, I think." They both regarded the sculpture. "She's charming, isn't she? I knew you'd like her."

Though the old man wore a cardigan with a high collar that was much too big for him, the musty heat made Lagarde almost dizzy. "How much?" he whispered.

"Let me see." As Gruen lifted the edge of the lead pan that Degas had used as the tub, his bony left hand crawled under like a spider. Slowly it withdrew with a yellow stub dangling a green string. "160,000. But minus the ten percent, it's yours for 144. A steal, let me tell you."

Lagarde was pale. His heart shook his chest.

"If it were a bronze, you couldn't touch it for under 750 these days. But it's wax and plaster. The way Degas is going, I ought to hold on to it. Give it five years, it'll double, triple, who knows? But forget the money. Just look at her."

Lagarde had not taken his eyes off her. She stared up at him over crossed legs, her left foot cupped in her right hand as she lolled in her bath.

"Too much? You could buy on time. By the month."

Her left hand held a sponge. Her hair was like a clump of wet, thick cloth. Lagarde was taking deep, quiet breaths, trying to calm himself. Degas had worked a reddish brown pigment into the wax to resemble bronze; why hadn't he cast the piece? Lagarde guessed without bothering to calculate that he couldn't afford it even if he sold everything: the house, the stocks, the car. "It's very nice, very fine. But I've really got to find Fernandez. It was a pleasure meeting you." Lagarde had already backed into the outer office and was feeling for the door. "Perhaps I'll stop back when I have more time." He closed the door before the old man could speak. His breath burst from him in little white clouds as he hurried down the cold hallway.

As the elevator descended, he leaned against a carved walnut panel. He left the papers for the ship chandler with the guard at the information desk.

                    * * *

Peter Lagarde busied himself for the next few weeks with a complex lawsuit arising from the grounding of a barge near White Castle in Iberville Parish. He had been accompanied on the site visit by a young Baton Rouge attorney representing some of the underwriters. She was a second-year associate named Lauren and, like him, a graduate of Tulane. The litigation kept them in frequent communication, and among the marine surveys, the depositions, and the motions for summary judgment, a friendship began to emerge. Lagarde found himself scheduling their appointments late in the afternoon so she might be more likely to stay for dinner. He surprised her with symphony tickets one night, but she couldn't stay—she had to prepare for a trial the next morning. He worried over whether he could give her a Christmas present without embarrassing her.

Just before the holidays, an envelope arrived for him at the firm. There was a Canal Street return address. Inside, a photocopied letter from the Gruen Gallery announced a Christmas sale. At the bottom of the letter was a handwritten note: "For tax purposes, I can let you have the Degas for $125,000 until the end of the year." He felt something like panic overtaking him. How had Gruen gotten his address? He remembered the business card he had offered the old man.

In fact, despite his work and despite his colleague from Baton Rouge, he had been unable to force the woman in the tub from his mind. At odd moments, he discovered himself imagining her. He had even spoken with a real estate agent and his broker. After expenses, he could expect $85,000 from the house and his investments. The car was only a year old; he would certainly clear $15,000. He had been relieved to realize that he really couldn't afford the piece. Where would he find $44,000? But now, thanks to Gruen's tax man, he was only $25,000 short, and Lagarde knew where he could find $25,000.

He picked up the phone and called his grandmother. He didn't mention the money. He wished Nana a merry Christmas and told her about his progress at Daigle, Johnson. He hinted at a romance with Lauren. He admitted that he couldn't get away to join his parents in New York for the holidays, but he knew they would understand. Nana insisted that he have Christmas dinner with her at the Wharton; he gracefully accepted.

He was ashamed even before he had hung up. But, he told himself, he wasn't going to ask his grandmother for the money because he wasn't going to buy the Degas. Even if it were the great investment Gruen suggested, it was insane for him to consider buying such a work of art. It would cost him everything he owned, plus a great deal more. And all he would have to show for it was an exquisite lump of wax.

That night, after a quick dinner at a new Mexican restaurant on Magazine, Lagarde stopped by the Tulane library. The reference librarian showed him the registers of prices paid at auction for artworks. Gruen had not exaggerated, but there was nothing like the maquette in the records. He could only guess that the enormous prices fetched by Degas bronzes could make his sculpture worth a quarter of a million in the right auction. Again, for the second time that day, he felt shame. But to his surprise, he realized that he was ashamed of thinking of his little bather in terms of money. He put his hands on the red cover of the closed volume before him and stared at his reflection in the window.

The next morning, Lagarde had coffee with Tommy Hinton, a friend in his firm's business section who specialized in estates. He explained his father wanted to surprise his mother with a fiftieth birthday present, a Degas sculpture. The colleague offered to check it out. "No sweat, we handle stuff like this all the time. You can't imagine the crap we have to do for the old farts we represent. Just get me the papers on it—and the price."

At lunch, he walked over to Gruen's. His heart was beating faster and faster as he rode the current of holiday shoppers. He noticed a legless beggar with a dog in the alcove of a bankrupt department store. The peeling sheets of brown paper revealed glimpses of mannequins in summer smocks; he recalled from his childhood the Christmas window displays of the store.

He pulled his coat closed against the cold, damp gusts. A ragged preacher with a plastic loudspeaker attached to his belt berated the crowds hurrying past. Lagarde tried to avoid the man's attention as he slipped into the Effinger Building.

As the old, ornate elevator creaked toward the eighth floor, he realized that he wouldn't have time for lunch. He was hungry, but this was more pressing.

The door to 815 was ajar. Lagarde peeked in. Gruen and another man were eating sandwiches on a crate. "Come in, come in," the old man insisted, rewrapping his food as he spoke. "This is my neighbor, Mr. Ruiz. He has the business next door." The lawyer nodded to the small dark man. "You're here for the Degas, am I right?"

"No, not today. I just wanted to ask you a few questions about it."

"Questions? Yes, ask me questions," the old man said, motioning to Ruiz to stay.

"First, could I have a copy of the papers?"

"The papers?"

"You know, to authenticate the piece." Lagarde saw the old man stiffen. "Not that there's any question."

The slightest smile creased Gruen's face. "Of course. I don't buy without papers." He turned to Ruiz and winked. "Well, maybe if it's really cheap, I make an exception."

"You have my address," the attorney reminded him.

"I'll put a copy in the mail this afternoon, no problem," the old man promised, still smiling.

"Also, I was wondering—and I'm not sure I want to go ahead with this—but I was wondering whether you needed all the money by the first of January?"

"December thirty-first. Not January."

Lagarde corrected himself. "Yes, all the money by the end of December?"

"If I wait until January, I may as well wait another year. Taxes. You're a lawyer; you know."

"Midnight on the thirty-first," Ruiz interjected.

"So you need everything?" Lagarde tried one last time.

Gruen shrugged. "Of course everything. If you want to buy on time, then we have to go back to the first price. But come see her again. Look here." The old man had shuffled into the back room and was struggling with the lid of the container.

"No, no, it's not necessary," Lagarde protested, weakening.

"Come, come see."

While Lagarde hesitated, Ruiz got up to view the piece.

"Oh, beautiful," he said with a vague Latin accent. "Look at her. And served up on a platter."

"It's a tub," Lagarde objected as he joined the two men peering into the low crate. The plaster podium of crumpled canvas on which Degas had set the piece swirled with the frozen folds of the cloth, like a woman's robe dropped carelessly on the bathroom floor. There was something terribly brazen—or innocent—about the girl.

"Oh, yes, a bath," Ruiz whispered. He reached into the box and stroked the bottom of her thigh with his finger. "Lovely, no?"

Lagarde was offended. It was ridiculous, he knew, but he felt a kind of jealousy overwhelm him. He repressed an urge to insult the little man.

Turning to Gruen, he asked, "Will you be here on the thirty-first?"

"Where else would I be?"

"I have to go. I'm late," Lagarde said, still flustered by his emotions.

"I'll see you then, yes?" The old man followed him with small steps out into the hall.

"We'll see," the attorney said as he hurried toward the elevators. "Maybe."

                    * * *

Lauren slept with Lagarde for the first time a week before Christmas. Two days of depositions from crewmen of the beached barge and its tug had been scheduled at Daigle, Johnson, and she had arranged to spend the intervening Thursday night in New Orleans. Finishing their work about eight, the two attorneys treated themselves to an expensive dinner in the French Quarter. They laughed easily with each other, and by the time one of them looked at a watch it was well past eleven. Lagarde offered to walk his colleague back to her hotel on Canal Street. She took his arm, and they huddled together against the cold wind that shook the shop signs of the Quarter. In the lobby of the hotel, Lauren kissed him on the cheek. He smiled as he waved good-bye from the revolving doors.

By the time they had concluded the last deposition late Friday afternoon, Lauren had already called her roommate in Baton Rouge to say she would not be home that night. In fact, she did not see her roommate again until Sunday evening, when, giddy and exhausted, she announced that she was in love.

For Lagarde, the weekend had disturbed and then simplified everything. The furtive glances across the conference table Friday morning, his clumsy invitation at lunch to stay through the weekend, the shy and tender smile with which she accepted, the interminable afternoon of lawyerly questions and answers, the confusion about what to do with her car at the hotel—everything, all the complexities and awkwardness and impatience of sudden love, fell with their clothes to the floor when at last, after dinner and a few fortifying drinks, the young couple shut the door of Lagarde's house behind them and put out the lights.

The next Thursday, Christmas Eve, the attorney slipped away early from the firm's holiday party to meet Lauren in Baton Rouge for dinner and to exchange gifts. Before he left, though, Tommy Hinton pulled him aside. "Listen, I got the report back from our appraiser this morning," his friend whispered conspiratorially over a half-empty glass of bourbon. "That statue, you know, for your daddy, it checked out. And it's worth at least 175, maybe 200,000. A hell of a deal." Clapping his friend on the back for the favor, Lagarde realized that he had almost forgotten about the sculpture during the last few days.

The following morning, snuggling beneath a comforter that had belonged to the girl's grandmother, the two lovers kissed and teased. Lauren wanted him to join her family for Christmas dinner that afternoon, but he had promised to celebrate the holiday with Nana at the hotel where she lived in New Orleans. "Well," said the young woman, struggling into her nightgown beneath the covers, "at least we can have a Christmas breakfast together."

By the time Lagarde had dressed, Lauren's roommate and her boyfriend had emerged from their room and were stumbling around the kitchen, begging for coffee. They had come in late, and so Lagarde had not yet met them. Stephanie, a friend from Lauren's undergraduate days at LSU, was a medical technician; her fiancé, Vic, was an intern at Our Lady of the Lake Hospital. The four shared a quiet breakfast. While Stephanie and Vic stared off into the flowering vines and blue lattice of the kitchen wallpaper, Lauren slipped her hand into Lagarde's beneath the table.

                    * * *

Nana was waiting in the lobby of the Wharton when her grandson arrived. "I would've come up and gotten you," Lagarde said, embracing the old woman gently.

"No, the reservations were for 12:30. I didn't want them to give our table away."

"Nana, it's just 12:30 now."

"Good, then we can go right in." She took her grandson's arm.

Seated near the small fountain at the rear of the dining room, Lagarde was pleased to be spending Christmas with his grandmother. With his parents' move to New York and the death of his aunt last year, he was the last of Nana's family still in the city. Sooner or later, his father would insist on bringing the old woman north to live with them. But for another year or two, she could manage on her own—with Lagarde's occasional help. Indulging finally in champagne and the restaurant's famously excessive desserts, grandmother and grandson enjoyed a merry afternoon, with the conversation somehow always returning to Lagarde's new friend in Baton Rouge. The young man insisted on paying for the meal, and Nana invited him up to her rooms for coffee.

As an ancient bellhop brought them to the top floor of the hotel in the small elevator, Lagarde's grandmother whispered discreetly how pleased she was that he had found a young lady. "It's about time," she said.

Lagarde protested that they had just met and who could say what would come of it.

Nana gave him one of the smirks he remembered from childhood. "Who are you trying to fool? You're going to marry this girl."

They had reached her floor. As the old woman stepped out into the hall, Lagarde stayed in the elevator. *She's right*, he thought to himself with a start.

The bellman turned to his passenger. "Top floor," he wheezed. "Going down."

Lagarde followed his grandmother to her door. The furniture from the big house on Prytania looked odd squeezed into the apartment. Nana had moved here a few years after the death of Lagarde's grandfather. Four or five other elderly New Orleanians kept apartments at the Wharton; it was an old tradition that only a few hotels in town still honored. She picked up the phone and ordered coffee from room service.

Lagarde had managed to avoid the subject of the sculpture, but as they waited for the coffee to be delivered, he offhandedly mentioned the Degas he had been offered. Nana, enamored of the French, recalled her honeymoon in Paris.

"Your grandfather never had a taste for it, but he bought me my little Renoir pastel as a wedding present. It was our last day before coming home. The weather was terrible, but we were walking on the Rue Rivoli when I saw it through a window. I dragged him into the shop. Oh, it made me weak, I loved it so much. But he said no, absolutely not. I was furious with him—what a spoiled young thing I was. Then, that night, when we got back from dinner, there was the little drawing propped against the pillow of our bed. He was such a stinker, your grandfather."

Lagarde tried to change the subject. The last thing he wanted was to trade on his grandmother's happy memories. But Nana refused to talk about anything else. She demanded all the details. She even dragged from him the financial arrangements he might make.

"So you need a loan of $125,000 by next week," the old lady said, nodding her head, "but you'll pay back $100,000 as soon as you sell the house."

"And the car and the stocks," Lagarde added, with growing anxiety.

"Why not?" Nana smiled mischievously. "Why not?"

Lagarde felt his heart beating too quickly in his chest.

"And I'll tell you what," his grandmother continued, "if you marry Lauren, the other $25,000 will be my wedding present to you." Then wagging her finger at him, she said laughing, "But if you don't get married, you'll have to pay back every penny." She instructed him to call Deacon Gilbert, the family's attorney, on Monday afternoon. "Deek'll make the arrangements," she promised.

After they had had their coffee, Nana took Lagarde into her bedroom to show him the Renoir. He had not seen it since he was a child. It left him, as it had his grandfather, absolutely cold. The pretty young girl, smudged in pink and purple and blue, touched nothing within him, but his grandmother, standing next to him, brushed tears from her cheeks with a pale, wrinkled hand.

      * * *

He had just gotten home from Nana's when there was a knock at the door. He peeked out through the living room window. "Surprise," Lauren shouted from the porch.

Once inside, she explained that she had gotten back to her apartment after lunch with her family and couldn't think of anything to do except to work on an admiralty case she was handling that involved a barge and a sandbar. So she had popped down to New Orleans to see if her cocounsel might want to spend the weekend collaborating with her on some legal research.

"Oh, I see. You want to get into my briefs, huh? Well, come on then," Lagarde agreed, pushing her into the bedroom, "we'd better get to work."

As the evening progressed to several courses of Chinese food, an old movie on cable, and finally a few hours of intermittent sleep in each other's arms on the sofa, their playfulness yielded to passion.

Lagarde woke to the rush of water. Wrapping himself in a blanket, he pushed open the bathroom door. Lauren, reclining in the huge, old tub with ball-and-talon legs, instinctively tried to cover her nakedness. Then she smiled at herself and shyly let her hands slip back into the water.

Dropping the blanket around his feet, Lagarde joined her in the tub. The water rushed up to her throat as he sat down across from her. She tried to lift her long hair out of the water; it lay along her shoulder like wet, dark silk.

"Give me your foot," he said.

She slid her foot along the porcelain until it slipped into the stirrup of his hand. Lifting it up on to his stomach, he cupped the top of it with his other hand and massaged it till she closed her eyes and sighed.

      * * *

As his grandmother had promised, her attorney had the check waiting for him when he called Monday afternoon. Deek knew better than to ask what the money was for. "Can you pick it up tomorrow?" the old lawyer wondered. "I was just leaving for the club."

So after lunch on Tuesday, Lagarde returned to work with a check for $125,000 in his pocket. He was most afraid that someone in the office might see it; such a check would be difficult to explain, particularly if he tried to tell the truth about it.

He drove around for a long time before going home that night. In fact, he even took a ride out to Lake Pontchartrain. He knew he was approaching the moment when he would have to make a decision. He had only two days left.

A 5 P.M. filing deadline for a motion in a wrongful death suit brought by the widow of an oil rig worker occupied the attorney's attention for most of the next day. By the time a messenger had hurried off with the motion, Lagarde was almost relieved to discover that it was too late to make it over to Gruen's.

That night, he had trouble sleeping. He would make up his mind to buy or not to buy the sculpture; then, almost asleep, he would have second thoughts and roll onto his back to rethink the whole decision. As he grumpily ordered coffee and a blueberry muffin at the breakfast shop in his office building on New Year's Eve, Lagarde made up his mind for the last time.

He called Gruen at ten o'clock and arranged to pick up *The Tub* at the end of the day. Having committed himself to the purchase, he grew more and more excited as the morning matured into afternoon and the afternoon steeped into early evening. By four, most of the partners had already left for the long weekend. A few minutes after the hour, Lagarde pulled out of the parking lot and fought the early traffic to the Effinger Building. Finally finding a space, he dumped a handful of change in the meter and hurried into the building.

Gruen, already in his worn overcoat, was waiting. Somehow, he had dragged the unwieldy crate into the front room. His daughter, he explained, was picking him up downstairs in fifteen minutes. He handed over the authentication papers.

"Well," said Lagarde, taking a deep breath, "here's the check." Endorsing it with his Montblanc, he presented the old man with the slip of paper he had carried in his wallet for the last two days.

"But the tax," stammered Gruen. "Where's the tax?"

"I thought it was included."

"Included? Do you think I could sell you a Degas for $115,000? Even a maquette?" The old man leaned against the crate.

"It's all I've got." Lagarde realized in a kind of terror that he was in danger of losing her, but he bluffed anyway. "If it's not enough, I'll understand." He held out his hand to take back the check.

The old man folded the check and put it in his shirt pocket. "You're robbing me," he complained.

Lagarde had seen this before in negotiations for settlements. He sensed that even without the tax, the dealer was still making a comfortable profit. The lawyer wondered how cheaply the old man had gotten the piece in the first place.

Now that he had the money, Gruen was impatient to close up. Still grumbling, he locked the door behind him as Lagarde struggled down the hall with the crate. He held the elevator for the young man, who carefully placed the container onto the carpeted floor as they made their slow descent. Gruen said nothing, and when the elevator doors opened on the first floor, he hurried off without even a good-bye.

Lagarde muscled the crate into the trunk of his car but had to use a rope to tie it shut. Driving home, he avoided as many bumps as he could, afraid he would find the sculpture cracked in half when he pulled into his driveway.

It seemed to take forever to get home, but once he did struggle through the door with the heavy container, he felt a secret joy begin to seep through him. He gently lowered his burden onto the floor. Unlatching the top and stooping over the statue, he felt the weight of it along his spine as he began to lift. He stopped and bent his knees. As the bottom of the statue cleared the edge of the box, he quickly set the sculpture down on a kilim he had gotten at auction. Lagarde hadn't considered where he might put the piece. He had very little furniture, though what he had was of value, antiques carefully collected in the dusty warehouses of the city's oldest dealers.

Surveying the room, he chose as the statue's pedestal the nineteenth-century gaming table he had found the year before at an estate sale. He covered the polished mahogany with a tablecloth and thick towels. Then he lifted the sculpture onto its center. He pulled the sturdy cockfighting chairs, upholstered in green leather, away from the table and adjusted the dimmer on the little chandelier. In the shimmering light of the crystal lamp, he admired *The Tub*.

Now that the work was his, he examined it more closely. He was shocked to discover the lips of a vulva pinched between her fleshy thighs and curls of thick hair scored across her pubes. But these were secrets, hidden by the bronze patina of the wax and the shadows of her raised legs.

For the first time, he touched the body of the bather. It looked so much like bronze, his fingers were surprised that the breast was not cool. The hardened wax of the figure felt like flesh grown suddenly taut under an unexpected hand.

Lagarde opened a small cabinet and withdrew a bottle of brandy. Pouring himself a snifter, he sat across the room admiring his sculpture. But in the midst of his pleasure, he began, inexplicably, to sadden.

Even after he had gone to his bedroom to dress for the evening, he could not shake the melancholy that had tainted his happiness. In fact, as he buttoned the leather thongs of his braces to the black, satin-striped pants and as he fumbled with the unfamiliar knot of a silk bow tie, his mood worsened, like the storm whipping out of the Gulf and across the marshes.

                              * * *

A cold rain lashed his windshield by the time he reached the interstate. Having promised Lauren that he would be in Baton Rouge by nine o'clock, he had to drive faster than he would have liked in such nasty weather. Her parents were hosting their annual New Year's Eve party, and she was eager for them to meet her new friend. Though he had hinted at his misgivings about being introduced to them at a party, Lauren was confident her mother and father would love him as much as she did. He almost hadn't noticed her use of "love." It was the first time either one of them had said the word. To his surprise, it left him not—as he would have expected—peevish, but rather calm, almost placid, as if it were the right word, after all, to describe the pleasure he felt in her company. It might have slipped by unnoticed in the distraction of his concern about meeting her parents if Lagarde hadn't caught Lauren's slight pause and sidelong glance as she said it.

He repeated her sentence as his car skimmed over the slick concrete of the highway.

                              * * *

"But why do you have to leave so early?" Lauren asked groggily. Then, sitting up in the bed and brushing the sleep from her eyes, she realized, "It's still dark outside."

As he gathered up his cummerbund and bow tie from the floor and stuffed them into a pocket of his dinner jacket, Lagarde explained that he had to go.

"I thought we were going to spend the weekend together," Lauren said, the hurt creeping into her voice. "Didn't you have a good time last night?"

Lagarde sat down beside her on the bed. "I had a wonderful time."

"Were my parents awful?"

"I love your parents," he said, then added after a pause, "and I love you."

Lauren strained in the darkness to see his eyes.

He bent and kissed her. "But I have to go," he whispered.

"At least let me make you breakfast."

He relented. "Just coffee."

They did not say much as they sipped from steaming mugs beneath the harsh kitchen light. Lagarde tried to find a way to explain why he had to return to New Orleans immediately, but with only a few hours sleep and still a bit dazed from the New Year's Eve festivities, he couldn't think how to make Lauren understand his anxiety about his statue.

In fact, he hadn't yet told her anything about the Degas. When he considered what he had done—spending $125,000 on a work of art—and even more when he considered what remained to be done—selling his house, his car, and his stocks to pay back his grandmother's loan—he began to see how foolhardy it would all appear to the woman whom, yes, he loved.

"I could come with you," she suddenly said, interrupting his thoughts. "We can call my mother from New Orleans and tell her we can't come to dinner. She won't mind; they're having a whole house of friends over to see LSU in the Cotton Bowl. It's just going to be a buffet."

"No, I wouldn't take you away from your family on a holiday," Lagarde protested. "Why don't you come tomorrow?"

"I can't. We have the firm's touch football game tomorrow. I have to play. Remember? You were going to be my cheerleader. Anyway, what's so important in New Orleans on New Year's morning?"

"I can't tell you. It's a surprise."

As they stood at the door, Lauren gave Lagarde a small, pouting kiss. He wanted to explain, but instead he hurried down the steps and out to his car.

Driving back to the city as dawn began to stain the horizon, he had a long conversation with himself, trying to ferret out the diverse sources of his worry. The most obvious was practical: he might not have insurance on the piece. It hadn't occurred to him that he might need a rider on his policy to cover such an expensive addition to his household furnishings, but at 4:30 A.M., tossing restlessly in Lauren's bed, the thought had suddenly pierced him. A second arrow of anxiety followed the first. The sculpture was still sitting on his dining room table, unprotected and exposed. His neighborhood, though relatively safe, had witnessed its share of crime since he had moved in. The piece might already have been stolen; surely burglars realized many people were away from their homes on New Year's Eve. Or it might even have been vandalized by teenagers hopped up on booze and drugs. Lying awake in the dark, Lagarde had taken a deep breath and made himself admit that his fears were exaggerated. Still, his insurance agent wouldn't be in the office until Monday; he decided he had to stay with the statue until then.

But money wasn't the only source of concern. He had felt guilty in Lauren's arms. In part, he was troubled by keeping a secret from her; however, he was too embarrassed and too uncertain of her response to reveal his purchase. There was another barb of guilt, though, that he was less ready to acknowledge. Smothering Lauren in his kisses, he had felt somehow unfaithful to the woman in *The Tub*. It was ridiculous, he knew, and as soon as he realized what had been rasping his conscience, it ceased to trouble him. But now, driving through the damp pine forests west of New Orleans, he recognized that he was as much owned by the work of art as owner of it. He could not imagine it as less than a petulant mistress, lolling indifferently in her bath. It was no mere lump of wax, of plaster, of canvas. It was a small, exquisite woman with a claim on him.

Lost in thought, he nearly hit an armadillo, dead on the highway.

                    * * *

When Lagarde left for work Monday morning, he hid the statue—replaced in its crate—among some empty boxes in the laundry room. Even once the insurance had been secured, Lagarde rarely removed the woman from her hiding place, particularly after his real estate agent began to show the house to prospective buyers.

It did not take long to sell the house, though the price was less than he had hoped. An antiques dealer made up the difference but left Lagarde with only a mattress, a chair or two, a small table. He waited until he had moved to his new apartment on the streetcar line before he sold his car. The stocks were worth a bit more than the last time he had checked, but with commissions and fees and all the unexpected costs of divesting oneself of material possessions, Lagarde found he still had to withdraw most of his $5,000 in savings to equal the $100,000 he owed his grandmother.

When he telephoned to let Nana know he'd sold his house, she dismissed his concerns about the money. "Just send the check to Deek after the closing," she said, making clear her indifference about the matter. But she was insistent on one point. "When am I going to get to see this beautiful woman of yours?"

"Well, I've got her in a crate right now," Lagarde said, trying to put his grandmother off.

"In a crate?" Nana repeated, horrified. "The poor girl. You should be ashamed."

Lagarde suddenly realized what his grandmother was talking about. "Oh, you mean Lauren."

"Of course I mean Lauren. You're not seeing someone else, are you?"

"No, no," Lagarde protested, "I thought you wanted to see the sculpture, the woman by Degas that I bought."

"Yes, her, too," the old lady said, still a bit disconcerted.

"I promise, as soon as I've got my new apartment all straight, you'll come for dinner. You can meet both women at the same time."

Nana laughed lightly. "So what did Lauren say when she found out you'd sold everything to buy a work of art?"

Lagarde coughed. "I haven't told her yet. I want it to be a surprise."

There was a silence on the other end of the line. Finally, the old woman said, "It's none of my business, of course, Peter. And I think it's utterly charming what you've done. And daring. But..."

"Yes," he said resignedly, "you're right."

                    * * *

He had joked to himself that he might have to marry Lauren just to avoid paying back the other $25,000 Nana had given him, but he began to wonder whether Lauren would have him after weeks of inexplicable behavior. She had sympathetically accepted one excuse after another. He was tired of worrying about a house; he preferred an apartment. His antique furniture was oppressive. He wanted a less cluttered, more minimalist look. The car was too much trouble, too ostentatious, and he insisted that the weekend trips to Baton Rouge he now made on the bus were preferable to driving—they gave him a chance to catch up on his reading. But when at last he allowed Lauren to see his bare new apartment, she betrayed her misgivings.

Standing in the doorway, she looked for something to admire in Lagarde's new place. Two wooden chairs faced each other across the gray carpet of an otherwise empty living room. There was nothing upon which to place the crystal vase she had brought as a housewarming present. She handed the wrapped package awkwardly behind her to Lagarde, who still stood in the hall.

"Let me show you the rest," he said without much confidence.

The gray carpet lapped at the white floor tiles of a tiny kitchen. A counter jutting out past the far wall of cabinets concealed a windowless dining alcove. There, a small black table plunged its stubby legs into another swatch of gray carpet.

Beyond lay the bath and bedroom, where a mattress sprawled on the floor. The phone rested on a book beside the simple bed.

Still holding the gift, he sighed. Lauren took his hand, and she made him sit with her on the edge of the mattress.

"I just want to tell you," she said, taking a deep breath, "that I've managed to save some money over the last two years. If you're having trouble right now, I want you to have it. It's not much—"

Lagarde interrupted her. "Thank you," he said.

"No matter how it happened—gambling, or whatever. It's yours, all of it."

Lagarde shook his head. "No, that's not it," he began. "I have to show you something." He stood up. "I want you to wait in here until I call you. OK?"

He closed the bedroom door behind him and unlocked the large hall closet, on which he had had a dead bolt installed before he moved in.

When Lauren emerged from the bedroom, Lagarde had extinguished all the lights except for three track lamps in the breakfast nook. In dimmed incandescence on the black table rested the sculpture. The shafts of muted light fell upon the wax face, a breast, and the legs of the nude woman. Slight shadows gave weight to her small body.

Lauren walked silently around the statue, once pausing to shyly touch the hand of the figure. Coming round to where she had started, she looked to Lagarde for an explanation.

"It's a Degas. It cost me everything." He couldn't bring himself to excuse it as an investment. "I just thought...." He stopped and sighed.

"She's exquisite," Lauren said. Her voice trembled as if she had been wounded in some way. "But you gave up everything for her."

Lagarde understood, all at once, that he was about to lose her. Without warning, he took Lauren in his arms, kissing her hard and unyieldingly as she tried to break free of him. He pressed her against the wall and slipped a hand inside her blouse. Then she was unbuckling his pants, pulling his shirt up. They fell to the floor and entwined beneath the indifferent gaze of the brazen nude woman.

Hours later, exhausted and bruised, the couple slept on the mattress in the back room. Just before dawn, Lagarde rolled awake from restless sleep and walked to the kitchen for water.

The dimmed lights still illuminated the statue. Naked, he stood before the work of art, his weariness swelling into fury over the sacrifices required of him by the woman in the tub, forever bathing, forever demanding his attention.

He began to see the folly of his devotion. For a moment, he could have done anything; he could have smashed the mocking face, the teasing body. But he was already too ridiculous, and he could not bring himself to hurt the beautiful creature.

He fled into the bedroom. The fringes of light from the other room cast themselves over Lauren, who had twisted free of the covers. The hair curling like cloth against the face, a breast cupped in her hand, the legs bent to expose the dark frills of her genitalia, a long arm dangling over the edge of the mattress onto the floor—Lagarde recognized, with a slight shudder, who lay asleep at his feet.

He wavered. "So this is love," he said, hopelessly, then knelt among the sheets frothing about her ankles and touched her.

Moira Crone (1952–)

Moira Crone was born and grew up in Goldsboro, North Carolina, a small tobacco farming town and home to Seymour Johnson Air Force Base. Like her character, Elizabeth in the short story, "There Is a River in New Orleans," Crone is "...a girl raised by a good family in a house on a corner in a dreamy southern town" (79), and like Elizabeth, her father was a lawyer. The summer before leaving Goldsboro for Smith College, where she planned to pursue a degree in painting, Crone attended the University of North Carolina. While there, she took a writing course, and her teacher was very enthusiastic about her work, even telling her that it was publishable. At Smith, Crone, having had no formal education in painting, discovered that she was not as developed an artist as her peers, but she was further encouraged in her writing by her instructor, the formidable V. S. Pritchett. But even before that, Crone discovered that she was a natural storyteller while spending time with her grandmother, a transplanted New Yorker. Crone writes: "after rounds of poker, gin rummy, and drags on her Pall Malls, I asked her to tell me stories. She didn't know how. I realized I did, and could teach her."[1]

As a teenager, Crone read and was excited by many authors, such as Reynolds Price, Truman Capote, Katherine Anne Porter, and later on in college, Isak Dinesen, D.H. Lawrence, and Carson McCullers, still one of her favorites. But it was not until she read Grace Paley that she felt "some kind of permission to write the way I wanted to, in a frank first-person voice.... She [Paley] was a liberation."[2]

After Smith, Crone went on to graduate from Johns Hopkins, and since then she has taught creative writing at several universities, but primarily at Louisiana State University (LSU) where she directed the Creative Writing MFA program from 1997-2002. Crone has published several collections of short stories, most recently the acclaimed *What Gets Into Us* about which Doris Betts writes: "Fayton, North Carolina, has here its own Sherwood Anderson as Crone interweaves four decades of a town's dreams and secret sorrows."[3] Fayton, North Carolina, was surely inspired by Crone's childhood in Goldsboro, and the collection of interwoven short stories about that small fictional town evokes the gentle profundity of the writer she so admires, Carson McCullers.

We see that same quiet profundity in her story from the 1995 collection *Dream State*, "There Is a River in New Orleans." The protagonist, Elizabeth, looks back on her recent life with her husband Gerald both before and after their divorce, but even further back to her childhood, growing up with a rather eccentric mother in a small southern town reminiscent of Crone's own Goldsboro. Crone nails this depiction of a mentally unbalanced mother who has real difficulty trying to cope with simply being a good wife and mother, and this character appears often in Crone's fiction. Elizabeth, in this short story, looks back on her childhood with such a mother and seems to learn from that reflection why her own marriage failed. However, she comes to terms with the fact that, even though she loves her husband, she is better off being a divorced mother. She achieves some sense of calm, as the last sentence in the short story suggests: "Still."

Crone also gives us a glimpse of New Orleans decadence in this story, when Elizabeth, while being chastised by Gerald for taking up smoking again, thinks how different he is "...from the men in this town, who seem to have a zest for things that will hurt them, who like to woo their own ruination and wish that you would come along. And if you won't willingly, they'll drag you." Elizabeth likes the excitement of New Orleans, while Gerald moves to Mobile, Alabama.

Moira Crone, in her essay, "The Art of Opening Up," writes: "In my experience, those in this country who still want to listen, who know those old codes, are almost always Southerners—whites and African Americans alike."[4] She is truly the voice of these southerners but also a voice of New Orleans and the New Orleanians about whom she writes. Her short stories have appeared in such journals as *The New Yorker, Mademoiselle, North American Review, Ploughshares, Southern Review*, and *New Orleans Review*. She has received numerous awards and grants for her writing, and in 2009, Crone received the Robert Penn Warren Award for Fiction from the

---

1   From Moira Crone's website, http://www.moiracrone.com.

2   Moira Crone, personal inteview, March 2012.

3   Moira Crone, *What Gets Into Us* (University Press of Mississippi, 2006), Back Cover.

4   Crone, interview.

Fellowship of Southern Writers for the body of her work.

There Is a River in New Orleans[1]

That night Gerald asks me a riddle: what is a river, really, its waters or its old banks?

We are in a restaurant. One of the waiters comes up to tell him he has a call. He hesitates. It would be rude to leave. He's a gentleman. I once enjoyed that. My father liked him. My mother, too, in her way. Gerald used to be my husband.

"Go," I say, "I know you'll be right back," which softens his face. We have issues to talk about tonight, what will happen to our daughter—but all I can think about is my mother, who isn't even alive. The July sun hasn't set yet. With Gerald gone I can see out the restaurant window that the Mississippi is winding through the city of New Orleans. You never see it at street level here, because the levees are in the way.

The banks last.

She was a beautiful woman, people said of my mother. She was from a good family, French Huguenot, rare and dark-eyed, and she was given to singing at the wrong times—at the table, in front of the help. Where I grew up people said that if my mother had been someone less mad, my father would have been governor, or something close. My father was considered by others long-suffering. He was a lawyer, a long-legged man who wore his seersucker suits loose. He even had ideas about progress of a kind.

Her soul was a bird closed up in a drawer.

Why do you sleep in daytime clothes, Gerald used to ask me. He thought that was low, which meant, I thought then, while we were breaking up, that he was disappointed a girl raised by a good family in a house on a corner in a dreamy southern town had not been brought up a lady and wouldn't forever act like one. Antique as that sounds. I don't act like a lady now, no, not ever, all my old friends who used to tell me to live a little in college would be proud of me. But truth be told, I wasn't raised at all. I grew like a stalk.

She'd drive away, sometimes, without telling the maid or us where, and then we'd wait at the kitchen table. It would be me and my younger brother and my sister, my father off lawyering, the maid's ride—a friend of hers or an ex-husband with a car—would have come to get her at five-thirty, and be long gone. We'd wait while the butter on the cooked carrots cooled to tiny yellow puddles. I can smell that kitchen, see the high ceilings, the top pantry cabinets filled with Limoges we never used. The smell of spicy beef, cooked ketchup, the sound of onions snapping in grease, the meat loaf blackening in the oven.

I believed things would turn out, and my mother would, she would, come back. But I didn't tell anybody this. I'd insist we play cards, war or old maid, and entirely ignore the hour, the facts. I knew the world was beneficent when I was thirteen, that it was beautiful if you knew where to look. My daughter Juliana is thirteen now, and she knows the same.

I'm supposed to be gazing down at the artistic veal medallions with a Madeira sauce just set before me by another waiter, but I look up and see Gerald, across the room. He startles. I've caught him being alone. It's a bad habit he must want to conceal.

When I was twenty-eight, I felt ninety, gristly and old, all these memories would bubble out of my bones when he moved towards me. I never told him what I was thinking then.

She didn't believe things could ever get better, my mother. Or ever change.

After I divorced, her old sadness came and stayed with me for its first long visit, it was unanticipated, this grief. After all, I had asked for the divorce. It visited me anyway, the sense of irretrievable ruin—my daughter's tears when she came home from kindergarten after Gerald moved out, her sleeplessness when she returned from one of her long stays with him, the open loss I saw when I faced my house's emptiness once he'd closed the door to take her the next time. When I was alone I'd cry over cheap things breaking, African violets that couldn't be brought back to life after being left too long, after being allowed, by my own negligence, to dry out. I felt closer to my mother than ever that first year after.

Mother was the essence of blue.

I don't say anything when he reaches the table.

"It's a client. I told him to call Monday. I told him I wasn't working."

"It's okay. I had a smoke," I say.

He frowns. I quit long ago, actually, before he married me. I don't know why I've started back.

We are here because of our daughter's school—it's a good one in New Orleans, private, but it stops at eighth grade, and she can go to a private high school or to the competitive public one she has qualified for, and Gerald, who lives now in Mobile, came over to discuss this.

He should have remarried, we both know that. Alabama has plenty of tanned women in sarong skirts who make a career of how they look, who are raised to serve their husband's interests, to drive jaguars and have gorgeous children who always sleep in nightgowns. New Orleans has even more. He could look. But when he comes to pick up Juliana I think he lingers unnecessarily at the door. He asked for a cup of coffee in my kitchen, recently. The drive back, he said, he didn't want to fall asleep. He sat down to drink it. He didn't have to do that. And we could have gone to any dive or café to discuss Juliana's schooling, but we are in this place which is so famous, on the top of a hotel, where we have so many waiters you have to shoo them away. He chose it. There could be several reasons. I should be trying to figure this out. It is another riddle.

He says, "You started up again?" in a tone I almost recognize as my father's—that Middle South Protestant resignation, so unlike the excitement I sometimes find in men in this town, who seem to have a zest for things that will hurt them, who like to woo their own ruination and wish that you would come along. And if you won't willingly, they'll drag you.

We discuss the schools—Newwell and McCollam, Trinity, the Catholic academies, the public school. He's more interested in the public one than I expected, not because he's cheap, but because it is "more like the real world," he's saying now, and he knows, he lives in the real world, more than when we were married. That's a consequence. So do I. So do I. Being divorced is more real than being married, these days.

I thought I had a reason to be optimistic. My mother always came back, sometimes after a day or two or three, but she came, to our kitchen, to Clara or Sophie or May, whoever was our maid that year—she fired many, and many left, because she was hard to work for, I guess that's clear. She looked beautiful to me at a distance, coming up the walk, her roundness swathed in some dark draped color, or black. She'd wear a jacket or she'd wear a hat. But something would be wrong close up.

My mother's looks comprised the state of the world to me then.

Lipstick smeared, a dirty blouse, a run in her taupe hose, up high on the calf by the seam. When I'd see the flaw, when she'd come home, just like I knew she would but didn't say—it might break the spell—my heart would sink, the universe would collapse. She'd stay up late drinking tea that wasn't really tea. She'd sit in a chair, her legs so far apart, I could see her garters. She didn't care. She smoked like a chimney.

The nothing that she claimed, at first, to be wrong, grew in the room. It grew the way shadows did in the afternoon, when the sun had abandoned the big windows, and slipped down below the rail on the porch.

"Your father," she'd say very late when we were alone, long after she'd given the maid extra money, handing no one an explanation. "Wants to own me where I live. He does. I'm not letting him. And where is he—where is he?"

Off being important, of course.

When we were in our twenties in Metairie, a suburb, Gerald would be dressing to go into New Orleans and leave me alone with Juliana and the other wives in that little complex with the flimsy wrought iron balconies, I'd tell him, "Being selfish is breathing to you," and he'd wave his long arms and put one hand behind his head and say, "How? Why do you think I work?"

"Are you BLIND?" I would ask Gerald, standing there in the doorway, the hanging ferns falling in my eyes, Juliana in my arms in the clothes she had slept in.

"Show me what I don't see," he'd say, "for crying out loud."

In one way, I didn't think a man, any man, could stand the truth.

In another, I didn't think I could risk telling it. "Elizabeth?" Gerald is speaking to me. "Did you want anything else? Earth to Elizabeth," he says, something from a sitcom, I'm sure, he watches them a lot, Juliana told me. When she visits him in Mobile, he doesn't cook. He takes her out to a little beignet and cafe au lait place they have in Mobile, so she will feel "at home"—she's a sophisticated young lady, now, she's a New Orleanian. He lets her drink *coffee.* He adores her.

"I'll have dark roast," I say. Back to the subject. "Her friends will probably all go to McCollam, except the really smart ones."

"My point," he says, "I want her to go to New England for college, I want her to be with the smartest ones. I mean Smith or Mt. Holyoke or even Yale, or Bryn Mawr," he says.

I don't say Bryn Mawr's in Pennsylvania. New England is really a state of mind, not a place, when you are this far south.

I can hear my father when he gets home at night, upstairs, shouting at Mother, "Do you have any idea how this looks? You think you are getting away with this?"

I run down the long hall. I'm holding my ears.

Gerald's standard line was, "Let yourself go."

"Go where?" I finally said back. "Don't tell me where to go." Where, in that apartment with its thin walls and its short hallway, and Juliana, a baby, two or three, ready to wail any minute, or come tell us her nightmares, and me wanting to know what they were, anything to get off the subject. The subject being where should I go according to him. According to him.

"It seems a little stacked," I say to Gerald. "You have made up your mind, haven't you?"

"I didn't think you wanted her to spend her high school years—" he starts in, hesitates.

"What?" I say in an old tone.

"Turning into some little, some purely social being. With the private schools, there's the danger—"

"What danger?"

"That she'll end up like we did, don't you think? Don't they all go to get ensconced in that? Marrying people just like themselves. From the same narrow world, not knowing there is any other? It's as if there's a spell on them, how people surrender to the past here, I am starting to think. It almost always wins."

And he's right.

But I am running down the hall, still, holding my ears. "Nothing's more important than for her to take herself seriously, I'm quoting," he goes on.

"Who said that?" I ask.

"You. I'm quoting you."

This is where I begin to know I don't know what will happen next. He is being very straight, very sincere. I can tell. Also kind.

There was a harshness back then, when we were breaking up, when she was five, an irony in his voice, when I said I had to take myself seriously, and couldn't be his little wife. And Gerald would say— "What do you mean 'go where?' That's not how I meant it."

"I know Juliana does take herself seriously," I say, putting my cup down in the saucer, causing the slightest splash, but Gerald does not seem to mind my lack of ladylikeness tonight. In fact I get the feeling he likes me just the way I am, looser all together and entirely on my own. That's what he had meant.

"I believe she does too," he says, being dear, "is there really anything to argue about?" He's smiling. His eyes are big. "Didn't you say she wants to go to the public school but she's not sure?"

Let myself go, I might go crazy. My mother did, quietly, in her room, finally—as long as she stayed in the house, okay. As long as she appeared in public in one piece now and then if my father wanted, then okay.

"Juliana knows what she wants. She takes after her mother," he says.

I'm not like my mother, I am thinking. She was the way all women were supposed to be—weak, hysterical, corrupt, ripe for slaps, escapist, Scarlett, Blanche, all that. I know this is the 1990s. But he's right, nothing ever seems to die out in New Orleans. Everything is chronic. Even the reign of those old gals. I really don't take after my mother. Especially since I'm on my own. I don't.

He grabs the check. The last time I let him buy me food was the day I saw the lawyer. But why not, I think. I don't protest. I feel odd, momentarily beyond it.

I'm also a little queasy, like, seasick.

"She's so amazing," he says, standing, "you've done an incredible job. You have. Listen."

And now, I don't want to argue with him, because we do agree, and it is Juliana. We stroll through that beautiful place, saying goodnight to so many waiters I feel embarrassed. I can tell I'm about to say something, either stupid or brilliant, I'm still not sure which. The urge is irresistible.

We glide down in the slow glass atrium elevator, and the lights lining the riverbank make a snaky cascade outside the window. "What has got you tonight, Elizabeth? What are you thinking about?"

I wish I could concentrate entirely on this extraordinary view, this height, this moment. We had our honeymoon near here at a little hotel, the Cornstalk. Once I remember, when he was with me, I leapt right out of myself, reaching blind, for every dimension of the room at once. I even found them. But afterwards, something had been stolen from me. I felt completely lost. "What is it, Elizabeth?" he asked me, just exactly what he's saying this minute. But he's not upset, right now. You can tell he just wants to know.

When I said and did certain things, when I told him to go, he acted like a man, out of pride. But his pride now breathes. I could walk right through it. And he'd still be there on the other side. I wish I didn't know this.

He was there when I had Juliana. He was there in the hospital's silly yellow paper gown, saying he wanted to be, watching me sweat her out, it felt like, terrible wave by terrible wave. And so I say, off the top of my head, I can't help it, as the elevator lands and opens into a lush green lobby, "You remember when she was born? You remember that day?"

"I do, I never saw you so happy," he says, just as the doors open, as we begin to stroll by the closing shops, the newsstands, the places that sell pralines and Tabasco. "I felt as if I had never made you happy any other time, it was the only day, her little face in that white blanket—" His voice cracks a little when he says this.

We push the brass and glass doors out.

Now we are walking on Royal, into the Quarter, where the past has a life of its own, so says the new slogan. And in the distance, a street saxophonist, but we can't see him. We are completely, impossibly alone.

I hear myself saying, "I wouldn't let you make me happy in those days."

"I know," he says, his face so sweet, so ready, I can hardly bear it. He waits a beat. He doesn't walk. He stands there, asking for my attention. "What's wrong with now?"

"I can't be sure," I have to say.

"Still?" he asks me.

That's when I get the answer. The river has to be its waters, where they go. It isn't its banks even here, where they make so much ado about shoring them up. The river floods. The levees crumble. The gates break down. New Orleans turns into Venice. There are boats in the streets, gondolas with paddle wheels, lovers serenaded by blues musicians, zydeco stars. Odds are sometime in my life this will happen. Some people might find it marvelous, I see that. And others would be overwhelmed, utterly overwhelmed.

Still.

Fatima Shaik (1952–)

Fatima Shaik grew up in the New Orleans 7th Ward, the setting of her 1987 short story included here, "Climbing Monkey Hill." In the story we meet the thirteen-year-old protagonist, Levia, who comes of age at the same time that legal desegregation comes to pass in New Orleans. Drawing on her own experience of growing up in this crucial time in the city's history, Shaik depicts the tense racial climate caused by local resistance to integration by the white community, which intensified the distrust in the black community.

Shaik, like Levia, was thirteen and living in the historic 7th Ward when Hurricane Betsy hit New Orleans in 1965, and in the story she uses Betsy to symbolize the racial storm that was taking place in the city. Shaik was also attending a black junior high school at the time and made the conscious decision to attend the white Dominican High School once the local schools were legally integrated. However, as much as this story may resemble Shaik's life, it is Levia's, not Shaik's story.

Shaik was born on October 24, 1952 to Mohamed and Lily Shaik. After graduating from Dominican, she attended Xavier University of New Orleans for two years before moving to Boston where she received her Bachelor of Science degree from Boston University in 1974. Four years later she received her Master's degree from New York University. Throughout her college career, Shaik worked as a writer/journalist for several publications, including the New Orleans *Times-Picayune* and the *Miami News*. She also worked as an editor for McGraw-Hill for over a decade before she began teaching writing, first at Southern University of New Orleans, then later at St. Peter's College in New Jersey, and Hunter College in New York City. As a freelance writer, her work has appeared in several national publications, such as *The New York Times* and *Essence* magazine. She has written four books, and is currently working on *Société,* a book about a New Orleans secret society of fifteen free men of color, which began in 1836. Shaik grew up as a New Orleans creole, but in fact, her paternal grandfather, from a small village near Calcutta, India, immigrated to the 7th Ward in the 19th century.

In "Climbing Monkey Hill," Shaik captures the close-knit neighborhood in which Levia lives. It is primarily an African American community, with the exception of one family, "the white country people around the block… a family of six pale, big-boned boys and girls." Levia liked maintaining "a friendly distance" from that family, and for a while thought perhaps forced integration was "unnatural." One night, Levia overhears the adults around the kitchen table discussing integration and gerrymandering, saying that because of the way New Orleans neighborhoods blend into one another, it would be almost impossible for "politicians… to be zigzagging that color line all through people's front porches to keep everyone separate and still follow the integration law." But we learn that it is not only a logistical problem but a cultural one as well and divided right along racial lines.

Shaik calls Monkey Hill "a guiding symbol" in the story, saying that Levia's trip to Monkey Hill represents Levia's rite of passage, her "uphill battle against racial prejudice, both white and black."[1] Monkey Hill, at 28 feet, was once the highest point in the city, which sits under sea level. It is manmade, a result of a 1930's WPA expansion of the city zoo at Audubon Park Uptown. It has long been a favorite playground for children in New Orleans, but Shaik calls it "a tenuous place; fun for children, but there could be danger."[2] In the story, Levia's mother leaves her in charge of the younger kids playing on Monkey Hill, and Levia hears the white parents saying of them, "Look at them little monkeys on Monkey Hill." On the drive Uptown to Monkey Hill, Levia notices the neighborhoods change and that "they were going to white places now… [where] anyone black who wore a uniform was welcome." Levia is well aware of the disparity between the Uptown, Garden District neighborhoods, and her own.

While the city learns to handle integration, so must Levia, begrudgingly: "Integration, that's all Levia heard and she was sick of it…. For years, Levia had looked forward to high school. But now the first question everyone asked her was whether she wanted to go to school among blacks or whites." Several occurrences help to make Levia's decision easier beginning with her trip to Monkey Hill: Hurricane Betsy and the bombing of the levees in

---

1   Fatima Shaik, Personal Interview, October 20, 2011.

2   Ibid.

the poor black neighborhoods to save the rich white ones; a fake bomb scare by some white teenagers at the rival black high schools' football game; her father carrying a gun to work in order to quell the racial tension. Through all of this, her parents leave her to make her own choice, and like integration, it is one she cannot escape.

Shaik's story offers a close look at the racial struggle in New Orleans in the 1960s through the eyes of a teenager who, like all teenagers, already has so much to struggle with. She finally must act, and she "abandons her hold on her childhood security... and the games on Monkey Hill."

Climbing Monkey Hill[1]

It was cause for embarrassment if black children climbed on Monkey Hill, even after they had integration. The boys and girls who ran from their nearby homes to play in Audubon Park after school did not arrive with their freedom only given the law.

When they ran up the hill, they were ridiculed by the parents who called down their own pale children. The adults stared at the black ones as if to see them for the first time. Although some were their over-the-fence neighbors, they replaced with bitterness the casual greetings of earlier times. "Look at them little monkeys on Monkey Hill," the parents agreed to each other over their children's heads. They spoke in a jovial way that encouraged their sons and daughters to adulthood by sharing the laugh.

Watching from a distance away, Levia knew what occurred. The adults stood confidentially close to one another, but arrogantly. Phases of sarcasm carried to her in the air, although only slightly because there was no breeze, as is usual in New Orleans in summer. Levia did not expect to hear more of their words because to shout at the children made the adults appear reckless under the law. She recognized they used their only remaining tool, ridicule, and, legally, the children were not bound to care.

Still, she held the hands of her brother and sister to keep them away from Monkey Hill. "Don't let yourself be a joke for nobody," she told them, just like her mother.

Levia's mother warned them not to wander too freely while she walked to get soft drinks. They were all safer if the children stayed on the blanket she placed on one patch of grass while she alone went to the concession stand.

But Levia now told her brother and sister to make them feel better, "Here, take some money and go get on a ride." She wanted them to know they could afford to go places. And she watched their figures walking away, like miniature adults hand in hand, little shadows of a man and a woman walking across a horizon sharp as tightrope while around them the world offered itself bleached and bare in the midday sun.

Levia sat on the scrap of lawn looking at Monkey Hill. It was a big lump in the middle of a flat, dusty field of Audubon Park, like one bucket of sand a child upends at the beach. Any grass planted once on Monkey Hill had died from the heat or underfoot from children running. Before development in this area, the park was a corner of swamp near the Mississippi River. It still had in spots the aura of unforgettable melancholy like most of New Orleans. But it took on an irony. Huge oaks with moss waterfalls fringed the dry field where Levia sat.

Monkey Hill was an even more incongruous site on the barefaced and dusty plain. Mud and river sand piled up about three dump trucks high, Levia figured. She pictured men in white uniforms building Monkey Hill and molding it with their hands to look like a giant, clay scoop of ice cream. After Monkey Hill took on popularity, politicians on television proclaimed it a site for the education and freedom of enjoyment of the children of New Orleans. Levia knew who they meant.

Anyone offered something by television in 1965 had to be only one race. And that specification excluded Levia, who was many things, but not white.

She was a girl who now at adolescence molded her two fat plaits into one rope of hair that followed her long neck and turned up naturally where her shoulders took hold. She was nearly as tall as her squat mother and glowed healthily like her dad.

"You're a miser's penny," he told Levia to let her know how precious and beautiful she was to him. She was copper-colored sometimes when he looked at her. Other times she showed more red or gold. He teased her, "Maroon," like that kind of person sold for a time in New Orleans after she ran very fast. So Levia was actually black and as yet a threat to the people who wanted only one kind of child on Monkey Hill and in Audubon Park.

But that didn't bother Levia. These days she cared less about what people thought and more about what she was feeling. Specifically, she wondered if Monkey Hill was high enough to see New Orleans in a different way.

No one in the city, adult or child who did not travel ever experienced both going up and coming down another side of a hill. The closest they ever got was the levee, which extended itself to one high point, then made a sheer drop. A child running against the breeze had to stop suddenly at the peak of enjoyment or fall into the river.

Levia once went alone to the levee. At the plateau was a path where people rode barebacked horses or walked south to the left and north to the right. Levia wondered how far they could go before the levee was no longer needed, either because the earth held back the water enough by itself or the waves of the Gulf took over.

Levia wished she could go to the river now. The day was so hot and uninspiring. The adults that Levia and her family joined in the park now bickered at a picnic table a hundred yards away. The topic, as usual, was who got hurt in civil rights demonstrations this week, and how everyone else should react. Levia just wanted to go some place where it was high, quiet, and she felt free. At thirteen, she wasn't anxious to join them.

Her mother said Levia should begin making decisions. The first one she gave her today was to watch the children near Monkey Hill. "Olevia, mind them till I come back. Show a little responsibility," her mother said. Levia felt responsible already. But she could not talk back. "Yes ma'am." That's all she was allowed to say as yet.

"Yes ma'am. No ma'am." Who gave Levia credit for thinking?

She felt she considered a lot but everyone said she was daydreaming. "Just a stage, you know," her mother told people all the time to explain Levia.

Levia had stared out the window this morning while they drove to Audubon Park. It was about one half-hour from their house.

The scene changed from small wooden homes that were painted to match the same shades in their gardens to half-block estates with stained glass windows and ironwork.

While they loaded the car to leave—shoving in the blanket and ice cooler along with a box of sandwiches their mother promised to bring for her friends—the neighbors came out to their porches and watched. They nodded approval, or showed envy at the picnic by waving down to them like shoo-fly, as the car drove off. The children were bound out of respect to reply to either greeting.

"Hello, Mrs. Dee. Hi, Brown. Good-bye, Irma Ann." They had to greet the neighbors each personally or the one they missed would try to convince even the others who got a hello that the children—because they were going to white places now—were growing stuck up.

By the time they neared Audubon Park, they could quietly look out the window. The houses here were so big, even if people wanted to they couldn't wave to their neighbors because no one could see from porch to porch.

Everyone called this area the garden district because the big plots displayed huge flowering trees. Not only did hundreds of flowers grow there but almost as many people were hired to take care of them. Levia's father, who knew people that worked outdoor parties in this area, said anyone black who wore a uniform was welcome here. In this neighborhood, no one flinched at the mention of slave quarters attached to a house.

Levia studied those estates in the city magazine that her mother ordered to come weekly to their home. And when she and her mother drove around, exploring the city, as they did often, Levia counted streets and streets of these massive and imposing buildings.

Some had four big, square, brick front-porch pillars, that her mother called, "grandiose Creole." Others had smooth, round, white columns, "southern Greek." Shingled roofs came down low to just top the cut-glass front doors that sparkled like diamonds.

Levia liked to believe these doors were locked like the treasure trunks in her mythology books and held great mysteries and came from secret places. But Levia's mother reminded her as they drove that everything she saw was the product of "hard work." And, occasionally, as they passed the houses, she said, "Slave labor."

But she didn't say that often because it stopped both of them from talking and she knew Levia liked to dream aloud.

"I'm going to have a big house on St. Charles Avenue someday."

Her mother said, "You better learn first to keep clean."

"And I'll have a library of books in two rooms and a horse in a stall near the back by the park."

"And who's going to pay you to waste time?"

The conversation usually developed into an argument soon after that or else Levia's mother ended it quietly, "My child, you can have anything that you really want."

Except recently, Levia wanted to go to the garden district by bus and walk around by herself as she did in her neighborhood. But her mother said, "That won't do." Because of integration, people in the city were angrier with each other than ever before. Levia considered going without telling. Their anger had nothing to do with her. She'd have to change buses and streetcars three times. Even the transportation system allowed for the separate traditions of New Orleans communities.

Different people did not live side by side. Instead, their houses were back to back. So there were white streets and black streets and most traffic followed the major white avenues, where Levia thought to get off and walk.

If she went on the bus, on entering she got a thin piece of tan paper to make the transfers. She had to be careful not to clasp it too tightly or sweat because it could melt in her hand. Many seats would contain workingmen who smelled strong from their day jobs and women with their arms draped tiredly over the back part of the chairs where their small children sat. Levia had to avoid the old ladies because no matter who sat next to them, they talked and she could miss her stop.

For the first transfer, she would be on Canal Street, where she could see anyone. A neighbor might tell her family. A stranger might hurt her. There were sailors and tourists, shopgirls and businessmen, teenagers much worldlier than Levia and foreigners who wanted to stop and talk.

But, they were dumb, people said, so conversation was pointless. Levia wasn't sure whether that was actually true. But it was safer, she felt, not to speak to anyone at all.

At Canal and St. Charles, where she boarded the streetcar, there would be a crush to get on. But by Magazine Street, all the pushy ones—men from the business district, transients, and the women who shopped in the expensive stores in the daytime, but who lived other places—would have left. Those remaining stayed in either big St. Charles houses or the small communities organized to serve them, located a couple of streets behind. Both of these people accepted their destinations with leisure. Some pulled down the wooden shade and dozed out of the sun, as the train rocked on the tracks to the end of the line.

The problems, Levia imagined, would come when the streetcar had only a few empty seats. A great deal of confusion occurred about who would sit first since the curtain was gone behind which black people sat. Now if a seat became open, a white person might come to the back of the bus to claim it or a black to the front. Both movements were considered rude if others in the predominant race in that section stood. Even a young boy would not get up for an old woman, unless they were the same.

Once, Levia's friends rushed to a seat to prevent a white woman from sitting. "Come. Here. Olevia," they called. "You shouldn't stand."

Levia repeated to herself, "Slave owner. Miss Anne. She's not so fragile." Levia wondered then, would her mother think this was rude or just?

Levia did not want to encounter trouble if she went by herself but she did want to take the ride. She knew her mother would say, "No. Everyone is just too upset now over integration." Integration, that's all Levia heard and she was sick of it.

New Orleans became possessed with the idea. It seemed good enough to think about, when it was planned. But now it just appeared too much trouble to Levia.

People were always protesting and others moved from places they lived all their lives. Where blacks and whites had lived willingly with their differences, now they were bitter. Too much change, Levia thought. Too much fighting, supposedly because of their children.

For years, Levia had looked forward to high school. But now the first question everyone asked her was whether she wanted to go to school among blacks or whites.

Next summer she'd have to make up her mind. "Does it matter?" she asked people who looked dumbfounded when they heard her reply. That was another occasion when her mother asked everyone to excuse her child. Then whoever posed the question to Levia in the first place would say she had a duty to her race. Of course, she had a duty. Levia understood that.

For what other reason would she be going to school at all? Lynne Carre's parents let her wear miniskirts and boots and date boys who were five years older, and Lynne said she wasn't going to school because she first had to please herself. Actually, she was pregnant last fall.

But Levia's parents "expected things" of her and a baby was not part of their plan. If fact, her father warned, "If I ever see you on the corner with those neighborhood bums, don't come home." So she didn't stay out late. Not that she thought he was fair. But she believed he would not let her back in the house and she couldn't figure out how she would take care of herself alone.

But everyone else made too big a deal of things she would do naturally, like go to high school, while Levia had better plans. For example, Levia made herself a promise to enjoy living day to day. And she was keeping it, not worrying too much, thinking about the things she wanted to do and not the requests of others, remaining free like a child.

She thought, this was the prime of her life, the summer beginning, and she was in the park. Levia lay in the sun, idly thinking, not anymore about her sister, brother, or mother. She took the quiet for granted, rested and watched the shadow of Monkey Hill grow as the sun marked time.

"New Orleans has too much of a mixed-up society to be bothered anyway," Levia heard one of the adults talk against integration at the kitchen table one night. "Now, who's going to tell me how they going to draw the line around here?" The grown-up said no one would want real race relations legalized: "With where the poor whites live and the St. Lima whites with black people from Corpus Christi Parish right back of them, politicians going to be zigzagging that color line all through people's front porches to keep everyone separate and still follow the integration law."

Levia listened to only this part of the conversation, then she went out into the backyard. Maybe it was unnatural to force people to change. She wouldn't mind people keeping a friendly distance like she did with the white country people around the block. They were a family of six pale, big-boned boys and girls whom she really didn't mind.

Once their pet armadillo climbed under her fence.

"Watch him, watch him now," the oldest boy told his sisters as he ran around the corner to get into Levia's yard. The armadillo buried itself into the mud where the chain link ended near the ground. The girls poked it with a stick to send it to their side. But their backyard was concrete. And the armadillo acted as if it were embarrassed to run away but obligated to go where it was greener because it burrowed under the grass behind Levia's house while they called it, going deeper and deeper into a hole.

The boy arrived with a wood and screen box, the kind, Levia knew, that was used to keep in pigeons. He stopped the armadillo by cornering it with a board. He kept blocking its moves until the animal tired of the places it originally wanted to go. Then he picked up the armadillo and showed it to Levia, "Look here."

She studied its slate-colored shell, long fingernail claws, and little unprotected parts around its legs on the underside.

"Won't hurt yer," he said by way of thanks. "You could come play with it if you want." Levia shook her head yes to be polite. But it seemed too unfair to both man and animal, she felt, to play with something that you had to catch.

Instead, in the evenings she played with the children in the houses that faced hers on the block. They attended the black public school up the street or went to Corpus Christi, the elementary attached to the church.

Their games were mostly inventions, like Coon Can where they hit a rolling ball with a stick and ran back and forth from one square drawn on the ground to another, scoring points. They played Red Light to see who could sneak to the light before getting caught or Fassé with each one keeping the ball from the others and a Hide-and-Seek called I Spy.

Before night fell, all the children sat on the steps and talked. Levia felt they made their own sidewalk family, besides being involved in separate ones at home. Elanore wanted to be everyone's mother with her bossiness, "Girl, you ought to take off that short skirt with them bony legs," "Johnson, come over here."

Philip was "do-fuss," the children said. He allowed his mother to tell the barber to cut his hair too short and one time he even showed them a part shaved crookedly right onto his scalp. Philip never spoke first to anyone and only talked back to Elanore if she pushed up against him. Once he told Levia that when he grew up he wanted to be a policeman.

"Why you want to do that, to have a gun?" she asked. "I'm sick of white people telling me what to do," he replied. Levia looked at him hard for a few minutes, then took up conversation with another child on the step. She didn't tell anyone Philip's desire and she even avoided Elanore some after that. Levia wasn't quite sure why. But Elanore, Levia sensed, would force Levia to choose sides. And all Levia knew was that she felt bad talking about white people all the time, as everyone did, and now she didn't feel good either talking with Philip.

Levia preferred to spend time with her cousins. Charlene was a cheerleader now for St. Augustine. The two black Catholic high schools, St. Augustine and Xavier Prep, had a football rivalry so intense that nothing else mattered for weeks in the neighborhood.

"Go, St. Aug.," people called from their porches to youngsters dressed in purple and gold. Young mothers balanced their baby-children on their hips as they stood outside the St. Augustine schoolyard fence watching the band practice in cavalier helmets. Girls not yet pregnant lingered with one arm hooked above their heads in the chain link to display themselves to the male musicians. Many a trumpet and saxophone player was inspired to further a musical career by the sight of female curves on the horizon, a line that stretched from the school's Hope Street to Law Street boundaries.

The night before the game, Charlene gave Levia and her friends a demonstration of cheerleading in the street. The boys who wanted to watch promised to keep an eye out for oncoming cars. Levia and the girls sat in a pyramid on the steps and waved their hands like paper shakers for Charlene to begin.

"We're really rocking them, really rolling, really pushing them down the field. Look at Purple Knights, a real swinging deal. We push them back, and roll them back, and knock them to the ground. Look at our team, we really rocking them down. St. Augustine. Go St. Aug. St. Augustine...." Every time Charlene said St. Augustine, the girls on the steps put their hands on their hips and directed their shoulders from one side to the other, like mini-Supremes.

Every cheer these days was a little angry with a newfound pride. Black cheerleaders had always done the latest dances and "finger-popped" while the bands played. However, they got a greater appreciation for the way they looked while dancing after they saw new, sophisticated female groups on television. But they also got laughed at during cheerleading competitions against the white schools. Their cheers were acrobatic, but the blacks' cheers were musical. The result was that the cheerleaders for St. Aug., Prep, and many others held their heads with a little higher tilt under bouffant hairdos that took advantage of their full hair, and they smiled a little less these days for every occasion.

On the day of the game, Levia accompanied Charlene. Then Levia took a seat near the top of the stadium. The air was clear and cool, hinting at the arrival of fall. The oppressive heat in summer, that made a poor choice of any seat close to the sun, was gone.

Levia looked across the field to Xavier Prep. Bodies rocked in unison as if pulled side to side by the music. Levia heard from the competition an occasional shrill snatch of trumpet or a couple of drumbeats. It gave her the feeling that she wanted to dance too, except she felt it inside, like a stirring in her body or a shiver in a place she could not locate. While she waited for the St. Augustine band to begin, she pulled against the collar of her sweater in a way her mother disapproved because she said it would stretch. But that made Levia relax a little and she looked more closely at the stands below her.

People brought umbrellas to open and bob with the band's music. Others waved white handkerchiefs in their enthusiasm. Like two hundred flags, an army of individuals bound by music and rivalry, they slapped the air to the right and left.

The movement was one of sureness. Levia felt part of a single voice raised for enjoyment of the day. Support for a team was so unlike Levia's picture of high school, if she had to go there under the laws of integration.

When she watched television at dinnertime with her parents, the white people protested blacks coming to their schools. "Two-four-six-eight, we don't want to integrate." Levia saw their spokesman address a reporter, "They will lower the standards in our classrooms to where our children couldn't learn anything."

"Why do we want to be where they don't want us, anyway?" Levia asked her mother.

"For the future, Olevia. Pass your plate." She went on serving dinner.

Levia's father said, "Education is the only way to move up. Whatever high school you go to, Levia, we want you to apply for college."

Levia remembered complaining, "Do I always have to think about this?"

But alone at the football game, Levia conceived an easy picture of high school. She would go to a black school and be safe, just like she was today, or all her life in her neighborhood, and with her family.

From her seat, away from the crowd, Levia saw her neighbors—Philip and his mother, Elanore and her boyfriend. Many other people looked familiar to her, like cousins, in shapes with rounded shoulders, in sun-lacquered hues and clothes she knew from the local stores. She nodded hello to a soft, masculine face that she recognized from the neighborhood or maybe he was even a cousin. But when he smiled, Levia saw from the crookedness of the teeth and the way the lips were hooked around them, he was no one she knew.

Still, he rose from his seat a couple of sections away and began walking over to her. Levia didn't know what to do. If she moved away, he would think she was rude. Plus, she already was sitting at the top, so she would encounter him if she tried any route to leave. She waited, pulling her sweater across herself with both hands, making an X. She was shivering when he arrived.

"Are you cold? What's your name?"

"I came to the football game with my cousin," Levia replied.

"I'm Roger. Want me to get you warm?"

"I have to go to the bathroom." Levia got up.

"What high school do you go to?" He caught her arm.

Levia shook herself away, rushing now, down the steps. She called back, "I'm just in eighth grade."

Levia hurried with her head down and her arms across her chest, to the bathroom under the bleachers. It was dimly lit and where ceiling lights were broken in places, electricity buzzed in the dark. She slowed her pace to think in the dark places because no one could see her there.

She was angry because he touched her arm. She wondered what she would do. He can't make me talk to him, Levia thought.

But she knew she felt bad because of her confusion. Other girls, like Elanore, could have been slick or jive.

"Does that feel good to you," Elanore had once replied to a boy who had pushed her up against the house. She told Levia the boy let her go right after that. "I didn't have to fight. You just got to be smart," she advised.

It was just the same with the white people, Levia thought. Always someone was telling her, "We have to outsmart them to get what we want." When people told her that, Levia could not remember a thing that she wanted from whites. How could she want anything that people were not willing to give? And if she got it because she was smarter, why didn't she have it all along?

It was very confusing even though her mother said, civil rights was a problem for white people because "then they will have to see we're the same."

A cheer went up from the stands above Levia's head. This year Xavier was winning. The championship moved between it and St. Aug. because they were so evenly matched.

Levia stood still and looked around her. Pretty high school girls flirted with boys in the bright places near the concession stands as they waited to get treated to soft drinks and sandwiches. They laughed with their faces tilted up, just so the light flattered the curves of their cheeks and slid over the bones in their jaws.

Levia considered that men challenged women just to see who would win. Another cheer broke from the stadium above her head. Levia tried to laugh like the girls did who were standing under the light. But she only succeeded in making a dumb sound like little grunts linked by a strained desire.

Suddenly people came running down the ramps of the stadium. "They say there's a bomb in the stands," someone yelled as he passed. Levia looked around for Charlene or anyone she thought she might know. She saw no one. So she ran with the crowd, out of the gates of the stadium into the parking lot.

People stood around looking confused and disappointed. Levia walked from group to group, peering into them to see who she knew. When she got farthest away from the stadium, she saw a motorcade coming. With horns blowing and convertibles alternately speeding up and screeching to a stop, crowds of white teenagers drove past shouting to the people who were leaving the game, "Dumb niggers. We fooled ya'll dumb niggers."

More protests were on the evening news during dinner. This time, mothers were crying and fathers were mad. "How can my child be safe anymore in her classes?" one woman said, full of tears.

"They just don't want our young men fooling with their girls," Levia's father called at the TV from his seat at the kitchen table.

"Marvin," Levia's mother told him, "please hold your tongue in front of this child."

"I'm going outside anyway," Levia told them. "I don't see how no boy can do anything to me that he wouldn't do to a white girl."

As Levia left, she figured she had said something right because she heard her mother catch her breath.

Ever since the game, Levia was wondering about the rules of being kissed. Was it like something you said you wanted to do? Or was it like being ambushed? People in the movies clung to each other, the man holding the woman's head in his hands as if something precious was there. Levia would have to think harder, like the women on TV, to be able to say the right things and get kissed for her smarts. She resented that people thought white girls would get kissed more than her. Levia felt she had just as much brains.

The question of school, too, still hung before her. But worst, her parents wanted her to consider going to a white school with all girls.

Levia saw them many times on the bus. They wore white blouses where the ironing seemed to melt by the afternoon and blue, pleated skirts that they rolled at the waist so short it called attention to their legs, yellow like chicken parts. Their mothers let them shave to their knees and many carried big, square, adult pocketbooks.

The girls at Xavier Prep were not nearly as free. A hint of wiped-off lipstick carried three afternoons of cleaning the nuns' windows, and any objection to punishment made a trip to confession necessary.

"You're not going to school to socialize," Levia's mother told her, "and you might make a few friends." That time Levia walked into her bedroom without answering. She did not tell her parents about the boys she saw pass in the car. She knew they would say "rowdies come in every color."

She was losing her arguments, too, about all white people because the whites who stayed in the Catholic schools had to agree with integration. The bishop threw out of the church that year any of the others who did not want to mix. It was un-Christian and un-Catholic, the bishop said.

Levia and her mother had seen it on television, and they cheered as the bishop refused to talk to the people who protested blacks entering.

"Finally, somebody is putting their foot down on real sin," Levia's mother said.

"It is never too late," Levia agreed. But now, as the decision acutely affected her, she wondered, what about blacks who did not want to go to school with whites? Was it as bad for black people to be against white people, as whites were against them?

Elanore said no, once when Levia asked her. "They be always on our case. Why you so polite to them? You some kind of Oreo, black on the outside, white on the inside. Or oleo, yellow all the way through."

Levia answered, "I don't like white people."

"So let's go then," Elanore called her along.

Levia had said, "I don't like white people," a little louder than she would have liked for her parents to hear. They told her because she had freckles from one Irish great-grandfather, that she should not be quick to draw lines. "You just focus on what is just and what is unjust," her father told her, "and don't choose your sides by the color of skin."

But wasn't it true that white people hated them because of appearance? "So why," Levia argued, "do we have to be nice?"

"It will keep you from being a fool to the wrong kind of people, girl," her father said like he didn't want to hear anything more.

But that day with Elanore, Levia did not hesitate to follow Elanore's convictions. She was dark and she had freckles too, like they could be sisters, she said, as she once flattered Levia.

"I know how we can get them," Elanore whispered after they entered Richards, the dime store around the corner on the white street. "I'm going to make a fuss with that woman at the cash register. You pick out some candy for me."

Levia got a few Tootsie Rolls, some gum, and a mint. Then she walked to the front. "That's the one with her," the saleswoman called to a man coming toward Levia as she saw Elanore run out of the door. "Check her pockets. You got money to pay for that?"

"But it's not for me."

"You think I'm going to put it back on the shelf?" the saleswoman glared.

Levia left with her pockets empty of change and a bag of candy in her hand. As she turned the corner, Elanore appeared from behind one of the shady oak trees. "You got some gum for me? You are some sucker." She stood with her hand on her hip laughing at Levia.

Levia drew back her arm and popped Elanore in the face with the candy bag. The candy flew out of the bag as it broke and stayed spread over the sidewalk because Elanore chased her all the way home.

When she got to her house, Levia went straight to her room, to be alone and to be quiet. Both the whites and her black friend had turned against her and she did not want to be around anyone anymore.

"Some people just want to stay stupid," Levia's father, with a drink in his hand, badgered her because she refused to discuss anymore where she was going to high school.

"Maybe I'll just get books and read at home," Levia said. "Oh, what we got here is a separatist," he called to the air. "You into black power or white?" "Daddy, shoot." Levia left the room. She didn't think she could learn at home. But she saw many people on television who took their children out of the public schools. Black parents who feared violence and insults took their children to schools formed by church parishes. Whites, who didn't want theirs to mix, formed small teaching groups at home.

All these adults claimed to be right. Others said, "Trust in God," for all answers. "His justice will reign," said one woman who came to Levia's door selling religious books. She dropped to her knees and prayed on Levia's wooden porch when Levia told her she'd better start to go home because the radio just predicted a hurricane on its way.

"God's going to wipe the slate clean," Levia's neighbor, old Mr. Gontier, stopped to tell her on the way to the grocery store.

He had seen many hurricanes, "Lola, Darleen, Sylve, Ethel, Darleen." Levia nodded her head with each one, especially for the hurricane he mentioned twice, thinking he might get the message that she had to go and was getting bored. But that just seemed to encourage him to go on.

"Out of respect," her mother said pay attention to old people. So Levia felt caught by his stories, and she blamed her parents for her delay now. "God always works in mysterious ways. But I'll tell you, He always sends a message for you while He's doing it. Something for you to learn from." Levia was beginning to back away from old Mr. Gontier, and he noticed. "Now you hear me well," he hollered. She had backed off far enough to be able to turn her face away with one last shake of her head, "yes sir."

Levia hurried to the Circle Food Store. The lines were long. Before any hurricane, people stocked up on canned food and candles, liquor, water, and ice. If she ran out of money, Levia wondered which of the necessities she should choose out of that group.

But her mother gave her enough to buy two bags of ice and four tall votive candles. They had enough, Levia guessed, of the rest.

While Levia waited in line, she watched old people gather under the arches right outside of the entrance door. Circle Food Store was more a tradition in the neighborhood than a full-service grocery. It was rambling building, erected in parts, like occasional Spanish memories, probably as the owners got more money in their cash registers. With several red-tiled roofs and upside-down U's linked side by side to make an open wall for a breezeway that extended over the sidewalk, the Circle gathered the old and the romantic. Nothing in the vicinity was new.

The checkout clerks were over sixty-five, the pigeons that lived under the arches were balding, and some boxes of food were usually damaged by rain or outdated and sold at discount. The floor was worn in spots from black-and-white linoleum squares to a smooth, sloping plywood.

The old people came to the Circle in numbers to discuss the hurricane and that too seemed right on time. Levia thought that a good wind could destroy either the building or the people with one gust. The idea made her wish that she had spent longer listening to Mr. Gontier.

"We will be closing in twenty minutes," an announcer said. The checkout clerks sighed and people began rolling their baskets quickly in Z patterns up the aisles. The way their carts jingled over the floor as the people shoved them, then crashed into others when their drivers left them, struck Levia as funny. "Miss, will you hurry up. Is something humorous here?" Before Levia answered, the clerk said, "Next."

The sky was dark by the time Levia reached her house. There were marbled patterns above her of black sky and white clouds, changing constantly with an unpredictable pace. "Thank God," Levia's mother stood on the porch. They closed the door and latched the long, cypress shutters behind them, just before the wind began shaking the wood.

First, it rained like a thunderstorm, except without lightning. Then, the wind hit the front of the house like someone was throwing debris. Soon a noise rose like all kinds of people shouting at once. But above it, Levia's family could hear the shutters of the house next door bursting against its own windows, garbage cans rolling down the pavement, car horns going off and on like bleating-sounds that made Levia think of the instruments in a band running away from the musicians. Tree branches scraped down the street like fabric being ripped. The lights went out.

Levia, her mother, brother, father, and sister moved into the same room and gathered around one votive candle. "First, let's say a prayer for the people who will suffer through this," Levia's mother said. "For the good and the bad, may they find Your Wisdom." The family said, "Amen."

The next morning a neighbor from across the street rattled the door blinds to wake them. Levia's father jumped from the floor. "Man, I thought you were the hurricane," he said after he opened the door.

"You got to see this, brother," the neighbor pointed to the corner as they walked away. Levia ran down the steps to follow. Water tapered off to become level with the street where it rushed into the drainage sewers about two blocks from Levia's house. Beyond that, St. Bernard Avenue was a canal. People had launched skiffs into it and were paddling downtown.

"They say it gets deeper and deeper farther back. To the ninth ward, it's over the roofs," the neighbor called to her father over the sound of others saying the same thing.

The street was also filled with children playing. They laughed and splashed in the shallow water as if all of a sudden God gave them a public pool. The city had ordered all swimming facilities closed a year earlier since too many people complained about such intimate mixing of whites and blacks. Levia's mother spoke to the television when she heard the reports, "That's OK, city, we always swim in the natural lake."

Neighbors, who had left their houses to stay with relatives during the storm, slowly returned. They carried stories up the street, crossing from porches on one side to those on the other.

The telephones didn't work.

"In the ninth ward, the water is over your house," one man said. "They claim lots of us drown." He carried the contents of his refrigerator, offering meat and eggs to families as he went along. "I rather do this," he said, "than to let it spoil."

Levia went to the corner to find other children. Only Philip was out. "They say Elanore's family went down to the ninth ward." Elanore's grandfather approached her house dressed in the suit and straw hat he wore every day to go to the horse races.

"They not home," Philip said and told the grandfather about the floods in the ninth ward.

Elanore's grandfather sat on the step with his head in his hands, "The white people done it."

Levia went to the edge of the water at St. Bernard Avenue and waded. Then, the water got too deep, near the curbs where the street sloped down or near intersections. So she swam. The water was brown like the river and it smelled like the London Avenue sewerage canal. People passed in small motorboats, making soft wakes. They shouted, "You ought to get out. This water's filthy."

But Levia wanted to swim downtown as far as she could. She could go two miles in the lake and had since she was little. This water was shallower and porches jutted above it along the way where she could rest.

Once when she stopped, bits of clothing and then a suitcase floated past. "Didn't get away fast enough," Levia thought, then she wondered where was the person they fit. The water held boards and tree branches, plastic toys and food, like a box of cereal. Levia watched most of the day from that porch about one mile from her house. She did not go further because all she saw ahead of her was just drifting and she decided not to just follow along.

When the radio came on in a couple days, reports said the levee had broken downtown. By that time, Levia and her family already heard a different story from people arriving in boats docked near their street. People said the levee was torn away by the city at a section in the ninth ward. That made the water pour into the black neighborhood and relieve the flooding of whites on the other side. Everyone who drowned during Hurricane Betsy was black, Levia heard. A movement began for revenge.

Elanore never appeared and Levia prayed constantly, asking God to forgive her for hitting Elanore in the mouth. Soon after, she saw Elanore getting out of a car. Levia ran up to hug her.

"Is you crazy?" Elanore jumped back waving her hand at Levia as if to drive away a bad smell. "Nobody got to worry about me, I could swim."

Elanore's mother told Levia that Elanore saved her grandmother as the flood rose. She pulled her in the water from the roof of a house to the three-story school building across the street.

"I'll tell you one thing, I'm not going to be nice anymore," Elanore said.

People sat on their porches more than usual for the next week while the telephones were out. Daily came news, less about dead people now, more that pet cats were bloated and found in backyards when the water receded, or new furniture was ruined with no insurance to pay for it, and of permanent watermarks near the ceilings of houses.

Where Levia disbelieved everything before the hurricane, now she listens to anything. "They say the Black Panthers are going to defend the ninth ward from now on," Levia told her mother, "and they're going to stop school integration."

"Cheer up," Levia's mother smiled. But Levia could not figure out what she meant. Levia was frightened like most of the old ladies she visited on the block. One told her, "I guess God just don't want people to mix. If He did, wouldn't he see to it that we could get better along?" Levia thought for a second that her father said people were together more at one time in New Orleans, until they started black and white separate justice. But Levia said nothing. The old woman kept talking, "I think them Black Panthers is right. We need protection."

"The Panthers say, if you don't put something black on house, you have no respect for the dead in the ninth ward and you will be hurt," Levia brought a new rumor home.

"That's crazy," Levia's father answered. "Who doesn't know we're for black people doesn't know us. So it's none of their damn business."

But in the same way that Levia brought the requirement to her house, other children and childish minds spread the rumor down the block. The neighborhood soon accumulated drapes of sympathy all day in varying degrees from solidarity to fear: Flags of red, black, and green hung out of some windows. Others hung pieces of black material, a coat jacket, a navy blue towel, and a black negligee appeared.

"What is she giving up for the revolution?" Levia's father called to his wife.

"Hush up," her mother laughed.

Levia followed her father into the bedroom and watched while he opened a dresser drawer and got out his gun. "I can take care of this family good enough."

But when they went to sleep, Levia took her grammar school uniform out of the closet. Although it was navy blue, she planned to hang it out on the porch. She unlatched the shutters and pushed the blinds open to see if anyone was outside. But the electricity had not yet been restored so there were no streetlights.

Levia tiptoed out to the porch, clutching her school uniform in her folded arms over her nightgown. To think of a place to hang it she sat on the steps. She tried to get her eyes to adjust to the darkness all around her. She could make out a few candlelit front rooms in the neighborhood where people sat up, or where they kept a kerosene lamp burning because they were afraid.

Levia felt cold sitting on the steps in her sheer gown. But she didn't want to go inside. There was something going on all around her, and Levia felt if she sat outside long enough she could smell it. The air held the salty moisture of breeze off the river, the rancid smell of moss and wet grass, and a tinge of something burning. Levia thought to hang her school uniform from the door. But then she remembered that she would have to wear it tomorrow and her father would be the first one out of the house. She thought maybe he was right about keeping the gun loaded. If the white people came inside, he would just blow them up.

"The big fish eat the little fish, and we, the people, eat all the fish," old Mr. Gontier joked with Levia as she watched him unload his boat. His nephews stood in the skiff on its bed pulled behind the car parked in the driveway. Mr. Gontier handed one of the older boys the garden hose to wash the stench of dead bait and catch out of the boat, while the other gave him the ice chest.

He dragged it into his unfenced front yard and took out fish one by one to show the children. "This here is my dinner. And this," he picked up a dead shrimp, "was his dinner." The children laughed as he made gulping noises and pointed to the fish.

But some fish were still alive. The children stared at their big, unblinking eyes and sighed while the fish drew air deeply through their gills. These produced a collective "Aw," in sympathy, speckled trout that lost their rainbow as soon as they were lifted out of the ice by the tail and croakers who made long, painful belches as they gasped and flopped slowly from one side to the other on the pavement.

"Ya'll too soft," Mr. Gontier fussed at them. "Where ya'll get hamburgers? From Old McDonald's cow!"

"Ugh," children groaned and covered their mouths. The old man continued, "And you know how they kill them, pow, they shoot them right in the middle of the head."

"I don't believe you," Elanore said. "Old stupid man," she called ahead of herself so he could not hear her as she went home. Levia decided it was time for her to go too. Philip remained next to the step until the sun went down and the old man said he had to go inside.

Levia went to the kitchen table, "Do we have to kill animals to eat?"

Her mother replied, "Well, there are some things that we grow. A person could eat vegetables and grains all the time."

Her father entered the room, "No. Listen to me child, in life you are either the hunter or the hunted."

"That's not true, Marvin," said her mother.

"You'll tell me then, if it's not man against animal, it's man against man. It's either kill or be killed, Darwinism, the philosophy of the hunter. Have people ever been able to get away from that? No, it's a jungle and until people first understand that it is, they will never get beyond it."

"Well, that's the survival of the stupid if you ask me," Levia's mother said.

"Thanks, answered her father. "What are we having for dinner?"

"Pork chops."

Levia ran out the back door, holding her stomach. "The poor pig."

Twilight was falling when she sat on the backyard steps. She tried to make out the outline of her things she enjoyed. The bay leaf and pecan trees, the tomato bushes, her mother's planters with pansies, the doghouse and the dog's silent pacing in his fenced off section.

She heard evening bugs around her. Something big like a bee flew near her head and she tilted her ears on an angle to the ground, and held herself stiff. After she relaxed, she stared at the dark grass. Its stillness was calming and every once in a while, she'd notice a faint little glow, a lightning bug, low to the ground. Levia stayed outside even though the mosquitoes were beginning to bite.

In the daytime, mosquito hawks ate the mosquitoes. Like flying dragons, someone once told Levia, mosquito hawks were all over the yard. She used to catch them by their transparent wings and feed them tobacco. Now she just liked to watch them. They were getting too fast for her, Levia's mother said, to encourage her to act more like a lady. And Levia began to take pleasure just noticing their prettiness. The mosquito hawks had different tints -some were shaded blue, some green, others black, silver, gold from their flat, fly noses to their crispy wings.

If she caught them, she did not see the color. She had to concentrate on keeping them still. Half the time the wings broke from the pressure of children holding. Most pinched the wings harder if the mosquito hawks tried to get away.

Once, Levia's mother caught Philip shaking a mosquito hawk by the fragile wings to make it release the tobacco in its mouth.

"Philip, what are you doing? You gave it to him. That thing didn't do anything to hurt you. So leave it alone."

Levia wondered as she began to go inside and slapped the mosquitoes now stabbing her arms whether to kill something that first comes after you was all right?

She hit at the site of a prickly pain and squashed the insect into a fragment of rolling fabric under her hand. When she tried to pick the dead bug off her arm, what she felt most was the wetness of her own blood.

Her cousin carried a gun with him all the time. "Once I was fishing," he said, "and I nearly got bit by a snake." He was a big man and a hunter like most of his friends. Sprouting along the walls of their houses were necks, faces and antlers.

He taught Levia how to shoot. "You don't have to act all the time like a girl," he said. "Besides, you'd better learn how to protect yourself." He placed his hand over hers as she held the base of the weapon. "Now hold it straight up and shoot it into the air."

Levia pulled the trigger. A vibration traveled from her wrist to the center of her chest. "There you go. Now that wasn't bad, was it? You want to do it again?" he asked.

Levia said no. He had shown her the proper way to load and carry the weapon. Shooting it once was all she could stand.

When he let her shoot, it was New Year's Eve night so no one noticed the ringing sound. In fact, shooting rifles and handguns were part of the fun in New Orleans. In neighborhoods where riflemen did not have time to buy blanks the sky rained buckshot.

Everyone drank and hugged out of tradition in the background. Overhead was pitch-black. But the shooters stood safe distances from each other, or in groups that would not face head on, and from the ends of their weapons, quick, deadly fires blazed. It was like one hundred matches lighted at once, or a burst of anger, a scar on the sky.

The children that year played a new game called "Killer." One girl's cousin brought it from California for the holidays. He lived in Watts. They would sit in a circle and wink at each other before another winked at them. Once you caught the wink of another, you were dead.

Levia played once and lasted a long time. But she did not like the way she felt during the game. "Come on, girl," the boy from Watts challenged her, "I could do better this time and it's more fun with lots of people."

"Didn't I tell you I don't want to play?" Levia pushed his shoulder away from her in the circle where they sat. But before he could push her back, tears came out of her eyes. She did not know why and they dried up immediately from her own shock.

The boy walked away from the other children, telling the others, "Where did you get this weird one?"

While the party was still going on, all the children were called into the front room. The television was on. "Look at Dr. King," the grown-ups were pointing. It was more news about civil rights, Levia thought. She didn't want to listen too long. But everyone was quiet. He was talking about marching for nonviolence. He kept using the words "Love" and "Peace."

"He don't know these crackers down there in New Orleans," one of the adults said. "I rather listen to Malcolm X." Then the adults began arguing and Levia returned to the other room. The children were talking about the same thing. "I'll rather see them all die," the boy from Watts said, "than to live with them."

By spring of her eighth grade year Levia had to start thinking about high school. Elanore would attend the junior high in the neighborhood for a couple years, she said. Philip told everyone his father wanted him to work.

Levia stopped going around them because they kept asking her what she was going to do, and bragging about their own choices, which Levia felt they had not really made. If they were telling the truth, she told herself, how were they able to decide so easily?"

Surprisingly, in one year, some parts of the city had gotten more accustomed to integration. But now pressure came from other sides. Her teachers encouraged Levia to be the first. "Go there and get on the volleyball team." Or, "It would be nice if they had a black girl debate."

Levia would have to fight for these things as well and she was not sure she even wanted to try. Others in her community showed her another way: That blacks did not need to be among whites at all. That made sense to Levia from the life she had experienced so far.

A man visited every Saturday morning selling Muhammad Speaks. He talked to Levia's mother at length each time. She liked the way he looked. He was dressed out of date as far as Levia was concerned —hair cut too short, a bow tie and a suit that was too shiny, especially for Saturday morning. But Levia enjoyed the way he paid attention to her.

"Good Morning, beautiful sister," he addressed her. "Is your mother here?"

On days that her mother was busy, he handed Levia the paper to bring inside and her mother swapped back to him the weekly newspaper of her Catholic faith. Levia wished she had something intelligent to say to Brother then. She had always sneaked out of mass so they couldn't talk about religion. But in Muhammad Speaks she had read the cartoons that called "shameless" the women who wore their dresses too short and tight. Levia had not yet developed a figure like in the cartoons but she did feel she could comment on that.

So the next time Brother came, Levia tried to seduce him into a conversation about clothes. She was standing in front of the house watering the garden. She was barefoot because of the especially warm spring day and had on a short play suit. Every few minutes she would run a stream of water across her legs and feet. That stopped them from scalding on the cement for a time.

"I think you are right about women not wearing their dresses too tight, Brother," Levia smiled and looked him in the eyes.

"That's right." He watched the blush on her shoulders down her long arms that ended at her thighs, to her toes.

"Are you cool or warm?"

"OK, I guess. But I think it's right about self-respect and the way ladies put on dresses. My parents always told me that."

"Is your mother home?"

"No, But you can talk to me."

"Give her this, beautiful sister. And if you want to have a conversation, there are many women who would like to give you guidance, if you wish to consider visiting the Mosque. In the meantime, young sister, be aware of yourself, like your mother says, and at least put on a dress."

Levia felt very hot. The soles of her feet burned. Suddenly she realized why. She had been standing the whole time with the water running into the bushes. She picked up the hose and now pointed it at the cement as the Brother left. Then she held it up like a fountain and let it shower her like when she was a little girl.

Charlene called to ask Levia what about going to St. Mary's. If she did go to St. Mary's like her cousin Charlene, Levia might be popular. St. Augustine picked most of its cheerleaders from there. It was a black, Catholic girl's school and having a cousin could help, especially since Charlene was awarded the title of school queen during her senior year.

Levia considered the possibility of an active social life based on her royal blood. She remembered Charlene's coronation in the auditorium. Folding chairs covered the floor except for a wide center aisle. Parents sweated in their Sunday clothes. Some women wore tall white hats iced with net in their college sororities' colors, while men had on shiny striped suits and several kinds of official emblem ties.

That day Levia sat on the aisle so she could photograph Charlene. Everyone smiled as much as the queen did as she passed them to the stage. Charlene was as gracious as if they all were her servants applauding. She waved her scepter like the bishop sprinkling out blessed water with a holy enthusiasm that the people shined under like they were catching some summer rain. Levia wondered if everyone felt like she did—that Charlene was looking just at them and if they looked back, they would have some of her beauty.

When Charlene arrived at her aisle, Levia snapped a picture and waved. Charlene stopped then and blew Levia a kiss. A sigh rose from the crowd, sweet like candy air floating up to the sky from the cotton-making machine. It was as if everyone puffing softly could make Charlene nicer.

Charlene got the most roses, red long-stemmed ones, of any of the girls on the stage. The runners-up received flowers according to rank and Levia took pictures of each one of them, even though the man sitting near Levia said, "Save your film for the best."

Later, after the photos developed, Levia pinned them to the bulletin board on her wall. While she studied and listened to the radio in the evening, she stared at them every day until she knew by heart what they all looked like.

She imagined that these girls were like starlets who were kissed in the movies, each one more favored than the next. The ones who were the least pretty were the least admired. The one who was beautiful, Charlene, was not only well-liked, but rich and famous.

But the day Levia was studying and thinking about going to high school and she looked at the pictures, an idea occurred to her. She was not nearly as pretty as Charlene. Levia glanced quick to the mirror; there was hardly a family resemblance. How would they know she and Charlene were related. And what if she told them and they could not see Levia was as pretty as her cousin, so they didn't care? What if people didn't like her still after they knew she had a famous relative? She would be a total failure.

Levia suddenly felt like a little fish in the high school pond, and already eaten by Charlene.

Levia sat still thinking with her hands on her books and listened to the radio. It played the Supremes' "Nothing But Heartaches." Then the Temptations came on with "Just my Imagination (Running Away with Me)," and then followed a new group called the Jackson Five.

Levia had danced to this music by herself many times around the room, pretending that she would grow up to be somebody that a special person would like. No one like that had yet arrived, although a kind of love life happened already for some of her friends.

Like Elanore. Levia hadn't seen Elanore for months. But someone told Levia that Elanore was sighted on Canal Street.

"She was sticking out this big." That person put their hands right about in the spot of a beer belly.

"Who is the daddy," Levia asked.

"Who you think," the other said, "Philip."

Levia wondered now how someone like Philip could be a good father at all. The men she imagined herself dancing with were at least a foot taller than Philip, broader and had deep voices.

"Why haven't I seen you before?" one whispered in her imagination.

"I guess because I'm inside studying a lot."

"There is nothing I like more than a woman with brains."

The handsome man pressed his hands softly against her head and tilted her up to kiss.

"I can spell constitution," Levia whispered back, "C-O-N-S-T-I-T-U-T-I-O-N." She returned to the lesson. There must be some benefit for spelling.

Her eighth grade teacher said that men liked women smart as much as they liked them pretty. Levia as yet saw no evidence of that. She saw that men just wanted the pick of the best women. But then they all had their definitions of best.

She had asked Philip once. He said, "I like them sexy." Brother said that women should not be sexy at all. And her father just said, "Stay a good girl." Levia did not know a woman yet whom she could be like and yet not compete with. Everyone wanted to tell her how to grow up. But Levia thought the grown-ups made too many rules about life, just like the white people.

The white people said blacks were lazy and ugly, athletic and stupid. Levia knew that didn't apply to her.

The radio announcer said it was 5:45. Looking out of her window, Levia felt that was about right, although she could never guess the time in early evening when the sun was no longer visible but the sky wasn't yet dark. It might actually be only a few minutes long. But Levia felt she spent several hours of every day in twilight.

Perhaps that was because she sat so long thinking about everything lately, particularly herself, not nearly as grown up as she wanted to be, but much more than a child.

She was tall and lean. Her face had pushed out in places that promised to be attractive. Her body even showed little bumps and curves, plumpness where she was once all hard running muscle.

But her thoughts seemed to grow only in spurts and then completely shrink, so that lately she had no control over her mind. Where she once had contentment, peace like her little brother and sister had who played and hummed all day to themselves, Levia now was uneasy. There was nothing to do. Nothing could hold her interest. Nothing satisfied. All one day she spent worrying over a cowlick that appeared in her hair. Then her knees ached all night. Her mother called that growing pains.

If hurt meant something was growing, Levia thought, so was New Orleans. Now people were breaking the windows of government buildings and setting houses on fire, in response, they said, to the hurricane. New Orleans ached all over from integration. Levia didn't know if it was worth all that much. Why couldn't everything have stayed soft and comfortable like when she was young and a baby?

Then, the family went on picnics out at the lake. In a special place, Levia learned to swim, between two identical pilings. They were actually broken telephone poles hammered into the lake's bottom for a construction that never came. They were the same because the tops of both of them had been split by lightning.

She was just a baby when her parents let her float inside a life preserver tied by string. They sat on the shore, on a step that rose out of the water, letting her paddle out with the soft tide, then reeling her back in. Only once did she get in trouble, when she drifted against a construction piling. She bumped it and tried to hold on. But her parents tried to pull her back, thinking she had just grazed it and was not clinging.

The life preserver got caught on a nail, holding her just at water level. Every time a wave passed her head went under and she had to hold her breath. She screamed for her parents in the wake of the water, when the low, sucking part of the tide came. A couple of times, she hollered too late and a salty flood filled her nose and mouth, and she was choking.

"I will die now," she remembered thinking. "My life is short." But she actually had no choice then.

Her mother arrived to take off the life preserver and wrap one arm around Levia to pull her to shore.

They continued swimming that afternoon, Levia's mother said so they would not become afraid. Her father, who never learned to swim, stood anxiously watching from the steps while holding the string and life preserver. From the water, Levia could hear him continue to curse the broken pilings and construction wood junked in the lake's "colored side."

Levia remembered those years when the lake was divided into separate areas where the blacks and whites swam. The white side had a sand beach. She could see it when they passed in the car. On the colored side, a slope into the water was built with tossed off street construction material-bricks, rocks, and broken oyster shells.

At the time, she thought the shells where pretty. But her cousin, the hunter, said, "That's because you were kid. We told you to swim over the shells to be strong."

Levia wondered, if she went to the colored side of the lake right now, how would she feel about it? There were lots of people who would probably be sitting there enjoying themselves.

That night before supper, Levia's father got a phone call from a man on his job. "Stay out of trouble," the voice had warned. Her father had told the family at the table. He made a joke out of it, "I was in trouble just by being born. I don't know what side's doing the calling." He explained at his job, there was continual fight between blacks and whites. "I try to stay out of it until it gets to me," he told the children. "Then I got to act."

Levia saw him in the morning, getting ready for work. He was taking this gun. She volunteered to get it for him. "I know how to handle one," she said.

Levia lifted the case from the drawer of her father's dresser. She set it on the bed and unzipped the leather holder. It opened like the inside of a small animal slit up from the belly to the throat.

The body of the revolver was a metallic brown. Levia brought it to the light to see it up close. With the white bulb shining hard, the gun appeared a mean grey, the color the bank looked that night when she and her father got there too late and were locked out.

She heard once on the radio that everything living has colors, like emotions. Peace is green and anger is red. She wondered how she looked in the light of the bedroom lamp, if it had the power to diagnose her feelings as it did with the turncoat gun. Levia wondered if people turned colors when they were afraid. Would a crowd of people marching, if incited, suddenly turn orange like a clamoring flame?

And were the colors of rage and happiness the same for white people and black, or were they darker and more melancholy for black people since they seemed sad more of the time? Or were colors just reserved for the halos of saints, glows that surrounded their heads on top of their hair?

As she was thinking and Levia's father watched, she loaded the gun. She took out the box of bullets from a different drawer. She broke the revolver like her cousin showed her and spun the chamber, putting in bullets one at a time like thumb tacks.

"You've done it correctly," he said. He had always told her that the gun was in the drawer for any time she needed it.

People have to defend themselves, Levia thought. If they didn't, who would? She thought that her mother would answer the question with God. Her father would say himself. Levia wondered who would defend her if either one of them died. Would she get married for her husband to protect her? Nobody like Philip would ever do, she thought. Nor would anybody who didn't think I was pretty enough.

After her father watched her load the gun, he left to the back of the house. Levia was placing it back into the leather case when she heard her mother begin arguing with him.

"Are you crazy, you going to be like the rest of these crazy men. Shooting at shadows? What is going on with you?"

Her father said, "I just got to show who the boss is around there. If I don't show some strength now, everybody will be able to push me."

"But a gun, Marvin," her mother said. "Isn't there something else you could do?"

"I thought integration was the answer. Hell, I pushed for it at the job. And now, everyone's turning against me."

Levia tried to listen now. She felt alone too most of the time. And for some reason, she was always afraid. But afraid of what? Certainly not whites. Not blacks. And yet something was always bothering her. Something that made her anxious. It was a feeling like a weak stomach. But she carried it around with her all the time, as if it were already a part of herself. Like no one could give her the definite truth, the right thing to do, yet they were asking her for it. What's good for the future? What's bad for it? Do you want to live around whites? Do you believe in killing for a just cause? What are the limits of race?

It was as if all the adults she knew became suddenly stupid but they continued to act. Big people shouting on television that they didn't want children to go into a restaurant or ride a bus. Her father kept his gun oiled. Her neighbors hung underwear on their porches now every time there was a thunderstorm. The city said it could not figure out how the levee broke.

And all of them were asking their children, what should we do? You are our future now. It seemed to Levia that the children were their present, were responsible for their own life-and-death decisions. Levia looked up from the gun, saw the picture of Charlene smiling from where she was pinned on the clothes closet, and then Levia couldn't ignore her own reflection in the mirror.

Maybe the truth always weighed on children. Mama said when she was a child she had to raise her brothers and sisters while her parents worked. She had to cook and clean and get them from school every day. She had to defend them from the bullies across the street, she said too. Once she said she hit a boy in the head with a baseball bat. "I never went to see what happened to him," she told Levia, "and I heard he was OK but I regretted it all my life."

"But wasn't it him or you, Mama?"

"The older I got the less I could tell."

Levia had just about finished zippering the gun case, but then she reconsidered. Her father just had to show he was powerful. So he could take his gun. But she would protect him. She would finally make a decision that would help her parents.

She opened the gun with both her hands, pulling the barrel apart from the body on both sides. She shook the bullets out to the floor where they hit soft like hail. Then she went into the back room where her parents argued.

"Here, Daddy," she gave it to him. He put it inside the waist of his pants under his coat jacket.

Levia felt good all day. She had made a decision. Like Martin Luther King, Jr., she thought, she would tell her parents later, she had decided on nonviolence.

She felt good until her father did not come home that evening. While she and her mother waited with dinner, they turned on the news. "Oh my God, Levia," her mother called her close to the television. There were pictures of violence and sounds of shots as the camera weaved through the crows. "That's Daddy's work," her mother said, "What should we do?"

Levia didn't know what to say. She just ran out the house.

"The white people," she said to herself, she kept repeating. "They killed my father."

She ran to the corner where the children were playing. But she had nothing to say. They just looked at her as she stood silently. She ran to her cousin's house, the hunter. But he wasn't home. "I'll get a gun and I'll kill them," she kept saying to herself. "I'll kill all of them." She ran around the corner where the white children lived. She shouted to them on their porches, "I hate you."

The boy heard her and came down the steps. "My father," she hollered and she began to run home. He followed her and by the time they arrived, people from her neighborhood were all gathered around her steps. Everyone was saying, "What's wrong?" They were talking to her mother who was looking for Levia. "What's wrong?"

"My child," Levia's mother gathered her close and held her.

They sobbed together on the steps of the house, while all the neighbors came near. The people were there from the front street where the blacks lived. And the children from around the corner brought their mother when they heard the news. "Oh my God," they were all saying, "dear God," when Levia said she had taken the bullets.

Then her father drove up.

Levia started open mouthed.

Her father thanked everyone for their concern. He had gone to another location for work. There was too much fighting on his job. He had experienced the worst and he wanted to move. He also admitted to his neighbors that he had taken a gun to work. "But I checked it before I got out of the car. And I found out it wasn't loaded."

Some of his neighbors laughed at his waving an empty gun around. Others looked horrified since they knew that aiming a gun at someone without the power to shoot was like suicide.

"I asked myself," her father continued his confession, "what if my child felt responsible since she gave me the gun this morning. What if I killed someone? Everyone now is too crazy. We have never hated each other before like this."

Old Mr. Gontier called from the back, "Amen."

"We got to act more civilized," he said. Then he opened the door of the house. "Anyone who wants to is welcomed inside," he told them. Slowly, the neighbors came to sit around the dinner table. Levia's mother gave everyone spoonfuls of rice and red beans that had been simmering.

People continued to come over all night, filtering in and out. People talked from the separate streets who never knew each other except by appearance. They introduced themselves by name. Mostly, the black people stayed. But the mother of the white country people from around the corner came bringing all of her children.

Levia made sandwiches, opened soft drinks, and cut cakes that people brought and served them around. As the crowd stayed in the back room of the house, the children her age gathered off to the side.

While they talked, Levia asked the others where they decided to go to school. Nobody liked where they were going, and they wanted to stay in the neighborhood. The white country boy said most of his friends left the public school because they were afraid of the blacks. Levia said she did not know where she would go yet, "But I think I want to where it's integrated."

"Why?" someone asked her. "Everyone just wants to fight now. Isn't it just too hard?"

"Not everyone," Levia said, "and only because things are important."

When the people were leaving the house, Levia thought she wanted to ask the boy more, about what things were hard for him. She wanted to ask him if he had ever climbed Monkey Hill, and how that felt. She thought maybe the next time. But not too long after that, his father moved their family out of the neighborhood. She never saw him again.

And as time passed, Levia began to think less about the games of Monkey Hill played by children, the running and climbing and fighting to get to the top. And she thought more about growing up, and how in the future people could be good, but never better than others.

Made in the USA
Columbia, SC
26 March 2019